Climbers and Hikers

# GUIDE to the

# WORLDS MOUNTAINS

(377 maps and 380 fotos)

SECOND EDITION

Kelsey Publishing Co.
310 East 950 South
Springville, Utah
USA   84663

First Edition April 1981
Second Edition March 1984


Copyright © 1981, 1984 Michael R. Kelsey
All rights Reserved

Library of Congress Catalog Card Number
83-083441

ISBN Number 0-9605824-2-8



Published in Great Britain/Europe by
Cordee
3a De Montfort Street
Leicester LE1 7HD
ISBN 0 904405 32 X

Distributed in North America by
ALPENBOOKS
Box 27344
Seattle, Washington 98125

Dear Climber of Hiker:
    If you have traveled in some far away place and have climbed a mountain which you believe to be additional good material for this book, please send a resume of your climb to the author at the address listed below. Include a map, and the following information; the mountains name, elevation and location; length of time needed for the climb; available transportation; weather information; any special equipment needed; and where is the best place and the last place to buy food. The author hopes to put out further editions of this book.
    Climbers, hikers and travelers are requested to send corrections, comments, suggestions, and orders for books to the author at the following address:

Michael R. Kelsey
310 East 950 South
Springville, Utah, USA
84663    Tele. 801-489-6666


**Front Cover**

1 Matterhorn—East Face, Switzerland
2 Barre des Ecrins—North Face, France
3 Volcanic Plug—Hoggar Mountains, Algeria
4 Masherbrum—Southeast Face, Pakistan


**Back Cover**

5 K-2—from Concordia, Pakistan
6 Egmont—East Slopes, New Zealand
7 Mt. Fray—North Face, Alberta, Canada
8 Buckskin Gulch of Paria River—Utah, USA
9 Chinchey—Southwest Ridge, Peru
10 Licancabur—Atacama Desert, Chile

# TABLE OF CONTENTS

## CHAPTER 7 MEXICO, CENTRAL AMERICA, CARIBBEAN .................................600

This is the Bugaboo Hut at Boulder Camp at about 2200 meters (Map 183).

The Confluencia Hut with Aconcagua in the background (Map 365).

# MAP SYMBOLS

Village or City .................................................

Buildings, Homes ............................................

Huts, Shelters, Refuges ................................

Campgrounds ................................................

Church .........................................................

Ranger, Guard, Warden Stations .....................

Buddist Temple · · · · · · · · · · · · · · · · · · · · · · · · · · · · · · ·

School ..........................................................

Roads-Paved ................................................

Road-Unsurfaced ...........................................

Roads-4WD ...................................................

Tunnels .......................................................

Trails ...........................................................

Routes .........................................................

Pass or Col ...................................................

Lakes ...........................................................

Peaks, and Ridges .........................................

Snowfields or Glaciers ...................................

Springs or Waterholes ....................................

Rivers ..........................................................

Intermittent Stream .......................................

Airport or Airstrip ..........................................

Railway ........................................................

Ski Lift or Tramway ........................................

Grassland ....................................................

Forest ..........................................................

Mines ..........................................................

Salt Flats ......................................................

Back-Country Campsite ...................................

Volcano .......................................................

Waterfalls .....................................................

Parking Place ................................................

T.V.-Radio Antenna .......................................

# MAP ABBREVIATIONS

Hut, Hutte, or Hacienda .................................... H
Lake, Lago, Laguna ...................................... L
Estancia .............................................. E
River, Rio ............................................. R
Creek ................................................ CK
Reservoir ............................................. R
Youth Hostel .......................................... YH
Campground ........................................... C.G.
Picnic Grounds ........................................ P.G.
Guard Station .......................................... G.S.
Ranger Station ......................................... R.S.
Quebrada ............................................. Q
4 Wheel Drive Road or Vehicle ......................... 4WD
Gasoline Stations (Iceland) ............................ G

-----

Author has climbed or attempted
 at least one peak on this map ..................... **MAP 21-1**
Author has visited the region
 of the map. but has not climbed .................... **MAP 105-2**
Author has had no personal experience
 with this immediate area .......................... **MAP 201-3**

## Utah Canyonlands

Narrow Canyon ...................................... ◁⊂⊃⊃⊃▷

Narrows ............................................. Ⓝ

Springs or Seeps .................................... Ⓢ ○

Pictograph or Petrogylph ............................. Ⓟ

Steep Escarpment ................................... ⊤⊤⊤⊤⊤

Spring, Intermittent ................................. Ⓢⱼ

Natural Arch ........................................ Ⓐ

Archaeological Ruins ................................ Ⓡ

## ACKNOWLEDGEMENTS

It's impossible to recall all of the thousands of people who in the past 10½ years have helped me with information concerning mountains, waterholes, travel problems, where to find the maps or books available, and so on. Nor is it possible to recount all the friendly people who invited me into their homes during bad weather, or under some other adverse circumstance. There are countless memories of people much poorer than I, who gave me gifts of food along the way to various mountains, but unfortunately they remain nameless. These people number in the thousands, and are scattered throughout the 100 countries I have visited thus far in my traveling and climbing career.

Some of those who I do remember because they gave so much of their time are as follows: Steve Tyler, the friend who originally got me interested in Mountaineering. Mitsuo Hiroshima, climbing leader of the 1977 Japanese K-2 expedition. Luis Fernando Toro, Colombian climber and Glenn Galloway, Peace Corps volunteer in Colombia, both of whom spent hours going over my Colombian maps. Marc Anderson, IAGS, Quito Ecudor, who helped me obtain maps of Ecuador. Doc Odle, John Greenough, and Stan Shepard, USA Embassy employees in La Paz, Bolivia, who assisted in information and transportation in the Cordillera Real. Tom Hendrickson, Cuzco, who gave his time and knowledge concerning the mountains around Cuzco. James Terry, IAGS, Lima, who helped obtain maps of Peru. Ralph Cummings, Argentine climber.

Also, David Taylor, Carlos Zarate and son, Rajan Nair, Asraf Aman, Renato Korell, John McGhee, Shabbir Hussain, Robert Brock, Bill Mahar, Brad Gilbert.

My father, Roland Kelsey, would not be considered a climber, but who at the age of 68 reached the top of Kings Peak, the highest summit in Utah. He died in 1975 while I was in Asia mountain climbing. He never tried in any way to discourage me from climbing solo.

And most important, the person who helped proof-read my entire manuscript which took into the hundreds of hours, and the person who sent and received my packages while I was overseas, and who helped keep me informed of all developments while traveling, my mother, Venetta Kelsey.

## ABOUT THE AUTHOR

The author experienced his earliest years of life in Eastern Utah's Uinta Basin, namely around the town of Roosevelt. Later the family moved to Provo, Utah, where he attended Provo High School, and later Brigham Young University, where he earned a B.S. degree in Sociology. Soon after he discovered that was the wrong subject, so he attended the University of Utah, where he received his Masters of Science degree in Geography, finishing that in June, 1970.

It was then that real life began, for on June 9, 1970, he put a pack on his back and started traveling for the first time. He has now (March 1984) been on the road on 13 different trips for a total of 81 months, and has seen about 100 countries.

The only places the author hasn't seen are (March 1984): parts of West and Southern Africa, parts of Eastern Europe, USSR, China, and Antarctica.

During these travels the author has been pre-occupied with two things—Geography and Mountaineering. These two subjects are now combined in this book. As for climbing mountains, the author feels he has climbed more mountains in more geographical regions of the world than any man. He has climbed solo on all climbs with the exception of early trips to McKinley, Huascaran, and Ambato. He has climbed (or attempted) 72 mountains in South America, and has attempted solo (with varying degrees of success), several peaks in Asia such as Tirich Mir, Rakaposhi, Gul Lasst, Masherbrum, Broad Peak, Nun Kun, and Annapurna II.

The author's goal, besides updating more editions to this guide, is to climb at least one mountain on every map shown in this book. As of this first edition, he has climbed or attempted peaks on 265 of the maps, or 70.5% of those covered in the book. In addition, the author has passed through areas covered by an additional 40 maps, making a total of 305 (81.1%) maps in this book the author has firsthand knowledge of.

# METRIC CONVERSION TABLE

| | |
|---|---|
| 1 Centimeter = .39 Inch | 100 Kilometers = 62 Miles |
| 1 Inch = 2.54 Centimeters | 1 Liter = 1.101 Quarts (US) |
| 1 Meter = 39.37 Inches | 1 Quart (US) = .908 Liter |
| 1 Foot = 0.3048 Meter | 1 Gallon (US) = 3.63 Liters |
| 1 Kilometer = 0.621 | 1 Acre = 0.405 Hector |
| 1 Mile = 1.609 Kilometers | 1 Hector = 2.471 Acres |
| 100 Miles = 161 Kilometers | |

## METERS TO FEET (Meters × 3.2808 = Feet)
## (Well-Known Places and Mountains)

100 m = 328 ft. ..................... Roma, Italy—98 m
500 m = 1640 ft. ..................... Innsbruck, Austria—610 m
1000 m = 3281 ft. .............. Calgary, Alberta, Canada—1068 m
1500 m = 4921 ft. ..................... Zermatt, Swiss—1554 m
2000 m = 6562 ft. .............. Nuwara Eliya, Sri Lanka—1830 m
2500 m = 8202 ft. .............. Addis Ababa, Ethiopia—2438 m
3000 m = 9842 ft. ..................... Quito, Ecuador—2850 m
3500 m = 11483 ft. .............. Lhasa, Tibet, China—3650 m
4000 m = 13124 ft. .............. Kings Peak, Utah, USA—4123 m
4500 m = 14764 ft. .............. Mt. Whitney, California, USA—4419 m
5000 m = 16404 ft. .............. Mt. Stanley, Uganda—5119 m
5500 m = 18044 ft. .............. Damavand, Iran—5671 m
6000 m = 19686 ft. .............. Kilimanjaro, Tanzania—5963 m
6500 m = 21325 ft. .............. Illimani, Bolivia—6402 m
7000 m = 22966 ft. .............. Aconcagua, Argentina—6959 m
7500 m = 24606 ft. .............. Gongga, China—7589 m
8000 m = 26246 ft. .............. Annapurna, Nepal—8078 m
8500 m = 27887 ft. .............. Kangchenjunga, Nepal-Sikkim—8598 m
9000 m = 29527 ft. .............. Mt. Everest, Nepal-China—8848 m

## FEET TO METERS (Feet ÷ 3.2808 = Meters)

| | |
|---|---|
| 1000 ft. = 305 m | 16000 ft. = 4877 m |
| 2000 ft. = 610 m | 17000 ft. = 5182 m |
| 3000 ft. = 914 m | 18000 ft. = 5486 m |
| 4000 ft. = 1219 m | 19000 ft. = 5791 m |
| 5000 ft. = 1524 m | 20000 ft. = 6096 m |
| 6000 ft. = 1829 m | 21000 ft. = 6401 m |
| 7000 ft. = 2134 m | 22000 ft. = 6706 m |
| 8000 ft. = 2438 m | 23000 ft. = 7010 m |
| 9000 ft. = 2743 m | 24000 ft. = 7315 m |
| 10000 ft. = 3048 m | 25000 ft. = 7620 m |
| 11000 ft. = 3353 m | 26000 ft. = 7925 m |
| 12000 ft. = 3658 m | 27000 ft. = 8230 m |
| 13000 ft. = 3962 m | 28000 ft. = 8535 m |
| 14000 ft. = 4268 m | 29000 ft. = 8839 m |
| 15000 ft. = 4572 m | 30000 ft. = 9144 m |

# Chapter 1 Introduction

The one principal objective of this book is to get the climber or hiker, on the right side of the mountain in question, and to the top via the normal or easiest route possible.

This book will not discuss the kinds of clothing and equipment needed for traveling or climbing, with the exception of such things as rain gear or ice ax and crampons when special conditions require them. Subjects such as geology, history and cultures of the people living in the areas surrounding the mountains, will not be discussed here, with only a few exceptions.

The book is set up this way. As each page is turned, one sees a map showing a peak or mountain range. On the opposite side is one page of written information about that particular map. There is sometimes a series of maps covering a large mountain system, such as the Andes, Himalayas, etc.

The subjects covered on each written page are in approximately the following order: the mountain type, whether a volcano—new or eroded, or some kind of folded and uplifted mountain range; the location of the peak or range, and elevations. Next, the length of time needed for the trip, or the number of days of food one should begin the trip with. This is always for the round trip—up and back—and from the last place motorized vehicles can be used, or from where the climber usually begins walking. Also stated, along with the amount of food needed, will be the *best place* in the region to buy food supplies, and the very *last place* some kind of meals can be found. Also discussed are the types of transportation available, whether buses, trains, trucks, your own car or hitch hiking (auto stopping). In other words, how to get from the capital city or some other large town, to the base of the mountain. Usually toward the bottom of each written page is something about the weather—the dry or rainy seasons, and whether hot, humid or cold, etc. Also discussed will be the possible need for ice ax or crampons, and whether the mountain has glaciers or snow fields; if there are huts or shelters on the mountain and if a tent is needed. The above subjects are covered on each of the written pages which accompany the maps.

The words "be careful" will not appear in this book—after this sentence. The author has made more than 99% of his ascents solo, and is still alive and well and is telling about it now. It will be assumed that anyone heading to the Andes, for example, will have reasonable climbing experience and will have partial knowledge of what kind of equipment is needed to hike or climb within such areas. Little or no extra caution is given to those attempting Everest, than to those hiking up Mt. Pelee in the Caribbean. It is assumed that the reader will recognize that Mauna Loa in the Hawaiian Islands will be much easier and safer than climbing in the Alps of Europe or the Karakorum in Pakistan. It will also be left to the climber who wants to attempt more difficult routes, to take a second look at the peak once he's there, or look up a more detailed guidebook on that particular mountain range.

Many of these maps are fairly detailed, especially when only one mountain is shown, such as Iliniza in Ecuador. On other maps, such as those in the Himalayas or the mountains of northwest Canada and Alaska, large areas of wild country are covered, and are not meant to be detailed maps, but instead should be used by the climber to get a generalized view of the region in question. The important thing is that the maps in this book will get a climber on the right side of the mountain and on either the right ridge or face, in order to make the easiest ascent.

In some cases the serious climber will want to buy additional maps of a range, especially if a difficult route is desired. To be quite honest, the author feels that if some details are lacking it makes for a more interesting climb—as opposed to having a guidebook in hand which describes in great detail every step or meter of the way. Most climbs the author has made have been done with little or no information, and usually with only a road map of a particular country in hand. This is the more adventurous way, although it can lead to an occasional failure.

Another important thing to remember is, that each map covers only so much territory, making it necessary for the reader to buy or obtain a national highway map. The maps in this book always include a larger city, or at least the last village on the route to the mountain or range. Therefore, if a national, state, or provincial road map is carried, no trouble should be found in getting to the right place.

This book is divided into 7 different chapters or regions of the world. There are 2 pages of introduction to each section, giving generalized information about each area.

An important aspect that must be discussed here is one of the big problems confronting travelers, hikers and climbers as they leave the borders of thier own country. It has to do with caring for one's personal belongings—money, travelers checks, cameras, pack, etc. One can't begin to describe the horrors involved when something of value is stolen—especially an entire pack!

The very worst places in the world for crime, especially those against travelers, are South America, then Mexico and Central America. These are followed by such places as Morocco, East Africa (Kenya), then Black Africa in general.

Other places are very safe—such as New Zealand, where open dishes are still used to hold money in newspaper boxes on the streets. This is a rare exception in this day and age.

Here are some generalized tips for traveling (more detailed information will be covered in the region of South America). Carry money, travelers checks, and passport in either a waist belt or a neck pouch—and make it as thin and unnoticeable as possible. Carry cameras or tote bags over the shoulder and not just in the hand. In other words, make it difficult to lay something down. When camping in the mountains and particularly on beaches or near towns and cities, put everyting securely in your tent at night and don't leave the tent unattended during the day.

Once on the road (in a new country), the first place one should stop is at the tourist office. These are located in virtually every country nowadays, usually at the international airport, as well as in the downtown section of the capital city. If you're in an area of the world where the language is a problem, you will need city and national road maps much more than ever. Tourist offices can give you most maps needed, as well as addresses of the national map making and selling institute, the names and addresses of mountaineering clubs, banks, embassies, airline offices, bus and train stations, truck loading areas, locations of the cheapest (or more expensive), hotels, etc.

Most expeditions take cartridge stoves to the Himalayas and Andes, but what happens when you run out of cartridges? Replacements can usually be found in places such as Kathmandu and Huaraz, but they're expensive and sources unreliable. The author has always used a kerosene stove and has never had trouble finding fuel in the 100 countries he has visited.

Ojos Del Salado to the left, scene from bridge over Agua Dulce (sweet water) (Map 362).

## Chapter 2 Europe

This chapter is the first of 7 in this book which covers the world. This part includes all the regions of Europe, and has 79 maps. Some of the areas included here are Greenland (because it's a state or province of Denmark), the Azores and Canary Islands, and from Spitsbergen to Greece. The Soviet Union will be included in the Asian chapter.

Most people in the developed world—North America, Europe, Australia and New Zealand, have at least one language which originated in Europe, so language in Europe is not the problem that it can be in other parts of the world. If a traveler has either English, French or German, he can usually get by just about anywhere, and if he has all three, then traveling is made very easy. The next best language is Spanish or perhaps Italian. Normally, people in the north of Europe speak from 3 to 5 languages. This is especially true in The Nederlands and Denmark.

It's difficult to make any generalizations concerning climbing here because of the vast distances covered by this chapter. Needless to say, the further north one goes, the colder and more miserable the weather becomes. If one is in Iceland, or other North Atlantic islands, rain gear is standard equipment, along with a sturdy tent.

If one is in the Mediterranean region, then it's going to be hot and dry in summer, but cool and wet in winter. There are no glaciers in Spain, Italy (excluding the Alps) or Greece. The majority of the maps in this section cover the Alps. Throughout the Alps one sees glaciers—some very small, especially on the southern slopes, but others rather extensive, such as in the Berner and Pennine Alpen of Switzerland. An ice ax and crampons should be standard equipment for the whole of the Alps—although on some of the easier and more popular peaks, there's a well beaten path in the snow to the summit and this equipment is sometimes not needed.

In some areas such as the Dolomite in northern Italy, one will have little use for ice equipment, but instead may want to take rock climbing gear along. The Dolomiti offers the best rock climbing in Europe.

Crimes against travelers are very unusual in Europe, especially in the northern parts. What is meant here is, someone getting into your tent, or picking your pocket in railway stations, etc. In places like Iceland, the Faroe Islands, Norway, crime is almost unheard—of. In all the author's travels in Europe he has lost nothing. While most people use the huts or refuges in the Alps, the author always camped—but never had anything taken from his tent. However, the author has always taken more precautions in the south of Europe. In southern Europe, it's best not to leave a tent for long periods of time. This region is very safe when compared to Latin America.

While the costs of transportation in Europe are very high, it's also possible to travel in this region very inexpensively—that's by auto stopping or hitch hiking. Auto stopping is very good in the Alps and all over northern and northwest Europe. The areas that are slow are the southern regions, generally the poorer countries.

For most people living outside the continent, special passes are obtainable for the system of railways throughout most of Europe. These passes are called Eurail Passes, and can be bought and used anywhere from 2 weeks to 3 months. If one is visiting all of Europe, then these passes are fine, but if you're going to the Alps to climb, and will spend time there, it's best to auto stop. In 1979, the author carried one, two or three signs—stating the name of the mountain, best-known town in the area of the mountain, and distance in kms (especially if the destination was near). Using this method, he made 21 ascents (or attempts) in 33 days, beginning with Grossglockner in Austria, and finishing with Ecrins, in France.

Typical of all of Europe, whether it be in the north, east, west or south, one can almost always find huts or refuges on the higher and more prominent mountains. This is one area of the world where one can climb without a tent.

Besides huts high on the mountains, Europe has many youth hostels. Most of these are found in the largest cities, but also in most of the important mountain resort towns as well. There's a fee for the membership card, but it's good for a year and allows one to use all International Youth Hostels in the world.

The further north one goes in Europe, the more expensive everything becomes. The further south one travels, the cheaper commodities are.

Matterhorn rises to the southwest of Zermatt (Map 48).

Milking a goat in the high alps (pastures) of Switzerland (Map 52).

## Trails of South Greenland

The area covered by this map is the extreme southern end of Greenland, but none of Greenland's famous ice cap is shown. This region is perhaps the warmest and most heavily populated of all of Greenland. Important towns in the area are Julianehab, the largest, and Narsaq. Other places indicated on the map are much smaller, and are populated almost exclusively by Eskimos.

For the tourist or traveler, the one place of prime importance is the airport at Narssarsuaq. It's the only airfield in the region, and is an important link to the outside world. This airfield was built during World War II, by the Americans, and was named Bluey West II. Nowadays, there's only the airport, Arctic Hotel (with small store, restaurant, and bookshop), Feldstation (which is a kind of youth hostel), and a small port area. A number of Danish workers live and work at Narssarsuaq, as Greenland is a territory of Denmark.

Few high mountains exist in the area covered by this map. For people wanting to travel to the more isolated areas of the island, helicopters or private boats must be hired for such trips. This involves time and great expense.

For those who can be satisfied with climbing shorter mountains or trekking, this region is excellent. The trails shown, for the most part, are sheep trails, which have evolved over the years. In recent years, the DVL (a Danish youth hostel and trekking type club) has painted stones and made markers along some of the more scenic routes. This same group, with headquarters at Feldstation, also has fixed up old houses in some areas, which can be used by anyone for a small fee.

To give an example of time and distance, the author took a tourist boat from Narssarsuaq to Kagsiarsuk, then had a leisurely walk of about 2½ days to Narsaq. From there a state-run ferryboat was taken back to Narssarsuaq (in about 1½ hours).

Even in summer, go prepared for wet and cool weather, and mosquitos! Fly to Greenland from either Iceland or Denmark (nothing going to or from North America as of 1979). Someone at the Arctic Hotel, Feldstation, or the tourist office at the airport can help with the latest information concerning trails, ferry boats, private boats, the whereabouts of small stores, use of mountain huts, etc.

**Map:** Tourist map—South Greenland, 1 : 250,000, and maps in **Atlas-handbog over Gronland.**

Just south of Kagsiarsuk, one still sees icebergs in the Fjord.

# Map 1-1, Trails of South Greenland

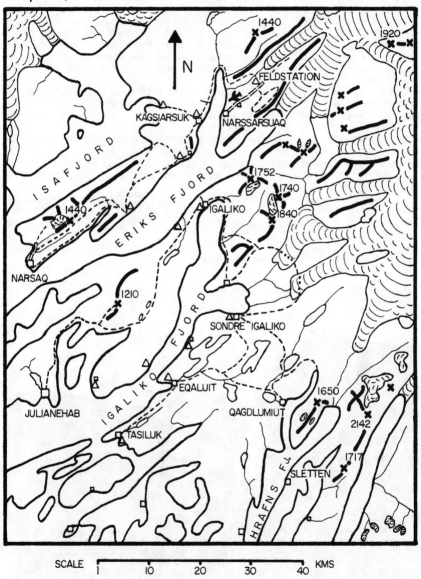

## Eiriksjokull, Iceland

In an area about 100 kms northeast of Reykjavik, and just a few kms due north of Geyser and Gullfoss, lies the Langjokull, the second largest ice sheet in Iceland. The highest peak in the region is not on or part of this glacier, however. The highest summit is the top of Eiriksjokull, 1675 meters, to the northwest of Langjokull.

Unlike some other mountain and glacier regions in Iceland, this area is relatively near some main roads, populated areas, and gasoline stations. For example, a straight line route between Husafell and Eiriksjokull is about 25 kms and the same is true from Gullfoss (the largest and most famous waterfall in the country) to Blafell. This means that the poor traveler or mountain climber can, with a large pack, walk to any point in the region covered by this map. For the foot traveler it would take two or three days to climb either Blafell or Eiriksjokull, and return to the main roads.

One can auto stop to Husafell (a bit slow there) and to Gullfoss. Lots of traffic going to Gullfoss and Geyser, as this area is the premier tourist attraction in Iceland. There's a gasoline station with small store at Geyser and Husafell. However, buy all supplies in Reykjavik for better variety and lower prices, if possible.

The track from Gullfoss to Hveravelar is quite good with large buses taking the more rugged "tourists" into that area. The huts shown on the map are available to anyone, but you must contact the Iceland Tourist Board in Reykjavik for reservations and other information concerning their availability and also the latest road (track) conditions. Good maps are available in the large bookstores in Reykjavik.

The worst part of a camping trip to Iceland is the bad weather, especially the high winds. Take a good tent and look for a sheltered spot to place it. Also, take clothing suitable for cold and wet conditions. July, August, and the first part of September are the best months to visit Iceland.

**Map:**   Adalkort Bl.5(Map 5), Mid-Island, 1 : 250,000, from Geodetic Institute-Copenhagen. Also 1 : 50,000 and 1 : 100,000 maps available.

This whaling station is on the coast not far from Eiriksjokull.

## Map 2-2, Eiriksjokull, Iceland

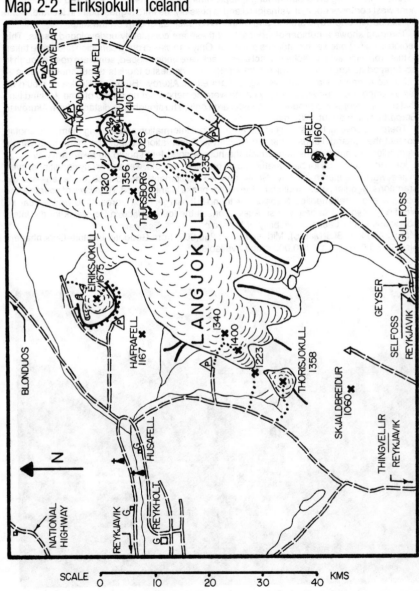

## Bardarbunga, Iceland

Featured on this map is a mountainous region in the very center of Iceland. The area surrounding Hofsjokull, or Hofs Glacier, is the most isolated in all of Iceland. The highest mountain in the region is Bardarbunga, approximately 2000 meters. It's located very near the northwest corner or edge of Vatnajokull and is possibly the third highest point in Iceland. It can be climbed in one day from the end of the 4WD track as shown on the map.

The map shows a number of "roads," but these are completely undeveloped tracks. This region is uninhabited and distances are great. Only vehicles in good condition should be taken to this area. However, despite the fact these tracks are undeveloped, some are good enough to accommodate large buses which take foreign and domestic tourists throughout the area.

For someone to walk into this region from either Akureyi, Burfell or Reykjavik would be almost impossible, unless a supply cache were somehow set up ahead of time. Iceland isn't that big, but people live around the coastal area only. The straight line distance from Akureyi to Bardarbunga is about 120 kms.

There are several tourist huts in the area. To get information about using them, one should contact the Iceland Tourist Board in Reykjavik. Reservations should be made in advance. Regardless of one's plans concerning the huts, a good tent should be *taken* anyway.

Iceland is notorious for bad weather so go prepared for cold, wet and windy conditions, even in the warmest month of July. Snow and ice equipment should also be taken—ice ax, crampons, goggles, etc.—if climbing the higher peaks is anticipated. Reykjavik of course is the best place to get all supplies. Maps can be found in the larger book stores. 4WD vehicles can be hired or rented, but at heavy cost. Again, consult the tourist office in Reykjavik for the latest conditions of the tracks, availability of huts, etc.

**Map:**   Adalkort Bl.5(Map 5), Mid-Island, 1 : 250,000, from Geodetic Institute-Copenhagen. Also 1 : 50,000 and 1 : 100,000 maps available.

This scene is from near Gullfoss, but is typical of Iceland.

## Map 3-3, Bardarbunga, Iceland

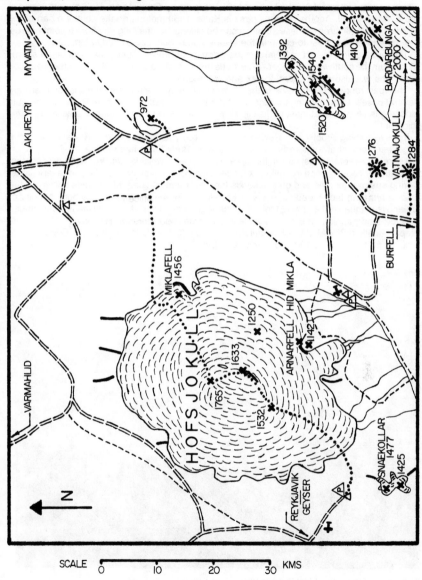

SCALE 0 10 20 30 KMS

## Hekla, Iceland

If you talk to someone from Iceland, they will tell you the most famous mountain on the island is Hekla. The reason for its fame is that it's the most active volcano on the Icelandic mainland. It last erupted in 1970. At 1491 meters, it has perpetual snow and is now building glaciers—but with no crevasses yet. Hekla is a good climb for the average traveler or tourist, but climbers would be more interested in the highest peak in the area—Godusteinn, 1666 meters, a part of the Eyjafjallajokull. Another famous peak is Katla, 1450 meters, on the southern part of the Myrdalsjokull. All three of these summits can be climbed in one long day from a point nearest the mountains. It is best to camp in the area so one could get an early start.

The weather in this part of Iceland is the worst in the whole country, as most of the storms come from the southwest. Raingear is perhaps the most important of all the equipment one can take. One will also need a tent, ice ax and crampons.

The road running through Vik is the national highway which circles the island. There are several buses a day passing through Vik, but the area is not that far from Reykjavik, so auto stopping is very good at least up to Vik. Beyond Vik auto stopping is more difficult, as traffic thins out.

If you're coming directly from Reykjavik to climb, buy your supplies there. However, Vik is the largest settlement around and has several stores. Burfell also has a store.

There are several tourist huts in this area and they are available. One would have to contact the National Tourist Office in Reykjavik for details on their availability, costs, and reservations. During summer months and on weekends they will be most used. Most roads shown on the map, other than those leading to Vik or Burfell, are for 4WD vehicles. The back country of Iceland is uninhabited and wild. Only vehicles in good condition should ply these wastelands.

Good topographic maps are available in the larger bookstores in Reykjavik.

**Map:**  Adalkort Bl.6(Map 6). Midsadurland, 1 : 250,000, from Geodetic Institute-Copenhagen. Also 1 : 50,000 and 1 : 100,000 maps available.

The coast just south of Hekla near Vik is very rugged.

## Map 4-2, Hekla, Iceland

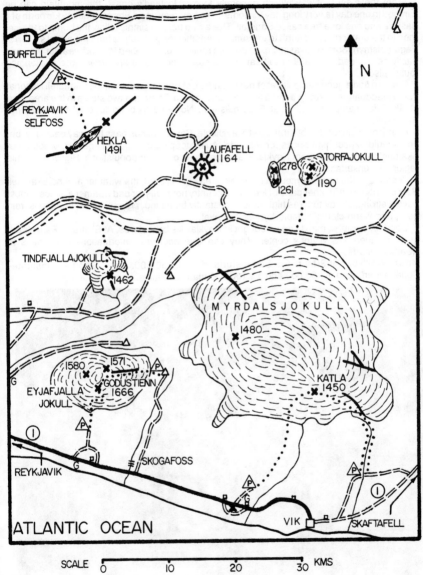

SCALE    0    10    20    30    KMS

## Hvannadalshnukur, Iceland

Near the south coast of Iceland, and at the southern edge of Vatnajokull, Iceland's largest glacier, stands the highest mountain on the island, Hvannadalshnukur, at 2119 meters. This peak is the highest of several summits which ring a very old and eroded volcanic crater, called Oraefajokull. There are three other peaks over 2000 meters on the same crater.

From the main highway, which generally follows Iceland's coast, the mountain can be climbed in one day (a very long day for some). The best way up begins at a point ½ km north of a pasture and one lone tree called Sandfell. There's no trail, so simply follow the hump to the ice, then to the crater rim, and north to the summit. Another longer route is from the petrol station at Fagurholsmyri. Some crevasses exist on both routes, but if climbed in good weather they can easily be avoided. The author felt safe in his solo effort. There are other more challenging routes also.

One can find a good campsite at or near Sandfell, or one may camp at the Skaftafell National Park Headquarters Campground a few kms up the road. There are two stores in the area; one at Skaftafell camp, the other at Fagurholsmyri. No need to bring food all the way from Reykjavik.

Along the main road public transport is available. Several buses pass this way each day, but one should expect high prices for that ride. Auto stopping in Iceland is generally good, but Skaftafell is a long way from Reykjavik and the areas of higher populations. Highways in this region are unsurfaced.

Because of the way the mountains in this area are situated, the weather around Skaftafell Park is better than in other parts of Iceland, a country notorious for bad weather. Climbers must have a strong, sturdy tent (as high winds constantly buffet the region), ice ax, crampons, rain gear, and warm cloths suitable for glacier travel.

Good topographic maps can be bought in Reykjavik's bookstores. At Skaftafell Park Head-quarters, there's a visitor's center. They can give additional information—from maps to weather reports.

**Map:** Adalkort Bl.9(Map 9), Sudausturland, 1 : 250,000, from Geodetic Institute-Copenhagen. Also 1 : 50,000 and 1 : 100,000 maps available.

From point 1848 on map, we see Hvannadalshnvkur in the distance.

## Map 5-1, Hvannadalshnukur, Iceland

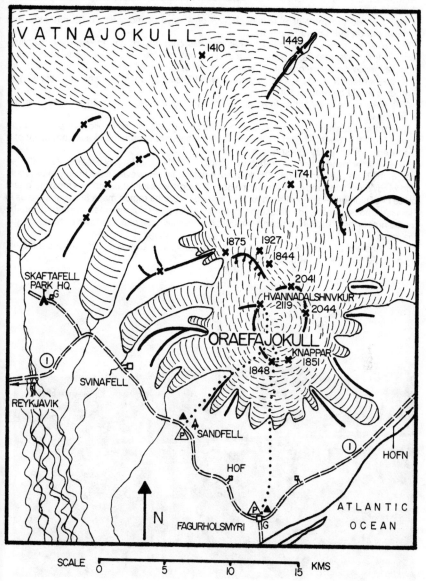

## Snaefell, Iceland

In eastern Iceland, just to the northeast of the large Vatnajokull (Vatna Glacier), stands a rather famous eroded volcano, Snaefell. It's one of the higher peaks in the country at 1833 meters. Because Snaefell stands "behind" the largest glacier in Europe, and is in its "rain-shadow," the snow line here is a bit higher than in the southwest part of Iceland. To climb Snaefell, it would take a 4WD vehicle and a couple of days from the town of Egilsstadir; or if one is using public transport or auto stopping, 3 or 4 days or more would be needed, from somewhere on the national highway.

If one is interested in venturing further into this cold desert, say for example, to climb Kverkfjoll, at 1920 meters, it would be a serious undertaking—a small expedition in fact. It would either cost a lot of money if you wanted to rent or hire a 4WD vehicle, or it would take a lot of time—perhaps 8 to 10 days if one were to walk! The distance from the national highway to Kverkfjoll would be around 100 kms.

The Askja Volcano is another famous mountain (in Iceland at least), which has been erupting in recent years.

There are buses running constantly on the national highway, but no public transport exists on any of the back roads—in fact it's completely uninhabited. Logurinin Lake is somewhat of a resort area with a small forest nearby.

The weather in these parts is probably the best in all of Iceland, largely because it's on the lee side of the island, and in the rain shadow much of the time. However, even in July expect cold and windy conditions and don't forget rain gear. A tough, wind resistant tent is a most important piece of equipment—along with ice ax and crampons. Look for good maps of various scales in Reykjavik bookstores, and contact the Iceland Tourist Board for information about using the tourist huts in the area. All food can be bought in Egilsstadir, the only real town or community in the region.

**Map:** Adalkort Bl.8(Map 8), Midausturland, 1 250,000, from Geodetic Institute-Copenhagen. Also 1 : 50,000 and 1 : 100,000 maps available.

This is the elevated roadway across the stream south of Skaftafell.

## Map 6-3, Snaefell, Iceland

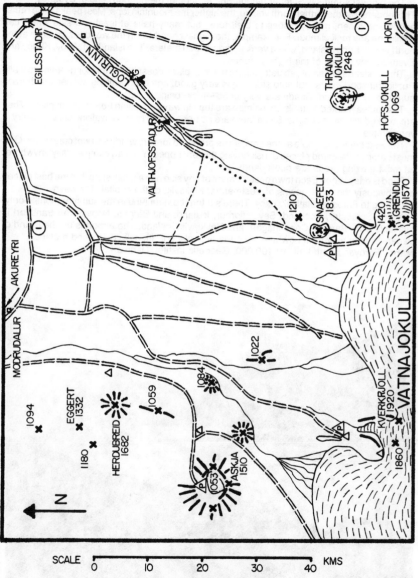

## Slaettaratindur, Eysturoy Island, Faroe Islands

In the stormy North Atlantic about halfway between Bergen Norway, Iceland, and Scotland, lie the Faroe Islands. Faroe consists of 18 islands with a land mass of about 900 sq. kms. The islands are made up of old volcanic lava, laid down in layers. Sandwiched between some of the lower levels are coal seams.

The highest summit is Slaettaratindur, 882 meters, at the northern end of Eysturoy Island. The tendency is, the further north you go, the higher the mountain tops. Most peaks have rather gentle and green, grassy slopes to their tops, but many have at least one side which can challenge any rock climber. For example, the highest headwall in the world is said to be at the north end of Kunoy Island, with a vertical drop of 820 meters. The islands of Vidoy, Kunoy and Eysturoy have most of the highest summits.

These islands are small, so getting from place to place doesn't take that long—even to walk. Public transport exists, but auto stopping is very good, and even walking will get you there in surprisingly little time. Roads are very good—most being paved.

The routes marked as trails on the map are the old ways of getting from place to place. They are marked with stone cairns. Since there are no trees on the islands, walking cross country is very simple.

The weather is miserable all the time, so be prepared for very windy and wet conditions. One must camp in sheltered places or risk having the tent ripped. You can camp literally anywhere, as most grazing areas are public lands.

Food is easy to get. Each town or settlement of any size has a small store, but the best places are obviously the larger towns of Vestmanna, Klaksvik, or the capital, Torshavn.

Getting to Faroe is relatively easy. There's a ferryboat running in the summer months only, between Scrabster, Scotland; Seyoisfjorbur, Iceland; and Bergen, Norway. Air transport is available from Bergen, Copenhagen, and Reykjavik, Iceland. The airport is on the island of Vagar—a long way from nowhere—but the only place in the islands to land a plane.

**Map:** Foroyar, North half, 1 : 100,000, Geodetic Institut, Danmark.

A typical scene in the Faroe Islands. Most mountains are rounded.

## Map 7-1, Slaettaratindur, Faroe Islands

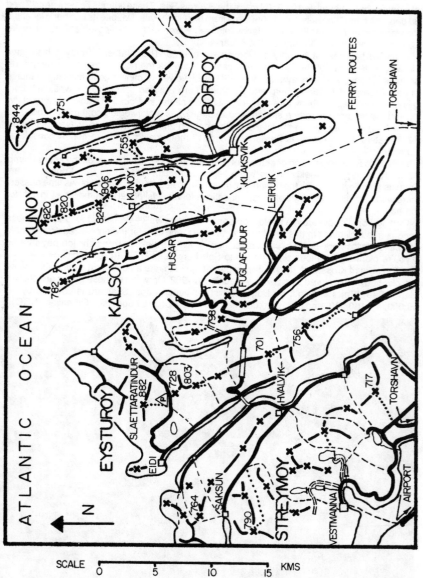

# Newtontoppen, Spitsbergen, Svalbard Is., Norway

Few people have heard of Spitsbergen, let alone know of its whereabouts. Even fewer people would consider mountain climbing there, but in this day and age of the airplane, almost any part of the earth is open and available to mountaineering.

Spitsbergen Island is the largest of the group of islands known as Svalbard. Svalbard is part of Norway, but is separated by 950 kms of the Barents Sea. These islands lie between 77 and 80 degrees north, and only about 1050 kms from the North Pole. Despite its northerly location, the warm ocean currents keep the islands relatively warm—at least ships are able to anchor at Longyearbyen for 3 to 4 months of the year.

Svalbard has been a territory of Norway since 1925. The Svalbard Treaty, which gave Norway sovereignty of the islands, also gave 41 nations the right to exploit its natural resources. Today, only Norway and the USSR are involved in mining coal, the only resource under development. Barentsburg and Pyramiden are Russian coal mining towns, with Longyearbyen the capital, the Norwegian administrative center and location of the only airport. Ny Alesund is an arctic research station, and Sveagruva is a Norwegian coal mining town.

The highest mountain on the island of Spitsbergen and all of Svalbard, is Newtontoppen, 1717 meters. Not far away is Perriertoppen, 1717 meters also, but is somehow considered number 2.

Getting to Spitsbergen and near the mountain is the problem, not so much the actural climb. As of 1975, regular weekly flights were begun from Tromso, Norway, to Longyearbyen. Tourists are allowed to visit the region, but must take their own food and tents. As time passes, there will surely be other kinds of accommodations for tourists, but at this time it's a trip only for the hardy.

Getting from Longyearbyen to Newtontoppen is a long walk—probably too long. For those serious about climbing in this or other remote areas, one can, for the right-sized pocketbook, find either helicopters, boats or snow machines, which can make the overland journey shorter. If you're planning a serious climbing trip to Spitsbergen, plan for arctic conditions.

In the area of Krossfjord, the northwest part of the map, are a number of peaks which were first climbed and explored by a Swiss expedition in 1962. Only part of those peaks are shown.

**Map:** See **"Spitsbergen"**, by Hugo Nunlist for better maps. Svalbard is covered by 1 : 50,000, 1 : 100,000, and 1 : 1,000,000 maps by the Norge Geografiske Offmaling (NGO).

Looking north from about the area of Mt. Michelsen.

## Map 8-3, Newtontoppen, Spitsbergen, Norway

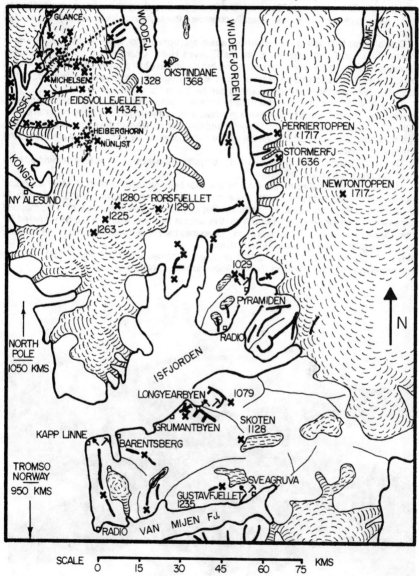

# Galdhopiggen, Jotunheimen, Norway

In the south central part of Norway, and to the northeast of Bergen, lie most of the higher mountains of Norway. These mountains and many glaciers lie, for the most part, at or near the heads of several large fjords, two of which are Nordfjorden and Sognefjorden, two of the longest fjords on the west coast of Norway. The highest summits are Galdhopiggen, 2469 meters, and Glittertinden, 2470 meters. Galdhopiggen usually appears as one meter shorter, but it has a rock summit and is generally considerd the highest peak in Norway and in all of Scandinavia.

Both of these high peaks can be climbed easily and from one location—or several. The most normal route up Galdhopiggen, is via the Gjuvvas Hytta. Gjuvvas is a hut or refuge with sleeping and food accommodation. From this hut it's an easy half day climb to the summit, via a trail. The mountain can also be climbed from the main highway and Elvesaeter (a holiday hotel complex). Still another route of approach can be found from Spiterstulen.

To reach Glittertinden, the most normal route is via Spiterstulen and the trail reaching the top. In two days, one can climb both of these mountains, from the single base camp of Spiterstulen. Still other ways would be from Visdalsaeter and Glitterheim. Most of the summits in this region are not so rugged or difficult. They have all been worn down by past and present glaciation, and many easy routes can be found.

The third highest summit in the area is Hurrungane; 2405 meters. It can best be climbed from near the place called Helgedalen.

All of the places marked on the map as towns or buildings are hardly that. Most are resort hotels, filling stations, or just a "wide place in the road," but not big towns. If you're planning to be in the area for several days and camping, buy all your supplies before reaching the mapped area—certainly before leaving Lom. Also, this area is very wet and cool, so be prepared for that. Better have ice ax and crampons too, sometimes they're needed. Anybody at the hotels or hut can help you with additional information.

**Map:**   Ardal, NP 31,32-11, 1 : 250,000, or others at scales 1 : 50,000 and 1 : 100,000 from Norges Geografiske Oppmaling (NGO), 3500 Honefoss, Norway.

F͏ m the top of Galdhopiggen, looking south.

## Map 9-1, Galdhopiggen, Jotunheimen, Norway

# Romsdal, Romsdalhorn Group, Norway

To hikers and rock climbers around Europe the name Romsdal is familiar. The name Romsdal comes from one very steep mountain summit called Romsdalhorn. It's nearly vertical on all sides and in some ways resembles the Matterhorn in Switzerland. Because of this one famous peak, the entire region has more-or-less taken on the name of Romsdal. This formerly glaciated mountainous area is located on the west coast of Norway, about 175 air kms southwest of Trondheim. It's also about 125 kms northwest of the main north-south highway town of Dombas. There is only one town of any importance on this map and that's Andalsnes.

Andalsnes is located at the head of Romsdalsfjorden, and is about 100 kms from the open seas of the west coast. The region has many prominent peaks and summits, but none are above 2000 meters. Romsdalhorn itself is only about 1550 meters, but its base is near sea level. The valleys have all been heavily glaciated and are "U" shaped. The rock is mostly granite, thus is seen many huge rock faces. This is one of the best rock climbing places in the world. The lower valleys are all green and filled with sheep and cattle during the summer months. The map the author used to create this one is the Alesund, 1 : 250,000 Joint Operations Graphic map. It's good to use to get an overall look at the entire region. But for greater detail on slopes and trails, it is recommended the four maps listed below be used. Also, for the serious rock climber, use the book entitled, "Walks and Climbs in Romsdal Norway", by T. Howard.

Most people reach Andalsnes via a good paved highway from Oslo by driving their car or possibly by autostop-hitch hiking. In summer there's a fair amount of traffic. One can also get from Oslo to Andalsnes via train. Andalsnes is a small town, but has food and gasoline stores, hotels, and campgrounds in the area. Food will be cheaper in Oslo.

For rock climbers, there are huts on top of Romsdalhorn, Store Trolltind, and Kongen, and another near Trollshig Pass (Bispen Hut). The locations of these huts indicates the more popular rock climbing areas. For hikers, there are trails-of-sorts in all valleys, but the most popular hikes are these. From Verma go to Reitan (16 kms), located on the south end of Lake Eikesda, take a ferry halfway up the lake, then walk west to Morstol. Also, a 24 km hike is from near Trollstigheiman east to Verma. And one from Berill to near Trollstigheiman. In July and August the weather is warm and better than in the Alps or in UK.

**Map:** Romsdalen, Valldal, Andalsnes, and Eresfjord, 1 : 50,000, from Norges Geografiske Oppmaling (NGO), 3500 Honefoss, Norway.

Romsdalshorn from Vegedal Seter.

# Map 10-3, Romsdal, Romsdalhorn Group, Norway

# Kebnekaise, Lappland, Sweden

In northern Sweden, not far from the Norwegian boarder, and about halfway between Kiruna, Sweden and Narvik, Norway, lies the highest mountain in Sweden, Kebnekaise, at 2117 meters elevation. This part of Sweden is known as Lappland. Because of the latitude, nearly 68 degrees north, one would expect to find a highly glaciated country, and for the most part, this is true. But, since the mountain range in which Kebnekaise is a part, is on the lee or rain-shadow side of the watershed, it is noticeably drier than the mountains which form the border of Norway and Sweden. The mountains on this map are higher than the border mountains, but the amount of precipitation they receive is less. However, there are still many streams, lakes and glaciers.

Kebnekaise is reached via Kiruna, Pirttivuopio (which is the end of the road), and the Kebnekaise Fjallstation. There's a trail to the top of the mountain which makes this climb very easy. Depending on one's fitness and pack weight, it should take somewhere between 3 and 5 days round trip from Pirttivuopio. Don't leave Pirttivuopio without making inquires or arrangements for the one lake crossing which must be made by *boat*!

There are a few trails in the area, and even a number of emergency type huts, scattered throughout the valleys. If you don't have a tent and are planning to use the huts, better inquire about them in Pirttivuopio before hiking.

Kiruna is a bigger town, and the last place in which you can do any shopping. Kiruna is on the main rail line connecting the iron mines in Sweden, with the open port at Narvik. There isn't much traffic between Kiruna and Pirttivuopio, but the road is reasonably good. During vacation time, July and August, there are many more travelers in the area, so auto stopping is possible.

Any of the mountains in this region can be climbed without crampons or ice ax, but it's recommended you take them anyway. Also, be prepared for cold, wet weather, and lots of mosquitos.

**Map:** Kebrekaise(29I), and Abisko(30I), from Generalstabens Litografiska Anstalt, Kart Centrum, Vasagatan 16, 11 20 Stockholm.

Got a foto? Please send to author.

## Map 11-3, Kebnekaise, Lappland, Sweden

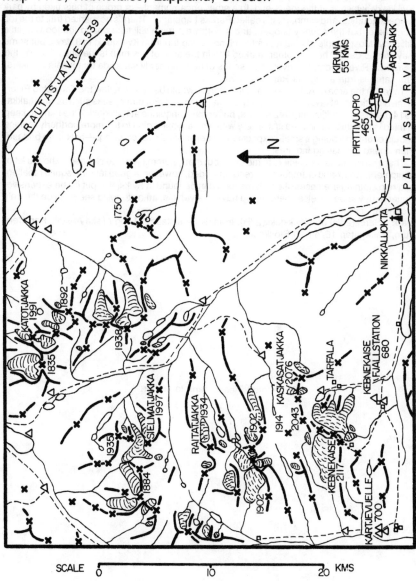

SCALE  0        10        20  KMS

## Partetjakka, Sarek Nat. Park, Lappland, Sweden

In northern Sweden, not far south of Narvik Norway, lie several groups of peaks which are the highest mountains in Sweden. Included on this map is part of the Sareks National Park, and the only access road from the south—which is Partetjakka, 2005 meters. Fortunately, this mountain is the most easily reached of all the higher summits. There's a good trail from Kvikkjokk, which is at the roads-end, to a small encampment—or group of huts used by park rangers, tourists, and climbers. It's called Pareks Lapplager. There's no marked trail to the top from there, but the country is open, and a northwest route will take one to the top with little difficulty. Most people should make the climb, round trip from Kvikkjokk, in 3 days, but some may want 5 days. The only other marked trail in the area of this map is the one following the Tarraatno River. Along this river are a series of huts, primarily set aside for tourists or hikers. The same is true along the Rapaatno River.

To reach the area of Akkatjakka, 1974 meters, it would be best to follow the Tarraatno River, in the direction of Alkavare, where a "rengarda" is located. For other peaks such as Apartjakka, 1914 meters, or Midtjisarki 1942 meters, better make inquiries at Kvikkjokk. One thing to keep in mind is that this whole area is still very wild, and anyone going to the more northerly regions should count on it being a small "expedition." Keep in mind river crossings—not all are bridged. Plan ahead by making inquires.

There are some large glaciers in the area, but many summits can be climbed without a lot of equipment. Ice ax and crampons are recommended, however. A good tent, mosquito repellent and rain clothing are necessities. Some food can be found in Kvikkjokk, but it'll be expensive. Better to buy supplies elsewhere. If you haven't a vehicle, auto stopping seems to be the only means of access.

**Map:** Sarek(28H) and Kvikkjokk(27H), from Generalstabens Litografiska Anstalt, Kart Centrum, Vasagatan 16, 11 20 Stockholm.

Got a foto? Please send to author.

# Map 12-3, Partetjakka, Sarek N.P., Sweden

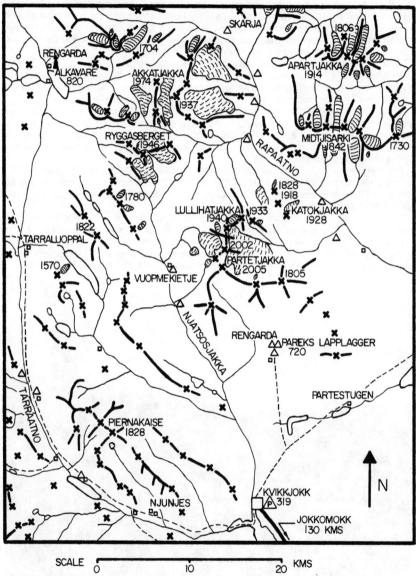

SKARJA

1806

RENGARDA
ALKAVARE
820

1704

APARTJAKKA
1914

AKKATJAKKA
1974

1937

RYGGASBERGET
1946

MIDTJISARKI
1842                    1730

RAPAATNO

1780

1828
1918

LULLIHATJAKKA  1933      KATOKJAKKA
1940                    1928

1822

2002

TARRALUOPPAL

PARTETJAKKA
2005      1805

1570

VUOPMEKIETJE

NJATSOSJAKKA

RENGARDA
PAREKS LAPPLAGGER
720

PARTESTUGEN

TARRAATNO

N

PIERNAKAISE
1828

KVIKKJOKK
319

NJUNJES

JOKKOMOKK
130 KMS

SCALE    0          10          20    KMS

## Carrauntoohil, Macgillycuddy's Reeks, Ireland

In the extreme southwest corner of Ireland, in Country Kerry, stands the group of mountains known as Macgillycuddy's Reeks. The summits aren't high, but they're the best Ireland has. There are two peaks over 1,000 meters, the highest of which is Carrauntoohil, 1041 meters, the number one peak of Ireland.

Ireland has a number of small mountain ranges scattered about the land, but a few more exist in the southwest, and Country Kerry. It's in this part that the more rugged territory is found. In central and eastern Ireland the mountains are smooth and rounded, as a result of the last glacier age. Other important mountain ranges in Ireland include the Mourne, Wicklow and Galtee Mountains. Hill walking is popular in all these areas.

Country Kerry is a tourist area—but it can't be that "paradise" as some call it, as the weather is too often terrible. Nonetheless, there are a lot of tourists, especially Americans, who return to their ancestral homeland. Tralee and Killarney are the tourist towns. Killarney is a good place to make one's first stop before doing some trekking or climbing in the Reeks.

Carrauntoohil can be approached from east, west, north or south, but the more normal way is via the youth hostel in the Black Valley. There's also another youth hostel, formerly a school, on the north slopes. This is the second most used route. However, the most scenic route and one that's amongst the more rugged sections of the mountain, is the approach to the mountain from the northwest and Breanlee Bridge.

Please note that the author has indicated routes for the most part, as opposed to actual trails. There are a number of sheep trails on the mountain, which are used by hill walkers, but oftentimes don't take you where you want to go. It's not difficult to travel cross-country, as the land is open and treeless.

Carrauntoohil can be climbed easily in one day from any direction. Keep in mind that although the mountains aren't big or rugged (except of the Coomlaughara Laugh Cirque), the way can easily be lost in the clouds, as the weather in the west of Ireland is typically very bad. It's recommended that a raincoat and rain pants be carried at all times while hiking in this area.

**Map:**   Dingle Bay,(20), 1 : 126,720, Ordance Survey of Ireland, Phoenix Park, Dublin.

Got a foto? Please send to author. Mourne Wall, Mourne Mts.

## Map 13-1, Carrauntoohil, M. Reeks, Ireland

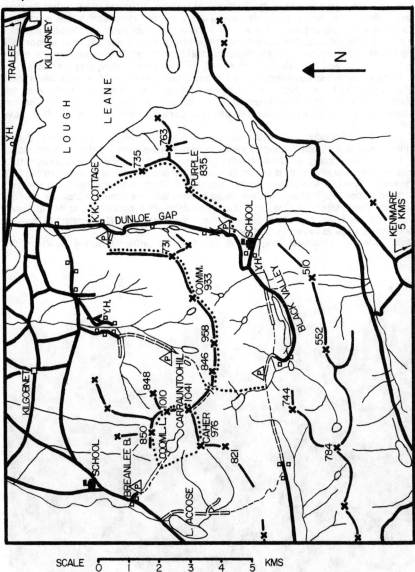

## Snowdon, Cambrian Mountains, Wales, UK

In the extreme northwest of Wales, and in the Cambrian Mountains, lies the highest mountain in Wales, Mt. Snowdon, 1985 meters. Of course it's not a high mountain, but it's famous, and a lot of people get to the top, either walking or riding the train.

Mt. Snowdon is now within the boundaries of the Snowdonia National Park. This national park includes a greater part of the Cambrian Mountains, the name of which has geologic connotations. The national park was created late in Welch history, so this area is not to be confused with national parks in other parts of the world, which have a wilderness aspect.

One can reach the top of Snowdon by using one of two different methods; ride a train or walk. For tourists there's a train running to the summit via Llanberis, with four stations enroute. Hikers or climbers can walk, despite the "iron horse", as there's a trail along side the tracks.

There's another trail beginning at the youth hostel on the east side of the mountain, marked 356 meters. On the southeast side, a trail begins near Plas Gwylnant. On the west and southwest sides, trails begin at Rhyd-Ddu, F. Uchaf, and the youth hostel near Llyn Cwellyn. There's at least five different routes. The climb can be made in one day from any of the above trails.

Just north of Snowdon, lies a 1000 meter summit named G. Fawr. It and two other peaks are in the center of a triangle formed by three mountain rescue posts, as shown on the map.

To the north of this group is the second highest peak of the Cambrians, C. Llywelyn, 1062 meters. There are several trails to near its summit, but one can also climb without a trail from the rescue post to the southwest. At the summit of F. Grach is a mountain hut or shelter.

If one is interested in obtaining maps, books or other literature about the Snowdon area, be sure and stop in Llanberis. One can find an information office, bookstores, as well as supermarkets in this tourist town. Rain gear is perhaps the most essential equipment to have, as Snowdon is know to have very bad weather.

**Map:** Snowdonia National Park, 1 : 126,720, from the Ordnance Survey, Southampton, England.

A typical scene in any mountains in the UK(Cairn Gorm).

# Map 14-3, Snowdon, Cambrian Mts., Wales, UK

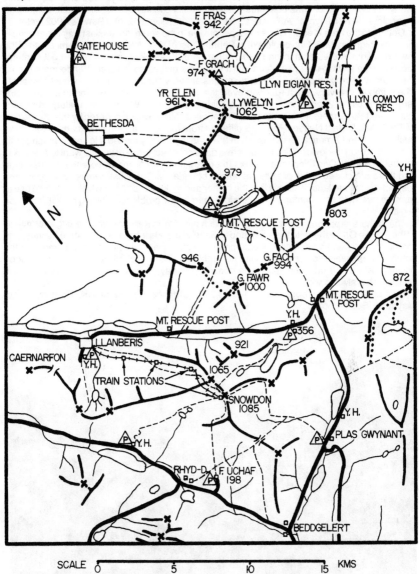

F. FRAS 942
GATEHOUSE
F. GRACH 974
LLYN EIGIAN RES.
YR ELEN 961
C. LLYWELYN 1062
LLYN COWLYD RES.
BETHESDA
979
N
MT. RESCUE POST
803
946
G. FACH 994
G. FAWR 1000
872
MT. RESCUE POST
MT. RESCUE POST
Y.H.
356
CAERNARFON
LLANBERIS
Y.H.
921
TRAIN STATIONS
1065
SNOWDON 1085
Y.H.
PLAS GWYNANT
Y.H.
RHYD-D
F. UCHAF 198
BEDDGELERT

SCALE  0        5        10        15  KMS

## Scafell, Lakes District, England, U.K.

This map covers the heart of the area known as The Lakes District. The Lakes District is located in northwest England, not far south of Scotland. More precisely, it's in the area between Motorway 6 (M-6) and the west coast, and to the south of the large city of Carlisle. These hills are called the Cumbrian Mountains, and reach their highest point in a peak called Scafell Pike at an altitude of 977 meters. The elevation is certainly not high by anyones standards, but they are some of the highest and best preserved hill sections in the UK. Other notable summits or highpoints are Helvellyn, at 949 meters; High Stile, 806; Pillar, 892; and Bow Fell, 902 meters.

Getting to the area is easy. Since most people live in the south, the easiest way to get there is via Superhighway M-6. One could exit at Penrith, east of Keswick, or get off not far south of the town of Windermere, located on Lake Windermere. Keswick is probably the most centrally located large town in the Lakes Area, but it's also the biggest tourist trap. Windermere is much the same way-very "touristy." These mountains are very subdued because of past glaciation. The summits are very much rounded over, the valleys are "U" shaped and there are many large valley lakes: Windermere, Ullswater, Thirlmere, Derwent Water, Wast Water, Crummock Water, and Buttermere, just to name the larger ones. All the region covered by this map is part of The Lakes District National Park. It's different from national parks in other parts of the world, such as in North America, in that much of the area is privately owned. However, much of this private land is in the lower valley bottoms and does not effect those of us who want to hill-walk in the back country. One thing to remember, there are many trails, many more than on this map, and there are closed gates or styles at fenced boundarys. One must always close gates and respect the private land. It seems that the higher and rocky parts, those which have little use to farmers, are held as common land, therefore there's few problems in hiking or walking these regions.

The authors experience went like this: He hitch hiked from Keswick, after getting information at the Tourist Office there, to the south and to Seathwaite. He left his pack in some bushes, and climbed in the rain and clouds to the summit of Scafell. He then returned and camped to the south of Seathwaite for one night with no problems. Then hitched out the next day. Good hitching. Any climb on the map can be done in one day. Take a waterproof tent and good raingear. It's always wet.

**Map:** Lakes District Tourist Map, 1 : 63,360, Ordance Survey of UK, Romsey Road, Maybush, Southampton.

This valley is just north of Scafell Pike. The main trailhead.

# Map 15-3, Scafell, Lakes District, England, UK

## Ben Nevis, Scotland, UK

In all of Scotland and Great Britain the highest summit is Ben Nevis, 1343 meters. This mountain is very near the city of Fort Williams, which in turn is located at the head of Loch Linnhe, near the west coast of Scotland. From Fort Williams, it's about 166 kms to Glasgow to the south, and about 125 kms to Inverness to the northeast.

Getting to Fort Williams is easy. Most tourists (and there's a lot of them), drive their own cars. This should make auto stopping good, but it's a little slow, as cars are often full. The other most popular way is by train. There's a new station, complete with shower facilities, at Fort Williams.

The "tourist route" up Ben Nevis, is via Fort Williams, a farm and parking lot called Achintee, then up a good trail on the west side of the mountian to the summit. One can also get on this same trail from the campground, caravan (trailer) park and youth hostel, as shown on the map. This is one of the most climbed mountians in the world.

To get to the northeast face, and the mountain rescue hut, there's a trail beginning on Highway A-82, just northeast of Fort Williams. It's this northeast face that has been the training ground for many of the great British climbers. On top is an old observatory, now in ruins, and a number of cairns.

Even if you're taking the "tourist route" go prepared for very cold and windy conditions near the top. Rain gear and gloves are essential. The west coast of Scotland has some of the worst weather conditions of any place in the world. Because of its northerly latitude—it can snow at the summit year-round.

In the vicinity of Fort Williams, there are a number of caravan parks, campgrounds and youth hostels. July and August are the warmest months—but are also the most *crowded*.

The map shows other summits in the region. Each peak will have some very easy routes, as well as some more difficult. Fort Williams has a tourist office at the R.R. station and bookstores which sell good maps and guidebooks. There's several supermarkets in town as well.

**Map:** Ben Nevis and Glen Coe, 1 : 63,360, from the Ordnance Survey, Southampton, England.

This steep gully leading off the summit is a winter challenge.

# Map 16-1, Ben Nevis, Scotland, UK

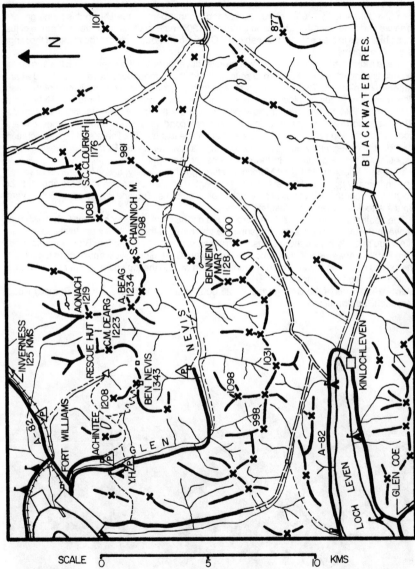

## Cairn Gorm, Grampian Mts., Scotland, UK

If we eliminate Ben Nevis, the highest summit in all of the UK, we would have the high tops in the Grampian Mountains of central Scotland as the highest. These Grampian Mountains are located in the north of Scotland, not far to the southeast of the city of Inverness, and to the west of Aberdeen. Closer to the area are the towns of Aviemore and Braemar. These two towns are both on this map.

The best known summit in the entire region is Cairn Gorm, at 1245 meters. But the highest is Ben Macdui rising to 1309 meters, the second highest peak in the UK. In this same general area we find a number of high tops in excess of 1200 meters. On some maps the name of just these high tops in the center of the map is the Cairn Gorm Mountains, but the whole of the range is the Grampians.

These mountains are made mostly of granite, but absent are the sheer pinnicles and spires we usually find in association with granite. Instead, these mountains have been rounded and flattened by glaciers. There are some steep sided canyons, mostly in the center of the map. These small rock outcroppings are used by rock climbers, and are similar to Ben Nevis in the area of Fort William. Even though the elevations are low, this is a northern latitude range, and at 57 degrees north one must expect very sevier winter conditions. Even in summer snow can and does fall on the top peaks. In fact, the weather can be just terrible. There's lots of preciptation, strong winds—espicially up high, and cool or cold temperatures. Remember these factors, especially if you're going out in the mountains for the night.

Between Aviemore and Loch Morlich and through all this valley, and in the area of Braemar, one finds many hectors of forests. Some are planted coniferous trees and others appear to be the natural vegetation, but this is only in the valley bottoms. Treeline is only about 500 meters. So it's a rocky, barren and desolate place.

The easiest approach is via Aviemore, found on the main highway number A-9, which runs between Perth, near Dundee in the south, to Inverness in the north. It's relatively easy to get lifts if you're on foot. And there's bus and train service too. If coming into Braemar, use roads from Perth and Aberdeen. If at Aviemore and you want Cairn Gorm, walk and hitch to the base of the ski lifts on the north slope of the mountain, then walk to the top on trails. Near the summit is an inn with food and drinks.

**Map:** High Tops of the Cairngorms, 1 : 25,000, from the Ordnance Survey, Romsey Road, Maybush, Southampton.

Cairn Gorm is near the center of foto. From Aviemore.

## Map 17-3, Cairn Gorm, Grampian Mts., Scotland, UK

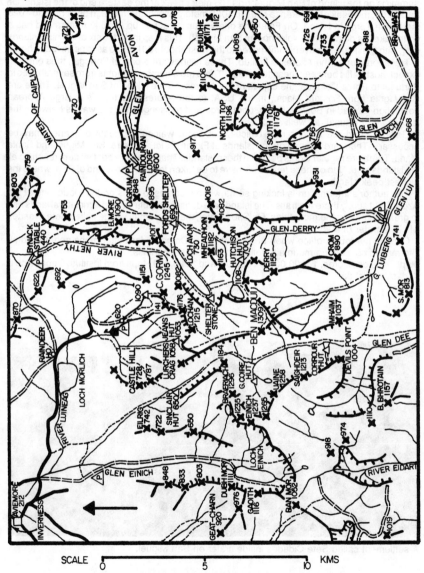

SCALE 0 · · · · 5 · · · · 10 KMS

## Volcan Pico, Isla Pico, Azores Islands, Portugal

The Azores Islands are located about 1600 kms east of Portugal and are a province or state of that country. This group of nine islands lie on, or just east, of the Mid-Atlantic Ridge. All the islands are volcanic and are a direct result of the activities of this great ridge. The highest summit lies on the island of Pico, that being Volcan Pico, 2321 meters. The second highest summit is on the island of San Miguel; an 1105 meter peak at the eastern end of the island. On Sao Jorge, the peak of Esperanza rises to 1066 meters, while another high peak rises to 1023 meters on Terceira Island. On Faial, the one volcano reaches up to 1043 meters and has a crater lake (as do two other volcanos on San Miguel). This map includes six of the nine islands only, with San Miguel conveniently moved to the west about 100 kms so as to be included here.

Transportation to the Azores is limited. These islands are a part of Portugal, thus one can expect most traffic between these two areas. There are a number of flights from several cities in Portugal to Ponta Delgada, the capital of the Azores, on the island of San Miguel. There are also flights from Boston, Mass., in the USA, to the Azores—as there's a large Azorean population located in Boston. Boats, both cargo and passenger, ply the waters between the islands and Portugal, as well.

Getting arond the islands isn't difficult, but some waiting for boats or planes may be necessary. There are airports on the islands of Flores, Faial, Terceira, Sao Miguel and Santa Maria. There are regular flights between these islands. There's a ferry boat system reaching all the islands also. One of these ferries will have to be taken to reach the island of Pico, where the highest peak stands.

The author's information is lacking some when it comes to trails on the mountains of the Azores, but surely there are trails. The islands are densely populated and agricultural lands rise to great heights on the mountains. On Sao Miguel, there's a small village called Sete Cidades within a crater of a volcano.

Contact the tourist office when arriving at Ponta Delgada, for better maps and additional information concerning mountain trails and ferryboat schedules.

**Map:**  Isla do Azores, 1 : 200,000, 1 : 50,000, and 1 : 25,000 Maps from Instituto Geografico e Cadastral, Lisboa.

A settlement called Sete Cidades inside crater on San Miguel.

# Map 18-3, Pico, Isla Pico, Azores Isl., Portugal

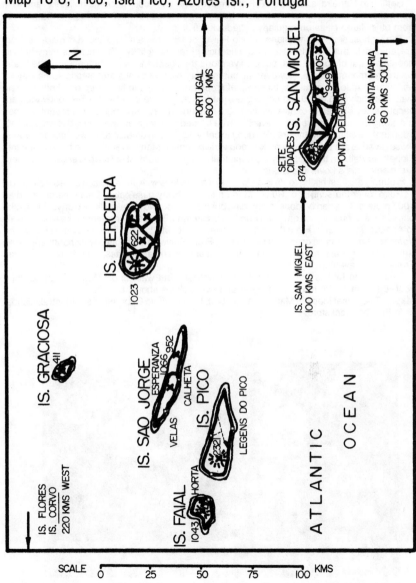

# Ruivo, Madeira Island, Portugal

The map shown here is of the small and remote island called Madeira. Madeira belongs to Portugal and is located several hundred kms southwest of Lisboa and some distance to the north of the Canary Islands. It sits alone with no other island neighbors, and is volcanic in orgin as are all of the middle and north Atlantic islands.

Getting to Madeira is easy but a bit expensive. One can book "package holidays" and fly in from most European capitals, or fly from New York, Portugal, London, Madrid, the Canarys, or from other large cities on regularly schedualed flights.

The highest peak on the island is Pico Ruivo, at 1861 meters. The island is made up from volcanic rock, but there is little or no evidence of recent activity. The island is fairly heavily populated, but of course most people live along the coast and not in the center of the island where the mountains are. However, all but the very highest slopes are used in some way for agriculture. At low elevations, all forms of crops are grown, and higher up one finds grazing livestock, including goats. Something unique to Madeira are its levadas. These levadas are various sized ditches or canals, which begin at springs or streams high on the mountain, then run along a contour line to areas which can be farmed and irrigated. Many levades are at about 1000 meters altitude. Many are also used to carry water to hydroelectric power stations. Along these levadas are trails which make good walking paths. Many levadas have been made into tunnels as well. On the map only the main trail around the summit of Ruivo is shown, but there are many trails all over the island.

Probably the best hiking route is as follows. It's a 16 kms walk from a place called Achada do Teixeiro, over the summit of Ruivo, then on to a highway pass called Encumeada, listed as 1007 meters. This can be done in one day, but most hikers would take it in two days. First, take one of several buses each day from Funchal to Santana. Then one can either take a taxi or walk to Achada do Teixeiro. From there to Pico Ruivo is about 5½ kms. There's a small hut not far from the summit that is open and free to use. From Ruivo, one can also walk south and climb Arieiro, 1800 meters, or continue on to the west and end up at the pass, or perhaps Curral Das Freiras or Boaventura.

Best time to hike is from March through October, but walking on Madeira can be done year-round. In cooler months, raingear and warm cloths should be taken.

**Map:**  Two-sheet maps of Maderia, 1 : 50,000, from Instituto Geografico e Cadastral, Lisboa, or in Funchal bookstores.

Typical Lavada or small canal makes an interesting hiking path.

Map 19-3, Ruivo, Madeira Island, Portugal

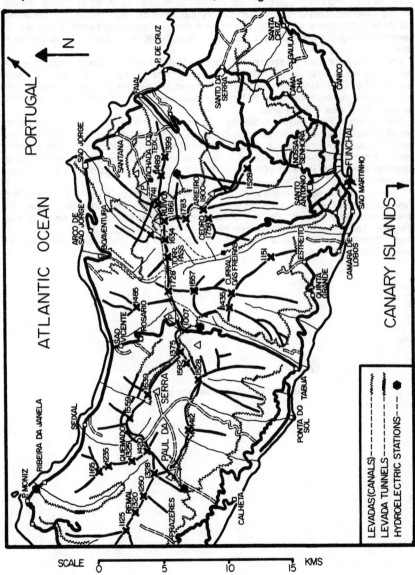

## Machachos, La Palma Island, Canary Islands

The Canary Islands, lying off the west coast of Morocco, but belonging to Spain, has seven main islands, all of which have been created by volcanic eruptions. The second highest mountain in the Canary's is Machachos, 2426 meters, on the island of La Palma. La Palma lies at the western end of the Canary group, and can be reached by ferries from other islands, namely Tenerife (Santa Cruz) and Gran Canary (Las Palmas). Also, one can fly to the island, but those flights come from other islands—the two previously mentioned. There are no international flights going directly to La Palma. Most flights to the Canary Islands begin in Spain.

Machachos is simply the highest point on the rim of an old volcano. A better way to describe this feature would be to call it a caldera—as that's the name given to the huge, 6 km wide chasm, at the center of the island. Most of the rim lies at, or above, the 2000 meter elevation. On the rim is a trail, beginning at the Refugio Forestal, and continuing north, then circling and decending just west of Los Lianos.

There are many approaches to the highest part. Perhaps the normal or most used route would be via El Paso, La Cumbrecita, the crater rim, and around to Machachos. One can also use the route passing through the small village of La Caldera. Still another possibility would be to walk right from the town of Las Nieves. This is a longer route with more vertical rise. A strong hiker can walk from El Paso to La Cumbricita, the crater rim, Machachos, down the west side of the crater and back to El Paso—in one long day.

There is some live water—a stream, in the heart of the caldera, but no water anywhere else. Take your own. All precipitation comes during the winter months, from November to May. The remainder of the year is very dry. Any of the towns named on the map have stores for food shopping. For further information, locate the tourist office in Santa Cruz.

**Map:** Generalkarte Tenerife(La Plama-Hierro-Gomera), 1 : 150,000, Mairs Geofraphischer Verlag, Stuttgart, Germany.

Got a foto? Please send to author.

# Map 20-3, Machachos, La Palma Isl., Canary Islands

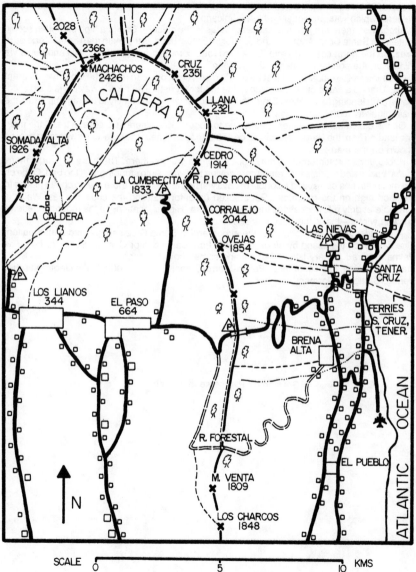

2028

2366

MACHACHOS
2426

CRUZ
2351

LA CALDERA

LLANA
2321

SOMADA ALTA
1926

CEDRO
1914

1387

LA CUMBRECITA
1833

R. P. LOS ROQUES

LA CALDERA

CORRALEJO
2044

LAS NIEVAS

OVEJAS
1854

SANTA
CRUZ

LOS LIANOS
344

EL PASO
664

FERRIES
S. CRUZ,
TENER.

BRENA
ALTA

EL PUEBLO

N

R. FORESTAL

M. VENTA
1809

ATLANTIC OCEAN

LOS CHARCOS
1848

SCALE    0          5          10   KMS

## Pico de Teida, Tenerife Island, Canary Islands

The highest mountain in Spanish Territory (including Spain itself) lies on the island of Tenerife in the Canary Islands. The mountain is Pico de Teida, at 3718 meters.

The Canary Islands are a group of 7 major islands which have developed as a result of volcanism. It's likely that at one time the highest summit on Tenerife was much higher than at present. The summits indicated on the map are those remaining peaks of an old and eroded caldera, which was previously a higher volcano.

Altogether, there are four main access routes to the caldera. One is a high mountain scenic route from Santa Cruz. Another, and possibly the most used, is the main road from Puerto de la Cruz, on the north coast of Tenerife. A third road comes in from Chio and still another is via Vilaflor on the southern flanks of the volcano.

Once inside the caldera and just below Pico de Teida, one can reach the top in two different ways. There's a cable car or lift going to the top for tourists. The hiker's way is via a dirt road, then a path leading to the Hielo Cave, the Refugio Altavista, and finally to the summit. From the main highway to the top is only 5 kms.

On the old caldera rim, where peaks rise to about 2500 meters, are several trails, the main one leading from the Parador Nacional de Las Canadas to near the hotel and swimming pool as shown on the map.

Public transportation may or may not exist when you get there. There are of course many tourist buses and tourists with rental cars driving that way. Auto stopping isn't too bad. Once on the mountain one can spend a couple of days walking around, but there are no cheap places to get food high on the mountain. Get stocked up before leaving the coastal cities. Water is available at only a few locations inside the caldera. Higher locations of the mountain receive snow in winter—that's the busy tourist season.

The tourist information offices at the airport and in Santa Cruz can give more informaiton. One can reach the island by air or ferry boat from Barcelona or Cadiz in Spain, or from Las Palma on Gran Canary Island, but nothing comes from Morocco.

**Map:**   Generalkarte Tenerife(La Palma-Hierro-Gomera), 1 : 150,000, Mairs Geofraphischer Verlag, Stuttgart, Germany.

Got a foto? Please send to author.

## Map 21-3, Teide, Tenerife Isl., Canary Islands

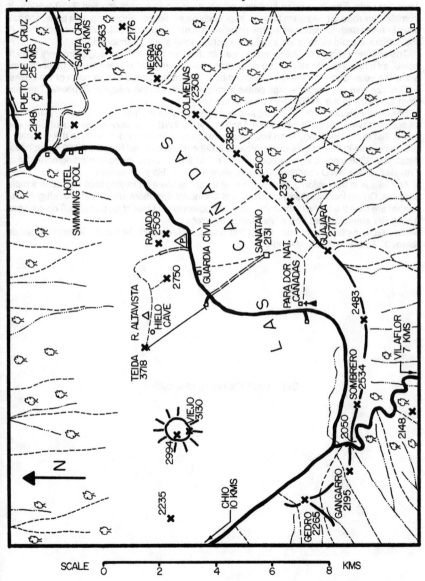

# Mulhacen, Sierra Nevada, Spain

The highest peak in Europe, outside the Alps, is in southern Spain and in the Sierra Nevada. This peak is known as Mulhacen, listed as being 3478 meters. To some people's surprise it's higher than any peak of the Pyrenees. It's located just southeast of the famous city of Granada.

There are a couple of main access routes to this mountain range. Perhaps best is the road from Granada. This is a good highway which leads up to a pass marked 3150 meters. In summer this road is used quite heavily, especially on weekends. From near this pass, one can walk in an easterly direction along the ridge crest, until the summit of Mulhacen is reached. At the top are the old ruins of an early observatory, long since abandoned.

The southern slopes of Mulhacen, as well as all other peaks in the range, are very easy to scale, as it has a gentle slope. The north faces are much steeper however, some containing snow the year-round. The only difficult climbing is from the cirque basins north of the peaks.

One can also approach the high peaks from the south, and the village of Capileira. The road from Capileira to the 3150 meter pass is not for the ordinary car.

Still another route from the south, and perhaps the "ruta normal" for Mulhacen, is from the village of Trevelez, at 1476 meters. Find and follow the 4WD road running west out of town, and follow that to the ridge top. Then walk along the crest of the ridge due north to the summit.

Other peaks in the range include: Veleta, 3392 meters, climbed from the 3150 meter pass; Alcazaba, 3366 meters, can be scaled from either Mulhacen or the road running north out of Trevelez, or the 4WD road heading southeast from the Hotel Alhambra.

Any village in the region of this map has at least one store for buying food and other simple supplies. On old Instituto Geografico maps of the mountains, there are shown two refugios, but neither are near the highest summits—they are obviously not meant for climbers. The area has a long dry summer from about May through October.

**Map:** Guejar sierra, Lanjaron, 1 : 50,000, Instituto Geografico National, General Ibanez de Ibero, 3, Apartado 3007, Madrid-3.

Got a foto? Please send to author.

# Map 22-3, Mulhacen, Sierra Nevada, Spain

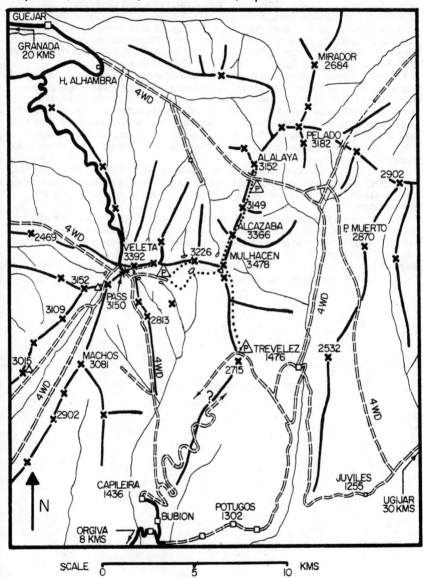

GUEJAR

GRANADA
20 KMS

H. ALHAMBRA

4WD

MIRADOR
2684

PELADO
3182

ALALAYA
3152

2902

4WD

2469

3149

ALCAZABA
3366

P. MUERTO
2870

VELETA
3392

3226

MULHACEN
3478

3152

PASS
3150

2813

3109

3015

MACHOS
3081

4WD

4WD

TREVELEZ
1476

2532

2715

4WD

2902

CAPILEIRA
1436

JUVILES
1255

UGIJAR
30 KMS

N

POTUGOS
1302

BUBION

ORGIVA
8 KMS

SCALE 0          5          10  KMS

# Tiro de Santiago, Picos de Europa, Spain

If you're traveling Europe and would like something a little different than the Alps or even the Pyrenees, you might try the Picos de Europa. This group or massif is located about halfway between Santander and Gijon. The mountain range along that coast is known as the Cordillera Cantabrica, and follows the coast from the end of the Pyrenees to the northwest corner of Spain. The Picos de Europa, located near the center, forms the highest section.

While some maps show Torro de Cerrado, at 2648 meters, as being the highest peak, the maps used by the author indicate that Tiro de Santiago, at 2670, is the highest of the group (there could be a misprint, as some people aren't happy with the Spanish maps). At any rate, there are several summits over 2600 meters, with some interesting hiking and climbing in the area. Few people outside Spain know of, or visit, this mountain region.

With the mountains so close to the coast, one could probably enjoy the trip more if a southerly approach were used. It's recommended to take the route from Potes, Espinama, and to Fuente (which is the end of the road and where a teleiferico is located). From this place, all the high peaks can be climbed, at least those east of the Rio Cares. Maps show 5 refugios or huts in this group, which means during the summer months a fair amount of visitors are in the area. From the Cabana Veronica (it's the refugio between Santiago and Blanca), any of the peaks can be reached in one day. One can also reach this same area from Arenas, on one of two routes leading south from that town.

To the west of the Santiago group is another high area, with the highest peak being Peña Santa, 2596 meters. It can be reached easiest from Soto, but the Instituto Geografico Nacional maps don't show that route accurately. The trails from Lago de Enol and from Cain de Abajo are more definite.

Count on the weather in the Pico de Europa being similar to the Pyrenees, but with more cloudiness and rain. The summer months are however, generally stable and dry. For best food selection, shop in some bigger town before reaching these mountains, as there are only villages in the immediate area of the peaks.

**Map:** Macizo Occidental and Naranjo de Bulnes, 1 : 25,000, Editorial Alpina, Apartado de Carreos 3, Granollers(Barcelona), España.

Got a foto? Please send to author.

# Map 23-3, Santiago, Picos De Europa, Spain

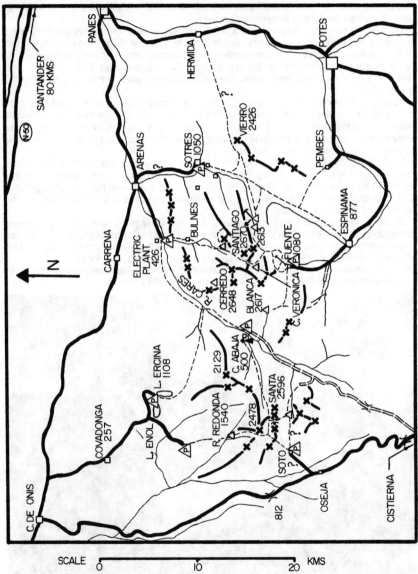

## Vignemale, Pyrenees Mountains, France-Spain

The map shown here is the first of 4 maps covering the Pyrenees Mountains which form the border between France and Spain. Included on this map are: Pic du Midi D'Ossau, 2884 meters, in the western portion; centrally located Balaitous, 3144 meters; and in the eastern portion of the map, Vignemale, 3298 meters, one of the better known peaks in all the Pyrenees. As with most of the Pyrenees Mountains, the rock make-up in this section is largely metamorphic, caused by the folding of the earth's crust.

The western half of this map includes a couple of lower passes, which have good highways built over them and even one railway tunnel (this one beneath the Col du Somport). As a result of these passes, access to the region is good. Any mountain summit included on this map can be climbed in one day from the trailhead at the end of the nearest road. This area is a skier's paradise, with at least four large resorts, three of which are located on the Spanish side of the border.

Access roads, trails and refuges are much more developed on the north or French side, than the Spanish side. On this map, there are almost no refugios on the southern slopes. It must be noted too that the most difficult climbing routes are nearly always on the north faces, where snow and glaciers have a chance to accumulate. The southern faces are generally more gently sloping and, of course, sunnier and drier.

To climb Vignemale, one can approach the mountains from Cauterets and Pont D'Espagne. From Pont, there's a well used trail to the east face of Vignemale and a couple of nearby refuges. This trail is part of the Grande Randonnee (GR), a series of trails linked together to form one long walk from the Atlantic to the Mediterranean coasts. Vignemale can also be reached via Torla on the Spanish side.

Balaitous can be approached about equally well from Gallego on the south or from Arrens and Migouelo on the north. Like Vignemale, Balaitous too has some small glaciers. To help you decide which route is best, contact people at a nearby refuge—they are normally the best source of information. Ice equipment is needed on some routes, but not all.

**Map:**  Pau-Bagneres de Lucho, #70, 1 : 100,000, from the Institut Geographique National, Service des Ventes et Editions, 107, Rue La Boetie, 75008 Paris.

This is a view of the North Face of Vignemale.

# Map 24-2, Vignemale, Pyrenees Mts., France-Spain

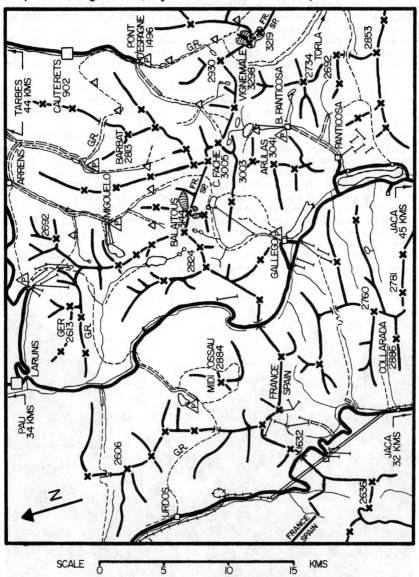

SCALE  0    5    10    15    KMS

## Perdido, Pyrenees Mountains, France-Spain

The second map in the series covering the major mountain summits in the Pyrenees Mountains, covers the peaks forming the Cirque du Gavarnie, Perdido (the highest peak on this map and the third highest in the Pyrenees), at 3355 meters, and the peak Lustou, 3023 meters.

On the south or Spanish side of the mountains, few large settlements exist, while on the north, or French side, there are several larger towns and small cities. They are Cauterets, Luz, Gavarnie, and Saulan. All these towns are built around tourism, especially Cauterets and Gavarnie (the most famous of all).

Most of the high peaks are within relatively easy reach of the tourist town of Gavarnie, so logically, this is the best place to begin a climb. Peaks such as Taillon, 3144 meters, and Marbore, 3248 meters, form part of the most famous cirque in the world. They, and even Perdido, can be reached from Gavarnie.

If you're looking for easier routes up these peaks of the cirque, it's best to go to the Spanish side. To climb Perdido, the easiest route would be from Bielsa, and Pineta, where there's a tourist hotel. Another possibility is via Broto and Torla, then up the canyon to the refugio—as shown on the map.

For the most part, the French side of the mountain is by far the most developed, with many ski resorts, hotels, restaurants, and refuges. Few mountain refugios exist on the Spanish side. The French side also has more and better developed roads and trails.

Keep in mind, if you're camping on the French side, a large part of the western half of this map is part of the Parc National des Pyrenees, and camping is forbidden. However, bivouacking (putting a tent up at night and removing it the next morning) is condoned.

If you plan to spend some time in the mountains, buy your groceries in Luz or Saulan. Higher up, the selection is poor and expensive. For the best information concerning trails, refuges, camping and routes, consult the tourist offices in the larger towns, especially Gavarnie, and the refuges in the mountains.

**Map:**  Pau-Bagneres de Lucho, #70, 1 : 100,000, from the French Institut Geographique National, Service des Ventes et Editions, 107, Rue La Boetie 75008 Paris.

Due south of Gavarne is the Cirque du Gavarne.

# Map 25-1, Perdido, Pyrenees Mts., France-Spain

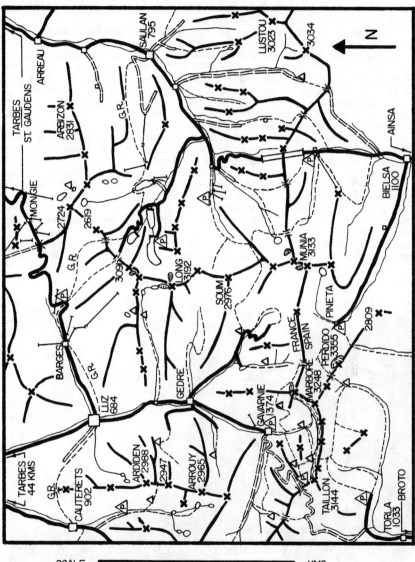

SCALE
0    5    10    15    KMS

## Pico Aneto, Pyrenees Mountains, Spain

Very near the geographic center of the Pyrenees Mountains stands the highest summit in the entire range, Pico Aneto, 3404 meters. As one might expect, most of the high peaks are on the boundary line between France on the north and Spain on the south. In most cases this is true, but in the region this map covers, the international boundary does not follow the line of highest peaks or the natural watershed. In the area of Luchon, the boundary turns north, then east, which puts the Vall D'Aran in Spain, not France.

Pico Aneto, and Posets, 3375 meters (the second highest peak in the Pyrenees) both lie south of the international boundary and the watershed and are within the boundaries of Spain.

The normal route for those climbing Aneto, is via Benasque and the Refugio Renclusa. From this last of several refugios on the mountain, the climb is made in one day. Enroute to the summit, a glacier must be crossed, so an ice ax and crampons are needed. It can also be climbed from the Refugio Cabana, located on the main highway, southeast of the peak.

To climb Posets, one has a choice of two routes. There's a trail from the village of Eriste (about 3 kms below Benasque), running to the northwest, then up either the south ridge or the east face of the mountain. Another route begins about 3 or 4 kms above Benasque. This trail begins at an old work camp, and follows the stream to the Refugio del Cantal. From that area to the top is a rough trail up a north faceing gully. To climb the south ridge, no special equipment is needed but the north route may require ice ax and crampons.

The only large towns in the immediate area are Benasque and Luchon. These are the best places to buy food and get the latest information about the conditions of the area. Each of these towns is big enough to have bookstores which sell more detailed maps of the region.

Winter time brings heavy precipitation, but the summers tend to be very dry and sunny. Expect slightly better weather on the southern slopes. One should also expect less improved roads and facilities on the Spanish side.

**Map:** La Vall D' Aran, Maladeta-Aneto, and Posets, 1 : 25,000, from Editorial Alpina, apartado de Correos 3, Granollers(Barcelona), Espana. Also, St. Gaudens Andorre, #71, from the Institut Geographique National, Service des Ventes et Editions, 107, Rue La Boetie, 75008 Paris.

Just south of Oo are interesting lakes and Mt. Perdiguru.

# Map 26-1, Aneto, Pyrenees Mts., Spain

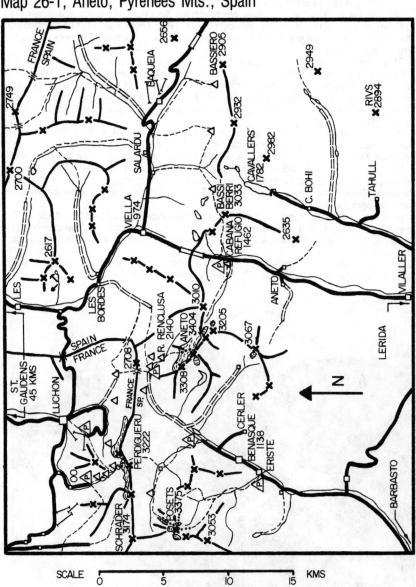

SCALE

0    5    10    15    KMS

## Estats, Pyrenees Mountains, France-Spain

This is the fourth map covering the higher portion of the Pyrenees Mountains. This map is centered on the tiny Republic of Andorra, which sits on the mountain tops between France and Spain. This country uses currency from both its neighbors, and both French and Spanish are national languages. Nowadays, the entire economy of Andorra is based on tourism.

The highest peak in the area does not border on Andorra, but France and Spain. Pico D'Estats, at 3141 meters, is the highest summit east of Pico Aneto. Estats can be reached from the north or south, with the northern route being used most, as there are more alpinists in France than in Spain.

This northern route is via Vicdessos, Auzat, Marc and finally up a road to where water is diverted into an electric plant pipeline. The trail passes several old stone huts, which can be used for free (but often aren't real good shelters, especially when it's raining), then it rises to the top of Mont Calm and finally to the top of Estats. It's a long one day hike from the area around Marc, so most people camp in the higher meadows. Vicdessos or Auzat are both good places to buy food.

From the south or Spanish side, Estats can be climbed via Sort, Alins, Areu and the head of that valley. Trails are shown beginning at the end of the road, but may or may not be in good condition. However, even if there's no trail, it's easy traveling in open country at that elevation.

Not far to the east of Pic D'Estats, is a high area with three large reservoirs and a number of good peaks. The refuge at the end of the trail above Cayane, is a popular place for hikers and climbers. These higher peaks, including Pic du Port, 2903 meters, can be climbed most easily from the Andorra side.

Access to most of the higher mountains on this map can be reached best from Andorra. The town of Andorra is a good place to buy detailed maps and get the latest information on trails, camping, the refuges, etc. There are no ice or snow routes in these parts, so only good boots are needed.

**Map:** St. Gaudens-Andorra, #71, 1 : 100,000, from the Institut Geographique National, Service des Ventes et Editions, 107, Rue La Boetie, 75008 Paris.

From the top of Mont Calm we see Estats to the North.

## Map 27-1, Estats, Pyrenees Mts., France-Spain

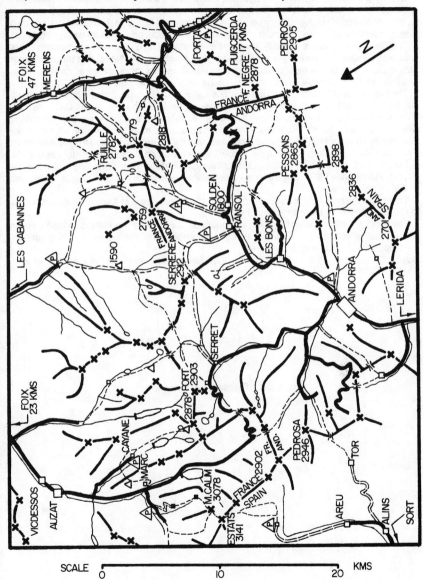

SCALE
0    10    20    KMS

## Monte Cinto, Corsica, France

In the Mediterranean Sea, southeast of France, is the French Island of Corse, or Corsica. This island is very mountainous, having peaks ranging up to 2710 meters, in Monte Cinto. Two maps will be used to cover the high mountains of this island.

Getting to Corse is not difficult. First, go to France. There are flights, from Nice and Marseille, to the airports at either Ajaccio or Bastia, the two largest cities on the island. Also, there are a number of ferries. Year-round ferry service is from Nice and Marseille, to the two main ports of Corse; Ajaccio and Bastia. Seasonal ferries sail from Toulon, on the south coast of France.

The climate of Corse is typically Mediterranean; that is, long, hot, and dry summers, and cool, wet, winters. The time of year with the heaviest percipitation is November through March. May or June may be the most pleasant time to visit Corse, as there are fewer tourists, cooler weather, and a little snow left on the mountains for a refreshing drink.

The highest peak is Cinto, 2710 meters. The easiest way to make this climb is via Calacuccia, the village of Lozzi, and past three bergeries, or refuges, one of which is Cesta, at 1575 meters. From there it's an easy climb to the top. Another route is via Asco, and Haut Asco, where is located a ski lift. From this valley one can use the route from the ski lift, or the one passing the Bergery Manica. Whichever route is used, it's a one day hike to the top and return. The north slopes of Cinto are the most rugged, while the south slopes are mostly free of cliffs.

For those interested in longer hikes, rather than just climbing, there's one long trail, called the Grande Randonnee (GR). This trail begins at Calenzana, passes Col de Vizzayona, and ends at Conca, far to the south.

Towns in the immediate area are small, but food can be bought at Asco or Calacuccia. Best to stock up at one of the main coastal cities.

There's one rail line linking the north and south coasts, but one would have to take a bus or auto stop to get near the mountains. Lots of young people are on the highways auto stopping in the busiest months of July and August.

**Map:**   Corse Nord, #73, 1 : 100,000, from IGN, Service des Ventes et Editions, 107, Rue La Boetie, 75008 Paris.

Got a foto? Please send to author.

## Map 28-3, Cinto, Corsica, France

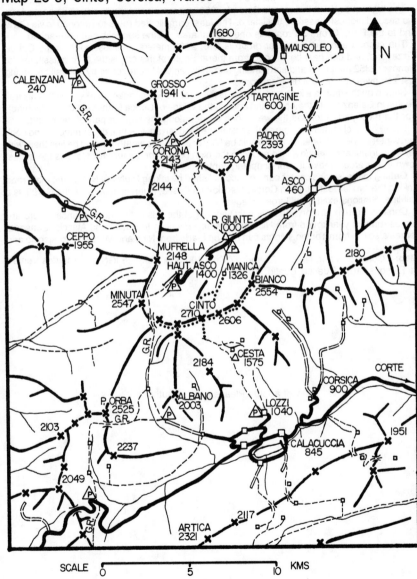

SCALE 0 ——— 5 ——— 10 KMS

# Rotondo, Corsica, France

Not many people consider the French Island of Corsica as much of a place for mountaineering, but the mountains there will surprise most travelers. This is the second of two maps covering the high peaks of the island. This map covers three groups, not far south of the highest summit on Corse, Cinto, 2710 meters.

The highest peak on this map is Rotondo, 2622 meters. It and the surrounding peaks form the second highest massif on the island. The least complicated route to Rotondo is via Corte and to the Berg. Grottelli. From this one central area, all the summits can be reached.

The second and much smaller group is Oro, 2389 meters. It is just north of the Col de Vizzavona, and can best be climbed from there. South of this col, is the third massif, that of Renoso, 2352 meters. It and surrounding summits can best be reached by the trail beginning just southwest of the Col de Vizzavona.

Shown on the map is a long trail, known as the Grande Randonnee, marked "GR". This trail begins in Calenzana to the north, and ends at the village of Conca further south (off the map). For the most part, it follows the watershed divide, along the highest part of the island.

Corse has a climate the same as the rest of the Mediterranian—hot, dry summers, and cool, wet winters. The best time to climb would be May or June. The weather would be fine then, with fewer tourists, and maybe a little snow on the high peaks, for dry throats. Corte is the largest town in the area—make it your shopping center.

Getting to the islands center can be accomplished by taking Highway N-193, the main road linking the two largest cities on Corse, Ajaccio and Bastia. Running alongside the N-193, is a rail line. Stations exist at all larger villages.

Corse is French territory, and the only way to get there is to first go to France. There are ferries running year round from Nice and Marseille, sailing to Bastia and Ajaccio. Seasonal ferries also run from Toulon. Flights can also be made from Nice and Marseille, to Ajaccio and Bastia.

**Map:**  Corse Sud and Nord, #73 and #74, 1 : 100,000, from the IGN, Service des Ventes et Editions, 107, Rue La Boetie, 75008 Paris.

Got a foto? Please send to author.

# Map 29-3, Rotondo, Corsica, France

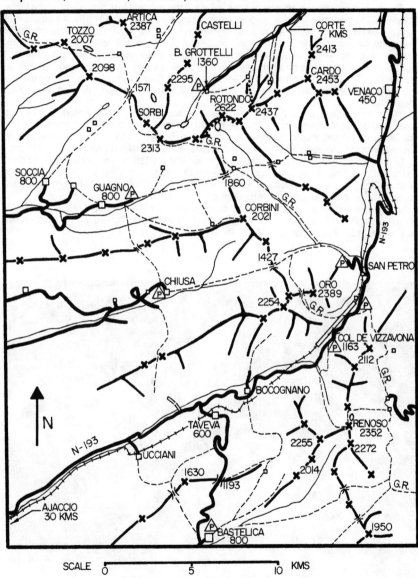

SCALE 0      5      10    KMS

## Argentera, Maritime Alps, France—Italy

From Mont Blanc, the highest mountain in Europe (located in the far northeast of France), to the Mediterranean Sea, the mountains gradually diminish in size. At a point about 50 kms from the sea, stands the most southerly "big mountain" in the Alps. This peak is Argentera, 3297 meters. Between it and the Mediterranean Sea there are no more 3000 meter peaks.

There are some definite advantages to climbing in this region. Most climbers go to the higher mountains further north for their holidays, so traffic on the trails is usually light. Argentera itself is fairly well known however, as it's on all highway maps of the region. A second advantage is the good weather in summertime. Long periods of sunny weather can be expected in the summer season. Almost all precipitation comes in the winter months in the form of snow.

The area around Argentera is rather isolated, as far as major highways and railways are concerned. The closest rail lines are in Nice, France and Cuneo in Italy. Buses can be taken to as far as St. Martin on the French side of the mountains. Auto stopping is rated fair in these parts.

In the immediate area of Argentera are several summits over 3000 meters. These high peaks can be approached best from the Italian side (as the entire mountain lies inside Italy) and the village of Valdieri, then to the Rifugios Remondino, Bozaro or Morelli. One can also ascend these peaks via Entraque and the Rifugio Genova, or on the French side by way of Boreon.

To the northwest of Argentera, is another 3000'er, Matto, 3088 meters. Climb it from Valdieri. In the southeast part of the map is another group of peaks—with Chafrion, 3073 meters, the highest. The basin which holds the Refuge Nice and a couple of lakes, would be a good location to place a camp and to make several climbs.

No real glaciers exist in the area, so all summits can be climbed without snow equipment.

**Map:**   Haut Pays Nicois, #9, 1 : 50,000, from the IGN and Didier Richard, Service des Ventes et Editions, 107, Rue La Boetie, 75008 Paris.

East Ridge of Weisshorn(Map 48).

## Map 30-3, Argentera, Maritime Alps, Fr-Italy

PAUR 2972

ISOLA 2000

3079

MATTO 3088

S. ANNA

FRANCE ITALY

VALDIERI 1368

CUNEO 35 KMS

R. BOZARO 2453

R. MORELLI 2400

ORIAL 2943

LANTOSQUE 13 KMS

BOREON

R. REMONDINO 2485

ARGENTERA 3297

NASTA 3108

IT. FR.

ENTRAQUE

ST. MARTIN

R. BOREON 1526

3054

R. GENOVA 1914

2987

R. COUGOURDE 2090

ITALY FR.

SAVINA 2821

G. VALERA

R. SORIA 1780

R. MADONE 1903

R. BIANCO

CHAFRION 3073

2549

R. PAGARI 2650

2828

CLAPIER 3045

LANTOSQUE 8 KMS

ST. GRAT

R. NICE 2232

R. VALMASQUE 2221

ITALY FRANCE

2755

SCALE    0         5         10   KMS

# Chambeyron, Cottian Alps, France—Italy

The mountains included on this map are of the southern part of the Cottian Alps. This area is about 100 kms from the Mediterranean on the Franch-Italian border. There are no really high peaks in the region, but a number of summits are over 3000 and up to 3400 meters. The highest summit is the Aiguille de Chambeyron, at 3412 meters. This peak is in France, but many peaks in the group are on the international frontier.

Getting into this area is reasonably easy. There are no railways close by—the closest being at Guillestre in France, and Cuneo, Italy. There's a major highway crossing the border at Col de Larche, which connects Barcelonnette and Cuneo. The area can also be reached from Guillestre and the Col de Vars.

The climate in the southern Cottian Alps is almost Mediterranean—that is, heavy snows or rain in winter, with long, dry, hot summers. One can expect long periods of good climbing weather during the summer months.

The best way to reach Chambeyron and others in that group is via St. Paul, Fouillouse and the Refuge Chambeyron. One could make a number of good climbs if a camp were set up near the lake above the refuge.

Another group of peaks nearly as high as Chambeyron, lie between Mortice and Font Sancte, 3169 and 3385 meters respectively. There are trails reaching the tops of these two summits. Font Sancte can be climbed from the Refuge Maljasset, while Mortice can be ascended from the same place or from Grande Serenne. There's also a trail running along the ridge crest, beginning at Col de Vars.

Most food and some supplies can be bought at Larche and Condamine-Chatelard, but for better selections stop in Barcelonnette. Shopping can also be done in Acceglio and Argentera, Italy. A bit further north is Briancon, where an alpin information office is located, as well as several large bookstores where detailed maps of this area can be found.

**Map:** Queyras and Haute Ubaye, #10, 1 : 50,000, from the IGN, and Didier and Richard, Service des Ventes et Editions, 107, Rue La Boetie, 75008 Paris.

North slopes of Pelvoux(Map 35).

# Map 31-3, Chambeyron, Cottian Alps, Fr-Italy

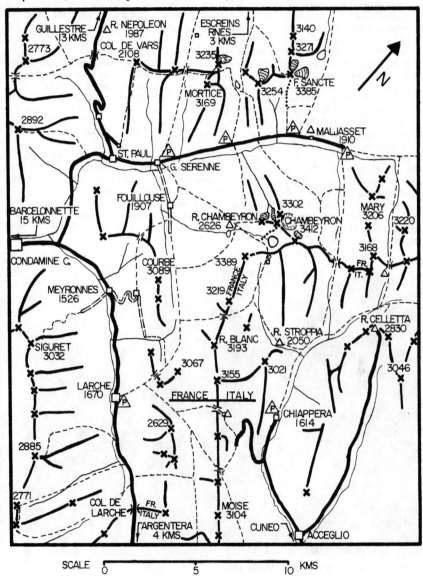

GUILLESTRE 13 KMS
2773
R. NEPOLEON 1987
COL DE VARS 2108
ESCREINS RNES 3 KMS
3235
3140
3271
MORTICE 3169
3254
F. SANCTE 3385
N
2892
MALJASSET 1910
ST. PAUL
G. SERENNE
P
P
BARCELONNETTE 15 KMS
FOUILLOUSE 1907
R. CHAMBEYRON 2626
3302
CHAMBEYRON 3412
MARY 3206
3220
CONDAMINE C.
COURBE 3089
3389
3168
FR. IT.
MEYRONNES 1526
3219
FRANCE ITALY
SIGURET 3032
R. STROPPIA 2050
R. CELLETTA 2830
R. BLANC 3193
3046
3067
3155
3021
LARCHE 1670
FRANCE    ITALY
2629
CHIAPPERA 1614
P
2885
2771
COL DE LARCHE
FR. ITALY
MOISE 3104
CUNEO
ARGENTERA 4 KMS
ACCEGLIO

SCALE    0        5        10    KMS

## Monte Viso, Cottian Alps, France-Italy

Near the center of the Cottian Alps (that part of the Cottian Alps which straddles the southern French-Italian border), is the highest mountain in all of the southern European Alps. This is Monte Viso, with an altitude of 3841 meters. The summit lies inside Italy about 3 kms, but part of this map includes mountains in France.

Even though the elevation is high, there are no real glaciers on the mountain—only a "handful" of small snow fields. Its southerly location puts it on the northern fringes of the Mediterranean Climate, which means almost all the precipitation comes in winter, while the summers are long, warm and relatively dry.

Monte Viso is relatively isolated, that is, there are secondary roads to near the mountain, but with no major highways nearby. The nearest railways are found near Guillestre in France and Saluzzo, 33 kms below Crissolo in Italy. Monte Viso is one of the better known mountains in Europe and is climbed by many. The generally fine weather is one of the reasons.

Viso can be approached from about 3 different directions, two of which are on the Italian side. The most used route is via Crissolo, Rifugios Re and Sella, then up the mountain on the southern side. The next best way would be from Casteldelfino, Castello, and to the southern face. On the French side one can get there via Guillestre, Abries, L'Echalp and the Rifugio Gagliardone.

Besides Monte Viso, there are other good climbs in the region. Several high peaks exist in the neighborhood of Rubren, 3311 meters. They can be reached from Chianale or Maddalena, both in Italy. Just north of this group is another massif with peaks Longe and Bianca, 3146 and 3059 meters. They can be climbed from either the French or Italian side.

The last places in which to buy food would be in St. Veran, Abries, Crissolo, or Casteldelfino. For the best information locally, contact someone at any "refuge" or "rifugio."

**Map:**  Queyras and Haute Ubaye, #10, 1 : 50,000, from IGN and Didier and Richard, Service des Ventes et Editions, 107, Rue La Boetie, 75008 Paris.

This is the upper south face of Monte Viso.

## Map 32-3, Viso, Cottian Alps, France-Italy

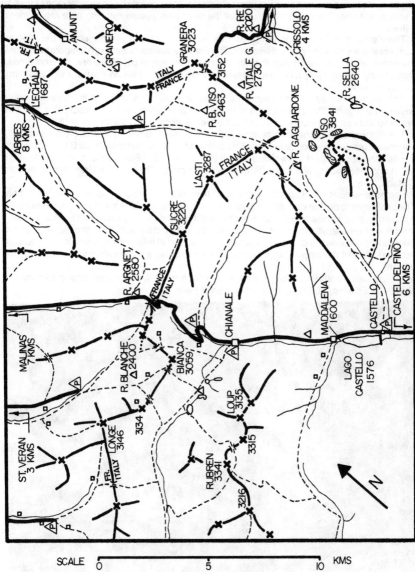

SCALE 0       5       10    KMS

## Bric Froid, Cottian Alps, France-Italy

To the southeast of Briancon and the Massif du Pelvoux, and northwest of Monte Viso, lies the northern sections of the Cottian Alps. Included on this map is part of the Parc du Quayras, a national and natural park. Internationally this area is unknown—most visitors being local French or Italians. The main reason for it being an unknown region is that there are no really high or well known mountains in the immediate area. Most people head for either the Massif du Pelvoux or Monte Viso—which means, for the most part, people climbing here are by themselves.

There's good skiing here in winter with as much sun as in any other part of the Alps. In summer there's even more good weather. The long dry summers with high temperatures, melt the heavy winter snows quicker than in the more northerly Alps. Therefore, the snowline is significantly higher. Only a couple of small snowfields exist, making it unnecessary to carry crampons or ice ax.

The region covered by this map is rather isolated, with no railways or major highways passing through it. The closest train stations are at Briancon and Guillestre. The highway reaching the central valley shown, is from either Briancon or Guillestre as well.

The highest peak in the area is actually Rochebrune at 3320 meters, but it is completely unknown outside the immediate area. This peak can be climbed from Col du D'Lzoard, or Les Fonds. Perhaps the best known mountain in the region is Bric Froid, 3302 meters. It has easy south and west faces, which can be approached from Le Roux on the French side, or from Cesana, Italy.

For those serious about spending time here, it might be best to buy a local map of the region. The best place to do that would be in Briancon, as it's in the center of a mountainous area and is a large city. It's also one of the centers of climbing and skiing activity in eastern France. Located there are several large supermarkets and a number of bookstores. It also has a tourist and alpin information office which is the best place to get any kind of information pertaining to mountain activities. Any of the larger villages shown on the map have small stores where food can be bought.

**Map:**  Queyras and Haute Ubaye, #10, 1 : 50,000, from IGN, Didier and Richard, Service des Ventes et Editions, 107, Rue La Boetie, 75008 Paris.

Small villages like this dot the landscape of the French Alps.

# Map 33-3, Froid, Cottian Alps, France-Italy

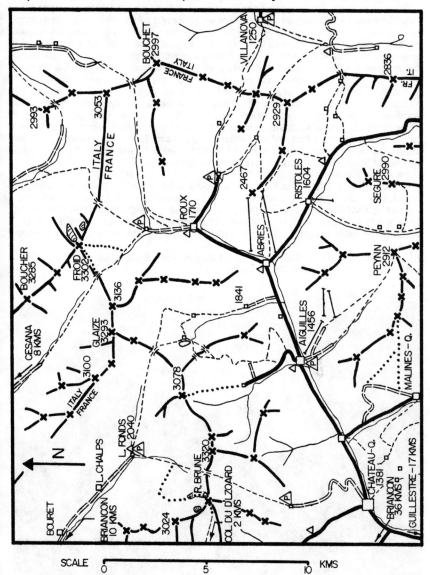

## Sirac, Dauphine Alps, France

At the extreme southern end of the Dauphine Alps, and the famous Massif du Pelvoux, is an area of small to medium-high mountains—as mountains go in Europe. These are the peaks just south of the really high and glaciated summits of the Pelvoux, and between the city of Gap and the town of Guillestre.

Because of its southerly location one can expect to find "good weather mountains." The climate in these parts is in contrast to the northern regions of the Alps. While heavy precipitation can be expected in winter, the same is true for sunshine in summer. The glaciers are small, with few crevasses. The Parc National des Pelvoux, is largely to the north of this map, but does extend south, almost to Orcieres. Camping in the national park is prohibited, but one can legally put up a tent at night and take it down next morning. This they call a "bivouac." The important thing is to keep it out of sight during the daytime hours, then there's never a problem.

Probably the best known peak in the area, though not quite the highest, is Sirac, 3440 meters. It can be climbed via either La Clot or Les Auberts, and the Refuge Vollonpierre. Someone at one of the refuges can indicate the "route normal" to nearby peaks.

The highest summit within the boundaries of this map, is Pic de Bonvoisin, at 3480 meters. It can be reached from La Clot and the Refuge Chabaumeau. This refuge is perhaps the best place in the region to set up a base camp from which to make several climbs. For most climbs over about 3100 meters ice ax and crampons will be needed

These mountains are far from any railways, the closest stations probably being at either Gap or Briancon. It's doubtful that public buses can be found to reach any place included on the map. Auto stopping is only fair in these parts, but in summer one can get around that way.

Both Gap and Briancon are larger cities, each having several supermarkets and bookstores. If one wants additional maps or other information about the mountains, these are the best places to get them, especially Briancon, which has an alpin information center and tourist office.

**Map:** Gapencais, #7, 1 : 50,000, from the IGN, Didier and Richard, Service des Ventes et Editions, 107, Rue La Boetie, 75008 Paris.

Near Ecrins. Looking south from the Refuge Glacier Blanc.

## Map 34-2, Sirac, Dauphine Alps, France

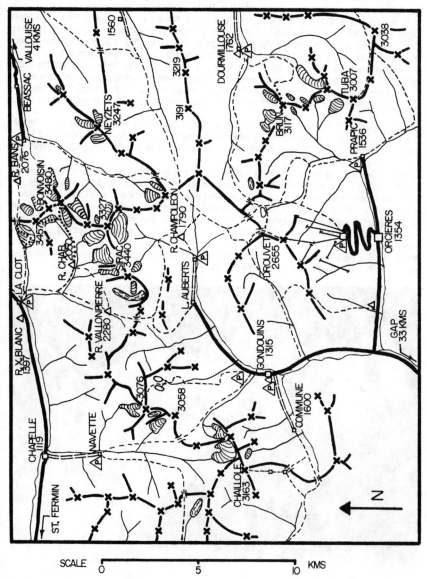

SCALE  0     5     10  KMS

# Ecrins, Massif du Pelvoux, Dauphine Alps, France

In the central regions of the Dauphine Alps, lies the Massif du Pelvoux. This high and heavily glaciated mountain complex lies entirely in France, with Briancon on the east, and La Grave and Col du Galibier to the north. There are abundant high and jagged peaks, and large glaciers with big crevasses. This may be the second best climbing area of France—the best is likely to be the area around Chamonix and the Mont Blanc Massif.

One can reach these mountains by trains to as far as Argentier and Briancon. Major highways penetrate to La Grave and Briancon, with secondary roads running up to Madame Carla, La Berarde and the refuges beyond Chapelle. The author found auto stopping very good in this immediate area, at least for people who appear to be mountain climbers.

The highest peak in the massif is Pic Lori, 4102 meters. It is the highest point in the group generally known as the Barre des Ecrins. The "route normal" to this peak (rather the nearby summit which is climbed most often called the Dome de Neige, 4015 meters), is via Madame Carla, and the Refuge Caron, then up the northeast face. A more difficult approach is via La Berarde.

Mont Pelvoux, 3946 meters, is climbed from Ailefroide and the Refuge Pelvoux, while Les Bans, 3669 meters, is climbed from La Berarde and the Refuge Pilatte. To the north is La Meije, 3983 meters. It is usually ascended from La Berarde and the Refuges Chatelleret and Promontorre.

There are too many mountains here to cover in just one page, but keep in mind there is hardly an easy route in the whole range. All require ice ax and crampons and some experience.

For additional information about routes to other peaks, contact the alpin information office in Briancon, or the "centre alpin" at La Berarde. Once on the mountain you should contact someone at the refuge nearest the climb you plan to make, concerning the route best for you. Briancon is a good place to buy the latest maps of the area, as well as shopping for food or supplies.

**Map:** Ecrins Haut Dauphine, #6, 1 : 50,000, from IGN, and Didier and Richard, Service des Ventes et Editions, 107, Rue La Boetie, 75008 Paris.

Barre des Ecrins to the left. Foto taken from Glacier Blanc.

# Map 35-1, Ecrins, Massif Du Pelvoux, France

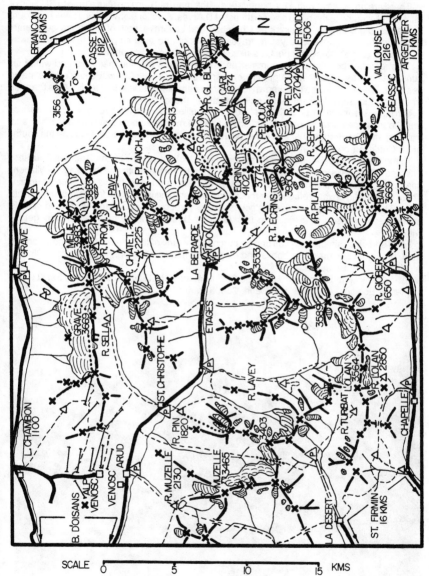

SCALE

0          5          10          15     KMS

## D'Arves, Dauphine Alps, France

This map covers the northern sections of the Dauphine Alps, which lie between Col du Galibier, Alpe D'Huez, and St. Jean. Within this area are two main groups of high peaks. They are Les Grandes Rousses in the western part and Les Aiguilles D'Arves in the east, just north of La Grave.

There are no railways within the boundaries of the map, but one can take a train to St. Jean or St. Michel, located to the north and northeast of D'Arves. A major highway runs between Bourg D'Oisans and Briancon, passing Lac Chambon and La Grave, both of which are good entry points to these mountains. If you're traveling on foot and auto stopping, this last highway mentioned is likely to be the best, as usually heavy traffic exists on it.

This region is popular during summer and winter. There are summer trails and winter ski runs, mainly in the area east of Alpe D'Huez, and to the north of La Grave. Because there are no really high peaks, this area is unknown to most climbers, and has little foot traffic. As is the case in all the other Alps, tourism is the only industry in these valleys.

The highest summit is one of the peaks of Les Aiguilles D'Arves, at 3510 meters. The normal route to these peaks is via Bonnenuit (located on the main road between Col du Galibier and Valliore), and the Refuge D'Arves. Other routes of approach might be from Rond on the south, or Le Chalmieu on the north.

To the west, Pic de Etendard, 3463 meters, is the highest summit of Les Grandes Rousses. This and other peaks in the group can be reached best from the south and the village of Mizoen, near Lac Chambon. If you're one who prefers to sleep in refuges, this is not your mountain. There is only one private refuge near the ski lifts, so camping is required for most climbs in this area. There are some fair sized glaciers in this group, so snow and ice equipment is needed—as opposed to climbing in Les Aiguilles D'Arves, where one can usually get by without.

Food and other simple supplies can be purchased in any of the smaller towns shown on the map, but to get equipment or books and maps, one must stop in Briancon, Bourg D'Oisans, Alpe D'Huez, or St. Jean.

**Map:** Ecrins Haut Dauphine, #6, 1 : 50,000, from the IGN, Didier and Richard, Service des Ventes et Editions, 107, Rue La Boetie, 75008 Paris.

Approaching M. Carla(Map 35).

# Map 36-2, D'Arves, Dauphine Alps, France

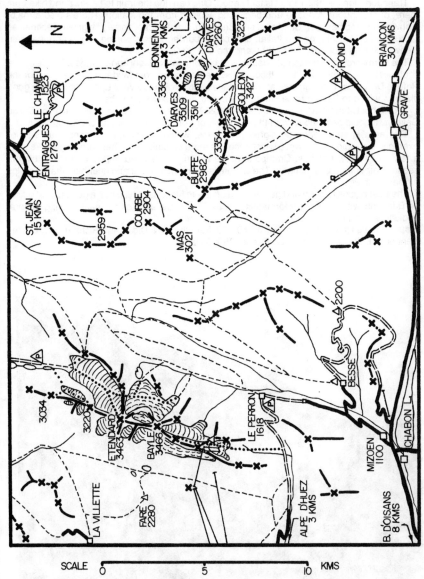

SCALE  0          5          10  KMS

## Mt. Thabor, Cottian Alps, France

The area just south of St. Michel and Modane, and immediately east of Col du Galibier, is the northern fringe of the Cottian Alps. The Cottian Alps are largely in Italy, but overlap into France as far as Briancon. The section shown on this map is the region surrounding Mont Thabor, 3207 meters. It is not the highest in the area, but is the best known.

Transportation into this region is fairly good. One can ride the train to La Praz and hike from there, or continue to Modane and beginning walking from the station. There's also a major highway running between St. Michel and Briancon. A major "secondary" highway reaches as far as Bardo Necchia, on the Italian side of the border. Auto stopping is good on the main highway linking Modane, St. Michel, and the Col du Galibier.

The normal route to the top of Thabor, is via Briancon, Nevachi and Granges. This is on the southeast side of the mountain. It could also be ascended from Modane and La Praz, or the Refuge Drayeres. The high area above Granges and the Refuge Valle Etroite, would be a good place in which to have a base camp, in order to make several climbs.

The highest summit in this area is Galibier, 3229 meters, located 2 kms due east of the Col du Galibier. It could be climbed from the Col itself, or from Plan La Cha, as shown on the map.

This area is surrounded by higher mountains, which makes it a bit drier, than say for example, the region to the west, which receives more precipitation. There are no glaciers, only a few small snow patches. Crampons or ice ax are not needed unless one is climbing in seasons other than late summer. The climate is definitely warmer and drier here than the Alps further north.

The best places to shop and get information are in Modane, which has a good tourist office, or Briancon with its alpin information office. These are both cities, each having several bookstores and supermarkets.

**Map:** Ecrins Haut Dauphine, #6, 1 : 50,000, from the IGN, Didier and Richard, Service des Ventes et Editions, 107, Rue La Boetie, 75008 Paris.

Looking south from near the R. Dent Parrachee towards Thabor.

## Map 37-2, Thabor, Cottian Alps, France

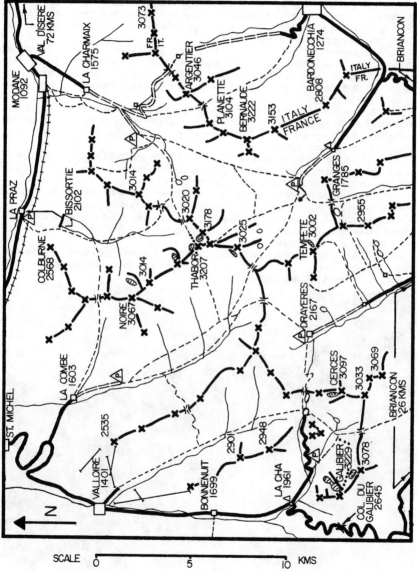

# La Dent Parrachee, Massif de la Vanoise, France

Large parts of the Massif de la Vanoise in the eastern French Alps, has been set aside as the Parc National Vanoise. A large section of this national park is shown on this map. This is the area immediately north of Modane, west of Termignon, and south of Pralognan. The region has a number of medium to high peaks and one very large glaciated area known as the Glaciers de la Vanoise.

Public transportation is fairly good to this area, at least the southern portion. A rail line stops about 1 km from the center of Modane, and from there one can walk to some of the mountains. One should be able to reach Termignon or Pralognan by bus. The author did just fine with a thumb, and a sign stating destination.

The highest summit in the area is La Dent Parrachee, 3697 meters, just west of Termignon and south of the Vanoise Glaciers. It can be reached beginning in Modane; then Aussois, past the ski slopes to the Refuge La Dent Parrachee, and then on a roughly marked trail northeast to the summit. With care, one won't need any snow or ice climbing equipment, as there's an "unkept" trail to the top.

To climb some of the peaks which form the western edge of the Glaciers de la Vanoise, one could approach from several directions, of which the Refuge Parrachee might be best, or from the Refuge L'Arpont as second best. There are many summits in this area over 3500 meters, all requiring ice ax and crampons.

To climb other high peaks such as Polset or Peclet (3534 and 3562 meters), one can walk from downtown Modane, past the Refuge L'Orgere and towards the Refuge Polset. This area also has a large glacier system, and the right equipment is needed.

Keep in mind that in France and all countries of Europe, camping within the boundaries of a national park is prohibited. However, one can get around this inconvenience by camping in a very isolated place or by bivouacking—that is, putting up a tent in the evening, and taking it down in the morning. This is legal, but sometimes not convenient. The thing they all dislike is to *see* a tent in the daylight hours.

Make Modane your shopping headquarters, for food, equipment and more detailed maps.

**Map:** Vanoise, #11, 1 : 50,000, from the IGN, Didier and Richard, Service des Ventes et Editions, 107, Rue La Boetie, 75008 Paris.

The southwest slopes of La Dent Parrachee.

## Map 38-1, D. Parrachee, Massif Vanoise, France

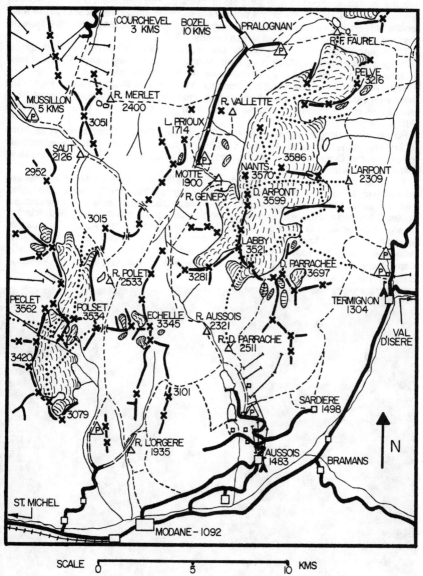

COURCHEVEL
3 KMS

BOZEL
10 KMS

PRALOGNAN

R.F. FAUREL

PELVE
3216

MUSSILLON
5 KMS

R. MERLET
2400

R. VALLETTE

L. PRIOUX
1714

3051

SAUT
2126

MOTTE
1900

NANTS
3570

3586

L'ARPONT
2309

2952

D. ARPONT
3599

R. GENEPY

3015

LABBY
3521

3281

D. PARRACHEE
3697

R. POLET
2533

PECLET
3562

POLSET
3534

ECHELLE
3345

R. AUSSOIS
2321

TERMIGNON
1304

VAL
D'ISERE

3420

R. D. PARRACHE
2511

SARDIERE
1498

3101

3079

R. L'ORGERE
1935

AUSSOIS
1483

BRAMANS

N

ST. MICHEL

MODANE - 1092

SCALE  0       5       10  KMS

## Albaron, Graian Alps, France-Italy

In the area to the south of Val D'Isere (perhaps France's most famous ski resort), and east of Col du Mont Cenis, is a group of high mountains, part of which form the French-Italian border. All the peaks are part of the Graian Alps, while only the western and northern sections are part of the Massif de la Vanoise.

In the area covered by this map there are no railroads. However, there is a major highway running from Mt. Cenis, Bessans, the Col de l'Iseran and to Val D'Isere. Buses run this route regularly. There's not a lot of traffic going over the pass between Bassens and Val D'Isere, so auto stopping on that particular route can be slow.

The highest mountain on the map is Charbonnel, 3752 meters. It's an isolated peak and not so rugged or glaciated as others in the area. As a result, it's not well known. The most likely route to the top of this peak is via Bassens and the Refuge Averole.

Some easy climbs can be found to the south of Val D'Isere, in the skiing areas. Pers, 3386 meters, is near the ski runs, but can also be approached from the Refuge Carro. Levanna, 3619 meters, lies on the international border and is usually climbed from the Italian side and the Rifugio Gervis.

Further south, along the border, is Albaron, 3637 meters. This is the most famous peak in the region. The "route normal" for Albaron, is via Bonneval, L'Ecot and the Refuge Evettes. Near the Lac du Mont Cenis, is Ronce, 3612 meters. This peak could be climbed best from the ski lift areas up from Adroit.

The snow line is higher here than in parts of the Alps further north. It's definitely warmer and drier around Bessans and that valley, than say for example the Zermatt, Switzerland region. Even so, most of the higher peaks support fairly large glaciers, especially on their northern slopes. Crampons and an ice ax are required on most peaks over about 3200 or 3300 meters.

Largest settlements in the area include Val D'Isere, Bessans, and Adroit. Food can be bought in any of these towns, but if you're looking for books or more detailed maps of the area, better to look in places such as Val D'Isere or Modan (located just off this map to the west).

**Map:** Vanoise, #11, 1 : 50,000, from the IGN, Didier and Richard, Service des Ventes et Editions, 107, Rue La Boetie, 75008 Paris.

The north face of Albaron from the Refuge des Evettes.

# Map 39-2, Albaron, Graian Alps, France-Italy

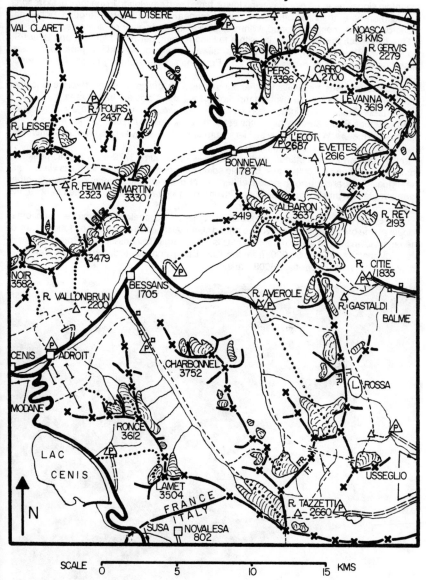

VAL CLARET

VAL D'ISERE

NOASCA
18 KMS
R. GERVIS
2279

PERS
3386

CARRO
2700

LEVANNA
3619

R. FOURS
2437

L'ECOT
2687

EVETTES
2616

R. LEISSE

BONNEVAL
1787

R. FEMMA
2323

MARTIN
3330

3419

ALBARON
3637

R. REY
2193

3479

R. CITIE
1835

NOIR
3582

R. VALLONBRUN
2200

BESSANS
1705

R. AVEROLE

R. GASTALDI

BALME

CENIS

ADROIT

CHARBONNEL
3752

L. ROSSA

MODANE

RONCE
3612

LAC
CENIS

USSEGLIO

N

LAMET
3504

FRANCE
ITALY

SUSA

NOVALESA
802

R. TAZZETTI
2660

SCALE     0          5          10          15    KMS

# Grande Casse, Massif de la Vanoise, France

In the area south of Bourg St. Maurice, west of Val D'Isere and north of Modane, is the Parc National Vanoise, covering a large part of the Massif de la Vanoise. Shown here is the northern portion of the park with highest peak, La Grande Casse, 3855 meters, at the south edge.

The higher and more remote regions have all been set aside as a national park. However, the mountain slopes near the highways and towns have been developed in the form of ski resorts, as much or more, than any other part of the European Alps. The areas around Tignes and Mancroix are the most developed. Winter is obviously the busiest of all the seasons.

One can reach this area by train, with a rail line running between Moutiers and Bourg St. Maurice, with Landry being the closest the railway comes to the national park boundaries. Buses can be found to reach Tignes and Pralognan. Auto stopping is good—by French standards.

Weather conditions are similar to other parts of the Alps, but generally a bit warmer and drier than areas such as those in Switzerland. Lots of full sized glaciers in this area.

La Grande Casse is the highest peak shown on this map. The normal route is via Prolognan and the Refuge Felix Faurel to the southwest of the peak. Just to the east of Casse is La Grand Motte, 3653 meters. What could be an ineresting climb is ruined by ski lifts (and a telepherique) that takes skiers to near the summit.

In the northern section stands another fine peak, Mt. Pourri, 3779 meters. This peak has some very good and difficult routes, but also some easy ones. The route normal is via Gurraz, the Refuge Turia, and the north slopes, either on rock or snow, whichever one prefers. Another normal route, but much more difficult and involving an ice fall, is via Landry, Les Lanche, the Refuge Pourri and the west face glacier.

For the best information concerning routes to other peaks, contact a refuge keeper or other people at one of the refuges near your planned climb. Also, good maps can be found in any of the larger towns in the area, notably, Val D'Isere, Bourge St. Maurice and Pralognan.

**Map:** Vanoise, #11, 1 : 50,000, from the IGN, Didier and Richard, Service des Ventes et Editions, 107, Rue La Boetie, 75008 Paris.

Looking south from Mont Pouri to the north slopes of Grande Casse.

# Map 40-1, Grande Casse, Massif De La Vanoise, France

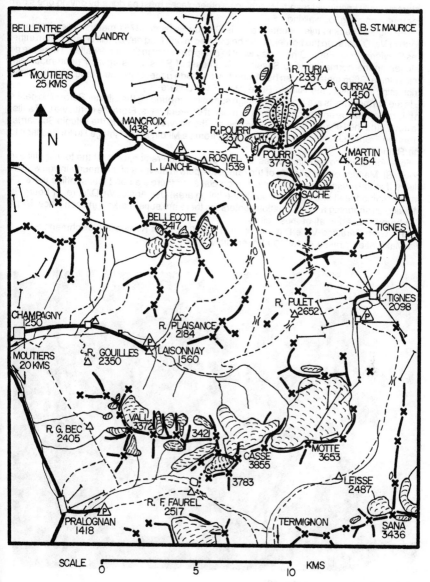

## Grande Sassiere, Alpi Graie, France-Italy

Included on this map is the mountain area north of Val D'Isere, southeast of Bourg St. Maurice, and west of Gran Paradiso, all of which is part of the Alpi Graie.

In this region there are no railroads—the closest one being in the Val d'Aosta, just to the north of this map, and at Bourg St. Maurice. Buses can be taken to Val D'Isere, which is an internationally known ski resort. Reaching all other places must be done by driving one's own car, auto stopping, or walking.

The highest peak in this mountain area is Grande Sassiere, 3751 meters. It lies just to the north of Val D'Isere, on the border. It can be climbed in one long day by a fit climber, from either Les Brevieres or Le Fenil. Others may want to camp one night in the upper valley. There are no refuges on the normal route to Sassiere. Southeast of Sassiere is another good mountain, Tsanteleina, 3605 meters. It can be climbed by the north ridge, or its south face, with the climb originating from Nial, the Rifugio Benevolo, or Val D'Isere.

In the northern parts are a number of high summits surrounding the Glacier Rutor. The peaks in this region can be approached from a number of different ways. From the north; via La Tauile, La Joux, and the Rifugio Deffeyes. From the southeast; via Bonne, and the Rifugio Scavarda. From the French side and the southwest, walk from Le Miroir, to the Refuge Ruitor and then to the Rutor Glacier.

For information concerning routes to other peaks in the region, contact the tourist office in Bourg St. Maurice or Val D'Isere, or the refuge keepers in the area of the mountain you want to climb. If in Italy, use Aosta as an information place, as there's a good tourist office there. Or contact someone at one of the rifugios in the Italian area. Use Aosta, Val D'Isere, or Bourg St. Maurice as shopping and information centers, as there are supermarkets in each place. Maps can be purchased in all of these cities.

**Map:** Gran Paradiso-Valle D'Aosta, #86, 1 : 50,000, from Kompass-Fleischmann S.a.r.l., Via-Max-Valier-Strasse 4, 139100 Bozen, Italy.

West face of Mont Pouri(Map 40).

# Map 41-2, G. Sassiere, Alpi Graie, France-Italy

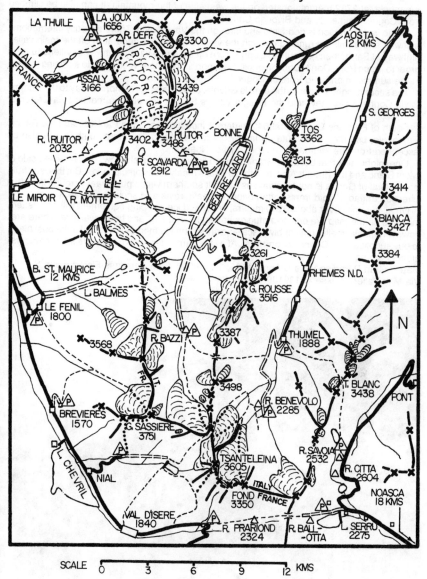

LA THUILE

LA JOUX
1656

R. DEFF.

3300

AOSTA
12 KMS

ITALY
FRANCE

ASSALY
3166

3439

S. GEORGES

R. RUITOR
2032

T. RUTOR
3402  3486

BONNE

TOS
3362

3213

3414

R. SCAVARDA
2912

BEAURE GARD

BIANCA
3427

LE MIROIR

R. MOTTE

FR.  IT.

3384

3261

B. ST. MAURICE
12 KMS

L. BALMES

G. ROUSSE
3516

RHEMES N.D.

N

LE FENIL
1800

3568

R. BAZZI

3387

THUMEL
1888

3498

T. BLANC
3438

PONT

BREVIERES
1570

G. SASSIERE
3751

R. BENEVOLO
2285

FR.  IT.

R. SAVOIA
2532

R. CITTA
2604

L. CHEVRIL

NIAL

TSANTELEINA
3605

ITALY
FRANCE

NOASCA
18 KMS

VAL D'ISERE
1840

FOND
3350

R. PRARIOND
2324

R. BALL
-OTTA

L. SERRU
2275

SCALE  0    3    6    9    12  KMS

# Gran Paradiso, Alpi Graie, Italy

In the area due south of Aosta and the Aosta Valley, is a group of high peaks and large glaciers now included in the Gran Paradiso Parco Nazionale. The highest summit is Gran Paradiso itself, at 4061 meters. It is one of the better known mountains in the Alps.

For those climbing Gran Paradiso, the normal route is via Pont and the Rifugio Vittio Emanuele, at 2732 meters, located on the west side of the mountain. It can also be climbed from Cogne, Valmaina, and Bivouac Carlo Po.

Public transportation is good into and through the Val d'Aosta. There's a busy international highway and a railroad running through the valley. To reach Cogne, turn off the main valley highway at Sarre, then go south to Cogne. Turn off the same valley highway at Villeneauve, in order to reach Pont. Don't count on public transport to the upper valleys. Auto stopping is good in the summer months to Pont or Cogne.

The second highest peak in the area is Grivola, 3969 meters. The normal way to this summit is via Cogne, Valnontey, and the Rifugio Vittoris Sela. It can also be reached via Creton or Rousse.

South of Pont lies Cliarforon, 3642 meters. Since it's near Gran Paradiso and the Rifugio Emanuele, use the same route up from Pont to the rifugio, then turn south. It can also be ascended from the southeast, via the town of Noasca.

One might think that because Gran Paradiso lies in the "rain shadow," or on the lee side of Mont Blanc and the French Alps, that these peaks receive less precipitation. But this isn't true, as the Gulf of Genoa is not far away; as a result southern winds push heavy clouds from that direction ahead of cold fronts, often bringing heavy rains and snow to this area.

On all summits over about 3200 meters, snow and ice climbing equipment will be needed. Included on the map are only two rifugios having food, drinks and beds available. There are, however, many smaller huts or bivouacs—as shown on the map. Aosta is by far the best place to buy supplies, with Cogne second best. At all the campsites shown there are small campers' grocery stores.

**Map:** Gran Paradiso-Valle D'Aosta, #86, 1 : 50,000, from Kompass-Fleischmann S.a.r.l., Via-Max-Valier-Strasse 4, 139100 Bozen, Italy.

The upper west face of the Gran Paradiso.

# Map 42-1, Gran Paradiso, Alpi Graie, Italy

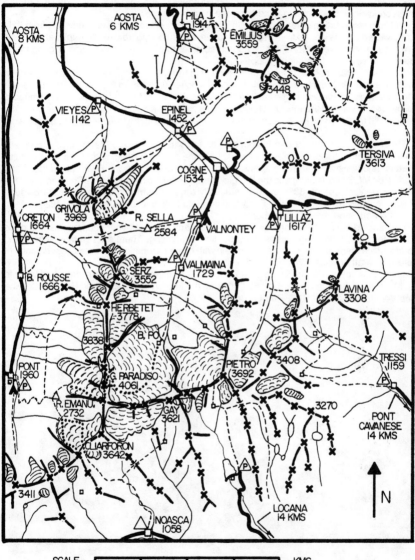

## Mont Blanc, Graian Alps, France-Italy

The Mt. Blanc Massif is a high and glaciated group of peaks which lies on the boundaries of three countries—France, Italy and Switzerland.

The hub or capital of this climber's paradise is Chamonix on the French side. Chamonix compares with Zermatt, Switzerland in size, elevation, proximity to some of the highest mountains in Europe, availability to climbing information, etc., etc. It's a real tourist trap, but interesting—and the climbing is perhaps the best in Europe.

Public transportation is very good to Chamonix. Besides super highways entering from Italy and Switzerland, as well as from France, there are trains coming from each country also. There are lifts in service year-round, for skiing and summer tourists, and even some cogged trains running to several of the higher slopes.

Mt. Blanc, 4807 meters, is the highest summit in Europe. The normal route can be done in several ways. Mountaineers can walk from Les Hoches up a trail to the Voza Station, then on the train tracks to the end of the line, and finally up the trail to the Refuge Gouter. From there follow a snow ridge to the top. Other people can either take a train all the way from St. Gervais, or ride a lift from the Les Hoches area to the rail line, then up to the Refuge Gouter, and beyond on foot.

Other peaks in the area can be climbed as follows: Peuterey, 3772 meters, is normally ascended from Rifugio Peuterey; Jorasses, 4208 meters, from Rifugio Jorasses; Geant, 4013 meters, is often scaled from the tramway (connecting Chamonix with Entreves, at the Italian end of the Mt. Blanc Tunnel) and the Rifugio Torino, or the alpinest route via Chamonix and the Refuge Reguin; Dolent, 3820 meters, is usually climbed from Pre du Bar, and the Bivouac Piorio; Noir, 3836 meters, from La Fauly and the Refuge Neuve, and Chardonne, 3824 meters, from La Tour, and the Refuge Albert I.

One should stop in Chamonix before beginning any climb. All your shopping can be done there; for food, equipment, maps, guidebooks—everything. There's a climbing school and tourist office there and those people can help with more information on routes, reservations of refuges, weather, etc.

**Map:**   Massiccio del Monte Bianco, #85, 1 : 50,000, from Kompass, Bozen, Italy. And Massifs du Mont Blanc-Beaufortain, #8, 1 : 50,000, from the French IGN, Didier and Richard, Service des Ventes et Editions, 107, Rue La Boetie, 75008 Paris.

From Mont Pouri, Mont Blanc rises to the north.

# Map 43-1, Blanc, Graian Alps, France-Italy

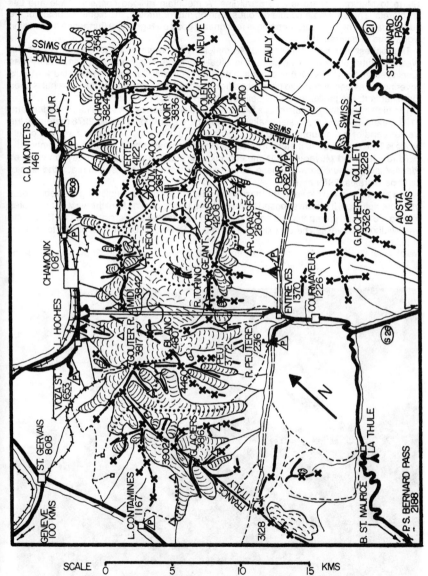

## Wildhorn, Berner Alpen, Switzerland

The region covered by this map includes the western end of the Berner Alpen. It's the area northwest of Sion and north of Martigny. By Swiss standards these would be considered small mountains, yet there's a couple of medium sized glaciers beneath the higher peaks.

Public transportation to and around the area is good. Busy Highway 9 runs in the valley from Sierre to Martigny. There is also a rail line. A mountain railroad connects Aigle and Les Diablerets. There's also a couple of roads running into or through the higher slopes. For the budget traveler on foot, auto stopping is reasonably good on Highway 9 (further east this same highway is numbered 19).

The highest summit is Wildhorn, 3248 meters. The normal route to Wildhorn is via the Wildhorn Hutte just north of the peak. The usual way to get to this hut is via a secondary road running south from Lenk. Or one can reach Wildhorn Hutte via Lauenen, on a multitude of trails covering the slopes. It can also be climbed from the Gelton Hutte, but normally this hut is used for ascents to the peaks around Arpelistock, 3035 meters.

The high massif to the south of Les Diablerets, is a ski resort by the same name. Oldenhorn, 3123 meters, is one of the easier peaks to climb. There's a refuge, marked 2278 meters, at the western end of the group, offering good climbing in the vicinity. The highest summit of this group is Tete Ronde, 3210 meters. It can be scaled most easily from the ski lifts or Oldenhorn.

To reach Grand Muveran, 3051 meters, take the trail running between Leytron and Les Plans. A similar route between these same two towns can also be used to reach the area of Dent de Moreles, 2969 meters.

The snowline is a bit lower here than in the east of Switzerland, indicating the region gets more precipitation. It's more exposed to the cyclonic storms coming from the west. Many routes require ice ax and crampons, but some do not. Except for the glaciers around Les Diablerets and Wildhorn, crevasses hardly exist. Sion, Aigle, or Bex would be the best places to shop for supplies.

**Map:**   Col du Pillon, #41, 1 : 100,000, from Eidg. Landestopographie, 3084 Wabern, Bern.

Camping east of the Matterhorn(Map 48).

# Map 44-2, Wildhorn, Berner Alpen, Swiss

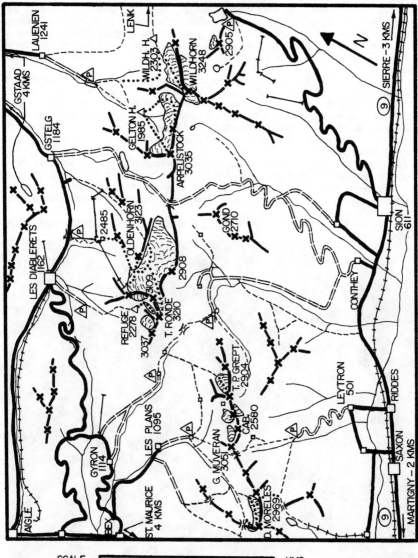

SCALE

0        5        10   KMS

# Bietschhorn, Berner Alpen, Switzerland

Located to the north of Visp and Sierre, and to the south of Bern in central Switzerland, is the central section of the Berner Alpen. This central part is just to the west of the highest portion of the Berner, which contains the famous Jungfrau and Eiger Peaks, and many more. This central section contains high peaks, but not of the same scale as those to the immediate east. In this middle part, the Berner Alpen can be seen narrowing down from about 25 kms in width to a single ridge about 10 to 15 kms wide.

Public transportation to the area is good. Running along side Highway 9 is an important international rail line. Train stations exist at several locations in the valley, including the most important stop, Brig (just off the map). From Brig one can board a train which runs through a tunnel coming out at Kandersteg, on the north slope of the range. If you're on foot and heading up some of these canyons, make a sign stating your destination. For short rides this helps a great deal.

The highest summit shown on this map, is Bietschhorn, 3934 meters. The normal route to this mountain is via Wiler, and the Bietschhorn Hutte. Blumlisalp, 3664 meters, is climbed via the trail where the Blumlisalp Hutte is located. A traverse can then be made of its' triple peaks.

Further to the west, one can easily ascend a number of peaks which surround a flat, snow filled basin, called the Glacier de la Plaine Mort. Wildstrubel, 3244 meters, is the highest peak of this group. One can reach the glacier rim from either the Montana ski area, or from Lenk and the Wildstrubel Hutte.

Don't forget your ice ax and crampons, as the snow line and glaciers in this region are lower than in other parts of the Alps, particularly those areas to the south in Italy. Brig, Visp or Sierre are larger towns, each having cheap food and other supplies at Migros Supermarkets, as well as several bookstores where the best maps can be found. There's also a tourist office in each city.

**Map:** Col de Pillon #41 and Oberwallis #42, 1 : 100,000, Eidg. Landestopographie, 3084 Wabern, Bern.

Bietschhorn in the central part of the Berner Alpen.

## Map 45-2, Bietschhorn, Berner Alpen, Swiss

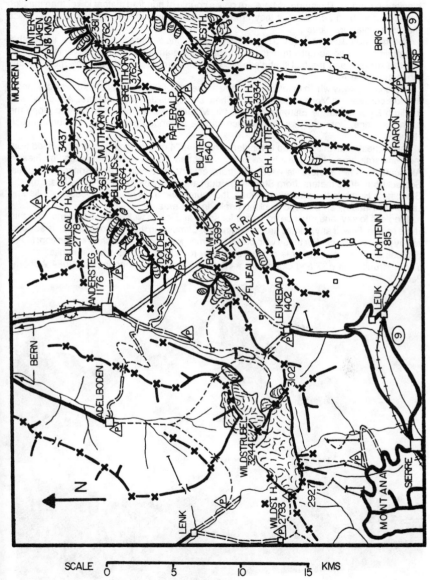

SCALE  0    5    10    15    KMS

# Jungfrau, Berner Alpen, Switzerland

The Berner Alpen in central Switzerland has some of the most famous mountains in the world. Names like the Eiger and Jungfrau top the list. Others like Wetterhorn, Schreckhorn, Aletschhorn, and Finsteraarhorn are a bit less famous—but almost as challenging. The part of the Berner included on this map is the highest part of the range, and includes the longest glaciers in Europe. The summits here are only a couple of hundred meters lower than the high peaks surrounding Zermatt, but they are directly in the path of the incoming storms, which makes the glaciers bigger.

The most noted mountain is the Eiger, 3970 meters, and especially its north face. It and other mountain faces rise abruptly from the lowlands in one giant step with no intervening foothills. For this reason, and the fact that it's in the heart of Europe, it is perhaps the most famous mountain in the Alps.

There is a railway which takes tourists to near the top of Eiger, under the summit of Monch, and to a col between Monch and Jungfrau. There stands the Junfraujoch Hotel. An "easy" way to climb Eiger is via the Eismeer Station, the Mittellegi Hutte, thence to the top along the northeast ridge. Both Jungfrau and Monch can be ascended easily from the Jungfraujoch Hotel.

The highest peak in this group is Finsteraarhorn, 4274 meters, and is normally scaled from the Finsteraarhorn Hutte, which, in turn, is reached from Belalp, Reideralp, or Fiesch. Aletschhorn, 4195 meters, is ascended from either Oberaletch or the Konkordia Huttes; Schreckhorn, 4078 meters, from Strahlegg Hutte; and the Wetterhorn, 3701 meters, from the Glechstein Hutte. In the easterly sections, the routes and trails reaching Dossen, Gulie and Lauteraar Huttes, can be used to climb peaks in that area.

Needless to say, one must be equipped for snow and ice as well as for rock climbing in this entire region. Few, if any, climbs are for beginners. Climbing in the heart of this area is as good as any place in Europe. For those who prefer to camp, go prepared for a short expedition. Make inquiries at the huts in the area of your climb, for routes up various other summits.

**Map:** Brunigpass #37 and Oberwallis #42, from Eidg. Landestopographie, 3084 Wabern, Bern.

Aletschhorn seen from the south on route from Belalp.

## Map 46-1, Jungfrau, Berner Alpen, Swiss

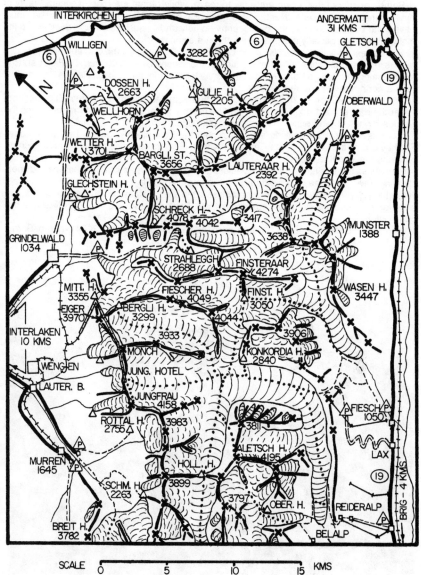

INTERKIRCHEN

ANDERMATT
31 KMS

GLETSCH

WILLIGEN

6          P          3282

6

19

OBERWALD

P          DOSSEN H.
2663

GULIE H.
2205

WELLHORN

WETTER H.
3701

BARGLI. ST.
3656

LAUTERAAR H.
2392

P

GLECHSTEIN H.

P

SCHRECK H.
4078          4042          3417

3638

MUNSTER
1388

GRINDELWALD
1034

P

STRAHLEGGH
2688

FINSTERAAR
4274

MITT. H.
3355

FIESCHER H.
4049

FINST. H.
3050

WASEN H.
3447

EIGER
3970

BERGLI H.
3299

4044

INTERLAKEN
10 KMS

3933

3906

WENGEN

MONCH

KONKORDIA H.
2840

LAUTER. B.

JUNG. HOTEL

JUNGFRAU
4158

FIESCH          P
1050

ROTTAL H.
2755          3983

3811

LAX

MURREN
1645

P

ALETSCH H.
4195

19

HOLL. H.

SCHM. H.
2263          3899

3797

OBER. H.

REIDERALP

BREIT H.
3782

BELALP

BRIG - 4 KMS

SCALE          0          5          10          15          KMS

# Grand Combin, Pennine Alps, Switzerland-Italy

The area directly west of Zermatt, Switzerland is covered on this map. It's also the region just north of Aosta, Italy; northeast of St. Bernard Pass, and south of Sion, Switzerland. This area is dominated by high peaks and large glaciers, and is at the western end of the Pennine Alps, which include many of the best climbs in the Alps.

Some portions of the region are easy to reach, while others are more isolated. Plenty of public transport from Aosta, over the St. Bernard Pass and to Martingy and Sion, but one must have a car or auto stop into the backcountry. In July and August it's easy to get lifts into the higher valleys, especially if one appears to be a climber.

The highest peak in the area is Grand Combin, 4314 meters. It's the only summit over 4000 meters in the group. It has two normal routes for the ascent. One is via Bourg St. Pierre and the trail reaching the Refuge Valsore. The other is via Villetta, Fionnay and the Refuge Panossiere, then a north approach to the summit.

Mont Blanc de Cheilon, 3870 meters, is climbed from Lac de Dix, the Refuge Dix, and from either the east or west ridge. Mt. Collon, 3667 meters, is usually climbed from Arolla and the Refuge Vignettes, and either the west or south ridge.

If one is interested in making several climbs, the best place might be the valley above Fionnay and in the vicinity of the Refuge Chanrion. This valley is less developed than some others in the Pennine Alps.

Go to these mountains prepared for glacier travel. If one desires more rock than ice and snow climbing, then go to the Italian side and into one of two valleys above Valpelline.

Martigny, Sion and Aosta are the largest cities in the area, so they would be the best places to shop for food, equipment, maps, guidebooks, etc. Each city also has a tourist office which is often helpful.

**Map:**  Val de Bagnes, #46, 1 : 100,000, from Eidg. Landstopographie, 3084 Wabern, Bern.

Mt. Velan as seen from the Refuge Valsore.

## Map 47-1, Grand Combin, Pennine Alpen, Swiss-Italy

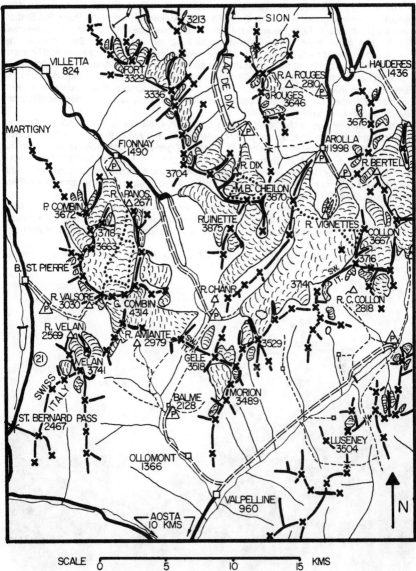

# Monte Rosa, Pennine Alpen, Switzerland-Italy

Possibly the premier climbing area in all of Europe is at Zermatt and the surrounding mountains. All the major summits in this ring of mountains are over 4000 meters and the glaciers as large as any in the Alps. Zermatt is undoubtedly the number one "tourist trap" in the Alps, and the Matterhorn is possibly the most fotographed mountain in the world. Even with all the tourists, the climbing is good and the area interesting.

The highest mountain in this region is Monte Rosa, with its loftiest peak, Dufourspitze, 4634 meters—second highest in Europe. One can walk or take the train to the Rotboden Station, then walk to the Monte Rosa Hutte, and to the summit from there. With an early start, one could take the train in the morning from Zermatt, make the climb, and return to Zermatt on the last train, but that would be a fast climb for the fittest climbers only! Nearby, Liskamm, 4527 meters, and others in that corner of the basin can also be climbed using the same approach route.

The Matterhorn (or Mt. Cervino), 4478 meters, can be ascended from Zermatt and the Hornli Hutte, or from the Italian side from Breuil and the Rifugio Abruzzi. Both routes have been modified with ropes, ladders or steel cables, with the Italian side having the most modification. The Italian Route is said to be the easiest.

Other mountains can be climbed as follows: Breithorn, 4159 meters, from either the Theodul or Mezzelama Huttes; Dent d'Herens, 4171 meters, normally from the Rifugio Aosta; Dente Blanche, 4357 meters, from the Refuge D. Blanche; Ober-Gabelhorn, 4063 meters, from the Rothorn Hutte—or direct from Zermatt for the more fit climbers; Nadelhorn, 4327 meters, from Mischabel or the Dom Huttes; Dom and Lenspitze, 4545 and 4294 meters, from the Dom Hutte and Randa. For more information about other climbs in the area, contact the tourist or climbers information offices in Zermatt.

The driving public must park vehicles in Tasch and walk or take the train from there. Only workers can drive cars or trucks to Zermatt. In Zermatt there are several supermarkets and hundreds of sport and bookshops—if better maps or equipment is needed. Equipment and guides can be rented also.

**Map:**   Val de Bagnes #46 and Monte Rosa #47, 1 : 100,000, from Eidg. Landestopographie, 3084 Wabern, Bern.

Monte Rosa's west face. Monte Rosa Hut near center of foto.

# Map 48-1, Rosa, Pennine Alpen, Swiss-Italy

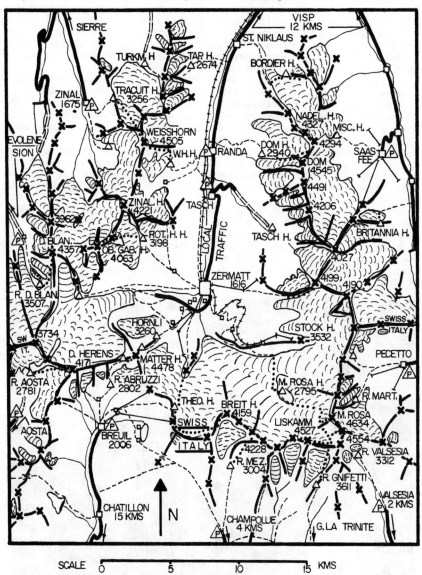

SIERRE

VISP
12 KMS

ST. NIKLAUS

TURKM. H

TAR H.
2674

BORDIER H.

ZINAL
1675

TRACUIT H.
3256

NADEL. H.
4327

MISC. H.

EVOLENE
SION

WEISSHORN
4505

W.H.H.

RANDA

DOM H.
2940

4294

SAAS
FEE

DOM
4545

4491

ZINAL H.
4221

TASCH

4206

3962

D. BLAN.
4357

ROT. H. H.
3198

LOCAL   TRAFFIC

TASCH H.
4027

BRITANNIA H.

OB. GAB. H.
4063

TASCH H.

R. D. BLAN
3507

ZERMATT
1616

4199   4190

3734

HORNLI
3260

STOCK H.
3532

SWISS
ITALY

SW

PECETTO

D. HERENS
417

MATTER H.
4478

M. ROSA H.
2795

R. AOSTA
2781

R. ABRUZZI
2802

THEO. H.

BREIT H.
4159

R. MART.

M. ROSA
4634

AOSTA

BREUIL
2006

SWISS
ITALY

LISKAMM
4527

4554

R. VALSESIA
3312

4228

R. MEZ.
3004

R. GNIFETTI
3611

VALSESIA
2 KMS

CHATILLON
15 KMS

N

CHAMPOLUE
4 KMS

G. LA TRINITE

SCALE    0        5        10        15    KMS

## Weissmies, Pennine Alpen, Switzerland

The mountains included on this map lie just south of Brig and east of Zermatt in southern Switzerland. While sections of Italy are shown, the highest summits lie in Switzerland.

This is a part of the eastern Pennine Alpen which has two peaks over 4000 meters, along with some "medium sized" glaciers.

Access to the area is easy, unlike many summits of the Berner Alpen just across the valley to the north. To the west of the highest peaks runs a road beginning at Visp, and is used mainly by skiers going to the Saas Fee ski resort. Running through the center of the area and to the east of the highest summits, is Highway 9, and the Simplon Pass. These two highways make for some short access routes to nearly all of the more interesting peaks. One can take a train as far as Brig or Visp in Switzerland, and to Varzo in Italy.

The highest peak of the group is Weissmies, 4023 meters. It's normally climbed from the Weissmies Hutte, then a northwest approach to the summit. From this same hut many people also climb the next two highest summits in the range, Lagginhorn, 4010 meters, and Fletschhorn, 3996 meters. Oftentimes, both of these peaks are climbed on the same day by doing a traverse, as shown on the map. Both peaks can also be scaled from the village of Simplon.

To the northeast of Simplon Pass is another smaller and less known massif, with Leone, 3553 meters, the highest in the group. It can be ascended from the Simplon Pass itself, or from a place on the main highway called Maderalp. Also, one can climb from the Italian side; from the town of Varzo, to the village of Ciameiaoero, located in a central position amongst the high peaks.

Still further to the northeast on this map is another small cluster of peaks, with Helsenhorn, 3272 meters, the highest. These peaks can be scaled from Binn, Switzerland or Ciameiaoero, Italy. Ice ax and crampons are needed here as on all peaks on the map.

Brig is the best place for buying food, equipment, maps and guidebooks. Brig, in the heart of a great tourist mecca, has all the amenities of a larger city.

**Map:** Oberwallis #42 and Monte Rosa #47, 1 : 100,000, from Eidg. Landestopographie, 3084 Wabern, Bern.

From summit of M. Rosa looking east. Weissmies right, Fletschhorn left.

# Map 49-2, Weissmies, Pennine Alpen, Swiss

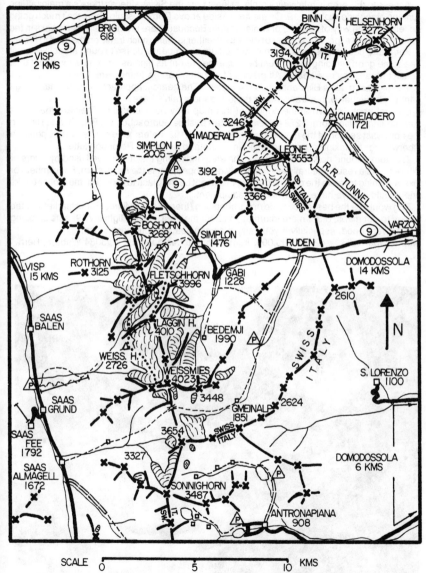

## Blinnenhorn, Pennine Alpen, Switzerland—Italy

To the northeast of the high peaks surrounding Zermatt, and to the southeast of the Jungfrau-Eiger Massif, is located the most easterly extension of the Pennine Alpen. This map includes the single ridge of peaks from about Brig to the Furka Pass, and to the southeast of Highway 19, the road connecting those two points.

Access to this area is relatively simple, at least from the Swiss side, as there's a main rail line running alongside Highway 19. On the Italian side above Domodossolo, there isn't much going on, either in the way of summer or winter sports. Because there are no really high peaks in the area, it's almost a forgotten corner of the Alps. Neither is there much traffic on the road to Riale.

For many people this area of small-to-medium sized peaks doesn't sound attractive, but it has some good climbing areas. Just because they're not as high as some nearby mountains, doesn't mean they're all easy. All grades of climbing can be found here.

The highest peak is Blinnenhorn, 3374 meters. The nearest approach is via a small village named Reckinger with a trail leading up to the mountain's base.

Several peaks shown at the bottom of this map may be interesting. They are the peaks surrounding Helsenhorn, 3272 meters, and can best be approached via Fieschi and Binn. In the northeast section of the map is located Rotondo, 3192 meters. One can reach this peak via Oberwald or by taking a trail beginning in Realp and ending at Rotondo Hutte.

The author found no ski lifts or runs in the area, indicating that it's not well used by skiers or climbers. As a result, the trails are not overly developed, nor is the hut system. For climbers or hikers wishing to leave the crowds behind, this might be the place to go to. For the higher peaks one should always have snow and ice equipment.

Brig would be the best place to do one's shopping (there's a big Migros Supermarket located there), to get maps, or for more information about the area. Along Highway 19, auto stopping can be very good, especially if you carry a sign indicating your destination.

**Map:**   Oberwallis, #42, 1 : 100,000, from Eidg. Landestopographie, 3084 Wabern, Bern.

Western glacier and face of Dom(Map 48).

## Map 50-2, Blinnenhorn, Pennine Alpen, Swiss-Italy

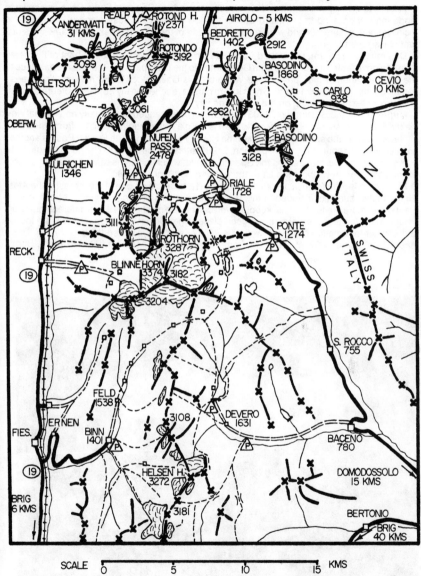

SCALE 0 5 10 15 KMS

## Dammastock, Urner Alpen, Switzerland

In central Switzerland, south of Luzern, and west of Andermatt, is an area of medium high mountains with a couple of glaciers that compare with the largest in Switzerland. Most of the high summits are along one long ridge, called Winterberg. Most peaks on this ridge are around the 3500 meter mark, including the highest in the area, Dammastock, 3630 meters.

Access to the region is good and simple. Trains run from Brig over Furka Pass and down to Andermatt, thence north to Altdorf and to the lowlands. It's a busy place, Andermatt and vicinity—both in summer and winter. It's in the heart of the Alps and has all the amenities of a first class resort town.

Dammastock is normally climbed from the Damma Hutte, located to the east of the peak. One can drive, auto stop or walk, from Goschenen to the Damma Hutte, then up the east face to the summit. Another high peak of the Winterberg is Gallenstock, 3583 meters. It's an easy climb from the Albert Heim Hutte, which in turn can be reached easily from the hotel-restaurant complex called Tiefenback, on the main highway.

Further north, the Sustenhorn, 3503 meters, can be ascended by the easy and normal way via the Susten Pass, Steingletscher and the Tierbergle Hutte. Another route is from Chelenalp Hutte, which is in the same valley as Damma Hutte. To the north of the Susten Pass is another smaller group of mountains, with Spannort, 3198 meters, as the highest. The normal route to its summit is on the trail that passes the Spannort Hutte, which in turn, is reached via Engelberg. From Engelberg town there's a lift to the top of a 3028 meter peak.

For someone interested in glaciers, the Rhone-Trift complex is one of the largest in the Alps. All the higher summits included in this map require an ice ax and crampons. At all the huts mentioned, there are full-time hut keepers who can advise climbers as to the different routes up mountains in the area. Andermatt is a good place to get local information, as there's a tourist and climber information office (as well as a climber's school) located there.

**Map:**  Brunigpass, #37, 1 : 100,000, from Eidg. Landestopographie, 3084 Wabern, Bern.

The east face of Galenstock as seen from near the Albert Heim Hutte.

## Map 51-1, Dammastock, Urner Alpen, Swiss

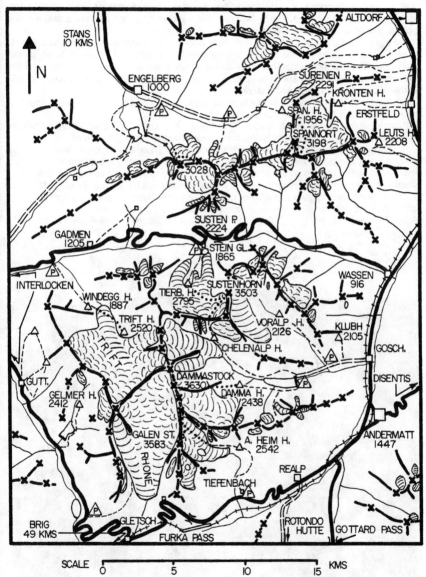

STANS
10 KMS

N

ALTDORF

ENGELBERG
1000

SURENEN P.
2291

KRONTEN H.

SPAN. H.
1956

ERSTFELD

SPANNORT
3198

LEUTS H.
2208

3028

SUSTEN P.
2224

GADMEN
1205

STEIN GL.
1865

WASSEN
916

INTERLOCKEN

WINDEGG H.
1887

TIERB. H.
2795

SUSTENHORN
3503

VORALP. H.
2126

KLUBH
2105

TRIFT H.
2520

GOSCH.

CHELENALP H.

T R I F T

DISENTIS

GUTT.

GELMER H.
2412

DAMMASTOCK
3630

DAMMA H.
2438

ANDERMATT
1447

GALEN ST.
3583

A. HEIM H.
2542

R H O N E

REALP

BRIG
49 KMS

GLETSCH

TIEFENBACH

ROTONDO
HUTTE

GOTTARD PASS

FURKA PASS

SCALE    0          5          10          15    KMS

# TÖDI, GLARNER ALPEN, SWITZERLAND

In central Switzerland in the area surrounding Disentis, lies the Glarner Alpen. By Swiss standards these mountains would be classed as medium sized. Because of this, the region is not as popular as other ranges in Switzerland for mountain climbing.

The area is easily accessible with a rail line passing through Altdorf to Andermatt, then over Oberalppass, to Disentis and eastward to Chur. Another rail line comes as far as Linthal in the northeast section of this map. The highway running east-west through Disentis is also a major route to the southern part of the country and northern Italy.

The highest summit in the region is Todi, 3614 meters. The author was told the most normal route to climb Todi was to pass through Linthal, then to the Gronhorn Hutte and finally up the east ridge. However, some literature says an easy route exists as shown on the map—via the Planure Hutte, Sandy Pass and then up from the west. Other good peaks in the Todi area are Bifertenstock, 3421 meters, and Clariden, 3267 meters.

Tgietschen, 3328 meters, is usually approached from the Cavardiras Hutte, while peaks in the region of the Etxli Hutte can be climbed from that hut.

To the south of Disentis stands Medel, 3211 meters. It is normally approached from a village just south of Disentis, the Medel Hutte, then a northwest route to the summit.

Most climbs in this region involve a combination of ice, snow and rock, so it's important to have an ice ax and crampons. Andermatt, Altdorf and Disentis are the largest towns in the area and are the best places to do the shopping. Each of these towns have several bookstores in which to buy better detailed maps or books, as well as food. Each town has a tourist office that can be of assistance in giving directions to mountains and routes. There's a mountaineering school and information office in Andermatt, which can also be of help.

**Map:**   Panixerpass, #38, 1 : 100,000, Eidg. Landestopographie, 3084 Wabern, Bern.

The northeast face of Tödi from above Linthal.

# Map 52-1, Tödi, Glarner Alpen, Swiss

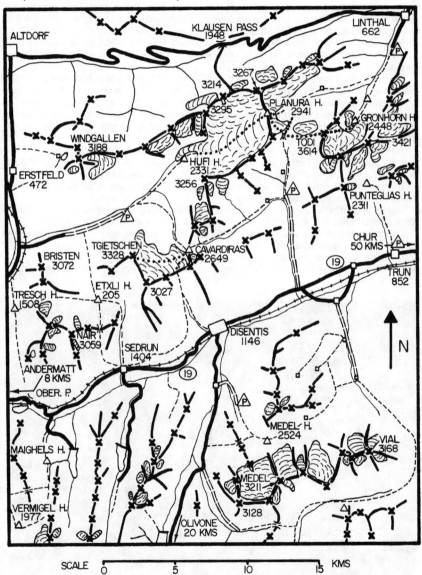

## Ringelspitz, Glarner Alpen, Switzerland

In an area west of Chur, in eastern Switzerland, lies a group of smaller and less climbed peaks which are part of the Glarner Alpen. By Swiss standards, these are small and insignificant mountains. However, there are some good climbs here, including some on ice, snow and glaciers.

For the most part there's one single ridge running parallel to Highway 19. This ridge and the surrounding valley area is a winter sports haven, with lifts and ski runs stretching from one end of the valley to the other. Most of the ski areas are concentrated above Flims. As one would expect, along with all the development, there are many dirt roads and trails on these slopes. From almost anywhere along Highway 19, one can find a road or trail by which to reach the peaks.

There are about three Swiss Alpine Club (SAC) huts in the area. These huts are open in the busy months of both summer and winter, and are attended to by a keeper. Usually some food and drinks can be bought in the huts. One hut is located above Tamins, on the trail and route to the highest peak in the region, Ringelspitz, 3247 meters. To the west a short distance, and in the valley above Vattis, is the Sardona Hutte. It is situated at the foot of Surenstock, 3058 meters.

Still further west is the Martinsmad Hutte, which is approached from the north and Elm. It's in a basin surrounded by rugged peaks, including the twin summits of Vorab, 3028 and 3018 meters. This mountain can easily be scaled from Flims and the ski trails.

To the south of Linthal is another summit, Hausstock, 3158 meters. It can be climbed from either Panix or Linthal, in one easy day.

Transportation to this area is good. There's a rail line running along Highway 19, connecting Chur with Disentis and Andermatt, to the west. Still another line ends at Linthal.

Chur is the largest town in the region, so make it your shopping headquarters. Locally, one can get additional information at hotels, the Chur tourist office, or at huts in the mountains. They may not be needed but ice ax and crampons should be taken along.

**Map:**   Panixerpass, #38, 1 : 100,000, from Eidg. Landestopographie, 3084 Wabern, Bern.

Swiss farm houses. A common scene in the Alps.

# Map 53-2, Ringelspitze, Glarner Alpen, Swiss

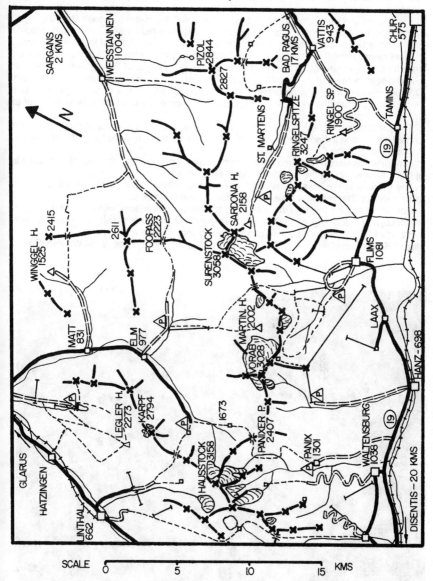

SCALE

0     5     10     15     KMS

# Adula, Adula Gruppe, Switzerland

In the southeastern corner of Switzerland, near the Italian border, and not far north of Bellinzona, Switzerland, is a small and little known group of mountains called the Adula Gruppe. Several of the peaks are of medium size, the others would be classed as small. As a result, they're almost unknown, despite the fact there's some good climbing on the higher slopes.

Transportation is not good close to this group. A rail line passes through Bellinzona and Biasca, then to Andermatt, and on to Chur. Otherwise, one must take a bus, or auto stop on either of the two minor highways located on the east and west sides of these mountains.

The highest summit in the region is Rheinwaldhorn, 3402 meters. This is more commonly known locally as "Adula," as this is in the Italian speaking sector of Switzerland. The easiest and shortest route to Adula is via Dangio, Soi, and two huts on the west side of the mountain. One can also approach the mountain from the east side using the trail passing the Zapport Hutte. On the north, the trail passing the Lanta Hutte could be used, but this route is not as convenient as the west side route.

The second highest peak is Guferhorn, 3383 meters. The easiest way up should be from the Lanta Hutte, using the northern approach. More difficult routes may be found if one used the Zapport Hutte or the Canalalp routes.

For someone wanting to climb a number of peaks from one base, the best cirque basin to operate from would be the one the Zapport Hutte is in.

The glaciers in the area are not big, but the larger ones have some crevasses, so it's recommended that climbers take along an ice ax and crampons.

Most of the smaller towns in the area have at least one small store, with Olivone, Malvagia, Mesocco, and Splugen being the best places to buy food. Bellinzona is about the only place in that part of Switzerland where one can find better maps of the area.

**Map:** Sopra Ceneri, #43, 1 : 100,000, from Eidg. Landestopographie, 3084 Wabern, Bern.

Homes with slate shingles, near the village of Dangio.

# Map 54-1, Adula, Adula Gruppe, Swiss

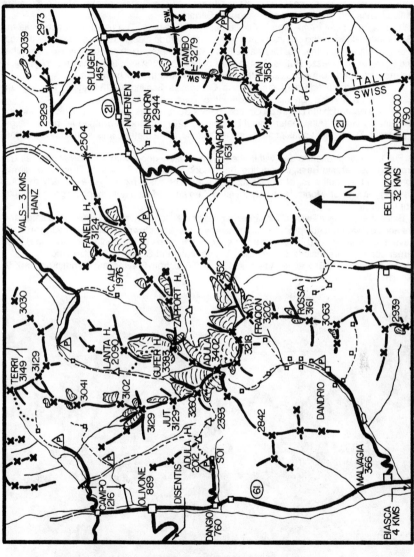

## Pik Bernina, Bernina Gruppe, Switzerland-Italy

Included on this map are the Bernina and Disgrazia Gruppes. They are located south of St. Moritz, Switzerland and north of Sondrio, Italy on the international border. This region is considered one of the best climbing areas in the Alps. There are many sharp summits, knife-edge ridges, and large glaciers with big crevasses. While there are some rather easy routes, there are many peaks with more difficult and challenging climbs. Among the more difficult ones are: Ferro, Rosso, Roseg and Bernina.

The highest peak in the area is Pik Bernina, 4049 meters. The usual approach is via the Bovalhutte—then a long one-day climb with a high altitude glacier traverse, and near the top, along a knife-edge ridge. Not far away is Palu, 3905 meters, which can be climbed from either the Boval or Diavolezza Huttes. To the west of Bernina is Roseg, 3920 meters. This peak is normally climbed from Pontresina, the Roseg Hotel and the Tschiera Hutte.

On the southern flanks of the Bernina Gruppe, is Scalino, 3323 meters. It's normally ascended via Sondrio, Chiesa, and from either Rifugios Cristina or Zoja.

To the west and in the Disgrazia Gruppe, Badile, 3308 meters, can be scaled via Masino and the Rifugio Gianetti. Its eastern neighbor, Ferro, 3267 meters, is climbed from the Rifugio Valsecchi. The highest peak of the group is Castello, 3392 meters, and is an easy climb from the Rifugio Allievi.

Public transportation to and within the region, is fairly good, with an international rail line crossing the Bernina Pass, connecting the Sondrio Valley with St. Moritz. There's no railway running to the southwest of St. Moritz, however. The main highways, especially the one passing through St. Moritz, is heavily traveled. The author found auto stopping good throughout the area.

Since there's few all-rock climbs in either group mentioned here, one must have snow and ice and cold weather equipment at all times. Any of the larger towns in the surrounding area will have supermarkets and bookstores (for even better maps of the peaks than this one). The larger communities include Sondrio and Tirano, Italy and St. Moritz, Switzerland.

**Map:**  Bernina und Engadiner Alpen, #51, 1 : 100,000, from Freytag und Berndt, Kohlmarkt 9, A-1010 Wien.

Pik Bernina from the glacier below Mt. Palu.

## Map 55-1, Bernina, Bernina Gruppe, Swiss-Italy

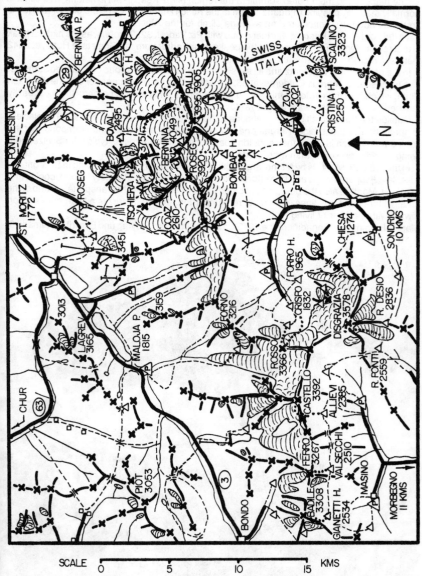

SCALE 0    5    10    15    KMS

# Kesch, Retiche Alpen, Switzerland

The Retiche Alpen is a rather indistinct mountain mass consisting of three higher areas or groups. The location of these peaks is to the northwest of Highway 27, and due north of St. Moritz, in eastern Switzerland. Also included on the map is part of the Languard Gruppe to the southeast of Highway 27.

The highest and most noted summit in the region is Piz Kesch, 3417 meters. This climb is normally made by passing through Bergun to the Kesch Hutte, thence up the glacier and to the northeast ridge. It's considered an average climb for the Alps.

To the northeast of Kesch is another group with Piz Vadret, 3229 meters, as the highest peak in that region. One can climb most of the peaks near Vadret from the Grialetsch Hutte, at 2542 meters. Enter this area from the Davos side.

In the area west of St. Moritz and its ski slopes, is another small group of glaciated summits. The highest peak there is Calderas, at 3397 meters. One can camp near or use the Jenatsch Hutte, which is in the center of this ring of high summits. This area is perhaps the most easily reached, since one can walk from downtown St. Moritz.

Outside the three small groups mentioned, there are many mountains but no other glaciers to speak of. For these higher areas one will need at least an ice ax and crampons, but if a southern approach is used, they shouldn't be needed. The weather is typical for Switzerland, being no drier or wetter than other parts.

In the area, St. Moritz is by far the largest city. One should plan to do shopping in St. Moritz as it has large supermarkets and bookstores, where one can find great variety of food, books, and maps. St. Moritz is also the best place to begin a climb because it's the transportation hub of the area, with rail and bus lines. One must remember too, that St. Moritz is a "rich man's resort town," with the cost of living high.

**Map:**  Bernina und Engadiner Alpen, #51, 1 : 100,000, from Freytag und Berndt, Kohlmarkt 9, A-1010 Wien.

Looking at the north face of Kesch.

# Map 56-2, Kesch, Retiche Alpen, Swiss

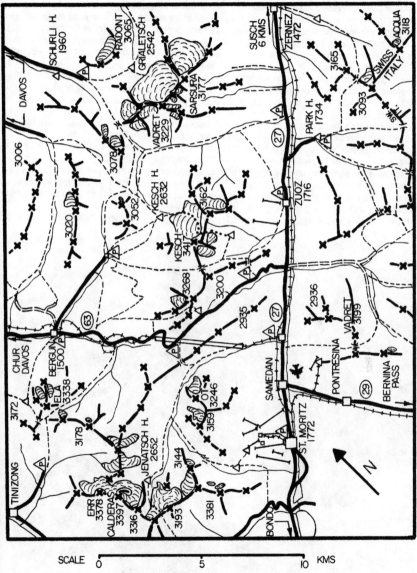

SCALE 0       5       10   KMS

## Piazzi, Languard Gruppe, Italy

The Languard Gruppe lies just east of the Bernina Gruppe and the Bernina Pass, and just west of Bormio and Sondalo, in northern Italy. Part of this group lies on the Swiss-Italian frontier, but is mostly in Italy.

For the most part these mountains are not as high nor as rugged and glaciated as its neighbors to the west (Pik Bernina). The glaciers which do exist are only remnants of their former past. Crevasses are either small or nonexistent. Perhaps the best thing about this area is that there are fewer hikers, climbers and rifugios in the region. Also, with mountains not quite so high, the weather is often better than, say for example, in the Bernina Gruppe.

The highest peak in the Languard Gruppe is Cima de Piazzi, 3439 meters. On its north flank is the area's largest glacier, Vedrette de Piazzi. To climb Piazzi, use this approach—Bormio, Semogo and Binacco (Rifugio) Ferrario at the foot of the glacier.

Another group of peaks lies in the center of the map. The highest summit there is Viola, 3384 meters; also Conca, 3166 meters; and Dozde, 3231 meters. The three huts or rifugios in the area are: Dosde, Falck, and Caldarini. One can get to these peaks from either Fusino or Semogo.

Still another small group is in the area of Paradisino, 3302 meters. Approach these peaks from the Swiss side and from the Rifugio Saoseo, not far from Bernina Pass.

There's public transport on the roads linking Bormio and Tirano, and Bernina Pass with Tirano, but neither highway is heavily used. Auto stopping is slow.

To be on the safe side, take along your crampons and ice ax, but if it's a south side ascent you plan to make, they may not be needed. For more information about routes locally, contact someone at the nearest rifugio. If you need better maps. stop at Bormio or Tirano in Italy, or St. Moritz in Switzerland (to the northwest of Bernina Pass).

**Map:** Bernina und Engadiner Alpen, #51, 1 : 100,000, from Freytag-Berndt, Kohlmarkt 9, A-1010 Wien.

North ridge of Roseg(Map 55).

# Map 57-2, Piazzi, Languard Gruppe, Italy

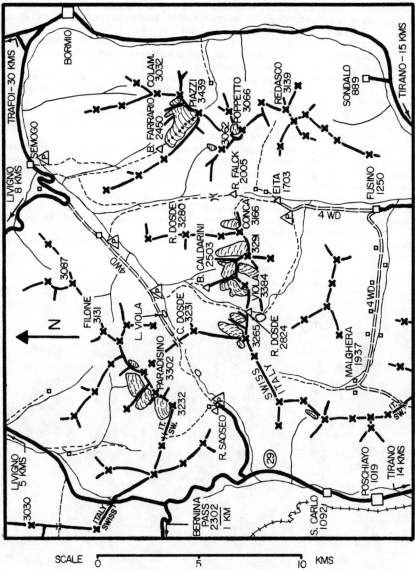

# Gruppos Adamello—Presanella, Italy

The area included on this map involves two groups of high peaks very near each other. They are the Gruppo Adamello and Presanella. This region is just west of Trento and to the southwest of Bolzano in northern Italy. Both of these groups are very near, but not actually part of, the Dolomiti system of the Alps further to the east.

On the Adamello side, Adamello Peak is the highest at 3554 meters. The normal routes to its summit are via the Lobbia Alto, or the Rifugio Trento. Both routes involve long glacier walks. A less popular route is via the Rifugio Predenzini. Care Alto, 3462 meters, at the southeast end of the group, is usually climbed from the Rifugio Care Alto.

Just across the valley to the east is the Gruppo Presanella, with its highest summit, Presanella, 3556 meters. It can be approached from at least three different directions. Perhaps the easiest way is via the Rifugio Presanella. Another possibility is from the Rifugio Stavel, located on the north side of the group. One can also make the climb from Rifugios Bedole and Trento, to the west of the peaks. By using these two rifugios, or camping in that area, both Adamello and Presanella peaks can be explored and climbed.

Both of the groups just discussed include glacier travel, so ice and snow equipment are needed on most climbs. There are many ski resorts in the area, particularly at Passo del Tonale. Many of the ski lifts operate the year-round.

One can expect public transportation to be available to Pinzolo and on the route from Vermiglio to Edolo. Edolo is the closest city to which trains make their way. These towns—Pinzolo, Edolo and Vermiglio are the biggest settlements in the area, so they are the best places to buy food supplies, including more detailed maps.

Generally speaking the weather in this part of the Alps is better than in the areas further north, therefore climbing is often more enjoyable. The system of trails and rifugios is very good in and around these peaks and mountains. People in this entire area speak Italian, as opposed to other mountain valleys to the north, where German is spoken.

**Map:** Brenta-Adamello-Presanella, #50, 1 : 100,000, from Freytag und Berndt, Kohlmarkt 9, A-1010 Wien.

Northern slopes of Presanella from near the Rifugio Stavel.

## Map 58-1, Adamello-Presanella, Italy

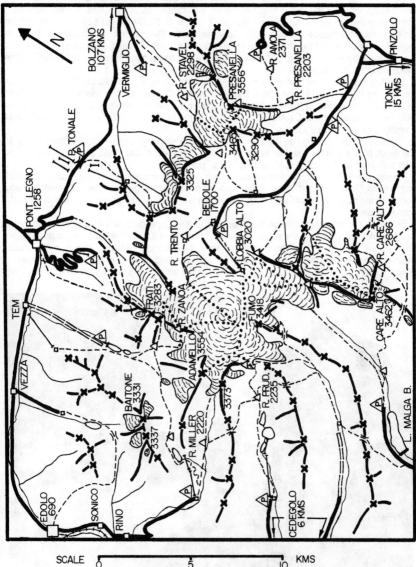

SCALE 0 5 10 KMS

## Ortler, Ortlergruppe, Italy

In an area to the west of Bolzano in northern Italy, is located the Ortlergruppe. This is a high and glaciated area and ranks as one of the best snow and ice climbing places in Italy. The highest summit is Ortler (in Italian, "Ortles"), 3902 meters. There are several other summits of 3700 meters and higher.

Ortler can be climbed from either Trafoi or Solden, and via the Payer Hutte, located on the north ridge. Beyond this hut is one section of "iron route," or steel cables. It's an interesting climb, despite the cables. Another nearby peak is Konigs, 3859 meters. It can be climbed from Solden and the Schauback Hutte, or St. Caterina and the Rifugio Pizzine, situated on the south side of the peak. Also from the Solden Valley, one can scale Vertain Spitze, 3544 meters. The normal route here passes the Zaytal Hutte. One can also reach the area by way of Prud and the Hochwand Peak, 3123 meters.

San Matteo is another high peak normally ascended from the Rifugio Branca. Other routes can be used—including the one from Cagolo. Zufritt, 3438 meters, can easily be climbed from either Zufritsee or the St. Gertraud side. Another easy climb is to Vioz, 3640 meters—a trail reaches its summit from Cagolo. There's also a trail to the top of Zufall, 3764 meters, from Cagolo and the Rifugio Larcher.

There is public transport on the main routes passing through Laas, including the railway. In the west, buses can be taken to as far as Bormio. The rest of the roads are mountain routes, with holiday travelers driving to resorts in the mountains.

The one best valley from which to climb several mountains is Solden, where a couple of small stores exist. Solden is a big winter resort, as are many other villages in these high valleys. Many people in the northern half of the Ortlergruppe are German speaking; people in the other parts speak Italian.

Being on the southern side of the Alps, the Otlergruppe generally has somewhat better weather than mountains to the north. However, there are still lots of big glaciers, so don't forget your ice ax and crampons. The biggest cities in the area are Bolzano, Italy and Innsbruck, Austria. If better detailed maps are required, one can find them in either of these places.

**Map:** Ortler, #46, 1 : 100,000, from Freytag und Berndt, Kohlmarkt 9, A-1010 Wien.

North ridge of Ortler from the Payer Hutte.

## Map 59-1, Ortler, Ortlergruppe, Italy

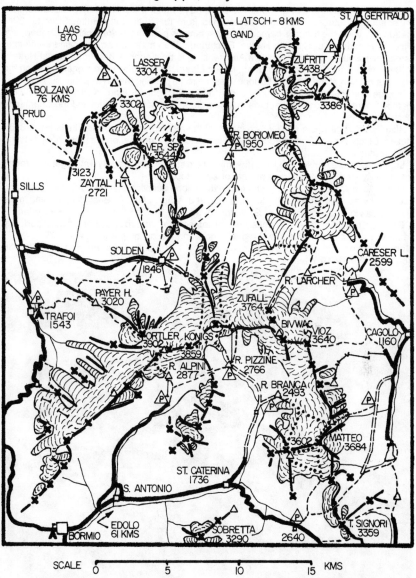

# Piz Buin, Silvretta Gruppe, Switzerland—Italy

The Silvretta Gruppe is located on the Swiss-Austrian border near the point where these two countries and Liechtenstein meet. Climbing routes are about equally distributed on both sides of the border, but the Austrian side may offer slightly easier and shorter routes to most of the summits.

The highest peak in this group is Piz Buin, 3312 meters. It's normally climbed from the Weisbadener Hutte, but can also be reached from the Shamanna Hutte. Silvretta, 3244 meters, for which the group is named and most famous peak in the area, can be climbed from either Weisbadener or Silvretta Huttes. Fluchthorn, 3399 meters, can be scaled from either Jamtal or Heidelberger Huttes, while Augstenberg is best approached from Jamtal Hutte.

For those wanting only rock to climb, try Piz Linard, 3411 meters, the highest peak on the map, but not part of the Silvretta Gruppe. Use the route passing the Chamanna (hut) Linard.

Included on this map, but actually a part of the Sesvennagruppe, is Piz Lischana, 3105 meters. There's only one real approach to this peak and that's via Scuol and the Chamanna Lischana.

Also included here is a peak which is part of the Albulagruppe. It is the Fluela Horn, 3085 meters. Climb this one from Wegehaus or Fluela Hospis. Inquire at one of these huts as to the exact route.

Little or no public transport exists in the immediate area. About the only way of getting around is to have your own vehicle or rent one, or auto stop.

In the vicinity, several small towns exist where food supplies can be bought—Susch and Scuol in Switzerland; or St. Gallenkirch, Galtur, and Ischgl in Austria. Best places to find maps of the area would be Innsbruck or St. Anton, Austria; or St. Moritz or Davos in Switzerland.

For exact routes high on the peaks, consult someone at a nearby hut. For the most part, any peak over about 3000 meters, will require snow and ice climbing equipment.

**Map:** Ratikon-Silvretta-Verwallgruppe, #37, 1 : 100,000, from Freytag und Berndt, Kohlmarkt 9, A-1010 Wien.

Buin and its northern slopes and glacier.

# Map 60-2, Buin, Silvretta Gruppe, Swiss-Austria

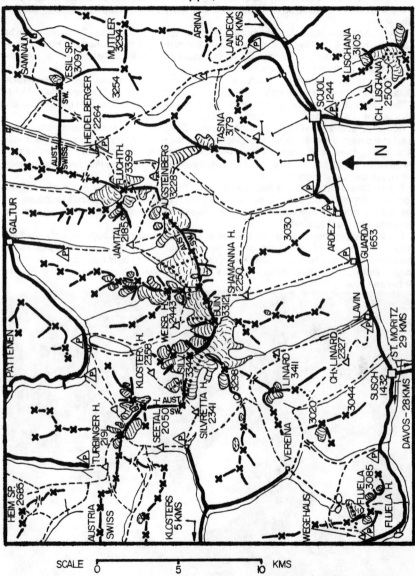

SCALE 0     5     10 KMS

# Kuchenspitze, Verwallgruppe, Austria

Located just to the north of the Silvrette Gruppe, is a little known massif called the Verwallgruppe. This cluster of peaks is immediately south of the Arlberg Tunnel and Pass, in extreme western Austria.

The peaks here are not as high as in other parts, but climbing may be more enjoyable since it's not quite as popular or crowded. It seems most people head for higher mountains elsewhere.

The highest peak in the Verwallgruppe, is Kuchen Spitze, 3170 meters. This summit can be ascended from either of two valleys. One can walk from Ischgl to the Darmstadter Hutte, thence to the top. One could also begin at St. Anton, walk or ride to the Konstaner Hutte, then the Darmstadter Hutte, and to the top.

Krenzjoch, 2919 meters, can easily be climbed from Himich or Kappl, then the Niederelbe Hutte, and by trail to the top. Patteriol, 3056 meters, is climbed from the Konstaner Hutte. Hoher Riffler, 3168 meters, can be acended from the area in which the Edmund Graf Hutte is located. This hut can be reached from Perpet or Pettneu.

Of the four above mentioned climbs, only Kuchen Spitze requires an ice ax and crampons, at least in the early summer. Later in summer, an all-rock route is possible. The same is true of other peaks; snow climbs early in summer—rock climbs later on. A fit climber can climb any of these peaks in one day from the lower valleys; however, most people take two days for each climb, spending one night in a hut.

At any of the towns or villages shown on the map, food can be bought. St. Anton is the biggest community in the region, so that's the best place to do shopping—for food and all supplies. For the best information concerning the higher routes, consult someone at a hut nearest the mountain you want to climb.

Public transportation is quite good. There is a rail line passing through St. Anton and the Arlberg Tunnel, as well as an international highway. Auto stopping is reasonably good as the main east-west road linking Innsbruck with Liechtenstein, is heavily traveled.

**Map:** Ratikon-Silvretta-Verwallgruppe, #37, 1 : 100,000, from Freytag und Berndt, Kohlmarkt 9, A-1010 Wien.

Northeastern slopes of Kuchenspitze.

# Map 61-2, Kuchenspitze, Verwallgruppe, Austria

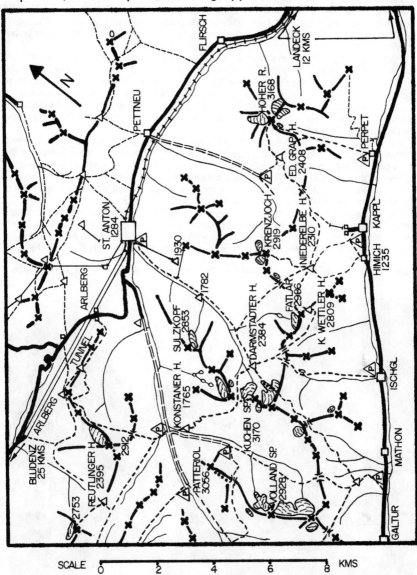

SCALE 0 2 4 6 8 KMS

## Wildspitze, Otztaler Alpen, Austria

To the southwest of Innsbruck lies the Otztaler Alpen, an area of high and glaciated mountains. The second highest peak in Austria, Wildspitze, 3772 meters, is located here. This group of mountains, the Otztaler Alpen, is covered in two maps. This one includes mountains in the western and northern portions, mostly west of Solden.

Access to the area is good, with an international highway running through Solden. Beyond Solden to the southwest, is Vent, the most convenient and centrally located village in the region for climbing purposes. Vent would make the best "base" for anyone wishing to make a number of climbs in the region.

Wildspitze can be climbed most easily from Vent and the Breslauer Hutte, but also from the Braunschweiger Hutte, located to the north. This latter route is much longer. From the Hochjoch Hopiz, or at least from that direction, one can climb Weisskugel, 3739 meters, or Dahmannspitze, 3401 meters. This is considered the "normal weg," for each mountain.

In the more northern area, Glockturm, 3355 meters, can be climbed from either the Gepatsch or the Hohenzoller Huttes. Wazespitze, 3533 meters, can be ascended from either the Verpeillhutte or Kaunergrat Hutte.

One is not obligated to use these huts of course, but they are good places to get the latest information on trail conditions and routes. One can camp anywhere on the mountain for the most part, but hut keepers generally frown on people camping too close to the shelters.

Besides the climbs just mentioned, there are many more in this area, most of which require snow climbing equipment (ice ax and crampons). The area to the left, or the southwest part of the map, is in Italy, but most climbs are made from the Austrian side.

Solden is a good place to stock up on food—as it's by far the largest town in the immediate area. There are also a couple of very small stores in Vent, as well as hotels and cafes. One will find public transport to Solden, but to nowhere else covered by this map. Auto stopping is usually very good, especially if one makes a sign indicating destination. Climbers have no problems getting lifts.

**Map:**   Otztaler Alpen, #25, 1 : 100,000, from Freytag und Berndt, Kohlmarkt 9, A-1010 Wien.

The Breslauer Hutte on the south face of Wildspitze.

# Map 62-1, Wildspitze, Otztaler Alpen, Austria

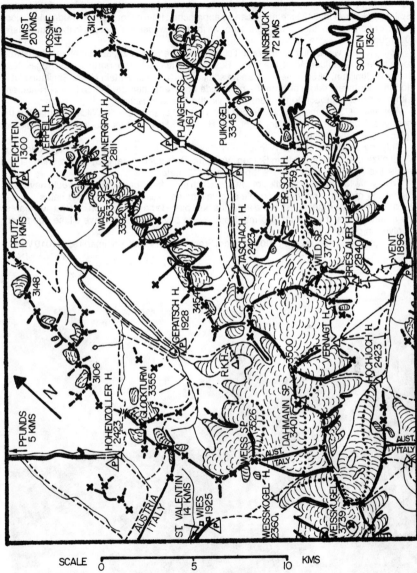

IMST 20 KMS · PIOSSME 1415 · 3112 · INNSBRUCK 72 KMS · SOLDEN 1362

FEICHTEN 1300 · ERPEL H. · PLANGEROSS 1617 · PUIKOGEL 3345

WASE SP. 3553 · KAUNERGRAT H. 2811 · 3391 · BR.SCH H. 2759 · WILD SP. 3772 · BRESLAIER H. 2840 · VENT 1896

PRUTZ 10 KMS · TASCHACH H. 2423

3148 · GEPATSCH H. 1928 · 3451

3106 · R.KH. · 3500 · FERNAGT H. · HOCHJOCH H. 2423

PFUNDS 5 KMS · N · GLOCKTURM H. 3355 · DAHMANN SP. 3410 · 3526

HOHENZOLLER H. 2423 · WEISS SP. 3526 · AUST. ITALY · AUST. ITALY

AUSTRIA ITALY · ST. VALENTIN 14 KMS · WIES 1925 · WEISSKOGEL H. 2360 · WEISSKOGEL 3739

SCALE 0 ____ 5 ____ 10 KMS

# Weisskugel, Otztaler Alpen, Austria-Italy

The Otztaler Alpen, a large group of high and glaciated mountains to the southwest of Innsbruck, will be covered in two maps. This map covers the southern section, which straddles the Italian-Austrian border.

One notable peak on the Italian side is Lodner Spitze, 3279 meters. The normal route to this summit is via Partschins, the Lodner Hutte, and the northwest ridge. To the north of Lodner Spitze, is Hochwilde, 3482 meters. It can be approached from either the Italian side, via Eisjoch Hutte, or from the Austrian or the north side, via the Hochwildehaus, located to the southwest of Obergurgl.

Going further west, the next important climb is Hintere Schwarze, 3628 meters. The normal route here is via Solden, Vent, the Martin Busch Hutte and either the north or west ridges. Next in line is Similaun, 3606 meters. It can be scaled via Karthaus, Rafein Hutte, Similaun Hutte, and the northwest ridge; or from the north side and Vent, then the Martin Busch Hutte, and either a direct approach to the summit or via the Similaun Hutte.

Weisskugel, 3739 meters, can be climbed via the Italian side (see Wildspitze map) or the northeast approach, via Solden, Vent, the Hochjoch Hospiz, over the long Hintereisferner (glacier), and the south ridge.

Only the southern route to Wildspitze is shown on this map—for the north approach see Wildspitze map. The route from Solden, Vent, the Breslauer Hutte, is by far the shortest and easiest to Austria's second highest peak, at 3772 meters.

If one were to choose one valley or town in which to make a "base camp," it would have to be the village of Vent. Vent has a couple of small stores, plus many hotels and cafes.

For directions to other peaks in the area, the best place to get information is at the hut nearest the mountain which you want to climb. Needless to say, one should have all the equipment involved in glacier travel.

**Map:**   Otztaler Alpen, #25, 1 : 100,000, from Freytag und Berndt, Kohlmarkt 9, A-1010 Wien.

Looking southwest from Vent with its picturesque church.

# Map 63-1, Weisskugel, Otztaler Alpen, Aust-Italy

SCALE 0 ____ 5 ____ 10 KMS

## Zuckerhutl, Stubai Alpen, Austria

In the region southwest of Innsbruck, Austria, is the high mountain range called the Stubai Alpen. There are a number of interesting peaks here, with varying degrees of difficulties. The highest of the group is Zuckerhutl, 3507 meters, and can be climbed from either Dresdner Hutte on the north, or Hildesheimer Hutte, on the southwest slopes.

Wilder Freiger, 3418 meters, is normally climbed from the Nurnberger Hutte, located north of the peak. Feuerstein, 3265 meters, can be scaled from either the Bremer or the Nurnberger Huttes.

Further north and to the west of the above mentioned summits, stands Wilde Leck, 3361 meters. The normal route to its summit is via the Amberger Hutte. Still further to the north is Schrankogel, 3486 meters. It can be climbed from either Amberger or Franz Senn Huttes.

If one prefers to do a lot of climbing, perhaps from one central location, the valley of Ranalt, with the Dresdner and Nurnberger Huttes, is the best choice. One drawback to this valley is the lack of any larger towns in which to do shopping. If you're going there, buy all your supplies in Innsbruck, located only about 30 kms away. If you prefer more detailed maps of the area get those in Innsbruck as well. While in Innsbruck, stop at the Austrian Alpen Club office near the center of town, for further information about routes, huts, etc.

Public transport is available to Solden, but there are no buses into the Ranalt area. For someone who looks like a climber, auto stopping is easy, especially if you hold a sign stating destination.

Most routes on the higher summits, in this region, involve some snow and glacier travel, so ice ax and crampons are required. On the other hand, if one of the normal routes is taken, oftentimes this equipment is not needed, as the way is very much a "well beaten path," right to the summit.

**Map:**   Stubaier Alpen, #24, 1 : 100,000, from Freytag und Berndt, Kohlmarkt 9, A-1010 Wien.

The north slopes of Zuckerhutl

## Map 64-1, Zuckerhutl, Stubai Alpen, Austria

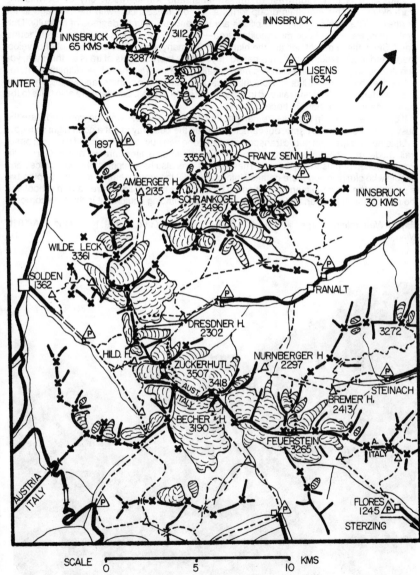

INNSBRUCK

INNSBRUCK
65 KMS

3112

3287

UNTER

3235

P LISENS
1634

N

1897 P

3355 FRANZ SENN H.

AMBERGER H.
2135

SCHRANKOGEL
3496

P

INNSBRUCK
30 KMS

WILDE LECK
3361

P

SOLDEN
1362

P RANALT

P

DRESDNER H.
2302

HILD. H.

ZUCKERHUTL
3507 3418

NURNBERGER H.
2297

3272

P

STEINACH

AUST
ITALY

BECHER H.
3190

BREMER H.
2413

FEUERSTEIN
3265

A.
ITALY

AUSTRIA
ITALY

P

FLORES
1245 P

STERZING

SCALE 0 5 10 KMS

## Zugspitze, Bavarian Alpen, Germany-Austria

After World War II, those who drew the boundaries pretty well eliminated the Alps from Germany (that's Deutschland). The German-Austrian border now follows the northern-most ridge of the Alps, putting Germany entirely on the "north slope." The highest summit in Germany, therefore, is on one of those ridges. Zugspitze, at 2962 meters, is that high point.

Zugspitze is just southwest of the summer and winter resort city of Garmisch—Partenkirchen. This mountain group forms a "U" or "horseshoe," with the drainage to the northeast. The rock climbing possibilities are tremendous, with all degrees of difficulty. Only problem is, it's near a large metropolitan area—Muchen. This makes the place a real "tourist trap." Since these mountains are the highest in Germany, one would expect a lot of development. And that's exactly what's happened. If you think there are lots of trails on this map, you should see some hiking and climbing maps available. Many trails have been eliminated here.

The area has many ski lifts and funiculars that are used both in summer and winter. There are even two funiculars and one railroad to the top of Zugspitze itself. But there are also trails to the summit as well—so there is hope.

If one is using huts in the area, remember that July and August—and the weekends, are the busy times. Few people camp, but camping may be the best way to get a good night's sleep.

Little need to mention public transport or where one can buy food. One could pick up a better trail guide in a bookstore which specializes in climbing literature in either Garmisch-Partenkirchen or Innsbruck, Austria. These two places also have alpen clubs, with offices and people who can give you more detailed information. Of the warm weather months, September is probably the most pleasant for outings in this area, as most children are back in school and the crowds much smaller. Little need for snow or ice climbing equipment in this little corner of the Alps.

**Map:** Wettersteingebirge, #34, 1 : 100,000, from Freytag und Berndt, Kohlmarkt 9, A-1010 Wien.

Austrian village to the south of Bavarian Alpen.

# Map 65-2, Zugspitze, Bavarian Alpen, Ger-Austria

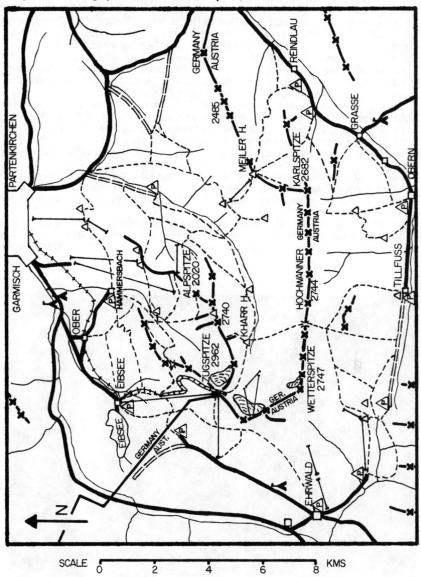

PARTENKIRCHEN

GERMANY
AUSTRIA

2485

MEILER H.

REINDLAU

GRASSE

OBERN

KARLSPITZE
2682

GARMISCH

OBER

HAMMERSBACH

ALPSPITZE
2020

KHARR H.

2740

GERMANY
AUSTRIA

HOCHWANNER
2744

TILLFUSS

ZUGSPITZE
2962

EIBSEE

EIBSEE

GER.
AUSTRIA

WETTERSPITZE
2747

GERMANY
AUST.

EHRWALD

N

SCALE  0    2    4    6    8  KMS

## Hochfeiler, Zillertaler Alpen, Austria-Italy

In an area to the southeast of Innsbruck lies the Zillertaler Alpen, which has a number of good peaks. The highest summit is Hochfeiler, at 3510 meters. The more normal way to climb this mountain is from the south or Italian side, via the Eisbruggjoch and/or the Hochfeiler Huttes. This part of Italy is known as Sudtyrol (South Tyrol) and is German speaking.

Along the same long ridge and to the east of Hochfeiler, stands Moseler, 3478 meters. It can be climbed from either Furtschagl or the Berliner Huttes. Next to Moseler stands Turnerkamp, 3418 meters. It's normally scaled from the north and the Berliner Hutte, but can also be approached from the south and the Neveser Joch Hutte at 2420 meters altitude. To the east of Turnerkamp are many other prominent peaks, all having some glaciation.

In the northern section of this map lies Olperer, 3480 meters. It's entirely within Austria and can be climbed from the Geraer or Spannagel Huttes. This area is much more developed having several ski lifts and is more of a winter resort than summer.

The two most common routes of approach to the Zillertaler Alpen are: from the south via Bolzano, Brixen, Bruneck, and to Luttach and Prettau. From the north the route is from Innsbruck, Wiesing, Zell, and Mayrhofen. Mayrhofen is the best place to make your headquarters if plans are to climb several mountains. It can be reached by road and train and is a big enough town to have ample book, food and sport stores. Auto stopping is also good to Mayrhofen.

If additional information is needed, contact the Austrian Alpen Club in Innsbruck—it's also the best place to pick up good maps. For any particular mountain the best place to get the latest information on trail or route conditions, is at one of the alpen huttes nearest the peak you plan to climb.

Most climbing is done during the months of July through September, but June is also good. Early September might be the very best, as children are back in school and the crowds smaller.
**Map:** Zillertaler Alpen, #15, 1 : 100,000, from Freytag und Berndt, Kohlmarkt 9, A-1010 Wien.

High mountain meadows are still trimmed with a sickle.

# Map 66-3, Hochfeiler, Austria-Italy

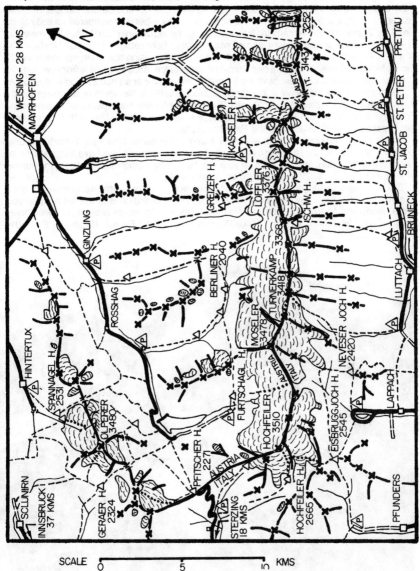

SCALE 0 5 10 KMS

## Hochgall, Rieserfernergruppe, Austria-Italy

Located on the border of northern Italy and southwest Austria, is a small mountain range known as the Rieserfernergruppe. It's not a large area, but has a couple of fairly high summits, with many easy routes and a few difficult ones as well.

The highest peak is Hochgall, at 3435 meters. Its north face has some tough routes, but the easy and normal way is from the eastern side, via the Patscher and Barmer Huttes. The route has some steep sections and part of it is on ice and snow—but it's considered an easy climb. From the Barmer Hutte one can also walk on a trail to the top of Lenkstein Peak, 3236 meters.

Another summit is Ruther Horn, sometimes known as Schneebiger Nock, 3377 meters. This is a very easy climb as there's a trail to the top—if one is using the south approach via the Gansebichljock Hutte. This route has almost no snow or ice. Another route is from the north via the Hochgall Hutte. One must have ice ax and crampons for one short section of this route.

There are two normal ways of approach to this area. From the south or southwest on the Italian side, one must pass through Brixen, Bruneck and Anterselva—thence to the mountains. From the Austrian or East Tyrol side, one must pass through Lienz or Matrei, then up a narrow secondary road to Erisbach and the Patscher Hutte.

This is a more remote area, with less traffic than in other parts of the Alps. There's little or no public transport and auto stopping a little slow. If doing the latter, always have a sign stating the name of the mountain, and last town on your trip. Many times a sign simply stating the number of kilometers (10 kms, 20 kms, and so on) works well.

The last places to shop in the area would be Bruneck, Lienz or Matrei. If one is unsure of the final route on the mountain, the best place to get that information is at the hut nearest your climb. June, July, August or September are the best months for mountaineering or hiking here.

**Map:**  Zillertaler Alpen, #15, 1 : 100,000, from Freytag und Berndt, Kohlmarkt 9, A-1010 Wien.

A  glacier on the northeast part of Hochgall.

# Map 67-3, Hochgall, Austria-Italy

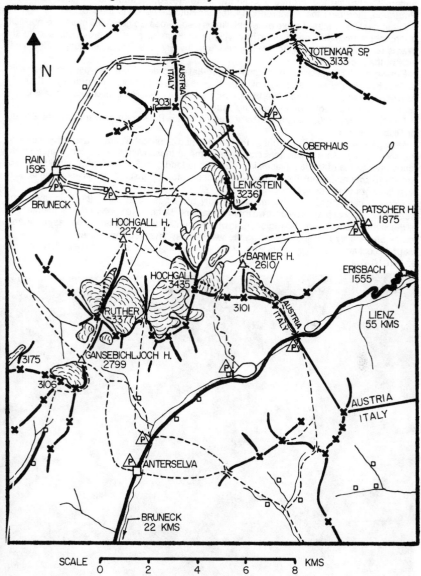

# Grossvenediger, Venedigergruppe, Austria

Included on this map are some of the highest peaks and largest glaciers in Austria. This is the area known as the Venedigergruppe. The highest peak is Grossvenediger, 3674 meters. It's located near the center of the group and is surrounded by glaciers, but is rated an easy climb. The normal route is from the north and the town of Neukirchen, the Kursinger Hutte at 2562 meters, then to the top. From the south the "normal weg," is from the towns of Matrei and Pragraten, then past the Johann and Defregger Huttes—hence to the top.

Other peaks in the area make excellent climbs also. Gross Geiger, 3360 meters, is normally approached from the north, from the village of Krimml, past Tauernhaus, and to the Warnsdarfer Hutte. It could also be climbed from the Essener-Rostocker Hutte on the south side of the area.

Rotespitze, 3495 meters, lies on the Austrian-Italian border. From the west and Italian side, drive to Kasern, then to the Lenkjochl Hutte, thence to the summit via the north ridge. From the east or Austrian side, drive to Hinterbichl, then walk to the Clara Hutte, and up to the pass on the north ridge, where both routes join leading to the summit.

Reichen Spitze, 3303 meters, can be scaled via Gerlos Pass or Krimml, and from the Zittauer or Richter Huttes.

Most people spend a night in one of these huts, then climb to the summit and return home on the second day. More fit climbers can make some of these climbs in one long day from the roads end. Some of the last places in which to buy food supplies are Matrei, Neukirchen, or Krimml. To get additional information and/or maps, stop in Innsbruck, the best place in all of Austria to get those things.

If one is climbing during the months of July or August, and using the huts, avoid the weekends, as local people overcrowd them at that time. Better take snow and ice equipment for all the higher mountains in this region. As in other mountain areas in Austria, the easy or normal routes are heavily traveled, so finding the way is easy, even on the glaciers.

**Map:** Glockner und Venedigergruppe, #12, 1 : 100,000, from Freytag und Berndt, Kohlmarkt 9, A-1010 Wien.

Northwest face and glacier of Grossvenediger.

# Map 68-3, Grossvenediger, Austria

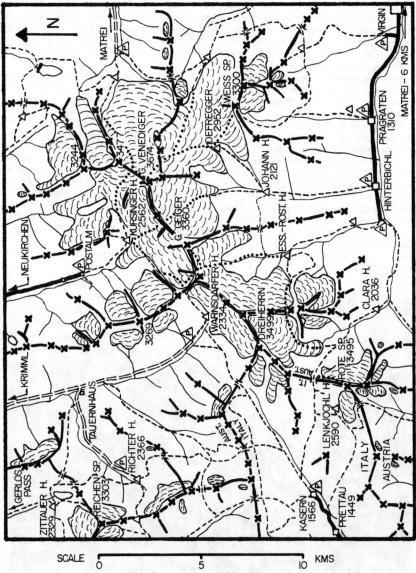

SCALE 0 5 10 KMS

# Grossglockner, Glocknergruppe, Austria

The highest summit in Austria is a mountain called Grossglockner, with an altitude of 3797 meters. It's also one of the better climbs in Austria. The normal route or "normal weg," has been made easy by a trail up a rocky ridge, then by hordes of people walking up a glacier, making a very good path in the snow. There's also a hut high on the mountain, which encourages some people who ordinarily would not be there to climb the mountain. Without the trail, snow path and hut, this would be a very good climb. Elsewhere on the mountain, very difficult routes exist.

The beginning of the trail to Grossglockner is at the Hotel Franz Joseph at 2451 meters. At that place there's a 4 or 5 level parking lot, needed to accommodate the thousands of tourists visiting the place each week. At this same complex, there are several small stores selling food and souvenirs, as well as prepared meals. There is no public transport to Franz Joseph, but auto stopping is easy.

From the parking lot, one can ride a lift *down* to the glacier, then walk over the ice to a ridge. There a trail begins, and follows first the ridge, then a route over snow to the Johann Hutte, 3454 meters, and finally to the summit. One can also ignore the lift and walk all the way, via the Hofmann Hutte.

Perhaps the second most important climb in the area is Grosswiesbachhorn, at 3565 meters. It's located a few kms north of Grossglockner, and to the west of the resort of Ferleiten. The normal way up this peak is from the northwest side and the Schwaiger Haus, at 2802 meters.

Both of these mountains and most others in the group, require at least an ice ax and crampons, as this is perhaps the most heavily glaciated area in Austria. Some of the places where food and supplies can be bought are: Mittersill, Lienz, Bruck, and the one place nearest the mountain, and a kind of climbers headquarters—Heiligenblut. This town has only one industry—tourism. It has many hotels, restaurants and small food stores. It is to Grossglockner, what Chamonix is to Mont Blanc, and what Zermatt is to Monte Rosa, only on a much smaller scale. For additional information, contact the tourist office in Heiligenblut, or the Austrian Alpen Club in Innsbruck.

**Map:**  Glockner und venedigergruppe, #12, 1 : 100,000, from Freytag und Berndt, Kohlmarkt 9, A-1010 Wien.

Foto taken from near the Hofmann Hutte.

# Map 69-1, Grossglockner, Austria

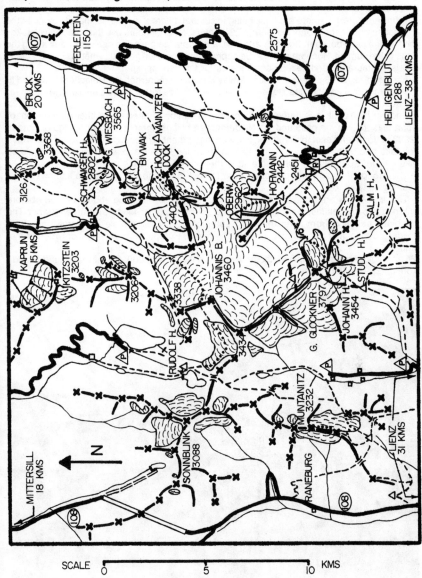

SCALE 0      5      10   KMS

## Hocharn, Goldberg Gruppe, Austria

Located in west-central Austria, just east of Heiligenblut and the highest summit in Austria (Grossglockner), is the Goldberg Gruppe. The group is not large in area or high in altitude, but there are some fair sized glaciers on the north-facing slopes.

If one is interested in doing several climbs or spending time in the area, the best place to go is the large basin on the north where Ammererhof is located. The highway route is via Taxenbach and Rauris.

From Ammererhof, there are trails going in several different directions, including one to the highest summit in the group, Hocharn, 3254 meters. Most climbers use this route, which takes them to the pass between Sonblick and Hocharn. From the pass one can walk north along the ridge to the summit. Hocharn can also be approached from Heiligenblut, where is located many hotels, restaurants, and several small stores for food shopping.

For Sonblick, 3105 meters, the normal way is from Ammererhof, the Rojacher Hutte, and to the summit, via a trail. No need for snow equipment on this route. There's also a lift to very near the summit.

Another high peak is Schareck, 3122 meters. It can be climbed from either Ammererhof or Sport Gastein, via the pass and the Niedersachsen Haus, then up the north ridge of Herzog (2933 meters), and east to Schareck. No snow equipment is needed for this route. However, if you take one of the other two routes as shown on the map, ice ax and crampons should be taken. From Sport Gastein, there's a lift to the top of Schareck.

The group can also be approached from Dollach and Innerfragant on the southwest and southeast sides.

This immediate area doesn't have any large towns, so shopping should be done before entering the mountains. Badgastein, Rauris, Heiligenblut or Lienz are larger towns. The climbing season is from June through September, but most people in Austria have their holidays during July and August, as does the rest of Europe. Huts are most crowded at that time.

**Map:** Goldberg-Ankogel, Radstadter Tauern, #19, 1 : 100,000, from Freytag und Berndt, Kohlmarkt 9, A-1010 Wien.

Main street in Heiligenblut, which lies west of Hocharn.

## Map 70-2, Hocharn, Goldberg Gruppe, Austria

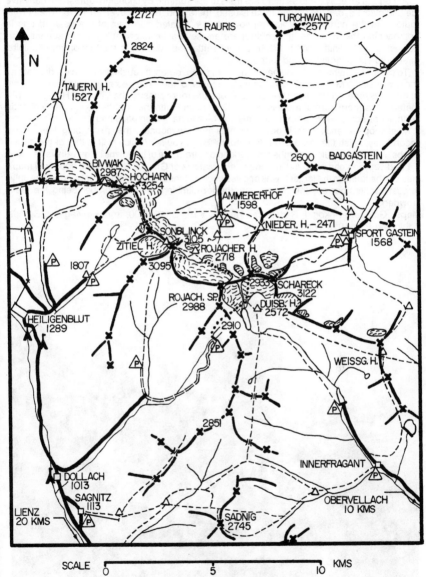

N

2727
RAURIS
TURCHWAND
2577

2824

TAUERN H.
1527

2600    BADGASTEIN

BIVWAK
2987    HOCHARN
3254

AMMERERHOF
1598

SONBLINCK
3105
NIEDER. H. – 2471

SPORT GASTEIN
1568

ZITIEL H.
3095
ROJACHER H.
2718

1807

2933    SCHARECK
3122

HEILIGENBLUT
1289
ROJACH. SP.
2988
DUISB. H.
2572

2910
WEISSG. H.

2851

INNERFRAGANT

DOLLACH
1013
SAGNITZ
1113
OBERVELLACH
10 KMS

LIENZ
20 KMS
SADNIG
2745

SCALE    0        5        10        KMS

# Ankogel, Ankogelgruppe, Austria

Almost due south of Salzburg and near the tourist resort town of Badgastein, is the last big mountain (or the most easterly big mountain) group in Austria. The best known peak here is Ankogel, at 3246 meters. However, the highest peak in this cluster is Hochalmspitze—3360 meters. East of Ankogelgruppe, the mountains are much lower elevation, and have no glaciers.

Ankogel is an easy climb as there are trails to the summit. By choosing routes, one can have ice and glaciers, or if the regular route is used, there's no need for even an ice ax. The normal route from the northwest is via Hannover Haus, located due east of the peak. If one is approaching the area from the south there are several ways of getting to the summit. The easiest is via Mallnitz, then the Schwussner Hutte, then directly to the top; or from Mallnitz, directly to Hanover Haus, and to the summit.

To climb Hochalmspitze, one has a choice of three routes. If you desire to have a dry path all the way, use the Mallnitz—Schwussner Hutte route, or the more westerly trail to the northwest of the Grossener Hutte. If you like glaciers, use the route passing the Villacher Hutte, at 2194 meters. The more normal route is via the Grossener Hutte then on the trail heading directly north. It has some snow to cross, so it may be best to have crampons and ice ax on this route.

Most people spend a night in one of the huts near the mountain they're climbing, then on the second day, finish the climb and return home. But if you're physically fit, either of the above climbs mentioned could be climbed in one long day from one of the towns in the valleys below.

Food supplies can be found in Badgastein, Mallnitz or Gmund. If you'd like good trail maps they can be found in the larger towns or cities such as Innsbruck, Salzburg, or Badgestein. July, August, September are the normal months for climbing, with September being the least crowded.

**Map:** Goldberg-Ankogel, Radstadter Tauern, #19, 1 : 100,000, from Freytag und Berndt, Kohlmarkt 9, A-1010 Wien.

Cows are curious, but seldom do damage to ones camp.

# Map 71-3, Ankogel, Ankogelgruppe, Austria

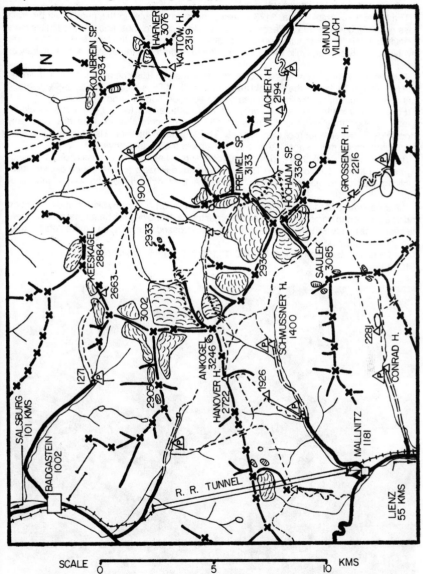

SCALE 0 _____ 5 _____ 10 KMS

# Tosa, Gruppo Brenta, Italy

Immediately east of the Gruppo Adamello and Presanella, and just to the west of Trento in northern Italy, stands the Gruppo Brenta. This rather small cluster of mountains is geologically part of the Dolomiti—most of which lies to the east of Trento and Bolzano and just south of the Austrian border. The rock here is dolomite, with many sheer faces. There are no glaciers in the Brenta, but some large snowfields exist.

The highest summit is Tosa, 3173 meters. The normal route up this peak is via the trails passing the Rifugios Brenta or Pedrotti. Both routes are steep climbs, and are rated a little more difficult than the "normal routes" up other peaks in the Alps. From the Rifugio Brenta the route involves a snow coulior, while the way from Rifugio Pedrotti, on the east slopes, is entirely on rock.

The second highest summit is Cima Brenta, 3150 meters. It can be ascended from the north and the Rifugio Tuckett or the Pedrotti area. Just south of Tosa is Cima Agola, 2953 meters. A trail reaches its top, via the routes passing the Rifugios Agostini and Apostoli.

If one is climbing in this central portion of the Brenta, an ice ax and crampons should be taken, although they may not be needed. Outside this central area there are few if any snowfields. The area is for rock climbing only. The weather in the Brenta is typically "Dolomiti," that is, with much more sunshine than in the Alps to the north and west.

The Brenta is a small area and is surrounded by good highways. Access is easy. A major highway runs from Trento, west to Tione, then north to Pinzolo and Madonna di Campiglio. Public transport is available in the form of buses. Auto stopping in northern Italy is only fair at best.

The area around Madonna di Campiglio, is a winter resort with many ski lifts and runs. Food and equipment can be bought in any of the larger towns. If one desires better maps of the area, the best place to buy is in Trento. The Brenta is criss-crossed with trails, so a more detailed map than this one may be desired.

**Map:** Brenta-Adamello-Presanella, #50, 1 : 100,000, from Freytag und Berndt, Kohlmarkt 9, A-1010 Wien.

The Dolomiti is one of the best rock-climbing area anywhere.

# Map 72-3, Tosa, Gruppo Brenta, Italy

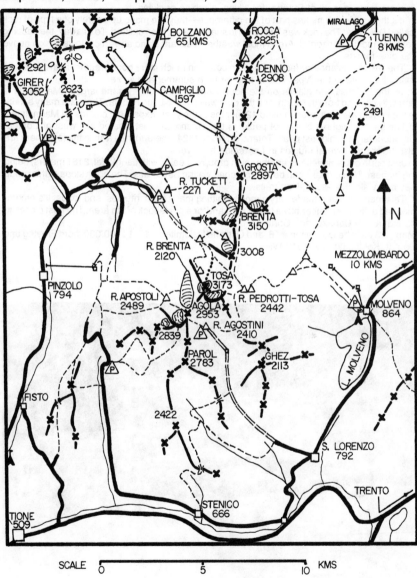

## Marmolata, Dolomiti, Italy

The Dolomiti, or Dolomites, are that part of the Alps lying just south of the present Austrian—Italian border, to the east of Bozano, and north of Belluno. The Dolomiti are not high when compared to other parts of the Alps—the highest peak being Marmolata, only 3342 meters. But they have distinctive qualities, which make them among the most attractive mountain areas in all of Europe, for hiking, climbing or skiing.

It's the rock which makes part of the difference—they are made up entirely of a type of rock called Dolomite. The rock was laid down in shallow seas, then uplifted. To this day, the bedding remains mostly horizontal. Areas most weather-resistant stand as vertical towers high above the pine forests.

The weather is another factor. One can count on much more good weather in the Dolomiti, than elsewhere in the Alps. This is true for both summer and winter.

In all the Dolomiti, the glacier on the north slope of Marmolata, is the largest. Marmolata is normally climbed from the north, and the dam which holds Lago Fadaia. There are many ski lifts in the immediate area and are used 12 months of the year. Expect big crowds on Marmolata!

The second highest cluster of peaks is the Tofano Gruppe, located just west of Cortina. Unfortunately, the highest peak, Tofano di Mezzo (3244 meters), has a lift to the top. There are also trails and several rifugios in the region however.

Just north of Campitello, is another high group of peaks, with Langkofel, 3181 meters, being the highest. These peaks can best be reached via the Sella Pass. The north slope of this group has many ski lifts—as well as trails.

This map has been made very simple, omitting many trails, rifugios, and roads. It's recommended a hiker or climber buy a better map and*or a guidebook of the area. The best places to do that are in Canazei and Cortina.

**Map:**   Westliche Dolomiten #16, and Ostliche Dolomiten #17, 1 : 100,000, from Freytag und Berndt, Kohlmarkt 9, A-1010 Wien.

The north face of Marmolata on a busy weekend.

# Map 73-1, Marmolata, Dolomiti, Italy

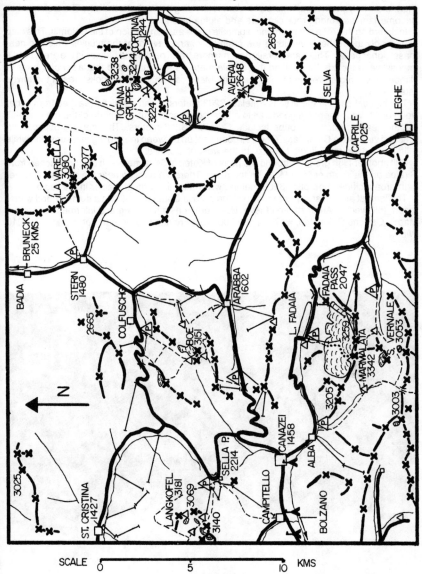

## Antelao, Dolomiti, Italy

The Dolomiti, or Dolomites, is that part of the Alps lying mostly to the east of Bolzano, south of Bruneck, and north of Belluno, in northeast Italy. The name Dolomiti, comes from a type of rock with a high limestone content. There are no granites, schists, or lavas here—only dolomite. The bedding or layers of rock are horizontal, with some portions more weather resistant. As a result, there are many prominent fingers of barren rock rising vertically to the sky. The Dolomiti has become famous among rock climbers and alpine hikers.

Included on this map are the higher summits of the eastern section of the Dolomiti. This map shows only the higher summits, a few main trails, and several of the rifugios which lie near these higher peaks. There are literally dozens more trails, peaks and rifugios in the area, but it's impossible to include them all on this simple map. It's recommended that a *serious* hiker or climber buy a more precise map of the area. Maps can be found in bookstores in the towns listed below.

The highest peak in the area is Antelao, 3263 meters. It can easily be reached from either Vodo or St. Vito. There's a good trail to a bivacco, or small hut, just north of the main peak.

Other easily reached groups include Cristallo, 3216 meters. This small group can be reached via the Tre Croci Pass. One trail goes right up between the two highest summits, while a lift ascends to the Rifugio Lorenzi, to the west of Cristallo.

Still another high group is around the peak of Kofel, at 3192 meters. It can be reached from Giralba on the south or from Moos on the north. There's a bivacco near the summit. Another high area includes Sorapiss, 3205 meters, which has the largest glacier in the region.

The largest and most important town in the area is Cortina—which is a summer and winter resort, followed by Auronzo, and Pieve. Use Cortina as a shopping and information center.
**Map:** Ostliche Dolomiten, #17, 1 : 100,000, from Freytag und Berndt, Kohlmarkt 9, A-1010 Wien.

More peaks north of Marmolata (Map 73).

# Map 74-3, Antelao, Dolomiti, Italy

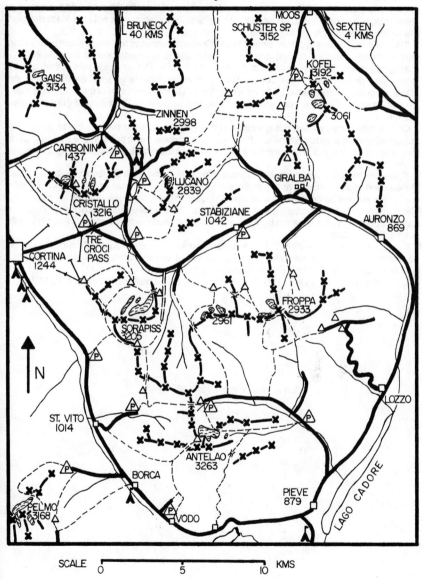

MOOS

BRUNECK 40 KMS

SCHUSTER SP. 3152

SEXTEN 4 KMS

GAISI 3134

KOFEL 3192

ZINNEN 2998

3061

CARBONIN 1437

LUCANO 2839

GIRALBA

CRISTALLO 3216

STABIZIANE 1042

AURONZO 869

TRE CROCI PASS

CORTINA 1244

N

FROPPA 2933

2961

SORAPISS 3205

LOZZO

ST. VITO 1014

ANTELAO 3263

LAGO CADORE

PELMO 3168

BORCA

PIEVE 879

VODO

SCALE 0 5 10 KMS

# Triglav, Julische Alpen, Yugoslavia

In the extreme northwest corner of Yugoslavia, where the boundaries of Italy and Austria now meet, is the highest mountain in Yugoslavia, Triglav, 2863 meters. The mountain is due south of the Austrian city of Villach, and southeast of Jesenice, the largest town in that part of Yugoslavia.

Triglav is part of the Julian or Julische Alpen. This part of the Alps now lies across the Italian-Yugoslav border, with about half lying in Italy. This map covers only the Yugoslav part where the highest summits are found.

The Julische Alpen are rather similar to the Dolomiti, further to the west in north Italy. The rock is largely limestone or dolomite, and is generally considered good for rock climbing.

In former times, the area was part of the Austrian Empire. The language tells of that, as four languages can be heard in the area of Triglav; Slavens (local language), Serbo-Croat (one official language of Yugoslavia), German, and Italian. On the Italian side of the border, the main languages spoken are German and Italian. In tourist areas a small amount of English is also spoken.

On the map, one can see many trails and mountain huts. All or most of the huts, but only about half of the trails are shown—as this area is criss-crossed with paths and is a popular area for the Yugoslav tourists. The Julische Alpen is perhaps the most easterly of the alpine regions of the Alps.

There are two main approaches to Triglav. One is from the town of Mojstrana, then via the place called Aljasev located at the end of the valley on the north side of the mountain. Trails lead to the summit on both the east and west ridges. There are several huts on the mountain. The area can also be approached from Bovec, Soca, and the valley just east of Na Logu. Either route is about the same distance from the mountain, and each requires about the same length of time for the climb.

If you prefer huts to camping, they are generally open from about July 1, through the end of September. Many of the huts offer sleeping and eating accommodations. Good public transport exists on all main roads in Yugoslavia.

**Map:**   Julische Alpen, #14, 1:100,000, from Freytag und Berndt, Kohlmarkt 9, A-1010 Wien.

Got a foto? Please send to author.

# Map 75-3, Triglav, Julische Alpen, Yugoslavia

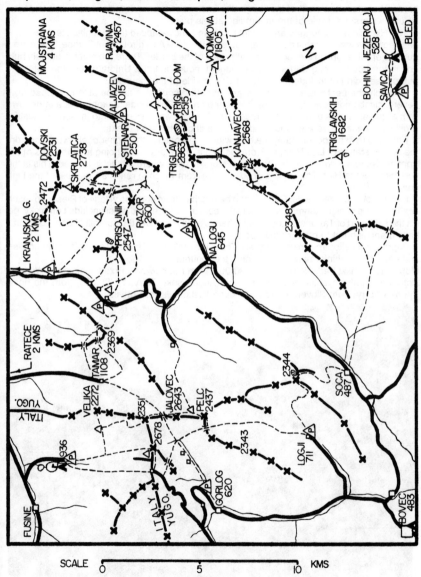

# Gerlach, Tatra Mountains, Poland—Czechoslavakia

The international boundary separating Poland and Czechoslovakia runs along the mountain tops, which include the Sudeten, West Carpathian and the East Carpathian mountains. About in the center of the West Carpathians, is located the highest portion of mountains in Eastern Europe and is called the High Tatra. This is a small massif in size and elevation, but it's the highest they've got. The highest summit is Gerlach, 2655 meters, located just inside the Czech border, but along the crest of the range (the international boundary does not conform to the natural watershed-divide of the mountains at this point).

The High Tatra is a rugged area, with alpine and snow-capped (but not glaciated) peaks. It has been developed a great deal, as are other parts of the Alps throughout Europe. There are a number of ski resorts in the region on both sides of the border. There are many mountain huts and resort hotels, along with a good network of mountain trails. Unfortunately, the maps the author used did not include much of the Czech side of the mountains.

Probably the best place to go to be amongst the mountains and be able to choose from several climbs and routes, would be Zakopane on the Polish side. Zakopane is a large town with all the amenities of a mountain resort city. In some ways it's similar to Innsbruck, Austria. From Zakopane, there are roads and trails leading to the high peaks.

From the Polish side, probably the best way of approach to the higher peaks would be from the border station of Lisa Polana. From that point, there are roads going to both sides of the frontier. There's a good road to the lake at Morskie Oko, where a hotel is located. This is the very heart of the High Tatra and is a good place from which to reach all, or most of the high summits.

If you're on the Czech side, Gerlach can be reached from near the village of Pleso. To reach another group of high summits, located to the east of Gerlach, and which include Lomnicky, go via the ski resort of Tatranska Lomnicky. There's a ski lift to near the summit of Lomnicky, and trails branching out to other rugged peaks.

Poprad and Zakopane are the largest cities in the region, and the best places to buy supplies and get additional information concerning the mountains.

**Map:**  Tatrzanski Park Norodowy, 1 : 30,000, from Panstowowe Przedsiebiorstwo Wydaw-nictw Kartograficznych, Warszawa, Poland. And Vysoke Tatry, 1 : 50,000, from the book **Vysoke Tatry,** from Slovenske Telovychovne Vydatatelstvo, Bratislava.

Tatra Mts. Cierny Stit-2434 meters left.

Map 76-3, Gerlach, Tatra Mts., Poland-Czech.

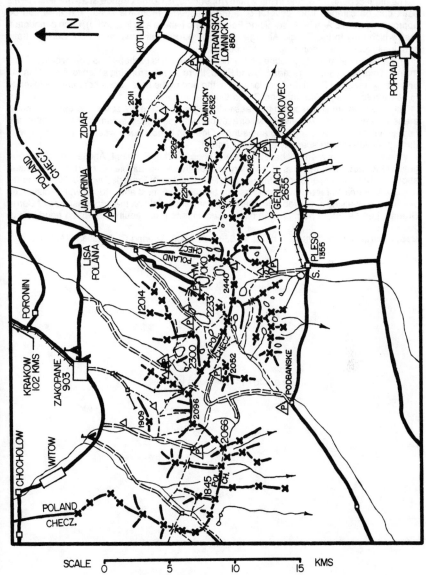

# Corno Grande, Gran Sasso, Alpi Appennino, Italy

The mountains forming the backbone of Italy and which run almost the length of the country, are known as the Alpi Appennino. They reach their greatest height in an area about 100 kms northeast of Roma, and are called the Gran Sasso d'Italia. The area has several ski runs, and can be reached easily from Roma via Autostrada 24 (A24).

The highest peak here, and in the whole Appennino, is Corno Grande at 2914 meters. This peak can be climbed from several different directions. From the south, the area can be approached from L'Aguila, Assergi and Font Cerreto (where a lift is located); or on a mountain road which runs to the Rifugio Albergo. From there, or lower down from Font Cerreto, trails eventually lead to the north side of the peak.

The area can also be approached from the north, which is perhaps less complicated. From the main highway (S80, or Strada 80) and Fano, there's a road running south to Pietra Camela and the ski resort of Pratti de Tivo, located at the end of the road. Trails here can be taken to Font Cerreto, Rifugio Albergo and Corno Grande.

This region is small compared to areas in the Alps, but there are some interesting climbing areas. The Autostrada 24 runs almost directly beneath the highest summits. Winter snows are heavy, but the summers are long and sunny. One can expect good weather from about May through October, with scarcely any precipitation.

When going to the area, it's best to stop and shop in either Fano or L'Aguila. The closer one gets to the mountain, the less of a variety of food there is available. For further information about local conditions, enquire at the rifugios, Font Cerreto, or Pratti de Tivo. Public transportation can found to as far as Fano and Assergi, but then one must auto stop or walk—distances are short, so walking's no problem. There's a small snow field on the northeast side of Corno Grande, but the *"route normal"* can be climbed with no more equipment that a good pair of boots.

**Map:** Carta Automobilistica D'Italia, #16, 1 : 200,000, Touring Club Italiano, Milano.

Got a foto? Please send to author.

## Map 77-3, Corno Grande, Gran Sasso, Italy

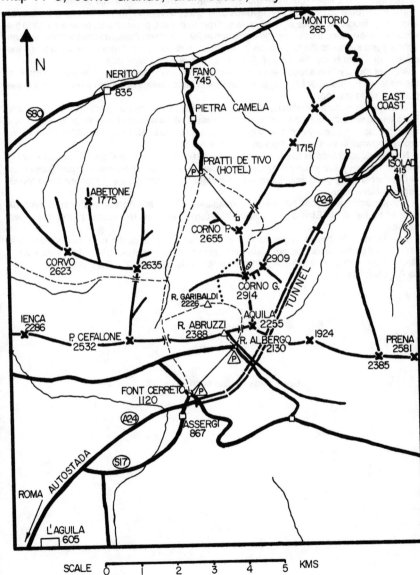

SCALE  0  1  2  3  4  5  KMS

## Mt. Etna, Sicily Island, Italy

Very near the east coast of the island of Sicily stands the highest mountain in Italy south of the Alps. This is Mt. Etna, reaching about 3340 meters. It's the most active volcano in Europe, and has been that way throughout written history. Despite its activity—or perhaps because of its activity, there are roads, trails, rifugios, lifts and an observatory on the mountain. It's a big tourist trap all the time—but even more so when the mountain is in full eruption.

The main route up the mountain involves driving to, then above, either Nicolosi or Zafferana, and to the Rifugio Sapienza at 1917 meters. From that point, one can walk or take the lift to the volcano observatory, located on the crater rim at 2942 meters. From the observatory one can walk around the rim to the highest point. Besides the observatory, there's also a rifugio on the crater's rim. Just below the Rifugio Sapienza, is located a resort hotel.

Another route, which is much less used, and the one to take if avoiding crowds is important, is the route via Fornazzo or Linguaglossa, and the Rifugio Citeli. From Citeli there's a trail to the crater rim and the top.

Etna is a dry mountain—that is, because it's a volcano, and made up of porus lava and ash, there are no streams high on the mountain. One must take a water bottle while on the climb, or if it's winter, spring, or early summer, snow can usually be found. Normally the mountain receives heavy snowfall in winter, but the summers are hot and dry.

No special equipment is needed—about any kind of shoe or boot will get you there (except in winter, of course). Early summer would be the best time to make the climb, with late September or October another good time. Each year is different, but normally the winter rains and snows begin in November.

One shouldn't go beyond Nicolosi or Linguaglossa without having food and/or other supplies needed for the climb. Etna is a one day climb from either of the two access points mentioned above.

On the main highways surrounding the mountain there is public transport, namely bus service; but getting up on the mountain will require one to have his own vehicle or auto stop.

**Map:**   Parchi Naturali D'Italia(Mt. Etna and others), Guida 2, 1 : 125,000, Instituto Geografico de Agostini, Novara.

Got a foto? Please send to author.

## Map 78-2, Etna, Sicily Island, Italy

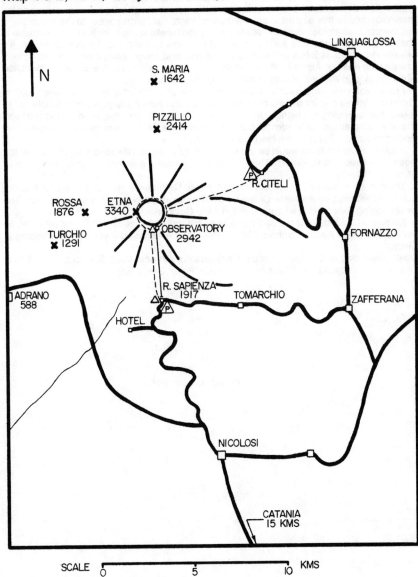

## Mytikas, Mt. Olympos, Greece

The highest mountain in Greece is Mt. Olympos, the highest peak of which is Mytikas, 2918 meters. This massif is located about 100 kms southwest of Thessaloniki, the largest city of northern Greece, and about 20 kms west of the main highway (E-92), which links the north of Greece with Athens.

On the mountain summits there have been found several very old ruins and remains dating back before Christ. Many Greek myths have come down through the centuries concerning the mountain, and to this day there are what some might call "pilgrimages" to the mountain.

Olympos is an alpine mountain, with several rugged peaks along a ridge. The normal route to the top is from the east and the resort town of Litochoran, at about 300 meters elevation. It's wise to stop there as it has restaurants, hotels and food shops. Also, there's an information office of the Hellenic Alpine Club located there. They can help out with additional information about trails, and the use of huts or rifugios on the mountain.

From Litochoran, the road continues on to the pilgrim's chapel or monastery called Dionisiou. Sturdy and fit climbers can make the ascent in one long day, but most people do the hike in two, spending one night on the mountain. One can camp or stay in one of the two huts. There's a marked trail to the summit, but it's not exactly a walk up. These peaks are impressive, and have some good rock climbing routes.

Another approach route would be from Ellasson, Kallithea and the road which ends near the base of Antonios, 2816 meters. There's a trail, at or near the end of that road, to the top of Mytikas.

The climate in this part of the world is called "Mediterranean," that is, it has long, hot, dry summers, with wet, cool winters. On the mountain of course, there's heavy snow in winter. The best climbing season is from June through early October.

No special equipment is needed if one uses the trail or "route normal." The area can be reached by either train or highway. Long waits can be expected if you're auto stopping in Greece.

**Map:** See map of Olympos in book, **Backpackers Greece,** Marc S. Dubin, Bradt Enterprises, Cambridge, Mass, USA and Chalfont-St. Peter, Bucks England.

Got a foto? Please send to author.

## Map 79-2, Mytikas, Mt. Olympos, Greece

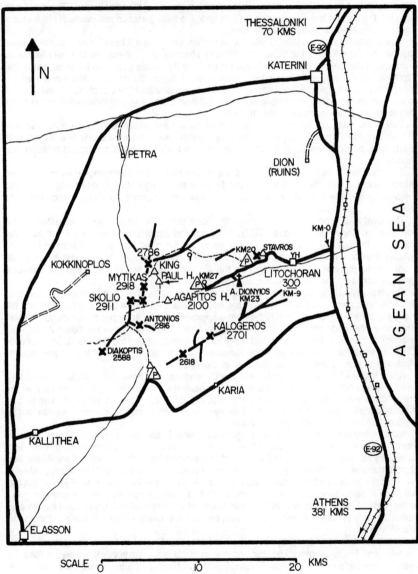

# Chapter 3 Africa

In this chapter covering Africa, are only 11 maps, as the continent has very little to offer in the way of climbing. Just about every mountain on the continent is included here.

It's difficult to make generalizations about the mountain types in Africa, but if one has to be made it would be that most have had their beginnings in the form of volcanism. About the only exception to this rule would be the Atlas Mountains of North Africa and the Ruwenzori on the Uganda-Zaire border. The mountains in East Africa, the Jebel Marra of Sudan, Tibesti of Chad, and Mt. Cameroun are all volcanos. In Ethiopia, the high plateaus are made of old lava and much of the Hoggar shows volcanic plugs.

The problems with languages are not what they could be if it hadn't been for the colonial period and the efforts of the British and French. Much of North, West and Central Africa were formerly under French control, so French is used by the native people in those areas as their "international language." Many other places such as Egypt, Sudan, East Africa and places in West Africa use English as their second language. In many countries, such as Nigeria, English is used as the only common language among different tribes. If you're fortunate to speak these two tongues, you'll have no problems while traveling in Africa.

Two of the most spoken native tongues in Africa are Arabic and Swaheli. Arabic is spoken throughout the Sahara and points north, as well as along the east coast of the continent. Swaheli is a mixed language which dominates East Africa, and is composed of about 40/ Arabic.

The weather in North Africa is controlled by the middle latitude cyclonic storm systems, which pass through the area from about November through May. These bring occasional heavy snows to the Atlas Mountains. Southern Africa experiences a similar situation during its winter.

The central portions of Africa, especially those within the tropics, are dominated by the Intertropical Convergence Zone (ITCZ). These are the equatorial jet streams which meander back and forth, north to south, during the year. For the most part, the wet season in Africa follows the sun—that is, when the sun is in the northern hemisphere, the rains are normally north of the equator. For mountains on the Equator, there two wet and two dry seasons, brought about by the north-south movement of the ITCZ.

Generally speaking, climbing difficulties in Africa are nil, but there are exceptions to this rule. For example, climbs in the Ruwensori are about equal to the best peaks in Europe, and Mt. Kenya is barely "soloable"—with the right equipment and by an experienced climber! There are some very good rock climbs in the Hoggar (and in the Dragensberg of South Africa—but that's not included in this edition), and some in the Ruwensori and that's about it. Snow and ice climbing equipment are needed in the Ruwensori and on some routes of Kilimanjaro and Mt. Kenya, and during some winter climbing in the Atlas.

Africa is one of the worst places in the world for travelers to have things stolen. Fortunately, most thievery occurs in the larger cities and on beaches. The main problem areas are where many tourists visit, such as Morocco and places in East Africa. Other countries such as Sudan, are completely different and very safe. See the chapter introduction for South America for tips on how to keep from losing your valuables.

Another generalization; in former English Colonies, public transportation is very good; in former French areas, it's very poor. It seems the British concentrated on building roads and especially railway lines, and the Franch did something else. Egypt, Sudan, East Africa and Nigeria have very good railway systems and bus service, while in French West Africa, railways are almost non-existent, and roads are nearly always dirt "tracks." However, if you've got the will to go to some far-out mountain range, you'll find a way. Auto stopping or hitching is good along parts of North Africa and in East and South Africa, but is almost unheard-of elsewhere. About the only private vehicles one sees on the roads in Black Africa are those belonging to missionaries.

For the most part public transport is cheap in the former English areas, expensive where the French were. There are almost no youth hostels in Africa, and what hotels there are, are usually expensive—that's in Black Africa. Sudan, Egypt and Morocco (in all Islamic countries) have many cheap hotels. If you're willing to eat food the natives eat, that can be cheap; but imported or European type food can be very expensive.

In East Africa, contact mountaineering clubs in the capital cities for further information about mountains in that region.

From the summit of Kibo, one has a good look down at Mawenzi (Map 88).

At about 3000 meters one must pass through a moss forest (Map 89).

## Toubkal, Atlas Mountains, Morocco

Most people think North Africa is as arid and dry as the Sahara Desert—but that's not true. There are some places, namely the high Atlas Mountains of Morocco, which have many streams, deep winter snows, and an invigorating climate. One of these places is on the route or trail to Toubkal, 4167 meters, the highest peak in Morocco and all of North Africa.

Toubkal and the Atlas are folded mountains with a variety of rock formations. The highest part is due south of Marrakech, about 60 kms by road. One could climb in the area from a number of directions, as there are sheep and goat trails criss-crossing the area, but the normal route is via Asni, Imlil (where the road ends), then by trail to the top. The author walked from Asni, and made the climb in 3 days, round-trip. But if one has less time, taxis can be hired at Asni for the trip to Imlil. The valley from Asni to Imlil is an oasis, with a fine stream of water, irrigated fields, and many trees. It's a nice walk.

At Imlil, the last village, one can find a small store or two, and buy enough basic food for the trip. For better variety, however, shop in Marrakech. Also at Imlil, is a climber's hut or refuge. Anyone can stay there—for a fee, of course. It was in good condition in 1974. From Imlil, the remaining climb can be done easily in two days.

Higher on the mountain is another refuge, at about 3000 meters. It's big enough to sleep perhaps 20 people. Apparently this mountain is climbed fairly frequently. There are no glaciers in the area, but snow stays late in the summer on the high summits. The best times to climb are from May or June, through October or even November. Heavy precipitation is often received in the winter months. There's a trail to the top which makes it easy, but it's a rugged area and more difficult routes can be found.

One can get to this area by bus or auto stopping from Marrakech. While in Marrakech, stop at the campsite or tourist office, to check on the condition of the huts, if you normally use huts when climbing. Last minute information indicates there are now 6 CAF(Club Alpine France) refuges located in the higher valleys of the Atlas. This 2nd map shows there locations.

**Map:** Michelin map 169, Maroc, 1 : 1,000,000; NH-29-3, 1 : 250,000 from US Army Defence Mapping Agency, Washington D.C., and a French IGN 1 : 100,000 map covering the Toubkal area.

A few kms below Imlil on the way to Toubkal, highest in the Atlas.

## Map 80-1, Toubkal, Atlas Mts., Morocco

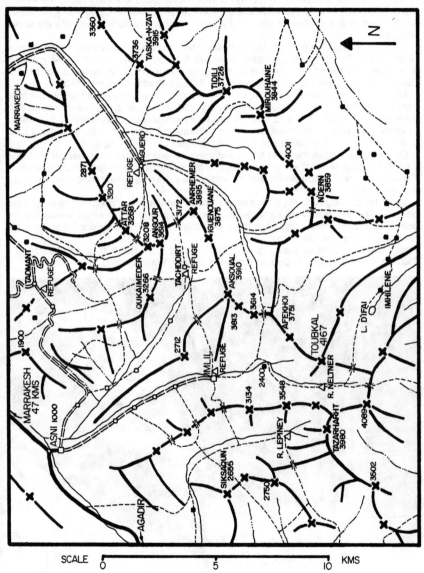

SCALE  0                    5                    10   KMS

## Khedidja, Djurdjura Massif, Atlas Mts., Algeria

Stretching almost halfway across North Africa, from the south of Morocco to Tunisa, are the Atlas Mountains. They reach their highest in Morocco with Toubkal, then gradually become lower to the east. But in about the center of the north of Algeria, is another high mountainous area known as the Djurdjura Massiff. The highest peak is Lalla Khedidja, at 2308 meters elevation. Another summit nearly as high is Timedouine, 2305 meters. It lies to the west of Khedidja about 12 kms. These mountains are not big by alpine standards, but the higher slopes are forested, with a mixture of trees and brush, and the very highest summits are above timberline.

Getting to the Djurdjura is easy. Not far to the north is the main coastal highway linking all of North Africa. To the south is another important highway running south of the divide or watershed. In the middle of the massif another good road runs from M'chedallad, north to Tizi Ouzou (located on the main coastal highway). This link-road is numbered N-30.

No public transport exists on N-30, with the exception an occasional taxi, but the main east-west highways on either side of the Djurdjura have much traffic. The author walked from the town of M'chedallad, up road N-30 a ways, then cross country finally reaching Tala-Rana. From there a trail exists which is easy to follow to the summit. After the climb, the author walked all the way back to M'chedallad on the road. This was all in one long day.

On the higher slopes there are brush and trees, as well as goats and shepherds. Above Tala-Rana, is a pine forest with wild monkeys, or maybe barbary apes—or something like that! Timber line is around 2100 meters, with the part above that altitude windy and barren, as on any high mountain.

M'chedallad is large enough to have several shops and stores, and good food selections can be found. The route is very dry, so carry enough water for the trip. In mid-winter, snows become deep, and in 3 or 4 of the summer months the temperatures are high, making fall or spring the ideal time to climb or hike in the Djurdjura.

**Map:** Michelin Highway map Algerie-Tunisie, #172, 1 : 1,000,000, and NJ-31-15, 1 : 250,000, from the US Army Defence Mapping Agency, Washington D.C.

Hoarfrost on the highest trees on the south slopes of Khedidja.

## Map 81-1, Khedidja, Djurdjura Massif, Algeria

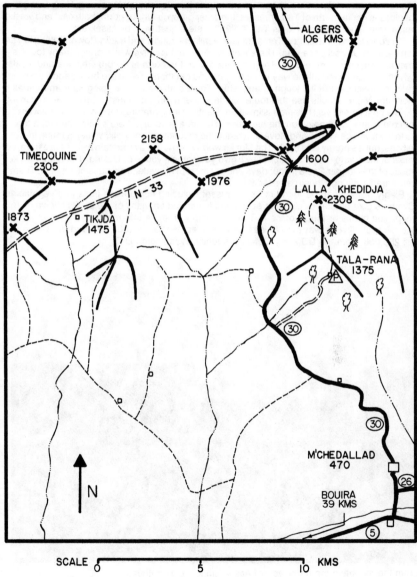

## Tahat, Hoggar Mountains, Algeria

For those people who want to climb or hike in unusual places, the Hoggar Mountains in south central Algeria, might be one place. Actually this region is more of a plateau than true mountains, as much of it appears similar to parts of the Colorado Plateau in the southwest USA.

Intermingled among the flat-lying beds are two separate groups of peaks which are actually the remains of volcanic plugs, again very similar to Devil's Tower in Wyoming, USA. One group of plugs is not far north of Tamanrasset; the other group is further north, both east and west of Assekrem. The highest peak is Tahat, 2918 meters, just west of Assekrem.

The only town in the area is Tamanrasset, a military, tourist and trading town. Getting to Tam isn't as difficult as it once was. There's an airport—an incentive which brings many tourists to the area, mainly from France. There's a road from the north and from Ghadaia and Insalah which may be paved all the way to Tam when you get there. There are buses and trucks, and private vehicles—but it's tough to auto stop. There's also a track leading up from Agades in northern Niger. Trucks use this route regularly, but overland tourists must travel in convoy.

The best time to visit this area is in winter. Daytime temperatures then are pleasant with cool or cold nights, depending on the elevation. The area is so dry, there's little need for a tent.

In Tam you can hire Land Rovers to reach the mountains—or walk. Water is found in 3 or 4 places, but it's hardly fit to drink. The Monks who live on top of a mountain called Assekrem, get most of their water from tourists. They'll give you some if you're out hiking. The author walked much of the Hoggar Circle in four days and got most of his water from passing tourists. There's more traffic during Christmas holidays.

Plenty of food can be found in Tamanrasset including some fresh fruits and vegetables. Climbers take note: rock climbing equipment is needed on many of the peaks shown on this map. The hotels or tourist office in Tam can help with more information.

**Map:**  Michelin Highway map Africa North and West, #153, 1 : 4,000,000, and NF-31-4 and 8, 1 : 250,000, from the US Army Defence Agency, Washington D.C.

From the mountain top hermitage of Assekrem looking southeast.

# Map 82-1, Tahat, Hoggar Mts., Algeria

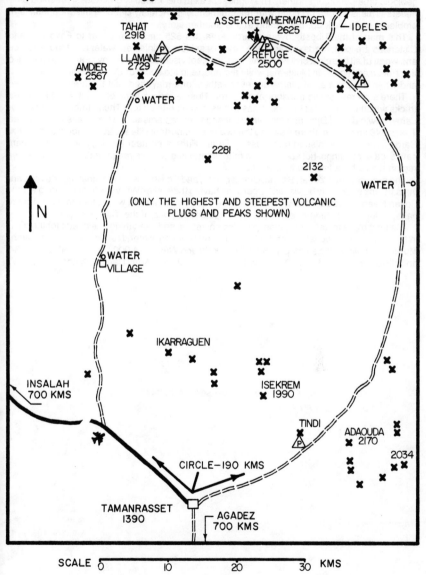

## Emi Koussi, Tibesti Mountains, Chad

In the very heart of the Sahara Desert and in the extreme north of Chad, is an area called Tibesti. This is a rugged mountainous region with many dry river beds called wadis and a number of relatively high mountains; most of which are a result of volcanism, during one geologic time period or another. The highest peak in the Tibesti is Emi Koussi reaching 3415 meters. This is a volcanic cone with huge dimensions. Actually climbing this mountain is no problem—it's a walk up, but getting to it is another story.

This map of the Tibesti covers a large area. It's 525 kms from Zouar to Faya Largeau! Distances are long, roads or tracks are never or seldom maintained, water and food is scarce, and worst of all there's a civil war there that has kept visitors out for many years. The people of the Tibesti are nomadic Moslems, while the people in the south of Chad are Black Africans. If and when the political problems are ever settled, one may then visit the area.

There's no real public transportation to the Tibesti—as we think of it, but there are cargo trucks which provide that service. Passengers always ride on top. These trucks begin in Fort Lamy, now called N'Djamena, and first proceed to Faya Largeau, where an airstrip is located. That's 948 kms! From there it's on to the two most important villages in the Tibesti, Zouar and Bardai. There's a furnished resthouse at Zouar. Further on near Bardai, one can find many caves, cave paintings, hot springs, and other interesting sites. If transportation was better, this region would be a fine tourist attraction.

The area between Zouar, Bardai, Chegar Teck, and Emi Koussi, is the most rugged area and the part which can only be visited by persons having their own 4WD vehicle or by hiring a Land Rover. Needless to say, one would have to be equipped with extra water, fuel, tools and spare parts, before attempting a journey to the unsettled regions of the Tibesti.

The best place to get information, permission, maps, and everything one needs for the trip is in N'Djamena, the capital of Chad. Plan your travels during winter, November through March.

**Map:**   Michelin Highway map #153, Africa North and West, 1 : 4,000,000. And NF-33 and 34, and NE-33 and 34, all 1 : 1,000,000, series 1301, from the US Army Defence Mapping Agency.

Got a foto? Please send to author.

# Map 83-3, Emi Koussi, Tibesti Mts., Chad

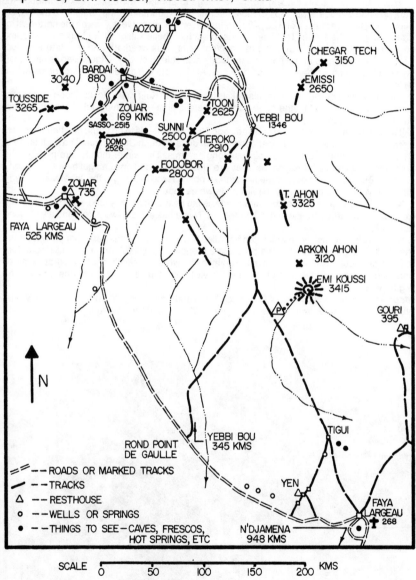

AOZOU

CHEGAR TECH
3150

BARDAÏ
880

EMISSI
2650

3040

TOUSSIDE
— 3265

TOON
2625

ZOUAR
169 KMS

SASSO—2515

YEBBI BOU
1346

SUNNI
2500

TIEROKO
2910

DOMO
2526

FODOBOR
2800

T. AHON
3325

ZOUAR
735

FAYA LARGEAU
525 KMS

ARKON AHON
3120

EMI KOUSSI
3415

GOURI
395

N

ROND POINT
DE GAULLE

YEBBI BOU
345 KMS

TIGUI

==— —ROADS OR MARKED TRACKS

— — —TRACKS

△ — —RESTHOUSE

∘ — —WELLS OR SPRINGS

YEN

FAYA
LARGEAU
268

● — —THINGS TO SEE—CAVES, FRESCOS,
HOT SPRINGS, ETC

N'DJAMENA
948 KMS

SCALE   0      50      100      150      200   KMS

## Jebel Marra, Sudan

To the people of western Sudan, Jebel Marra is a region, rather than a single mountain. It includes a number of villages and several stream valleys, which encircle an old, eroded volcanic caldera. On the southern rim of the caldera is the highest summit in the area, at 3042 meters. This crater holds two lakes—one salty, the other fresh water.

There are many trails leading from one village to another, therefore trekking through the canyons and villages is perhaps of more interest than mountaineering. Getting to the highest summit will take perhaps 4 or 5 days from either Nyertete on the west, Suni on the northeast, or Kalu Kitting on the south. There are roads to each of these villages with trucks coming and going on market days. Kalu Kitting has a Wednesday Suk (market), and Nyertete and Suni have a few fruits, nuts and other meager foods available each day. Other villages have their own suks, each on a different day of the week. At Nyertete is a government experimental fruit farm.

The route used by the author for his trek, is the one from Kalu Kitting to the Trongtunga area. However, his guess is that the route from Nyertete is best—if reaching Jebel Marras highest summit is important.

It's wise to stay near a stream or on any good trail, as water is to be found nowhere else. It is warm the year-around, the rainy season is from June through September. The vegetation is typically "Savannah", with green places along streams. The winter months are perhaps the best time for a visit to this region, as skies are always clear, and one can get by without a tent. Remember, water and heat are the two biggest obstacles to trekking in the Jebel Marra. Carry plenty of water and continually inquire of its whereabouts.

Nyala, located at the end of the railway line, is the best place to buy food—also it's the place to inquire about trucks going to the Jebel Marra. Nyala has at least two hotels and a very good daily suk.

Nyala is also the last place which can be called "civilization." Things get rather primitive once the rail line is left behind—but the people are friendly and helpful. An important stop before leaving Khartoum, is at the Lands and Survey office where relatively good topographic maps can be purchased. At the time of the author's visit, the map covering the northern half of the region was out of stock.

**Map:**  Michelin Highway map #154, Africa North and East, 1 : 4,000,000. And ND-35-M, and ND-34-I, 1 : 250,000, from Lands and Survey Office, Khartoum, Sudan.

This is Jebel Marra from the south and near Kalu Kitting.

## Map 84-1, Jebel Marra, Sudan

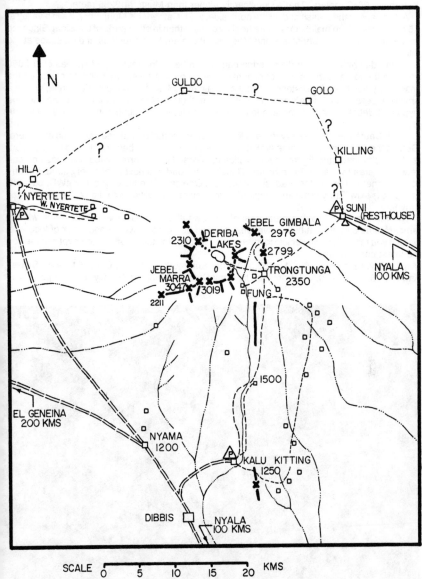

## Jebel Musa (Mt. Sinai), Sinai Peninsula, Egypt

In the heart of the Sinai Peninsula is a group of mountains the Christian world knows as Mt. Sinai. The Moslems know the same mountain as Jebel Musa. In Arabic the name Musa, means "Moses." It's the most famous peak in the area and one of the best known in the world, but it is not the highest in the region. To the southwest about 3 kms is the highest summit, Mt. Katernina, 2642 meters. That's significantly higher than Musa, at 2285 meters.

At the base of the massif and on the north side, is St. Catherine's Monastery. It's in a valley at 1570 meters, which makes for a more healthy climate than in other parts of the Sinai. Since the mountain is sacred to Christians and Moslems, there are both churches and mosques at the site.

In one day both Musa and Katherina can be climbed. One route up Musa has over 3000 steps to the top and thousands of pilgrims have made this ascent over the 14 centuries the monastery has been in existence. There's a trail from Musa to the top of Katherina, where a small chapel stands. There's another route connecting the Monastery with Katherina; this one bypasses Jebel Musa. It's possible to make a circle route and climb both summits, all in one day.

At St. Catherine's Monastery there is limited accommodation, but one can camp anywhere. Getting there may present some problems. In recent years it has been controlled by Israel, but that has changed, and Egypt now occupies the Sinai. Under normal circumstances one can reach the area by way of Elate or Abu Rudeis. The road has never been very good, but bus tours go there often, so the road isn't really bad. One can drive his own car or 4WD, but auto stopping is slow. Entry to the area depends largely upon the political situation at the time of your arrival.

The Sinai is desert, with a great deal of good weather. It's never very cold, but in winter, temperatures can drop at high elevations. It would be best to have a good stock of food and water if you take your own vehicle to this region. Check at the tourist offices in Egypt or Israel for the latest conditions.

**Map:** Egypt Highway map, 1 : 750,000, from Kümmerly und Frey, CH-3001, Bern, Swiss. And NH-36-   , 1 : 250,000, from the US Army Defence Mapping Agency, Washington D.C.

St. Catherines' Monastery at the foot of Jebel Musa (Sinai).

## Map 85-3, Musa (Sinai), Sinai Peninsula, Egypt

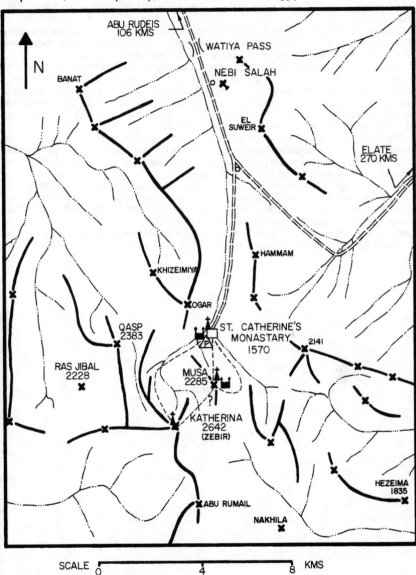

## Ras Dashen, Semyen Mountains, Ethiopia

The highest point in Ethiopia is the mountain of Ras Dashen, 4550 meters. This is hardly a mountain, but rather only the highest point on an escarpment or plateau. Geologically, this area was once the scene of many volcanic outpourings laid down in horizontal beds. Later there was tilting and uplifting and still later—which brings it up to the present—there has been erosion causing this great escarpment. It has some similarities to parts of the Colorado Plateau in the southwest USA.

Climbing Ras Dashen is more of a trek than a climb. In some ways it's very similar to trekking in Nepal—there are lots of up and down trails, and many small villages along the way, where one can see many rather primitive people living in a basic agricultural economy.

The shortest and simplest way to reach the mountain is to proceed to the village of Debarech, located on the main highway linking Addis Ababa, Gondar and Asmara. From there, one of many trail heads in a east, northeast direction to the village of Geech. The main trail then heads east to a pass near the high point of Buahit, 4437 meters. Not far beyond that the trail winds down to the bottom of the Mayschaha River Gorge, then there's a long uphill grade to the pass just west of Ras Dashen, at about 4300 meters, and an easy scramble to the summit.

This trek will take about a week roundtrip. It's best to buy your food and fuel supplies in one of the larger cities—such as Gondar, Asmara or Axum. As mentioned previously, there are many small villages en route, so one need not starve to death if supplies run out, but only the barest necessities will be found in the mountain villages.

Remember, this entire trek is at high elevations, and although it's in the tropics, cold temperatures exist there, especially since there's a great deal of cloud cover higher up. The best months for climbing are September to December. For additional information, contact the Semyen Mountain National Park, headquartered in Gondar.

**Map:** Hoch Semyen, 1 : 50,000, Boyerisches Landesnermessungsamt, Muchen. And Michelin Highway map Africa North and East, #154, 1 : 4,000,000.

Got a foto? Please send to author.

# Map 86-3, Ras Dashen, Semyen Mts., Ethiopia

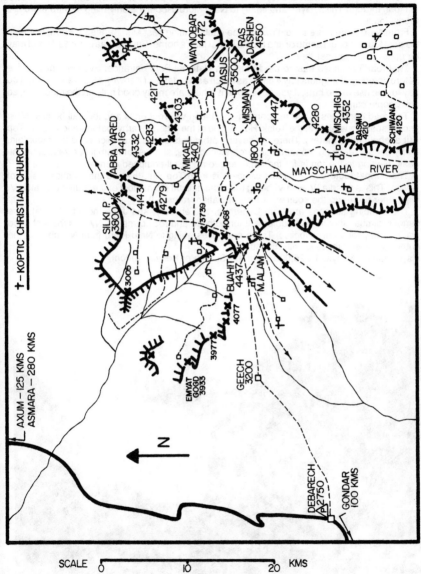

## Batian Peak, Mt. Kenya, Kenya

Mt. Kenya is located due north of Nairobi about 175 kms, and near the center of Kenya. Mt. Kenya, with its twin summits, Batian, 5201 meters, and Nelion, 5190 meters, is the second highest mountain in Africa. Like most of East Africa's high mountains, it too is an old and eroded volcano. In fact, it's so old that only the throat or plug remains.

Getting to the mountain is easy. There's a very good paved highway running north out of Nairobi, through Thika, Nyeri and finally to Naro Moru. About the only thing at Naro Moru is a tourist lodge.

From Naro Moru there's a dirt road to the east, running past Mrs. Kenealy's Farm, where in the past tourists could camp or find rooms in that lady's home. But she was old in 1974 and may be gone when you get there.

That road continues east to the Mt. Kenya National Park entrance. Everyone pays a fee before entering (foreigners pay 4 times as much as residents of Kenya!). This is also where you pay for the use of the huts, if you have no tent. There are many good huts on the mountain, so few people camp.

The road continues to the meteorological station where it ends and the trail begins. Most people spend one night in the Teleki Hut, or one of the others nearby, before reaching the Top Hut at about 4800 meters. There are several other huts on the trail which rings the mountain. Many people reaching the mountain are trekking only, so most of them just hike around the peak. Getting to the top is for the experienced and well-equipped climbers only.

The normal route used by most climbers is from Top Hut, then up the southeast side of Nelion. This is rated a IV, with VI being the most difficult pitch. Most of the routes are rated V. One other route, up the southwest face of Batian, rates a IV.

The climbing seasons are from December to February, and June through August. The serious climber should take equipment for both ice and rock climbing. Nyeri is the last good place to buy food and supplies. There are buses going to Naro Moru from Nairobi, but the author got lifts both ways with his thumb.

**Map:**   Mount Kenya, 1 : 25,000, from the Survey of Kenya, Nairobi.

Top Hut to the right on ridge, with Batian and Nelion left.

# Map 87-1, Batian, Mt. Kenya, Kenya

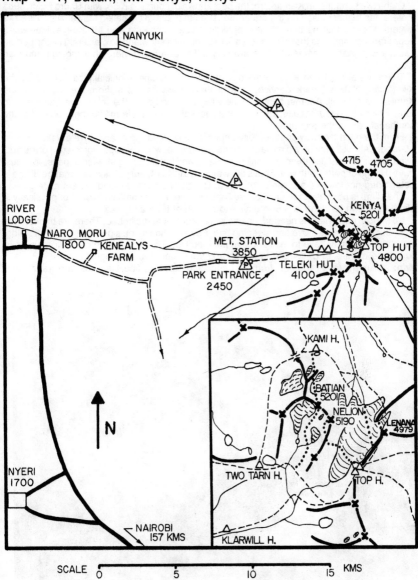

## Kibo, Mt. Kilimanjaro, Tanzania

One of the most awesome and spectacular mountains in the world is Kibo, which is the highest of the two summits forming Mt. Kilimanjaro. The mountain is located in northern Tanzania, near the Kenya border. It rises from the dusty plains at an altitude of about 1000 meters, to nearly 6000 meters, in a distance of about 30 kms.

Of the two summits on Kilimanjaro, the best known of course is Kibo, with Uhuro Point, 5963 meters, the highest place on the crater rim. The other summit is called Mawenzi and is 5149 meters. Mawenzi is the third highest peak in Africa, after Kibo and Mt. Kenya. Mawenzi's appearance is similar to that of Mt. Kenya. It has very little snow and no glaciers. The top portion has many pinnacles, some of which are very difficult—a much more challenging climb than Kibo.

There are about three trails to the mountain, but only one is officially sanctioned by the Kilimanjaro National Park Service. One of these trails comes in from the north and the Kamwanga sawmill. Another begins at the village of Kombo, on the southwest. But the main route which all the tourists use, and by far the best trail, is the one from Marangu, located on the southeast part of the mountain.

From the main highway south of Kilimanjaro, turn north at Himo, and drive or take a bus to Marangu. About 3 kms up a dirt road is the park entrance, where you pay for the use of the huts (whether or not you use them, you still must pay!), and before being allowed to pass, you must have a guide or porter with you. That's the way it was in 1974, but policies can change (If one is determined not to have a guide or porter, a way can be found around the entrance gate!).

The climb is normally made in 5 days. That's for the unacclimatized hiker. For physically fit climbers, it can be done in 3 or 4 days—to the top of Kibo and back.

No special equipment is needed, unless an unusual route is climbed. There are bunks in the huts, but you'll need a stove and sleeping bag. Pay attention to the sign, "last water." It's a dry mountain. You may have to melt snow at the Kibo Hut. The best time to climb Kilimanjaro is during the months of December to March and from June through August.

**Map:** Kilimanjaro, 1 : 100,000, from the Lands and Survey Office, Dar es Salam, Tanzania.

A look at Kibo from the Mawenzi Hut. The saddle is in between.

## Map 88-1, Kibo, Mt. Kilimanjaro, Tanzania

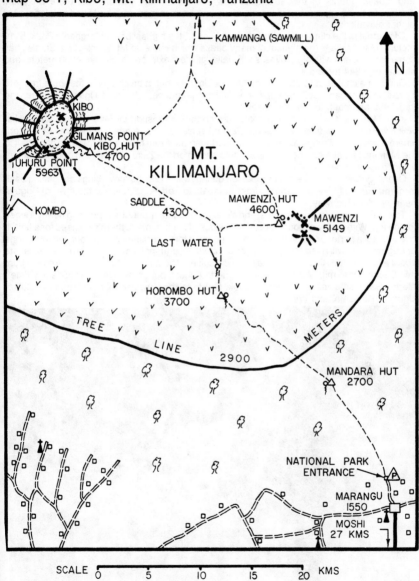

# Margherita, Ruwensori Mountains, Zaire—Uganda

Some of the most unique mountains in the world are found in East Africa and the most peculiar of them all are the Ruwensori Mountains sitting on the Zaire-Uganda border. These mountains are mostly known for their strange animal and plant life. The plant life seems to "go crazy" above the 3000 meter level, as one finds giant groundsel (up to 12-14 meters), heather and lobelia. Plants of this size exist nowhere else in the world. Also, there are giant earthworms—nearly a meter in length, along with strange monkeys, birds and antelope, all at higher elevations.

Of interest to the climbers are the glaciated peaks, the highest being Margherita Peak, 5119 meters. Margherita is the highest of many peaks which make up Mt. Stanley. Mt. Stanley has some real glaciers with big crevasses. Smaller glaciers exist on Mt. Speke, 4890 meters, and Mt. Baker, 4844 meters.

One has a choice of climbing from Zaire or Uganda, but at this moment the route from the Zaire side looks bad—politically speaking, but things change. In the past, Uganda has been the traditional approach to the Ruwensori.

In 1974 during the author's trip, there was no public transport in Zaire—only a few trucks, which were very few and far between. Several vehicles a day made it to the area of Mutsori, where there is the Virunga National Park Headquarters. From Mutwanga there's a good trail to the Moraine Hut at 4400 meters. All shelters shown on the Zaire side were in good condition, with stoves and beds (1974).

On the Uganda side, interest dropped off during Amins rule, but now things are getting back to normal. Buses take passengers from Kampala to Fort Portal, then to the town of Bugoye near the main highway.

To enter this area from either side, and climb one mountain, count on spending nearly a week for the trip. With plenty of good huts on both sides of the mountain, there's no need for a tent. If one desires a porter or guide (there's really no need for either) they can be found in Mutwanga or Bugoye. One will need rain gear, extra dry clothing, crampons and ice ax. These peaks rate about even with the Alps, as to some route difficulties. The driest times to visit the area are from mid-December to mid-March, and from June to August, but expect wet conditions any time.

**Map:** See Osmaston and Pasteurs book, **Guide to the Ruwenzori,** from Mountain Club of Uganda, Kampala, and West Col, UK.

Margherita Peak, highest part of Mt. Stanley with heavy rhime or hoarfrost.

# Map 89-1, Margherita, Ruwensori Mts., Zaire-Uganda

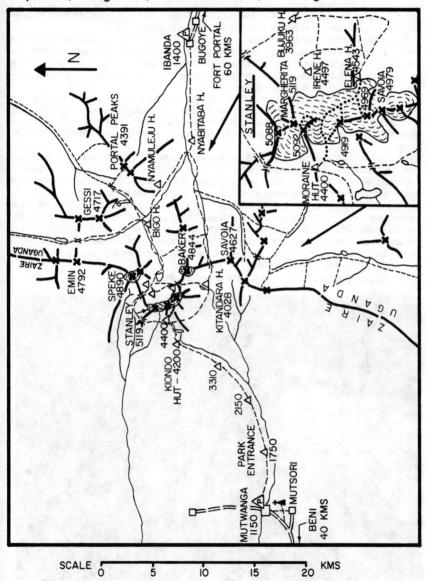

## Mt. Cameroun, Cameroun

In the extreme western part of Cameroun, very near the Nigerian border, stands one single mountain which rises above the tropical forest just a few kms from the Gulf of Guinea. This a Mt. Cameroun, at 4070 meters.

Most people will enter Cameroun by air at Doula, the capital; but others may come by land, perhaps from Nigeria as did the author. From Doula, or from the main highway linking Doula with Nigeria, go west to the mountain town of Buea. There's a good surfaced highway to Buea which is easy to reach—either by bus, truck or auto stopping.

Buea is the starting point for climbing Mt. Cameroun. Located there are several shops and a market place, with many fruits and vegetables that Europeans are accustomed to. Because Buea is at an altitude of 1000 meters it has a cool climate. It is also in that part of Cameroun that was once under British control; therefore many people still speak English, as opposed to the rest of Cameroun which is French speaking.

People wanting to climb the mountain are required to hire a guide! A guide is definitely *not* needed as the trail to the top is very good, but the police say you must pay for, and have the guide along anyway! A similar situation exists all over Black Africa. However, if one wishes to climb free of this extra burden, the police checkpoint can be skirted, and the climb be made alone.

About 3 hours from Buea is a hut and the last water to be found on the mountain. You must carry water from this point for the rest of the hike. At about 3200 meters is another hut (made of aluminum) which will sleep about 10 people. It's not fancy, but it keeps out the weather. Most people sleep there one night, then reach the summit and return to Buea the next day.

The weather at the summit can be very cold, so go prepared. The author remembers the winds at the very top as being among the strongest he has ever encountered. That was at the end of January, 1974. These winds were felt at the summit itself, while about 100 meters below that last cinder cone, there was just a breeze. Keep in mind however, that while in the rain forest above Buea, you're in the tropics with its normal heat and humidity, so short pants are recommended for that part of the trip.

**Map:** Michelin Highway map, Africa Central and South, #155, 1 : 4,000,000.

This tin shelter at 3200 meters is large enough for 10 people.

# Map 90-1, Mt. Cameroun, Cameroun

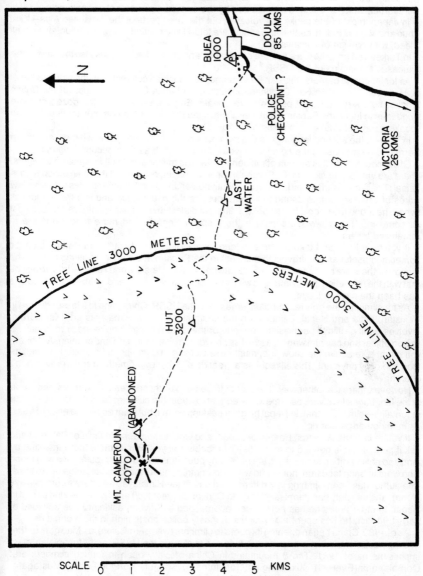

# Chapter 4  Asia

This chapter on Asia has a total of 50 maps. Included here are the countries of Turkey and the USSR in the west, Korea, Japan and Taiwan, in the east. Indonesia and the Philippines are included in the chapter on the Pacific.

This is such a large area, it's impossible to make any generalizations on the mountain types, but there are some volcanos and a lot of mountain ranges, such as the Himalayas and Karakorum, which are folded and caused by the apparent movement of continents.

In Japan, most of the peaks are volcanic, but the three parts of the Japanese Alps—Kita, Chuo and Minami (north, central and south), are folded and uplifted. Taiwan's mountains are all folded, with no sign of volcanism.

In Turkey and Iran, there's a mixture of volcanos and crustal folding, as is also the case in the Caucasus Mountains of the USSR.

As for language barriers, this can be for some, the most difficult region of the world to travel in. However, the Indian Sub-Continent (including Sri Lanka-Ceylon) was part of the British Empire, so every educated person there speaks English. Because of the dozen or more languages in India, the Parliament in New Delhi uses English as the common tongue. English speaking travelers have no problem in India.

In Turkey, the second language is German, as a result of so many Turkish men working in Germany. All the rest of the countries involved use English as their second language.

Of the countries in this section of the book, Taiwan is the most difficult for western travelers. There are virtually no signs in the European-used alphabet, not even at the main bus station in Taipei. The author had to stay in a sort of, "youth hostel" in Taipei for several days to learn a few words of Chinese, before daring to venture out into the countryside and into the mountains (where he found the people there spoke a different dialect than in the capital!). Japan is almost as confusing, but a few more people there speak English, and more road signs are in romanized letters.

If you're in India and take the time to learn some Hindi (it's "Urdu" in Pakistan), then it's sometimes useful as one travels to the west in the Persian and Arabic speaking areas. The reason is, there are many common words between Arabic, Persian, and Hindi—Urdu. It may be that with the revolution in Iran, all signs which western travelers can read, will be taken down, as has been the case in Libya.

As for climbing, the only real problem areas lie in the USSR, China, and to a lesser degree in Pakistan, India and Nepal. Climbing on the south slope of the Himalayas and Karakorum, involves getting official permission from one of the governments. You're required to have a liaison officer and pay him wages, as well as provide him with tent, food and clothing. All porters you might take above the snow line, must have clothing and equipment provided, as well as food and daily payment. This all requires a great deal of money, something small groups don't often have.

However, there's another way. The author traveled to all these areas by land, learned some of the languages involved, became knowledgeable about the customs, and then went into the mountains—simple as that! In Nepal he got a trekking permit, but went above the ends of trails, as many other people do.

If you're in North America, Europe or Japan, and write to someone in India or Pakistan and ask if permission is needed to trek—they'll probably say yes! But if you're there traveling by land and not importing food—there are never any questions asked. The problem lies with those who want to bring food from home and who know nothing about the local language or customs. The author has been climbing in 7 different regions of the Himalayas and Karakorum (always alone), and has only had permission to go to Concordia (near K-2) and had a trekking permit in Nepal. In other areas he has never been approached by anyone asking to see any kind of permit. In fact, he has spent many nights at lonely police posts high in the mountains.

As of 1980, China began opening its doors to climbers (with permission), as Mao gets further into the past. Permission will have to be received to climb in the USSR; and Afghanistan looks impossible as of 1981. The 8 mountains in China officially open to foreign climbers are: Qomolangma(Everest), Xixabangma(Gosainthan), Kongur, Kongur-Tiubie, Mustagata, Bogda, Anyemaqen, andGongga(Minya Konka).

Thievery is almost unheard-of in Asia, but in Turkey and Korea, one should take a little extra precaution. The author has never met anyone who has had things stolen from his pack, but has encountered con-men twice—in Istanbul and Delhi.

Always make a tourist office your first stop in any country, to obtain maps, and get the latest information concerning transportation, hotels, market places, map offices, etc.

Bamiyan and the 52 meter high statue of The Buddha in the cliff face (Map 107).

Solo climbers are greeted by everyone in the village of Hushi (Map 111).

## Mt. Elbrus, Caucasus Mountains, USSR

Between the Caspian and Black Seas in the southern part of the USSR, lie the Caucasus Mountains. These mountains span the entire distance between these two great bodies of water, and form a natural barrier—both culturally and climatically, between the steppes of Russia and the mountainous regions of Georgia, Armenia and Azerbaydzhan in the extreme south of the USSR.

The highest mountain in the entire range is Mt. Elbrus, 5633 meters. Mt. Elbrus is an old volcano, but still retains enough of the conal shape to make the climb technically easy.

The normal route to the top of Elbrus is via Baksan, the Baksan Valley and the end of the road—a place called Itkol; then by trail up to a hut at 4160 meters, called the "Refuge of Elevan." From the hut to the top is a long hike, but not difficult.

Another very famous peak included on this map is that of Ushba, 4710 meters. This is considered to be the "Matterhorn of the Caucasus." The summit has two peaks with the south peak higher by 4 meters. The mountain can be climbed from the north or south, but a south route seems less complicated. Climbs can be made from the Seti Mestra and Mazeri area.

Another famous area for climbing includes a pair of 5000 meter peaks; Rustiveli, 5201 meters, and Dykh-Tau, 5198 meters. These two peaks are generally climbed from a northerly approach, and from the towns of Nal Chik and Bezingi. From Bezingi, the route heads southwest and up the Bezingi Glacier.

Keep in mind, most of these peaks are of the highest grades of difficulty and require all the equipment needed for difficult snow, ice and rock climbing.

Now the problem of getting into the area and the USSR. To get a visa, one must make all reservations and pay for everything before that visa is given. Normally, all climbing expeditions must apply for and receive special permission, in order to climb in the Caucasus Mountains, or anywhere else in the USSR. See more details on the Kazbek map.

The following maps have information dating from the 1940's.

**Map:** See maps from US Army, series 1301, NK-38, and series N501, NK-38 1, 4, and 5. Or see the two maps from the Austrian Alpine Club on the central Caucasus Mountains.

One of the best climbs in the Caucasus is Dykh-Tau.

## Map 91-3, Elbrus, Caucasus Mts., USSR

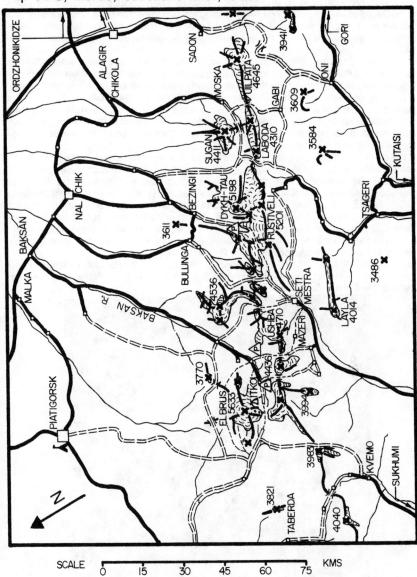

SCALE    0    15    30    45    60    75    KMS

## Kazbek, Caucasus Mountains, USSR

This is the second of two maps covering most of the higher portions of the Caucasus Mountains. This section is the central Caucasus and includes perhaps the second most famous mountain in the range, Kazbek, 5047 meters.

Kazbek is one of the most easily reached of all the high and important summits in the Caucasus. From the large city of Ordzhonikidze, on the north slopes and due north of Kazbek, is the Georgian Military Road or Highway running south to the city of Tbilisi. This is a good road and the only major highway across the Caucasus. At one point it runs about 10 kms to the east of Kazbek. It's possible to climb the mountain from this highway, but there are other routes as well.

One possibility is from the village of Zemo, on the south slopes, and still another is from the tourist town of Karmadon (possibly named Dargavs) to the north of the peak. Keep in mind that Kazbek is not an easy climb. It will require snow and ice equipment and experienced climbers.

Climbing and traveling in the USSR is more different than in other countries. One must first make out a schedule or program of travel that must be approved by, and reservations made with, Intourist, through a representative travel agency. If you want to climb in the Caucasus, Intourist can make those arrangements. You'll probably be required to have guides, and do it their way—all in group fashion.

But there is another possibility. There are several places in the Caucasus where any tourist can drive his own car and stay in hotels. This normal tourist route is through (see Elbrus map) Piatigorsk, Baksan and to Itkol, near Elbrus. Also, from Baksan, Ordzhonikidze, Gizel, and finally to Karmadon, north of Kazbek. Also, by the Georgian Military Road from Ordzhonikidze to Tbilisi and Erevan, or to Gori and the Black Sea coast. One can camp or stay at bungalows or hotels in these places. If, you're at Itkol (near Elbrus) or Karmadon, it seems possible that a climb could be made without official permission—as long as your reservations were made for the hotels there. Get Intourist information about these driving routes, and for climbing permission at any tourist agency specializing in Russian travel.

**Map:** Tbilisi, NK-38, 1 : 1,000,000 or Gora Kazbek, NK-38-5, 1 : 250,000, both from the US Army Defence Mapping Agency, Washington D.C. Also, the Austrian Alpine Club prints two maps of the Central Caucasus.

The twin summits of Ushba to the east of Elbrus (Map 91).

# Map 92-3, Kazbek, Caucasus Mts., USSR

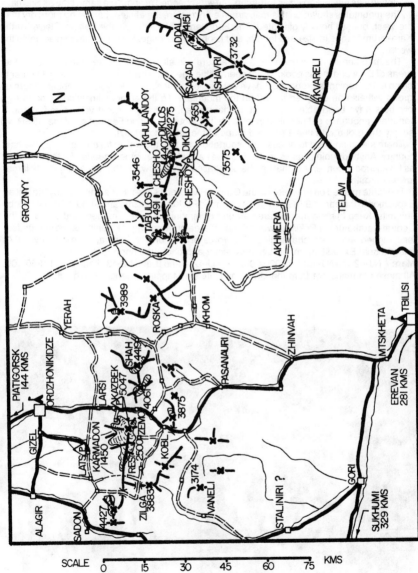

## Pik Kommunizma, Pamir Mountains, USSR

The highest peak in the Soviet Union is Pik Kommunizma, 7495 meters. It lies in the center of the area of Soviet Central Asia, known as the Pamirs, or the Pamir Knot. This mountain was for many years called Pik Stalina, but since that era in Russian history has gone, so has the name. The second highest summit in the region covered by this map, is Pik Lenina, 7134 meters. This mountain was earlier known as Kaufman, but was changed at about the same time as Stalina.

The mountains shown on this map are in a dry region, the eastern part being more dry than the west, but still heavily glaciated. The Fedchenko Glacier rivals the Baltoro Glacier of the Karakorum Range in size and length, and is one of the longest middle latitude glaciers in the world.

The map here is not intended to be as accurate in all aspects, as are maps of many other areas of the world in this book. There seems little need for a great amount of detail. In order to climb in this region, a group must have permission, which may take years to obtain. A foreign group will also be escorted to and on the mountain. To the author's knowledge, no foreign climbers have been able to go at it unchaperoned. In the event that you or your group is fortunate enough to get permission to climb, the Mountaineering Federation of the USSR will supply the group with latest detailed maps of the area (hopefully).

There's also no need to discuss transportation, as that too will be taken care of by the host country. Anybody going there should of course have all the equipment needed for the climb, but as far as food is concerned, that can be purchased in Moscow, Dushanbe, or any of the larger towns enroute.

The route marked on the map, via the Garmo River and Glacier, is the one used by the British Expedition in the early 1960's, when they climbed Pik Kommunizma and at least 3 other nearby summits. Keep in mind that the area around Kommunizma is very rugged, and similar to the Central Karakorum in Pakistan while the high area surrounding Pik Lenina is more rounded, less rugged, and less challenging. The route shown on Pik Lenina, is that of the 1974 International Expedition on the Lenina Glacier approach (the north route).

**Map:**    NJ-42 and NJ-43, 1 : 1,000,000, and NJ-42, 4 and 8, and NJ-43, 1 and 5, at 1 : 250,000. All these old maps are from the US Army Defence Mapping Agency, Washington D.C.

The northern slopes of Pik Kommunizma.

# Map 93-3, Kommunizma, Pamir Mts., USSR

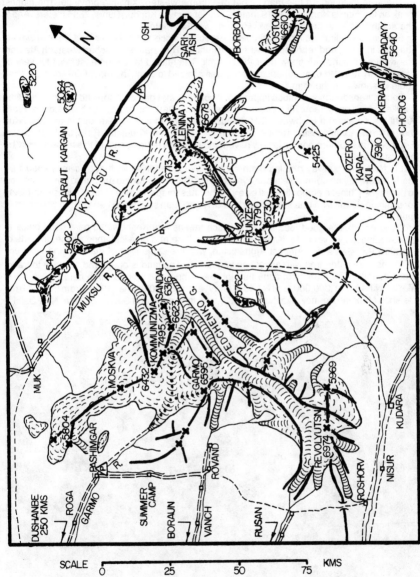

# Kongur, Muztaghata Mountains, China

The area included on this map is that of extreme western Xinjiang province. The highest peak on the map is Kongur at 7719 meters. Not far away is Kongur Tiubie, 7595 meters. And to the south is the third highest peak, Muztaghata, 7546 meters.
allowed to climb Mt. Everest in August, 1980, which has really opened the door to climbing in China.

The area included on this map is that of extreme western Xinjiang province. The highest peak on the map is Kongur at 7719 meters. Not far away is Kongur Tiubie, 7595 meters. And to the south is the third highest peak, Muztagata, 7546 meters.

Few western climbers have been here, especially since 1950. Tilman and Shipton were in the area in 1947, and reported rather easy climbing. They had approached Mustagh Ata from the west and found soft snow near the summit. They failed to reach the summit for various reasons. In July, 1980, an American group was allowed to climb the mountain—on skis. Their route is shown on the map.

Today, transportation is much improved. If you're in that part of China and planning to climb it's likely you'll be in Kashi (the western name is Kashghar) before any climbing is done. From Kashi the Karakorum Highway (KKH) heads southwest to a large lake known as Bulun Kul, then on to the south passing Tash Kurghan, and eventually to Khunjarab Pass, on the Pakistani Frontier. The southern portion is now paved and soon the entire length of this highway may be hard surfaced.

It is from this highway running north-south in Western Sinkiang, that all climbs should be made. There are no up-to-date maps available, but if you're fortunate enough to get permission to climb, the Chinese authorities will give you the latest maps. Inquire at any Chinese Embassy for climbing permission (the author used old US Army map series 1301 and 501 in creating this map).

China now has a good food industry, which means that Kashi would be a good place to buy all supplies for your trip. Kashi is similar in culture and physical appearance, to parts of northern Pakistan and northeast Afghanistan, with the same type of markets and produce.

This is a very dry area with almost no vegetation. The land is open, and it's easy to travel cross-country. The months of June through September are best to climb here.
**Map:**  NJ-43, 1 : 1,000,000, and NJ-43, 6 and 7, at 1 : 250,000(series 1302), from the US Army Defence Mapping Agency, Washington D.C., and the Lands and Survey of India, New Delhi.

Mustagata from the north. Route is up long ridge.

## Map 94-3, Kongur—Mustagata, China

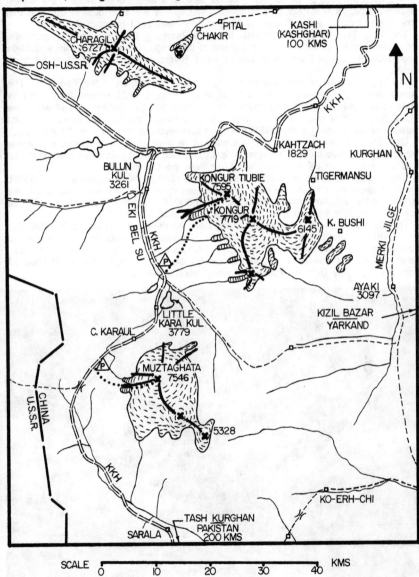

## Pobeda, Tian Shan Mountains, USSR-China

The map shown here of the Tian Shan Mountains is of a very small scale and hardly intended to be used as a climbing map. However, it does show the mountains in relation to the nearest towns and villages.

Little is known of the Tian Shan in the west, with only one group of western explorers having seen the area at the beginning of this century. It wasn't until 1943 that the highest peak, Pobeda, 7439 meters, was discovered and its true elevation determined. Until that time it was thought Khan Tangri, at 6995 meters, was the highest of the range.

The Tian Shan extends in an arch from the Pamirs in the southwest, to about the Mongolian border in the east. To the south of the range is the Tarim Basin and Takla Makan Desert, one of the driest places on earth. Rivers flowing to the south end in sand dunes.

The region shown on this map is the highest and widest part of the Tian Shan. The surrounding region is very rugged, with the Muzart Pass at 3630 meters, being the only route in use between north and south. For the most part the glaciers, two of which are about 70 kms long and among the largest in Asia outside the Karakorum, run east and west. That section lying in the USSR has been extensively studied by Russian scientists.

Until the late 1970's, China has not allowed western climbers into their mountains. However, since Mao's death, changes have taken place and some chance now exists that western groups can climb in the Tian Shan from the Chinese side.

If by chance you are able to obtain permission to climb, either from China or the USSR, those people should supply the latest maps of the region. The only maps available to the author are the U.S. Army map series 1302, at 1:1,000,000, and the U502 series, 1:250,000 scale. These date back to near the end of World War II.

The route used first in climbing Khan Tangri was via the Innultchek Glacier in 1936. This was a Russian group, with one Swiss climber. It appears that Pobeda could be climbed from either side of the border, with perhaps the Chinese side being the easiest of access.
**Map:** NK-44, 1301 series, 1 : 1,000,000, and NK-44, 1, 2, 5, and 6, all at 1 : 250,000, all from the US Army Defence Mapping Agency, Washington D.C.

From the slopes of Pik Lenin one sees Kongur in China (Maps 93-94).

## Map 95-3, Pobeda, Tian Shan, USSR-China

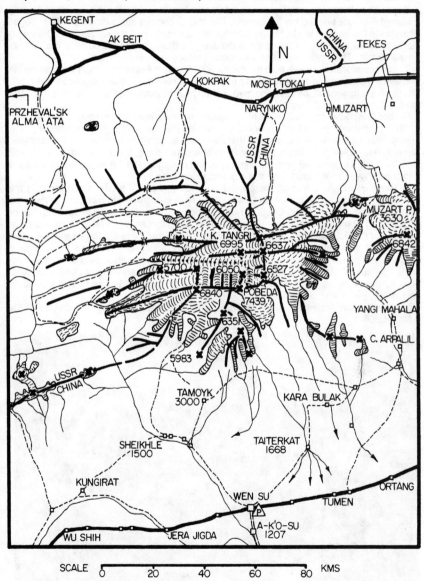

# Bogda, Tian Shan, China

As of 1980, there were 8 mountain peaks or areas in China that were open to foreigners. They include: Qomolangma (Everest), Xixabangma (Gosainthan), Kongur, Kongur-Tiubie, Muztagata, Bogda, Anyemaqen, and Gongga (Minya Konka). The one covered here is Bogda Shan, at 5445 meters. Of all the peaks you can now climb legally in China this one is the lowest elevation and the most northerly.

Bogda Shan is conveniently located about 60 kms from the end of the railway line in Xinjiang (Sikiang) Province and the city is Urumchi. The map shows the approximate position. Bogda Shan lies in the Bogda Uula or Range, which is at the eastern end of the Tian Shan (Heavenly Mountains). To the North of the range is the Junggar Basin, and to the south is the Turpan-Toksun Basin. This latter basin has elevations below sea level.

The information here comes from the book, *High Mountain Peaks in China,* published by the Chinese Mountaineering Association. It's in both Japanese and English languages, has fotos, and some sketchy maps. By using the map and the text, the author has compiled this map. The road to the Base Camp may not be.

Guided groups can go into this mountain region, and since independent travel is now allowed in China, it seems certain that anyone can now visit the area with little or no difficulty. The principal objective for most tourists, and there seems to be growing numbers, is the lake named Tianchi (Heavenly Pool). There are somekind of facilities there, but it's uncertain what. And there's a 10 km motor road from the lake to the foot of Bogda. But it may not reach the Base Camp as shown on the map. The scale is approximate as well.

In summer, July and August, there must be a fair amount of tourist traffic going in the direction of Tianchi, so this is the best time to climb. The trip begins in Urumchi, that's where the buses or trucks can be found. Once at Tianchi, one can walk to the base of the mountain or perhaps find a bus load of other climbers or tourists going that way. The Base Camp area is at the edge of the Daweigu Glacier, at about 3650 meters. From there the routes shown on this map should be fairly accurate. This north slope gets a lot more rain and snow, thus a coniferous forest at lower elevations and glaciers higher up. The south slope is much drier. The author guesses it may take a week to make this climb. In July and August, food may be at Tianchi, but stock up in Urumchi. Most rain comes in summer. Will need snow climbing equipment, ice ax and crampons.

**Map:** Book-*High Mountain Peaks in China,* Chinese Mountaineering Association, ISBN 4-8083-0056-7.

From Tianchi (Heavenly Pool) we see the high peaks of Bogda to the south.

# Map 96-3, Bogda, Tian Shan, China

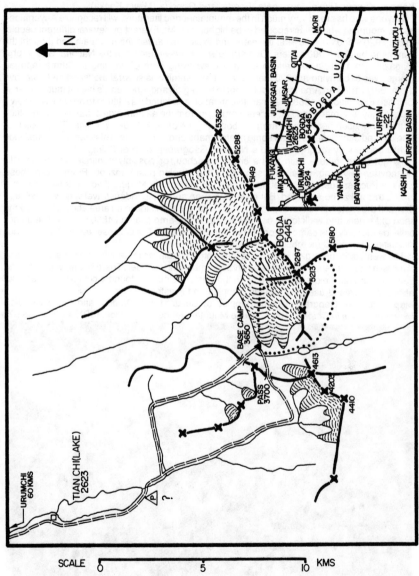

# Anyemaqen, Jishi Shan, China

This map shows one of the 8 mountains in China which were opened to foreign climbers in 1980. This is Anyemaqen with an altitude of 6282 meters. It lies in southeastern Qinghai Province, which is northeast of Xizang or Tibet. The massif is called the Jishi Shan, which is a mountain range at the eastern end of the Greater Kunlun Shan (Mountains). The other 7 mountains in China open to climbing are: Qomolangma (Everest), Xixabangma (Gosainthan), Kongur, Kongur-Tiubie, Muztagata, Bogda, and Gongga (Minya Konka).

Anyone who has read very much in the mountaineering literature, will recognize Anyemaqen as the mountain which was reported to be higher than Mt. Everest by several different people. In the 1920's and 30's, several travelers and explorers viewed the mountain and thought the summit to be over 9000 meters. One article was even written up in the National Geographic Magazine. In 1944, an American airplane crew flying from Chongqing to Burma reported themselves to be flying at 9000 meters, and the summit was several thousand meters above them! But in 1948 an American group went to the region and reported it's height much lower. A Chinese Expedition in 1960, made an investigation and found it's altitude to be what we know it today. They also made the first ascent, coming in from the eastern side of the mountain. Much of the information here comes from the book, *High Mountain Peaks in China.* This book is in English and Japanese, and has some sketch maps and good fotos. This map is a compilation of this books very rough map and a National Geographic map of China.

To get there, take a train to the city of Lanzhou, or possibly continue on the train to Huangyuan or Xining, which is a secondary line running past Lanzhou. From one of these cities, a truck or bus must be found to finish the trip to near Maqen. If you're traveling with a group, this will all be arranged. But nowadays, free and independent travel is now possible in China. If the route of the first expedition is to be taken, then stop in an area about 30 to 40 kms short of Maqen, and walk to the northwest to a Base Camp at about 4800 meters. The author believes that only one camp beyond Base Camp is needed. The Chinese reported some minor difficulties, but put 8 members on the summit in one day.

The weather in this region is similar to the central Himalayas in Nepal; that is, the best time to climb is in late April and May, and again in September and October. There is heavy precip in the summer months. Below 3200 meters on the eastern slopes is found a coniferous forest, but above is grassland used by nomadic peoples and livestock.

**Map:** National Geographic Map, Peoples of China, 1 : 6,000,000, and the book, *High Mountain Peaks in China,* by the Chinese Mountaineering Association, ISBN 4-8083-0056-7.

The northeast face of Anyemaqen and the Varma Glacier.

# Map 97-3, Anyêmaqên, Jishi Shan, China

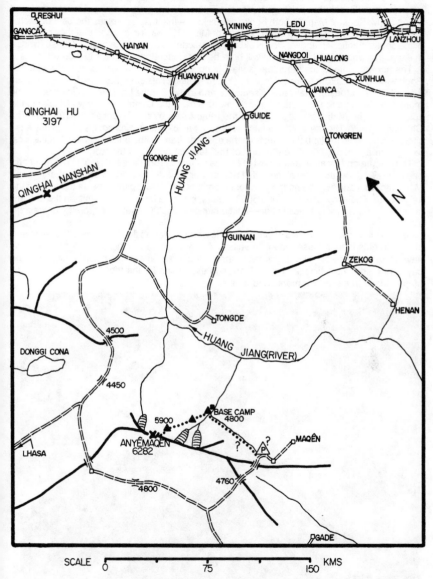

RESHUI
GANGCA
HAIYAN
XINING
LEDU
LANZHOU
NANGDOI HUALONG
HUANGYUAN
XUNHUA
JAINCA
QINGHAI HU
3197
GUIDE
TONGREN
GONGHE
HUANG JIANG
QINGHAI NANSHAN
GUINAN
ZEKOG
HENAN
TONGDE
4500
HUANG JIANG(RIVER)
DONGGI CONA
4450
BASE CAMP
4800
5900
LHASA
ANYÊMAQÊN
6282
MAQÊN
P ?
?
4800
4760
GADE

SCALE 0          75          150 KMS

## Gongga, Hengduan Mountains, China

The map here has been created for the most part by using two maps from two different books. First, is *Men Against the Clouds* (Mountaineers, Seattle) the story of the 1932 American Expedition which conquered Gongga (Minya Konka) on the first try. And from a new book from Japan entitled *High Mountain Peaks in China* (People Sports Publishing House of China). This book lists the 8 peaks of China now open to foreign climbers. They are Qomolangma (Everest), Xixabangma (Gosainthan), Kongur, Kongur-Tiubie, Muztagata, Bogda, Anyemaqen, and Gongga (M. Konka). Maps in both books are lacking—this map combines the best of each.

For those with permission to climb Gongga or Minya Konka, it is advised that they read both of the books mentioned above. One is old and American, the other is new and Chinese (written in Japanese and English), but they will both help in understanding the situation there.

The normal route to the mountain is via Chengdu, the capital city of Sichuan Province of Southwest China. From there to Yachow (Yaan), Luting, Tatsienlu (Kangting), over the pass west of Djezi La (pass), finally over Tsemei La and to the Gompa Lamasery at the base of the mountain. From there the route follows the north side of the Gongba (Gongga) Glacier to the col, then up the northwest ridge. This is the route taken by the Americans in 1932 and the Chinese in 1957. There's a difficult pitch or two, but as big mountains go, it's a relatively easy climb. It's possible to climb the peak from the east and from Taitho and Mosimien, but the local relief is great—about 6000 meters, one of the deepest gorges in the world.

The climate and weather are almost the same as for the Himalayas of Nepal. The monsoon begins in mid June and ends at the last of September. The dry season is from October through May, with April and May being the warmest months. One should plan to be on top around the 1st of June. The snow line is around 5000 meters, but it's a bit lower than this on the eastern face as a result of more precipitation—a little higher than 5000 meters on the dry or western side.

As with all or most mountains of China and the world, expect to find livestock, shepherds and shepherd huts high in these mountain valleys. For the last part of the climb, expeditions will have to use horses or yaks up to base camp. Of course, after permission is granted, and payment made, the Chinese hosts will arrange everything for the trip.

**Map:** Maps in the above mentioned books.

Gongga (Minya Konka) from the southwest. Northwest ridge on left.

## Map 98-3, Gongga, Hengduan Shan, China

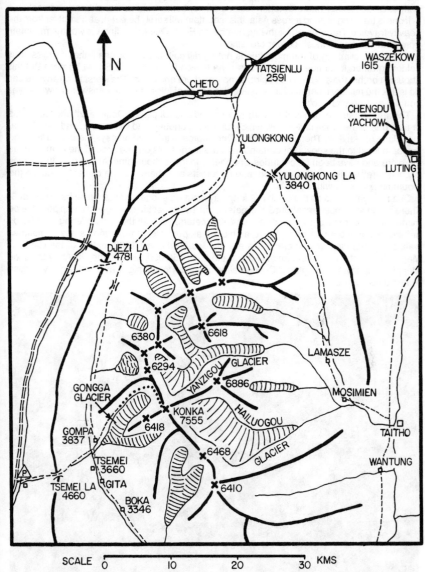

N

WASZEKOW
1615

TATSIENLU
2591

CHETO

CHENGDU
YACHOW

YULONGKONG

LUTING

YULONGKONG LA
3840

DJEZI LA
4781

6380

6618

LAMASZE

6294

YANZIGOU GLACIER

GONGGA
GLACIER

6886

MOSIMIEN

GOMPA
3837

HAILUOGOU

6418

KONKA
7555

TAITHO

TSEMEI
3660

6468

GLACIER

WANTUNG

TSEMEI LA
4660

GITA

6410

BOKA
3346

SCALE    0        10        20        30  KMS

## Agri Dagi (Mt. Ararat), Turkey

Agri Dagi, 5165 meters, is located in extreme eastern Turkey, only a few kms from the borders of both Iran and the USSR. Few people in the Christian world know this mountain by Agri Dagi, that's the Turkish name. Most people know it as Mt. Ararat.

Agri Dagi is an old volcano, but with little erosion. It still remains an almost perfect cone. To the southeast, stands Little Agri Dagi, at 3926 meters. It too is a volcano with perfect conal shape. Since neither has erupted in historic times, both would be considered dormant.

If one is traveling by land across Asia, this mountain will surely be seen, as it's not far from the heavily traveled Trans-Asian Highway, numbered E-23. One has a fine view of the mountain from near the Iran-Turkish border crossing.

The actual climbing of the mountain is not so difficult, but rumor has it that permission is seldom granted to climbers to enter this zone (which is so near the Soviet border.) But this shouldn't bother the adventurous spirit. Simply go there and climb. The *worst* thing anyone can do is ask the military if permission is needed! In cases of this nature, the answer is always "yes you do, and no you can't"!

The author's suggestion is, that you buy your food and supplies in Dogubayzit, then auto stop or take one of the small taxi-buses, which run from Dogubayzit to the border, and get off near the village of Ganikor. Then start walking. One source of information says there's a trail to the top, or at least to the snow. For certain, there are many trails on and around the mountain, as there are and have been for centuries, shepherds in these mountains. At any rate, the area is dry, the weather nearly always good, and no forests anywhere, so one can set sights on the mountain and walk with ease.

One may be able to do the climb in 2 long days, but it's suggested that plans be made for 3. There's a good campsite at about 3000 meters, but it's suggested the highest camp possible be made, at or near the snowline, or about 4000 meters. With all those wandering shepherds around, camp should be as high and as hidden as possible. Unguarded camps sometimes walk away. Both ice ax and crampons are needed for the last 1000 meters of the climb.

**Map:** NJ-38, 1 : 1,000,000, and NJ-38, 1 and 2, 1 : 250,000, all from the US Army Defence Mapping Agency, Washington D.C. and a simple Turkish tourist highway map from any Turkish tourist office.

Agri Dagi (Ararat) to the left, and Little Agri Dagi right.

# Map 99-2, Agri Dagi (Ararat), Turkey

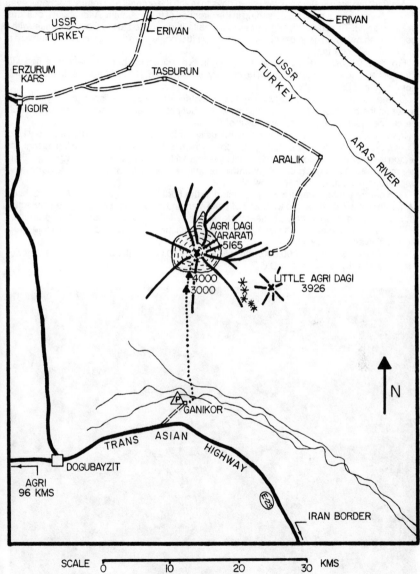

## Suphan Dagi, Turkey

In extreme eastern Turkey, not far from the Iranian border and just north of Lake Van is located Turkey's second highest mountain, Suphan Dagi, 4434 meters. It's about 200 kms southwest of Agri Dagi, or Mt. Ararat.

Suphan Dagi is a very old and eroded volcano. Not too much of the conal shape is left today, but there's still a crater at the summit filled with snow.

Making the climb is simple. It takes two days to reach the summit and return, from Adilcevas. From 'Cevas there's a dirt road heading in the direction of the mountain. After about 6 or 8 kms, the road splits. The one on the right goes to a small village nestled at the mountain base, with a good spring nearby. These people appear to have just come from the Ukraine or someplace to the north! Strange faces.

From this village there are many trails going in every direction, but don't be concerned with that, just walk towards the summit. The country is not rugged, nor is it forested. In fact, there's not a tree or bush in sight.

On the south slopes at about 2800 and 3000 meters, are a couple of springs. This is the last water on the mountain. The upper part is steeper but not difficult. The author believes it could be climbed just as easily from the town of Sarisu.

In winter time the area can have trememdous snow fall, but for the most part, it's a dry land. During the months from June through October, which is the best time to make the ascent, the region is very dry. One could probably get by without a tent during this time. A warning—there are many sheep and goats on the mountain, usually tended by teenage boys—so don't leave unguarded camps, especially at low altitudes!

One can reach this area from Agri, located to the north on the main Trans-Asian Highway (A-23), or from Tatvan, at the west end of Lake Van and on the main railroad line connecting Istanbul and Teheran. Plenty of cheap hotel space in Tatvan, and a good bazaar or market. Adilcevaz is a larger town with many shops. It's not difficult to find buses or trucks running from Agri to Tatvan, via Adilcevaz.

**Map:** Tabriz, NJ-38, 1 : 1,000,000, and NJ-38, 1, 1 : 250,000, both from the US Army Defence Mapping Agency, Washington D.C.

From the steamer on Lake Van looking north at Suphan Dagi.

## Map 100-1, Suphan Dagi, Turkey

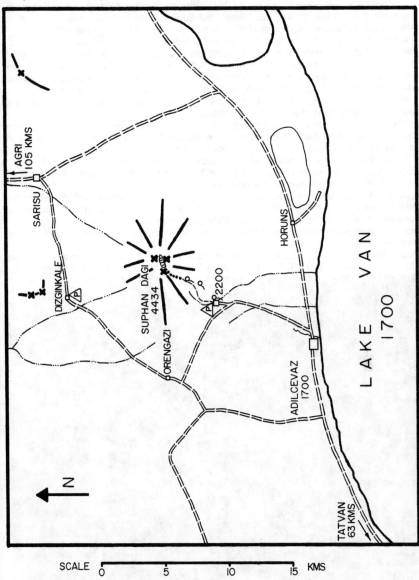

SCALE 0  5  10  15  KMS

## Jabal Hadur, Hijaz Asir Mountains, Yeman

In the southwest corner or the Arabian Peninsula is a highland area, which for the most part, is in the country of Yeman. These mountains stretch all the way from the Gulf of Aquaba to the Gulf of Aden, and are called the Hijaz Asir Mountains. They reach their greatest height between the cities of Sana and Taizz with the highest peak of all, Jabal Hadur, 3760 meters, southwest of Sana.

Visiting this area is not difficult normally, but politics play an important role in whether or not you enter. Tourists are allowed into Yeman, but South Yeman or Aden, seems to be on a different political course, and more difficulties may be found in entering that nation.

Although Yeman is right next door to Saudia, its culture and way of life are vastly different. The one major factor in that difference is the mountainous condition of this region. Because of the mountains there is more precipitation, more plant and animal life, and thus more agriculture and people. Agriculture and attachment to the land is more common in Yeman than in Saudia, where the nomadic way of life has been most common. The reasons for mentioning these facts is to let the reader know that this area can, and does, hold a much denser population than is found in any other part of the Arabian Peninsula.

The mountains in Yeman are not forested, but many areas have been terraced, like the rice paddies of southeast Asia. There isn't much water, but they grow coffee, grains, fruits and vegetables. The population of Yeman is about 6 million.

With all those people, it is surely more easy to climb these mountains than if it were bone dry and unpopulated, as most of us imagine it to be. Most rain falls from November through about April (wintertime), which may be the best time to climb.

Jabal Hadur can be climbed easily in one day from the place called Zayland, located on the main highway that links Sana to the port of Hodeida. All of the roads are near the higher summits—shown on the map—as most of the population lives on or near the mountains. Access is reasonably easy to most of the high peaks. Special equipment needed might be extra water bottles.

**Map:** Michelin Highway map, Africa North and East, #154, 1 : 4,000,000 and maps 687A and 687C, series 1404, 1 : 500,000, from the US Army Defence Mapping Agency, Washington D.C.

Terraced villages in the Hijaz Asir Mts. south of Dhamar.

220

## Map 101-3, Hadur, Hijaz Asir Mts., Yeman

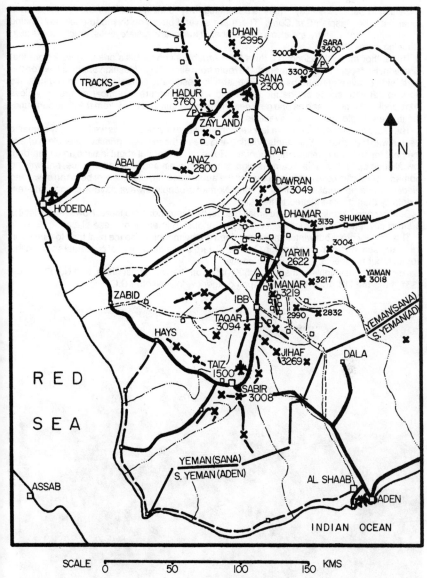

TRACKS

DHAIN
2995

SARA
3400

3000

3300

SANA
2300

HADUR
3760

ZAYLAND

DAF

ANAZ
2800

ABAL

DAWRAN
3049

HODEIDA

DHAMAR
3139

SHUKIAN

3004

YARIM
2622

YAMAN
3018

3217

MANAR
3219

ZABID

IBB

2832

2990

TAQAR
3094

YEMAN(SANA)
S. YEMAN(AD)

HAYS

JIHAF
3269

DALA

TAIZ
1500

SABIR
3008

N

RED

SEA

YEMAN (SANA)
S. YEMAN (ADEN)

AL SHAAB

ASSAB

ADEN

INDIAN OCEAN

SCALE  0      50      100      150   KMS

## Sabalon Kuh, Iran

The third highest mountain in Iran is Sabalon Kuh, 4821 meters. Sabalon is a very old and eroded volcano, located in the extreme northwest of Iran, not far from the USSR border. It's also located about halfway between the southern part of the Caucasus Mountains of the Soviet Union and the Elburz Mountains of north central Iran. However, it belongs to neither of these mountain ranges.

Getting to Sabalon is easy. There is a main highway running from Tabriz to Ardebil, then to Astara, on the Caspian Sea Coast. There are several buses on this road each day, linking Tabriz with Ardebil. There are also a fair number of trucks and private autos, which makes auto stopping a possibility.

The author made the climb in 4 days from Ardebil, all on foot. It's one long walk from that direction. He recommends to others that a route from either Nir or Meshkin Shahr, a town on the north side of the mountain, be used. The land in these parts is treeless, with rolling hills. It's easy to set your sights on the mountain and walk. There are a number of stream valleys surrounding the peak, and as one gets nearer the mountain and away from the plain surrounding it, there is plenty of water available.

There are also many trails and a few very small villages in the area, as well as many nomadic people with their round "Yurt" tents. Visiting and seeing these more "primitive" people is one of the best reasons for climbing the mountain. However, be careful about leaving an unguarded, low altitude camp. If your last camp is high on the mountain and in a hidden place, and with no nomadic camps in view, it may be safe; but the author recommends the tent be taken down and hidden, while you make the final ascent. Nomadic people always have a slightly different mentality than those attacted to the land.

Both Nir and Meshkin Shahr are small places, but food shops are there. However, Ardebil is a small city, and Tabriz a lot bigger. Do your shopping in either of these places.

This is a dry area, but winter snows get deep on the mountain, so the best time to climb is in the warm season from June through October. There's a small amount of perpetual snow on the summit, but no special equipment is needed.

**Map:**   Iran tourist highway map, 1 : 2,500,000, from Iranian tourist office, and NJ-38, series 1301, from the US Army Defence Mapping Agency, Washington D.C.

Sabalon  Kuh in the far distance, an old and eroded volcano.

# Map 102-1, Sabalon Kuh, Iran

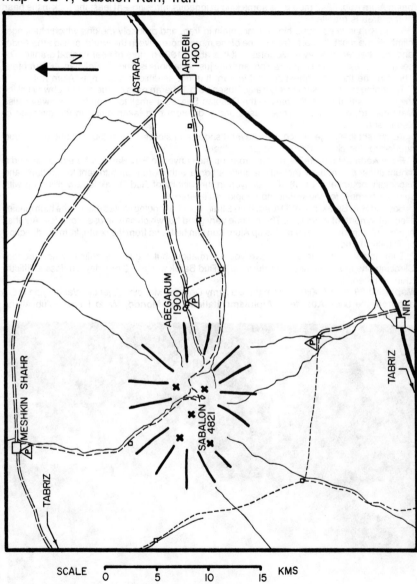

## Alum Kuh, Elburz Mountains, Iran

The Elburz Mountains, which form an arc around the south end of the Caspian Sea in north Iran, are a strange mixture of tectonics, or mountain building processes. In the center of the range is Damavand, a volcano still having some life left, then to the west (and to the northwest of Teheran) is a totally different kind of mountain mass. This massif, with the highest summit being Alum Kuh, 4840 meters, is some kind of igneous intrusion—at least the rock in the heart of this area is granite.

Alum Kuh is the second highest mountain in Iran, and probably the one which challenges climbers the most. Its north face is one of the more impressive in the world, outside the Andes and the Greater Himalayan Mountains. It has about 1000 meters of near vertical granite. The second highest summit in this region, and one just as famous is Takht-e-Soliman, 4650 meters. This may be the 4th highest summit in Iran. It is not as difficult a climb as Alum Kuh.

Reaching the area is relatively easy. Buses from Teheran pass on the main highway linking the capital with the "north coast"—the Caspian Sea. At a small town on that highway called Marzanabad, one must change buses and a different one taken going in the direction of Kedarasht.

Kedarasht is a large village, with several shops and stores. The author bought all the food needed for the climb in two of the shops there.

From Kedarasht, there's a rougher road up the canyon to Rud Barak, where one can find a mountaineer's bungalow (actually a guide's home with extra rooms to rent to climbers, and especially potential clients!). The canyon in the vicinity of Rud Barak is now filling up with summer homes, for the well-to-do people in Teheran.

Beyond Rud Barak is a 4WD road, then a trail. The challenging routes exist in the high glacier filled basin north of Alum Kuh. There's one very good hut which can be used for a fee. Another higher hut is in ruins. Easier routes up Alum Kuh can be found from the south, from the direction of Tanakrud and beyond.

That guide in Rud Barak can give you information, but a guide is definitely not needed. Climbing one mountain and the return trip to Rud Barak will take 3 or 4 days, unless a difficult route is taken.

**Map:** NJ-39, 1 : 1,000,000, from the US Army Defency Mapping Agency, Washington D.C., and from the book **Atlante di Alpinismo Italiano nel Mondo,** Mario Fantin, Club Alpino Italiano.

The North Face of Alum Kuh is one of the best climbs in west Asia.

# Map 103-1, Alum Kuh, Elburz Mts., Iran

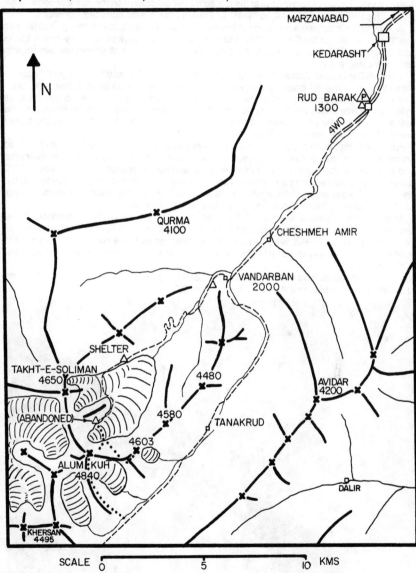

MARZANABAD

KEDARASHT

RUD BARAK P
1300

4WD

QURMA
4100

CHESHMEH AMIR

VANDARBAN
2000

SHELTER

TAKHT-E-SOLIMAN
4650

4480

(ABANDONED)

4580

4603

TANAKRUD

AVIDAR
4200

ALUM KUH
4840

DALIR

KHERSAN
4495

N

SCALE 0    5    10 KMS

## Damavand, Elburz Mountains, Iran

In the central regions of the Elburz Mountains of north-central Iran, is located Iran's highest mountain, Damavand, 5671 meters. The Elburz Mountains form the shape of a crescent at the south end of the Caspian Sea. Almost all mountains in this area are folded and uplifted; however, Damavand is a volcano. There are no records of the last eruption, but there's hot steam and sulfur gases coming out at the top, so this would place it on the active or semi-active list. It's located about 100 kms northeast of Teheran, on a hard surfaced highway.

Getting to the mountain is easy, as this highway is one of two main roads linking Teheran with the "North Coast," or the Caspian Sea and lowlands It's a busy road with many buses, trucks and cars using it. Auto stopping isn't too bad here, but in Iran, not all drivers are familiar with travelers using a thumb.

To climb Damavand, stop at the village of Raineh on the south or southeast slopes. There's a small bazaar or market place, and a few shops where food can be bought; however, much better selections can be found in Teheran. From Raineh, one can walk up the road, as indicated, or hire a taxi, which takes you to another small village higher on the mountain. The author found it more of a military camp than village. Coming from the mountain the author bought food in one small shop there.

From the camp, there are several roads and many trails in the area, so one should first head up and to the left, in a northwesterly direction. There's a very good trail, used both by shepherds and climbers, which leads to the Iranian Mountaineering Federation Shelter at about 4470 meters (take a sleeping bag and stove). The beginning of this trail may be difficult to find, but once on it, it's easy going. Have a full bottle of water with you before leaving the military camp, as there's none on the mountain, and it's warm at the low elevations.

At the hut, there's snow nearby, which can be melted for water—or in the afternoons some snow-water can be found. For most people, it's a two-day climb from Raineh, but because of its elevation, some may need three days. In late summer or early fall no special equipment is needed—except for a large water bottle. Iran is a dry land, with most precipitation coming in the winter months.

**Map:** Iranian tourist map of Iran, 1 : 2,500,000, and NJ-39 and NI-39, 1 : 1,000,000, from the US Army Defence Mapping Agency, Washington D.C.

Damavand is Irans highest mountain. It's just northeast of Tehren.

## Map 104-1, Damavand, Elburz Mts., Iran

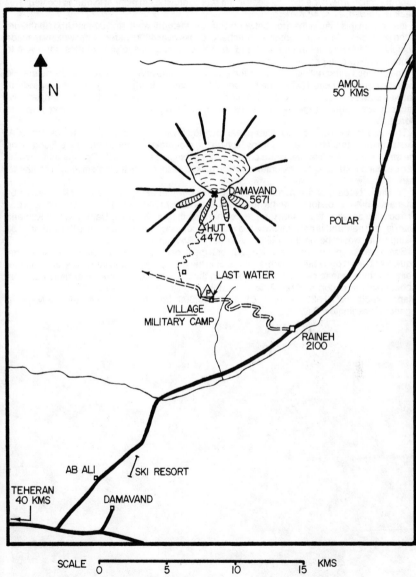

N

AMOL
50 KMS

DAMAVAND
5671

POLAR

HUT
4470

LAST WATER

VILLAGE
MILITARY CAMP

RAINEH
2100

AB ALI

SKI RESORT

TEHERAN
40 KMS

DAMAVAND

SCALE  0      5      10      15    KMS

## Zardeh, Zagros Mountains, Iran

In western Iran near the border of Iraq, is one of the most extensive mountain ranges in the world. From the area where the borders of Turkey, Iraq and Iran meet, southeast to the region of Bandar Abbas and the Straits of Hormuz, is one continuous mountain chain. Various groups of peaks are lumped together and called the Zagros Mountains. The part of most interest is the central section where the highest peak in the range, and the 4th highest in Iran, is located. This peak is Zardeh, at 4548 meters.

Included in this map is the area between Dorud in the northwest, and Isfahan and Shahrkurd in the southeast. This area contains a number of peaks over 4000 meters, all of which are made of highly folded and upturned rock bedding. The stream drainage pattern runs northwest to southeast, between parallel ridges.

The author's personal experience in the area was a climb of Shotaran Kuh, 4328 meters. He rode the train from Dorud (where he had bought two days of food), and got off at a village about halfway between Dorud and Azna. He then climbed halfway up the mountain and camped. The next day was spent for the climb and the return to the highway. He then hitch hiked back to Dorud.

The area is dry, having a similar appearance to Nevada's mountains in the western USA, except in the Zagros there are no trees high on the mountains. Wooded areas are found along the streams, but the mountains are covered with grass and short brush. Springs and streams can be found near all higher mountains, which makes water less of a problem than in southeast Iran.

To climb Zardeh, and a number of other peaks in that area, the starting place would by Isfahan. A bus can be found for the ride to the large town of Shahrkurd. From there either a bus or truck can be taken to Farsan, then somewhere north to the Kuhrang Dam area (the Kuhrang Dam is very new and is not shown on this map; its exact location is unknown to the author). The hiking route would be on the trail to the south of Raugunsk.

Some peaks in this area are rugged, but most can be climbed easily without special equipment. Most precipitation comes in winter in the form of snow, with late spring and summer being the best time to climb. The best place in the area to get additional information, at least about public transport and hotels, ets., is at the tourist office in Isfahan.

**Map:** NI-39 and NH-39, series 1301, 1 : 1,000,000, from the US Army Defence Mapping Agency, Washington D.C.

From Dorud we see to the southeast Shotaran Kuh (Camel Mountain).

# Map 105-1, Zardeh, Zagros Mts., Iran

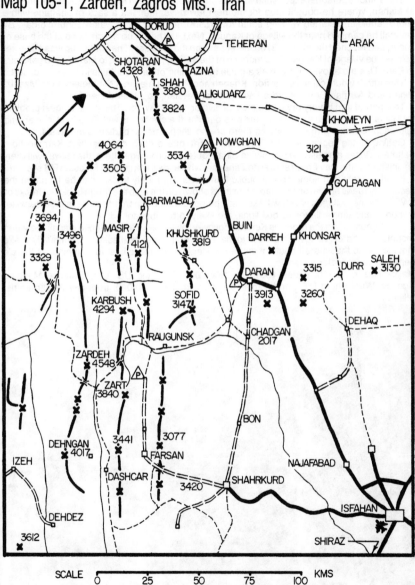

# Hazar, Southern Plateau, Iran

In the southeastern section of Iran are many high mountains—the highest of which is Hazar, 4420 meters. This region is south of the city of Kerman, which is on the main highway crossing central and eastern Iran, linking Zahedan. This highway from Teheran is paved all the way.

The author's personal experience with this area was like this: In March, 1975, he got off a bus at Mahan, where he bought food for the next few days, then left a sack of baggage with a shopkeeper, and started walking south towards Kuh-i-Jupar. That was around mid-day. By nightfall he camped near the village of Kanuas. Next day he set up a high camp at the base of Jupar, and reached the top of a 3700 meter peak on the third day. The final camp was again set up near the village of Kanuas. The morning of the 4th day, he returned to Mahan, and got a bus to Bam. Use the above example as a guide in reaching other mountains in this vast desert.

The author would climb Hazar from Khaneh and Rayin; Lalezar, 4374 meters, from Mashiz, Nigar, and Azghar. Better learn a few words of Persian, you'll need them!

This part of Iran is very dry with almost no live or running water. This is the biggest problem with climbing here, but that dry climate also benefits the climber as well. The land is open and approach routes are made easy as there are no deep gorges, badlands or forests.

Getting to the region is easy. There are many buses each day reaching Kerman from Teheran. Buses also use the Kerman to Sirjan route. When you get there, the railway will likely be finished all the way from Teheran to Zahedan, where it will link into the Pakistan RR system.

It's also likely that some sort of public transportation, if only trucks, can be found on the secondary roads shown on the map. Most trails shown on the map are rough tracks for trucks or 4WD vehicles. Villages which will likely still be populated are named on the map; otherwise, symbols indicating villages or buildings, are likely to be abandoned.

The biggest city in the region is Kerman, followed by Mahan. Shop in these places. Between mountains and*or villages, it's best to have several water bottles full. Continually make inquiries as to the where-abouts of the next water. Springtime is best for climbing, as there's generally more water available.

**Map:** Hazar, NH-40, series 1301, 1 : 1,000,000, from the US Army Defence Mapping Agency, Washington D.C., and Iranian tourist map, 1 : 2,500,000, from any Iranian tourist office.

Southwest of Mahan is the village of Kanuas with Kuh-i-Jupar beyond.

# Map 106-1, Hazar, Southern Plateau, Iran

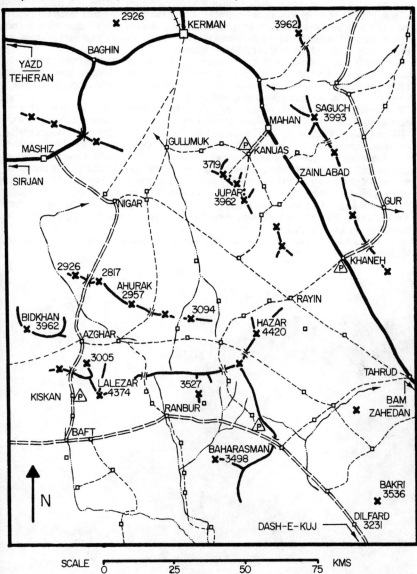

## Shah Fuladi, Koh-i-Baba Mountains, Afghanistan

From one location in central Asia, often called the Pamir Knot, several mountain ranges radiate out in different directions. They are the Pamirs, Tien Shan, Kun Lun, Karakorum, Himalayas, Hindu Kush, and finally the Koh-i-Baba. The Koh-i-Baba is the smallest range of the group and has no really high summits.

The highest peak in the Koh-i-Baba is Shah Fuladi reaching to 5143 meters. Getting to the area may or may not be difficult, depending on the political situation at the time. But in times of political stability, one can take a bus or truck from the capital of Kabul, and reach Bamiyan in one day. Bamiyan is the number one tourist attraction in Afghanistan. Located there are two huge statues of The Buddha (one is 52 meters high) carved out of a cliff. There are other nearby ruins, having to do with the raids of Ghengis Khan.

Bamiyan is a large village, with a good bazaar and a number of small hotels and eating places. There are also first class accommodations on the hill near the airport. Buy all your food in Bamiyan (plan on a minimum of 4 or 5 days), then walk, hire a taxi, or get a ride on the occasional truck going in the direction of Fuladi village.

This part of the journey is best seen and enjoyed on foot. Along the way are numerous homes and irrigated fields, and some ruins dating back to the same time as the statues at Bamiyan.

Beyond Fuladi, which is the final village and the last shop where some basic foods can be purchased, there's a 4WD road a short distance, then numerous trails. Once in the mountains, forget the sheep and goat trails, and make your own way. In the foothills, beneath the higher summits, one can find many stone livestock shelters—simple rock fences forming circles. As the weather is very dry much of the year, these are usually good for sleeping. However, it's recommended a tent be taken, as it can get cold at night, even in summer.

The north faces offer some snow and ice climbing, and also many rock routes. The climbing season is from June to October. Almost no precipitation is received during that time, as Afghanistan is a very dry land.

**Map:**  Kabul, NI-42, series 1301, 1 : 1,000,000, from the US Army Defence Mapping Agency, Washington, D.C.

These peaks and glaciers are just east of Shah Fuladi (north face).

Map 107-1, Shah Fuladi, Koh-I-Baba, Afghanistan

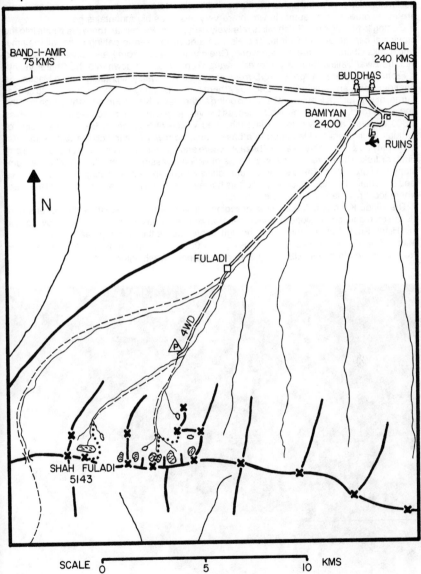

# Tirich Mir, Hindu Kush Mountains, Pakistan

The Hindu Kush Mountains, for the most part, form the boundary between Afghanistan and Pakistan. They also hold one of the most famous mountain passes in the world, Kyber Pass. The area shown here however, is not Kyber Pass, but the region further north around Tirich Mir, 7706 meters, the highest peak of the Hindu Kush.

Tirich Mir could be climbed in two to four weeks from Chitral, depending on one's fitness, and acclimatization prior to the climb. It is the most difficult climb in the entire mountain range. There are many other nearby summits which are very easy—as big mountains go.

Getting to the region of Tirich Mir is relatively easy. From Peshawar, there are flights into the provincial capital town of Chitral. There's also a good road—and getting better all the time, which links Chitral with the outside world. One can take a bus from Rawalpindi or Peshawar, into the Swat Valley, then to Dir, over Lawarai Top Pass, and down into the Chitral Valley.

From Chitral there's a "good" 4WD road, heading up the valley eventually linking Mastuj, the Shandor Pass, and finally Gilgit. Each day there are jeeps using this road. One should stop at Kurgh, or with luck, a jeep might be found going all the way to Kosht. From Kosht, which is at the end of the road, a trail begins, which passes the village of Otool, then crosses the Terich Pass (3800 meters), and down to the last inhabited village of Shahgrom. Beyond the fields of Bandok, a climbers trail leads up to a base camp, from which many climbs can be made.

Chitral has a fine market place or bazaar, where enough good food can be found to make any climb or trek. There are also several hotels of various classes and comforts to choose from. Many are very cheap. There's also a tourist office which can be of assistance in rounding up a jeep or porters however, is on the mountain at the end of the road, where local people know the trails better.

The Hindu Kush is a "good weather region." It's dry with good weather the general rule. However, higher on the slopes the weather always deteriorates. Winter climbing is now done in the Hindu Kush, but normally June through September is the climbing season.

**Map:** The Pamirs, NJ-42, 1301 series, 1 : 1,000,000, from Lands and Survey of India, New Delhi, or from the US Army Defence Agency, Washington, D.C.

From Ghul Laast, 6665 meters, looking east at Tirich Mir.

# Map 108-1, Tirich Mir, Hindu Kush Mts., Pakistan

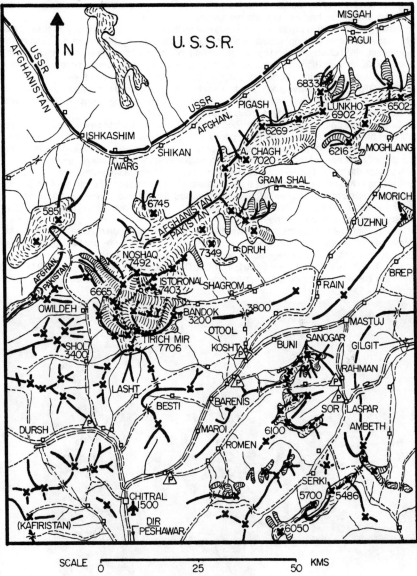

## Koyo Zom, Hindu Raj Mountains, Pakistan

The main mountain mass shown on this map is the Hindu Raj Range. It's located in northern Pakistan, and sandwiched in between the Hindu Kush and the Karakorum Mountains. Part of the Hindu Kush is shown in the upper left hand corner of the map. For mountaineers this is an unfamiliar area. The main reason is there are no peaks over 7000 meters, the highest being Koyo Zom, listed at 6872 meters. Despite the fact there are no really high mountains in the area, good climbing can be found. It's also an interesting region to do some trekking, as good weather is the rule, bad weather the exception.

When comparing this range with other regions in Asia, it is relatively easy of access. By far the easiest way of gaining access is via Gilgit, located about 20 kms off the map to the southeast. Gilgit can be reached by air from Rawalpindi, or by a good paved road, known as the KKH, or Karakorum Highway. Gilgit is a large town with many government people and a good market place. Everything needed for climbing or trekking can be found there.

From Gilgit, jeeps (always jeeps) can be found carrying cargo and passengers to the various sections of the Hindu Raj. The tourist office can assist in locating transport. Tractors with trailers are also used, but they're slow, tiresome, and dusty.

Larger towns on the map are Gupis, Pingal, Yasin, Gakuch, and Ishkuman. These and other villages have small shops selling basic goods. Many of the villages have resthouses, owned and operated by the government. These are clean, comfortable and cheap; and if desired, the Chokidar, or keeper of the resthouse, will prepare Pakistani meals at low prices.

To reach the highest peak, Koyo Zom, look for jeeps going to Yasin. From there, walk to near the village of Nialthi, then turn north. It could possibly be reached from the village of Karkot, but a pass would have to be crossed if this route were used. It could also be reached from the north, near the village of Pechus. Pechus can be reached by walking from Imit, on the southeast, or Mastuj to the southwest (off the map).

July through September are the best weather months. The monsoon rains seldom get this far north, so that's not a big factor to climbers. These late summer months are best in other ways as well, for fresh fruits and vegetables begin to ripen about July 1.

**Map:**   The Pamirs, NJ-43, series 1301, 1 : 1,000,000, and NJ-43, 13 and 14, 1 : 250,000, all from the US Army Defence Mapping Agency, Washington D.C., and Lands and Survey of India, New Delhi.

The author used this Zuk in reaching Masherbrum (Map 111).

# Map 109-2, Koyo Zom, Hindu Raj Mts., Pakistan

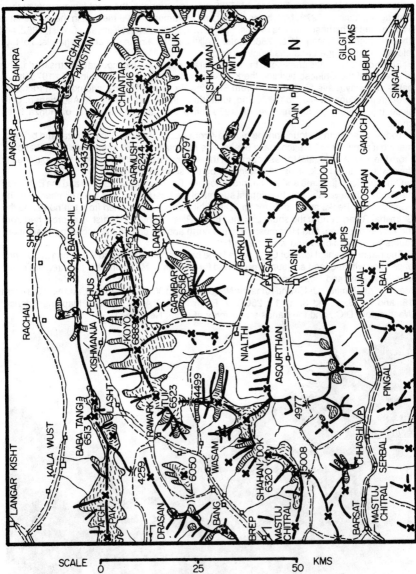

SCALE 0    25    50    KMS

# Rakaposhi, Karakorum Mountains, Pakistan

The area covered by this map is a vast region of northern Pakistan and includes the most northerly and westerly parts of the Karakorum Mountains. In the center of the map is the Hunza Valley with its capital, Baltit.

Some of the highest summits in the area include Kampire Dior, 7142 meters; Batura, 7785 meters; Shispar, 7619; and Ultar, 7398 meters. These are all north of the Hunza Valley. Other peaks south of Hunza are: Rakaposhi, 7788 meters—probably the most famous mountain in the region; Minipin, 7273; Malubiting, 7291; and Haramosh, 7406 meters. In the area east of Hunza are the highest summits on this map: Trivor, 7720 meters; Kunyang Chhist, 7852; and the very highest, Distaghil Sar, 7885 meters. All the mountains in this area, regardless of their elevation, are rugged and challenging climbs.

Some of these peaks are among the easiest of access of any big mountains in the world. This is a result of the Chinese building the Karakorum Highway (KKH), finishing it in 1978. It is a paved highway (paved in Pakistan) from Sinkaing Province of China, into northern Pakistan, through the Hunza Valley to Gilgit, and south through the Indus Valley to Abbottabad. Only since the opening of this highway in 1978, have the peaks to the east of Hunza been challenged.

Today, buses can be found on the highway from Abbottabad, to Gilgit, Hunza, and beyond, making it convenient to reach many peaks. The mountain easiest to approach is Rakaposhi. From the village of Jogalot to base camp, on the southwest side of the peak, is a couple of easy days with a large pack. It was first climbed by the southwest ridge.

Other peaks in the area and their approaches are: Batura, from the Batura and the Baltar (on the south) Glaciers; Shispar, the highest summit of the Pasu group, has been climbed from the Pasu Glacier. Peaks such as Trivor and Distaghil Sar can be reached from the north and the Shimshal River, or from the south and the Hispar River. Kunyang Chhist, is approached from the Hispar drainage, and Haramosh from the north and Barche. In the upcoming years more routes will be explored and written about.

The regional capital town of Gilgit has a large bazaar or market place which can supply any expedition with the food and supplies needed for any climb. Most climbs in this area are made in July, August and September.

**Map:** The Pamirs(NJ-43) and Khasmir(NI-43). Series 1301, 1 : 1,000,000, and NJ-43, 14 and 15, and NI-43, 2 and 3, all 1 : 250,000. From the US Army Defency Mapping Agency, Washington, D.C., and the Lands and Survey of India, New Delhi.

From Baltit, in Hunza Valley, looking at north slopes of Rakaposhi.

# Map 110-1, Rakaposhi, Karakorum Mts., Pakistan

SCALE

0   10   20   30   40   KMS

# K-2, Karakorum Mountains, Pakistan

In northern Pakistan along the Chinese border, stands the Karakorum Mountains. Within this range are 4 of the 14 summits in the world over 8000 meters elevation. These peaks are: K-2, 8611 meters, second highest in the world, climbed first in 1954 by an Italian expedition; Hidden Peak or Gasherbrum I, 8068 meters, number 11 in the world, first climbed in 1958 by Americans; Broad Peak, 8047 meters, 12th in the world, climbed first in 1957 by an Austrian team; and Gasherbrum II, 8035 meters, number 13, and climbed by an Austrian group in 1956. All of these summits are within about 30 kms of each other. No other place in the world has so many high mountains so close together.

The normal route used to climb all these peaks, and many more in that central region, is from Skardu (reached only by air—at least until 1980). From Skardu, one must hire a jeep for the 83 km trip to Dhaso. From Dhaso, and with porters going at *their speed*, it's 10 days to Concordia.

The normal camping places near villages are: Chapo, Chango, and Askole—where a police check post is located. After Askole it's wild country, with the following campsites: Korofone, Bardumal, Piau, Lilihua, Urdukas, Goro and finally Concordia. These campsites must be used—unless you're prepared to put porters in tents.

The part between Korofone and Bardumal can be bad! Early in the season, one can wade the river, but later, in July and August, another route must be taken. At times in the past there has been a bridge at Jola, but if there isn't one there, it's a long walk upstream to the Panmah Glacier and back.

Other important peaks are: Masherbrum, 7820 meters, climbed via Khapalu and Hushi; Saltoro Kangri, 7742 meters, from Khapalu, Gama, and the Siachen Glacier; Chogolisa, 7654 meters, climbed from Concordia; Ogre, 7285 meters, climbed from the Panmah or Biafo Glaciers.

The author bought most of his food in Rawalpindi, where the flights to Skardu originate, but some was purchased in Skardu—for his solo attempts of Masherbrum and Broad Peak. Skardu has several hotels—some very cheap, others expensive. The tourist office can help find porters and jeeps if needed. Many passenger jeeps reach Khapalu, also Shigar.

**Map:** The Pamirs(NJ-43) and Khasmir(NI-43). Series 1301, 1 : 1,000,000, and NJ-43, 15(and 16?), and NI-43, 3 and 4, 1 : 250,000. All maps from the US Army Defence Mapping Agency, Washington D.C., and Lands and Survey of India, New Delhi.

From near Concordia, K-2 center and Broad Peak right.

# Map 111-1, K-2, Karakorum Mts., Pakistan

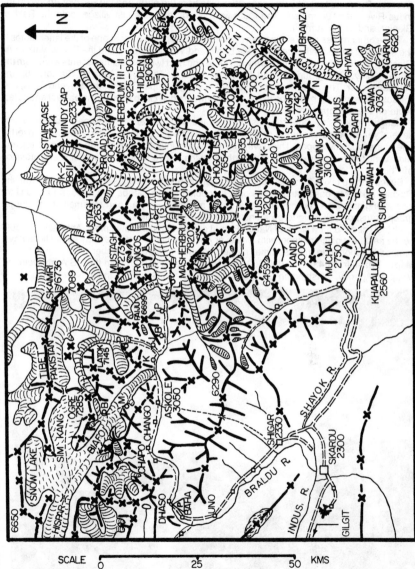

SCALE   0        25        50   KMS

# Nanga Parbat, Himalayan Mountains, Pakistan

The 9th highest mountain in the world is Nanga Parbat, 8125 meters, located in northern Pakistan. Although it's not far from the central Karakorum and the high peaks there, it's not part of that mountain system. Instead it belongs to the Himalayas, and is at the extreme western end of the range. It is also the most westerly of all the 8000 meter peaks.

Nanga Parbat was first climbed by a German team in 1953, not long after the conquest of Everest. The route taken by that expedition was from the north and the Rakhiot Bridge on the Indus River, at 1194 meters. The route went up to Tato—the last village, onto the Rakhiot Glacier, and to the summit.

Three other routes have since been climbed and it appears at least one of the latter routes is the easiest. The second ascent was via Bunar and Valley, Zangot, and the Diamir Valley and Glacier, reaching the top on the northwest face. The next two successful ascents were from the Rupal Valley. One group climbed from the village of Rupal, the Bazhin Glacier, and the southeast spur. The other was done via Rupal village, Rupal Glacier, the Mazeno Pass, and the southwest ridge. Those who made the southwest ridge climb said it is the easiest and safest route on the mountain.

Nanga Parbat is for sure the easiest of all the 8000 meter peaks to gain access to. For several years the Karakorum Highway (KKH), which was built by the Chinese—was closed to foreigners, but is now open. This paved highway starts in Abbottabad (north of Islamabad), and runs along the Indus River to Gilgit, then through the Hunza Valley, and into Sinkiang province of China.

Buses can be taken from Rawalpindi and Abbottabad to all points along the KKH. From the Rakhiot Bridge to base camp takes only a couple of days. Jeeps can be found at Bunji for climbs originating on the southeast side of the mountain—if your party is small. If it's a larger group, transport will have to be found in either Gilgit or Chilas.

All food needed for a climb of Nanga Parbat can be found in Rawalpindi. Abbottabad would be the next best place to shop, with Chilas or Astor the last resort. Previous expeditions have climbed the mountain in all summer months—June through September.

**Map:** Khasmir, NI-43, 1 : 1,000,000, and NI-43-6, 1 : 250,000, from the US Army Defence Mapping Agency, Washington D.C., and the Lands and Survey of India, New Delhi.

The northwest face of Nanga Parbat from Gilgit-Rawalpindi flight.

Map 112-2, Nanga Parbat, Himalayas, Pakistan

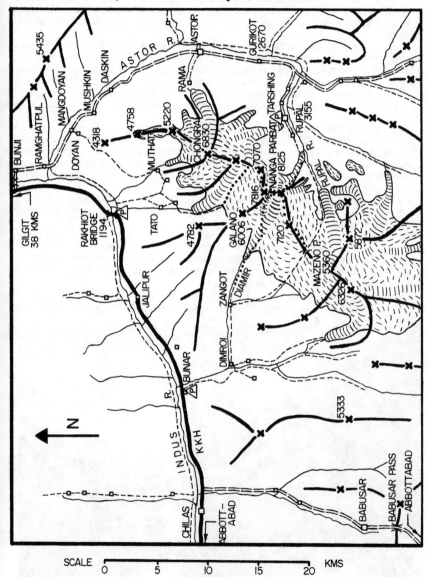

SCALE  0   5   10   15   20   KMS

## Nun Kun, Himalayan Mountains, India

The region covered by this map is that part of India just to the east of Srinagar and the Vale of Khasmir. The highest peak in the area is Nun Kun at 7135 meters. This part of the Himalayas is totally within the boundaries of India, so no political conflicts arise. Another important and challenging peak is Bremeh, 6575 meters.

There are two ways of approaching Nun Kun. The author walked from Kishtwar on the south, before the road from Srinagar to Leh was open to foreigners. Beginning with a 48 kg pack, it took 8 days to arrive at the mountains lower slopes, a distance of about 150 kms. This route is also used to reach Bremeh. At Sondar, inquire as to what nullah or canyon to use to reach Bremeh.

If you're using this route to Nun Kun, you'll pass villages of Palmar (the end of the road), Ikhala, Sondar, Hanzal, and Marwa. Then the route heads up the Krish Nullah past hot springs (Garumpani), and the last inhabited village of Metwan. Later, at the cemetery of Furiabad, it may be necessary to cross the river on a snowslide if it's early in the season. Metwan villagers usually erect a new bridge each year, when the water level drops. There are shepherd huts all along the way up to very near the mountain. One can buy some kind of food in all the villages enroute.

The route from the north is now the normal route. This begins in Srinagar with buses or trucks heading for Leh. Stop in Kargil, and look for jeeps or other 4WD's traveling south in the direction of Parkutse. There's little traffic on this 4WD road, but if you can find a cargo-passenger carrying vehicle, it'll save a long walk. From Parkutse, most expeditions head straight south and up the Parkutse Glacier. This puts climbers on the west side of the twin peaks of Nun, 7135, and Kun, 7077 meters.

It's also possible to continue east to the next village of Guimatung, 3820 meters, and climb south from there. This is up the Shafat Glacier, but subsidiary peaks will have to be climbed before reaching Nun Kun.

As with the southern route, any of the villages enroute can offer some food. Many have schools and/or resthouses which climbers or trekkers can use. The southern slopes are pine-tree covered and much wetter than the areas to the north. The best time to climb here is July through mid-September. All food for the trip could be bought in either Kishtwar or Kargil, but Srinagar, Jammu or Delhi are better places.

**Map:**   Khasmir, NI-43, series 1301, 1 : 1,000,000, and NI-43, 7 and 11, 1 : 250,000. From the US Army Defence Mapping Agency, Washington, D.C., and Lands and Survey of India, New Delhi.

South of Nun Kun on the Kishtwar route. Kun Nun is left of peaks.

## Map 113-1, Nun Kun, Himalayas, India

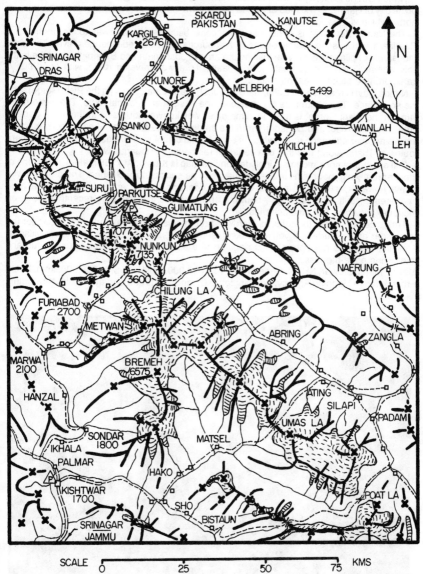

SCALE 0        25        50        75   KMS

## Nanda Devi, Himalayan Mountains, India

Some people are surprised to learn that the highest mountain in India is "only" 7816 meters elevation. That mountain is Nanda Devi. It seems that all the world's 8000 meter peaks, of which there are 14, are in two groups—one is along the Nepal-Tibetian border, the other is in northern Pakistan in the Karakorum. In between is India, with not one 8000'er!

Nanda Devi is located just west of the area where Tibet, Nepal and India meet, and just east of the city of Hardwar. The map of Nanda Devi shows India exclusively, except for the extreme north, which is Tibet or China.

The Nanda Devi area is rather easy of access, because not far away to the northwest is Badrinath, which is the source, or one of the sources of the sacred Ghanges River. There are thousands of pilgrims each year visiting the area of Joshimath and Badrinath, to bathe in the holy waters. Therefore, to Joshimath at least, it's a well traveled route, with good public transport, and plenty of eating places.

Nanda Devi is reached via Delhi, Hardwar, Joshimath, Lata, Deodi (in the Rishi Gorge), and the south face. The south face is considered the easiest and normal route. The same route through the Rishi Gorge, is used to climb other well-known mountains in the same general area, such as Trisul and Dunagiri. From the south, and the towns of Almora and Kapkohte, there's another approach route, which is used for the climbing of Nanda Kot and the southern routes of Trisul. Along this trail is a series of resthouses or bungalows.

Still another famous mountain included on this map is Kamet. At 7756 meters, it was one of the first really big mountains in the Himalayas to be successfully climbed. The problem with Kamet however, is the fact it's on the Chinese border and getting permission to enter that area has been difficult or impossible. About the only climbers into this area recently have been Indian expeditions. But times change.

Trains can be taken to as far as Hardwar and maybe a little beyond, then buses for the remainder of the journey. If you're trekking, some food may be found at the lower villages. Trekking is not as developed or as popular here as in Nepal, but can be just as fun and interesting none-the-less.

**Map:** Manasarowar, NH-44, Series 1301, 1 : 1,000,000, or NH-44-6, 1 : 250,000, from the US Army Defence Mapping Agency, Washington D.C., and Lands and Survey of India, New Delhi.

North ridge of Nanda Devi.

# Map 114-3, Nanda Devi, Himalayas, India

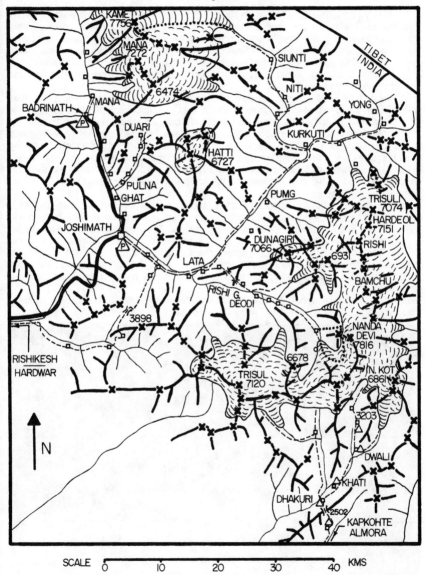

KAME
7756
MANA
7272
6474
SIUNTI
NITI
TIBET
INDIA
YONG
BADRINATH
MANA
KURKUTI
DUARI
HATTI
6727
PULNA
GHAT
PUMG
TRISUL
7074
HARDEOL
7151
JOSHIMATH
DUNAGIRI
7066
RISHI
6931
LATA
BAMCHU
RISHI G.
DEODI
3898
NANDA
DEVI
7816
6678
N. KOT
6861
TRISUL
7120
3203
DWALI
KHATI
DHAKURI
2502
KAPKOHTE
ALMORA
RISHIKESH
HARDWAR

N

SCALE   0   10   20   30   40   KMS

## Jumla Trek, Karnali Province, Nepal

The focus of attention on this map is not the high peaks, but an interesting trek into western Nepals Karnali Province. This isn't to say there are no mountains which will interest climbers, but there are simply no big name mountains here. The highest summit on this map is Kanjiroba at about 7045 meters. In the same group are several other peaks just under the 7000 meters mark.

Jumla is the zonal headquarters of the Karnali Province located in extreme western Nepal. To get to Jumla one must walk about 2 weeks from Pokhara to the east, or about one week from the end of the road at Surkhet. Or one can fly to Jumla from Kathmandu. There are regular flights from Kathmandu, but they are difficult to arrange, partly because there aren't that many, and because of weather. If you want to fly into this region and can't get on a Kathmandu flight, might try other flights originating from Nepalgani, located on the India-Nepal border, or from the before-mentioned town of Surkhet.

The western part of this map connects to the western part of the Dhaulagiri map at the place called Dune. If you intend to walk from Pokhara, then you must begin the trek by using the Annapurna map, then the Dhaulagiri, and finally this one. It's a long walk from that side!

The main reason some trekkers come to Karnali is to see the people and an interesting place called Rara Daha, or Rara Lake. Rara Lake is at a cool and delightful 3000 meters, and the mountain sides are covered with pine, fir, spruce and other trees. This is an area of relatively low population, thus the lake and surrounding hills are now part of a national park. If you want to camp at the lake for several days, then go to the south shore, which has more virgin forest and better camping places.

If you should fly to Jumla, take in as much food and supplies as possible. Because this area is so isolated, it's difficult, if not impossible to bring many supplies in. So once there you'll have to have your own or buy locally, which has chronic shortages. There is a bazaar in Jumla with rice, wheat, potatoes, beans and other fruits and vegetables in season. Information from one source, *Trekking in Nepal,* S. Bezruchka, says one should have a tent, as it isn't the custom of the people in these parts to have guests into their homes. The weather is good from about March to June, and again from September to November. Winter treking is possible in the lower altitudes.

**Map:** Guide Map of Nepal, 1 : 506,880, Natraj Tours and Travel, Kathmandu, or Manasarowar, 1 : 1,000,000, NH-44, US Army Defence Map or Lands and Survey of India.

If you're trekking and going "native" in Nepal, this is typical scene.

Map 115-3, Jumla Trek, Karnali Province, Nepal

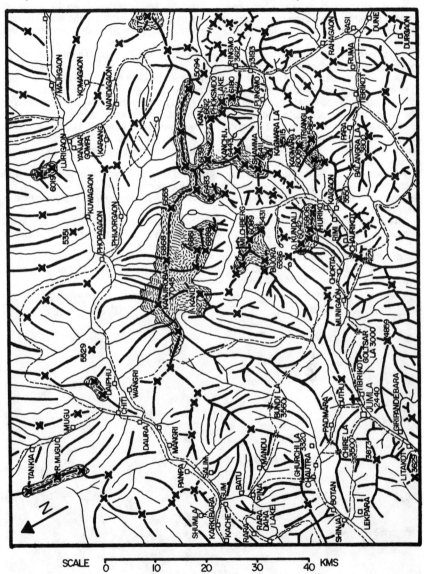

SCALE 0 10 20 30 40 KMS

# Dhaulagiri, Himalayan Mountains, Nepal

The 6th highest mountain in the world is Dhaulagiri, 8167 meters. This mountain is located in north central Nepal, not far to the northwest of Pokhara, and just across the Kali Gandaki River Gorge west of Annapurna. Dhaulagiri was first climbed in 1960 by a Swiss team. Of the fourteen 8000 meter peaks in the world, only Gosianthan was first climbed at a later date. The normal route to its summit is one of the more difficult of all the 8000'ers.

As of 1979 the only route that had been successfully climbed is the one up the northeast ridge. Few others have even been attempted. The route used in getting to the mountain has always been from Pokhara, Tirkhe, Tukuche, the French Col, the Northeast Col and finally the northeast ridge.

The time involved in reaching the Tukuche area would be about a week or a little more, but to get to base camp, which involves going over two passes, takes closer to two weeks.

Always plan to spend time in Kathmandu. Some of the things that must be done there are: get a trekking visa; food—of which there is plenty for any climb; a small language dictionary or phrase book, and additional information from the trekking organizations (as to the conditions of the trail on the approach route, and what local foods can be found enroute). Many people who go trekking now eat the local food along the trail—as every small village has a tea house and families who rent rooms. As time goes on, and as climbing parties get smaller, climbers too are using more local foods. Importing food into the country is costly—in time, money and headaches!

For climbers, the best times to climb are April and May, and the end of September and October. For trekking, and at lower elevations, only the months of June, July and August are too rainy and wet. Trekkers who stay in the lower valleys, find mid-winter an enjoyable time to visit Nepal.

There are plenty of buses running from Kathmandu to Pokhara, along with trucks and small aircraft. Pokhara is another fine place in which to spend a little time, as there's a number of cheap but clean hotels and many food shops and tea houses.

**Map:  Pokhara to Jomosom,** trekking map, 1 : 60,000, printed in Kathmandu, and NH-44, 1 : 1,000,000, and NH-44-16, 1 : 250,000, from the US Army Defence Mapping Agency, Washington D.C., and Lands and Survey, Kathmandu.

From the north, Dhaulagiri left, Tukuche right.

# Map 116-3, Dhaulagiri, Himalayas, Nepal

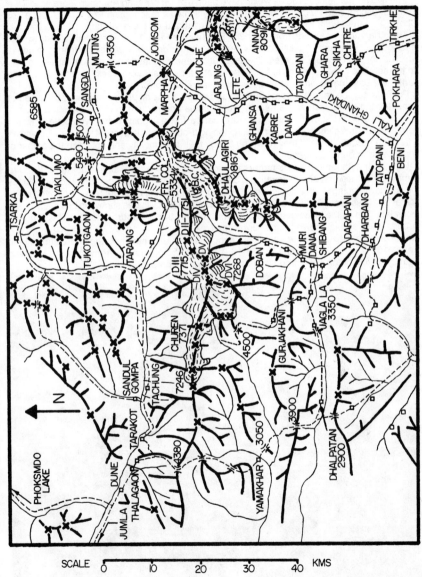

SCALE 0 10 20 30 40 KMS

# Annapurna, Himalayan Mountains, Nepal

One of the most famous big mountains in the world is Annapurna, standing 8091 meters. It's the 10th highest and was the first 8000'er to be conquered; that was in 1950 by a French Expedition. Of all the big mountains, or at least the 8000'ers in Nepal, Annapurna is the closest to any road or highway.

The two normal access routes which have been used in climbing Annapurna are as follows: The first ascent was made on the north face, which was reached via Pokhara, Ghansa and Choya, and the Miristi Khola. The route then zigzagged up the north face.

The other route was made from Pokhara, Birethanti, and the Modi Khola which leads to what is called the "sanctuary," a kind of box canyon, surrounded by a wall of mountains, much of which is not far below 8000 meters. It was a British team that made one of the best climbs ever up the southeast face. Getting to this base camp takes less than a week, but the route to the north face base camp area, will take a week or a little more.

Pokhara can be reached from Kathmandu by bus, truck or plane. However, the weather regulates the flying part, so it's usually more simple and reliable to make the trip by bus.

It's a good idea to spend some time in Kathmandu. If you're going to trek, you have to get the permit there. Solo climbers or other small climbing groups, can usually get in some climbing on a trekking permit; that is, if they're willing to buy their food locally and not go to the bother of importing it through customs.

May 20 or 25th, and mid-October are the times set aside for the summit attempts, if you're climbing. For trekkers, at low elevations, September through May are generally good. Besides the normal camping gear, a complete rain suit for both you and pack are required—even in the so-called dry season. Food and shelter can be found in most villages shown on this map. This is especially true of the villages on the trail which circles the Annapurna Range. This is a very popular hike, and is known as the "Jomsom Trek".

**Map: Pokhara to Jomosom,** trekking map, 1 : 60,000, printed in Kathmandu, and NH-44, Series 1301, 1 : 1,000,000, and NH-44-16, 1 : 250,000, from the US Army Defence Mapping Agency, Washington D.C., and Lands and Survey, Kathmandu.

From Pokhara on a sunny morning. Looking north at Annapurna 11 (R).

# Map 117-1, Annapurna, Himalayas, Nepal

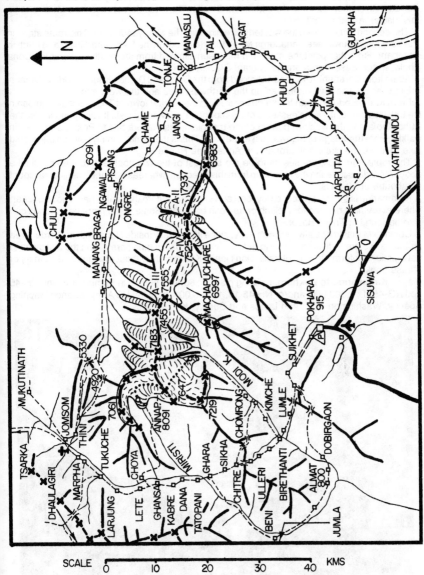

SCALE

0    10    20    30    40    KMS

# Manaslu, Himalayan Mountains, Nepal

The 8th highest mountain in the world is Manaslu, at 8156 meters. It's in Nepal, and just south of the Nepalese-Tibetan border. If one were to go to a point about halfway between Kathmandu and Pokhara, then go due north to near Tibet, there would be Manaslu.

There are two main ways in which to reach Manaslu. The route taken by the Japanese who made the first ascent in 1956, was from Kathmandu, Trisuli Bazar, Arughat Bazar and the Buri Gandaki River, then Sama and the Manaslu Glacier. The route they took to the summit was up this glacier, and the north face.

The second route is from the westerly direction and the Marsyandi River. This route starts in Pokhara and Sisuwa (see Annapurna Map), then to Khudi on the Marsyandi River, and north to Darapani. From that point the mountain has been climbed from the southwest and the Dona Khola, with a Base Camp on the Thulagi Glacier.

Again from Darapani, it has been climbed from the Dudh and Domen Kholas, and the Domen Khola Glacier. The final route was up the northwest face and the west ridge.

From Kathmandu one can take a bus or truck to the market town of Trisuli Bazar, and begin the trek from there, if it's the east side of the mountain you want to visit. If you intend to visit the Duhd Khola and the western portion of the mountain, then take a bus to Pokhara and begin walking from the village of Sisuwa, just to the east. This is the same starting point as one would take to make the circle trek around the Annapurna Range.

The route from Pokhara seems to be the shortest of the two approach routes. It will take about 7 to 9 days to reach the mountain from this direction, whereas from the Trisuli area, count on about 8 or 10 days.

Kathmandu is the best place to buy food and supplies, but Pokhara also has a good bazaar, where everything needed for a climb or trek can be found. Some of the more basic foods can also be found in Trisuli Bazar.

Going to Manaslu has always been easy, since it's actually inside Nepal with no border area problems. Kathmandu is the place to get your trekking or climbing permit, and the last place to get additional information about trails. Don't leave Kathmandu without a language dictionary or phrase book.

**Map: Kathmandu to Pokhara,** trekking map, 1 : 60,000, printed in Kathmandu, and NH-45 and NG-45, 1 : 1,000,000, and/or NH-45-13, 1 : 250,000, from the US Army Defence Mapping Agency, Washington D.C., and Lands and Survey, Kathmandu.

Manaslu, first climbed by the Japanese, from the east.

## Map 118-3, Manaslu, Himalayas, Nepal

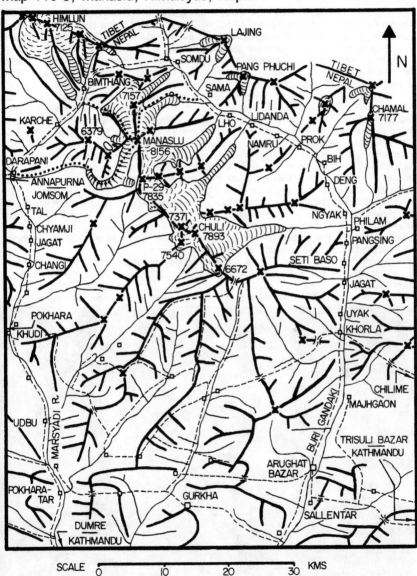

# Xixabangma, Himalayan Mountains, China (Nepal)

The 14th highest mountain in the world is Xixabangma, 8013 meters. This peak is located just inside the Tibetian or Chinese border, perhaps 3 or 4 kms from Nepal. However, this map shows little of the approach to the mountain. Instead, it concentrates on the areas between the Nepal-Tibetian border and Kathmandu. This is a popular trekking area for those with short holidays.

Until the late 1970's and early '80's, it was impossible to climb in China or Tibet, but in 1980, Messner was allowed to climb Everest from the Chinese side. It's now likely that permission can be obtained to climb Xixabangma, and from the Chinese side. Chinese climbers scaled Xixabangma in 1964, via a northeast glacier and ridge.

Besides Kathmandu and some trekking trails between that city and the border, it also includes the following mountains: Jugal Himal (Big White), 7083 meters; Langtang Himal (Kyungka Ri), 6979; Langtang Lirung, 7245; and Ganesh Himal, 7150 meters.

One could walk right from downtown Kathmandu, to any part of this area, but it's not pleasant walking at such low elevations. The best thing to do is to take a truck or bus to places like Trisuli Bazar, which is the normal approach route to all the mountains previously mentioned, with the exception of Xixabangma and Big White. By taking a truck or bus to Chautara, one can reach the south slopes of Big White.

Up until now there has been but one type of climbing expedition—the kind which brings all food supplies from Japan, Europe or North America, and whose pocket books have been heavier than their packs! That is slowly changing. Also there are two kinds of trekkers; those who hire porters to carry most of their baggage and all their food (which comes from far away at home); and those who "go native." These people who go native, eat local food, purchased at the village tea shops, now found in most villages. Most of these trekkers sleep in small "hotels, " or homes along the way. The point being made here is that one doesn't have to go to all the bother of bringing food from home—to trek or to climb in Nepal. Kathmandu has a good selection of foods for any climb.

When applying for a trekking permit in Kathmandu, all the latest information about routes, food availabilty on the trails, better maps, bus information, etc., will come available.

**Map:** NH-45 and NG-45, 1 : 1,000,000, and NH-45-13, 1 : 250,000, from the US Army Defence Mapping Agency, Washington D.C., and Lands and Survey, Kathmandu.

Under clear Tibetian skies we see the north slopes of Xixabangrna.

# Map 119-2, Xixabangma, Himalayas, China (Nepal)

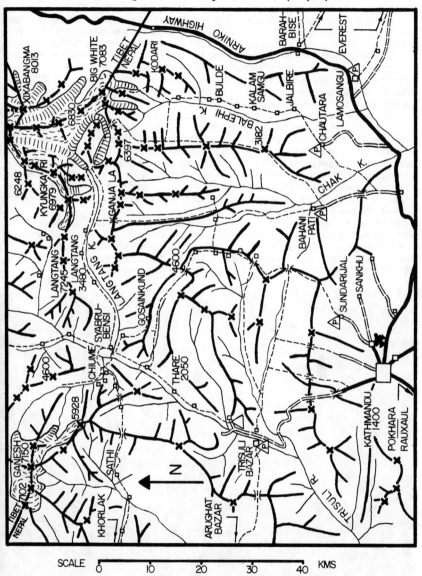

SCALE 0 10 20 30 40 KMS

# Everest Trek, Himalayan Mountains, Nepal

This map shows the route that has become famous in mountaineering circles throughout the world. It's the route that's been used since about 1950 for all expeditions heading in the direction of Mt. Everest and other high summits nearby, which form the "roof of the world." Today it's used by literally thousands of trekkers from every part of the world, who want to set foot on the highest mountain in the world. It's not difficult to go either by land or to fly to Kathmandu—obtain a trekking permit, and walk to the Mt. Everest Base Camp.

The best time to make this trek is in the months April, May, September, October, and November. However, if you're out to trek only, and will stay at lower elevations, the winter months can also be good. For climbing, the months just mentioned—that is, the Pre-Monsoon and Post-Monsoon periods, are the best times. Most people now consider the Post-Monsoon (end of September and October) season to be the most stable, weather-wise.

Anyone with hiking or backpacking experience can make this two-week-plus walk to the area of Mt. Everest. It's an up-and-down route, requiring more determination than anything else. It's a good way to get in shape and lose weight.

Before beginning the trek, do these things in Kathmandu: get a trekking permit; pick up information booklets at various trekking agencies which describe the route in more detail; buy a small language phrasebook—and start learning simple phrases immediately; buy food, for the trek and for the climb; and if desired—make arrangements for porters (all the names and addresses of all these organizations will come to you as you begin the process of getting the trekking permit). Big expeditions have always carried all their own food, but now little tea houses are scattered along the trail where local food can be found for those alone or with small groups. In Namche Bazar, near the Base Camp, one can find enough good food to climb Everest—believe it or not!

Daily buses can take you from Kathmandu to the start of the trail at Lamosangu, and if you wish, it's now possible to return by air from Lukla. Small hotels, or homes with rented rooms are found all along the trail—but take a tent anyway. Have good boots and rain gear.

**Map: Lamu Sangu to Mt. Everest Trekking Map,** printed in Kathmandu, and NG-45-2, 1 : 250,000, from the US Army Defence Mapping Agency, Washington D.C.

Cho Oyu, ranked 7th highest in the world, seen from Tibet (Map 121).

## Map 120-3, Everest Trek, Himalayas, Nepal

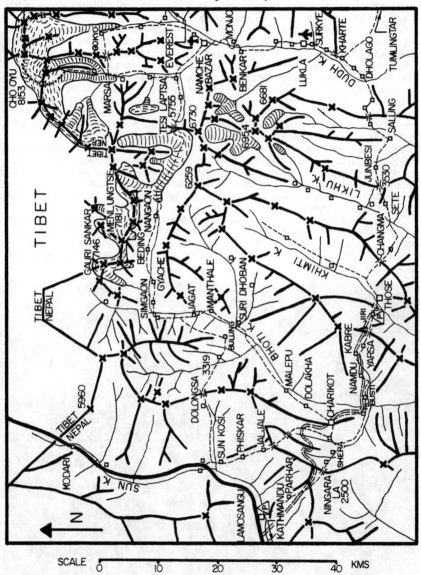

SCALE 0   10   20   30   40 KMS

## Mt. Everest, Himalayan Mountains, Nepal-China

The previous map covers the Everest Trek from Lamosangu to Namche Bazar, located two to three days walk from the Everest Base Camp. This map covers the area north or above Namche Bazar, and includes the 1st, 4th, and 7th highest mountains in the world. These are Mt. Everest, 8848 meters; Lhotse, 8511; and Cho Oyu, 8153 meters. To reach any of these mountains and many more high ones in this area, one is required to use the same route in reaching Namche Bazar. From Namche, the route divides, with most foreigners walking in the direction of Mt. Everest Base Camp at about 5350 meters.

Getting to this area is easier now than in previous years. Most people make the almost two-week walk from Kathmandu (Lamosangu to be exact), to Namche. However, it's now possible, in good weather at least, to fly to Lukla—a couple of days south or below Namche.

In this immediate area, Namche is the best place (the only place) to stock up on any last minute needed supplies. One can actually find enough good food here to climb Everest—but all expeditions still bring all their food from Europe, Japan or North America. In Namche one can find roasted nuts and grains, canned foods of all kinds, potatoes and other vegetables (in season), dried milk, ground cereals (for making hot porridge), kerosene, etc. For the latest information about what exactly is available in Namche, contact some of the trekking agencies in Kathmandu. You may want to buy some items in Kathmandu.

On Everest itself, the normal route is via the South Col (the original conquest route taken in 1953). Most expeditions have used that route, although nowadays, other more difficult routes are being attempted. Lhotse, which is actually the south peak of Everest, was first climbed in 1956 by a Swiss group that later climbed Everest while on the same expedition. They gained the top via the Western Cwm and a coulior on the northwest face. South face routes on Lhotse are some of the best in the world.

Cho Oyu was first climbed in 1954 by an Austrian team, along with two Sherpas. The route they used involved going over the Nangpa La or Pass, into Tibet, then climbing the west ridge.

**Map:** Mt. Everest, NG-45-2, 1 : 250,000, from the US Army Defence Mapping Agency, Washington D.C., or Chomolongma-Mount Everest, 1 : 25,000, from Freytag und Berndt, Kohlmarkt 9, A-1010 Wien.

Everest in center, with the Rongbuk Monastery to the left.

# Map 121-3, Everest, Himalayas, Nepal-China

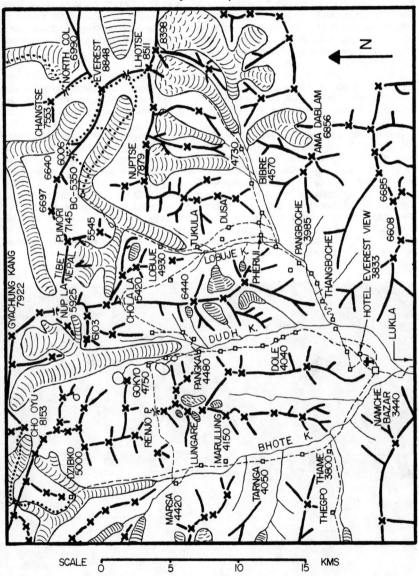

SCALE 0 — 5 — 10 — 15 KMS

## Makalu, Himalayan Mountains, Nepal-China

The big mountain to the east of Everest and Llotse is Makalu, 8481 meters, and is the 5th highest mountain in the world. It was first climbed in 1955 by a French team.

There are two possible routes by which to reach the base of Makalu. The map here shows the more normal route. It begins in the southern Nepalese town of Dharan or Dharan Bazar. The first part of this trail is the same route as used to approach Kangchenjunga (see Kangchenjunga map for the beginning of this trek), located further to the east. From Dharan, to a small village called Hile (where the routes to Kangchenjunga and Makalu split), takes 2 to 3 days, depending on the climber. Then the route goes to the left and northward to the mountain, all the time following the Arun River Gorge. Higher up this same river gorge, the name changes to the Barun Khola.

A second possible approach would be from Lukla Airport, which is south of Everest, and is an important and well used airfield (often used by Everest trekkers). From Lukla, the trail heads south, then turns east at a village called Kharte, and links up with the Dharan-Makalu trail just north of Tumlingtar. It is here that an airstrip is located. It's possible that a small aircraft can be hired in Kathmandu to land at Tumlingtar.

Before going to Dharan one must first stop in Kathmandu to get a trekking permit. It doesn't take much time, only a day or two. In the meantime you can go shopping for food, fuel, a phrase book, etc. Throughout Nepal, most people use kerosene stoves for cooking, and that fuel can be found in many villages. Needless to say, a kerosene stove is the best one to have in Nepal (as well as throughout the less developed world).

The climbing months are April, May, end of September, and October. Buses can be found in Kathmandu or Rauxal (Indian border), for the ride to Dharan. Kathmandu has bookstores and other places in which to buy more detailed maps and get the latest information on the trails, food availability on the trail, etc.

**Map:** NG-45, 1 : 1,000,000, and Kangchenjunga, NG-45-3, 1 : 250,000, from the US Army Defence Mapping Agency, Washington D.C.

Makalu is to the southeast of Everest and 5th highest in the world.

## Map 122-3, Makalu, Himalayas, Nepal-China

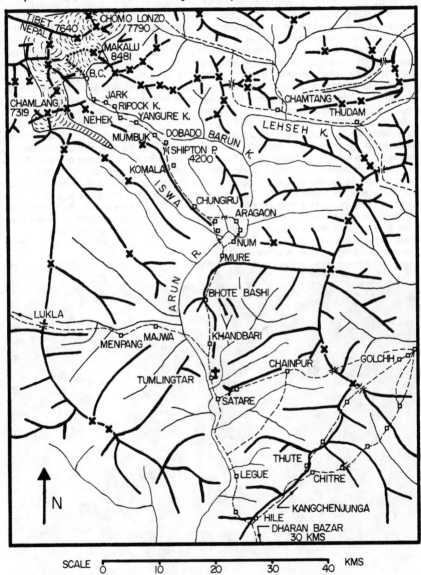

# Kangchenjunga, Himalayan Mts., Nepal-Sikkim

The third highest mountain in the world is Kangchenjunga, 8598 meters. It's located on the border of Nepal and Sikkim, and north of Darjeeling (northern India) about 80 kms. Kangchenjunga was first ascended in 1955 by a British group. It is the furthest east of the 8000'ers, and is the last really big peak in the Himalayas going east.

The route covered on the map is the one from the Nepal side, and the town of Dharan Bazar. One must look at the political situation in India, Nepal and Sikkim, then decide which route will be open—this one through Nepal, or another from Darjeeling. Politics change, and so may the approach route. The way used by the 1955 British Expedition was from Darjeeling, but they crossed over the Nepal border and made the ascent from the Yalung Glacier and the southwest face (the last of their climb is the same as is shown on this map). That expedition took 10 days to reach the base of the mountain. The route described here may take slightly longer.

Getting to Dharan, or Dharan Bazar, can be done from Kathmandu or the border town of Rauxal (India-Nepal). Small, overcrowded buses make this trip—which is one long ride. One might also catch a truck going that way—sometimes they are better than buses.

As for food, that can all be bought in Dharan or Kathmandu. Kathmandu has good enough food selections for climbing any mountain in the world. As one is trekking (or climbing) local food can be bought in the villages enroute. While it's different than the menu you're accustomed to, it is adequate. "Going native," is half the fun of being in this part of the world.

If one needs porters, they can be found in Dharan, or at points along the way. Porters do not need special equipment to reach the place called Oktong, but above that, special arrangements have to be made for "high altitude porters" (HAP's). Kathmandu is a necessary stop—not only for the best food selections, but for your trekking visa as well. Best months for climbing are April and May, the last of September, and October. The monsoon season is from June through early September. During all months, go prepared for wet conditions.

**Map:** Kangchenjunga, NG-45-3, 1 : 250,000, or NG-45, 1 : 1,000,000 from the US Army Defence Mapping Agency, Washington D.C.

South face route up the south face of Kangchenjunga.

## Map 123-3, Kangchenjunga, Himalayas, Nepal-Sikkim

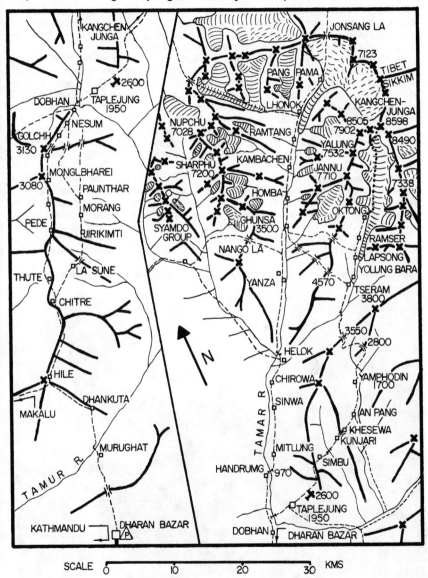

# Adams Peak, Sri Lanka (Ceylon)

One of the easiest, and for sure, one of the most interesting climbs you'll ever make is the one to the top of Adams Peak on the island of Ceylon (now called Sri Lanka). Adams Peak, 2233 meters, is a sacred mountain to the Buddhists. They believe The Buddha was there and left the impression of his foot in the rock at the summit. This could be the most climbed mountain in the world.

Adams is located northeast of Ratnapura, the gem capital of Sri Lanka, and southwest of Hatton, another important town in the highland region. From Ratnapura and Hatton, there are dozens of buses daily, in fact about one every half hour, going to both Carney and Dalhouse. These places are the trailheads on either side of the mountain.

The shortest trail to the top is from Dalhouse, which is at a higher elevation than Carney. From Dalhouse there is a cement staircase to the summit, complete with handrailings and electric lights. The trail from the Carney side is not as well developed—at least there's not quite so many cement steps, but it does have electric lights from top to bottom. The reason for the lighting on these paths, is that many people make the pilgrimage at night, when it's cooler. The humidity and heat on this tropical island are terrific!

Along the trails, particularly on the Carney side, are "trail vendors"; people with small shops or refreshment stands. No need to burden oneself by carrying food on the mountain. These people sell both food and soft drinks—all of which is carried to the mountain on someone's back.

At several locations, mostly on the Carney side, are pilgrim shelters, used as resting stops. These are large buildings with cement floors and roofs, but with open sides to allow for air movement. There'e never a charge for using the shelters—as they are public property. On the Carney side there are several small streams along the path. Drinking water is no problem. On top there's a shrine, covering the "footprint," and a place where Buddhist monks live.

The author recommends a traverse of the peak. Nothing special is needed for the hike—as thousands do it weekly, including very old people and people walking barefoot. An interesting hike.

**Map:**  NB-44, 2 and 6, 1 : 250,000, US Army Defence Mapping Agency, Washington D.C.

Foto taken not far above Carney on the south trail to Adams Peak.

## Map 124-1, Adams Peak, Sri Lanka (Ceylon)

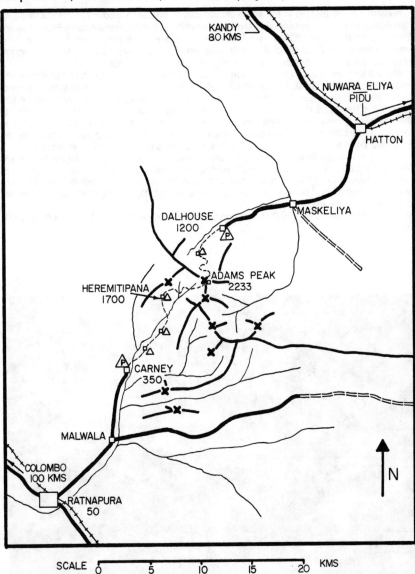

KANDY
80 KMS

NUWARA ELIYA
PIDU

HATTON

MASKELIYA

DALHOUSE
1200

ADAMS PEAK
2233

HEREMITIPANA
1700

CARNEY
350

MALWALA

COLOMBO
100 KMS

RATNAPURA
50

N

SCALE  0    5    10    15    20    KMS

## Pidurutalagala, Sri Lanka (Ceylon)

The mountains on the island of Ceylon, or in the Republic of Sri Lanka, are not high or rugged, but they are interesting. One of the main reasons for going to the mountains or highland areas, is to get up and away from the tropical heat and humidity. One fine place to do that is to visit the town of Nuwara Eliya and the highest peak on the island, Pidurutalagala, 2524 meters.

Nuwara Eliya is located in the south central part of Sri Lanka, about 70 kms southeast of Kandy, the old capital, and not far east of Hatton, which is on the route to Adams Peak. Nuwara Eliya is a hill-station at 1900 meters, in the middle of one of the most important tea growing areas of the world. Because of its altitude and refreshing climate, it's also a tourist hangout. Most tourists are Sri Lankans, as few foreigners know of the place.

About 3 kms immediately north of town is Pidurutalagala, or "Pidu" for short. From the north end of town near a hospital, there's first a street, which leads to a trail, and ends at the summit of Pidu. The walk is only about 5 kms and can be completed in a couple of hours. At one point, just beyond the Ramboda Pass, is a small stream where good water is found. The final portion of the trail is on grassy slopes, whereas lower on the mountain a virgin rain forest is found. In locating the trailhead, just ask anyone where the trail to Pidu is, and they'll show you. All educated people in Sri Lanka speak English, so communication is not at all difficult.

Getting to Nuwara Eliya is easy. There are many buses running to this region from every direction, including Kandy, Hatton and Colombo (the capital). Bus service in Sri Lanka is very good. In Nuwara Eliya there is a variety of accommodations, from the most expensive to very cheap resthouses, or in people's homes with rooms for rent. It's not a big town, but it has all that is needed for a pleasant stay.

**Map:**   NB-44, 2 and 3, 1 : 250,000, from the US Army Defence Mapping Agency, Washington, D.C.

There's one small spring on the trail to Pidu.

## Map 125-1, Pidurutalagala, Sri Lanka (Ceylon)

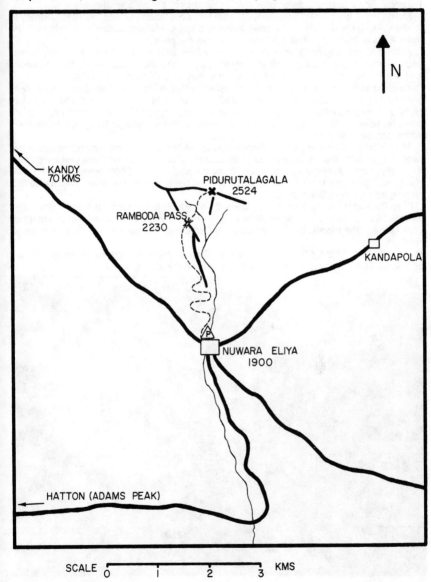

KANDY
70 KMS

PIDURUTALAGALA
2524

RAMBODA PASS
2230

KANDAPOLA

P

NUWARA ELIYA
1900

HATTON (ADAMS PEAK)

N

SCALE  0   1   2   3   KMS

## Yu Shan, Central Range, Taiwan

Yu Shan or Jade Mountain, 3997 meters, is the highest mountain in Taiwan and all of east Asia. It is built of metamorphic rock, as are all the mountains in Taiwan.

Getting to Yu Shan is an adventure in travel. There's only one way to the mountain and that's from Chaiyi. At Chaiyi is the beginning of the old narrow gage railway linked to Alishan. Alishan is formerly a lumber mill town and the railroad was used to haul trees and lumber down to the lowlands. Some lumber activity still exists in the region, but on a smaller scale.

From Chaiyi, the slowest and cheapest train takes 5½ hours to make the 70 km journey to Alishan. Along the way are many small towns and stops, where food can be bought from the train. A faster train takes half the time—at double the price.

Alishan is now a tourist town sitting at a refreshing 2274 meters. There are many hotels, youth hostels, eating places, and Buddhists temples. Not far away is the largest tree in Taiwan, and one of the largest in the world outside the state of California in the USA.

To climb Yu Shan, one must walk from Alishan to Yushan Ko, along an old unused railway line. Yushan Ko is at 2550 meters, and KM 82 (Alishan is KM 70). Yushan Ko is hiker's hut, or better still, a summer hotel. It has food available, beds and bedding, and running water—all for a fee. However, for the budget traveler, there are two work crew huts (in 1977) near Yushan Ko, which can be used for free.

From Yushan Ko, there's an old lumber road to the Tartar Ka Saddle, where the actual trail begins. The trail is newly built, and has been blasted out of the sheer rock-face in some places. It's a very good trail, all the way to the top. Along the way, at about 3400 meters, is the Pai Yun Hut or Refuge. It can sleep about 50 people in bunk beds, complete with bedding. It also has running water and cooking facilities.

From Pai Yun Hut to the top is a scramble with many trails to choose from. From Alishan, this hike will take 2 or 3 days, round-trip, depending on one's physical fitness, and time of departure from Alishan. The months of May and June, or October and November are the best times to climb Yu Shan.

**Map:** NF-51-1, 1 : 250,000, from the US Army Defence Mapping Agency, Washington D.C., and some Taiwanese mountain hiking maps, but they're all in Chinese.

Near Pai Yun Hut the trail is cut from solid rock.

# Map 126-1, Yu Shan, Central Range, Taiwan

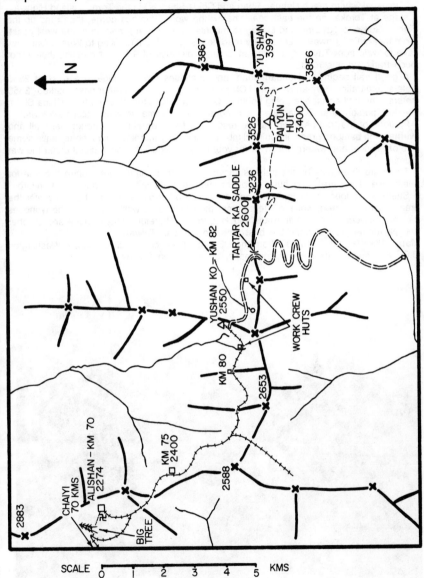

## Chida Shan, Central Range, Taiwan

Chida Shan, 3605 meters, is the highest summit in vicinity of the Hohuan Shan ski resort. This area of high peaks is about 20 to 30 kms south of Lishan and the still higher mountains of Hsuih Shan and Lam Whoa Shan, Taiwan's second and third highest peaks. As with most or all of Taiwan's mountains, Chida Shan is made up of metamorphic type rock, something like the Toroka Gorge, not far to the northeast.

The usual way to reach Hohuan Shan and Chida Shan, is via the Trans . .Island Highway. It starts at Toroka, on the east coast, below the world . .famous gorge, then runs up the Toroka Gorge to Tayuling and Lishan (a mountain resort town), and on to the west coast. From that main highway, a secondary road heads south from Tayuling to Wushi. One may have to walk from Tayuling to Hohuan Shan, a distance of 9 kms. Normally, there's not much traffic on this road.

A good trail begins at Hohuan Shan, and continues down a ridge to a pass at 2850 meters, separating Hohuan Shan and Chida Shan. Then at still another pass marked "3350 meters," the trail splits, one going south to Chida Su Shan, the other north to Chida Shan. The last portion near Chida Shan is a ridge-walk in some very beautiful meadows.

Portions of the trail between the ski resort and the Twin Huts is through very tall and overhanging bamboo grass. If you're climbing in the early morning hours, better have some kind of raincoat and waterproof cover for your pack, as you'll drench yourself under the wet brush.

There are three huts on the trail, as shown on the map. All three are open and free for public use. They are good huts, made of steel and aluminum, but have no furniture.

Streams are found near the huts, and at several other places on the trail. In winter the area is snow covered, while in late summer the island is hit with typhoons. The typhoons cause landslides on mountain roads, blocking traffic. Therefore, May or June and October and November are perhaps the best times to climb in Taiwan.

**Map:** NG-51-13, 1 : 250,000, from the US Army Defence Mapping Agency, Washington D.C., and some Taiwanese hiking maps, but they're in Chinese.

From the summit of Chida Shan looking southwest to Chida Su Shan.

## Map 127-1, Chida Shan, Central Range, Taiwan

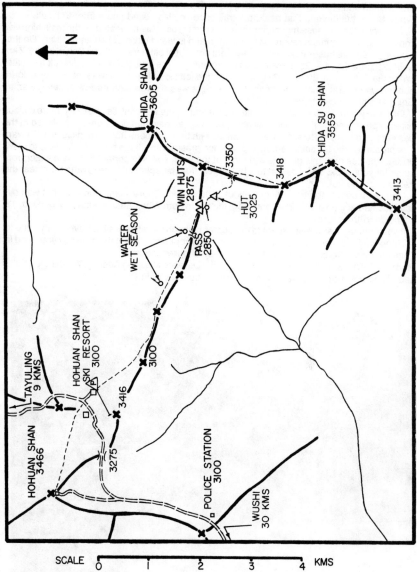

N

CHIDA SHAN
3605

CHIDA SU SHAN
3559

3350

3418

3413

TWIN HUTS
2875

HUT
3025

WATER
WET SEASON

PASS
2850

TAYULING
9 KMS

HOHUAN SHAN
SKI RESORT
3100

3416

3100

3100

HOHUAN SHAN
3466

3275

POLICE STATION
3100

WUSHI
30 KMS

SCALE  0    1    2    3    4    KMS

## Lam Whoa Shan, Central Range, Taiwan

In the northern part of Taiwan's Central Range, and northeast of Lishan, stand the third and fourth highest mountains in Taiwan. They are Lam Whoa Shan, 3740 meters, and about 5 kms to the south, Jong Yong Gien Shan, 3703 meters. These peaks consist of metamorphic rock of various kinds.

From the town, or rather the military camp of Suien, it's a two day climb (round – trip) to Lam Whoa Shan and probably 3 days to Jong Yong Gien Shan. There's a good trail as far as Lam Whoa Shan, but beyond that peak, the trail becomes less used and harder to locate.

To reach either of these mountains, one must first reach Suien, located on the main highway connecting the mountain resort town of Lishan and lowland cities of Ilan and Lotung. On that highway there are buses every hour or two, but not a lot of other traffic. From Suien, it's a 6.7 km walk to the trailhead at 2300 meters. The beginning of the trail can be a bit difficult to locate. When the author was there (1977), the trail on the left side of the road, was marked by colorful ribbons on several small pine trees. On the right was a large pine tree, with several small Chinese signs and ribbons.

Once on the trail there should be little trouble finding the way, but it's one of the more difficult hikes experienced by the author. All along the way, at least that part from the trailhead to the peak marked 3140 meters, the trail is marked with bright ribbons from hiking clubs in Taiwan. The problem is the tall and overhanging bamboo grass. With a large pack, it's not easy to crawl under. Besides that, this grass is wet most of the time, so it's important to have a waterproof cover for your pack. You'll be wet too, but largely from perspiration. Carry water from near the trailhead to the hut.

On the mountain, the tree . .line is about 3100 meters. There's one aluminum hut with dirt floor, located at timber line. The route from the hut to Lam Whoa Shan is easy, but beyond, it's unknown to the author.

If you're there in summer expect to encounter typhoons—with possible travel delays due to rain and landslides on the mountain roads. If this is your first climb in the area buy your food in Taipei. Or if you're coming from the south, buy supplies in Lishan.

**Map:** NG-51-13, 1 : 250,000, from the US Army Defence Mapping Agency, Washington D.C., and hiking maps from Taiwanese alpine clubs, but they're in Chinese.

The lower part of the trail to Lam Whoa Shan is covered with Bamboo grass.

# Map 128-1, Lam Whoa Shan, Central Ra., Taiwan

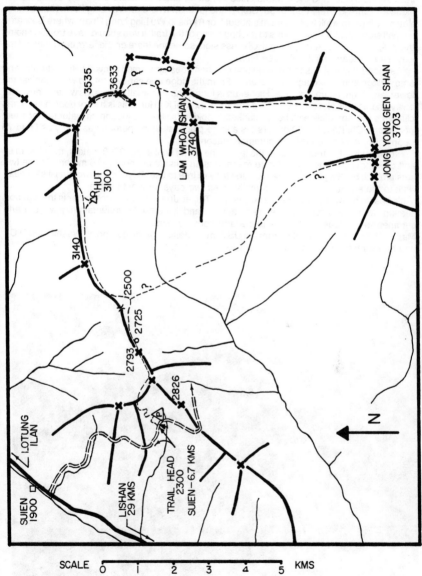

3535
3633
LAM WHOA SHAN 3740
JONG YONG GIEN SHAN 3703
HUT 3100
3140
2500
2725
2793
2826
LOTUNG ILAN
LISHAN 29 KMS
SUIEN 1900
TRAIL HEAD 2300
SUIEN — 6.7 KMS
N

SCALE 0 1 2 3 4 5 KMS

## Hsuih Shan, Central Range, Taiwan

Hsuih Shan, 3884 meters, is the second highest peak in Taiwan, and is one of the most climbed on the island. There's a very good trail to the top—and with none of the tall and overhanging bamboo grass to fight through, as is common on other nearby mountains.

The approach is from two directions. First, from the south and the resort town of Lishan; and from the northeast and the lowland cities of Lotung and Ilan. There are many buses on this highway, running every hour or so. Stop at the junction where the Wu Ling Farm road begins. You may have to walk from there. It's about 5 or 6 kms to Wu Ling Long Chan, where is located a small store, then another 3 kms to the beginning of the trail. If you should have trouble finding the trail, which is marked by a small Chinese sign, someone there on the farm can point out the way. (A tip—learn a little Chinese fast!)

The good trail first passes several homes, then goes up a small canyon with a stream, and onto a ridge and an old agricultural area. From the ridge one can see an old water tank at the lower left. Continue up the ridge. Higher up is found another small stream, as water is never far away on this trail. Not far beyond the stream is the Chi Ka Hut. This is a very good hiker's and climber's hut, complete with beds, blankets, cooking facilities, and running water (all for a fee, of course). Chi Ka (at 2500 meters), is a large place, sleeping perhaps as many as 50 to 75 people, but is open during the summer season only.

From Chi Ka, the trail winds up the last of the ridge, until about 3200 meters, then it's an up and down trail until the two huts are reached at an altitude of about 3175 meters. These two huts are old, but they keep the rain off and they're free to use. Beyond the two huts it's an easy walk to the summit. This climb normally takes two days for most people.

It's best to buy your food in either Lishan, or Taipei. June through September is the typhoon season, with heavy rains, sometimes causing landslides on the mountain highways. Early summer and October and November are the best to climb.

**Map:**  NG-51-13, 1 : 250,000, from the US Army Defence Mapping Agency, Washington D.C., and hiking maps from Taiwan, but they're in Chinese.

Looking along the east ridge to the summit of Hsuih Shan.

# Map 129-1, Hsuih Shan, Central Range, Taiwan

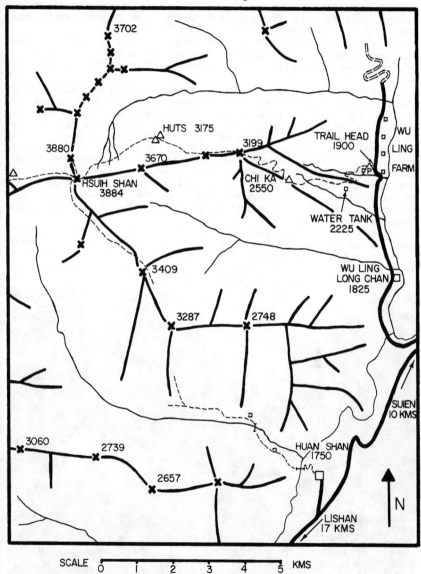

## Sorak San, South Korea

Sorak San is not the highest mountain in South Korea, but it offers some of the best camping and climbing possibilities in the country. The summit is at 1708 meters. Sorak San and the surrounding peaks are made up, for the most part, of granitic type rocks and others normally associated with igneous intrusions.

Sorak San is located on the east coast, not far north of the large city of Kangnung, and just west of Sogcho. Kangnung is on the main rail lines and motorways serving the country. From Kangnung to Sorakdong travel many buses, as that town, at the entrance to the Sorak San National Park is a real tourist trap.

In Sorakdong are dozens of hotels, restaurants and souvenir shops. Beyond Sorakdong, are many trails—most of which are over-used. The one main trail leading to the hostel and eventually to Sorak San, has a variety of small shops offering food, souvenirs and anything that will sell.

The hostel just mentioned is similar to the mountain huts in the Alps and in Japan, with food and beds available. Another hut, marked at 1075 meters, is not as fancy, but food can be found there. When the author was there during the month of September (1977), someone had pitched a tent right on the summit of Sorak San and was selling soda pop, candy and other goodies. Needless to say, there is no problem finding food in these mountains.

All trails which cross difficult places, have been fixed with ladders, ramps and bridges—something like the Dolimiti of north Italy. In some of the more remote areas of the park are several Buddhist temples. The water in all streams is generally good.

The mountain tops are generally rather smooth, as if they had been run over by glaciers, but the main canyon leading to Sorak San has many good rock climbing possibilities. Camping is regulated, so it's advised to ask questions before dropping a tent. Beware of leaving your camp unguarded.

Bus service exists on almost all roads in Korea, making travel easy. One fast hiker could easily walk from Sorakdong to Pyeongchondi in one day, then get a bus from there to the next destination. Two days is more pleasant however, especially if visiting temples is important.

**Map:** Guide Map of Climbing Mt. Seolag(Sorak San), 1 : 75,000, Jung-Ang Map & Chart Service, 125-1, Gongpyeong Dong, Jongro-Gu, Seoul.

"Iron Routes" in the gorge north of Sorak San.

## Map 130-1, Sorak San, South Korea

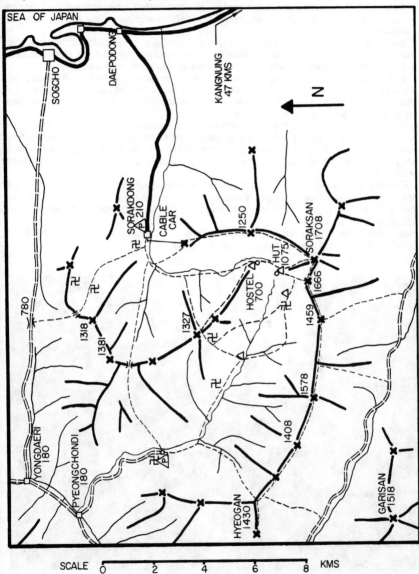

## Odaesan, South Korea

Of the four mountain areas in South Korea covered in this book, Odeasan is the lowest mountain, only 1563 meters, and is possibly visited the least of the four. However, that doesn't make it the least interesting. In fact, the Buddhist temples in these mountains are as interesting as in any of the mountains of Korea, with the exception of Sogri San (which is not covered here).

Odaesan and the surrounding mountains are heavily forested, from top to bottom. Nowhere in this area do the summits rise above the tree line, with the exception of the last few meters on Odaesan.

Getting to this area is easy, as with all the mountain areas of Korea. Odaesan is located just north of the Yeongdong Expressway—the one linking Seoul with Kangnung and the east coast. Auto stopping on the expressway is good, but on all side roads it's impossible.

If you're coming from Seoul by bus, they'll probably set you off at, or near, the Daegwan-ryeong ski resort. From there you'll have to catch another bus to Ganpyeongri and the "last bus stop," in the main valley leading to Odaesan. If you're coming from the Kangnung side, there are many local buses going to the same area.

At the last bus stop there are several small shops, eating places, and yogwans (small inns or hotels). This is the last place in the valley where one can surely buy food and accommodation. Further up the road there's a campsite (and possibly a store?). As for camping, it can be done any place, but beware of leaving unattended camps, as Koreans are not at all like the Chinese or Japanese.

From the last bus stop it's a 2 or 3 hour walk to the Sangweon Temple. That's where the main trail to the summit of Odaesan begins. Enroute, hikers pass two more temples before reaching the top. This trail is good, but others in the area may not be so used. During summer and early fall, all facilities are open.

**Map:**  Guide Map of Climbing Mt. Odae(Odaesan), 1 : 75,000, from Jung-Ang Map & Chart Service, 125-1, Gongpyeong Dong, Jongro-Gu, Seoul.

Trail to Odeasan is forested and has many rest stops.

# Map 131-1, Odeasan, South Korea

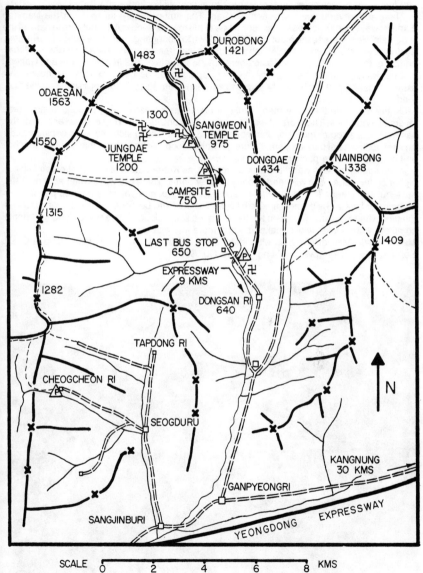

# Jidi San, South Korea

In south central Korea, not far from the southern coast, is located one of the largest national parks in that county. Within this park is the second highest peak in South Korea, Jiri San, 1915 meters. The national park has the same name.

As is true of all national parks in South Korea, transportation to even the most remote areas is very good. In a land where private autos are almost nonexistent (except in the big cities), there are large buses making several daily runs to almost all backcountry villages.

There are several ways to reach Jiri San. The author began in Jinju (on the Namhae Expressway) to the southeast, and took a bus to the town of Jongsan, literally at the base of the mountain. He traversed the mountain coming down to Yonggang, then got a bus to Tabri. Later, another bus was taken to the Namhae Expressway (the one running across the southern portion of the country). One can also approach the mountain area from the north and Gaheding, but it is recommended that the southern approaches be used, as they are nearer the expressway. Auto stopping on the expressways in Korea is good, but impossible on the side roads.

On the mountain there are many well used trails, as Koreans being Buddhists, are great lovers of mountains. There are at least two good huts on Jidi San. These however are not the same as huts on other more popular mountains in Korea. These lack any real sleeping places and are, for the most part, only small stores. Plenty of food can be found in these huts, either hot and cooked or of the packaged or snack variety.

In the stream valleys water is never a problem, as Korea gets a fair amount of rainfall; but higher on the ridges one will need to carry a water bottle. There is always water at or near the huts, but sometimes that is rain water, and if it's a dry period you may have to pay for it.

Spring or fall may be the best time to hike, but the huts may be closed. The summer season is the time when Koreans get out on the trails. On the south slopes, there's one Buddhist temple complete with monks, which makes the trip more interesting.

**Map:** Guide Map of Climbing Mt. Jiri(Jiri San), 1 : 75,000, from Jung-Ang Map & Chart Service, 125-1, Gongpyeong Dong, Jongro-Gu, Seoul.

This is the hut and hut keeper just west of Jiri San.

## Map 132-1, Jiri San, South Korea

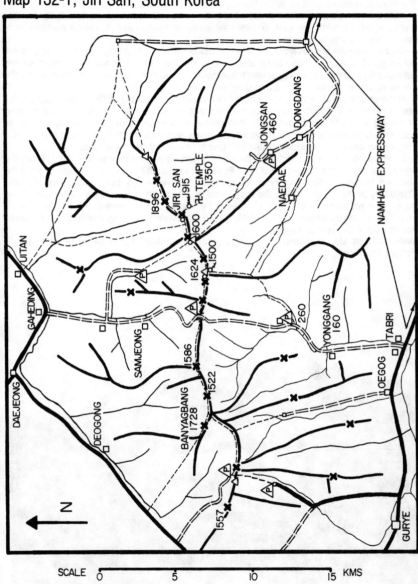

SCALE  0     5     10     15  KMS

## Halla San, Cheju Island, South Korea

In the channel separating Korea and Japan are many islands, one of which is Cheju. Like several of the islands in that channel, it is a volcanic island. The surface is pocked with cinder cones, some old, some very recent. The "island" is not yet considered "dormant". The highest summit on Cheju, and the highest mountain in South Korea, is Halla San, 1950 meters. Like all the mountainous regions in South Korea, it's a national park.

Halla San can be climbed in one day if one of the two western routes is taken. The three other routes—from the north, the east, and the southeast—are longer and may require an overnight stay on the mountain for some.

On the mountain are several huts; some rather good, and which you have to pay for; others not so good, and are in need of repairs. At any rate one can spend a night on the mountain without a tent. At most huts, especially those higher on the mountain, food can also be bought. These huts are similar to those in Japan and Europe.

At the beginning of each trail, is a house or park entrance gate. Everyone must pay a small amount to enter. They will give you a small map, and any information needed as to the opening or closing of huts and food availability. If you're there during the summer or holiday months, all huts should be open and serving food. For those wishing to camp, that can be done anywhere. The author camped inside the crater with plenty of water in two nearby ponds.

There are two ways of reaching Cheju Island. One is by air (unfamiliar to the author), the other is by ferry. One ferry route is from Pusan on the southeast coast, the other is from the southwestern town of Mogpo. From Mogpo there are two ferries daily, each taking 7 hours. Cheju City on the north shore is the ferry terminal, and a good place to visit. There are many buses running from Cheju City to all parts of the island, and expecially to Seogwipo. These buses can drop you off at any of the trail heads. Expect wetter and warmer conditions on Cheju Island than in the rest of Korea.

**Map:** Tourist Map of Cheju, 1 : 100,000, from Jung-Ang Map & Chart Service, 125-1, Gongpyeong Dong, Jongro-Gu, Seoul.

Wide angle lens sees entire crater at top of Halla San.

# Map 133-1, Halla San, Cheju Island, South Korea

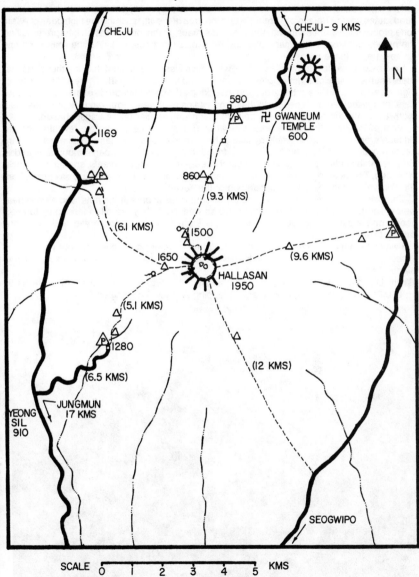

## Daisetsuzan National Park, Hokkaido, Japan

Daisetsuzan National Park, located at the center of Japan's northern island of Hokkaido, has perhaps the best hiking and scenic attractions of any of the national parks of Japan. All the peaks in Daisetsuzan Park are volcanic and in one stage or another—some old, some new. The highest summit in the park is Asahi, at 2290 meters. Several others rise above 2200 meters.

The high peaks of this national park are surrounded by many access roads, but the most used routes are the Sounkyo, Teninkyo, and the area of the lift, reaching the high peak of Asahi (one problem the author had with the Japanese maps, is that one needs an interpreter to find the names of places—few maps use any Romanized characters. That's the reason so few names are on these maps).

Hokkaido is the "last frontier" in Japan, with much less development than in other parts, but there seems to be a lot of development in and around this national park. There are a number of sight-seeing and ski lifts in the area, and that, coupled with the hundreds of buses and private cars, brings thousands of people to these mountains each year. Sounkyo is right on the main highway and is the easiest access point to reach with regular public transportation.

Most of the trails are above timberline and on higher places, therefore few streams are encountered—but water is easily available. Hokkaido is not a dry island. Within the park are several huts or shelters, similar to those found in other parts of Japan's mountains and in Europe. At the huts, some food can be purchased—sometimes hot meals, sometimes snack-type food. The sleeping places are large communal rooms, with the sleeping areas raised from the floor. The author found no separation of the sexes.

Camping is strictly regulated, with nearly all campsites at or near the huts, and always near water. The trails in the northern section are so well used, they are often fenced in, to keep people on the path. On the southern end, where there is much less foot traffic, trails are more difficult to keep track of.

Always have along some good rain clothing and a water-proof cover for your pack. Also, expect much cooler temperatures on Hokkaido, than in the Japanese Alps to the south on the island of Honshu.

**Map:**  Daisetsuzan National Park, 1 : 50,000, printed in Japan(all Japanese). Also, NK-54-9, 1 : 250,000, from the US Army Defence Mapping Agency, Washington D.C.

One of several volcanic cones in the Daisetsuzan National Park.

# Map 134-1, Daisetsuzan N.P., Hokkaido, Japan

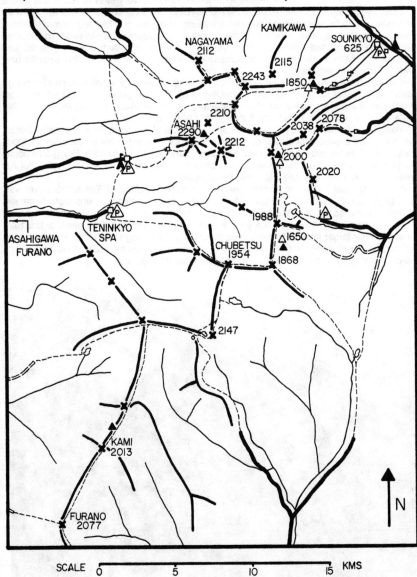

SCALE 0   5   10   15   KMS

## Tateyama, Kita Alps, Honshu, Japan

The map here includes most of the northern half of the Kita or Northern Alps. All the mountains coming under the name "Japanese Alps" are on the island of Honshu—same island as Tokyo and Fuji San. The highest mountain in this region is Tateyama with 3015 meters elevation.

As is the case with all the Japanese Alps, this area too, is very easy to reach and from a number of different directions. To get to the highest peak, the easiest approach is from the area of Takayama on the west, then by bus, or hitch hiking, to the resort of Murodoh. From Murodoh to the top is a one day hike. In fact, all of the summits in that region (the ones west of the Kurobe Dam), can be reached in one day from Murodoh. Another approach is from Omachi, and Ohgizawa, but this involves a boat ride across the lake behind Kurobe Dam. This is not the best route to reach Tateyama.

If an interesting hike is your goal, rather than climbing the very highest peak, then a long ridge walk might be just for you. From the town Ohgizawa, one can get to the top of a long ridge, which runs north to the high peak of Shirouma and town of Sarukura, and further. To walk this distance is to walk almost half of the total length of the Kita Alps.

Along this ridge are found many huts or shelters, most of which are small "hotels"—that is, there is space available for sleeping, and where one can buy either hot meals or snack food. Near by each hut is usually found a place to camp, generally for a small fee. Being on a ridge, water is difficult to find, but the hut keepers catch and store rainwater. When rain is plentiful, it's free, but in dry periods a small fee may be charged.

Another approach might be from the north and the town of Unazuki. The author never was able to get details, but there's a railway from Unazuki to Keyakaidaira. It undoubtedly serves tourists in summer, but if not, one could walk the tracks to reach the trails further up the canyon.

If you're planning to take and cook your own food, buy it in Omachi, Takayama, or Unazuki, or some other larger town before reaching the trails. June through mid-October is the hiking season here, with early October being one of the favorite times because of fall colors.
**Map:**  Kita(North) Alps, 1 : 100,000, printed in Japan in Japanese.

From Hotaka, looking north along prominent ridge (Map 136).

# Map 135-3, Tateyama, Kita Alps, Honshu, Japan

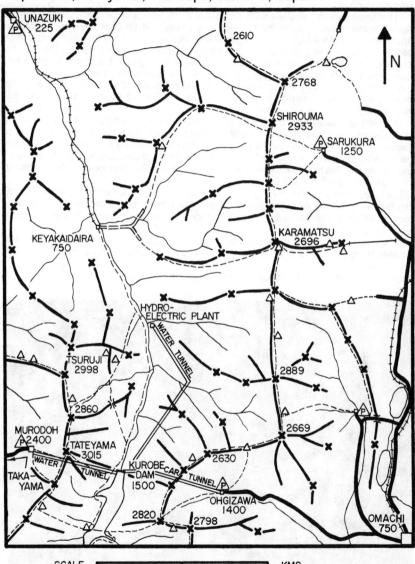

UNAZUKI
225

2610

2768

SHIROUMA
2933

SARUKURA
1250

KARAMATSU
2696

KEYAKAIDAIRA
750

HYDRO-
ELECTRIC PLANT

WATER TUNNEL

TSURUJI
2998

2889

2860

MURODOH
2400

2669

TATEYAMA
3015

WATER TUNNEL

KUROBE
DAM
1500

CAR TUNNEL

2630

TAKA-
YAMA

OHGIZAWA
1400

OMACHI
750

2820

2798

N

SCALE    0        5        10    KMS

## Yari Dake, Kita Alps, Honshu, Japan

Yari Dake, 3179 meters, is one of the highest peaks in Japan and is certainly one of the most impressive. It is the "Matterhorn" of Japan and is perhaps the most famous mountain there—next to Fuji San. The Kita or North Alps are folded and uplifted mountains composed mostly of metamorphic rock—as opposed to the volcano of Fuji San. None of the Japanese Alps are volcanic in origin.

In the same area as Yari Dake is Okuho Dake, at 3190 meters, Japan's third highest summit. Access to this southern part of the Kita Alps is very easy, and it is visited by more people than any other region of the Japanese Alps. The route involves taking a bus from Matsumoto (most people take a train to a point a few kms west of Matsumoto, then buses) to the resort of Kamikochi, a distance of about 45 kms. Hitch hiking is very good—but only to a point 6 kms short of Kamikochi. At that point, private autos are not allowed to pass—only buses.

At Kamikochi are many shops, stores, hotels and campsites. It's very beautiful, but a real tourist trap. From Kamikochi it's hiking the rest of the way. There is a narrow road to Yokoh, but that's limited to hotel deliveries only.

To climb Yari, about three leisurely days are needed, and by making one camp at Yokoh. To climb Okuho, about two days are usually enough. Most people doing this hike, camp at Kalasawa (camping is in designated areas only in this national park!). For those with more time, the following route is recommended: Kamikochi, Yokoh, Kalasawa, Okuho, Yari Dake, Yokoh and Kamikochi. This hike would take most people four days. The ridge top between Okuho and Yari Dake is rugged, but well used.

The valley camps have plenty of good water available, but it's rain water at the ridge camps and huts—sometimes for a fee. Most huts offer everything for the lite traveler who wants comfort in the hills. Special equipment must include a raincoat and cover for the pack, as heavy rains come often.

June through October are the favorite months for visits to the southern Kita Alps, with October being the most colorful and fotogenic—and at times the most crowded. Don't forget your camera.

**Map:** Kita(North) Alps, 1 : 100,000, printed in Japan in Japanese.

Holiday camping at Kalasawa. Too many camps!

# Map 136-1, Yari, Kita Alps, Honshu, Japan

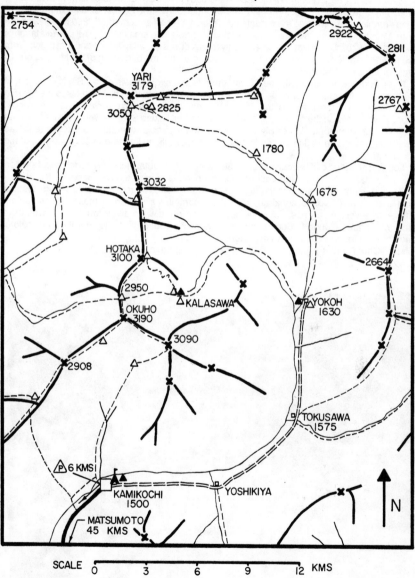

SCALE 0   3   6   9   12  KMS

## Komaga Dake, Chuo Alps, Honshu, Japan

The Chuo or Central Alps of Japan are located on the island of Honshu, just west of the Minami or Southern Alps and Fujisan, and not far south of the Kita or North Alps. The highest summit in the Chuo Alps is Komaga Dake, rising to 2956 meters. The Chuo Alps are part of the national park system which includes all of the high and important mountains in Japan.

Getting to the region of the highest peaks is easy. The normal route of approach is via the small city of Komagane, located next to the Chuo Expressway. After exiting, there are two roads running west and into the mountains. There's a resort area marked "850 meters" on the map. Located there are several hotels, eating places, and a small store. The power station is the end of the road for private vehicles—only tourist buses are allowed beyond that point. From the power plant to Shirabi Daira—the end of the road and the beginning of the lift, is about 15 kms, or about a 3 hour walk.

If you take the lift like most, you'll finish the ride in a cirque basin called Senjojiki, at about 2600 meters. If you'd rather walk, there's a good trail beneath the lift, which takes the hiker to Senjojiki as well. From the top of the lift there are many trails fanning out to all parts of the range, most of which are on the ridgetops. That part of the trail linking Senjojiki with the shelter or hut marked "2800 meters," is heavily traveled, even by people wearing fine clothes (such as business suits!) The trail is fenced in to keep all the traffic in line and to save the rest of the mountain.

Lodging and food can be found at all locations along the route, including the top-most shelter, Senjojiki, the resort area, and best of all at Komagane, where a supermarket is found.

If you're planning to sleep in the higher shelters or huts, you must have your own sleeping bag and stove (if you're cooking). Meals are sometimes served in these high mountain huts—for a very high price. Camping is permitted but always away from the crowds or in designated areas. June through October is the hiking season with October the most coloful month. Hitching to this area is very good.

**Map:**   Chuo(Central) Alps, 1 : 50,000, printed in Japan in Japanese.

Many people take the lift to Senjojiki, then hike to the summit.

## Map 137-1, Komaga, Chuo Alps, Honshu, Japan

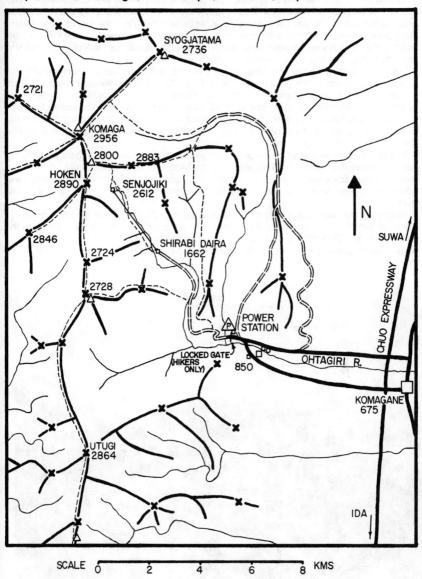

# Kita Dake, Minami Alps, Honshu, Japan

The Minami or Southern Alps of Japan are on the big island of Honshu (as are all the Japanese Alps), just west of Kofu and northwest of Fuji San. The highest peak in the entire Minami Alps is Kita Dake, 3192 meters. It's also the second highest in all of Japan—only Fuji San is higher.

Getting to this region is fairly easy. A bus can be taken from the city of Kofu to Ashiyasa and into the mountains to Hirogawara. Buses may have to be changed at Ashiyasa. It's also possible to hitch hike to any point on this road, especially if you're a foreign visitor to Japan. Many people make a traverse of the ridge tops. In fact, you haven't much choice in the matter as almost all trails are on the ridge tops. These ridge walks and climbs are fine for sightseeing and fotography, but sometimes bad for camping and finding water.

The author walked the trail from Hirogawara to Narada, taking two days. All or most of these huts are very similar to those in Europe. Inside the shelters, the middle section of each large sleeping room is for walking and shoes, the raised outer portions are for sleeping, eating and cooking. Generally the huts are large enough for 50 to 100 people. One can buy snack foods, or order a hot, prepared meal. Most hikers take along a small stove and cook for themselves. Each hut has facilities for catching and storing water. Normally they'll give you all the water you want, but in dry periods you may have to pay for it.

The Minami Alps are part of the national park system, so things like camping are regulated in crowded areas. Normally, campsites exist near the huts, but the hut keepers usually charge a fee. If camping, place your tent well, as high winds are common on these ridges. Japan is a wet country so a good waterproof tent is required, as is some kind of rain gear for you and your pack.

During the summer season, say from mid-June through October, there are many people in the mountains hiking, taking fotos, etc., especially on weekends. October can be cold on the high peaks, but it's a coloful season, with generally fewer people about.

**Map:**  Minami(South) Alps, 1 : 100,000, printed in Japan in Japanese.

The summit of Kita Dake looking north along ridge.

# Map 138-1, Kita Dake, Minami Alps, Honshu, Japan

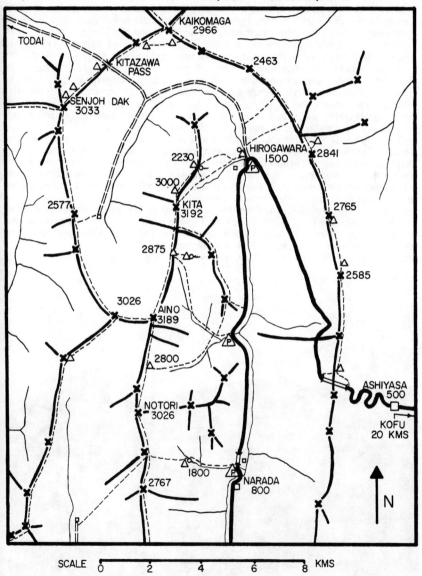

## Akaishi, Minami Alps, Honshu, Japan

The map here includes the southern half of the Minami or South Alps, on the Japanese Island of Honshu. This area is west of the city of Kofu and the volcano Fuji San. The highest and the best known of the peaks in the region is Akaishi, reaching 3130 meters. Unlike Fuji San and many other Japanese mountains, the Minami (as well as the Kita and Chuo Alps), are folded and uplifted mountains, consisting of metamorphic rock.

One might spend one or several days in the area. For example, to walk or hike from the north around Shiomi, to the south and the Hatanagi Dam, would take two or three days. However, most people would have little difficulty climbing Akaishi in one day from Koshibuyu.

There's a number of huts in the mountains, most of which provide food of some kind, and a place to sleep. The sleeping place is usually one large room for everybody, with the sleeping part raised above the floor half a meter. You sleep on mats, and your shoes or boots stay on the floor. Those familiar with Japanese customs know the situation. Sometimes hot meals can be ordered, but most food sold in the huts is the snack variety. The author recommends you have all your own food—it's very expensive in the huts. In many cases, the drinking water is rain water, caught and stored. In dry periods, a fee may be charged for it. Most huts are on the ridge tops, as are most trails. This situation is true for most Japanese mountains.

Reaching this section of the Minami Alps is not as easy as in other mountainous regions. There are simply no major highways in the immediate area. However, there's a good secondary road on the west side of the range and there are public buses on that road running as far as the place called Koshibuyu—at least in the summer season. On the south, there's a good paved road to the Hatanagi Dam. From there north, it's a poor motor road. All the trails in the area are well used, especially the one to Akaishi.

Camping is usually done at or near the huts, sometimes for a fee. Japan receives a great deal of rain, so waterproofs are required. Some kind of language phrase book would be helpful—not many hikers out there understand English (their second language). Auto stopping or hitch hiking is good in Japan, especially for foreign visitors.

**Map:** Minami(South) Alps, 1 : 100,000, printed in Japan in Japanese.

Shelters, or huts like this, are on all high mountains in Japan.

# Map 139-2, Akaishi, Minami Alps, Honshu, Japan

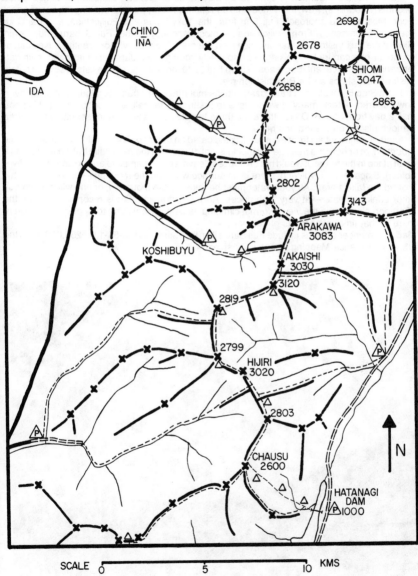

# Fuji San, Honshu, Japan

One of the most famous mountains in the world and by far the best known in Japan, is Fuji San, 3776 meters. It's location is in the south central part of the island of Honshu, not far west of Tokyo. Fuji is a semi-active volcano which hasn't erupted in recent history. It has an almost perfect conal shape, and is likely the most fotographed mountain in the world.

Each year the mountain is climbed by thousands of tourists, climbers, and most of all, pilgrims (Buddhists). Few, if any mountain can claim so many people reaching the summit each year. Most people approach Fuji San from the Tokyo side and Fujijoshida, and the Chuo (central) Expressway. From Fujijoshida the most used route is the "Fuji-Subaru Line," beginning at the Fuji Visitors Center, as shown on the map. From the visitors center, buses can be found, or one can try hitch hiking (it's especially good for non-Japanese) from the main gate entrance. This excellent road leads to Step 5 at 2270 meters. Step 5 consists of several hotels, restaurants, shops and a Buddhist temple.

From Step 5, a well used trail zigzags up the mountain. This trail has pilgrims' shelters every few hundred meters, many of which have refreshments for sell. Most people climb it in about half a day from Step 5. On top there are three temples and a weather observatory situated at various places on the crater's rim.

Another main route is from the south, as indicated on the map. There's also a trail circling the mountain, at or near the tree line. Camping is not allowed on the mountain, but if one can find a quiet place in the forest, it would not be noticed (leave a clean campsite and no one should ever object). Since this is a volcano, there is no surface water on the mountain—except far below, around the lake's area. All your water must be taken to the mountain, or one will have to buy other drinks or water—at very high prices. An early morning start is recommended, as the afternoon clouds ruin the view. Normal climbing season is from June to September. If you're there at that time, expect lots of company.

**Map:** A number of maps include Fuji San, all in Japanese, and NI-54-1, 1 : 250,000, from the US Army Defence Mapping Agency, Washington D.C.

Fuji San as seen from the north and Lake Kawaguchi.

# Map 140-1, Fuji San, Honshu, Japan

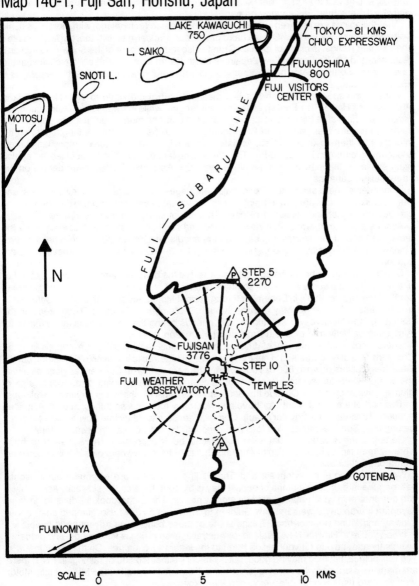

# Chapter 5 The Pacific

This section of the book has a total of 30 maps, covering Indonesia, The Philippines, Papua New Guinea, Australia, New Zealand, and Hawaii.

About half the total number of mountains in this region are volcanic, the others are folded and uplifted. Most—or perhaps all—of the summits in Indonesia, are volcanic related. Some are very old and have lost all their conal shape, others are still active. Indonesia probably has more active volcanos than any country on earth.

The Philippines are really an extension of the Indonesian Archipelago, with most of its peaks volcanos as well. Papua New Guinea has a great deal of volcanic activity too, but Mt. Wilhelm in the Bismark Range, is made of granite. Granite also forms the core of the Snowy Mountains in Australia and Mt. Kosiusko. New Zealand's North Island is made entirely of volcanic ash or lava, but the Southern Alps on the South Island, are "real" mountains—like the Himalayas or European Alps.

For anyone speaking English this is a pleasant part of the world to visit. New Zealand, Australia and Hawaii use English as the mother tongue, while in Papua New Guinea and The Philippines, English is the second language and the only common "lingo" used by people from varous parts of either country. In PNG there is said to be 717 different languages, so it's important for them to know English. Actually, Pidgeon English—a mixure of many languages, is becoming common in PNG today. The dominating language in The Philippines is Tagalog (very similar to Indonesian), but everyone there speaks some English, even people on the street selling bananas.

In Indonesia, there seems to be one major language—Indonesian, but a few people speak Dutch, and even more are now learning English. In virtually every bookstore in the country, one can buy an English-Indonesian dictionary. Their script is the same as used here.

As for weather, remember that New Zealand and southern Australia are dominated by the movement of cyclonic storms, the same as the middle latitudes in the northern hemisphere. Their winter is the rainiest season, at least in Australia. New Zealand seemingly never has a dry season.

One thing to remember in the tropical areas, is that the heaviest rainfall follows the sun. For example, when the sun is at its most southern point in the sky, it means that it's raining in areas south of the equator that's in December through about March. Areas north of the equator, have a rainy season from about May or June through September or October. Those areas on the equator generally have two wet and two dry periods during the year. This is the same as for Africa and partially true of South America (the Amazon Basin).

There's not much in the way of difficult climbing in this region, but one exception is in the Southern Alps of New Zealand. These peaks have altitudes up to just over 3700 meters, but Mt. Cook has glaciers down to 600 or 700 meters. The best climbs on Cook are as good as any in the world, when all factors are taken into account—weather, height of snowline, size of glaciers, avalanches, etc. Outside the Southern Alps, most climbs in this region are walk-ups.

This part of the world is safe for travelers. Not many tourists lose things, and when it does happen, it's usually the traveler's fault. Common sense should dictate how to care for one's belongings, See the introduction to South America, for the ultimate in security steps.

Getting to these various countries is not difficult, but is expensive. There are—or perhaps were—cheap flights from London to Australia, but to or from anywhere else in this region, one has to pay full airfares.

Within the islands of Indonesia and The Philippines, there are of course some flights between the larger cities, but the cheapest way is by boat. It's also the slowest—especially if you get on a ship which makes several stops enroute. The author took 16 days to go from Jayapura in Iran Jaya (western New Guinea) to Surabaya on Java. He "jumped ship" about midway and found a faster boat. Taking some of these boats is an adventure in travel.

When you're in Hawaii, New Zealand, or Australia, hitch hiking is very good—and probably necessary after paying for your airline ticket to the latter two countries. On the major roads in The Philippines, hitching may be good, but it's usually either too hot, or raining. In PNG, there are many missionaries who will stop for a thumb. If that doesn't work, the PMV's (Public Motor Vehicles) are usually available—though rather expensive.

The two "cheapest" countries in this region for travelers are The Philippines and Indonesia. Hawaii is likely the most expensive place, but one can camp on beaches and hitch hike, bringing the cost down.

The Wilhelm Hut located at Lake Piunde on the trail to Mt. Wilhelm (Map 157).

The best hike in the world, the Kokoda Trail, begins at Owens Corner (Map 158).

## Mt. Pulog, Luzon Island, Philippines

For people accustomed to a temperate climate, the most interesting and desireable place in all The Philippines to visit, is the highland areas of northern Luzon Island. Interesting places to see are the rice terraces of Banawe, summer capital of Baguio, the Kabayan Valley, and Mt. Pulog, 2930 meters—the second highest peak in The Philippines.

The place of attention on this map is the area surrounding the Kabayan Valley. Not only are there two of the highest mountains in The Philippines located there, but some interesting cultures and mummy caves to observe.

To reach this area, take one of the two regularly scheduled daily buses running from Baguio to Kabayan town, a distance of 85 kms. Get off at the Ellet or Kinayang Bridge. From that point, there's a good trail all the way to the top.

At first the trail passes rice terraces and farms, then at Ellet, turns right, and up a pine-tree-covered ridge (without water) to the village of Ambukot. From that point there's an old road (apparently coming from the other side of the mountain?) which ends at a pass between two hills, where the latter part of the trail actually begins. This trail leads to villages on the eastern side of the mountain, but also to the summit.

Above about 2500 meters the area is almost continually in cloud cover, therefore the trees are draped with moss. Above about 2700 meters, the moss forest is left behind, and the open and windy grasslands continue on to the summit. Remember, the dry season is from Octover to May; and that water is found only at Ellet Bridge, Ellet, Ambukot, and at a spring 2625 meters.

Besides climbing and viewing the various valley cultures, visiting some of the mummy caves is a must. On the mountain sides around Kabayan, and in natural caves, are many wooden boxes containing mummified remains of the valley's former inhabitants. Stop at the municipal hall in Kabayan to see a small museum, and get information as to the locations of nearby caves. Someone is always around to show you. Kabayan is the best place to buy food in the valley, but each village usually has a small store.

**Map:** Dagupan City, 2507, or NE-51-13, 1 : 250,000, from the Coast and Geodetic Survey, Manila. Also, Philippine Motorist's Road Guide, from Petrophil Corporation, Manila.

The best part of visiting the Kabayan Valley are the burial tombs.

# Map 141-1, Pulog, Luzon Island, Philippines

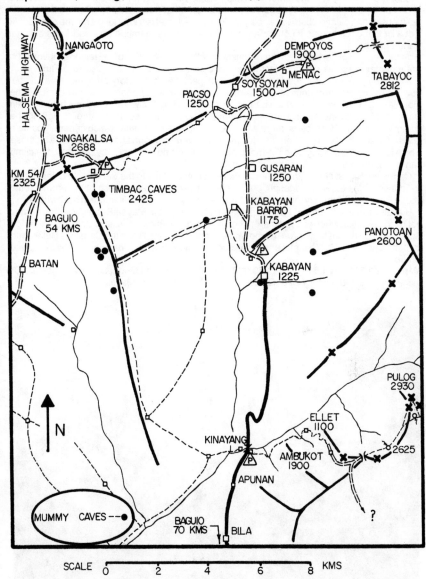

# Volcan Mayon, Luzon Island, Philippines

One of the most perfect volcanic cones in the world is located on the southern end of the island of Luzon in The Philippines. This is Volcan Mayon, just northwest of Legaspi. The approach is one of the simplest of any of the bigger mountains in the under-developed world.

One can reach the area by either bus, train, or plane, from the capital of Manila. You'll probably be coming from the direction of Manila; if so, stop at the town of Ligao. From there take a bus or "Jeepney" on the road to Tabaco, but get off at the junction where the road to the resthouse and volcano observatory begins. This paved road is 8 kms long and one can usually get a lift to the resthouse. If not, it's an interesting walk past bamboo huts and fields of sugar cane and abaca.

At the volcano observatory is a small museum with an explanation of the tectonics involved in the mountain's upheavals and destruction (and an explanation of the Cagsawa Ruins).

At one time there was a road up the mountain past the observatory for some distance, but now it's overgrown and unuseable. However, a fair number of people are now climbing the mountain, so there is a trail, at least to as far as the Buang Gully. This gully is where the rain waters race down the mountain during stormy periods. It makes an easy route right to the summit. At about 1300 meters, there are several potholes in the gully, which generally contain good drinking (rain) water. At about 1800 meters, several platforms have been made for those who wish to camp one night on the mountain, but there's no water nearby. Actually, the climb can be made in one day from the observatory.

On the southeast side of the mountain there's another route to the top (as told to the author by tourist office people in Legaspi), but surely it's overgrown, as is much of the normal route above the observatory. Try this way only if you're looking for a real adventure in bushwhacking!

Buy all your food in either Ligao, Legaspi, or Tabaco, as the Mayon Resthouse may or may not be in operation when you get there. The dry season for this area is from December through April, but expect rainshowers on the mountain at any time. Don't miss the Cagsawa Ruins, with its half buried church. This place is reminiscent of the Paracutin Volcano and the San Juan Church in Mexico.

**Map:**   Map 2516,(NB-51-11), 1 : 250,000, from the Coast and Geodetic Survey, Manila. Or the Philippine Motorist's Road Guide, Petrophil Corporation, Manila.

North face of V. Mayon, from the Volcano Observatory.

## Map 142-1, Mayon, Luzon Island, Philippines

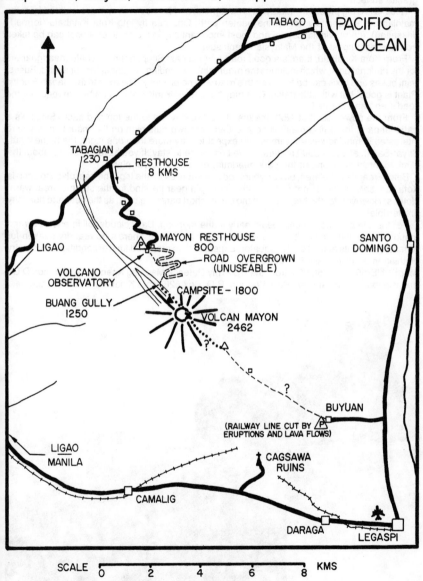

## Mt. Kinabalu, Borneo, Malaysia

On the north end of the island of Borneo, stands one of the highest and most impressive mountains in the Pacific. This is Mt. Kinabalu, rising to 4102 meters. This mountain is an igneous intrusion, not large by some standards, but impressive in that it rises so high and all alone. The top-most part is somewhat of a plateau, with a number of pinnacles rising from the granite surface.

Access is a big problem—Malaysia is so remote, and Borneo is even more isolated from the mainland. It is definitely not on the beaten path. One can fly into Kota Kinabalu (formerly Jesselton), the provincial capital and most important city in the area, or a boat can be taken from the east coast of the Malaysian Peninsula.

From Kota Kinabalu, there's a good road running past Simpangan Kinabalu (headquarters for the national park, which includes the mountain) and ending at Ranau, further inland. Buses, mini buses and taxis can be found on this road with no difficulty. The road to the Sabah Electric Plant is good, but with little traffic. One may have to walk this last section before reaching the road's end and the trail.

From the power plant at 1825 meters, it's a two-day trip to the top and back. Since it's a national park, the trail is maintained and there are two huts high on the mountain. If you're interested in making several climbs and expect to stay more than one night, the highest hut, Sayat-Sayat, at about 3800 meters, is the best place to stay. If you have questions about the climb, contact someone at the park headquarters or the power plant.

Before reaching the area, buy all your food and supplies for the trip. The best place to shop is Kota Kinabalu. A tent is not needed, but good rain gear is—and for the summit area, warm clothes. However, for the beginning of the climb, short pants are best, as the heat and humidity are terrible.

For the climb to the summit, begin early in the morning. Daily clouds roll in and cover the mountain, making it difficult to find the way back to the hut. There's no real dry season for Kinabalu, as it sits almost on the equator. Expect and go prepared for wet conditions. Extra dry clothing in a plastic sack is a good idea.

**Map:**  NB-50-7, 1 : 250,000, from the US Army Defence Mapping Agency, Washington D.C., and Kinabalu National Park, Park Warden, P.O. Box 626, Kota Kinabalu, Sabah, Malaysia.

The summit plateau of Kinabalu is solid granite with spires like this.

Map 143-3, Kinabalu, Borneo, Malaysia

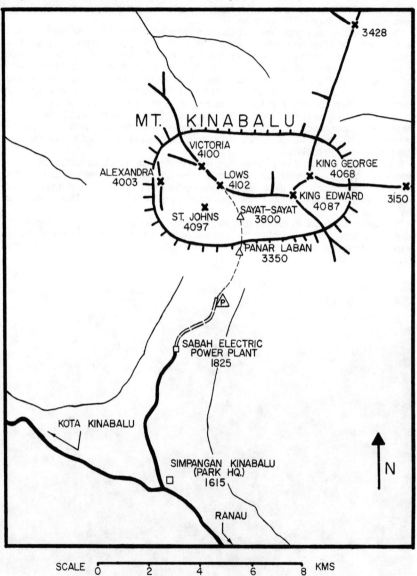

# Marapi, Sumatra, Indonesia

The island of Sumatra is Indonesia's most westerly island, and it—like nearly all of Indonesia—was "born of fire"; that is, it was created by the outpourings of volcanic lava and ash. Along the southwestern coastal area of Sumatra lies a chain of volcanos, some very old and some still active.

One of these volcanos is Marapi, at 2891 meters. Nearby, just across the valley is Singgalang, 2877 meters. In the valley between these two peaks, is a major highway and railroad linking Padang with Bukittinggi.

The information here comes from a tourist who spent several weeks on Sumatra, and who climbed to the top of Marapi in 1977. If you're coming from the west coast and the large city of Padang, there's a narrow-gage railway running as far as Payakumbun, as well as a good highway. The area is heavily populated, so there's no problem finding buses or trains. Stop at the village of Kota Baru, then walk straight east about 2 kms, to where some kind of experimental farm is situated (it may be just a farm or plantation). From the road junction, turn right or south, and follow that road to a bridge and building on the left, or east side of the road. The trail going to the top begins at that building. (Old topo maps of the area show a trail to the top from the village of Kubutjabadak; it's entirely possible the informant's directions were wrong and the correct route is through Kubutjabadak, rather than the one just described and on the map. Make inquiries at Kota Baru.)

There's never, or at least very seldom, any water beyond the last village on the volcanos in Indonesia. There is apparently water at the bridge mentioned above, but certainly none beyond that point. Have at least one liter of water at the beginning of your hike. From Kota Baru, it's a one-day climb, and is apparently easy with a reasonably good trail to the top. This, according to the informant.

This region is virtually on the equator, with the climate classified as "Tropical Rainforest." This means heavy rainfall throughout the year, with no pronounced dry period. Go accordingly.

**Map:** Padang, SA-47-3, 1 : 250,000, from the US Army Defence Mapping Agency, Washington D.C.

Rice patty scene from Indonesia.

## Map 144-3, Marapi, Sumatra, Indonesia

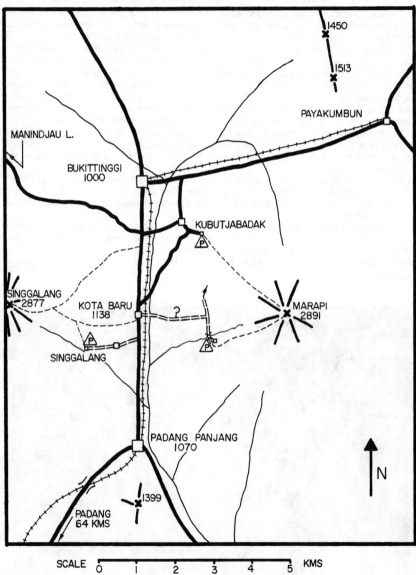

## Kerintju, Sumatra, Indonesia

The highest mountain in Indonesia (not counting the peaks of Irian Jaya) is one of hundreds of volcanos which make up the Indonesian landscape. This is Kerintji, 3809 meters, located not far from the west coast on the island of Sumatra. Sumatra is not as populated as Java, but near the mountain, especially on the north and south sides, are heavily populated farmlands. The higher sections of the mountain are forested.

One source of information says to take the road northwest from Sungaipenuh about 30 kms, to a village called Krisik Tuo, south of the peak. From there it's 8 hours to some kind of shelter or bush hut, then 4 hours to the summit, making it a two day climb from Krisik Tuo.

Using the author's personal experiences in other parts of Indonesia, this is what he recommends: Take a bus or bemos (cargo and passenger carrying truck) which runs from Sungaipenuh along the heavily populated valley south of Kerintji. Stop at one of the larger villages near the end of the good road, and make inquiries as to where the trail begins. On old topographical maps of the area, a trail is shown, but not a village named Krisik Tuo. Making inquiries is difficult unless you first learn a few words of Indonesian. Be sure and buy a small language dictionary (English-Indonesian) found in virtually all bookstores in the country.

The same old U.S. Army maps show another trail to the summit, this one from the north, and the village of Timbulan. The north route may be just as good. A hike from the north is perhaps longer, will take two days, and one will have to have a tent for an overnight stay on the mountain.

Whichever route is taken, water will likely have to be carried from the last village, as there's never any running water high on these volcanos. The larger towns of Sungaipenuh and Muaralabuh are the best places to shop for food, but smaller villages nearer the mountain also have small shops.

The climate in these parts, only 2 degrees south of the equator, is classified as "Tropical Rainforest," which means there's no dry period in the year. Go prepared for wet conditions, with a pack cover and extra dry clothes in a plastic sack.

**Map:** Paiman, SA-48-13, 1 : 250,000, from the US Army Defence Mapping Agency, Washington D.C.

No foto, but this is typical street scene in Indonesia.

## Map 145-3, Kerintji, Sumatra, Indonesia

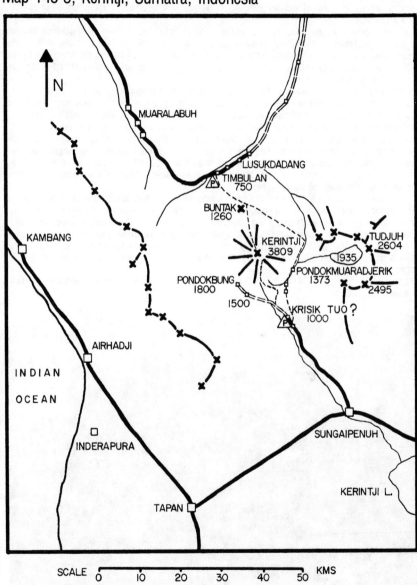

N

MUARALABUH

LUSUKDADANG

TIMBULAN
750

BUNTAK
1260

KAMBANG

KERINTJI
3809

TUDJUH
2604

1935

PONDOKBUNG
1800

PONDOKMUARADJERIK
1373

2495

1500

KRISIK TUO?
1000

INDIAN

OCEAN

AIRHADJI

INDERAPURA

SUNGAIPENUH

KERINTJI L.

TAPAN

SCALE  0   10   20   30   40   50   KMS

## Merbabu and Merapi, Java, Indonesia

Located in central Java are two very interesting mountains very near each other. The highest of the two is Merbabu, at 3142 meters. The other is Merapi, at 2919 meters.

Since the mountains are so near, and the trail to the top of each begins in the same village, one might as well climb both peaks while in the area. The village is Selo, located between the two summits and at a cool and delightful 1500 meters. Even if one doesn't mountain climb, this is a fine place to visit.

Getting to Selo is easy. Your journey will likely begin in the tourist town of Jogjakarta, located to the south of these mountains. Take a large bus from Jogjakarta to Solo and then to Boyolali. From Boyolali, take another smaller bus or truck, known as "bemos," to the town of Cepoco (Chepoco), and finally to Selo. In Selo, there are several stores and many roadside "restaurants." Plenty of food around.

In 1977 near the police station, there was a man who hired himself out as a guide, and whose home was a kind of Losmen (like an inn or boarding house). One can rent a room in the mans house, without obligation to hire him. A guide is definitely not needed for these hikes.

To climb Merapi, walk from the center of Selo about 2 kms west, then at Jalan (street) Merapi, turn south. After about 2 more kms the street ends and the trail begins, which zigzags up the northeast face of the mountain. There are several trails at the beginning, but higher up they combine into one good one. There's a crater at the top, still emitting smoke and fumes. Periodically it erupts and its lava can be seen from Jogjakarta. The last water is at the junction of Jalan Merapi and the main highway.

To climb Merbabu, go east from the town center to Jalan Merbabu, and walk north for 2 or 3 kms, to where the road ends in a couple of very small villages. From the end, or near the end of the road, there are several trails going up and west to a ridge top. Once on the ridge, it's easy to find the one trail to the summit. This trail is well used by local farmers who climb to the upper slopes to cut wood. On top of this highly eroded volcano, is a small platform and some kind of shrine, probably pre-dating the Dutch period. Wear light clothing for the hike, but carry a lite jacket for the summit.

**Map:** Jogjakarta, SB-49-14, 1 : 250,000, from the US Army Defence Mapping Agency, Washington D.C.

Merapi as seen from summit of Merbabu. Selo is to the left.

# Map 146-1, Merbabu-Merapi, Java, Indonesia

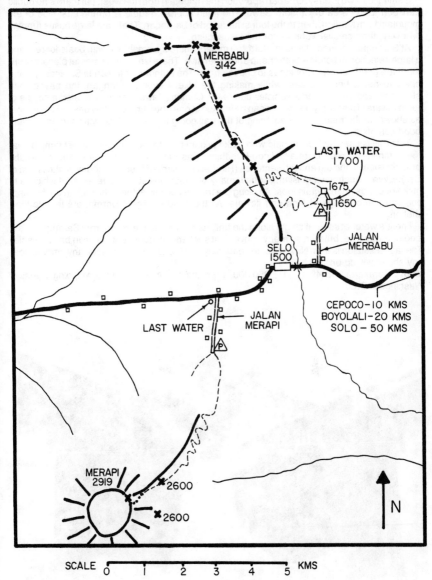

## Lawu, Java, Indonesia

Mt. Lawu, at 3265 meters, is one of the more interesting mountains on the island of Java. Like all mountains on this most populated of Indonesian islands, it's an old and eroded volcano. It still retains a symmetrical shape, but is heavily forested and hasn't seen any activity in hundreds of years.

Getting to Lawu is easy. One can approach the mountain from the west, but there's no public transport to the area of Cemoro Sewu. The main approach route is on the east side of the mountain from Madiun, then to the tourist hill resort of Sarangan. There are large buses running part way, then smaller vehicles for the last section.

At Sarangan, located at a delightful 1250 meters, there's a small lake with boats for rent and a large selection of hotels—both cheap and expensive. There isn't a large market place, but still there are good selections of foods to choose from. The author recommends Sarangan as the place to make headquarters, while making the hike. Beyond Sarangan, the paved road steepens, and only powerful vehicles can reach Cemoro Sewu, where is located a couple of radio towers. This is only 5 kms and can be walked in one hour. Immediately beyond the bridge, as shown on the map, is the beginning of the trail going to the top. It is well used and in very good condition.

This trail is used by local people who make pilgrimages to the Hindu-Buddhist temple near the summit, marked "Darma." Hindu-Buddhism was the religion of Java before the Arabs brought Islam in the 8th and 9th centuries (Hindu-Buddhism still survives today on the island of Bali). Even though Java is Islamic today, many old traditions still survive—one of which is to make offerings on mountain tops. All along the trail, especially at the huts marked on the map, one can see offerings of food and flowers. All these huts, except Darma, are lean-to type shelters.

There's water at several points along the trail, as marked on the map. From Sarangan, it's a long one-day hike, but with so many convenient shelters, an overnight stay can be enjoyable. The rainier season is from November to about May, but the climb can be made any time. Almost any shoes will do on this hike.

**Map:** Surakarta, SB-49-15, 1 : 250,000, from the US Army Defence Mapping Agency, Washington D.C.

This is the Dharm at the summit of Lawu.

## Map 147-1, Lawu, Java, Indonesia

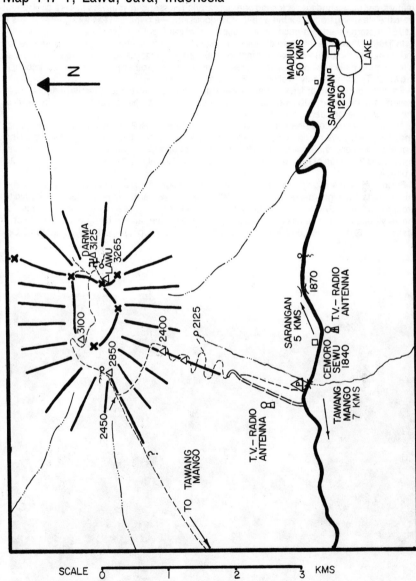

N

MADIUN 50 KMS

SARANGAN 1250

LAKE

ARMA 3125

LAWU 3265

3100

2400

2850

2450

2125

1870

SARANGAN 5 KMS

CEMORO SEWU 1840

T.V.- RADIO ANTENNA

TAWANG MANGO 7 KMS

T.V.- RADIO ANTENNA

TO TAWANG MANGO

SCALE    0    1    2    3    KMS

## Arjuno, Java, Indonesia

Climbing Arjuno is one of the more enjoyable trips in all of Indonesia. It too is a volcano; but this one is very old, has lost much of its symmetrical shape, and is heavily forested.

Access is easy. There's a very good paved highway from Surabaya to Malang, south of Arjuno. From the town of Pandaan, is another paved road to the hill station of Tretes. There are many small buses and trucks (called bemos) carrying passengers there, as this is a cool retreat from the steaming tropics for the well-to-do Indonesians—as well as a few foreigners. Tretes is at 750 meters, making it necessary to use blankets at night for sleeping.

In Tretes, there are many small hotels, ranging in price from cheap to rather expensive (by Indonesian standards)—as well as many souvenir shops, restaurants, and stores. There's also a fairly good market place, but the prices are higher than in other places on Java. Nothing is grown at Tretes—its only livelihood is tourism.

From the upper part of Tretes, there's a very good trail leading to the summits of Arjuno, 3340 meters, and Welirang, 3200 meters. This trail is used mostly by porters and miners who work at the sulfur mine or quarry, very near the top of Welirang.

At about 1600 meters, there's a small bush hut and spring. At 2450 meters is another spring, and the miners have made many small and very crude huts that they use while working on the mountain. Beyond the miners camp the trail divides; one goes to the mine on Welirang, the other leads to the top of Arjuno. From about 2300 to 3000 meters, the mountain is covered with a pine forest.

From Tretes, it's a long one day hike. For some it might be best to camp or use one of the miner's huts one night, making the walk in two days. At lower elevations, the heat and humidity are terrific. The author recommends some water be carried between waterholes. Because of the very good trail, the climb can be made at any time of year, and with any kind of foot wear.

**Map:** SB-49-16, 1 : 250,000, from the US Army Defence Mapping Agency, Washington D.C.

At 2400 meters is a miners camp in a pine forest on Arjuno.

# Map 148-1, Arjuno, Java, Indonesia

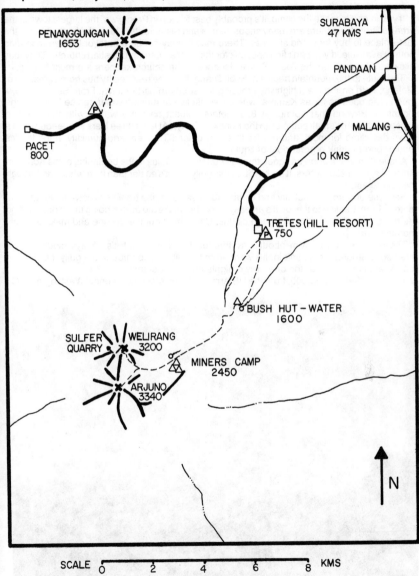

## Semeru, Java, Indonesia

If you're in Java and have time to make only one climb, head for Semeru, 3677 meters, the highest mountain on Java. For many years the mountain has been very active, and the chances are it'll still be that way when you get there. The author was there in 1977 and was literally chased from the summit by thundering explosions of gases and ash. The night before, solidified chunks of lava rolled down from the summit, all the way to his camp, located at 1700 meters.

If you intend to make the climb, it's probably best to stop in Pronojiwo, the largest town in the area. In Pronojiwo, there are many shops, stores and restaurants. This is the best—but not the last—place to buy food and supplies. There may or may not be a hotel or losmen (boarding house) available. If you can't find one, ask for the Kristian gereja (Christian church). They may allow you to sleep on the floor. All over Indonesia, the church keepers are most helpful.

The route to the mountain begins at Supit Orang. It can be reached by bus from Lumajung or Malang, both on the main highway crossing the southern part of Java. From Supit Orang, a rough road goes as far as Kamera, where the last live or running water can be found on the mountain. Beyond that spring, at 825 meters, expect no more water (with the possible exception of some small potholes in the Kobokan Gully). At least three liters are needed, as it's a two day climb for most, and maybe three for others. The heat and humidity of the tropics require one to drink a great deal of liquid.

Above Kamera, a good trail goes through sugar-cane fields to the beginning of the Kobokan Gully, at about 1200 meters. It's a bit rough this gully, but it's easier than bushwhacking through the rain forest.

Because of Semeru's activity and continuous lava flows, the treeline is down to about 1700 meters. From treeline to the top it's an easy climb, but make *big tracks* going up, in order to find the route back down in the afternoon clouds. Camp at about the treeline and make an early morning start.

The drier season is from about May through November, but it's always cloudy in the afternoons around the mountain. It's warm from the villages up through the gully, but cold on top. A tent is needed for the one or two nights on the mountain.

**Map:** SC-49-4, 1 : 250,000, from the US Army Defence Mapping Agency, Washington D.C.

Semeru is an active volcano, with smoke rising from the summit.

Map 149-1, Semeru, Java, Indonesia

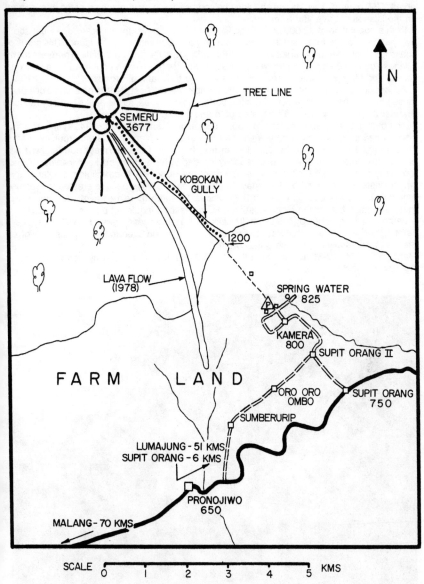

SCALE  0  1  2  3  4  5  KMS

# Raung-Merapi, Java, Indonesia

At the extreme eastern end of the island of Java are located several volcanic cones or mountains. The highest of these is Raung, 3334 meters, one of the highest on the island. This mountain appears to be the youngest of the group, as it still retains a crater at the summit and has a more symmetrical shape.

Other summits are Diampit, 2839 meters; its nearest neighbor, Rante, 2644; and Merapi, about 2750 meters. This Merapi shouldn't be confused with several others of the same name on the islands of Java and Sumatra.

With a population of 80,000,000 on the island of Java, one might expect villages just about everywhere. For the most part this is true, but only as far as water is to be found. This group of peaks is surrounded by villages up to, but not far beyond, the last water hole. There are many villages south and east of Rante, west of Raung, and there's even a populated area between Raung and Merapi. In these areas, there are many trails and dirt roads.

According to the maps and one tourist office employee, the best place to go to climb one or all these peaks is the Jampit region. From this coffee growing area, all the peaks can be reached. Another possible approach is from the south and the Sumberbulu area.

The best map available (which is 1:250,000 scale and dates from the 1940's) shows a trail from Jampit to near a lake on the west side of Merapi, then south to Sumberbulu. For sure there's some kind of a trail to the top of Merapi from that lake. These old maps don't shown trails on these mountains (or any others personally climbed by the author), but keep in mind, that not too many centuries ago, all of Indonesia was of the Buddhist-Hindu religion, similar to that which exists on the island of Bali today. Buddhists have always been interested in reaching mountain tops and erecting temples on high places. So surely there are trails to the tops of all of these summits, but for the exact location one will have to inquire at places like Jampit.

Jampit can be reached by bus or small trucks, which carry passengers. One will find shops in Jampit; but if you're going that way, it's best to buy your food in Situbondo or Wanusori. High on the summits it's always wet, so go accordingly.

**Map:** SC-49-4, SB-50-13, and SC-50-1, 1 : 250,000, from the US Army Defence Mapping Agency, Washington D.C.

This is the Kobokan Gully on Semeru with potholes and water (Map 149).

## Map 150-2, Raung-Merapi, Java, Indonesia

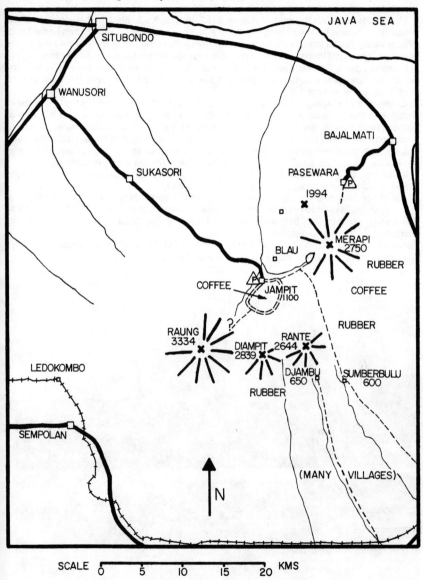

## Batur Caldera, Bali Island, Indonesia

The second of two main mountain areas on Bali Island in central Indonesia, is the Batur Caldera located in the northeastern section of the island. This caldera is undoubtedly one of the larger ones in the world—about 15 kms across. Within the crater is a large lake, several villages, roads, and in the very center a new volcanic cone named Batur, at 1717 meters. It's still considered active with lots of new lava on its south side (1977). The entire caldera is forested, inside and out, except on recent lava flows.

The highest peak on this map is Abang, 2152 meters. It's located on the east side of the crater rim. There was no confirmation, but the author was told of a trail leading to the top of Abang, along the rim from the Penelokon area. This is more than likely true, as the area is fairly well populated, and there are more and more tourists visiting the crater all the time.

Reaching Batur Peak is easy. From the lake, one can follow one of several trails going around the lake, until a convenient route or trail can be found to the peak. There are several faint trails to the summit.

Either of these peaks can be climbed easily in one day from the town of Penelokon. Penelokon can be reached from Denpasar (Balis capital) or Singaraja, by hourly buses or bemos (small truck-buses, for cargo and passengers). Penelokon is at 1340 meters, therefore a cool retreat from the tropics. There are a number of small hotels and losmen (small boarding houses, with meals—if desired), small stores and market place. It's a good place to spend some time, as well as a safe place to store baggage while out hiking or camping.

Inside the caldera is Batur Lake, which is heavily fished. One can rent a boat or have a fisherman take you around. An interesting place to visit.

The rainier season is usually from November through April or May, but rain can come at any time. An umbrella is good—for the rain or sun—whichever plagues you at the time. Getting to Bali is easy, either by ferry from Java, by boats from other islands, or by planes landing at the international airport at Denpasar.

**Map:** Singaradja, SC-50-1, 1 : 250,000, from the US Army Defence Mapping Agency, Washington D.C., or one of many tourist maps of the island of Bali.

Batur Lake and volcano inside the Batur Caldera.

Map 151-1, Batur Caldera, Bali Isl., Indonesia

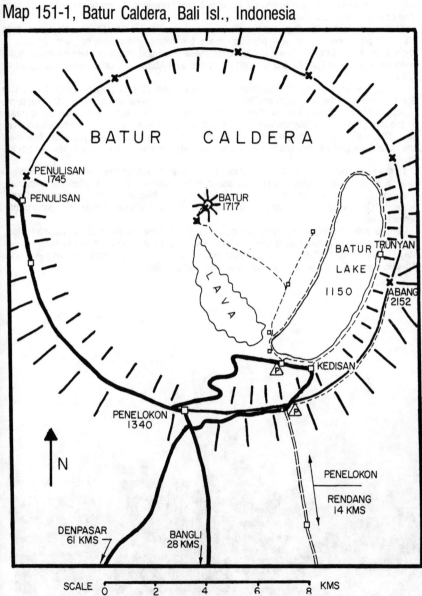

## Mt. Agung, Bali Island, Indonesia

One of the most interesting places in the world is the small island of Bali, just 3 kms east of Java, in Indonesia. The culture found on this one island and nowhere else, is a strange mixture of Buddhism and Hinduism. The island is literally covered with statues of gods and demons, which are evidence of the influence of those two great religions. Every home, office building, and road junction has them.

The reason for mentioning all of the above, is to make the point that a lot of foreign tourists visit this place each year, and although there are higher mountains on other islands in Indonesia, a bit more emphasis is placed on these summits. There are two main mountain areas of interest on Bali. One is the Batur Caldera and Abang; the other is Mt. Agung, 3142 meters.

Agung is a volcano, still in a state of semi-activity, and still retaining its conal shape. The lower portions of the mountain are heavily forested and farmed (up to about 1000 meters).

Agung can be climbed from the Besakih town and temple, just to the southwest of the peak. In the town, there are many souvenir shops and small places to eat. There's also a losmen or two. These are like boarding houses which offer a bedroom and meals if you wish. Normally they are someone's home and therefore are relatively clean and comfortable, and best of all, cheap.

To the right side of the temple is a trail heading almost straight up the mountain, but passing several homes and another temple at about 1200 meters. The trail gradually becomes overgrown, but those who persist can make it through. Because of the tropical heat and humidity it's generally good to wear lite clothing, but this trail has sharp grass—so long pants are advised.

Go to Besakih from Denpasar on a bemos or bus, sleep there one night, and get an early start the next morning. Take at least one liter of water, as there's none on the mountain.

**Map:** Singaradja, SC-50-1, 1 : 250,000, from the US Army Defence Mapping Agency, Washington D.C., or one of many small tourist maps of Bali.

Agung Volcano rises behind the Besaki Temples.

# Map 152-1, Agung, Bali Island, Indonesia

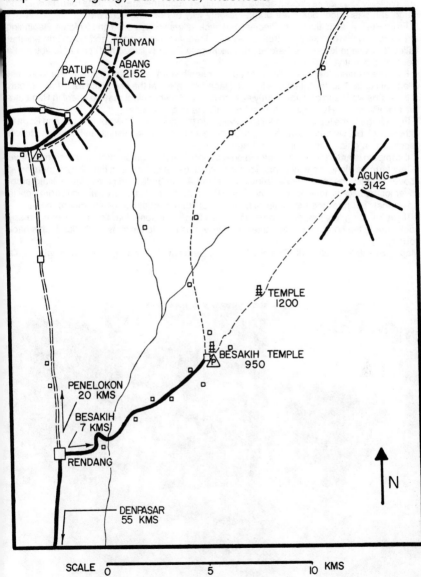

TRUNYAN

BATUR LAKE

ABANG
2152

AGUNG
3142

TEMPLE
1200

BESAKIH TEMPLE
950

PENELOKON
20 KMS

BESAKIH
7 KMS

RENDANG

DENPASAR
55 KMS

N

SCALE  0          5          10  KMS

## Rindjani, Lombok Island, Indonesia

On the island of Lombok, just east of Bali in central Indonesia, lies the second highest volcano in all of Indonesia, Rindjani, 3727 meters. The following information is supplied by William R. Mahar who climbed the mountain in 1977.

From the coastal town of Lombok, which can be reached by boat from other islands, buses are available to as far as Pringgyabaya and finally Pesugulan—the end of the road. Inter-island cargo and passenger boats are about the only way of reaching Lombok.

From Pesugulan to the top of Rindjani and back, takes about 4 days and 3 nights. Beginning at Pesugulan there is an easy trail to follow. It leads up over a pass, and down into another valley to a village known as Sembulun. The Kepala Desa (village chief) can help you find a sleeping place if you have no tent.

From Sembulun, the trail continues south (or southwest) for about 10 kms to the mountain village of Raga. This trail steepens toward Raga, which lies at the end of the trail. The last part of the trail is well used and apparently easy to locate. Another night may be spent in Raga at a farm family home. Remember, a small donation is in good taste.

From Raga to the top is about 4 kms—straight up the mountain. This last part beyond Raga is without trail, but with the mountain so near there should be little difficulty in finding the top. If necessary, a guide can be found in Raga.

If camping is anticipated, food should be purchased in Pesugulan, otherwise one may have to pay farmers along the way to provide food. While traveling between the villages mentioned above, at least one liter of water should be taken. An umbrella and some kind of waterproof cover for the pack is advised, as Lombok is in the humid tropics. The dry season is from April to November, but near the mountain rain can be encountered almost every day of the year.

If you're doing this trip, don't forget to buy an English-Indonesian dictionary, found in any bookstore in the country. Having at least a few words of Indonesian is essential for this back country trip.

**Map:**  SC-50-2, 1 : 250,000, from the US Army Defence Mapping Agency, Washington, D.C.

Idol makers on the island of Bali (Maps 151-152).

# Map 153-3, Rindjani, Lombok Island, Indonesia

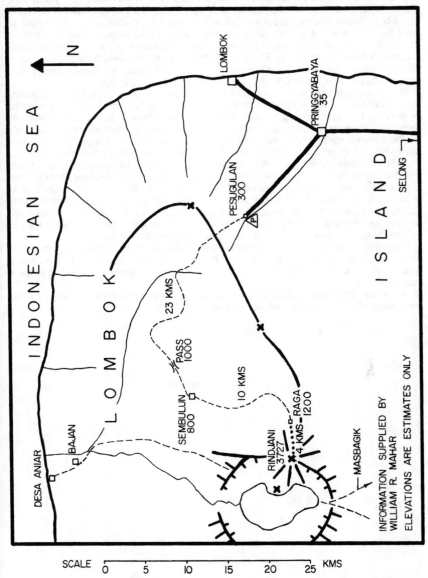

# Puncak Jaya, Sudirman Ra., Irian Jaya, Indonesia

The mountains included on this map are those in the highlands of Indonesias Irian Jaya-that's the western part of the island of New Guinea. Apparently the name of the range is the Sudirman Range. Others call it the Snowy Range. There are other conflicts concerning the names of the highest peaks. Evidently the highest summit is now called Puncak Jaya, at 4884 meters. This is the local or Indonesian name, but we all know it as Carstensz Pyramid. The second highest mountain is called Carstensz Timor, or as most say, East Carstensz Top, at about 4880 meters. The third best known summit is Naga Pulu, at 4862 meters. Some sources call it Sukarno Peak. Not only are the names in confusion, but elevations as well. Most maps of the area list P. Jaya as 5020 meters. But since the best maps are from the book, *The Equatorial Glaciers of New Guinea,* by G. E. Balkema, those names and elevations are used here. Balkemas' maps apparently come from the U.S. Army Joint Operations Graphic Series 1501, sheets SB53-4 (Timuka), and SB53-16 (Hitalipa), at scale 1 : 250,000.

The normal route into these mountains is from the highland town of Ilaga. There's an airstrip there serving a mission. Flights originate from Jayapura, Irian Jayas capital city located on the north coast, then from the larger town of Wamena, east of Ilaga, or from Mullia to the north. From Ilaga, there are two tracks leading west; a northern route, one heading for Ugimba; and a southern track or the highlands track which first heads southwest out of Ilaga. This latter route seems the best. Porters can be found in Ilaga for the four or five day trek to the mountain base.

Once in the area of the snow peaks, there are easy routes and difficult ones. Naga Pulu and the peak shown as 4700 meters, can both be climbed from the notch called New Zealand Pass, at about 4500 meters. To climb Carstensz Timor, cross over the N. Z. Pass, and make a camp in the Meren Valley (south of N. Z. Pass). Then cross over a small ridge and climb up the Carstensz Glacier to the top. The easy route up Puncak Jaya is to round the mountain and come in from the south face. All easy routes are south face approaches. The North Face of Puncak Jaya is the best and most difficult route in the range (all rock).

There's a copper mining town very near the base of the high peaks, but the company people there are not friendly to hikers and climbers. But if you could use the Tembagapura route, it would make an easy approach. The drier season is from May to November, and bring supplies from Jayapura.

**Map:** Book—*The Equatorial Glaciers of New Guinea,* Balkema, Rotterdam, 1968? And the maps mentioned above if they are obtainable.

Got a foto? Please send to author.

Map 154-3, Puncak J., Sudirman Ra., Irian J., Indo.

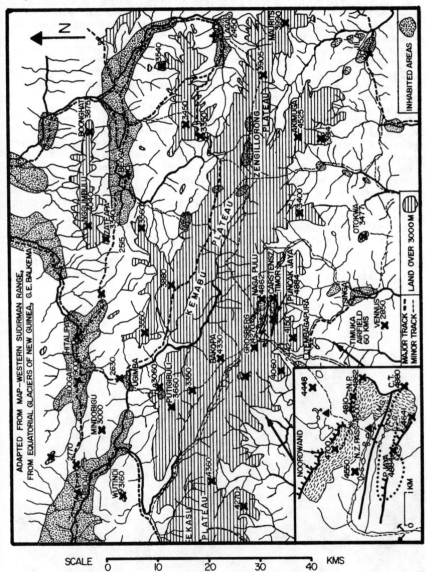

## Mt. Giluwe Central Range, Papua New Guinea

Mt. Giluwe, 4368 meters, located in the heart of the Papua New Guinea highlands, is a very old and highly eroded volcano, similar to Mt. Hagen. This mountain is high enough to have occasional snow showers at the summit and evidence exists of glaciation during the last ice age.

Mt. Giluwe can be climbed at any time of year, but there is a wetter period from about December through March. The route used by the author is via Tombul and Kargoba. PMV's (small passenger carrying trucks) can be taken from Mt. Hagen town to Tombul and with luck, on to Kargoba. However, there's not much traffic on the last 25 kms. Along this road, some fruits or vegetables may be purchased from people living in grass huts. An interesting walk.

Once at Kargoba (a high altitude agricultural station), one can walk near the fenced area in a southeasterly direction, until the forest is reached. The trail should be visible, but if you have difficulty, there is always someone around the station who can put you on the trail. The author found the first one and a half kms overgrown, but beyond that it was a good trail. He had no guide and no trouble; however, guides can always be found for the doubtful!

The huts shown on the map are bush huts and in no way resemble the climbers hut on Mt. Wilhelm; but one could get through a night in one of them. A tent is strongly recommended. The author did the climb in two very long days from Tombul—walking all the way (two 12 hour days!). A strong climber, with an early start, could climb Giluwe in one day from Kargoba.

The last place to buy food is at Tombul, but Mt. Hagen town has a couple of small supermarkets. Water is no problem on this mountain, as you will pass 3 streams between Kargoba and the summit. Raingear will keep one dry from the wet undergrowth, but would be hot and cause much sweating. It's recommended a change of clothing, kept dry in a plastic bag, be taken and used at night.

The top-most part of Giluwe is steep and one has to search a bit for the route, but no great difficulties should be found. Hopefully there will be enough people climbing the mountain since PNG's independence in 1975, to keep the trail open and clear.

**Map:** Lake Kutubu, SB-54-12, and Karimui, SB-55-9, both at 1 : 250,000. Old maps from the US Army Defence Mapping Agency, Washington, D.C., with newer ones by the Royal Australian Survey Corps, Port Moresby or Canberra.

Highest summit of Giluwe is in the center.

## Map 155-1, Giluwe, Central Ra., P. New Guinea

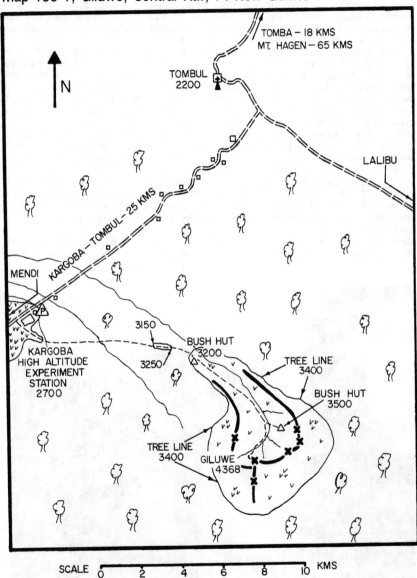

TOMBA — 18 KMS
MT. HAGEN — 65 KMS

TOMBUL
2200

N

LALIBU

KARGOBA — TOMBUL — 25 KMS

MENDI

3150

BUSH HUT
3200

TREE LINE
3400

3250

BUSH HUT
3500

KARGOBA
HIGH ALTITUDE
EXPERIMENT
STATION
2700

TREE LINE
3400

GILUWE
4368

SCALE   0   2   4   6   8   10   KMS

## Mt. Hagen, Central Range, Papua New Guinea

In the heart of the highlands of Papua New Guinea (which is the eastern half of the island of New Guinea) stands one of the higher mountains in the country, Mt. Hagen, 3778 meters. Mt. Hagen is not to be confused with the town of Mt. Hagen, which is about 50 kms to the east and which is the most important settlement in the western highlands.

Papua New Guinea (PNG), was a protectorate of Australia up until 1975, with most Australians finally leaving the country by 1978. Since that time it's likely that not many people will use the trail to the top of Mt. Hagen. It may in time, as fewer people use the trail, become overgrown. But it was a pretty good trail when used by the author in 1977.

The trail begins about half a km up the road from the Tomba sawmill. It passes several huts (or houses), then a swamp before it enters the forest. It's a muddy trail, used much more at the bottom than the top. There are two clearings in the forest before the trail enters the higher grasslands at about 3400 meters. The trail is reasonably good at this point, but again, only climbers (usually foreigners) use the upper sections. The hike can be done in one long day from Tomba, but if you decide to do it in two days, plan to camp high on the mountain where water is available. Most of the trail is on a ridge, with no water in the middle sections.

Getting to the highlands is easy. There are buses taking passengers from Lae on the coast, to Mt. Hagen town. From Mt. Hagen to other places, one must look for PMV's (Public Motor Vehicles), which are normally pickup trucks carrying cargo and passengers. One may also get a ride from missionaries, of which there are many in this land of bushmen.

At Tomba there's an Adventist church and a small shop or two where some food can be found (but it's best to buy food in Mt. Hagen town where there's several supermarkets). The dry season is from about May through November, but expect wet conditions any time. For those afraid of becoming lost, there will be plenty of volunteers to be your guide; however, guides are definitely not needed.

**Map:** Ramu, SB-55-5, and WABAG, SB-54-8, 1 : 250,000, from the US Army Defence Mapping Agency, Washington D.C., and the Royal Australian Survey Corps, Port Moresby or Canberra.

The author camps at the Adventist church in Tomba below Mt. Hagen.

Map 156-1, Hagen, Central Ra., P. New Guinea

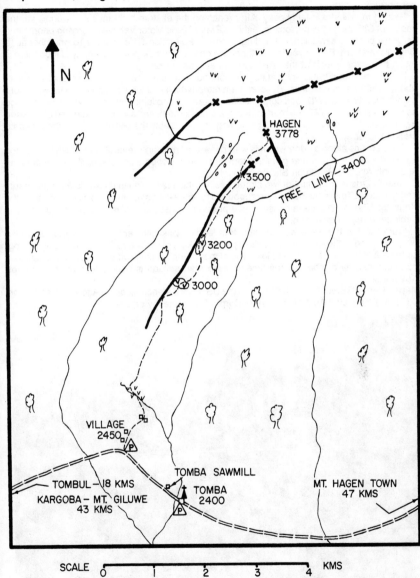

# Mt. Wilhelm, Bismark Range, Papua New Guinea

The independent Republic of Papua New Guinea occupies the eastern half of the island of New Guinea. This is a rugged and mountainous country, with the highest peak being Mt. Wilhelm, 4510 meters. Its location is north of Goroka and Kundiawa, northwest of Lea, and southwest of Madang (the latter two cities are on the coast) in the Bismark Range. The higher portion of the mountain consists of granitic type rock, which offers many good climbing possibilities.

Getting to Wilhelm is fairly easy. After reaching the eastern highlands and Kundiawa, the capital of Chimbu province, look for either a PMV (Public Motor Vehicle—carrying people and cargo) or perhaps a missionary heading north in the direction of Keglsugl or Toronambanau (a Catholic mission). Before you leave Kundiawa do your shopping, as the variety of food there is much better there than at the small store near the mission.

For the most part traffic ends at the mission, but there's a road on to the Keglsugl airstrip at about 2480 meters elevation. Beyond the airstrip (which is often used by climbers with more money than time) a 4WD road continues into a sawmill and lumbering area (which will change as time passes). In 1977, the road ended at a small stream, and a well-marked and often-used trail began. The trail is maintained by somebody—probably the people running the research station higher up.

The trail runs along a ridge-which is waterless, until reaching several small bush huts on the terminal moraine of a former glacier. From that point it's open grassland until the climbers hut and High Altitude Research Station is reached.

Lake Piunde is in the first of two cirque basins which rank high in the world for their beauty and grandeur. To use the hut, you're supposed to make the payment and pick up the key at the Keglsugl Airstrip caretakers house. If you prefer, it's possible to sleep free in the porters hut behind the research station.

From the hut there's a well marked trail leading past the remains of an old Japanese warplane, and to the summit. The yellow paint, marking poles and rocks, stands out in the fog, so there's little chance of getting lost. The climb normally takes two days from Keglsugl. The mountain can be climbed at any time, but the drier season is generally from May through November.

**Map:**   Ramu, SB-55-5, 1 : 250,000, from the US Army Defence Mapping Agency, Washington D.C., and the Royal Australian Survey Corps, Port Moresby or Canberra.

High on the slopes of Wilhelm is the wreckage of Japanese war plane.

## Map 157-1, Wilhelm, Bismark Ra., P. New Guinea

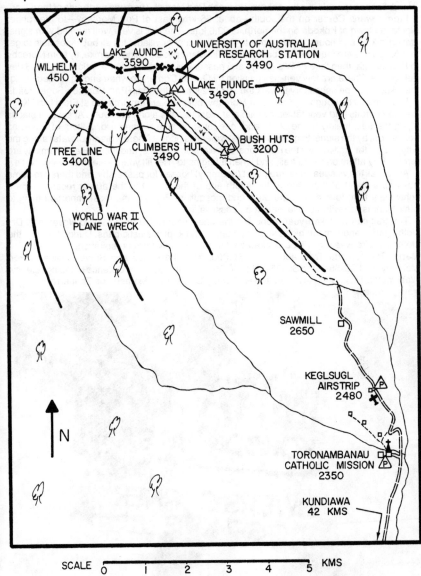

UNIVERSITY OF AUSTRALIA
RESEARCH STATION
3490

LAKE AUNDE
3590

WILHELM
4510

LAKE PIUNDE
3490

BUSH HUTS
3200

CLIMBERS HUT
3490

TREE LINE
3400

WORLD WAR II
PLANE WRECK

SAWMILL
2650

KEGLSUGL
AIRSTRIP
2480

N

TORONAMBANAU
CATHOLIC MISSION
2350

KUNDIAWA
42 KMS

SCALE 0 1 2 3 4 5 KMS

## Kokoda Trail, Papua New Guinea

The Kokoda Trail of Papua New Guinea, while not classified as a mountain climb, must be covered here, as it is one of the great "adventures" in the world of trekking. The Kokoda Trail is a "National Walking Trail," created by the Australian government during their stay in PNG.

The Kokoda Trail was a military battleground during World War II, but now it's used by occasional tourists, foreign businessmen and diplomats, and by the local people crossing the island. For poor people, it's the only way to reach Port Moresby from the north side of the island.

From Owens Corner on the south—about 65 kms east of Port Moresby—to the rubber plantation town of Kokoda on the north, is 93.6 kms. The trail is very well marked with signs, stating in kms and hours, the distance to the next water or village. It's all but impossible to get lost. No guides are required, but being fairly fit is. Many people doing this hike, fly from Moresby to Popondetta, then take PMV's (cargo and passenger truck) to Kokoda, where the 5 to 8 day trek begins. There are few vehicles passing by Owens Corner, so when ending (or beginning) the hike, it may be necessary to walk the 10 or 12 kms to the main Port Moresby-Sogeri road.

Food should be bought in Kokoda or Moresby, but there are small stores at Efogi I and Kagi, and some fruits and vegetables available at most villages along the route. At several places along the trail, mainly at the south end, one must be able to carry 1 or 2 liters of water, as pointed out by the signs, to get over several waterless ridges. There's plenty of water along the way, but as the trail follows the ridge tops, there are no streams, and the heat and humidity are terrific. Pay attention to the trail, and when it begins to rise, fill your canteen or water bottle.

Almost all the villages have free guest (or empty) houses for passersby, and there are some bush huts (most of them are at the south end of the trail), but the author recommends a lightweight tent, to keep out the bugs and mosquitos. Perhaps the most important thing to remember is, go with as little weight as possible.

The trail can be hiked year-round but the drier months are from May to November. Dry clothing to change into at night, should be taken and kept in plastic bags. During the day, the clothes you're wearing will be soaked continually—mostly from perspiration.

**Map:** The Kokoda Trail, about 1 : 150,000, from the Lands and Survey Office in Port Moresby, and SC-55-3 and SC-55-7, 1 : 250,000, from the US Army Defence Mapping Agency, Washington D.C., and Royal Australian Survey Corps, Port Moresby or Canberra.

Signs like this are seen all along the Kokoda Trail.

# Map 158-1, Kokoda Trail, Papua New Guinea

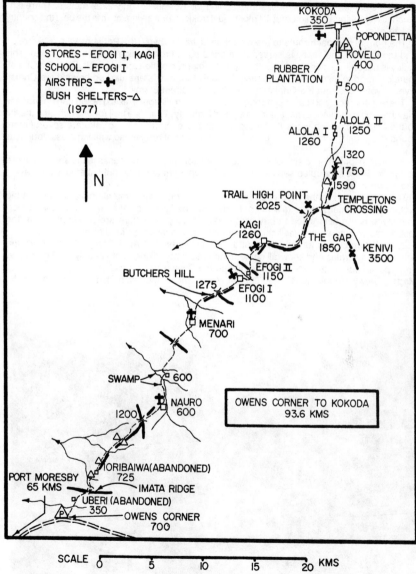

STORES — EFOGI I, KAGI
SCHOOL — EFOGI I
AIRSTRIPS — ✈
BUSH SHELTERS — △
(1977)

N

KOKODA
350

POPONDETTA

RUBBER
PLANTATION

KOVELO
400

500

ALOLA II
1250

ALOLA I
1260

1320

1750

1590

TRAIL HIGH POINT
2025

TEMPLETONS
CROSSING

KAGI
1260

THE GAP
1850

KENIVI
3500

BUTCHERS HILL

EFOGI II
1150

1275

EFOGI I
1100

MENARI
700

SWAMP

600

NAURO
600

1200

OWENS CORNER TO KOKODA
93.6 KMS

IORIBAIWA (ABANDONED)
725

PORT MORESBY
65 KMS

IMATA RIDGE

UBERI (ABANDONED)
350

OWENS CORNER
700

SCALE   0    5    10    15    20   KMS

## Kosciusko, Snowy Mts., New South Wales, Australia

Australia is the flattest of all continents with almost no mountains. There are a few hills in the southern and northern parts of Western Australia, and others scattered "thither and yon" throughout the land, but none can compare with the Snowy Mountains.

The Snowy Mountains are located south of Canberra—the national capital, in the state of New South Wales—not far north of the Victoria state line. These mountains aren't big by anybody's standards, the highest summit being Mt. Kosciusko, only 2229 meters. There isn't much of a challenge for climbers; it's mostly just trekking or walking, but it is the best the country has to offer.

The normal approach route to the mountain is via Jindbyne, the Perisher Village ski resort and the Chalet. The valley is served by a good paved road which is open year-round. This valley is not only a skier's paradise, but is a summer recreation area as well. From the Chalet, there's a road to just below the summit, but only tour buses are allowed beyond the Chalet. Even if you walk from the Chalet, it's not far, only about 8 kms.

There's another road passing through the Threadbo Village. This ski resort can be reached via Khankoban or Jindabyne, again on a good highway. There's a trail (or one can take the lift) to the ridge top, which leads to the top of Kosciusko. North of Kosciusko are several other rounded summits with a number of trails. The area is not rugged, so walking cross-country is easy.

Public transportation is almost nil. In the ski season there will be buses in the area, but there seems to be no scheduled service. Hitch hiking appears to be the only alternative to having one's own vehicle.

There are hotels in the area open year-round, but one can camp almost anywhere. A big problem in summer are the millions of bush flies—by far the most ever seen by the author! Jindabyne is the best place to buy groceries and supplies. There are eating places at the resorts, as well as some small shops, but they have only snack food at high prices.

Precipitation comes at any time, but the winter months of April through October are the wettest. Heavy rains and snowfall come during this time. Hiking boots and fly swatter are the only special equipment one needs to hike in the Snowy Mountains.

**Map:** Snowy Mountains, 1 : 250,000, from the Snowy Mountain Hydro-electric Authority, Canberra.

Threadbo Village and ski runs just south of Kosciusko.

## Map 159-1, Kosciusko, S. Mts., N.S. Wales, Aust.

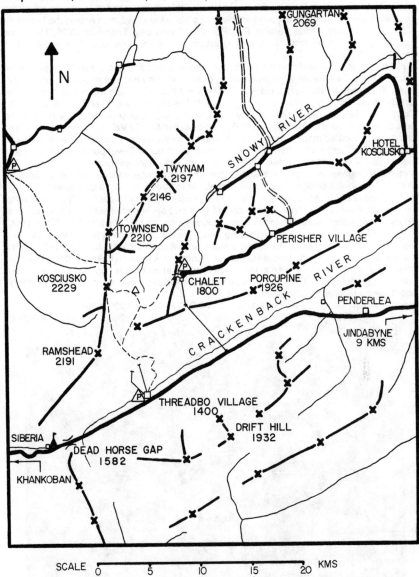

N

GUNGARTAN
2069

SNOWY RIVER

HOTEL
KOSCIUSKO

TWYNAM
2197

2146

TOWNSEND
2210

PERISHER VILLAGE

KOSCIUSKO
2229

P
CHALET
1800

PORCUPINE
1926

CRACKENBACK RIVER

PENDERLEA

JINDABYNE
9 KMS

RAMSHEAD
2191

THREADBO VILLAGE
1400

DRIFT HILL
1932

SIBERIA

DEAD HORSE GAP
1582

KHANKOBAN

SCALE 0   5   10   15   20   KMS

# Tasmania National Parks, Tasmania, Australia

The map here is actually 3 maps in one. Most of Tasmanias national parks and protected areas are shown. They are the Cradle Mtn—Lake St. Clair National Park, the Central Plateau Wildlife Sanctuary, Central Plateau Protected Area, the South West National Park, Mt. Field National Park, and Hartz Mtn. National Park. In no way should the reader use this map for hiking. This is merely an introduction to what is available on the island of Tasmania just off the southeast coast of Australia. If you're anticipating a trip to the island, then write to the Tasmania National Parks and Wildlife Service, P.O. Box 210, Sandy Bay, Tasmania, 7005. They send free information and brochures, as well as lists of books and other useful information. See below to find maps.

For hikers and especially climbers, the most interesting region is in the northern part of the mapped area. This seems to be where most of the trails and tracks are located, and a lot of lakes. This Central Plateau has many summits over 1300 meters and the overall height of the land is much higher than the rest of Tasmania. In this region the best place to hike is in the Cradle Mtn. and Lake St. Clair N. P. Drive or hitch hike south out of Burnie to reach one of the best developed parts of the National Park, a place called Cradle Valley. There's a chalet and campground located there with many trails. Another easily reached recreation area is Rowallan, on the northern end of Lake Rowallan. Drive south out of Devonport to get there. From either of these two just-mentioned locations, one can walk on tracks south past Mt. Ossa, 1617 meters, the highest peak on the island, and to another popular trailhead known as Derwent Bridge. At Derwent Bridge are a visitor center, campground and boating facilities.

Going to the south, and to an area not far to the east of Hobart (the capital city of Tasmania), we find Mt. Field N. P. Featured here are ski runs and several shelters and lodge facilities. There are also some well developed trails, including one going to the top of Mt. Field West.

In the southwest corner of this map is the South West N. P. It's the largest of the parks, and the most pristine and remote. Begin from a trailhead just north of Hartz Mtn. N. P. and walk in a circle eventually ending the trek at Ramsgate. Scotts Peak Dam on Lake Pedder is the most popular camping site in Tasmania. Remember, the weather here is cool and very wet. Take appropriate equipment. No water problem, it's everywhere. Hike from December through about March (similar weather to south island of N. Z.)

**Map:** Contact Lands Dept., Hobart, for 1 : 100,000 and 1 : 50,000 maps.

Lake Dove and Cradle Mountain.

# Map 160-3, Tasmania N.P., Tasmania, Australia

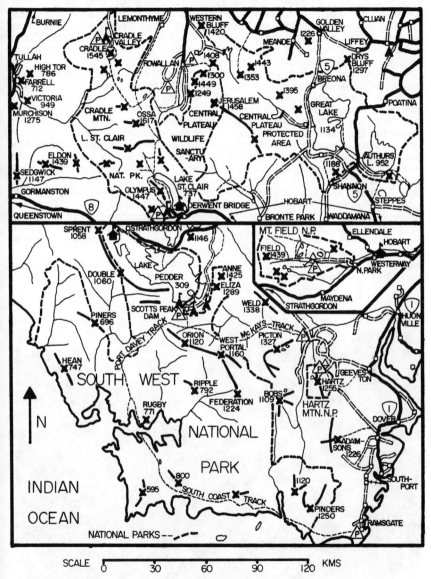

# Milford Track, South Island, New Zealand

Featured on this map is one of the best known hiking trails or tracks in the world. This is the Milford Track, located on the south island of New Zealand. Besides the Milford Track, there are several other trails or tracks in the area. They are shown on the map as the Greenstone, Routeburn, Hollyford, Big Bay and the Martins Bay Track. The reason the Milford Track is best known is because of the scenery and the ease of transport to both ends of the trail. Approximatley half of the map (western) shows portions of the Fiordland National Park. This national park covers the better part of the southwest coast of the south island. Fiordlands name tells the story. This part of N.Z. has many inlets or Fiords, and has a similar climate to that of Norway or British Columbia. The reason for all the Fiords is a result of the last ice age when many glaciers carved these canyons which are now lakes or inlets.

The Milford Track is normally a three day hike, or "tramp," as it's refered to in New Zealand. One can do the trek either beginning at Milford Sound or the Eglinton Flat Campground. About half way along the hike is Mackinnon Pass. The hike is totally in wooded areas, except on the pass, and the track has 11 huts scattered along the way. Most people use these huts as opposed to camping. The weather is usually bad, thus little camping. Some of these huts are operated by the Government Tourist Bureau, Dunedin, while others are part of the national park hut system. For these, make payments and reservations at the Fiordland National Park Board Office in Te Anau. Te Anau is a summer tourist spot on the main road leading to the Milford Sound, and is on the shores of Lake Te Anau. For the latest information, maps and books about this part of N.Z. see N.P. headquarters in Te Anau. Because this is a very popular summer fun spot, one must never go there from mid-December on through February, until reservations are made for the huts ahead of time. The very busiest time is from mid December through mid January. At this time most New Zealanders take holiday.

Hitch hiking in New Zealand is very easy, but in remote areas, long waits must be anticipated. Inquire in Te Anau or Queenstown about public transport into Milford Sound or Glenorchy regions. Beware of bad weather and take proper rain gear.

**Map:** Fiordlands National Park, 1 : 300,000, Dept. of Lands and Survey, Wellington or Te Anau. Other scale maps also available at Park Headquarters, Te Anau.

Lake Wakatipu and Queenstown not far from the Milford Track.

# Map 161-3, Milford Track, S. Alps, New Zealand

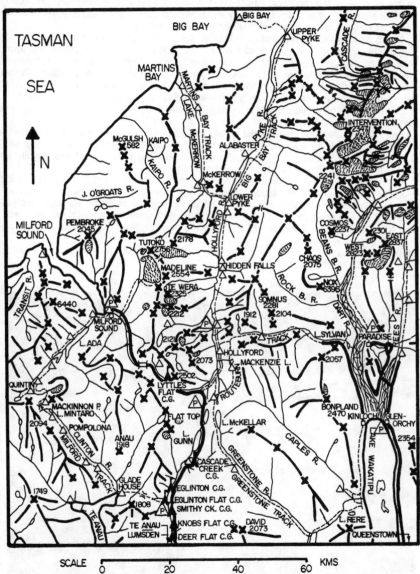

TASMAN

SEA

N

BIG BAY

BIG BAY

UPPER PYKE

MARTINS BAY

MARTINS BAY TRACK

LAKE McKERROW

McGULSH 582

KAIPO

KAIPO R.

ALABASTER

PYKE R.

BIG BAY TRACK

INTERVENTION 2341

McKERROW

J. O'GROATS R.

LOWER PYKE

2241

MILFORD SOUND

PEMBROKE 2045

COSMOS 2237

2301 EAST 2337

HOLLYFORD R.

BEANS B. R.

WEST 2823

TUTOKO 2756

2178

HIDDEN FALLS

CHAOS 2075

MADELINE 2554

NOX 6396

TRANSIT R.

TE WERA 2325

6440

2212

SOMNUS 2281

ROCK B. R.

1912

2104

DART R.

MILFORD SOUND

L. ADA

2121

TRACK

L. SYLVAN

PARADISE

REES R.

2073

HOLLYFORD

MACKENZIE L.

2057

QUINTIN

2502

LYTTLES FLAT C.G.

ROUTEBURN

BONPLAND 2470

MACKINNON P.

L. MINTARO

FLAT TOP

KINLOCH GLEN-ORCHY

2094

POMPOLONA

CLINTON

ANAU 1918

L. GUNN

L. McKELLAR

2354

CAPLES R.

MILFORD TRACK

CLINTON R.

CASCADE CREEK C.G.

GREENSTONE R.

LAKE WAKATIPU

GLADE HOUSE

EGLINTON C.G.

GREENSTONE TRACK

1749

EGLINTON FLAT C.G.

1808

SMITHY CK. C.G.

TE ANAU

TE ANAU LUMSDEN

KNOBS FLAT C.G.

DAVID 2073

DEER FLAT C.G.

L. RERE

QUEENSTOWN

SCALE

0        20        40        60        KMS

# Mt. Aspiring, Southern Alps, New Zealand

On New Zealand's South Island and running the full length of it, is a folded, uplifted, and heavily glaciated mountain range, known as the Southern Alps. They are just as rugged, even more glaciated, and have more bad weather, than the Alps of Europe. In the southern portion of this range stands one of the better known peaks in New Zealand, Mt. Aspiring, 3025 meters.

In times of good weather—which is seldom, and if you have your own car or vehicle (in which to get as close to the mountain as possible), it could be climbed in three days. However, weather almost never allows for such a quick ascent, so plan on spending time in one of the huts waiting for a break in the weather, then make a run for it.

The route to the top involves passing through the tourist town of Wanaka. This is the last settlement on the approach route, so have all your food and supplies before leaving town. Wanaka is also the headquarters of the national park in which Mt. Aspiring is the central attraction. It would pay to stop at the park headquarters for current information, especially that having to do with the use of huts. The huts on the mountain are operated by the park service and reservations are needed for using them—especially during the busy season. The busy season is from about mid-December through late January. That's when all, or most, New Zealanders have their holidays.

From Wanaka to the Raspberry Hut or Aspiring Station, is around 50 kms. If you haven't a car, it's a long walk; but during the summer there's some traffic on this otherwise lonely road, and getting a lift *isn't too difficult* (the last information given the author is the Raspberry Hut no longer exists—but it's location is still shown on the map).

The nomal route is via the Raspberry, Aspiring and the Colin Todd Huts. From Colin Todd Hut it's mostly a rock climb, but ice equipment is needed to pass over the Bonar Glacier. Because of the terrible weather one will likely encounter, make sure you have a good supply of wool clothing and rain gear. Summer time is usually best for climbing but good weather spells can come at any time. Because of the changable weather, few people camp on the high mountains in New Zealand.

**Map:** Mount Aspiring National Park, or Aspiring #SI06 and Earnslaw #SII4, from the Lands and Survey Dept. of New Zealand, Wellington.

The Hermatige at Mount Cook village.

# Map 162-3, Aspiring, Southern Alps, New Zealand

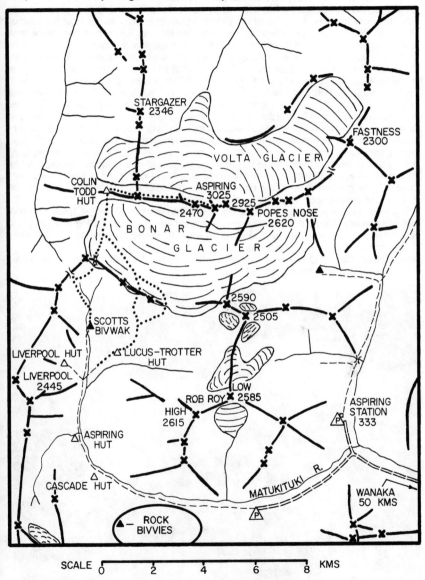

STARGAZER
2346

FASTNESS
2300

VOLTA GLACIER

COLIN
TODD
HUT

ASPIRING
3025

2925

2470

POPES NOSE
2620

B O N A R

G L A C I E R

2590

2505

SCOTTS
BIVWAK

LIVERPOOL HUT

LUCUS-TROTTER
HUT

LIVERPOOL
2445

LOW
2585

ROB ROY

HIGH
2615

ASPIRING
STATION
333

ASPIRING
HUT

CASCADE HUT

MATUKITUKI R.

WANAKA
50 KMS

▲ - ROCK
BIVVIES

SCALE  0    2    4    6    8  KMS

## Mt. Cook, Southern Alps, South Island, New Zealand

Mt. Cook is the highest and perhaps the most challenging mountain in New Zealand. It lies in the central part of the Southern Alps on the South Island, and is not far from the storm-battered west coast. If everything was favorable, it could be climbed in 3 days—but people who have been so fortunate, are few and far between. Most people take at least 10 days of food and supplies, and plan for a long wait for that good weather period.

Don't underestimate Mt. Cook and its nearby peaks. Forgetting the ease of access, mountain huts, and low elevation—it is of Himalayan proportions. From the base of the Tasman Glacier to Cook's summit is nearly 3000 meters. The weather is very bad most of the time, glaciers are extensive, and there are many crevasses and avalanches.

Regular bus and airline service exists to Mount Cook town, located in the valley below Mt. Cook. There are hotels, a youth hostel, campground, stores, park headquarters and even guide services available. All food can be bought at Mount Cook, but it's expensive.

There are many huts in the nearby valleys and mountains. Seldom do climbers use tents, unless they're preparing for an expedition to Patagonia or some other god-forsaken place. One must inquire about these huts at the park headquarters and make a payment for their use, as is customary for all national park huts. Expedition type clothing, including a lot of wool, must be taken. For the serious climber, February or March are usually the best months for climbing, but good weather periods can come at any time. Right now winter climbing is becoming popular.

Huts are usually equipped with stoves and fuel and often left-over food from previous parties. Each hut of any importance, is also furnished with a radio, which is used by climbers and park rangers in the evening of each day. Good maps guide books and further information can be found at the park headquarters located at Mount Cook.

For hikers there's a very most popular trek or walk known at the Copeland Track. This hike begins or ends at Mount Cook and runs to the West Coast Highway ending near the place called Karangarua. There are four huts along the way—Hooker, Copeland, Douglas Rock and the Welcome Flat Hut. It's an easy two day walk.

**Map:** Mount Cook and Westland National Parks, 1 : 100,000, from the Lands and Survey Dept. of New Zealand, Wellington.

Looking up the Tasman Glacier from near the Plateau Hut on Mt. Cook.

## Map 163-1, Cook, Southern Alps, New Zealand

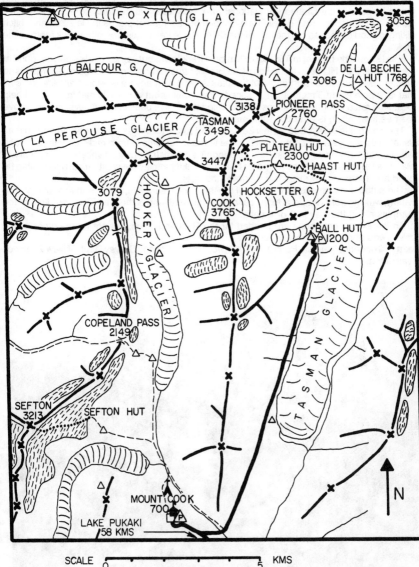

## Ruapehu, North Island, New Zealand

The three peaks of Tongariro, Ngauruhoe, and Ruapehu are all part of the Tongariro National Park. As with most (literally all) of the mountains on the North Island of New Zealand, these too are volcanic cones. Ngauruhoe had a thunderous eruption in 1976, but Tongariro and Ruapehu are apparently dormant. All three peaks can best be reached from the highway connecting the hamlets of National Park and Turangi.

Ruapehu is the highest and most developed—having several ski lifts, and many private and public lodges. At the Chateau or National Park Headquarters, a store, garage and service station can be found. Tour buses are available, but as in most places in New Zealand, hitch hiking is good on the road to the Top of the Bruce. Little traffic exists on other back roads in the park.

Food should be bought in Turangi or National Park town, but some supplies can be found at the National Park HQ., and at the Top of the Bruce. Streams abound everywhere, so water is no problem. Many huts exist throughout the park as well as many trails. Most trails are "poled," that is, a pole about 3 meters tall is placed on the trail about every 100 meters or so, to help locate the route in foggy conditions. These poled trails have been prepared everywhere above the tree line, which is at about 1000 meters.

The weather is always bad in New Zealand, so it's best to take along more wool clothing than usual, plus rain gear. The very busiest time in the mountains is from mid-December through late January. This is when most New Zealanders and Australians take vacations. February or March is perhaps the very best time for trekking or climbing, as the weather can more often be good and there are fewer people to crowd the huts.

The author recommends a traverse of the three main summits, from north to south (or vice versa), walking from Ruapehu to the car park at the north end of the area. One can climb all the summits along the way in 3 or 4 days.

An ice ax and crampons are needed for the Ruapehu climb, but not for the other peaks unless you're planning a winter ascent.

**Map:** Tongariro National Park, 1 : 80,000, from the Lands and Survey Dept. of New Zealand, Wellington.

From Top-of-the-Bruce looking at Ngauruhoe to the north.

Map 164-1, Ruapehu, North Island, New Zealand

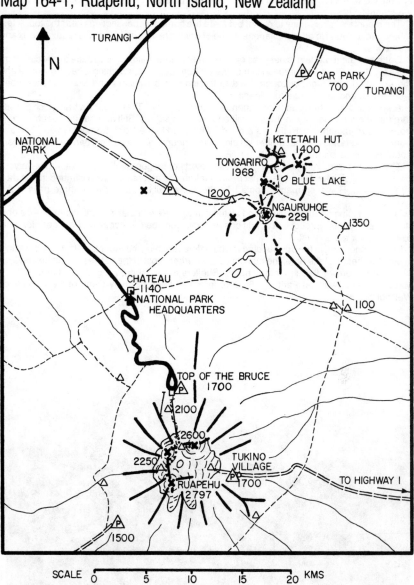

## Mt. Egmont, North Island, New Zealand

On the North Island of New Zealand, very near the west coast and the towns of New Plymouth and Stratford, lies one of the most symmetrical volcanos in the world. Its name is Mt. Egmont, and it rises from virtually sea level to 2510 meters. Despite its relative low elevation, it is crowned with snow throughout the year and even has some real "live" glaciers at and near the summit.

The mountain is very easy to climb, but there are some steeper sections near the top. A few routes can be found to offer challenges, some of which are very icy. All routes require ice ax and crampons.

Getting to the mountain is easy, as climbers have three main access roads to choose from. Possibly the most used approach is the one up from Stratford, reaching Stratford House and the ski resort at Manganui Lodge. Next to the lodge is a climbers and skiers shelter, open year-round, and free to use for sleeping.

A second route is the road from Kaponga to Dawson Falls. Then there's a trail which passes three shelters on the way to the summit on the south slopes. Still another approach route is from New Plymouth, where there's a good 28 km road to the North Egmont Chalet. The trail from this lodge joins another trail which circles the mountain. The summit can be reached from about any place on this loop trail.

There's no public transport to any of these resorts or lodges, so it's necessary to have your own car, or hitch hike. No matter what route is taken, the mountain can be climbed in one day, start to finish. However, many people hike the circle trail and take two or three days in the process.

The worst thing about this climb and all the climbs in New Zealand, is the weather—it's one storm after another. Expect wet conditions and you won't be disappointed. Rain gear for both you and pack are a must.

Do your shopping in the surrounding towns before reaching the mountain. If you're planning to use the shelters, take note; the busiest season, when most of the natives are on holidays, is from mid-December through late January. Shelters are most crowded at that time.

**Map:** Egmont National Park, 1 : 60,000, from Lands and Survey Dept. of New Zealand, Wellington.

Mt. Egmont from one of many dairy farms in New Zealand.

## Map 165-1, Egmont, North Island, New Zealand

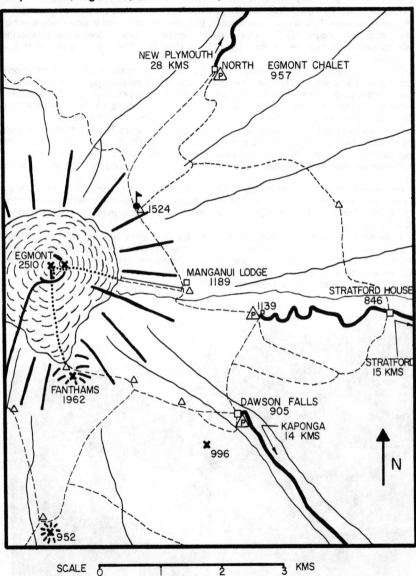

NEW PLYMOUTH
28 KMS

NORTH EGMONT CHALET
957

1524

EGMONT
2510

MANGANUI LODGE
1189

1139

STRATFORD HOUSE
846

STRATFORD
15 KMS

FANTHAMS
1962

DAWSON FALLS
905

KAPONGA
14 KMS

996

N

952

SCALE    0       1       2       3   KMS

## Matafao, Tutuila Island, American Samoa

Near the center of the Pacific Ocean and the island group known as Polynesia, is Samoa. Of the five or six islands in the Samoan group, only one is American Samoa. Two larger islands to the west form what is now known as Western Samoa. Western Samoa is independent, whereas American Samoa on the island of Tutuila, is administered by the USA.

This map covers the central part of Tutuila where all the higher mountains lie. Like most of the Polynesian islands, Tutuila is volcanic in orgin. Evidence of this is seen in the excellent harbor afforded by Pago Pago Bay. This is the remains of an old crater with steep sides. Most of the islands' population lives around the edge of Pago Pago Bay. The seat of government is at Fagatogo.

Tutuila is a rugged and mountainous island, but elevations are not great. The island is only about 30 kms long and very narrow. The highest summit is Matafao rising to over 500 meters. To some this seems like nothing, but they rise from sea level very quickly—Matafao being only one km from tidewater. Because this peak is the highest on the island and because the area is the source of drinking water, there are a few trails about and one to the summit.

There are three possible routes of approach to the top of Matafao. The topo maps show trails beginning at Fagaalu, Fagatogo, and from near the pass marked 181 meters, but doesn't show any going to the summit. However, there is a trail to the top, and it's shown on this map in it's approximate location. The region around Matafao is steep and heavily forested, as is all of the island.

Another interesting hike is to the top of Alava. From the village of Pago Pago, walk or hitch hike up the road to the pass, then turn right and walk along the ridge road (now only a trail) to the top. At the summit of Alava is a television transmitter and the top terminal of a cable car which runs from Fagatogo.

There are a couple of other hikes beginning from Pago Pago Bay. One trail goes to Vatia, another goes to Afono, both on the north coast. Another trail connects these two villages. This would make a nice day hike taking in both Afono and Vatia. Keep in mind that Samoa is warm and humid and recieves about 5 meters of rain each year.

**Map:**  Tutuila Island-American Samoa 1 : 24,000, USGS.

Pago Pago Bay and Matafao from the summit of Alava.

Map 166-1, Matafao, Tutuila Island, Amer. Samoa

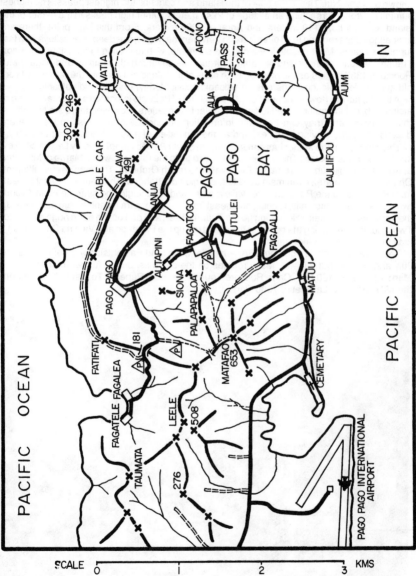

## Orohena, Tahiti, French Polynesia

Of all the South Pacific islands, the island of Tahiti is probably the most famous and legendary of all. It's truly a paradise with sandy beaches, coral reefs, old ruins, soft sea breezes and even some fairly high mountains.

The Island of Tahiti is actually in two parts, connected by a narrow isthmus. The larger part is known as Tahiti Nui. This is the bulk of the island and contains the highest peaks. The highest summit is Orohena reaching an altitude of 2241 meters. Other high peaks in the center of the island are Pito Ito, 2110 meters and Aorai at 2066 meters. From this high point, there are eminating ridges running in all directions. In between the ridges, are deep river valleys with fast running streams. Most people live along the shoreline, with few living in the islands' interior. The smaller part of the island is Tahiti Iti. It too has several high summits and ridges, with Rooniu at 1332 meters as the highest. Both parts of the island of Tahiti are the remains of very old and eroded volcanos. There is no volcanic activity today, only the old volcanic rock.

In the capital city (town—population about 20,000) of Papeete is located a mountaineering or alpine club, but the author failed to get an answer to two letters. However, there are two official tourist offices, and they can help with information not included here. Also in Papeete are dozens of hotels, varying in prices, and all the amenities of a large tourist congregation.

The information the author has comes from the *South Pacific Handbook,* by Dalton-Stanley, and the map listed below. The above book says to go to the ruins known as Marae of Mahaitea at KM 39, and hike up the Temarua River valley to reach Orohena. The map seems different. On the map there are seven main trails to the region of Orohena. They are from west to east: from Punaauia up the Punaruu River valley: a trail and road beginning near the Faaa Airport; two roads, turning into trails, running southeast from Papeete; a trail running from near Arue up the north ridge of Aorai; trail running up the Tuauru River; and one up the north ridge of Pito Ito. Two other trails reaching the center of the island run up the Papenoo and Vaihiria Rivers. It's 11 kms from Oriaroa to Lake Vaihiria.

Reach Tahiti by plane from the USA, Australia, Chile (and Easter Island). Drier months are July and August, but still wet. Many refuges on the summits, but no further information.

**Map:** Tahiti, 1 : 100,000, Carte Routiere Touristique, from Papeete Tourist Offices, or from the IGN, 107 Rue La Boetie, 7500 Paris.

Scenes like this are common on Tahiti (foto from Moorea Island).

Map 167-3, Orohena, Tahiti, French Polynesia

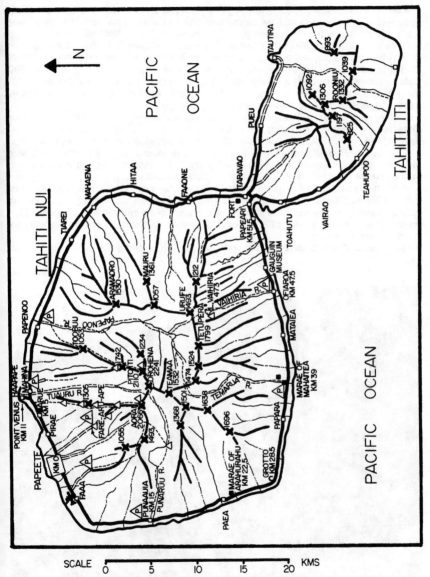

# Mauna Loa, Hawaii, Hawaiian Islands, USA

The second highest mountain on the big island of Hawaii is Mauna Loa, a huge dome of a mountain which is actually a shield volcano. Shield volcanos are different than some others, in that the lava flowing from them is very viscous and creates a broad, gentle sloping mountain. These differ from other volcanos such as Fuji, Rainier, or Ararat, which are much steeper and conal shaped.

Mauna Loa is an active volcano, erupting every few years, sometimes issuing lava from the summit crater—sometimes from the much lower Kilauea Crater, to the east. The summit and eastern portions of the mountain are part of the Hawaii Volcanos National Park.

There are two main routes up the mountain. The most used route, but which is the longest, is the trail beginning at the end of the road, not far from the Kilauea Crater. From the end of that road (marked 2000 meters), the trail winds its way over lava to the Red Hill Cabin, at about 3000 meters. This takes one day for most people. The next section is from Red Hill to the summit. Many people stay in the summit cabin overnight which makes the journey longer, but usually more enjoyable. This climb takes most people 3 or 4 days from Kilauea.

Another route is via the Saddle Road—connecting Hilo and Waimea, and the US Weather Observatory. The good road ends there. A closed gate bars the way to motor vehicles just beyond the weather station. One can take either the road or trail, and make this hike in one day.

If you take the Red Hill route, there is rainwater stored in tanks at the cabins. The park service strongly recommends that the water be boiled, or purified with tablets. There is no live water or springs on the mountain, so begin your hike with a full canteen.

Public transportation in the area is on the main road that passes the Kilauea Crater and on the Saddle Road. If you have no car then hitch hiking is your best bet. Hitching is easy in all of Hawaii. Sometimes one can get a lift from park rangers to the end of the road marked 2000 meters. Buy your food in Hilo or Kilauea, and for additional information see the national park headquarters at Kilauea.

**Map:**  Hawaii, sheets 2 and 3, 1 : 100,000, from the USGS, and any Hawaii state highway map.

Red Knob Hut on the northeast slopes on Mauna Loa.

Map 168-1, Mauna Loa, Hawaii Isl., Hawaii, USA

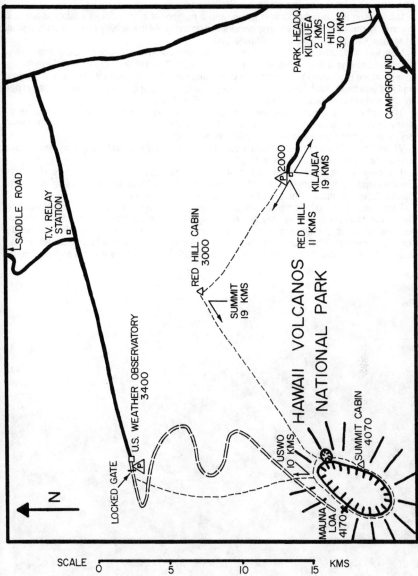

SADDLE ROAD

T.V. RELAY STATION

PARK HEADQ.
KILAUEA 2 KMS
HILO 30 KMS

CAMPGROUND

2000

KILAUEA 19 KMS

RED HILL CABIN 3000

RED HILL 11 KMS

KILAUEA 19 KMS

SUMMIT 19 KMS

U.S. WEATHER OBSERVATORY 3400

HAWAII VOLCANOS NATIONAL PARK

LOCKED GATE

USWO 10 KMS

SUMMIT CABIN 4070

MAUNA LOA 4170

N

SCALE   0        5        10        15   KMS

# Mauna Kea, Hawaii, Hawaiian Islands, USA

The highest mountain in the Pacific Basin, with the exception of peaks in New Guinea, is Mauna Kea, a 4206 meter shield volcano on the big island of Hawaii in the Hawaiian islands.

The entire chain of islands known as the Hawaiian Islands are made up of volcanic outpourings throughout the past millions of years. The oldest rock material is found in the islands to the northwest; the youngest to the southeast. The youngest or newest island of them all is Hawaii, sometimes known as the Big Island.

Mauna Kea is a huge mountain mass, with a number of cinder cones scattered about its summit. At this time the mountain is considered dormant. All the activity has now shifted south of Mauna Kea to its sister peak, Mauna Loa.

Most will be disappointed to find there's a road to the summit of Mauna Kea. But, there's also a trail, and no one is forced in any way to ride to the top. The trail on the map (and there may be others on the mountain?), begins at the picnic and camping site near Halepohaku. It's a good trail and well used. At about 3500 meters there's an old mine or quarry, used in the ancient past by the native Hawaiians as a place to mine their ax heads.

The trail ends at a road near the summit. One must walk the last 2 kms on a road to the astronomical observatory. There are several telescopes at this University of Hawaii Observatory. The highest summit is very near all the telescopes.

Water can be found at the summit area, at the supporting research station of Halepohaku, and at the ranch near the Saddle Road.

This area can be reached from either Hilo on the east coast, or Waimea to the west, via the Saddle Road running between Mauna Kea and Mauna Loa. There is limited bus service on the Saddle Road, so most visitors rent cars. Hitch hiking is very good.

These islands are within the tropics, so any month is a good time to climb—however, from December to February snow may fall at the higher elevations. With a close look, one can observe evidence of past glaciation, and to this day there is still some permafrost under the surface at the top. The best and only places to buy food for this hike is at Waimea or Hilo.

**Map:** Hawaii, sheet 2, 1 : 100,000, from the USGS, and any Hawaii state highway map.

From the top of Mauna Loa one can see cinder cones on Mauna Kea.

Map 169-1, Mauna Kea, Hawaii Isl., Hawaii, USA

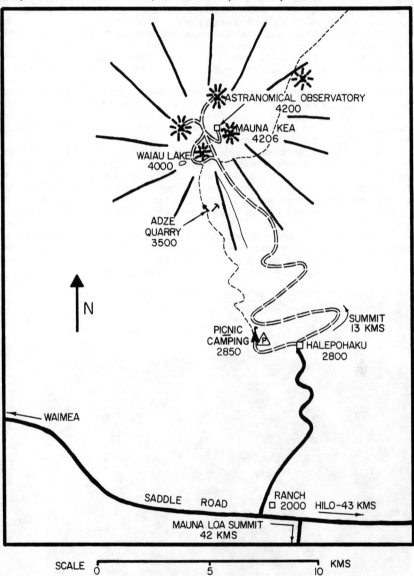

## Haleakala, Maui, Hawaiian Islands, USA

The entire chain of the Hawaiian Islands, is made up of volcanic outpourings. The oldest and most eroded islands are in the northwest with the younger or newer islands in the southeast. The youngest island and the one with the most recent volcanic activity is the biggest island of all, Hawaii. It's the last of the chain, and has the least amount of erosion. The next to the last island in the chain, and the next to the youngest, is Maui. It's on Maui that we find the second highest group of peaks in the island chain. The mountain we're concerned with here is Haleakala, or more specifically the Haleakala Crater.

This is an old and eroded volcanic cone or crater, that still retains the look of activity. Within the giant crater are cinder cones of multicolors which form a desolate landscape. The highest point on the rim is the Puu Ulaula overlook, sometimes known as Red Hill, at 3055 meters. Unfortunately, there's a good road to the top of that point which makes it less than a thrilling climb.

This entire crater is within the Haleakala National Park, therefore very much protected. There's a good road winding up the northwest side of the mountain to the crater rim, which brings thousands of people to the area. At the rim is a visitor center, where you can get all the information needed for a day-hike or an overnight stay in the crater area. The trails within the crater are well marked and well used.

For those with more time than the average tourist, an overnight stay is recommended. There are three cabins or huts within the crater. At times these can be crowded, so advanced reservations are required. If you're there during the busy season, June through August, or in mid winter, plan on carrying a tent. At each cabin or campsite there is rainwater stored in tanks, but which must be boiled or purified before use. The author recommends the hike from the rim to the Paliku Cabin, then down the south face of the mountain to Kaupo. This could be done in one long day.

Don't wait 'till the mountain to buy your food. There's little if any there. Be prepared for possible cold and wet weather, and carry a full canteen of water at all times. There's no public transport to the rim, but hitching is good all over Hawaii.

**Map:**  Maui, 1 : 62,500, USGS, and any Hawaii state highway map.

Haleakala Crater. Note the many small cinder cones inside.

Map 170-3, Haleakala, Maui Island, Hawaii, USA

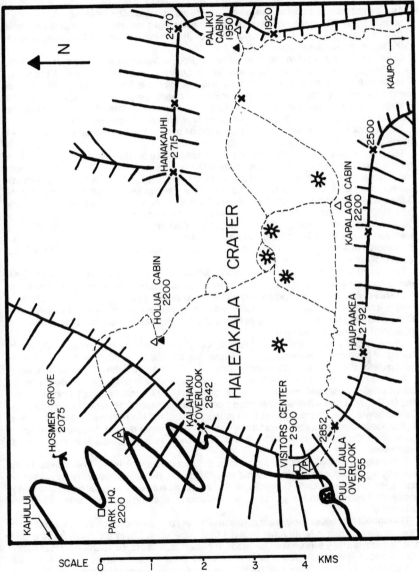

# Chapter 6 North America

The maps included in this region of the world are of North America—Canada and the United States. Altogether there are 118 maps here.

In this part of the world, the mountain type which dominates the scene is the uplifted and folded variety, caused by the wrinkling of the earth's crust and by the movement of the continents. There is some volcanic activity, but it's concentrated mostly along the Northwest Coast of the USA, and in Alaska—west of Cook Inlet and Anchorage.

As with most folded mountain ranges around the world, many of those in this section consist of granitic type rocks at their centers. Some of these ranges include the Sierras of California, Tetons and Wind Rivers of Wyoming, parts of the Purcells of British Columbia, and Mt. McKinley in the Alaska Range.

Great limestone ranges include the Canadian Rockies which extend southward into Montana. Ranges composed of quartzite rock are in Colorado and in Utah's Uinta Mountains.

In North America the one and only language to speak of is English. The British influence completely overpowered all others in this region. In Canada, the province of Quebec is officially French speaking, which has caused problems in Canada in the late 1970's. Most Canadian government documents, with maps as a good example, are in both English and French.

Throughout the entire region there are hundreds of native Indian languages, but they are slowly dying, and will surely die out completely one day.

This entire region is under the influence of the middle latitude jet streams and cyclonic storm system, much the same as in Europe. In winter time, the storm systems tend to move south, and at times move from the Pacific on shore to California (California has a Mediterranean type climate), then east across the USA. A second winter pattern shows storms moving from the Gulf of Alaska, to the Northwest Coast of the USA and into the Intermountain Region, thence to the east. Another familiar winter pattern sees the storms move through B.C. and Alberta in Canada, and down (south) the east side of the Rockies into the plains of the USA and eventually east to the Atlantic. This pattern leaves the Western USA warm and dry. The coasts of Oregon, Washington, British Columbia, and southern Alaska, are termed the "West Coast Marine Climates," and are very wet.

The mountains with the greatest climbing difficulties lie in Alaska and the Yukon. Great names such as McKinley, St. Elias, and Logan dominate all other mountains in the region. This is an area of little population and great distances. The largest glaciers on the continent lie here, making it necessary to use small aircraft to either land on glaciers with men and supplies, or to air drop supplies to climbers waiting on the mountains. Practically every mountain requires an expedition to reach the summit.

Those places which stand out as great rock climbing areas, are the Sierras of California, Tetons of Wyoming, the Sawtooths of Idaho, the Bugaboos of BC, and the Cumberland Peninsula of Baffin Island—Northwest Territories. These are just the more important ones.

If someone prefers cooler weather and snow and ice climbing, then areas along the USA-Canada border and northward are the best places. If a person enjoys hiking on trails—and for the most part warm weather, then places like Colorado, Utah, Nevada, Wyoming and California are best. The southwest USA is a dry region, but the high peaks always have an alpine appearance about them and there's always some water nearby. The winter months of from about October through May, always bring snow to the mountains in the American Southwest.

Generally speaking, climbers camping in the mountains can leave their camps in the morning and return in the evening to find everything safe. But as the population increases, so does theft. In places such as California, be slightly more cautious about leaving a camp all day unattended. However, thievery is still generally uncommon, and in areas of small population it's unheard-of.

Throughout the region public transportation is rather poor; the reason is, everyone has a car. The highway system in North America is the best in the world. There are railways in the USA and Canada, but they service very few areas of interest to climbers. Bus service is much better, but still it doesn't compare to other parts of the world. Simply stated, one will have to have a car or hitch hike. Foreign travelers who plan to stay long periods of time sometimes buy used cars, which are very cheap. Others may rent new cars. However, if one is on foot, it's possible to get to about any mountain in this region by using the thumb, especially in the months of June through August.

The summit ridge of Mt. Timpanogos during a mid-winter climb. (Map 257).

Mt. Temple as fotographed from near Lake Louise (Map 192).

## Gerdine, Chigmit Mountains, Alaska, USA

This is the first in the series of maps covering the mountains of Alaska and northwest Canada. It includes the higher peaks to the west of Anchorage and the Cook Inlet, and south of Mt. McKinley. The highest summit in this region is Gerdine, at 3841 meters. South of Gerdine is Spurr, 3375 meters. In the middle sections of the map are Telaquane, 2849 meters, and at the southern end Redoubt, 3109, and Iliamna, 3084 meters. The last two summits are volcanos.

These mountains lie in an almost uninhabited area with only a few kms of roads. On the one hand, Cook Inlet acts as a barrier, but on the other hand, it is a means of access to this roadless area.

Access is the major difficulty, but this problem can be overcome by having a little money to hire a small plane or boat. There are many glaciers in the area, and several lakes and inlets, which can provide landing sites of either ski planes or planes equipped to land on water. Best places to look for aircraft of this kind would be first in Anchorage, then Kenai or Soldotna as shown on the map.

Boats can also be found in these same places, to cross the Cook Inlet. The more northerly of the mountains such as Gerdine have to be reached by plane.

Generally speaking, the Cook Inlet and region is considered a bad weather area. Cyclonic storms from the Gulf of Alaska and the southwest, invade southern Alaska frequently. For all lower altitudes rain gear is essential. Alaska is famous for its mosquitos, so have a good supply of repellent as well.

All, or most of the summits of importance are glaciated, so snow and ice equipment is needed. It may also be necessary to buy or rent a radio in Anchorage, on which to place important calls. There's no problem finding the radios, planes and boats, as Alaskan life is geared for using this equipment.

There's no need to bring all your food to this north country, as Anchorage and other large communities have well stocked supermarkets. For the best maps of the mountains see the Geologic Survey in Anchorage.

**Map:** Tyonek, Lake Clark, Kenai, and Iliamna, 1 : 250,000, 1 : 62,500 maps from USGS.

Mt. Hunter left, Foraker right. South and west of Mt. McKinley (Map 172).

## Map 171-2, Gerdine, Chigmit Mts., Alaska, USA

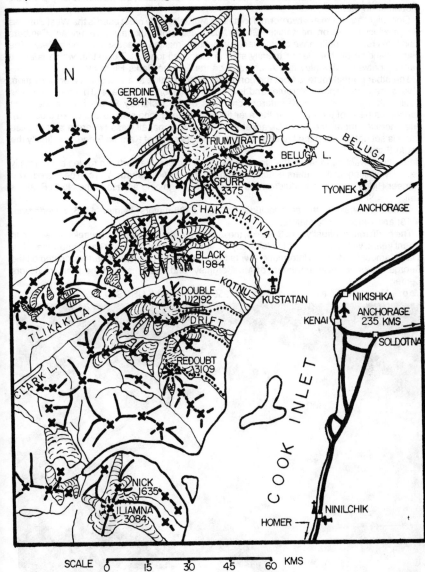

SCALE 0 15 30 45 60 KMS

# Mt. McKinley, Alaska Range, Alaska, USA

Mt. McKinley's south peak is 6195 meters, and is the highest summit in North America. McKinley is part of a large national park which covers much of the Alaska Range.

McKinley has a snow line beginning at about 1400 and continues to about 6200 meters, an elevation difference of 4800 meters. This is considered the greatest in the world. The main reason of course, is the fact that it lies at 63 degree north latitude, the most northerly of any big mountain on earth.

One might say there are two normal routes up McKinley. The most used is the West Buttress Route, which begins on the Kahiltna Glacier, just outside the national park boundary. Climbers using this route usually have only 2 weeks vacation—making it necessary to fly halfway. The planes landing on the glacier usually start in the small town of Talkeetna, which is about halfway between McKinley and Anchorage on the George Parks Highway.

The other normal route is from the north and Wonder Lake, at about 600 meters elevation. This is the more "sporting" route, and is for those with longer holidays. This route involves wading through about 25-30 different channels of the McKinley River—one of the most dangerous parts of the trip (near the river find a 2-3 meter long stick to use when crossing). Then across tundra, the small Clearwater River to McGonagall Pass (where a sort of base camp is set up), then up the Muldrow Glacier, the upper part of Karsten Ridge, and finally the South Summit.

For those wanting to reach the North Peak, 6058 meters, the northern routes are normally used. By walking up the Peters Glacier, the north face or Wickersham Wall can be scaled. The Pioneer Ridge, west of the Muldrow, has been used in gaining access to the North Peak as well.

Other high peaks in the area include: Foraker, 5303 meters; Hunter, 4445; Silverthrone, 4015; and Carpe, 3802 meters.

The north routes usually take 3 weeks, the airlift route about 10 days to 2 weeks. However, in recent years, with the coming of "Alpine Style Climbing," these times are being shortened. For a large amount of detailed information, write to or stop at, the park headquarters located on the George Parks Highway northeast of Mt. McKinley, and 112 kms from the Eielson Visitors Center.

**Map:**  Mount McKinley National Park, 1 : 250,000, from the USGS.

Foto taken from the lower part of the Pioneer Ridge, and North Peak.

## Map 172-1, McKinley, Alaska Ra., Alaska, USA

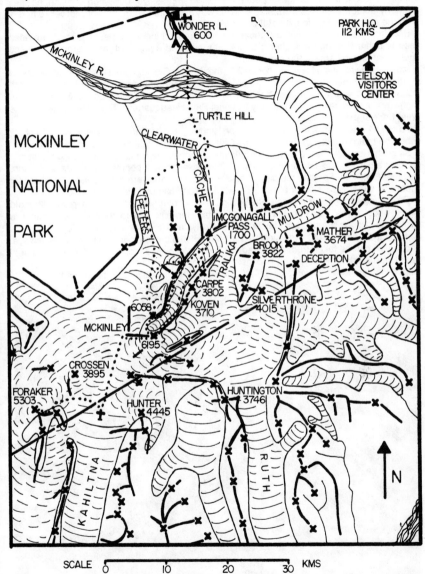

WONDER L.
600

PARK H.Q.
112 KMS

McKINLEY R.

EIELSON
VISITORS
CENTER

TURTLE HILL

CLEARWATER

MCKINLEY

NATIONAL

PARK

PETERS

CACHE

TRALIKA

MULDROW

MCGONAGALL
PASS
1700

MATHER
3674

BROOK
3822

DECEPTION

CARPE
3802

KOVEN
3710

SILVERTHRONE
4015

6058

MCKINLEY
6195

CROSSEN
3895

HUNTINGTON
3746

FORAKER
5303

HUNTER
4445

RUTH

KAHILTNA

N

SCALE  0        10        20        30   KMS

# Mt. Hayes, Alaska Range, Alaska, USA

Shown on this map is the central and eastern portions of the Alaska Range, and the area east of Mt. McKinley National Park.

The highest and most famous mountain in the region is Mt. Hayes, 4189 meters. It's considered one of the best climbs in the state. To the west of Hayes is Mt. Deborah, 3823 meters. The elevations of these peaks aren't too impressive, but when considering their northerly latitude, they present obstacles in the way of weather and glaciation, not very different from the much higher summits of the Himalayas.

Because of the tremendous distances involved in reaching these peaks, aircraft are often used to either land on the higher glaciers with men and equipment, or to airdrop food and equipment to climbers on the mountains.

Most people climbing Hayes either walk to the Susitna Glacier from a place called Denali, or are flown in to that same general area. Two approach routes are possible in reaching Mt. Deborah. One is to walk up the Yanart River and Glacier, beginning on the George Parks Highway not far south of Mt. McKinley National Park Headquarters. The other route is up the West Fork of the Susitna River, beginning at Denali.

To climb in the area east of the Richardson Highway, on the Cannel Glacier and Mt. Kimball, either the main highway or the trail to the Chisna or Dempsey area can be used for access.

Since this area is close to McKinley Park, the rangers there could help in locating a pilot and plane to airlift supplies into the mountains. Otherwise, contact people in the area of Paxson, Delta, or Big Delta. For sure the distances are long, but planes are not absolutely required for access to either Hayes or Deborah. The whole expedition can be done on foot.

The only towns in the area are Delta or Big Delta, all other places on the map are either old mines, ghost towns, roadside gas stations or cabins for rent. Generally the climbing season is from June through August, but May brings long days and good weather, and September has perhaps the least amount of snow on the ground. Buses can be found on the main highways, and a train can be taken from Anchorage to Fairbanks, with a stop at Mt. McKinley National Park Headquarters. Hitch hiking is considered good in Alaska.

**Map:**  Healy and Mt. Hayes, 1 : 250,000, USGS. Also 1 : 62,500 maps available.

Mt. Deborah from the south. Normal route is from the left.

# Map 173-2, Hayes, Alaska Ra., Alaska, USA

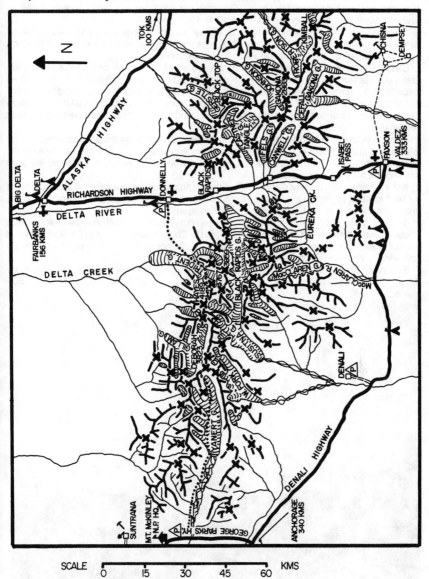

# Blackburn, Wrangell Mountains, Alaska, USA

In southeastern Alaska (not counting the panhandle), in the area east of Glennallen and Copper Center, and south of Slana and Tok Junction, are the Wrangell Mountains, one of Alaska's most extensive and highest mountain ranges. The highest summit in the range is Mt. Blackburn, 5037 meters. Second highest peak on the map is Mt. Bona 5006 meters, though some people may consider this peak a part of the St. Elias Mountains, which extends further to the southeast and includes Mt. Logan. Probably the most famous, and certainly the most visible mountain in the range, is Mt. Sanford at 4941 meters.

This map, like the others of the state of Alaska, covers a large area and does not show accurately glaciers or prominent ridges—but does show a generalized view of the area which will give a potential climber a good idea of what to expect.

Climbing is different in Alaska than in other areas of the USA or Canada. The great distances, lack of roads and trails, and large rivers, all combine to make almost any climb an expedition. As a result of these factors most climbs are made with the help of airplanes. With the highest concentration of light aircraft in the world, it's not difficult to find a pilot and plane to drop supplies into an area, or to land food, supplies and climbers onto back country glaciers or snowfields.

If you're planning to take a plane or have supplies airdropped into these mountains, look for planes and pilots at Copper Center, Glennallen Junction, Glennallen, or other nearby airfields. Anyone in this region can help locate qualified pilots, who in turn will assist in determining good landing places on the glaciers.

If one is determined to do it overland, then these routes may be used. For Mt. Blackburn, the easiest route of approach is from the south and somewhere between Strelna and McCarthy, along the old railway bed connecting old mining areas.

To climb Wrangell or Drum on foot, the closest routes from the south may be best, but may require taking a boat or raft of some kind to cross the Copper River. To reach Sanford, the least complicated route seems to be from Nebesna—at least there are no large streams to cross. By following river channels, muskeg and tundra can be avoided.

Best place to get supplies is in Anchorage, but Glennallen Junction has a couple of stores.

**Map:** Gulkana(s), Nabesna(s), Valdez, and McCarthy, all 1 : 250,000, USGS. Also 1 : 62,500 maps.

From the Tok Cut-off Highway, Sanford dominates the scene.

# Map 174-2, Blackburn, Wrangell Mts., Alaska, USA

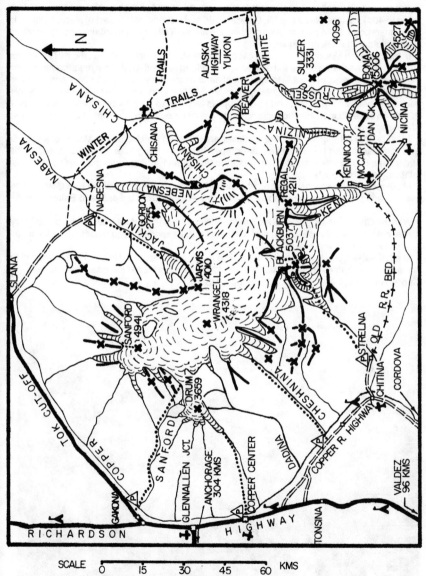

## Marcus Baker, Chugach Mountains, Alaska, USA

In south central Alaska, running from Anchorage to about the border of the Yukon Territory of Canada, are the Chugach Mountains. These mountains follow the coast and are the first of Alaska's mountains to be hit by the storms sweeping in from the Gulf of Alaska. This map covers the western half of the Chugach, the part from Anchorage to Valdez and the Richardson Highway.

There are some well known summits in this area, the most famous of which is Marcus Baker, rising to 4017 meters. Nearby is Mt. Goode, 3235 meters, and not far east of Marcus Baker, is Mt. Witherspoon, 3665 meters. Also on this map are the Talkeetna Mountains, located north of Jonesville and the Glenn Highway.

In the Chugach Mountains, as is the case in nearly all mountains in Alaska, most of the higher summits are reached with the aid of airlifts, in one form or another. If there are smooth landing places on a glacier, it's possible to land a light airplane there and unload climbers and supplies. This is what is done on the south slopes of Mt. McKinley. In other cases climbers take light packs and walk into the area, and have supplies dropped to them by parachute. Either way, it makes an expedition much shorter, and works well for those who have only a couple of weeks of holiday time.

Most people climbing in the Marcus Baker area, end up walking up the Matanuska Glacier with light packs, and have supplies air-dropped higher on the glacier. The bottom end of the Matanuska is only a few hundred meters from the Glenn Highway, and makes this mountain relatively easy to reach.

Mt. Goode can be approached from the Matanuska or the westerly flowing Knik Glacier. The final routes up both peaks are shown on the map—Goode from the east and Baker from the southwest.

With the Chugach being coastal mountains one must expect bad weather. There are long dry spells, but these are the exception and not the rule. Full expedition equipment is needed for all climbs. Sometimes winter weather is best.

In all of Alaska, Anchorage is the best place to shop for supplies. No need to import food to this area. Check the American Alpine Club Journal for additional information on routes.

**Map:** Anchorage and Valdez, 1 : 250,000, USGS. Also, 1 : 62,500 maps available.

The Nelchina Glacier comes from the heart of the Chugach Mts.

# Map 175-1, M. Baker, Chugach Mts., Alaska, USA

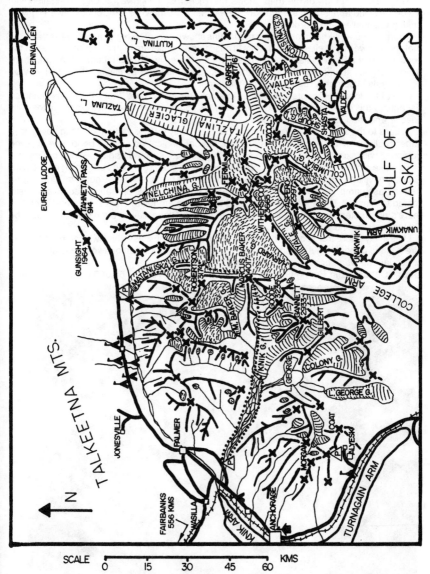

# Mt. Millar, Chugach Mountains, Alaska, USA

The map on the opposite page is of the eastern half of the Chugach Mountains, which lie along the Gulf of Alaska. The eastern portion of this map is of the area very near the boundary of Alaska and the Yukon Territory of Canada. Also, towards the eastern section of the map is the boundary of the Chugach and St. Elias Mountains.

The western portion of the map shows the Richardson Highway linking Glennallen with Valdez and the terminus of the Alaska Oil Pipeline. Also shown is the Copper River Highway linking Glennallen and Cordova.

There are no well-known or famous mountains shown here. The highest is Mt. Millar, at 3354 meters; followed by Stellar, 3130 meters. These two summits are high points on a ridge on the south side of the Bagley Glacier. Because there are no really high mountains in the area, there have been few attempted climbs; therefore, little information is available. There still may be some "firsts" left in this rugged and remote area.

One of the longest glaciers or ice fields in Alaska is located here, that's the Bagley Glacier. Essentially this same river of ice extends from Mts. Logan and Hubbard in the east, to the Mills Glacier and the Copper River Highway.

Access to the area can be done on foot, but that's only for those who have long holidays. If either Stellar or Millar were to be attempted, the only logical way would be to have a plane equipped with skis, fly in and land on one of the glaciers, such as Bagley, Bering or Guyot.

To make a climb a bit more of a climb, it's possible to carry light loads beginning on the Mills Glacier, or villages of Chilkat or Yakataga, and have the remainder of the supplies air-dropped near a base camp. Some kind of radio would be needed for this operation (radios are easily rented in Alaska). The state of Alaska, and the Yukon are full of bush planes and pilots, so there's no problem finding and lining up air transport. Glennallen or even Cordova would be likely places to find such a plane.

Little if any public transportation exists in the area. One must have his own car, hitch hike, or hire a plane or boat to get around. To have a successful climb, plan on two weeks at least, as continual bad weather makes fast climbing impossible.

**Map:**   Cordova and Bering Glacier, 1 : 250,000, USGS. And 1 : 62,500 maps available.

Eastern face and glacier of Mt. St. Elias (Map 177).

# Map 176-1, Millar, Chugach Mts., Alaska, USA

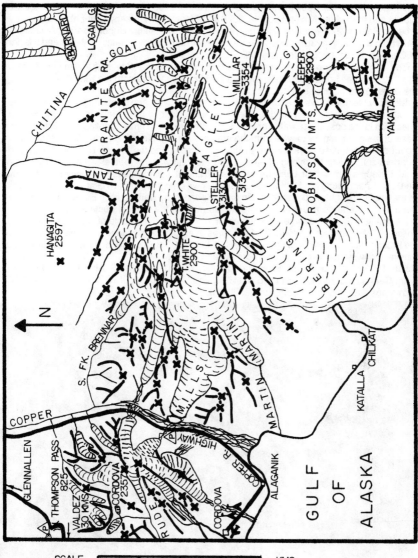

SCALE  0   15   30   45   60   KMS

## Mt. Logan, St. Elias Mountains, Yukon, Canada

The highest mountain in Canada, and the second highest mountain in North America, is located on this map. This is Mt. Logan, rising to 6052 meters. Logan lies in about the center of the St. Elias Mountains, which extend over the area from about Mt. Huxley in the west, to Glacier Bay (see Fairweather map). Haines and Skagway are in the southeast, and the Alaska Highway forms the northeastern boundary.

The second highest peak in the area is Mt. St. Elias, 5490 meters. It lies on the boundary of Alaska and the Yukon. Next is Lucania, 5228 and Steele, 5074 meters. Other high peaks in the area are Bear, 4527; Wood, 4843; Walsh, 4506; Vancouver, 4786; Hubbard, 4558; Alverstone, 4421; and Kennedy, 4238 meters. As is the case with all other mountains in Alaska and this part of Canada, these are isolated and difficult of access.

The original climb of Logan was in 1925, from the Alaska side and the mining town of McCarthy, up the Logan Glacier to the north side of the mountain, to the King Col, then along the ridge to the highest summit.

Most people nowadays fly onto the glacier with all supplies, and climb from this normal route, or others, such as the East Ridge. It has also been climbed from the south and the Seward Glacier. It is still possible to walk from the McCarthy area, and have supplies air dropped at the base of the mountain, or to walk from the area of Kluane Lake to the base of the mountain, in about one week or 10 days. Inquire at Haines Junction and the Kluane National Park Headquarters concerning the hiring of aircraft and the best walking routes.

Most people climbing St. Elias are flown from Yakutat onto the Malispina Glacier, south of the peak. Climbers taking Mt. Hubbard are usually flown onto the Hubbard Glacier south and west of that peak. It might be possible to climb Mt. Kennedy by walking from Haines Junction, but there are some large rivers in the area, which may be the biggest obstacle.

Haines Junction is the largest community in the area, with a couple of stores, gas stations, police (RCMP), and road crews. The best maps available can be found at the headquarters of the Kluane National Park, just northwest of the Junction. There's daily bus service all along the Alaska Highway, as well as to and from Haines, Alaska.

**Map:**  Bering Glacier, Mt. St. Elias and Yakutat, 1 : 250,000, USGS. Also 1 : 62,500 maps. From Canada Mount St. Elias(115B & 115C), and Kluane Lake(115G & 115F), 1 : 250,000, from Maps Canada, 615 Booth Street, Ottawa.

Mt. Logan left, King Peak on the right. King Col center.

## Map 177-2, Logan, St. Elias Mts., Yukon, Canada

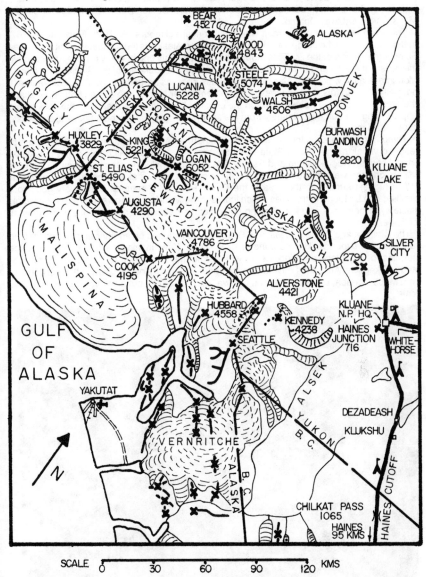

BEAR
4527

4213

WOOD
4843

ALASKA

STEELE
5074

LUCANIA
5228

WALSH
4506

BAGLEY

HUXLEY
3829

KING
5221

ST. ELIAS
5490

LOGAN
6052

BURWASH
LANDING
2820

KLUANE
LAKE

AUGUSTA
4290

SEWARD

VANCOUVER
4786

KASKAWULSH

SILVER
CITY

MALISPINA

COOK
4195

2790

ALVERSTONE
4421

KLUANE
N.P. HQ.

HUBBARD
4558

KENNEDY
4238

HAINES
JUNCTION
716

WHITE-
HORSE

GULF
OF
ALASKA

SEATTLE

YAKUTAT

ALSEK

DEZADEASH

KLUKSHU

VERNRITCHE

YUKON
B.C.

B.C.
ALASKA

HAINES CUTOFF

CHILKAT PASS
1065

HAINES
95 KMS

N

DONJEK

YUKON LOGAN

ALASKA

SCALE  0        30        60        90        120   KMS

# Fairweather, St. Elias Range, USA-Canada

This is the eight of nine maps covering the mountainous regions of Alaska, the Yukon and northwestern British Columbia.

All of these maps are small scale, that is, they show a large area; therefore, after getting in mind which mountains are to be attempted, more detailed maps will have to be found. Contact the US Geological Survey, in Anchorage, Alaska; the Kluane National Park Headquarters, Haines Junction, Yukon; US Geological Survey, Federal Center, Denver, Colorado; or Canada Maps Office, Ottawa, Ontario.

There are two areas of this map which will concern climbers. First, Mt. Fairweather, 4671 meters, located on the border of British Columbia and Alaska, is the highest summit in the area. Fairweather is part of the St. Elias Mountains, which is only one of many ranges running down the coasts of Alaska and British Columbia. It is also on the boundary of the Glacier Bay National Monument, all of which is in Alaska, and includes all areas around Glacier Bay. Fairweather is normally climbed this way. Planes are taken from either Haines or Yakutat, both in Alaska, to the area around Cape Fairweather, on the coast of the Gulf of Alaska. Then the walk inland, approaching the summit ultimately from the southwest. Serious climbers take 2 to 3 weeks of supplies to the area.

The other main area is the Juneau Icefields, north of Alaska's state capital. Juneau can be reached via air or the Alaska State Ferry System, which runs to all points along the Alaska coast between Kodiak Island and Seattle, Washington, including stops at several Canadian cities along the way. If you're taking a vehicle on that ferry, make reservations in advance.

The highest summit in the area is the Devils Paw, 2617 meters. Some very good rock climbing can be found in this area which includes the Mendenhall Towers. There are also big glaciers, so both rock and ice climbing equipment is needed for some peaks of the Juneau Icefields.

The Chilkoot and White Passes, and Skagway are included on another map. Plenty of food supplies can be found in Haines, Juneau, or Skagway. Keep in mind that this area is one of the stormiest of any place on earth. Better weather seems to come in the winter months.

**Map:** Skagway, Atlin, Mt. Fairweather and Juneau, USGS. And Skagway, Atlin and Juneau, from Maps Canada, 615 Booth Street, Ottawa. All 1 : 250,000, but also available in 1 : 62,500 scale.

The northern slopes of Mt. Fairweather.

# Map 178-1, Fairweather, St. Elias Ra., USA-Canada

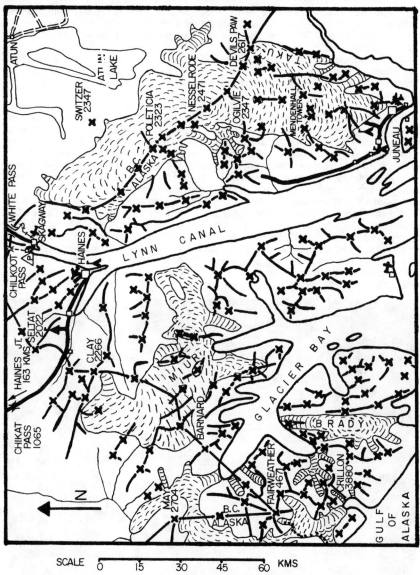

SCALE  0   15   30   45   60   KMS

## Chilkoot Trail, Alaska—B.C., USA-Canada

The Chilkoot Trail involves little if any mountaineering, but the historical significance of the "Gold Rush Trail of 1898" is worth taking a look at. The trail is 53 kms long and takes many people 3 days for the walk; but others do it in 4 or 5, especially if a family with children is involved.

One should begin in Skagway. It's not the exact beginning of the trail, but there's an office of the Gold Rush Historic Park there, which should be your first stop. Park rangers offer free movies of the historical aspects of the trail, Skagway, White Pass Railroad, and the entire Gold Rush scene of 1898. They can also give you trail guides and other information needed concerning the hike.

Getting to Skagway is now a lot easier than in the not too distant past. It can be reached by ferry from the towns and cities of the inland passage of Alaska and British Columbia; by train from Whitehorse—capital of the Yukon; and as of 1978, by highway from Carcross and Whitehorse.

Most people doing the hike begin at Dyea, and end the trip at Bennett Lake and railway station. From there, they either return to Skagway by train, or go on to Whitehorse. There are trains arriving at Bennett about noon every day. If your hike ends in Bennett, buy your ticket in Skagway before starting the hike. The price of the ticket includes your sourdough meal, which is served to every passenger on every train, at around noon each day at the Bennett station. Arrive at the station before noon on any day, have your meal, and get on the train. Remember, stop at the Historic Park office for the latest information concerning the train schedules. There is no road to Bennett, so one must take the train or walk from that area.

Equipment and gear needed for the hike would include: waterproof tent, warm sleeping bag and clothes, rain gear, gloves, good boots and a camera. There are shelters in the Canyon City area (Km 11), at Km 17, and at Lindeman City (Km 42). Park rangers can be found at Sheep Camp Shelter (Km 17), and Lindeman City. If you're on the Canadian side, information can be obtained at the RCMP in Whitehorse or Carcross, or at the train station in Whitehorse. Hikers are requested to report to emigration and customs when arriving at either Skagway or Whitehorse after the hike.

**Map:**   Skagway, 1 : 250,000, USGS, and several 1 : 62,500 maps.

An 1898 foto of the Golden Staircase, up to the top of Chilkoot P.

## Map 179-1, Chilkoot Trail, Alaska-BC, USA-Canada

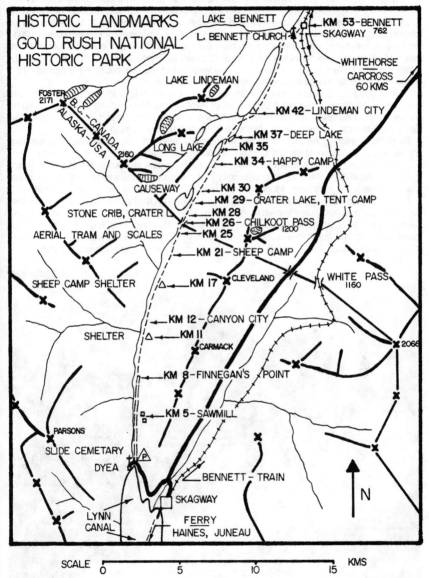

HISTORIC LANDMARKS
GOLD RUSH NATIONAL
HISTORIC PARK

LAKE BENNETT
L. BENNETT CHURCH

KM 53-BENNETT
SKAGWAY 762

WHITEHORSE
CARCROSS
60 KMS

LAKE LINDEMAN

FOSTER
2171

B.C. - CANADA

ALASKA-USA

2160

KM 42-LINDEMAN CITY

KM 37-DEEP LAKE

KM 35

KM 34-HAPPY CAMP

LONG LAKE

CAUSEWAY

KM 30

KM 29-CRATER LAKE, TENT CAMP

STONE CRIB, CRATER L.

KM 28

KM 26-CHILKOOT PASS 1200

AERIAL TRAM AND SCALES

KM 25

KM 21-SHEEP CAMP

SHEEP CAMP SHELTER

KM 17 CLEVELAND

WHITE PASS
1160

KM 12-CANYON CITY

SHELTER

KM 11

CARMACK

2066

KM 8-FINNEGAN'S POINT

KM 5-SAWMILL

PARSONS

SLIDE CEMETARY

DYEA

P

BENNETT - TRAIN

N

SKAGWAY

LYNN
CANAL

FERRY
HAINES, JUNEAU

SCALE   0        5          10         15   KMS

# Asgard, Baffin Island, N.W. Territories, Canada

One of the most unusual and far out places on earth for climbing is in the Northwest Territories of Canada, and more precisely, on Baffin Island. Much of this island is covered with ice, but the coastal areas, for the most part, resemble parts of southwestern Greenland, having some grassy places, but with swampy muskeg dominating the river bottoms.

The best known part of Baffin Island is called the Cumberland Peninsula. It's here at the head of the South Pangnirtung Fjord, that is found a group of peaks which rank among the best in the world for rock climbing. The highest peak in the region is Tete Blanche, at 2156 meters, but the best known and the most spectacular is the flatopped—twin summits of Asgard, rising to 2011 meters. By most standards these are not high, but they're just above the Artic Circle, in a very isolated place, and rise vertically from about 400 meters. These peaks have been shaped by glaciation and have many sheer walls. In some ways they resemble peaks in Patagonia and in Yosemite Park, as the best ones are made of solid granite.

Unless you have a boat of your own, the only way to reach this area is by plane. There are flights from Montreal to the small settlement of Pangnirtung. Pangnirtung is a former eskimo settlement, but is now a bit of a tourist place—with a hotel, campground, a small "supermarket", and the headquarters of the Pangnirtung National Park located there.

From Pangnirtung, one can walk—but most groups hire a boat or snowmobiles, to get from the airfield to the head of the fjord. This cuts down the walking distance enormously.

From the head of the fjord, where is located a national park shelter, to the area of Summit Lake, is about 40 kms. This is a difficult journey as there are large streams to cross and plenty of marshy muskeg to negotiate. Mosquitos in summer make this trip even more miserable.

Parks Canada has erected shelters at Summit Lake and at the head of Owl Valley (the exact locations of these huts is not known to the author). The area has only about one month of fine weather each year, so go prepared for wet, cold and windy conditions. Inquire at the national parks office for the latest information on all facets of climbing in the area.

**Map:** Pangnirtung, 1 : 250,000, from Maps Canada, 615 Booth Street, Ottawa.

Asgard with its famous square top.

# Map 180-3, Asgard, Baffin Isl., N.W. Terr., Canada

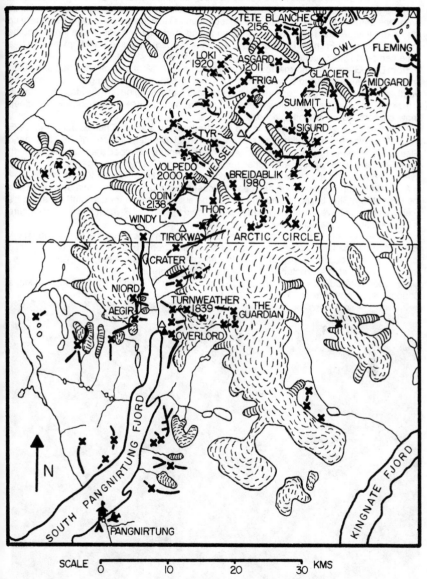

TETE BLANCHE 2156

OWL

FLEMING

LOKI 1920

ASGARD 2011

FRIGA

GLACIER L.

MIDGARD

SUMMIT L.

SIGURD

TYR

WEASEL

VOLPEDO 2000

BREIDABLIK 1980

ODIN 2138

THOR

WINDY L.

TIROKWA

ARCTIC CIRCLE

CRATER L.

NIORD

AEGIR

TURNWEATHER 1839

THE GUARDIAN

OVERLORD

N

SOUTH PANGNIRTUNG FJORD

KINGNATE FJORD

PANGNIRTUNG

SCALE 0    10    20    30 KMS

# Waddington, Coast Range, B.C., Canada

Mt. Waddington, at 4017 meters, is the highest mountain in British Columbia and in the Coast Range of Canada. Waddington lies about due north of Vancouver Island, and near the west coast of B.C. The mountain is very remote and difficult of access. Because of the wild nature of the region, very few attempts have been made to climb the peak.

The normal route of approach is by sea and the Knight Inlet. Most people doing this climb will likely begin in Vancouver, or at one of many small harbors along the coast of Vancouver Island. From one of these places, one must locate a boat and sail to the northwest and eventually up the Knight Inlet. At the head of this inlet is an abandoned lumber camp. From the camp, the route heads up the Franklin River and Glacier. It takes about 3 days to walk from the inlet to a base camp on Dais Glacier.

From Dais Glacier, the normal route is up the south face. Most groups have had extra food and supplies airdropped to a camp near the peak. It appears that with good luck from the weather, this climb could be done in less than 10 days, but this region is in the storm track much of the year, so plan on a longer stay than 10 days. The ultimate route up the peak involves steep snow couliors, so go equipped accordingly.

A second route up Waddington is via the Tiedemann Glacier. One expedition in 1975 (AAJ-1976) was flown into the area and left at a small lake near the end of the Tiedemann Glacier. From there they walked up the glacier and eventually climbed the peak via the north ridge. They also had supplies airdropped near a place called Rainy Knob. That particular group eventually traversed the massif and came down the Franklin Glacier to Knight Inlet.

As of 1980, apparently no one had been succesful in climbing the mountain by walking into the region from Bluff Lake. The maps used by the author shows a road to Bluff Lake, but it's likely more roads have since been made further down the Mosley River. If that is so, the future may see more groups walking in from the north.

For someone interested in climbing around the Homathko Icefield, the normal approach route seems to be from the Chilko Lake and Nine Mile Creek (both to the east of Homathko Icefield). One group traversed the icefield and came out on the Heakamie Glacier. They finished the trip at Waddington Harbor, at the head of Bute Inlet.

**Map:** Mount Waddington, 92-N, 1 : 250,000, and 92-N-3 and 6, both at 1 : 50,000, from Maps Canada, 615 Booth Street, Ottawa.

The west face of Waddington. Not an easy climb.

# Map 181-3, Waddington, Coast Ra., BC, Canada

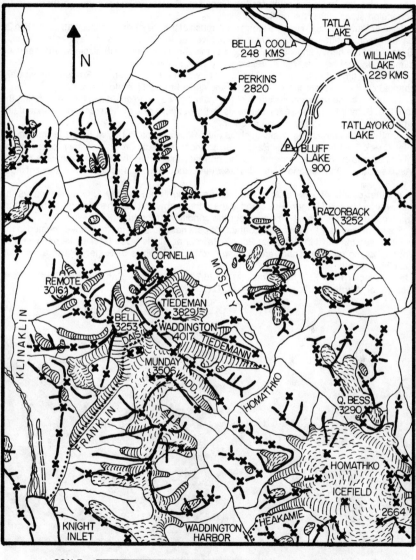

N

TATLA LAKE

BELLA COOLA 248 KMS

WILLIAMS LAKE 229 KMS

PERKINS 2820

TATLAYOKO LAKE

P BLUFF LAKE 900

RAZORBACK 3252

CORNELIA

MOSLEY

REMOTE 3016

TIEDEMAN 3829

BELL 3253

DAIS

WADDINGTON 4017

TIEDEMANN

KLINAKLIN

MUNDAY 3506

WADD.

HOMATHKO

Q. BESS 3290

FRANKLIN

HOMATHKO

ICEFIELD

2664

HEAKAMIE

KNIGHT INLET

WADDINGTON HARBOR

SCALE    0    15    30    45    KMS

# Glacier National Park, Selkirk Mts., B.C., Canada

Glacier National Park of British Colombia, is located west of Banff, in the Selkirk Mountains. There are no dominating summits here, but a number of peaks over 3300 meters are found in an area south of National Highway 1, and other areas to the north of the highway, over 3200 meters.

Highway 1 cuts through the middle of the park, affording good access, at least near the road. This is also the main rail route for the Canadian Pacific Railroad, although there are no scheduled stops within the park.

Glacier Park seems to lie in the storm track much of the year, having precipitation on 15 to 20 days of each month, with lesser amounts received during the months of May through August. Because of the heavy snowfall, 12 percent of the park is covered with glaciers. Snow and ice climbing is most popular, but there are some rock routes as well.

Access is limited to a handful of trails, all of which are well marked. Some of these trails marked on the map are fire-break roads and closed to public motor vehicles.

To reach the higher summits south of the main highway, one could use the trail running the length of Beaver River. However, the trail is on the opposite side of the river from the mountains and that river may or may not be fordable.

Another way of reaching peaks such as Fluz, Wheeler and Purity, would be to walk up the Flat Creek Trail to Flat Creek Pass, then to Incomappleux Creek and east to any of the glaciated peaks. However, it appears the normal route to the three peaks mentioned is via Asulkan Creek, Asulkan and Donkin Passes, the Bishop Glacier, thence to any or most of those peaks.

Another couple of trails exist to the high peaks north of Highway 1. One trail leaves the highway just north of Rogers Pass, and leads to the Hermit Hut, which sleeps about 8 persons. Inquire at Rogers Pass or Glacier about the condition of the hut.

For more maps and information, contact the park headquarters in Revelstoke, located to the west, or see the warden's office at Rogers Pass or at Glacier. Use Revelstoke or Golden as your shopping centers. There are lodging and dining facilities at Rogers Pass, as well as gasoline, but little else.

**Map:** Glacier Park-British Columbia, 1 : 126,720, from Maps Canada, 615 Booth Street, Ottawa, or Wardens Office, Rogers Pass, B.C.

This is the Hermit Hut not far above Rogers Pass.

# Map 182-1, Glacier N.P., Selkirk Mts., BC, Canada

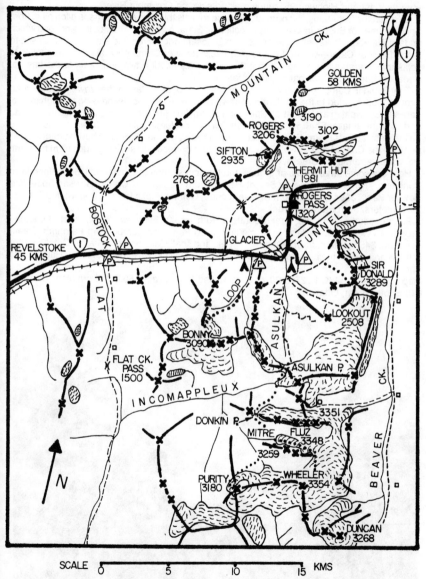

# Bugaboos, Purcell Range, B.C., Canada

The Bugaboo Group is a small cluster of sheer granite spires, which rate among the best rock climbing areas of Canada, North America, and the world. Probably the most famous peak in the group and on this map, is Bugaboo Spire, rising to 3186 meters.

The area covered here is located in the northern Purcell Mountains, south of Glacier National Park (B.C.), west of Radium Hot Springs, and north of Kootenay Lake. Most access roads are from the east and Highway 95, running along side the Columbia River.

To reach the Bugaboos, the normal approach route is this. Drive, or perhaps hitch hike, from Spillimacheen or Brisco, in a westerly direction up Bugaboo Creek. This is a logging road which ends at Bugaboo Forks, where is located the Gmoser Lodge. From there a good trail is used to reach Boulder Camp—about 4 hours with pack. Boulder Camp now has a large shelter to accommodate about 50 people. From this shelter it's about a two-hour walk to the base of Bugaboo Spire and Snowpatch, 3064 meters.

The Boulder Camp route is also one of the traditional routes to the Vowell and Conrad Groups, both located to the north and northwest of the Bugaboos. By passing through the col between Snowpatch and Bugaboo Spire, one can make a glacier traverse to the northwest and end up at the smaller Shaft %7 Hut. This shelter, which sleeps only about 8 persons, is located on the west face of Osprey Peak and east side of Malloy Glacier. From this hut one can climb all peaks in the Conrad and Vowell Groups. One can also reach these two groups from the north via Vowell and Malloy Creeks.

Here are some other peaks or groups and the access routes: Ethelbert, 3159 meters, from Dunbar or Templeton Creeks; Septet Peaks, from Templeton Creek; Howser Spire and Howser Peak, 3094 meters, from Gmoser Lodge; Quintet Peaks from G. Lodge; and Taurus, 2972 meters, from Frances Creek.

Further south, climb the Four Squatters from Healy; Eyebrow, 3354, from Horsethief Creek—as well as Stockdale, 3125 meters; climb Peter and Jumbo from Farnham Creek; Farnham, 3458 meters, from Horsethief Creek; and finally Mcbeth from Glacier Creek. Plenty of snow and rock climbing here, but bad weather too. Buy food in either Golden or Radium Hot Springs.

**Map:** Lardeau, 82-K, 1 : 250,000, or 82-K-10 and 15, both at 1 : 50,000, from Maps Canada, 615 Booth Street, Ottawa.

From the Bugaboo Lodge we see Bugabbo G. and Snow Patch, right.

# Map 183-1, Bugaboos, Purcell Ra., BC, Canada

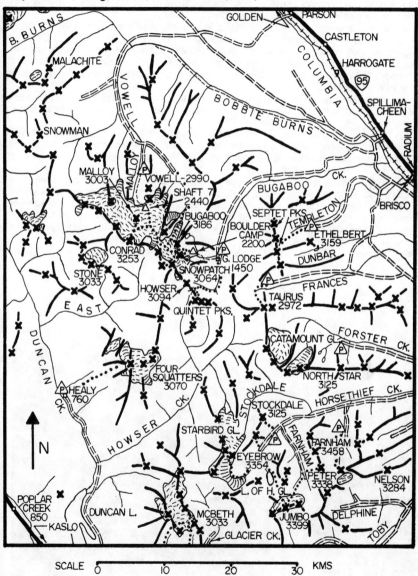

B. BURNS
GOLDEN
PARSON
CASTLETON
HARROGATE
95
SPILLIMA-CHEEN
RADIUM
MALACHITE
VOWELL
BOBBIE BURNS
COLUMBIA
SNOWMAN
MALLOY 3003
MALLOY
P
VOWELL 2990
SHAFT 7 2440
BUGABOO 3186
BUGABOO CK.
SEPTET PKS
TEMPLETON
P
BRISCO
BOULDER CAMP 2200
ETHELBERT 3159
CONRAD 3253
P
B.G. LODGE 1450
DUNBAR
STONE 3033
SNOWPATCH 3064
HOWSER 3094
P
FRANCES
EAST
QUINTET PKS.
TAURUS 2972
CATAMOUNT GL.
FORSTER CK.
P
DUNCAN CK.
FOUR SQUATTERS 3070
NORTH STAR 3125
STOCKDALE
HORSETHIEF CK.
P
HEALY 760
STOCKDALE 3125
FARNHAM 3458
P
HOWSER CK.
STARBIRD GL.
FARNHAM
P
N
EYEBROW 3354
PETER 3338
NELSON 3284
POPLAR CREEK 850
DUNCAN L.
L. OF H. GL.
DELPHINE
KASLO
MCBETH 3033
JUMBO 3399
GLACIER CK.
TOBY

SCALE 0    10    20    30    KMS

## Stalin, Stone Mt. Provincial Park, B.C., Canada

At about Km 645 (Mile 400) along the Alaska Highway, sits Summit Lake in the heart of the Stone Mountain Provincial Park. Immediately on either side of Summit Lake, are easy climbs up to just over 2100 meters. For the people driving the Alaska Highway, climbing one of these summits could be an excellent break from the monotony of that long drive. Some of these nearby peaks take only about half a day for the trip. Summit Lake has a highway maintenance shop, and a gas station-cabins-store complex.

To the south and southwest of Summit Lake, are a number of glaciated peaks with elevations of about 2750 to 2900 meters. They include Yedhe, Roosevelt, Churchill, and Stalin the highest, at 2896 meters. It's not as easy getting to these peaks as to those near the highway. For a 1966 expedition to this region, the use of float planes made it easier. It's possible to fly to Tachodi and Wokkpash Lakes, or possibly to a landing strip built for a copper mining operation east of Roosevelt Peak.

If hiring a plane is too expensive, there was at one time a 4WD road built along the west side of Racing River, to the previously mentioned copper mine, but there were no bridges as of 1966.

For the person who wants to hike into this back country, it's a long way, but easy on that old road; or if going cross-country, it's not too difficult either, as the brush is low and scattered. Trees are non-existent above about 1400 meters. To the copper mine is around 50 kms—or perhaps a 3 or 4 day walk with heavy pack.

The glaciers are extensive enough to be of concern for the solo climber, so go with care. There's also no corner grocery store, so do all your shopping in Ft. Nelson, or points south.

Winter climbing—using skis and perhaps sleds for supplies, might be easier than in summer, with no river-fording problems. One can get maps of the area at Whitehorse, Ft. Nelson, St. John, or Dawson Creek (beginning of the Alaska Highway). Weather is essentially bad much of the year so prepare for that. Hitching is generally good on the Alaska Highway.

**Map:**  Tuchodi Lakes, 94-K, 1 : 250,000, from Maps Canada, 615 Booth Street, Ottawa.

On top of St. Paul Mountain just off the Alaska Highway.

# Map 184-1, Stalin, Stone Mt. P.P., BC, Canada

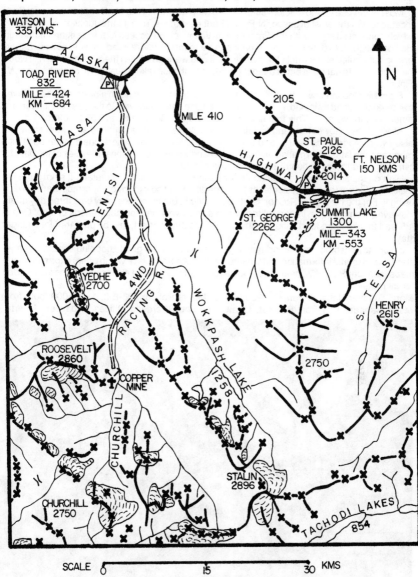

WATSON L.
335 KMS

ALASKA

TOAD RIVER
832
MILE—424
KM—684

P

N

MILE 410

2105

YASA

HIGHWAY

ST. PAUL
2126

FT. NELSON
150 KMS

TENTSI

2014

P

ST. GEORGE
2262

SUMMIT LAKE
1300
MILE—343
KM—553

S. TETSA

YEDHE
2700

4WD

RACING R.

WOKKPASH LAKE

HENRY
2615

ROOSEVELT
2860

1258

2750

COPPER
MINE

CHURCHILL

STALIN
2896

CHURCHILL
2750

TACHODI LAKES
854

SCALE  0          15          30  KMS

## Mt. Robson, Robson Provincial Park, B.C., Canada

Mt. Robson is the highest mountain in the Canadian Rockies at 3954 meters. Robson is a magnificent peak, standing for the most part alone, and towering over its neighbors. As with the other Rocky Mountains in Jasper and Banff National Parks, it is made up of limestone, which has been folded and uplifted. Robson is presently capped with, and surrounded by, many glaciers.

Most of the peaks and glaciers seen on this map are part of the Mt. Robson Provincial Park, located just to the west of Jasper N.P. and northeast of the Tete Jaune Junction. Highway 16, which connects Jasper with the Fraser River Valley, offers access to this park and mountain. Besides Highway 16, access to the park can be made by the railroad as well; however, there are no scheduled stops within the park itself. If one were arriving in the area on a train, it would be necessary to get off at either Jasper or Valemount, then take a bus, drive, or hitch hike to Mt. Robson.

From Mt. Robson town, there's a short road (2.4 kms) running north along the Robson River, to a parking lot and trailhead. From this trailhead one can easily walk to the base of Robson and other sites in the park. This trail is heavily used up to Berg Lake, at 1638 meters.

At Mt. Robson town, food and gasoline are available, but in very limited amounts. There are also two campgrounds nearby and a visitor information center, where one can get additional maps and the latest information on trails, snow and weather conditions, the rules of the park for climbers, and the condition of the hut on the mountain.

High on the south ridge is located the Robson Hut, at about 2440 meters. It's not large, so make inquiries at the visitors center as to its condition and how many other climbers are already using it. For the most part, Robson is a two day climb, but for some it may be a three day affair. However, weather is an important factor and can be very bad for long periods of time. One is advised to take extra food if the weather looks less than perfect, and be prepared for a longer stay.

Jasper town would be an important stop, because it has a good shopping center, a ranger station, and tourist information and weather offices. Another place which offers information and maps is Jasper Park HQ., near Moose Lake (on Highway 16). Ice ax and crampons are needed for all routes.

**Map:** Jasper National Park, 1 : 250,000, or Mount Robson, 83-E-3, 1 : 50,000, both from Maps Canada, 615 Booth Street, Ottawa, or from Wardens Offices in Jasper, Alberta.

This is the north slopes of Mt. Robson, from Berg Lake.

# Map 185-1, Robson, Robson P.P., BC, Canada

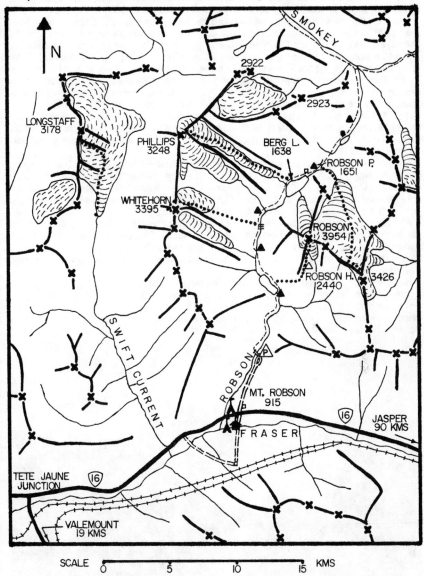

# North Jasper National Park, Alberta, Canada.

The map included here is of the northern half of Jasper National Park and the better part of Mount Robson Provincial Park. Jasper is entirely in Alberta, while Robson is in B.C. (For details on Mount Robson see the previous map). This region is due west of Edmonton, Alberta, and directly northwest of Banff National Park. It's also just north of Jasper townsite. This region has some of the highest peaks in the Canadian Rockies, but the emphasis here is not on the climbing of peaks so much as in some of the best backcountry hiking in Canada.

The one major hike on the map is often called the North Boundary Trail. It begins (or ends) at the Celestine Lake Trailhead, located about 45 kms north of Jasper townsite, and ends (or begins) at the Mount Robson Trailhead. The walking distance is about 150 kms. The well-used and well-maintained trail runs up the Snake Indian River, passing Snake Indian Falls after about 20 kms. All along the way are small wardens' cabins, used by wardens in trail maintenance. They are closed to the public. Eventually one crosses Snake Indian Pass, at 2019, then descends to Twintree Lake, and up the Smokey River. This is where the trail passes the best scenery and the highest mountains, but which is often cloud-covered. Finally over Robson Pass, 1651 meters, past Berg Lake and Mount Robson, and to the trailhead. This hike can be covered in about 6 days by very determined hikers, but a week to 10 days is more common. Because of the length of the hike, expect some bad weather enroute, and always expect foul weather around Robson.

For those with less time, there are some alternative hikes. From the Devona Trailhead, one can walk along the CNR tracks for 11 kms to the Miette Warden Cabin, where the trail up Moosehorn Creek to Moosehorn Lakes begins. One can follow this trail further on to Rock Lake, or walk south following Snake Indian River back to Celestine Lake. This loop is about 100 kms, with the distance to Moosehorn Lakes about 35 kms.

Another alternative would be to hike up the Moose River from Moose Lake, eventually joining the trail up Smokey River, and ending at Mount Robson. One can also hike to the top of Pyramid Peak, just above Jasper. For Pyramid, first drive to Pyramid Lake, the end-of-road. Walk up the fire road to near the fire lookout, but turn left or west on a road going to the tramway, then route-find to the summit.

See the visitor information center in Jasper townsite for hiking and camping restrictions and weather inform. Jasper town has all services and facilities, but is crowded in July and August, which are also the best weather months.

**Map:** Jasper National Park, 1 : 250,000, from Wardens Offices in the park, or from Maps Canada, Surveys and Mapping, Ottawa, K1A OE9.

An easy climb not far from Jasper is Pyramid Peak.

# Map 186-1, North Jasper Nat. P., Alberta, Can.

SCALE

0    5    10    15    20    25    KMS

# Edith Cavell, Jasper Nat. Park, Alberta, Canada

The mountains and valleys on this map are found in west central Jasper National Park, which is located in the Canadian Rockies due west of Edmonton, Alberta, and directly south of Jasper townsite. The highest summit and the best known peak on the map is Edith Cavell, at 3363 meters. Not far below is Mt. Fryatt, 3361 meters. There are a number of peaks above 3000 meters here and some good sized glaciers, especially the ones around Mt. Hooker. The climbs are mostly difficult and made for experienced mountaineers.

Access to most peaks in this area is via Highway 93A, which begins about 7 kms south of Jasper, and runs south to Athabasca Falls, where it joins Highway 93 running to Banff. To climb Edith Cavell, drive south from Highway 93A on the Cavell Road to Cavell Lake. The normal route goes up the western slopes of the ridge to the east of the lake. From the ridge top the route turns south and follows this ridge which eventually turns west to the summit. One can also climb the southwest ridge, which is reached via Astoria and Verdant Creeks.

To climb Fryatt, drive west and north from Athabasca Falls on Highway 93A, until reaching the Geraldine Fire Road (about 1 km). Drive this road (then trail) south and up Fryatt Creek to Fryatt Lake, where is located a climbers' shelter named Vallance Hut. The normal route runs to the northwest up the headwaters of Fryatt Creek to the pass or col on the south ridge. From there route-find north to the summit veering to the west side of the summit. The same south ridge can also be gained via the Whirlpool River and Divergence Creek. From this same base camp-area climbers can also climb Christie, Lovell and Belanger Peaks.

To climb Hooker, Evans, Kane, Serenity, Oates and others in the area of Athabasca Pass, drive to Moab Lake and walk up the Whirlpool River. Hooker, Evans and Oates can all be ascended by using a base camp located on Scott Creek and the lake in that basin.

Another popular climbing area is in the region of Amethyst Lakes. Park at the parking lot at Cavell Lake, and walk up the Astoria River to Amethyst Lakes or to the Wates-Gibson Hut 3 or 4 kms to the south of the lakes. Peaks such as Eremite and Parapet can be climbed from the hut.

Be sure and stop at the wardens office-visitor center in Jasper before entering any of these areas, and get the latest word on river crossings and to buy better maps. Jasper has a weather station, railway depot, and plenty of food and book stores.

**Map:** Jasper National Park, 1 : 250,000, from Wardens Offices in the park, or from Maps Canada, Surveys and Mapping, Ottawa, K1A OE9.

The 1300 meter north face of Edith Cavell.

# Map 187-2, Edith Cavell, Jasper N.P., Alb., Can.

MOUNT ROBSON

BEAVER L.

P | MALIGNE R.

N

JASPER 1050

16

TEKARRA 2688   2774

MEDICINE LAKE 1450

2791

ROCHE N.

MEADOW

2464

2000

MALIGNE L. 1671

MARMOT 2608

P

ATHABASCA R.

93A   93

MANX

PORTAL

LECTERN

MAJESTIC 3086

MACCARIB

ASTORIA R.

MOAT L.

AMETHYST LAKES 1750

CAVELL

P

E. CAVELL 3363

MOAB L.

ATHABASCA FALLS 1300

THRONE

P

PARAPET

P

2984

SCARP

FREMITE

ELEPHAS

RIVER

GERALDINE LAKES

BANFF

SIMON CK.

1370

DIVERGE

FRYATT 3361

FRYATT

CHRISTIE 3103

SUNWAPTA FALLS P

BEACON   NEEDLE

MIDDLE WHIRLPOOL

2827

3161

BELANGER 3109   LOVELL

LICK CK.

ATHABASCA R.

WHIRLPOOL

SCOTT

MALLARD

LICK

CATACOMBS

R. COX

LICK

EVANS   OATES

ALNUS CK.

DRAGON

CATACOMBS 3292

KANE

HOOKER

SERENITY

FORTRESS

BROWN 2799

ATHABASCA PASS

WOOD

FORTRESS L. 1336

SCALE   0   5   10   15   20   25   KMS

# South Jasper Nat. Park, Alberta, Canada.

The area covered by this map is the southern half of the Jasper National Park in western Alberta. This region is immediately north and northwest of Banff National Park. The highest summit in the area east of the Icefields Highway (93) is M. Brazeau, at 3470 meters. Next highest is Poboktan Peak rising to 3323 meters. The higher peaks to the west of Highway 93 are covered in the mapped area of Mt. Columbia.

Climbing in this area is not as popular as it is in the higher peaks to the west and along the continental divide. Keep in mind, these peaks and valleys are at slightly lower elevation than those to the west—therefore, it's noticeably drier with generally sunnier skies. As a result, for most people this region has the potential to be a more enjoyable place to visit, hike and climb. Noticeable differences too in the vegetation. The forest is more open, with grass in between trees, as opposed to brush mixed with trees in the British Columbia forests. Climb Brazeau from Miligne L. and Coronet Creek, the west face and south ridge. Climb Poboktan from Poboktan W.S. and Creek, and the southwest slopes.

For those hardy souls interested in long marathon hikes, the hike from the trailhead near Nigel Pass to the Beaver Creek Picnic Grounds near Medicine Lake might be the one for you. It's 176 kms long and would take most people 8 to 10 days to complete. From Nigel Pass (actually Camp Parker) the trail leads down the Brazeau River, up the Southesk River, then down Medicene and Rock Rivers, and finally past Jacques Lake to Beaver Creek P.G. This is the best opportunity to see real wilderness in Jasper Park. But it's a very long hike and in places the trail may be overgrown and hard to locate—but it is there.

A much shorter, but equally satisfying trek, is one beginning at Camp Parker and ending at Maligne Lake. This trip is about 90 kms, and will take from 4 to 6 days to complete. It could also end at Poboktan Warden Station, or begin at the warden station and end at Maligne Lake. By taking in a trek through either Jonas, Poboktan or Maligne Passes, true wilderness areas can be seen along with snow capped peaks and glaciers. This series of trails is used much more and is in better condition than the South Boundary Trail (Camp Parker to Beaver Creek P.G.).

Best to stock up on food and supplies before entering the national parks. But if you need supplies, then Jasper townsite or Lake Louise or Banff can be used. For further information about these trails, the best place to inquire is at the Visitor Center in Jasper but also at the Icefield Center and at the Poboktan Warden Station.

**Map:** Jasper National Park, 1 : 250,000, from Wardens Offices in the park, or from Maps Canada, Surveys and Mapping, Ottawa, K1A OE9.

Peaks like this are common in areas east of Nigel Pass.

# Map 188-1, South Jasper Nat. P., Alberta, Can.

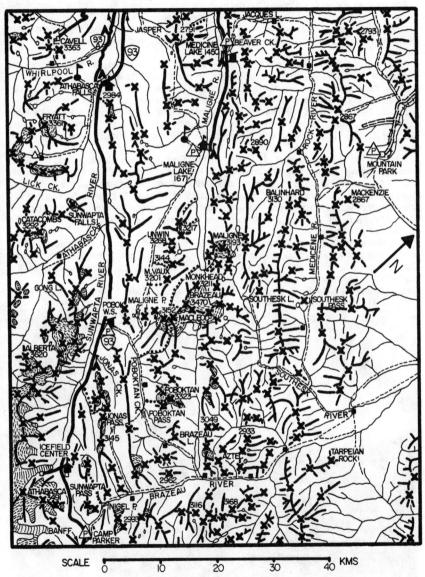

SCALE  0   10   20   30   40  KMS

# Columbia, Jasper Nat. Park, B.C.—Alb., Canada

Mt. Columbia, 3748 meters, is the second highest summit in the Canadian Rockies with only Mt. Robson being higher. It, like so many of the peaks in the Canadian Rockies, has some very difficult routes, but also has a walk-up route, via the Athabasca Glacier and the Columbia Icefields.

The Columbia Icefields include all the glaciers in the vicinity of Sunwapta Pass and Mt. Columbia. It's the largest amount of ice in the Canadian Rockies.

Access to Mt. Columbia, along with other high summits in the area, such as The Twins, Snow Dome and Kitchener, is via the same route—the Athabasca Glacier. This glacier can be reached by car on a good paved highway not far from Sunwapta Pass. Near the bottom end of Athabasca Glacier, there's a lodge, visitors center, and snowmobiles that ply the glacier with tourists.

Access to the Clemencia Icefields and Mt. Tsar, is via the Sunwapta Falls Bridge, the Athabasca River and the Chaba Creek. Keep in mind that with all the snow and ice and glaciers, these peaks are some of the most rugged and most difficult to climb in all of Canada. Needless to say, these peaks are for well equiped and experienced groups. For less experienced climbers and hikers, might try some of the peaks to the east of Highway 93—the Icefields Highway. Weather is generally better the further east one goes, therefore, camping and climbing are more enjoyable around Sunwapta Peak. Routes are shown to the better known peaks.

This area in the southern part of Jasper National Park is heavily glaciated, and has large rivers—along with some tricky river crossings. In the back country there are very few bridges, which means crossing the larger streams can be difficult and hazardous. As a result, climbing in many places is a small expedition, despite the fact that Highway 93 extends the length of this north-south valley, which parallels the crest of the Rockies. Remember, for climbing in the area west of Highway 93, use one of two main river crossings: the Athabasca Glacier and the Sunwapta Falls Bridge.

For national park and topographic maps of the region and information (especially about bridges and stream-crossings), stop at the warden's office in Jasper, or the visitors center just north of Sunwapta Pass. Jasper town is a good place to stop and shop, as it's a railhead and the only important town in the entire area.

**Map:** Jasper National Park, 1 : 250,000, from Wardens Offices in the park, or from Maps Canada, 615 Booth Street, Ottawa.

Mt. Athabasca is very near the Icefields Highway.

# Map 189-1, Columbia, Jasper N.P., Alberta, Can.

SCALE  0   5   10   15   20   25   KMS

## Forbes, Banff National Park, B.C.—Alberta, Canada

Forbes Peak, 3628 meters, is the highest summit within the confines of this map. The area included is the northern section of Banff National Park, with a small portion of Yoho N.P., north of Field. Most of the higher peaks lie to the west of the Icefields Highway, or Highway 93, but some over 3300 meters exist on the east side of the road. Despite having a major highway nearby, the area has few trails, and access can be difficult. The problem is that two large rivers must be crossed, the Bow and Mistaya, before the higher peaks west of the highway can be reached. For the most part these streams are braided—so with care and selection (and late in the season), they can be negotiated. However, river crossings are always a problem to consider, therefore the summits in this area are seldom climbed or even attempted.

The rock is stratified limestone, similar to that found in most other parts of the Canadian Rockies. The Freshfield and Lyell Glaciers and the area around Forbes Peak are the largest glaciers in Banff Park.

When climbing the higher peaks, one must have ice ax and crampons, along with adequate rain gear. Weather is generally better in July and August, but snow conditions should be better in August and September.

Golden, Jasper, Banff and Lake Louise are the only places to buy supplies in the area. To get better maps, especially topos, stop at any warden's office, especially the one at Lake Louise. They can inform you of the park rules and can help in finding the best routes into the area shown on this map. Maps can also be bought at all park entrances.

For those interested in climbing Forbes only, the southeast side of the mountain is best. One should cross the Mistaya River, then hike on a trail up Howse, Freshfield, then Forbes Creeks. For a crack at both Forbes and Lyell, cross the Saskatchewan River on a foot bridge near the junction of Highways 11 and 93, then hike up Howse Creek to a point about 3 kms west of Glacier Lake for a good campsite. Getting to a base camp above Glacier Lake will take about one day for the hike. The same is true for the length of time needed to reach a campsite on Forbes Creek.

**Map:**  Banff National Park, 1 : 190,080, and Yoho Park, 1 : 126,720, both from wardens offices in both parks, and from Maps Canada, 615 Booth Street, Ottawa.

An easy climb fairly near the highway is Sarback.

# Map 190-1, Forbes, Banff N.P., BC-Alberta, Can.

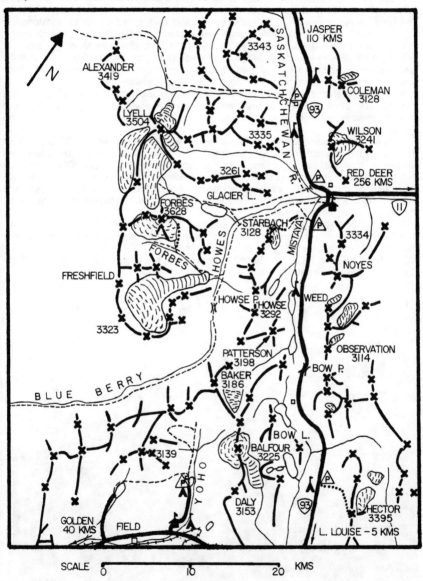

## Hector, Banff National Park, Alberta, Canada

Included on this map is the eastern-most part of the Banff National Park, from Highway 1 and 93 (or Windermere Parkway) to near the eastern border of the park. The highest summit in this area, and the highest summit east of the Windermere Parkway, is Mt. Hector, at 3395 meters. This peak is very near the main highway, and is an easy climb because of good accessibility. The second highest peak on this map, and one that takes nearly two days to reach the base of, is Mt. Willington, 3367 meters.

All of these mountains are composed of layered sedimentary rocks, such as limestone and dolomite. Much of the rock is fairly crumbly, but in places it makes for good free climbing.

Highway 1 in the south and Highway 93 in the northern sections make for easy access—at least near the highway—but beyond these main roads it is wilderness. However, the trails in the area are well marked and fairly well used. There are wardens cabins at regular intervals, which are used in trail maintenance, fire control and for emergencies.

All trailheads on the main highways are well marked and include parking lots. As time passes, more of the streams are being bridged with permanent structures, but some more isolated streams must be waded. This can be one of the big dangers to climbing in the Canadian Rockies.

July, August and early September are the best times to climb. For supplies, it's usually best to stock up before entering the park, but food can be purchased at Banff, Lake Louise and Jasper. At all national park entrances, and at Lake Louise and Banff Wardens Offices, one can buy good maps. Park wardens can also assist with information on trail conditions and camping and hiking requirements. On most north faces, one will need an ice ax and crampons, but in late summer, all-rock routes can be found to most peaks. A rain sheet for the tent and a waterproof for you and pack, are essential.

Trains can be taken to Banff and Lake Louise, as well as buses on Highway 1, that run the same route. During the summer months, hitch hikers line the main routes in Banff National Park, but hitching is generally good despite the crowds.

**Map:** Banff National Park, 1 : 190,080, from wardens offices in the park and from Maps Canada, 615 Booth Street, Ottawa.

A look at the north ridge of Mt. Hector.

# Map 191-1, Hector, Banff N.P., Alberta, Canada

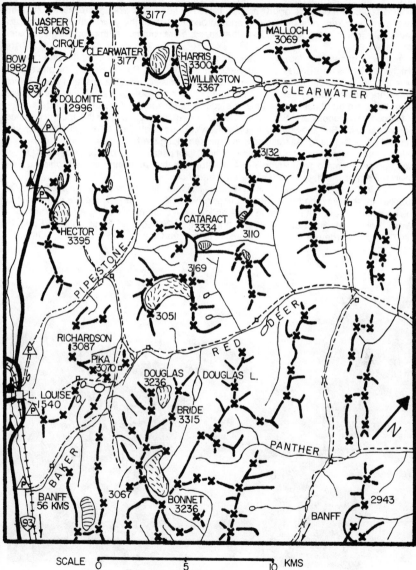

JASPER 193 KMS
CIRQUE
CLEARWATER 3177
3177
BOW L. 1982
HARRIS 3300
MALLOCH 3069
WILLINGTON 3367
93
CLEARWATER
DOLOMITE 2996
P
3132
P
HECTOR 3395
CATARACT 3334
3110
PIPESTONE
3169
3051
DEER
RICHARDSON 3087
RED
P
PIKA 3070
DOUGLAS 3236
DOUGLAS L.
L. LOUISE 1540
P
BRIDE 3315
PANTHER
N
BAKER
3067
BONNET 3236
2943
BANFF 56 KMS
BANFF
93

SCALE 0     5     10   KMS

## Temple, Banff National Park, B.C.—Alberta, Canada

Mt. Temple, at 3547 meters, is the highest summit in the vicinity of Lake Louise and on this map. The mountains in the Lake Louise area are among the most famous and most fotographed of any mountains in the world. With the Canadian Pacific Railroad first running through the region in about 1890, it became one of the first alpine climbing areas in North America.

The peaks are composed of sedimentary rock—mostly limestone, and are capped with glaciers, with some rather extensive. All types of climbs are possible, from easy walk-ups to the most difficult, both on rock, or on snow and ice. The larger glaciers are crevassed, so some care must be taken. Avalanches can and do occur much of the year, with the storm track seemingly right over the area. Bad weather seems more common than good, so go prepared for that.

Access is generally good, with Canadian Highways 1 and 93, running through the area (Highway 93 runs north to Jasper from Radium). Mts. Victoria, Popes, Huber, and other peaks west of Lake Louise can be approached from either Louise or from the west and Lake O'Hara. There are huts at Abbot Pass and at the head of Lake Louise—in the valley of Six Glaciers. Also, there are good camping sites and a couple of huts and lodges at Lake O'Hara.

For climbing Goodsir and Sharp, use Ottertail or Tumbling Creeks for the approach routes. For access to Mt. Ball and Stanley, try either Hawk or Red Earth Creeks. All these trails are well marked and often used. All trailheads are marked along the highways.

For more information about the use of huts, campsites and conditions of trails, snow, weather, and for more detailed maps including topographic, stop at the wardens office at Lake Louise, Field or Banff, or at any of the park entrances.

Towns just outside the park, such as Golden, Radium, or Calgary should be used to buy all supplies for the climbing trip, as food is expensive inside the park. There are some all-rock routes in the region, but it's best to have an ice ax and crampons along on any climb.

**Map:** Yoho Park and Kootenay Park, both at 1 : 126,720, and Banff National Park, 1 : 190,080, all at wardens offices in each park, or from Maps Canada, 615 Booth Street, Ottawa.

Lake Louise is the most popular destination in the Canadian Rockies

Map 192-1, Temple, Banff N.P., BC-Alb., Can.

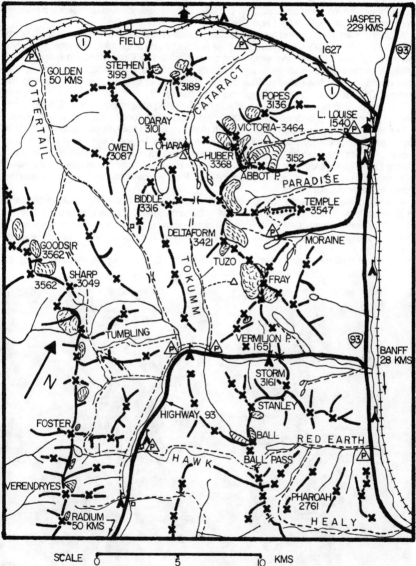

## Assiniboine, Banff Nat. Park, B.C.—Alb., Canada

Assiniboine is one of the premier climbs in the Canadian Rockies, and in all of Canada, for that matter. It's the highest peak between the Can-Am border and the Canadian Pacific Railroad line near Lake Louise. Most of the area on this map is Banff National Park, but Assiniboine is part of its own provincial park.

As with all the Canadian Rockies, the peaks in the Assiniboine area are composed of limestone. Glaciation is not extensive, but care must be taken because of the threat of avalanches from hanging glaciers. Only climbers with experience and confidence should try this climb, and only with proper equipment.

Access is normally on one of two routes. The easiest and shortest access route is via Spray Reservoir, where there's a poor road along the northwest side of the lake. From there it's a one day hike up Bryant Creek, over either Wonder or Assiniboine Pass, thence to Magog Lake. There, a lodge or climbers shelter and a campsite, are located. From Magog Lake, the normal route heads for the hut between Sturdee and Assiniboine, then up the north ridge to the summit. The southwest face is the second easiest way.

The Alpine Club of Canada maintains a hut at the 2650 meters level above Magog Lake, which sleeps 12. Stop at Banff and get the latest information concerning the use of this hut.

The other main access route is via Canadian Highway 1, about 10 kms west of Banff, then via Brewster Creek, Allenby Pass, and Assiniboine Pass to Magog Lake, where the routes previously mentioned can be taken. This Brewster Creek route takes at least 2 days to reach Magog Lake. Park wardens or other people in either Banff or Canmore can give you the latest information on roads, trails, snow conditions, etc. Park wardens can sell you more detailed maps, including topographics.

As for food and supplies, it's best to buy them in Calgary or some other town outside the park. In Banff National Park supplies can be found at Canmore, Banff or Lake Louise but prices are high. Weather is usually best in July and August—snow is better in August or September. Count on bad weather. Have rain gear, along with ice ax and crampons, as well as cold weather clothing.

**Map:** Banff National Park, 1 : 190,080, or 82-J-13, 1 : 50,000 from park wardens offices, or Maps Canada, 615 Booth Street, Ottawa.

A good look at Assiniboine from near Magog Lake.

Map 193-1, Assiniboine, Banff N.P., BC-Alb., Can.

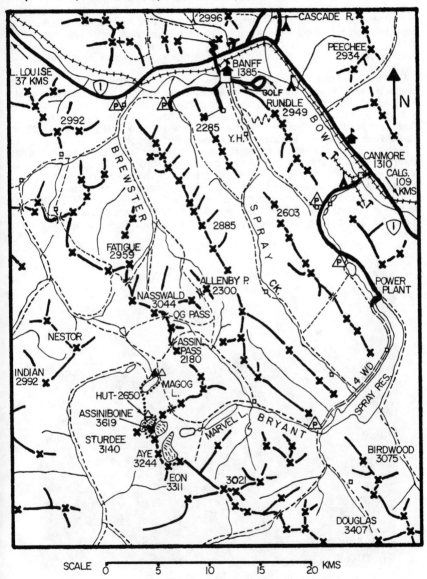

# Mt. Olympus, Olympic Mts., Washington, USA

Mt. Olympus, 2428 meters, is the highest summit in the mountainous area of northwestern Washington state known as the Olympic Mountains. Much of the area is now the Olympic National Park. It's also a peninsula, surrounded on three sides by water—the Pacific Ocean and Puget Sound. The Olympic Mountains are not volcanos, but are of the uplifted variety, as are the Northern Cascades, to the east. They're made mostly of limestone.

The number one influence on the physical makeup of the area, is the weather. This region is one of the wettest places in North America—and in the world for that matter. The peaks are not especially high, but receive enormous amounts of rain and snow during the year. For climbers the weather should be the number one concern. Rain gear is essential. One must expect bad weather, even in summer—although in the summer months long periods of good weather are a regular occurrence.

For those interested in climbing Mt. Olympus, there are three possible access routes. The longest is via the Elwha and Boulder Creek Roads. This route begins not far to the southwest of Port Angeles, on Highway 101. The next route is also via Highway 101, then Soleduck River and Soleduck Campground. Paths from these two trailheads join onto the third route or Hoh Trail coming up the Hoh River, which is the easiest route of access. The Hoh area is 32 kms east of Highway 101, and includes a visitors center and campground.

At the head of the Hoh River, is the Glacier Meadows Ranger Station and campsite. For all of the above routes, it's at least 3 days for a round trip climb of Mt. Olympus—if one has three days of good weather. It's one long day in, one day for the climb, and one day out—from any of the access routes. Crampons and ice ax are essential for climbing in these mountains.

Towns with some kind of shopping facilities in the area are; Port Angels, Forks, Hoquiam and Aberdeen. For further information, maps and books about the Olympic National Park, stop at the Elwha, Soleduck or Hoh Ranger Stations, or the National Park Headquarters in Port Angeles.

**Map:** Olympic National Park, 1 : 125,000, USGS or from any ranger station in the park.

From near Appleton Pass looking at Mt. Olympus.

# Map 194-1, Olympus, Olympic Mts., Wash., USA

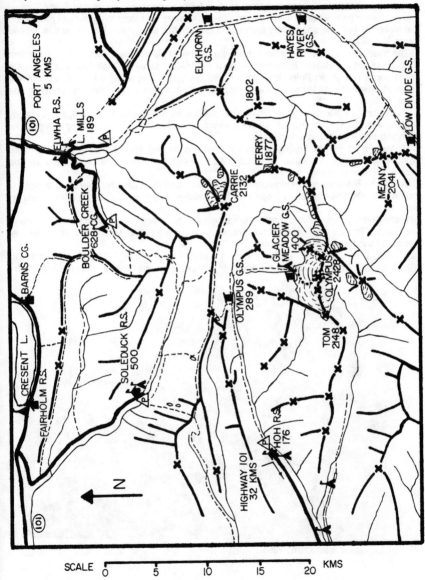

## Mt. Baker, Cascade Mts., Washington, USA

Mt. Baker is one of the higher of the volcanic mountains in the American Northwest. Its altitude is 3286 meters, and it is highly eroded and glaciated. Its location is due east of Bellingham, west of Mt. Shuksan, and not far south of the Canadian border.

Mt. Baker offers both easy and challenging routes. The mountain is climbed often, but not nearly as much as other peaks in Washington, such as Mt. Rainier.

The easiest and most common access route is from the north via Glacier and Glacier Creek; then to the car park, where the trail begins. The trail heads southeast to the area of the Kulson Cabin, not far from the snow line. Most people camp in this area, then climb to the summit and return the next day.

The second most common route is from the northeast side of the mountain and the Austin Pass ski resort and Baker Lodge area. From the ski resort, take the Chain Lakes Loop Trail to about 2 kms past Artist Point, then the left trail to Camp Kiser, about 8 kms. Then continue along Ptarmigan Ridge to the summit. Most people do this climb in two days also, camping one night at Kiser.

Regardless of the route taken, crampons and ice ax are required. Since this is a stormy region, wool clothing is generally better than those made of synthetics. Having rain gear for both you and the pack are important.

Highway 542, the one linking Bellingham with Glacier and Austin Pass, is open the entire year. This road is used in winter by skiers at Austin Pass, which provides the mountain a good access route even for winter climbing.

There's no public transportation on this highway, so one must have his own car or travel "by thumb". Weekends, especially those with fine weather, are busy, so getting a lift should be easy.

There's no big town in the immediate area, but small stores can be found at Kendall, Deming and Glacier. There's a ranger station at Glacier, where more detailed maps and more information about the mountain can be found.

**Map:**  Mt. Baker, and Mt. Shuksan, both 1 : 62,500, or Concrete, 1 : 250,000, from the USGS, or Mt. Baker—Snoqualmie National Forest, from the Glacier Ranger Stations.

Mt. Baker from Camp Kiser.

# Map 195-1, Baker, Cascade Mts., Washington, USA

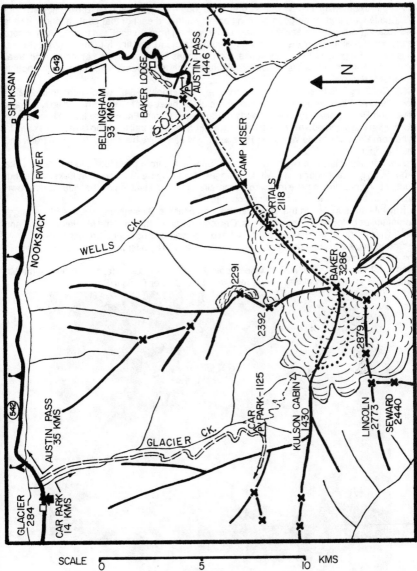

SCALE 0 _____ 5 _____ 10 KMS

## Mt. Shuksan, Cascade Mts., Washington, USA

For those interested in some good, challenging snow and ice climbing, the Northern Cascades have much to offer. Mts. Shuksan and Challenger (2783 and 2511 meters elevation) and others in this area, offer both good snow and ice and some rock climbing, in a wilderness setting. The Northern Cascades are not volcanos as are much of the rest of the Cascades, but instead, are uplifted and eroded.

Access to Shuksan, is the same as one of the routes used to reach Mt. Baker. However, for Mt. Challenger, and some good climbing areas south and east of that peak, a longer hike is necessary. Shuksan can easily be reached by walking from Austin Pass to Lake Ann, where many people camp. From there climb to the summit plateau, and finally to the summit pyramid. This route first goes to the north slopes, then switches to the south side of the summit area, where the final ascent is made. One could also reach the mountain from the north and the Nooksack River.

Mt. Challenger is best reached via the same road, Highway 542, which goes to Mt. Baker Lodge and Austin Pass. However, turn off this main highway and follow a dirt road up Nooksack River and Ruth Creeks, to where it ends at Hannegan Camp. From there the trail leads over Hannegan Pass and down the Chilliwack River. Further on, a trail leads up Brush Creek and to Whatcom Pass. From the Whatcom Pass area, one can make his way to Whatcom Peak and Mt. Challenger.

Another possible route of approach to Mt. Shuksan is from the south and the Baker Lake area, but this is a longer route. Mt. Challenger could also be reached from Baker Lake, but some bushwhacking may be involved. Generally speaking, climbing on the mountains shown on this map are not for the beginning climber.

Buy all your supplies in the Puget Sound area either at Bellingham, or some of the larger communities before arriving in this area. One can buy some things at the Mt. Baker Lodge and at Glacier (north of Mt. Baker), but they have little variety and things are expensive.

Crampons, ice ax, rain gear and a tent are essentials. The best weather generally comes in the summer months.

**Map:** Mt. Shuksan, and Mt. Challenger, both 1 : 62,500, or Concrete, 1 : 250,000, or the Mt. Baker—Snoqualmie National Forest map, from the Glacier Ranger Station.

Mt. Challenger from near Whatcom Pass.

414

# Map 196-1, Shuksan, Cascade Mts., Wash., USA

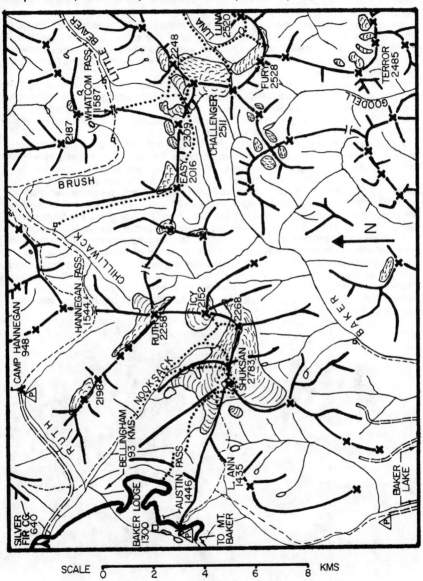

SCALE 0 2 4 6 8 KMS

# North Cascades National Park, Wash., USA

Covered here are the Northern Cascade Mountains of Washington state, and nearly all of the North Cascades National Park. The park boundary and the USA-Canadian border run together along the top of the map. Included here are Mts. Shuksan, Challenger and Terror—all of which are included on the previous map, Mt. Shuksan. The intention here is to give the climber and hiker an idea of the trail situation in the national park and access routes to some of the more popular and well known peaks.

Backpacking is probably the most popular sport in the park. If it is possible to arrange for transportation, then here are some long, one-way hikes. One could park at the Ross Dam on the North Cascades Highway (Highway 20), then walk to Big Beaver Creek, thence northwest to and over Beaver, Whatcom and Hannegan Passes, and end the trip at Camp Hannegan, a distance of about 77 kms, or about 4 to 5 days.

Another fine hike would be to begin at Manning Park in southern B.C. From Manning Park find your way to the Hozomeen Campground next to Ross Lake just south of the border, then hike south to the North Cascades Highway, a distance of about 50 kms. Another long hike would be to walk from Stehekin on Lake Chelan north to Diablo Lake. The problem with all the above hikes is returning to ones car afterwards.

Beginning in this region and extending north into B.C., is the Pacific Crest Trail. This trail or system of trails now runs as far as southern California. It's indicated on the map by a heavy dotted line. An easy place to intersect this trail is at Rainy Pass, at 1481 meters altitude.

Access to climbing areas is as follows: Shuksan, from Austin Pass and Lake Ann; Challenger, from Camp Hannegan and Whatcom Pass, or Big Beaver Creek on the east; Fury and Luna, from Big Beaver and Luna Creeks; Terror, from either Goodell or Stetattle Creeks (where some bushwhacking may be necessary); Eldorado, from Cascade Creek and Marblemount; Goode, from Rainy Pass and Bridge Creek; and Boston from Diablo Lake and Thunder Creek.

The main entrance to the park is at Marblemount. That's a good place to buy better maps and get more information. (In the east stop at Concrete for further information). Buy your food and supplies before reaching the park. Hiking and climbing season is from June through mid-Octover, but the eastern side has generally drier weather and more sunshine. The Cascades Highway is closed in Winter. Access to Stehekin is via ferry boat and Chelan.

**Map:** North Cascades National Park, Wash., 1 : 250,000, from the USGS, or information centers at Concrete or Marblemount.

Monte Cristo peak. This area is one of the most popular.

Map 197-1, North Cascades Nat. Park, Wash., USA

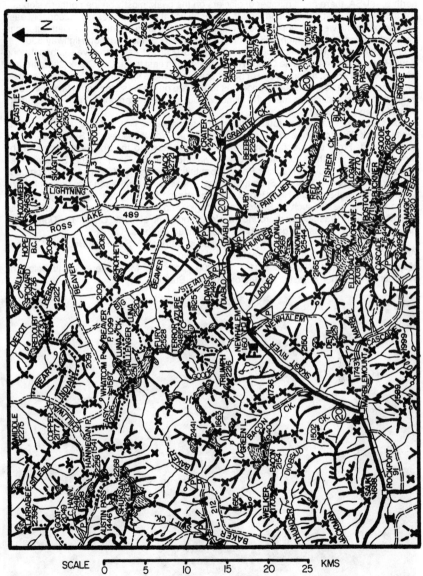

SCALE  0  5  10  15  20  25  KMS

# Glacier Peak, Cascade Mts., Washington, USA

Glacier Peak, 3222 meters, is one of the better climbs in the state of Washington. It involves some wilderness hiking and a variety of routes, some very easy—some harder. Most of the routes involve snow and ice climbing. Glacier Peak is an old and eroded volcano, having had its last eruption about 10-12,000 years ago. Since it's one of the highest mountains in the northwest USA, there are a number of glaciers on the peak, mostly on the northern slopes.

It's location is east of Everett in the Mt. Baker National Forest. Access is reasonably easy with almost all the westerly approaches beginning from the town of Darrington. Darrington can be reached from the Arlington Exit of Interstate Highway 5, then east on Highway 530.

From Darrington, the shortest route to the summit of Glacier Peak, is to drive southeast along Sauk River, to where the White Chuck River enters, then east to the Owl Creek Campground, where the trail begins. It's only a one or two hour walk to where the Kennedy Shelter is located. From there the easiest and least dangerous routes are on the west and south faces. In some years it may be possible to make the climb without ice ax or crampons, but this equipment should always be taken.

The second best approach route is nearly the same as the first, but instead of turning up White Chuck River, continue southeast along the Sauk River, then finally up Sloan Creek to the campground. From the campground, routes can be taken to the southern portion of the mountain. Still another approach route is via the Suiattle River to the Sulpur Creek Campground, then south to Glacier Peak. From this same trailhead, one can also approach other popular summits such as Spire and Dome. These same peaks can also be reached via Lake Chelan, Stehekin, and High Bridge. By using the road running past High Bridge, one can approach other peaks such as Boston, and Magic, and Sentinel. One of the most popular climbing areas in Washington is around the old mining camp of Monte Cristo. The Dome Peak and Monte Cristo areas are generally for experienced climbers.

The last good place to buy food and supplies is Darrington. See Fred Beckys "Cascade Alpine Guide" for much more information on this region.

**Map:** Glacier Peak Wilderness, 1 : 100,000, from the Mt. Baker—Snoqualmie and Wenatchee National Forests, Darrington Ranger Station.

Glacier Peak from the northwest.

# Map 198-1, Glacier, Cascade Mts., Wash., USA

SCALE

0    10    20    30    KMS

## Mt. Rainier, Cascade Mts., Washington, USA

Mt. Rainier is the highest peak in Washington State, in the northwest USA, and in the entire Cascade Mountains. It too is one of the volcanos which dot the northwest landscape. It's dormant now, but has some fumerals in the summit crater, indicating some activity remains. It still has the crater on top, which indicates it is still a youthful volcano. The glaciers are extensive and have done a fair amount of erosion. Mt. Rainier is now a national park.

When taking all things into account, Rainier has the best snow and ice climbs in the USA, with the exception of some Alaskan mountains. Rainier's glaciers are often the training ground for expeditions heading for the Himalayas and Mt. Everest. There are guide services available, and since it's in a national park, there are a lot of rules, regulations and restrictions concerning mountaineering.

There have been many people lost on the mountain, so don't take it lightly. It's in the cyclonic storm track much of the year, and weather is the big killer. Rainier is definitely a bad-weather mountain.

The mountain has two main access points—the Paradise Lodge and Sunrise. The "tourist route" is up from Paradise—first on a trail, then on snowfields to Camp Muir. This is one day. The second day is for the summit climb.

From Sunrise, one can take a trail to Camp Schurman on the northeast side of the mountain, then to the summit. Both of these access points offer easy climbs, along with many more difficult routes as well.

Pay attention to the weather forecasts issued by the ranger stations, at both Paradise and Sunrise. These offices also offer both topographic and national park maps and the latest information on routes, snow conditions, and the number of people on the mountain.

Don't plan to buy food and gasoline in the park as it's very expensive. Do your shopping before entering the area, such as in Yakima, Seattle, Tacoma or Portland. Wool clothing and ice ax and crampons are a must, along with other expedition type clothing, especially if the weather looks less than perfect.

**Map:**  Mt. Rainier National Park, 1 : 50,000, from the USGS, or at park visitor centers.

East ridge of Mt. Rainier. Route goes up rocky rib.

# Map 199-1, Rainier, Cascade Mts., Wash., USA

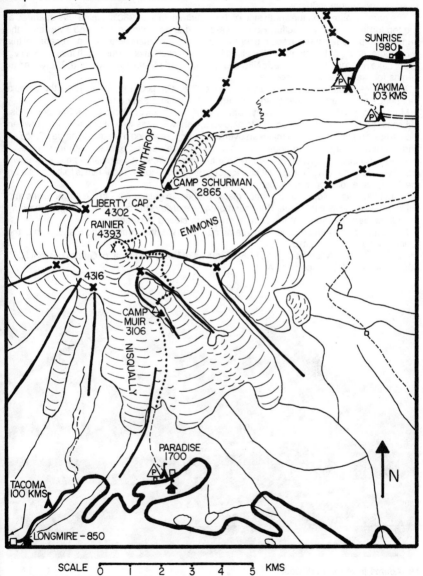

SUNRISE
1980

YAKIMA
103 KMS

CAMP SCHURMAN
2865

WINTHROP

LIBERTY CAP
4302

RAINIER
4393

EMMONS

4316

CAMP
MUIR
3106

NISQUALLY

PARADISE
1700

TACOMA
100 KMS

N

LONGMIRE – 850

SCALE   0   1   2   3   4   5   KMS

## Mt. Adams, Cascade Mts., Washington, USA

Mt. Adams is the second highest mountain in the northwest USA, and the state of Washington, at 3758 meters. It is a moderately eroded volcanic cone with a number of extensive glaciers. The territory surrounding the mountain is the Mt. Adams Wilderness Area, and is one of the more inaccesible volcanic mountains in the northwest. The immediate area is almost unpopulated, but places outside the Wilderness Area have been, and continue to be, used by the lumber industry.

The normal route is on the south side of the mountain. In the 1930's a mine was operated at the top for the recovery of sulfur. Horses were used to haul miners' food and supplies to the summit camp. Today one can see the remains of a cabin and mine near the top. Because of this easy route, some of the glamor of the climb has been taken away. This south face route is via Trout Lake and forest service roads N80 and N81, to Morris Creek Campground. There the trail begins for the route up the mountain.

The other standard route of approach is via the Killen Creek Campground. From this camp a trail heads south and southeast, to the summit. It too is an easy and safe route.

Most people do the climb in one day from either Killen Creek or Morris Creek Campgrounds, but some go higher on the mountain, to at least the snowline (as water is hard to find between the camps and the snow) and make an overnight camp, reaching the summit on day 2. Ice ax and crampons are standard equipment, but may not be needed on the south face route.

There's no public transport anywhere near the mountain, so it's a must to have one's own car. If you don't have a car, the best chance of getting close to the mountain is to hitch hike on the Trout Lake road on weekends.

Trout Lake has a store, but is a small place. It's best to get supplies in the larger towns and cities before arriving in this area. Summer months are always the best for climbing, particularly on Adams because some of the access roads are closed in winter.

For updated information concerning camping, trails, weather reports and maps, stop at the ranger station in Trout Lake.

**Map:** Mt. Adams Wilderness, 1 : 31,680, Trout Lake Ranger Station, or Gifford Pinchot N.F., 500 West 12th St., Vancouver, Wash.

Mt. Adams from the northwest.

# Map 200-2, Adams, Cascade Mts., Wash., USA

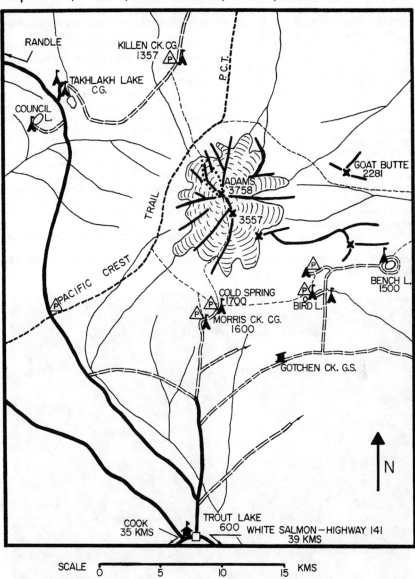

RANDLE

KILLEN CK. CG.
1357

P.C.T.

TAKHLAKH LAKE
C.G.

COUNCIL
L.

GOAT BUTTE
2281

ADAMS
3758

TRAIL

3557

PACIFIC CREST

BENCH L.
1500

COLD SPRING
1700

BIRD L.

MORRIS CK. CG.
1600

GOTCHEN CK. G.S.

N

TROUT LAKE
600    WHITE SALMON – HIGHWAY 141
39 KMS

COOK
35 KMS

SCALE    0        5        10        15        KMS

## St. Helens, Cascade Mts., Washington, USA

The map of Mt. St. Helens shown here was made in 1979 and shows the mountain as it was then. The dark line on the map shows the area most affected by the 1980 eruption. Since that activity to the time of this writing, the entire region has changed. There is not one building or road left on the map! There seems little sense in making a new map, as the mountain is still puffing smoke and could blow up again at any time.

It was late March, 1980 that smoke was first sighted near the summit. This was the first time for activity since 1857. The final blast or explosion was on May 18, 1980. That eruption killed nearly 70 people who were camping and taking fotographs in the region at the time.

As the map shows, the height of the mountain was listed at 2950 meters, but that has now dropped by about 200 meters, leaving the summit at about 2750 meters. Before this last eruption, there were many small glaciers flowing from the top, some large enough to have sizable crevasses. All the old snow and ice was either blown off the mountain or has melted. Now, new glaciers will slowly be forming on the higher parts of the peak.

Before 1980, there were many tourist facilities around the shores of Spirit Lake, including several lodges, a YMCA camp and an information center, set up and operated by the forest service. Now nothing remains of these buildings and facilities. A lake remains, but its appearance has changed greatly.

Since the explosion was on the north face, all trees north of the peak for about 25 kms, were blown down by the hurricane-force winds that accompanied the explosion. On the west, south and east sides of the mountain, things are still pretty much the same as before 1980.

No one can predict the future of this mountain, but chances are that it'll be designated some kind of national park or monument. It's likely, too, that new roads will be built into the area of Spirit Lake—not to make the area a scenic recreation area that it was—but to allow visitors to view nature's destructive powers.

Until these roads are built, climbers will have a longer walk to the mountain. The route from Castle Rock still will likely be the best approach route.

**Map:**  Mt. St. Helens-Spirit Lake, 1 : 62,500, (old map), but new ones at Gifford Pinchot N.F., 500 West 12th St., Vancouver, Wash.

Mt. St. Helens and Spirit Lake before the 1980 eruption.

# Map 201-2, St. Helens, Cascade Mts., Wash., USA

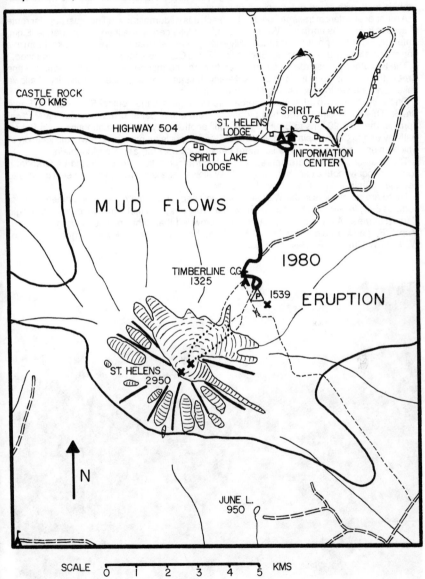

CASTLE ROCK
70 KMS

HIGHWAY 504

SPIRIT LAKE
975

ST. HELENS
LODGE

SPIRIT LAKE
LODGE

INFORMATION
CENTER

MUD FLOWS

1980

TIMBERLINE C.G.
1325

1539

ERUPTION

ST. HELENS
2950

N

JUNE L.
950

SCALE  0  1  2  3  4  5  KMS

# Matterhorn, Wallowa Mts., Oregon, USA

In the extreme northeast corner of the state of Oregon is the Wallowa Mountains. These mountains are not high or rugged, nor is the area large—but it is wild. The higher and centralized portion of these mountains is designated as the Eagle Cap Wilderness Area. The highest peak is known as the Matterhorn, reaching 3050 meters. Several other summits in the group are near the 3000 meter level. A large part of the Wallowa Mountains is made up of granitic rock, with some outcroppings of limestone.

A number of different trails can be used to reach this wilderness area. The most popular route of access is from the north and Wallowa Lake. This lake can be reached via La Grande, Elgin, Enterprise and Joseph, with the road finally ending near a ski resort at Wallowa Lake. From this one main trailhead, peaks such as Sacajawea, Eagle Cap and Aneroid can all be approached.

The two other access routes can be used from the north; one's from Lostine—and Lostine Creek, the other is up Hurricane Creek. Nearly the same route as used in reaching Wallowa Lake can be used to reach these two stream valleys.

On the south are two other main approach roads. One is to the Boulder Park resort on Eagle Creek. This creek can be reached by driving from either Baker or La Grande, via Medical Springs, then the 20 kms to Boulder Park. Still another way into the mountains is via Baker, Halfway and to Cornucopia at 1450 meters. Cornucopia is an old mining town, the location of which gives the best access to southern peaks such as Krag and Red Mountain.

The nearest cities that are served with public transportation are Baker and La Grande. If you're on foot without a car, then the road to Wallowa Lake is the route with the best chance to get a lift. Other access roads have less traffic.

There are no glaciers in the Wallowas and no need for any ice or snow equipment, except perhaps early in summer. Most peaks have both very easy and more difficult routes. The Eagle Cap Wilderness Area is more quiet and less crowded than other places in Oregon.

**Map:** Eagle Cap Wilderness, 1 : 62,500, from the Joseph or Wallowa Ranger Stations, or Wallowa-Whitman N.F., Baker Oregon.

Matterhorn Peak (in clouds) as seen from Ice Lake.

# Map 202-1, Matterhorn, Wallowa Mts., Ore., USA

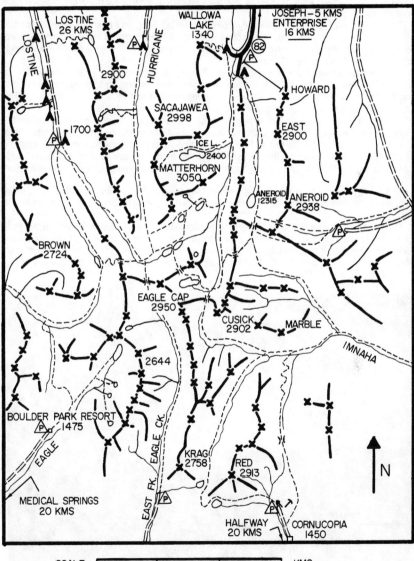

LOSTINE
26 KMS

WALLOWA
LAKE
1340

JOSEPH – 5 KMS
ENTERPRISE
16 KMS

LOSTINE

HURRICANE

2900

82

HOWARD

SACAJAWEA
2998

EAST
2900

1700

ICE L
2400

MATTERHORN
3050

ANEROID
12315

ANEROID
2938

BROWN
2724

EAGLE CAP
2950

CUSICK
2902

MARBLE

IMNAHA

2644

BOULDER PARK RESORT
1475

EAGLE

EAST FK. EAGLE CK.

KRAG
2758

RED
2913

N

MEDICAL SPRINGS
20 KMS

HALFWAY
20 KMS

CORNUCOPIA
1450

SCALE    0          5          10          15    KMS

## Mt. Hood, Cascade Mountains, Oregon, USA

Mt. Hood, reaching 3425 meters, is the highest peak in the state of Oregon, and one of the highest in the northwest USA. It's a volcanic mountain with an almost perfect conal shape. The mountain has not erupted in man's memory, but some hot gases and steam still vent in places, indicating it is not yet completely dead.

Hood is one of the most climbed mountains in the USA. The reasons are: it's near a large metropolitan area—Portland, Oregon; the area has good access roads; and the south face route is rather easy and safe.

Reaching the mountain is generally from two ways. First, most people come from the Portland area, via Highway 26. The second main route is Highway 35 coming from the north and Hood River City, located on the Columbia River. These roads converge on the mountain at a place called Government Camp.

The main or normal route for most people climbing the mountain is via Government Camp and the Timberline Lodge. At this lodge are rooms, restaurants, small gift shops and an office of the Mt. Hood National Forest, which gives out information and sells maps of the area. The rangers prefer hikers to sign in before the climb, but that's not required.

The south face or Mazama Route begins at the Timberline Lodge, and follows to the east or right side, of the ski lift. Beyond the lift, which operates the year-round, a trail heads straight for the summit, via the right side of a subsidiary peak known as the Hogback, then up a steep and icy coulior. Another route from the south heads further to the right or east, and up a kind of ridge called Castle Crags. This route is a bit more difficult. Ice ax and crampons are required for both routes.

The climb can also be made from the Hood Meadows ski resort, and the Cloud Cap area, located on the northeast side of the mountain. This is more of a glacier route than others on the mountain.

There's always water available at the resorts shown on the map—however, above the ends of the roads there's little or no running water, so a canteen is recommended. Do all necessary food shopping before reaching the area, as there isn't much to buy, on or near the mountain.

**Map:** Mt. Hood Wilderness, 1 : 62,500, from the Timberline Lodge Visitor Center, or Mt. Hood N.F., Portland, Oregon.

Mt. Hood from just above the Timberline Lodge.

# Map 203-1, Hood, Cascade Mts., Oregon, USA

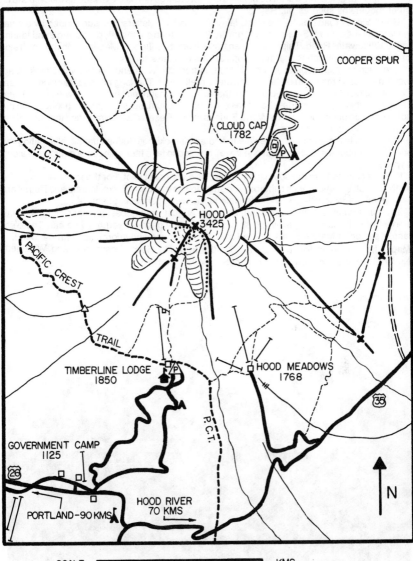

COOPER SPUR

CLOUD CAP
1782

P.C.T.

PACIFIC CREST

HOOD
3425

TRAIL

TIMBERLINE LODGE
1850

HOOD MEADOWS
1768

35

P.C.T.

GOVERNMENT CAMP
1125

N

26

PORTLAND-90 KMS

HOOD RIVER
70 KMS

SCALE 0          5          10  KMS

# Jefferson, Cascade Mountains, Oregon, USA

Mt. Jefferson is the second highest mountain in Oregon and is one of the many volcanos of the northwest USA. Jefferson at 3200 meters altitude is one of the older and more eroded volcanos in the area. Because of this erosion, some difficult routes exist on the mountain. However, the poor rock eliminates good rock climbing. The north and east sides of the mountains are glaciated, but these glaciers are not as large nor as crevassed as those found on other mountains such as Mt. Rainier.

Good access roads make the climb fairly easy, but Mt. Jefferson is surrounded by a small wilderness area. From Salem, take Highway 22 east, then southeast, past Detroit and Idanha to the Whitewater Road. This road—then trail—leads to Jefferson Meadows on the north side of the mountain, which is the more popular of the access routes.

The second most popular approach route is from the west and the Pamela Creek Road, located about 3 kms south of the Whitewater Creek Road. This logging road takes one to near Pamela Lake, where many people camp, then climb the mountain on the southwest side. There are many other access roads—from the north and the south, but they are much longer. On the northeast side of the mountain is Warm Springs Indian Reservation, eliminating that side of the peak as an access route.

At times in late summer, it's possible to find an all-rock route to the summit, eliminating the need for crampons and ice ax, but one is well advised to take these pieces of equipment along anyway.

If one is coming from the south, use Sisters as a shopping spot. For those coming from the north or west, try Salem or its suburbs. The small towns of Marion Forks, Idanha and Detroit are very small roadside villages and offer little in the way of shopping centers.

The three summer months of June, July and August are the best weather months. A fair amount of traffic is on Highway 22, so hitching is fairly good—if you have no car. There's a ranger station at Marion Forks where forest service maps and information can be found.

**Map:** Mt. Jefferson Wilderness, 1 : 62,500, from Mt. Hood, Deschutes, and Willamette National Forests, and any of their ranger stations.

Mt. Jefferson from the trail northwest of the peak.

# Map 204-1, Jefferson, Cascade Mts., Ore., USA

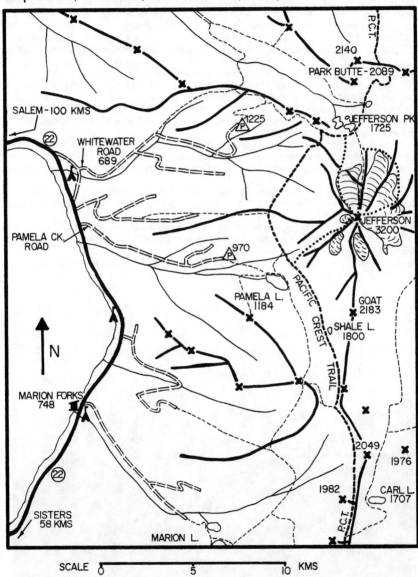

P.C.T.

2140

PARK BUTTE – 2089

SALEM – 100 KMS

22

JEFFERSON PK
1725

1225
P

WHITEWATER
ROAD
689

JEFFERSON
3200

PAMELA CK.
ROAD

970
P

N

PAMELA L.
1184

PACIFIC CREST TRAIL

GOAT
2183

SHALE L.
1800

MARION FORKS
748

2049

1976

22

1982

CARL L.
1707

SISTERS
58 KMS

MARION L.

P.C.T.

SCALE 0        5        10 KMS

# Three Sisters, Cascade Mts., Oregon, USA

The Three Sisters Peaks are a group of three volcanic cones, due west of Bend, Oregon in the central Cascade Range. Access is quite good to this area, with Highway 242 on the west, while to the south is the Cascade Lakes Drive, beginning at Bend.

Best ways into the peaks are from Lava Camp Lake and Frog Camp, both located near Highway 242. These routes are the best approaches to North Sister Peak, 3077 meters. On the south, trails begin at Devils Lake and on Fall Creek. These two routes are the best for approaching the highest of the peaks, South Sister, 3158 meters.

On the east side, one can approach the area from Sisters Town, by driving south on a good dirt road about 21 kms, to the Pole Creek Spring Trailhead. By continuing further south on this same road from Sisters Town, one can reach the Three Creeks Trailhead and Lake. This is one of the longer routes into the Three Sisters Wilderness Area.

Shopping areas can be found in Bend, with a large business district; and at Sisters Town, 34 kms northwest of Bend and northeast of the Sisters Peaks.

There are forest ranger stations in both Bend and Sisters Town, where one can get the latest information on trails, roads, weather and snow conditions, and where the latest maps of the national forest can be bought.

Of the four major summits in this area, North Sister is the oldest volcano and the most eroded, therefore the one having the most difficult routes. In late summer one can usually find an all-rock route up any of these peaks, but an ice ax and crampons should be the standard equipment.

The best weather conditions usually exist in the summer months, but September and October often have good weather as well. Normally, the 9 months, excluding summer, are subject to continuous cyclonic storm activity.

If you're on foot with no car, buses can be taken to and from Bend and Sisters Town, but probably nowhere else. Highway 242 and the Cascade Lakes Drive are fairly busy, so with a sign stating your destintion, hitching can be good.

**Map:**  Three Sisters Wilderness, about 1 : 95,000, from the Deschutes and Willamette N.F., and any nearby ranger station, especially at Sisters and Bend.

North Sister from the north. Right hand ridge is normal route.

# Map 205-1, Three Sisters, Cascade Mts., Ore., USA

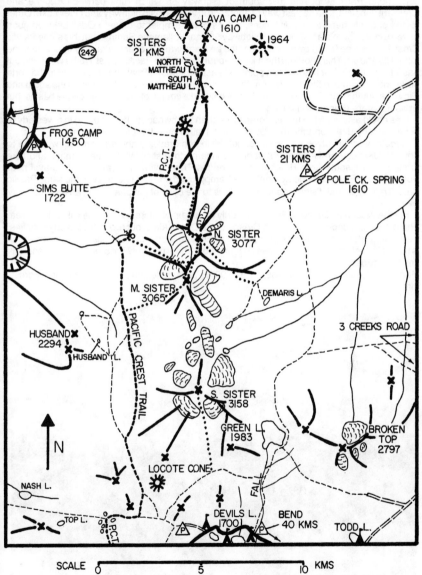

LAVA CAMP L.
1610

1964

SISTERS
21 KMS

NORTH
MATTHEAU L.
SOUTH
MATTHEAU L.

(242)

P.C.T.

SISTERS
21 KMS

FROG CAMP
1450

POLE CK. SPRING
1610

SIMS BUTTE
1722

N. SISTER
3077

DEMARIS L.

M. SISTER
3065

3 CREEKS ROAD

HUSBAND
2294
HUSBAND L.

PACIFIC CREST TRAIL

S. SISTER
3158

BROKEN
TOP
2797

GREEN L.
1983

N

LOCOTE CONE

NASH L.

FALL

DEVILS L.
1700

BEND
40 KMS

TODD L.

TOP L.

P.C.T.

SCALE  0          5          10  KMS

# Diamond, Cascade Mountains, Oregon, USA

Located near the center of Oregons' Cascade Range is the Diamond Peak Wilderness Area. Within this small primitive area is Diamond Peak, rising to 2665 meters, the highest in the immediate area. This wilderness area is so small, that a strong hiker with small pack can walk across it in one day. The area is full of small lakes, but few have fish.

Diamond Peak is located just south of Highway 58 which runs between Eugene and Crescent Junction. The easiest way of appraoch is via this main highway and Odell Lake. Other routes offer shorter walking distances, but it's much simpler to drive to Odell Lake on good paved roads. There's a trailhead on Highway 58 near Willamette Summit, but this same Pacific Crest Trail can be found by parking near the lake and walking over the railway tracks near the tunnel as shown. This shortens the hike by about 2 kms. The Pacific Crest Trail is well kept, but has little traffic. Follow this trail to a point just east of Diamond Peak then route-find to the north ridge, thence south to the summit. Another easy route would be to walk further to the south and climb the south ridge. There are small snow fields in a couple of north facing cirque basins, but in some years dwindle to nothing.

One could also walk the trail to Yoran Lake, then bushwhack (which is easy) in a westerly or southwesterly direction until the Pacific Crest Trail is met, then to the summit.

A route which involves less walking, but driving on graveled and dusty roads, would be to drive to Oakridge on Highway 58 about 40 kms northwest of Willamette Summit, and take forest road 21 south from Hills Creek Reservoir. This paved highway turns to gravel near Summit Lake. From near the Summit Lake Campground one can find and use the same Pacific Crest Trail. This time it's only about 6 or 7 kms to the base of the peak itself, an easy half-day hike for many.

For the most part Diamond Peak is the only mountain of interest within the wilderness area. There are a few cabins around both Crescent and Odell Lakes, but few places to buy supplies. Buy those before entering the region, either at Eugene, Bend, or Oakridge. Because the peak is not really high, an all rock route can be found from about mid-July on, so ice ax and crampons are not needed.

**Map:**   Diamond Peak Wilderness, 1 : 62,500, or Willamette and Deschutes National Forest maps.

Diamond Peak Massif from Yoran Lake.

# Map 206-1, Diamond, Cascade Mts., Oregon, USA

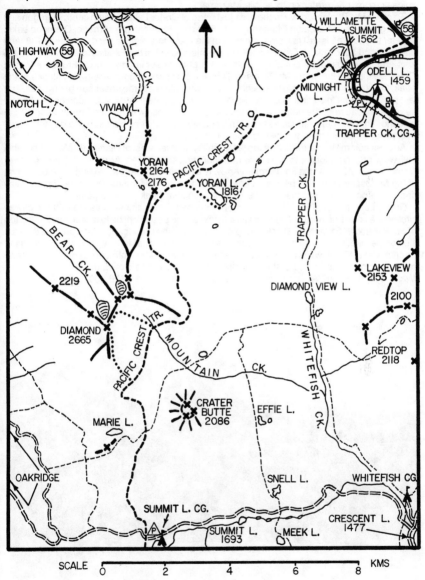

HIGHWAY 58

WILLAMETTE SUMMIT 1562

N

ODELL L. 1459

MIDNIGHT L.

NOTCH L.

FALL CK.

VIVIAN L.

TRAPPER CK. CG.

PACIFIC CREST TR.

YORAN 2164 2176

YORAN L. 1816

TRAPPER CK.

BEAR CK.

2219

LAKEVIEW 2153

DIAMOND VIEW L.

2100

DIAMOND 2665

PACIFIC CREST TR.

MOUNTAIN CK.

WHITEFISH CK.

REDTOP 2118

CRATER BUTTE 2086

EFFIE L.

MARIE L.

OAKRIDGE

SNELL L.

WHITEFISH CG.

SUMMIT L. CG.

SUMMIT L. 1693

MEEK L.

CRESCENT L. 1477

SCALE 0 2 4 6 8 KMS

# Thielsen, Cascade Mts., Oregon, USA

The one major peak shown on this map is Mt. Thielsen at 2799 meters. This is one of the lesser known of the old and eroded volcanic summits in the Cascade Range of the American Northwest. Also shown is Mt. Bailey, 2549 meters, just across the valley from Thielsen. And included is the Crater Lake National Park, which is actually the remains of a much higher volcanic cone often referred to as Mt. Mazama.

To climb Mt. Thielsen, drive to the area just north of Crater Lake in south central Oregon and to a large recreation area on Diamond Lake. From the southeastern corner of Diamond Lake, look for the Mt. Thielsen Trail. One can park at the lakeshore highway or on Highway 138 (and save walking about 1 km). From the lake to the intersection of the Pacific Crest Trail is about 5 kms and is well used, as climbing Thielsen is a popular summertime hike. From the Pacific Crest Trail, continue on the Mt. Thielsen Trail which zig zags up the southwest slopes of the peak. One has to go more or less straight up the scree slopes to the upper part of the peak. The last part steepens to a scramble, and the last 15 meters is near vertical, but can be climbed by nearly all because of the nature and composition of the rock which is the former throat of the volcano. That last part is much easier than it first appears. Up and back is half a day for almost everyone. Total length of the hike is about 6 to 7 kms.

Another summit with a trail to the top is Mt. Bailey, located west of Diamond Lake. To find this trail walk or drive along the paved road connecting the Broken Arrow and Thielsen View Camprounds. About 3 kms from Broken Arrow is a forest road and just beyond is the beginning of the Mt. Bailey Trail. This hike is another easy half day hike for most. From the top of Bailey one has a good view of Thielsen, the most spectacular peak in these parts.

Crater Lake National Park has little to offer the hiker and climber because of the highway circling the lake. But there are some trails and hikes. The best might be to take the trail to the top of Scott Peak, 2721 meters. This trail begins just east of the Cloudcap parking area on the east side of the lake. One could also walk from the rim to Timber Crater, as well as hiking along the Pacific Crest Trail which connects Crater Lake and Mt. Thielsen. There are many campgrounds in the area, but the entire region is popular and crowded.

**Map:** Rogue River, Winema, or Umpqua National Forests, 1 : 125,000.

Mt. Theilson from the west and Diamond Lake.

## Map 207-1, Thielsen, Cascade Mts., Oregon, USA

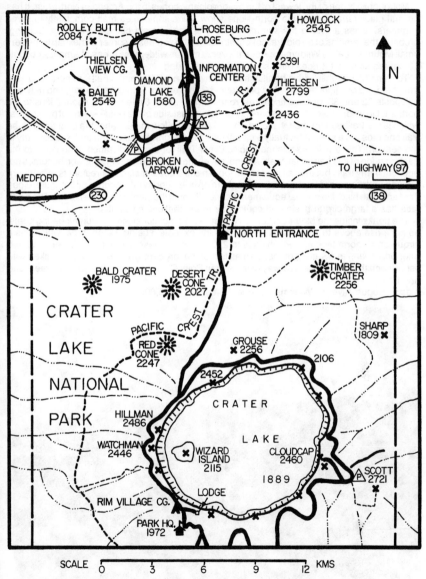

## McLoughlin, Cascade Mts., Oregon, USA

In southern Oregon not far from the California state line, stands another of the lofty volcanic cones which are part of the Cascade Range. This is Mt. McLoughlin rising to 2894 meters. The exact location is west of Klamath Lake, northwest of Klamath Falls and just north of Highway 140.

McLoughlin is one of the lowest of the major volcanic cones in the American Northwest. It has no real glaciers, and even the north-slope snow fields sometimes melt completely in some summers. It has a trail to the summit where one finds an old cement and stone building, probably the remains of an old fire lookout station. In the southeast corner of the map is the very small Mountain Lakes Wilderness Area. It's very small as wilderness areas of America go, only 10 square kms, but it does offer some interesting hiking.

To climb McLoughlin, drive or hitch hike northwest out of Klamathc Falls, or north and east from Medford on Highway 140. At a point about 2 kms east of Fish Lake Turnoff, and between mileposts 32 and 33, one will find forest road number 3650. Drive or walk about 5 kms to the northeast to where is seen a large parking lot on the west side of the road—a kind of picnic area, which is the trailhead for the Mt. McLoughlin Trail. Just a few meters after the beginning of the trail one crosses a stream (actually a canal) which is the only water on the trail, except early in the season. This trail intersects the Pacific Crest Trail for a short distance, then leads to the eastern ridge of this half conal peak. As one leaves the trees, the trail zig zags and becomes not one, but many trails but they all lead to the top. This is a popular climb for residents of southern Oregon and the author found 30-35 hikers there on one Sunday afternoon in mid-August. Good Trail and nice hike. No special equipment needed if doing the climb in summer or fall. The north face has a large cirque basin and could offer more challenging climbs.

The peaks inside the Mountain Lakes Wilderness are not considered mountaineering goals, as none rise above the tree line, with perhaps the exception being Aspen Butte, which has a cirque on its north face and which rises to 2502 meters. These summits are all rounded and offer only hiking in a setting of many small lakes, the larger of which have been stocked with fish. Reach this area easiest by way of the Aspen Point Campground or the Varney Creek road and trail.

**Map:**  Rogue River or Winema National Forests, 1 : 125,000.

Mt. McLaughlin from the northeast. East ridge to the left.

438

# Map 208-1, McLaughlin, Cascade Mts., Ore., USA

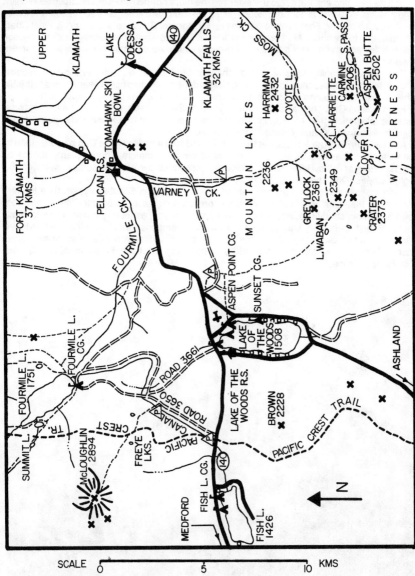

SCALE 0  5  10 KMS

## Mt. Shasta, Cascade Mts., California, USA

Mt. Shasta at 4317 meters, is the highest peak in northern California and is the second highest in the American Northwest. Of all the volcanos in the Cascade Mountains, only Rainier is higher. Shasta is an almost perfect volcanic cone, and not very old. However, it has not erupted in human history.

Shasta has glaciers, but not to the extent as the more northerly mountains, such as Rainier. The glaciers exist on the northern slopes, while the south face is largely free of snow and ice, at least in late summer. For the most part, the region north of Shasta is of the Marine West Coast Climate; that to the south, Mediterranean Climate. Summers are hot and dry, but it's far enough north to escape the real long periods of drought which are common in central and southern California.

The normal climbing season is June through September, with the remaining 8 months subject to frontal passages. However, climbing is done at all times of the year, thanks to the Ski Shasta resort located on the south face, which offers a good year-round approach.

From Shasta City, one can drive about 23 kms to the ski resort, on a wide, paved highway. Most people park at the resort parking lot and hike along the lift to where it ends, then over the ridge to Avalanche Gulch, thence to the summit.

Another normal route is to park at Bunny Flat, and take a trail to Horse Camp Lodge, then to the summit of Shasta, or its western sister, Shastina, 3759 meters. There's plenty of water at the ski resort and the Horse Camp Lodge, but otherwise there's little surface water on the higher slopes. One should carry water above these points.

Food, gasoline and other supplies should be purchased in Shasta City, which is the last place to do that. One should also stop at the forest ranger station in Shasta City for the latest road and snow conditions, as well as forest service maps, especially if one wants to climb routes other than those mentioned above. Ice ax and crampons should be taken, even on these "normal routes," although in late summer it can be an almost all rock and scree route.

**Map:** Shasta, 1 : 62,500, from the USGS, or the Shasta National Forest map, from Shasta City Ranger Office.

This is the south face and ridge of Mt. Shasta.

# Map 209-1, Shasta, Cascade Mts., California, USA

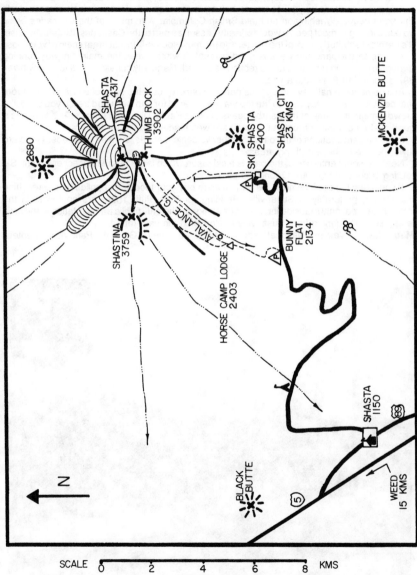

# Lassen, Lassen Volcanic N.P., California, USA

Lassen Peak standing at 3188 meters elevation, is the highest peak within the boundaries of the Lassen Volcanic National Park. Because it had its most recent eruption in 1914 (activity lasted for 7 years), the mountain has been made into a national park. This park is located in northern California, between Redding and Susanville, on US Highway 89.

In some respects this peak belongs to the Sierra Nevada, which include the high peaks south of this area. In other ways it seems to belong to the Cascade Range, which extends north through Oregon, Washington and into British Columbia. With much of the Cascades being volcanic in origin, most people would classify Lassen as part of the Cascades. If this is the case, it's the most southerly peak of the range, and the most southerly in that great chain of volcanos.

Access to the park and peak is good, except in winter when the main highway running through the park in a north-south direction, is closed. Generally speaking, this road (Highway 89) is open 7 or 8 months a year.

At a point about halfway through the park is a parking lot at the base of Lassen Peak. From that point it's a very easy walk to the top via a well cared for and well used trail. If you don't like crowds, might try some of the nearby peaks such as Eagle, Diller and Loomis. The park has a good system of trails throughout, and all are well marked and looked after.

In the eastern sections of the park are other volcanic features, such as lava beds. There are fewer people in these outlying areas.

Near the south entrance of the park is a ski resort which is the best winter access point. Ski touring is popular in winter around the park.

If you expect to spend time in the park, plan to buy your food and supplies before reaching this region, preferably in Susanville, Redding, or Red Bluff. There are no towns in the immediate area, only roadside inns and gas stations. The only public transportation in the area is bus service, running from Susanville to Red Bluff the year-round.

**Map:**   Lassen Volcanic National Park, 1 : 62,500, from the USGS or the Park Visitor Center.

Mt. Lassen from the northeast. Route is on the left skyline.

# Map 210-1, Lassen, Lassen N.P., Calif., USA

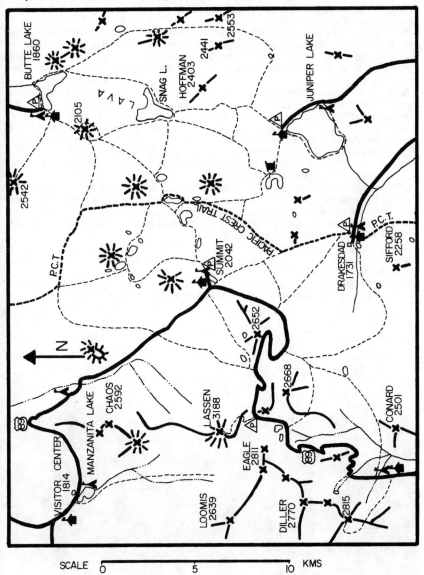

## Mt. Lyell, Sierra Nevada, California, USA

This is the first of 6 maps covering the high peaks of the Sierra Nevada in California. At the center of this map is Tioga Pass, which links Yosemite National Park with Lee Vining, located on the eastern side of the Sierras. In the north of the map is Conway Summit; in the south is June Lake.

Like all the Sierras, this part is made up mostly of metamorphic type rock, along with some granite. The entire range has been uplifted and folded, and are mountains in the truest sense. There are no volcanic peaks in this region.

If you haven't your own transportation, reaching the area can be a problem; except on the main road, which is California Highway 395. There's regular bus service on this highway—which runs from Reno and Carson City, Nevada, south to Bishop and through the Owens Valley to as far as San Bernardino. If you haven't a car then using the thumb is one other alternative.

Some of the areas which will interest climbers and hikers, are as follows. In the north are the mountains around the Virginia Lakes, including Dunderberg, which is the most northerly of the higher peaks of the Sierra. The peaks in this area are not difficult to climb. In the next canyon south of Dunderberg is a road up to Lundy Lake. This road runs into the mountains for about 10 kms but there aren't many high summits in the area.

One of the best access roads is Highway 120 crossing the Tioga Pass. From this pass a number of summits can be climbed, including Conness, North, Dana, and Gibbs. Dana is the second highest peak on this map, at 3995 meters.

Still further south are more peaks which can be approached from the June Lake Loop Road. Some of the higher summits here are Wood, Parker, Kolp, Kuna, Rodgers and Lyell at 3998 meters (the highest peak on the map). If you dislike crowds, don't plan to stay in the area of the June Lake Loop; it's always congested, usually with retired people. Other access points, with fewer people, are Walker and Parker lakes.

Lee Vining is the largest settlement in the area, with Mono Lake next. Get forest service maps and further information at the ranger station near Lee Vining, and the one west of Tioga Pass, just inside Yosemite Park.

**Map:** Yosemite National Park and Vicinity, 1 : 125,000, or Inyo National Forest, from any nearby ranger station. Several USGS maps also cover this area.

From the top of Dunderberg looking south towards Mt. Dana.

# Map 211-1, Lyell, Sierra Nevada, Calif., USA

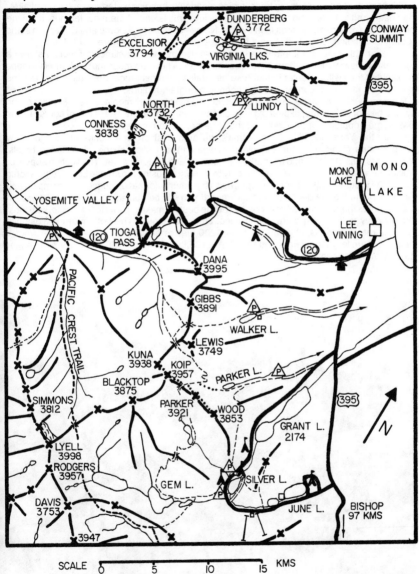

# Yosemite National Park, California, USA

This map is the second of a series of 6, covering most of the high regions of the Sierra Nevada of California. Five of these maps follow the main or highest crest of the range, but this one includes a section to the west of the divide, on the San Joaquin Valley side. This map is of the Yosemite Valley and the Yosemite National Park, one of the best known and most visited of the national parks in the USA.

This region is known for its big trees, alpine meadows, hanging waterfalls, and most of all for the sheer granite cliffs facing the Yosemite Valley. This is one of the most famous, if not *the* most famous rock climbing area in the world. Names such as Half Dome and El Capitan stand out in the climbing journals as some of the best rock climbs anywhere.

However, this map is not intended for serious use by the rock climber; it merely shows a generalized view of the southern 2⁄3 of Yosemite Park. There are much more informative maps available at the visitors center in the Yosemite Valley, at most ranger stations throughout the part, and at ranger stations in the neighboring mountain regions.

For those who like peace, quiet, and solitude, it's best to go someplace else. For those who want to hike or rock climb, expect big crowds and many regulations. All of this of course is due to extreme popularity of the area and the large population in California.

Within the Yosemite Valley itself—that's the area east of Arch Rock—are found many campgrounds, picnic sites, horse stables, a village with post office, chapel, clinic, lodge, hotels, restaurants, gas stations, and the park headquarters and visitors center. The section above, or east of the village itself, can be reached only by walking or using the shuttle buses. One should stop at the visitors center to obtain maps and all the latest information concerning camping and climbing within the national park. Be aware that you will be subject to many regulations.

Oftentimes the spring or fall seasons can be the best for making a visit to Yosemite, with most of the heavy traffic being there during June, July and August. The bottom of the Yosemite Valley is rather mild, as it's at a rather low 1200 meters elevation.

**Map:** Yosemite National Park and Vicinity, 1 : 125,000, from the USGS and any park ranger stations or visitor centers.

Rugged peaks in the northeast part of Yosemite N. P.

# Map 212-3, Yosemite National Park., Calif., USA

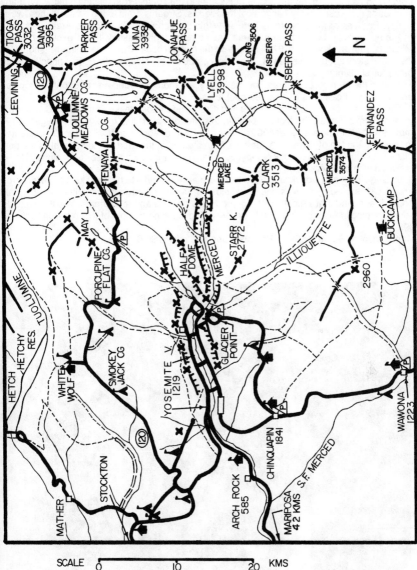

SCALE 0       10       20   KMS

## Morgan, Sierra Nevada, California, USA

This is the third in the series of 6 maps which cover the higher sections of the Sierra Nevada of central California. On the north is the Minerets and the Mammoth Mountain ski lodge, and on the southern end is Tom's Place and Rock Creek. This region is about halfway between Yosemite National Park and Bishop, which lies toward the northern end of the Owens Valley.

On the east side of the main crest of the Sierras is Highway 395. This very good highway runs from Reno on the north, to the Los Angeles area in the south. From this main highway, many side roads run west into the canyons of the Sierras. Streams drain to the east into the Owens Valley. Portions of the mountains here lie within the John Muir Wilderness Area.

The northern portion of this map area has no really high peaks, with the exception of the Minarets, with an elevation of 3744 meters on the highest peak. The name "Minaret" should tell the whole story about these peaks. They are a group of very steep and jagged pinnacles which make for challenging rock climbing.

Around the Mammoth ski area, the mountains are more subdued and offer only a crowded environment of campers and retired people.

The one area of perhaps most interest to hikers and climbers alike, is the Rock Creek area, west of Tom's Place. The highest peak in this group and on this map, is Mt. Morgan, 4191 meters. Others in the area over 4000 meters are, Hilgard, Abbott, and Mills. If you're interested in reaching the top of many high summits, then the end of the road on Rock Creek is the best place to begin. One can count 9 campsites in the Tom's Place-Rock Creek area alone. It too is crowded with campers.

McGee Creek and Convict Lake are two more access points to high peaks. Within this area are no glaciers—only a few small snowfields. There are no large communities nearby, only Tom's Place, and that's mostly just a group of gas stations and restaurants. You'll have to do your shopping in Bishop to the south, or Lee Vining to the north, both of which are on Highway 395.

**Map:** Inyo or Sierra National Forests maps and also USGS maps.

Yosemite Falls and Yosemite Point Buttress to the right (Map 212).

# Map 213-2, Morgan, Sierra Nevada, Calif., USA

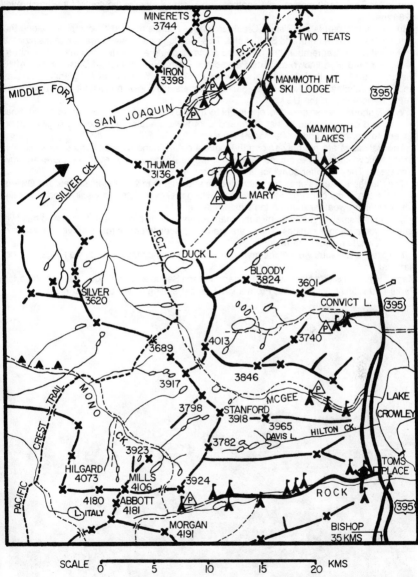

MINERETS 3744

TWO TEATS

P.C.T.

IRON 3398

MAMMOTH MT. SKI LODGE

395

MIDDLE FORK

SAN JOAQUIN

MAMMOTH LAKES

SILVER CK.

THUMB 3136

N

P.C.T.

L. MARY

DUCK L.

BLOODY 3824

3601

SILVER 3620

CONVICT L. 395

3689

4013

3740

PACIFIC CREST TRAIL

MONO CK.

3917

3846

3798

MCGEE

STANFORD 3918

LAKE CROWLEY

HILGARD 4073

3923

3782

3965

DAVIS L.

HILTON CK.

TOMS PLACE

MILLS 4106

3924

ROCK

4180

L. ITALY

ABBOTT 4181

P

395

MORGAN 4191

BISHOP 35 KMS

SCALE  0    5    10    15    20  KMS

## North Palisade, Sierra Nevada, California, USA

This is the fourth in a series of 6 maps covering most of the Sierra Nevada of California. This map covers the area west and south of Bishop, the largest and best known of the towns in the Owens Valley. The Owens Valley lies just east of the main crest of the Sierras, and runs in a north-south direction.

In the northwest section of the map is the Pine Creek area above Rovana. The highest peak here is Mt. Tom, 4162 meters, with another high summit further to the south, Mt. Humphreys, 4264 meters.

In the middle part is the Bishop Creek drainage. There's at least 11 campsites along the creek and at Lake Sabrina and South Lake. This is a highly congested area during the months of June through September, but is a good place to begin a hike or climb into the northern sections of the area known as "The Palisades." From the area around Darwin Peak, 4216 meters, south to South Palisade (not shown on this map), is one high wall of granite pinnacles and peaks culminating in North Palisade, 4342 meters. It's one of the best rock climbing areas in the Sierras and in the USA.

With Bishop Creek so crowded, one might try the Big Pine Creek Canyon. There are summer homes and one campsite in that area, and a lot fewer people. Big Pine Creek gives good access to North and Middle Palisade Peaks.

The Palisades are not only among the highest peaks in the Sierras, but also possess the largest snowfields. None are considered to be real glaciers however, as there are few crevasses. They do offer some ice and snow routes.

The Sierras' eastern slopes are much steeper and drier than the western slopes. The Owens Valley is one of the driest places in America, which makes for lots of sunshine and generally better climbing weather than on the western slope.

Bishop is a small city, with many supermarkets and a large business district. It also has two national forest ranger stations. These are the best places to obtain forest service maps, and more information about the region.

The area to the southwest of the main divide shown on the map is part of the Kings Canyon National Park.

**Map:** Inyo and Sierra National Forest maps, or the Sequoia and Kings Canyon National Parks and vicinity, 1 : 125,000. From a local ranger station or visitor center in Bishop.

Looking to the southwest of Bishop at the Palisades.

Map 214-1, N. Palisade, Sierra Nevada, Calif., USA

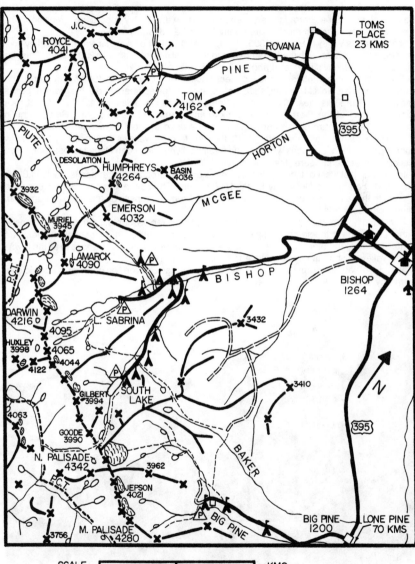

## Split Mt., Sierra Nevada, California, USA

The area covered by this map is from Middle Palisade Peak (4280 meters) and Birch Creek, south to the Independence area, with Symmes and Independence Creeks. The only town in the area is Independence, formerly a ranching community, but which now derives its livelihood from tourism.

Like all the maps in this Sierra Nevada series (with the exception of the one of Yosemite National Park), it covers the high crest of the range and the valley immediately to the east. The eastern slopes of the Sierra fall very steeply to the Owens Valley floor along a fault line. The western slopes descend much more gently to the San Joaquin Valley.

In the Owens Valley is Highway 395, linking Reno and the Los Angeles area. The valley floor is about 1200 meters, with the higher peaks to the west reaching about 4200 meters. This rise takes place within a distance of about 12 to 15 kms.

The crest of the mountains in the Independence area is dotted with 4000 meter peaks, the highest of which is Split Mountain, 4286 meters. It sits at the southern end of the group of peaks known as "The Palisades." This group of steep granite pinnacles is one of the finest rock climbing areas of the Sierras. These peaks can be reached via Birch and Red Mountain Creeks. The roads are dirt and gravel, but can be used by most passenger cars.

There are many side-roads leading off to the west from the valley's main highway. The valley floor is private land, but signs will be posted, telling if you can or can't legally cross to the Inyo National Forest land nearer the mountains.

In the area just west of Independence, there's another group of higher peaks, such as Black Mt., 4051 meters, and University Peak, 4156 meters. The best and most used access road leading to these peaks is up Independence Creek. From a campsite on this creek, a number of climbs can be made.

For further information and forest service maps of this region, contact the ranger stations at either Lone Pine to the south, or Big Pine or Bishop to the north. A number of guidebooks are written covering the Sierras, and they are available in book and souvenir shops in all the towns in the valley. Bishop is the best place to shop.

**Map:** Inyo National Forest     or the Sequoia and Kings Canyon National Parks and vicinity, from any local ranger station or the visitor center in Bishop.

Cinder cones along the fault line in the Owens Valley.

# Map 215-2, Split, Sierra Nevada, Calif., USA

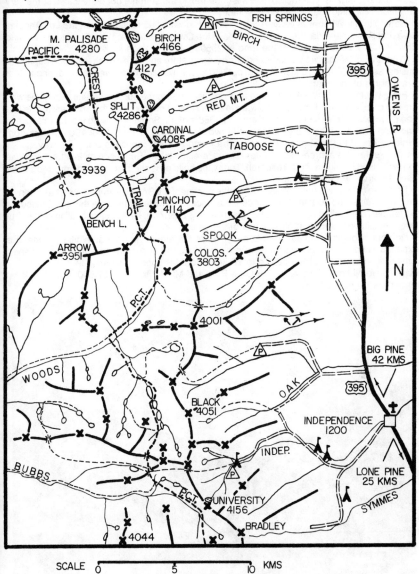

## Mt. Whitney, Sierra Nevada, California, USA

This is the 6th map of the series covering the Sierras of California. The highest mountain on this map is Mt. Whitney, 4419 meters. It's the highest peak in the Sierras as well as in the continental USA.

Whitney is located at the southern end of this range, with the physical makeup being mostly granite and quartzite type rock. There's a good trail to the summit, but there's also some very good rock climbing routes on the east face.

Getting to Mt. Whitney is easy. A major route, Highway 395 runs between the Los Angeles area and Reno, Nevada, passing Lone Pine in the Owens Valley. At Lone Pine, turn west and drive the 21 kms to the end of the road at 2550 meters, a place known as Whitney Portal.

Whitney Portal has two campgrounds and a small store and cafe, which are open during the busiest season. There are also several parking lots, which are full on weekends during four or five months of the year.

From Whitney Portal, the very good and well used trail to the summit begins. Along the way are two camping sites, for those who want to spend more time than one day in the area. The first one is Outpost, the second is Trail Camp, at 3658 meters. Some people do the 19 kms hike in one long day, but others prefer to do it in two. The vertical rise is about 1900 meters from Whitney Portal to the summit. Water can be found at many locations along the way.

At the summit is a three-room stone building, erected by the Smithstonian Institute, and was formerly used for high altitude research. Today the building is still in good condition, and can be used for an emergency shelter.

Because Whitney is the highest peak in the continental USA, it is climbed about as often as any mountain in the country. Weekends are especially crowded from June through October or November, depending on the weather (each year is different). Heavy snows fall in winter, but little precipitation comes at other times of the year.

Do your shopping no later than Lone Pine, as the store and cafe at Whitney Portal are expensive and lack variety. If you're traveling without a car, buses are the only public transport available on Highway 395. Hitching to Whitney Portal is good on weekends.

**Map:** Inyo National Forest, or Lone Pine and Mt. Whitney, 1 : 62,500, from any local ranger station or the USGS.

Mt. Whitney from just above Lone Pine in the Owens Valley.

# Map 216-1, Whitney, Sierra Nevada, Calif., USA

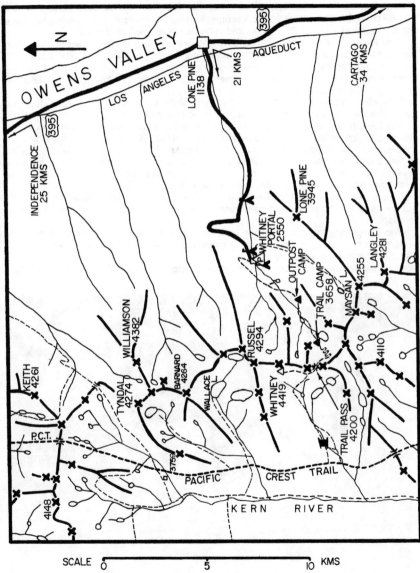

# White, White Mountains, California, USA

White Mt., 4342 meters, is the highest summit in the range known as the White Mountains. This dry mountain range is located just east of Bishop and the Sierra Nevadas in central California. These mountains form the western boundary of the Basin and Range system which covers most of Nevada and western Utah. It's been folded and uplifted, and consists of many different rocks. Many old mines are scattered about the region.

White Mt. itself is rather easy to approach, as there are two research stations on the mountain—one is 8 kms from the top, the other is at the summit itself. From the locked gate to the top, is about 13 kms. Only authorized vehicles are allowed beyond the gate.

Don't forget to have a full tank of gasoline and extra water, especially if you're planning to camp near the locked gate or in the Bristolcone Pine Forest, just to the south. In that forest are picnic sites, *but no water!* There are several small springs in the area, as shown on the map, but this is a very dry region, even at high elevations. The access road from Westguard Pass is good, but very steep in places.

If one wants to climb some of the northerly peaks, Morris Creek is perhaps the best approach route. This road leaves Highway 6, about 2½ kms north of the California fruit inspection station.

There are many dirt roads leading from Highways 6 and 3A, to the base of the mountains. Because of the dryness of the region and lack of forest in most areas, walking into the mountains is not difficult, even without trails. Boundary Peak, 4006 meters, is listed as the highest peak in Nevada. A recommended hike is from north to south—or vice versa, along the crest of the range. There's no trail, but it's not a difficult hike. You'll likely be alone, as most everybody else is across the valley to the west, in the Sierra Nevadas.

If you're planning a crestline hike, keep in mind the scarcity of water. Late spring or early summer would be the best time to make such a walk, as there would be some remaining winter snows.

Before beginning any climb in these mountains, stop at one of the ranger stations or the visitors center in Bishop for forest service maps and further information about access roads and the Birstolcone Forest.

**Map:**  Inyo National Forest, or White Mtn. Peak and Barcroft, 1 : 62,500, from any local ranger station or the USGS.

Bristlecone Pines in the southern parts of White Mountain.

# Map 217-1, White, White Mts., Calif., USA

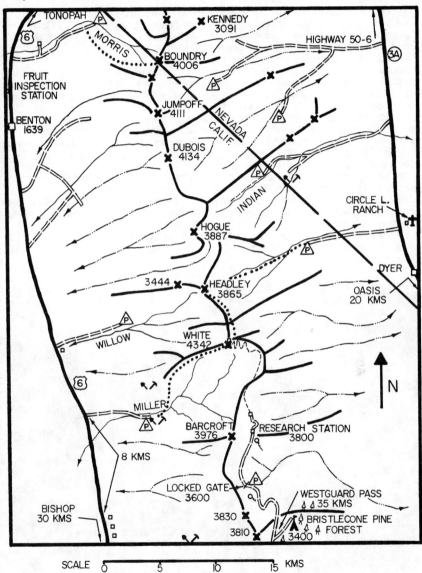

TONOPAH

US 6

MORRIS

FRUIT
INSPECTION
STATION

BENTON
1639

KENNEDY
3091

HIGHWAY 50-6

3A

BOUNDRY
4006

P

JUMPOFF
4111

NEVADA
CALIF.

P

DUBOIS
4134

P

INDIAN

CIRCLE L.
RANCH

HOGUE
3887

P

DYER

3444

HEADLEY
3865

OASIS
20 KMS

P

WILLOW

WHITE
4342

N

MILLER

P

BARCROFT
3976

RESEARCH STATION
3800

6

8 KMS

LOCKED GATE
3600

P

WESTGUARD PASS
35 KMS

BISHOP
30 KMS

3830

3810

3400

BRISTLECONE PINE
FOREST

SCALE  0        5        10        15   KMS

# Toiyabe Dome, Toiyabe Range, Nevada, USA

Toiyabe Dome, sometimes called Arc Dome, is 3590 meters high and the highest summit in the Toiyabe Range of central Nevada. These are folded mountains, composed mostly of quartzites. Toiyabe Dome is a rounded mountain with no difficult routes. The only rock climbing possibilities are about 3 or 4 kms up South Twin River from the road's end. At that point solid canyon walls offer some rock climbing.

To reach the summit of Toiyabe Dome, where the ruins of an old US Army Heliograph Station are found, drive to the Columbine Campground, on Steward Creek. Reach the Columbine Campground by driving south from Austin Nevada, to the Reese River Guard Station, about 65 kms. From there, continue up Steward Creek on a reasonably good road to the campground. From Columbine one has a choice of two trails.

Another route is via the Reese River Valley and the Cow Creek Road, beginning just north of the Cloverdale Summit. This country is mostly open with trees and sagebrush interdispersed, making for easy cross-country travel, even without trails. Either of these two routes to the summit can be hiked easily in one day.

A longer route, but perhaps more scenic, would be up the South Fork of South Twin River. This trail is well used and easy to follow. All the trails in this range (as with most other mountains in Nevada) are used and maintained, not by the forest service—but by cattle and cattlemen and in October, by deer hunters. For a good 2 day hike, try a loop, using the South and North Twin Rivers and climb Toiyabe Dome at the same time.

The east side of this range is easily reached via Highway 8A or 376, from either Tonopah on the south, or Austin on the north. Both of these towns mentioned have forest ranger stations, where more maps and information can be found. They are also the best places to get food, gas and other supplies. Nearer the area, one can get limited food and gas at Carver and Round Mountain, both old mining towns.

Climbing season is from June through October, in most years.

**Map:**  Toiyabe National Forest, Northern Section, 1 : 125,000, from the Tonopah or Austin Ranger Stations.

Relics of the gold rush days are seen in South Twin Canyon.

# Map 218-1, Toiyabe D., Toiyabe Ra., Nev., USA

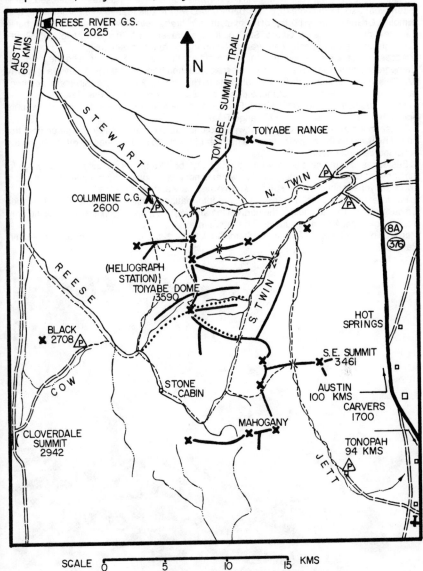

REESE RIVER G.S.
2025

AUSTIN
65 KMS

N

TOIYABE SUMMIT TRAIL

STEWART

TOIYABE RANGE

N. TWIN

COLUMBINE C.G.
2600

8A
376

REESE

(HELIOGRAPH
STATION)
TOIYABE DOME
3590

S. TWIN

HOT
SPRINGS

BLACK
2708

S.E. SUMMIT
3461

COW

STONE
CABIN

AUSTIN
100 KMS

CARVERS
1700

CLOVERDALE
SUMMIT
2942

MAHOGANY

TONOPAH
94 KMS

JETT

SCALE 0     5     10     15  KMS

## Bunker Hill, Toiyabe Range, Nevada, USA

Bunker Hill, at 3498 meters, is the highest peak in the northern half of the Toiyabe Range in central Nevada. The range at this particular point is very narrow with short canyons on either side. Other higher peaks in the area are Toiyabe Peak in the north, at 3290 meters, and Toiyabe Range Peak in the south, at 3341 meters.

Running the full length of the range is the Toiyabe Summit Trail. This trail is little used, but in recent years some maintenance has been done, with the increased interest in hiking and climbing. On the southern portion of the map, the trail pretty well follows the summit ridge, but in the area of the Kingston Guard Station, it is a gravel road. In the area of Big Creek Campground, it again becomes a trail, heading in a northerly direction.

Access to the area is good and easy. The old mining town of Kingston, and the Kingston Campground and Guard Station are all best approached from the east, and Nevada Highway 8A. This road puts one at the foot of Bunker Hill and its 3474 meter southern neighbor (apparently unnamed). Both of these peaks can easily be climbed in one day.

To the south, the Cottonwood Creek Road, which is a 4WD road in its higher sections, puts one within easy reach of Toiyabe Range Peak.

These mountains are not very big or wide, so one can climb any peak in the range from the paved highway on the east. There are a number of short, 4WD roads leading off this highway, up to the canyon mouths.

Best times to climb here is from June through October. Summers are long and hot, so go to the canyons which afford water. Usually, water is not found high on the mountains—but in the lower canyons, appearing as springs and flowing only a short distance.

For forest service or topo maps, and more information, contact the District Forest Ranger Office in Austin, Nevada, just to the north of the area on this map. Austin is also about the only place to get gas, food and supplies, in the entire area.

**Map:**  Toiyabe National Forest, Northern Section, 1 : 125,000, from the Tonopah or Austin Ranger Stations.

The trail to Wheeler Peak runs along the north ridge. (Map 224).

## Map 219-1, Bunker Hill, Toiyabe Ra., Nev., USA

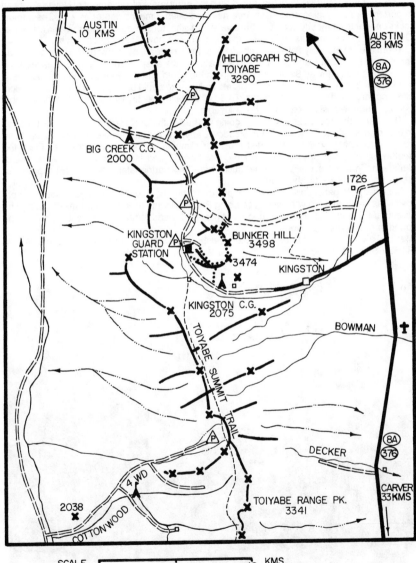

AUSTIN
10 KMS

AUSTIN
28 KMS

(HELIOGRAPH ST.)
TOIYABE
3290

N

8A
376

BIG CREEK C.G.
2000

1726

KINGSTON
GUARD
STATION

BUNKER HILL
3498

3474

KINGSTON

KINGSTON C.G.
2075

BOWMAN

TOIYABE SUMMIT TRAIL

DECKER

8A
376

CARVER
33KMS

4 WD

COTTONWOOD

2038

TOIYABE RANGE PK.
3341

SCALE  0        5        10  KMS

# Mt. Jefferson, Toquima Range, Nevada, USA

Mt. Jefferson, which has a couple of summits or peaks reaching to 3600 meters, is the highest mountain in all the central Nevada ranges. It's located in the Toquima Range, which is due north of Tonopah and Highways 6 and 96, and south of Austin and Highway 50. To the east is the Monitor Range, to the west the Toiyabe Range. All of the ranges in the Tonopah district are included in the Toiyabe National Forest.

The Toquima Range is forested, and during the early years of settlement of Nevada, was an important lumber-cutting area. This area has long been a mining center as well. The summit rocks appear to be mostly quartzite, but a variety of other rock formations exist within the range. Old mining towns such as Belmont and Jefferson, are now largely ghost towns.

There are several ways of approaching the summit plateau, but perhaps the best all-around route is via Pine Creek and Campground, located on the east side of the range. This area can be reached via Highway 82, from Tonopah on the south, or from Highway 50 and the Austin area on the north. By using the Pine Creek Trail, a hike could be made, in a circular fashion, climbing three of the highest summits. To do all three in one day would be too much for most people, but a two day hike would be enjoyable.

There are other routes as well. A trail going up the South Fork of Moores Creek, will take one to the north peak. From the south, the Meadow Canyon Road can be taken in order to reach the south peak (which may be the best route for climbing all the higher summits). From the southwest, one can drive about 10 kms east from Round Mountain to the historic site of Jefferson. From there, one can easily "bushwhack" in a northeasterly direction to the peaks, or use a trail as shown on the map.

Best places to get supplies are in Tonopah or Austin (there are forest ranger stations in both towns, as well), with the very last place being Round Mountain. Have a full tank of gas and be prepared for long dusty rides, on good, but graveled roads. Water is not plentiful, but can be found in all the main canyons.

**Map:**  Toiyabe National Forest, Northern Section, 1 : 125,000, from the Tonopah or Austin Ranger Stations.

Looking south at the south peak of Mt. Jefferson.

## Map 220-1, Jefferson, Toquima Ra., Nevada, USA

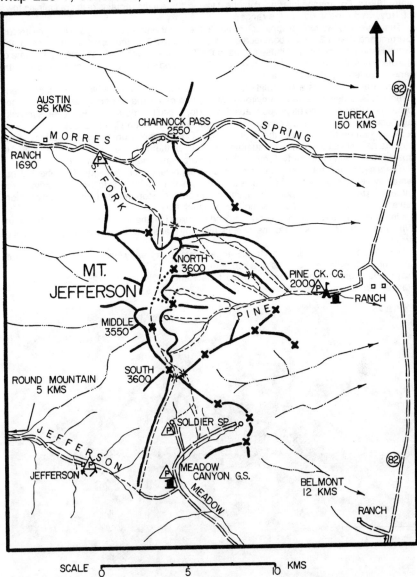

N

82

AUSTIN
96 KMS

EUREKA
150 KMS

CHARNOCK PASS
2550

S P R I N G

M O R R E S

RANCH
1690

P

S.

F O R K

NORTH
3600

MT.
JEFFERSON

PINE CK. CG.
2000

P

RANCH

MIDDLE
3550

P I N E

ROUND MOUNTAIN
5 KMS

SOUTH
3600

SOLDIER SP.

P

JEFFERSON

P

JEFFERSON

MEADOW
CANYON G.S.

P

82

BELMONT
12 KMS

MEADOW

RANCH

SCALE   0            5            10   KMS

## Troy Peak, Grant Range, Nevada, USA

Troy Peak listed at 3435 meters, is not a high mountain—even by Nevada standards, but because of its isolation, the chances are good you won't find other climbers or backpackers in the area to spoil an interesting climb. This is one place where a hiker can get away from it all.

On top of Troy Peak are the remains of an old US Army Heliograph Station, dating back to the early 1880's. For anyone interested in ghost towns, there's the remains of the old mining town of Troy, on the west side of the range.

There are only two logical approach routes to the Grant Range, and they are from the area of Current and Warm Springs, both located on US Highway 6, to the north and the west of the Grant Range. From either of these places, go to Troy ghost town and a bit beyond, to some of the old mines. From the end of the road, make your way up either Troy or the highest peak in the range, Whitepine, at 3444 meters.

The Grant Range is a bit isolated, yet there are major highways within 50 kms in any direction. Because of its desert environment and lack of any real streams, there's an absence of towns in the area, and no paved roads directly to, or into the mountains. However, even with all these minuses, there is one campground (forest service) on Cherry Creek.

Water can be a problem in the Grant Range. One must rely on only a few springs in the mountains, especially in the late summer and fall, as there is no "live," or running water to speak of. In spring and early summer there's more water available, however.

There's not much traffic around the mountains, especially once Highway 6 is left behind, but what travelers there are would probably stop for someone hitch hiking to Troy. Sometimes, the more remote the area, the better the hitching can be. It's recommended, however, that hikers have their own vehicles when visiting these mountains.

One is well advised to stock up on food and supplies in either Las Vegas, Ely, or Tonopah. What may appear to be small towns on state highway maps, may only be a crossroads, ranch, or ghost town.

Best time of year to climb in the Grant Range, is late spring, early summer, or fall. With a bit of snow around, water will be less of a problem.

**Map:** Humboldt National Forest—White Pine Ranger District, 1 : 125,000, from the Ely Ranger Station.

Bristlecone pines are the oldest living thing (summit of Troy).

# Map 221-1, Troy, Grant Range, Nevada, USA

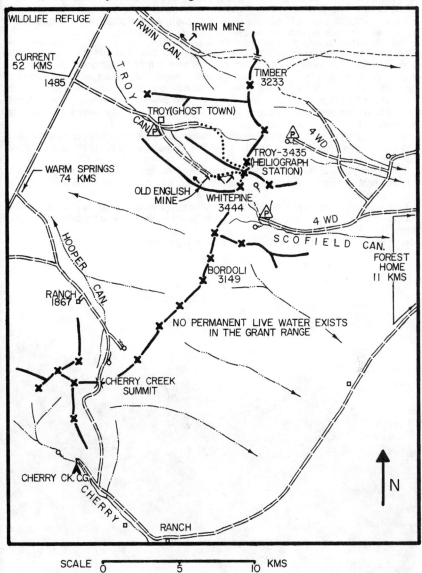

WILDLIFE REFUGE

IRWIN CAN.

IRWIN MINE

CURRENT
52 KMS

1485

TROY

TIMBER
3233

TROY(GHOST TOWN)

CAN.

P

4 WD

P

WARM SPRINGS
74 KMS

TROY-3435
(HEILIOGRAPH
STATION)

OLD ENGLISH
MINE

WHITEPINE
3444

P

4 WD

SCOFIELD CAN.

BORDOLI
3149

FOREST
HOME
11 KMS

HOOPER CAN.

RANCH
1867

NO PERMANENT LIVE WATER EXISTS
IN THE GRANT RANGE

CHERRY CREEK
SUMMIT

CHERRY CK. C.G.

N

CHERRY

RANCH

RANCH

SCALE    0          5          10    KMS

## Current Peak, White Pine Mts., Nevada, USA

Current Peak with 3510 meters elevation, is the highest summit in the White Pine Mountains. These mountains are located in east central Nevada, southwest of Ely and the Ruth Copper Mine, and west and northwest of US Highway 6.

The White Pine Mountains are similar to all the mountains in Nevada and western Utah. They run north-south, and are covered with a pine and spruce forest at higher elevations.

The central portion of the White Pines is composed of solid and largely unfractured, limestone, which dips about 45 degrees to the east. The upper east portion of Current Peak has some steep and smooth sections, which makes a climb interesting.

The White Pine Mountains and Current Peak are relatively easy to get to. There are three approach roads to the eastern side of the range, all of which take off from Highway 6. One route is the road running alongside Current Creek. It may have some bad sections, but it's the most direct to Current Peak. Park your car near the pass marked 2490 meters, and route-find from there. There's no trail to the top, but there's no need for one, as a good route is easy to find.

The second best approach is to leave Highway 6, and drive up White River, along which are located two campsites. At the junction marked 2140 meters, drive south and park somewhere northeast of the main peak.

Nevada is a dry state, but these mountains are high and large enough to produce sufficient water to feed three streams adequate for small fish. Camping in the White Pines is quiet and free, with few visitors.

The nearest town in the area is Ely, about 60 kms to the northeast. That's the best place to buy supplies, as it's the biggest town in eastern Nevada. If you're coming from the west, stop and shop in Tonopah.

For forest service maps and the latest information on roads and campsites, see the rangers stations in Ely or Tonopah, or possibly the Ellison Guard Station in the northeast section of the range.

**Map:** Humboldt National Forest—White Pine Ranger District, 1 : 125,000, from the Ely Ranger Station.

From the road junction marked 2140 meters, a look to the southwest.

# Map 222-1, Current, White Pine Mts., Nev., USA

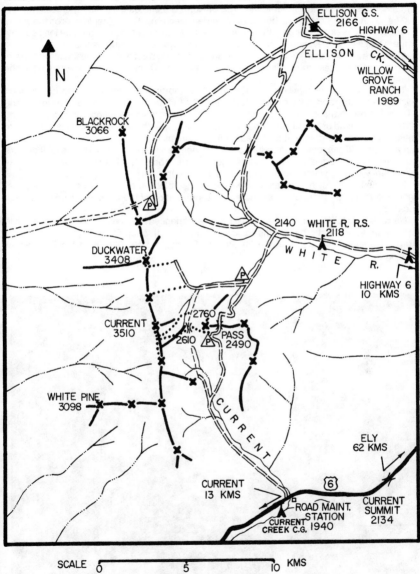

## North Schell, Schell Range, Nevada, USA

The Schell Range is located in extreme eastern Nevada not far from the Utah state line. It's also just east of Ely and McGill, and west of Mt. Moriah and Wheeler Peak. The highest peak on the range is North Schell, 3623 meters. Next is South Schell, at 3587 and Taft, 3577 meters.

Like all the mountains of the Basin and Range Province of western America, the Schell Range runs north-south, is long and narrow, and is forest covered. One can find various kinds of rock in these mountains, but in the area of North Schell Peak, it's mostly limestone.

The summits are not rugged, but mostly rounded over. From Cleve Creek Peak on the south, to about Bird Creek on the north, there are no real passes or low points on this one long summit ridge. Despite the elevation of this range, there are few large cirque basins.

There are a few trails in the Schell Range, and for the most part only local residents use them. From any of the access roads shown on the map, it's an easy one day hike to the summit of one or more peaks.

To climb North Schell, drive out of Ely and McGill north on Highway 93, then turn east on Highway 486, the road leading to the west side of the range. Turn east again at the sign stating "Timber Creek," and drive to the end of the road. There are two campgrounds and a small stream at the head of this canyon. From the road's end, take the trail to the north, and at one of many locations, head up and to the east for the summit.

Few if any difficult routes can be found in the Schell Range, but some north or east faces are steeper. The only equipment needed is a good pair of boots, and a tent if "over-nighting" is expected. Running water can be found in all major canyons.

Ely is the largest town in the area, making it the best place to shop. It's also the place to get more maps and/or information, as there's a ranger station of the Humboldt National Forest located there.

Heavy snows fall in winter, but very little rain is experienced in summer. Best times to climb in this range, as in most others in the region, is from June through October.

**Map:** Humboldt National Forest—Ely Ranger District, 1 : 125,000, from the Ely Ranger Station.

A scene from the summit of North Schell, looking south.

Map 223-1, North Schell, Schell Ra., Nevada, USA

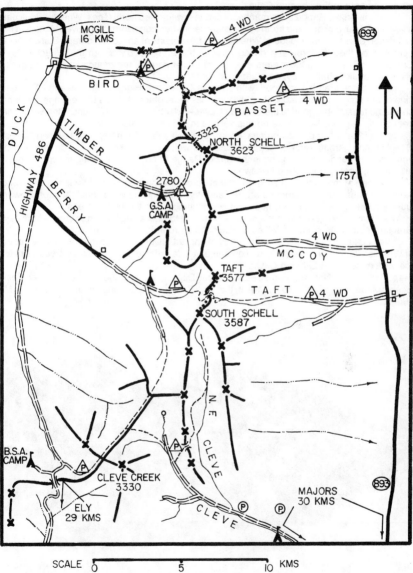

## Wheeler Peak, Snake Range, Nevada, USA

Wheeler Peak, at 3982 meters elevation, is located in the Snake Range of eastern Nevada, not far from the Utah-Nevada state line. Within this mountain range is the Lehman Caves National Monument, just off US Highway 50-6.

The Snake Range is similar to other mountain ranges in the Great Basin of Utah and Nevada, in that it has been uplifted and folded, and consists of quartzite and limestone, with some marble present in the Lehman Caves area.

Within the Snake Range are a number of cirques, with steep north faces. Wheeler Peak has a very impressive cirque and north face—especially when consideration is given to the fact it's in a desert environment. On top of Wheeler are the remains of an old Heliograph Station, once operated by the US Army and dating back to the early 1880's. From the Wheeler Peak Campground, at near 3000 meters elevation and just north of the mountain, one can easily climb the peak in half a day, on a very good trail.

Access to the area is very good, with Lehman Caves and Highway 50-6 nearby. The east side of the range is much easier to get to and has most of the streams in the range. Hitching should be reasonably good to the Lehman Caves—which is open year-round; otherwise, one needs his own vehicle. There's no bus service in the immediate area.

Food and supplies can be purchased in Baker, Nevada, 8 kms east of Lehman Caves. Gasoline and garage services are there also, as well as a forest ranger station. No special equipment is needed for climbing in the Snake Range or on Wheeler Peak, except for those attemptimg some north facing headwalls.

In this part of the American west and the state of Nevada, sunny weather is the rule—bad weather the exception. Summers are hot and dry, with only an occasional thunder shower. During some winters however, heavy snows accumulate in the higher areas.

A recommended hike, if time is available, would be to walk along the range crest—from say, Granite Peak in the south, to Wheeler Peak Campground, in the north.

Of particular interest to some, is the stand of ancient bristolcone pine trees within the cirque of Wheeler Peak. For further information and an explanation of the bristolcone trees, contact the visitors center at Lehman Caves.

**Map:** Humboldt National Forest—Ely Ranger District, 1 : 125,000, or the Wheeler Peak Scenic Area map. Both are found at the Ely Ranger Station and Lehman Caves N.M. Headquarters.

The north face of Wheeler East Peak.

# Map 224-1, Wheeler, Snake Range, Nevada, USA

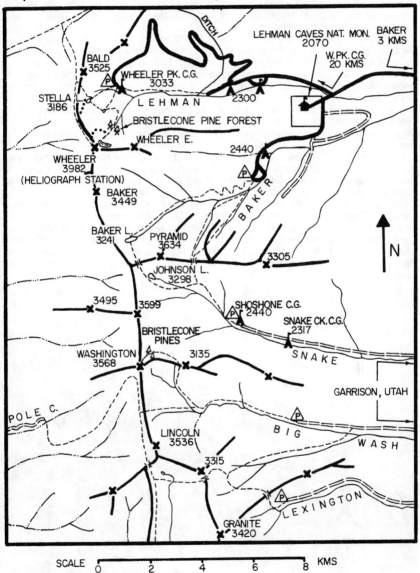

## Mt. Moriah, Snake Range, Nevada, USA

Mt. Moriah, 3674 meters, is technically part of the Snake Range, same as Wheeler Pk., but in reality it's a mountain and range in itself. The thing that separates these two high summits (Wheeler and Moriah) is US Highway 50-6, and the Sacramento Pass.

Mt. Moriah is a folded and uplifted mountain, composed mostly of limestone, but has outcroppings of various other rocks. All routes to the main summit are easy, but the North Peak, at about 3640 meters, has a good cirque and headwall on its northwest side. The steeper sections of this headwall are made up of smooth, solid limestone, which could present challenging routes to rock climbers.

There are three popular entry points to the Mt. Moriah Massif. First, on the southeast side, is Hendrys Creek. One can reach this canyon from a point very near the Utah-Nevada state line on Highway 50-6. From that point drive north about 13 kms to a junction. From near the junction, turn northwest on a 4WD road, which enters the mountains. This route involves the longest hike of the three major entry ways, but is also the most scenic. Plenty of water is available in Hendrys Creeks.

The easiest route—from the standpoint of roads and length of hike, is probably up Negro Creek. Drive about 12 kms north from Highway 50-6, then east toward a ranch and the major canyon. A 4WD road continues further, but cars must be parked at a good campsite about 6 kms east of the ranch. Most healthy climbers can do this hike in one long day.

The last route and the best one for reaching the "Tableland," is up the Four Mile Road and Canyon. This road can be reached by driving about 6 kms further north from the Negro Creek turnoff, then turning east and going as far as one's vehicle will allow. From there a trail is used to reach the table, or high, flat plateau, and the north peak area.

Each of the above mentioned routes have plenty of water available, along with good campsites. One should stock up on supplies in either Delta, Utah or Baker, Nevada, located to the east, or if one is coming from the west, at Ely, Nevada. No special equipment is needed, but a good-running vehicle is. Normally, the time of year to climb is from mid-June through October. You'll not find other hikers in these mountains, as they're unknown outside of Nevada.

**Map:** Humboldt National Forest—Ely Ranger District, 1 : 125,000, from the Ely Ranger Station.

From the western slopes of Mt. Moriah looking at the summit.

# Map 225-1, Moriah, Snake Range, Nevada, USA

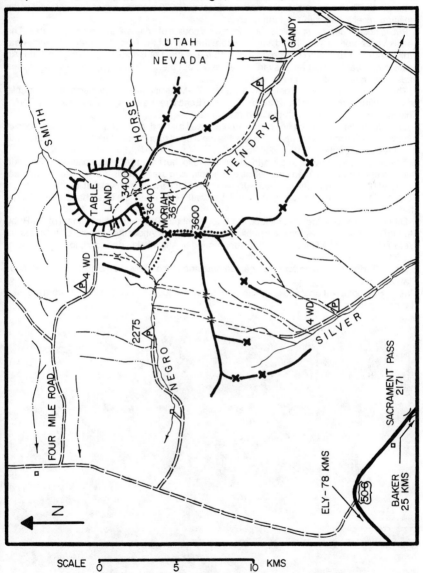

UTAH
NEVADA

GANDY

SMITH

HORSE

HENDRYS

TABLE
LAND
3400

3640
MORIAH
3674
3600

4 WD

NEGRO
2275

SILVER
4 WD

SACRAMENT PASS
2171

FOUR MILE ROAD

ELY-78 KMS

BAKER
25 KMS

506

N

SCALE 0        5        10  KMS

# Ruby Dome, Ruby Mountains, Nevada, USA

Ruby Dome, at 3471 meters altitude, is the highest summit in the Ruby Mountains located in northeast Nevada. The Ruby Mountains are fairly rugged—perhaps the most rugged in all of Nevada. The rock appears to mostly quartzite, but with some granite. There are "U" shaped valleys and many cirque basins, often holding small lakes. It's evident that because of its more northerly position, the area receives much more precipitation than the central Nevada ranges to the south. The timberline is also much lower (about 3200 meters), indicating that most of the moisture received falls in the form of snow.

Public access can be a problem, but there are a couple of easy ways to get into the area. The best is via Lamoille Creek Road, which enters the heart of the Ruby Mountains Scenic Area. From a number of sites on this road, one can reach most of the summits worth climbing. An eastern approach would be easy in some cases, but the foothills are covered with ranches under private ownership, with no public access.

The western side is also largely private, but the Te-Moak Indian Reservation has given public access for the area east of Lee. One can drive up Echo Creek aways, then hike to Ruby Dome. This is the best way in which to climb the Dome.

Trails in the Ruby Mountains Scenic Area are well marked, and because of the nearness of Interstate 80 which runs through Elko, are the most used of any mountain area in Nevada (with the possible exception of Wheeler Peak).

The best place to buy food, gas and supplies is Elko, but Lamoille has a small store. Roads in the area are generally paved and well used, compared to gravel roads in other Nevada ranges. The road up Lamoille Creek has heavy traffic (heavy for Nevada highways at least) in summer. For those on foot and hitch hiking, the Lamoille Creek Road offers the best chances of getting a lift into the mountains.

Other mountains in the area include the East Humboldt Range to the northeast of the Ruby Mountains; however, they too have public access problems. About the only way of access is via Wells and Angle Lake Road. From the campground at Angle Lake, one can find several peaks to climb.

More information and better maps can be obtained in the Wells, Lamoille, and Elko Ranger Stations.

**Map:** Humboldt National Forest—Ruby Mountains Ranger District, 1 : 125,000, from the Elko Ranger Station.

A look at the south slopes of Mt. Thomas.

# Map 226-1, Ruby Dome, Ruby Mts., Nevada, USA

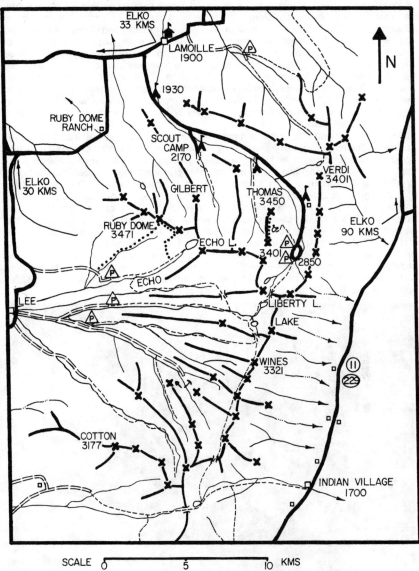

N

ELKO
33 KMS

LAMOILLE
1900

1930

RUBY DOME
RANCH

SCOUT
CAMP
2170

ELKO
30 KMS

GILBERT

THOMAS
3450

VERDI
3401

RUBY DOME
3471

ECHO L.

3401

ELKO
90 KMS

2850

ECHO

LEE

LIBERTY L.

LAKE

WINES
3321

11
229

COTTON
3177

INDIAN VILLAGE
1700

SCALE  0          5          10   KMS

## Matterhorn, Jarbridge Mountains, Nevada, USA

Few people know of a small wilderness area in the northeast corner of the state of Nevada. The one I'm referring to is the Jarbridge Wilderness, which covers the higher parts of the Jarbridge Mountains. This mountain region is located near the Idaho line and due north of Elko and Wells, Nevada. At the northwest boundary of the wilderness, is the very small community of Jarbridge, a former gold mining center, but which is now nearly abandoned. Jarbridge town has a small store for buying simple supplies, but sells no gasoline. To reach this area, one can either drive north out of Elko, or south out of Twin Falls Idaho. Of the two routes, the Idaho road situation is much better, as the road does not involve going over any major or high passes. For this route, take US Highway 93 south out of Twin Falls, and pass through Rogerson and Three Creek (where is located the last gasoline station). The pavement ends at Three Creek. From there to Jarbridge town is a well graveled road. If you're coming from the south and the Elko area, then drive north on State Road 51, eventually turning right or northeast on a gravel road leading to Jarbridge. The problem with this route is that one must go over two high passes on less than perfect dirt roads which are open for only 3 or 4 months each year. But in summer most vehicles can make it.

Once in the area and ready to climb, drive south out of Jarbridge town up the Jarbridge River past several campgrounds to the end of the road, where there is a parking lot and trail register. If you want a quick climb of the Matterhorn, the highest summit in the range at 3304 meters, then simply walk and do a little bushwhacking up the prominent ridge between Snowslide and Dry Gulches. This takes one to the summit with the least amount of walking. The author did this hike, then returned down Dry Gulch, where he found water about half way down. This route makes the climb a half-day hike for a fast and strong climber, but it's a fairly steep climb. For slower hikers it's a full day-climb. One could also walk further up the Jarbrige River to the Norman Mine and Jarbridge Pond, then walk north along the summit ridge, over Cougar Peak and to the Matterhorn. Another route would be to climb first Jarbridge Peak from the Success Mine or the town of Jarbridge, then walk south along the ridge to the Matterhorn. Camp anywhere in the canyon bottoms—lots of water. Climb from mid-June to October (Idaho route).

**Map:** Humbolt National Forest, 1 : 125,000, Elko Ranger Station. Also Jarbridge, 1 : 62,500, from USGS, or Elko Ranger Station or Jarbridge town store.

Matterhorn is not a rugged peak, except for the north face cirque.

# Map 227-1, Matterhorn, Jarbridge Mts., Nev., USA

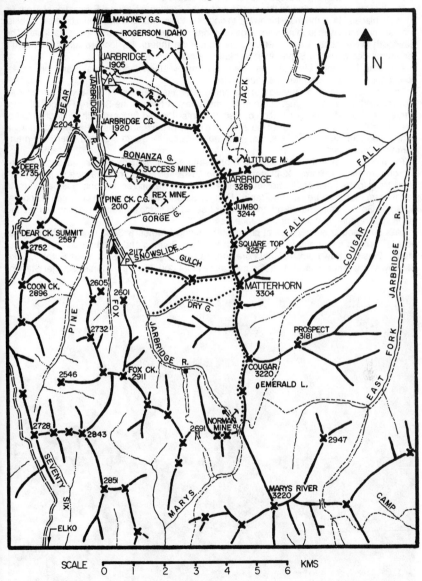

SCALE 0 1 2 3 4 5 6 KMS

# Thompson, Sawtooth Mountains, Idaho, USA

Included on this map is the Sawtooth Range, located in central Idaho, just southwest of the resort town of Stanley, and about 100 kms northwest of Ketchum and the Sun Valley region.

These are some of the most spectacular mountains in the USA, at least when viewed from Stanley. They offer some of the best rock climbing possibilities in the country as well. However, there is one problem—the place is over-run with tourists.

Much of the area included on this map is part of the Sawtooth National Recreational Area. As a result, places along the main highway, linking Sun Valley with Stanley and ultimately Challis, are very crowded with lodging places, gas stations, campsites, and other tourist facilities. The Sawtooth Wilderness Area is affected as well, even though it's located further north. It's recommended a visit in September be made, rather than mid-summer.

The area is a rock climber's paradise, with many steep jagged peaks and pinnacles, composed mostly of granite type rock.

The only settlement of any size in the entire region is Stanley. It has several stores, gas stations and restaurants. Just south of the main part of town is the Stanley Ranger Station. There's also another ranger station or visitors center located further south at Redfish Lake. These are the logical places to get more detailed maps of the mountains, as well as information concerning camping regulations, etc. Take note—because it's so crowded, there are many camping restrictions.

The highest peak in the Sawtooths is Thompson Peak, at 3285 meters. In that same cluster of high summits is Williams, 3242 meters; Baron, 3142, and Heyburn, 3119 meters. Maps don't show trails to the base of Thompson on either side, but walking cross-country is easy; first in sagebrush, then pine trees. The Stanley Ranger Station would be one access point; another would be Goat Creek; and still another is Iron Creek. This same central cluster can be reached via Wapti, on the west side of the range as well.

Less spectacular is the group of peaks surrounding Cramer, at 3268 meters. The shortest access route to this group is from the east and Hell Roaring and Pettit Lakes.

**Map:** Boise or Sawtooth National Forest maps, 1 : 125,000, or USGS maps Stanley, Lake Stanley, Warbonnet Peak and Mt. Cramer, all at 1 : 24,000. From the Stanley Ranger Station.

One of the best mountain views in the USA is from Stanley.

# Map 228-1, Thompson, Sawtooth Mts., Idaho, USA

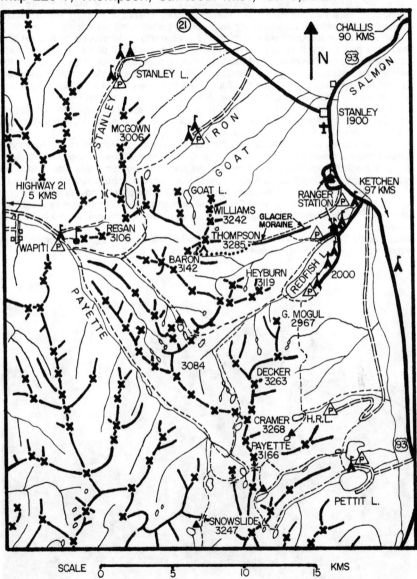

## White Cloud Peaks, Idaho, USA

The White Cloud Peaks are part of the Sawtooth National Recreational Area, located east of Stanley and north of Sun Valley, in central Idaho. The highest summit in the area is Castle Peak, at 3602 meters. Much of this area is composed of granitic type rocks; as a result, one can find many old abandoned mines, most of which are located in the northern parts.

This range is not a part of a wilderness area, but is rather wild none-the-less. There are many lakes, which makes fishing the number one recreational activity in the region. The mountains themselves, are not as rugged as their neighbors to the west, the Sawtooths.

Access is reasonably good, but one must drive several kms on dirt roads in order to get near the higher peaks. One thing to remember; there are thousands of people in the area each summer visiting the Sawtooths, so if you want to avoid crowds, approach the group from the east side and the road leading up the East Fork of the Salmon River. However, the easiest way to reach the highest peaks is via the 4th of July Creek Road, which begins about 5 kms south of Obsidian. It ends after 15 kms, in the area of 4th of July Lake.

On the East Fork of Salmon River, a good road leads as far as the Livingston Mine, but this is a long way from the highest point in the region, Castle Peak. To climb Castle, walk up the trails following either Little Boulder or Wickiup Creeks.

The places to buy supplies are Stanley, Challis or Ketchum. For more information and more detailed maps of this entire area, stop at the Yankee or Stanley Ranger Stations, or the visitor center at Redfish Lake. If you're coming from the south and the Sun Valley side, stop at the National Recreation Area Headquarters, about 15 kms north of Ketchum, also on Highway 93.

This region is especially crowded during the summer months of July and August, so the best time for hiking or climbing in the White Cloud Peaks is from the first of September, or after Labor Day weekend (an American holiday the first Monday of September), through the first part of October.

**Map:**   White Cloud Peak Area, or Challis National Forest, both 1 : 125,000, from any local ranger station, especially the Stanley Ranger Station.

Castle Peak is the highest summit of the White Cloud Peaks.

# Map 229-1, White Cloud Peaks, Idaho, USA

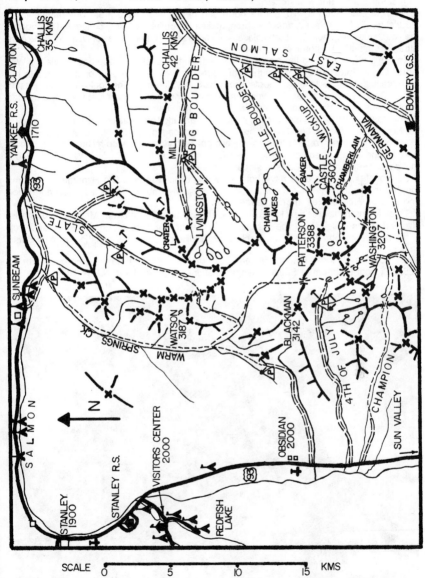

SCALE    0    5    10    15    KMS

## Hyndman Peak, Pioneer Mountains, Idaho, USA

Hyndman Peak, at 3682 meters, is one of the highest peaks in Idaho, and the highest in the region east of Sun Valley in an area known as the Pioneer Mountains. Also included on the map are parts of the Boulder Range with high peaks, Ryon, Kent, and Glassford.

This entire area is folded and uplifted, with lots of metamorphic rock such as quartzite, along with some granite and limestone.

Much of this region is wild, but it's not a part of any wilderness area. Unfortunately, the "tourist trap" of Sun Valley, near Ketchum, makes the entire area very congested throughout the year. However, there are some places with access to 4WD vehicles only, making the area attractive despite the hordes of tourists.

To climb Hyndman and the high summits nearby, the least used approach is via the Wild Horse Creek Road to the campground. This route involves a longer drive on gravel roads, but it's more scenic and with fewer people. From the Sun Valley side, one could drive northeast to Corral Creek, then walk east to Hyndman. Possibly the easiest and most used approach to Hyndman is via Gimlet, and the road leading up Hyndman Creek.

For those preferring the more solitary route up Kent and Ryon peaks, use the road going up the North Fork of the Big Lost River. This is not a good road for most cars, but few people use it. However, the easiest route to these same two peaks is via the Sawtooth National Recreation Area Headquarters, then north to near the LDS summer camp, and finally to West Pass. From this pass, simply route-find up the slopes to the east.

All mountains in this area have both easy and difficult routes. Old Hyndman has some tougher routes, but the rock is not the best for artificial climbing. There are a few north face snow fields, but ice axes are not needed.

Three towns in the area best for buying food and supplies are Ketchum, Mackay, and Challis. Hitching to Sun Valley should be easy, any time of year. For more information and maps, stop at the ranger stations in Ketchum, Mackay, or Challis, or at the guard station on Wild Horse Creek.

**Map:**  Challis National Forest, Eastern Half, or the Sawtooth National Forest, both 1 : 125,000, from Ketchum or Stanley Ranger Stations, or at Sawtooth N.R.A. HQ.

Hyndman Peak from the north. This is the north ridge.

# Map 230-1, Hyndman, Pioneer Mts., Idaho, USA

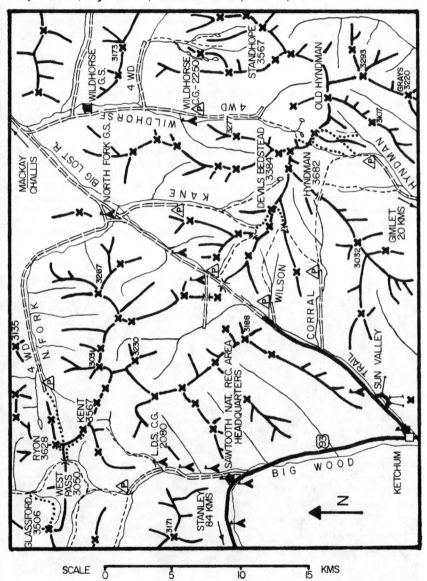

## Borah Peak, Lost River Range, Idaho, USA

Borah Peak, at 3858 meters, is the highest summit in Idaho. It's located in the Lost River Mountains northwest of Mackay. In this mountain range are several other high peaks, making it the highest group of peaks in Idaho. Two of these peaks are Leatherman and Breitenback, both of which are about 3700 meters.

These mountains rise abruptly from the valley, especially on the southwest side, where fault lines mark the landscape. Rocks consist of various types, including limestone and quartzite.

Any of the peaks which parallel US Highway 93, can best be approached from this highway. There are few, if any, trails into the range; but there are numerous short, 4WD roads leading up to the canyon mouths.

As one drives along the southwest slopes of the Lost River Range on Highway 93, one can see signs posted which indicate the names of the creeks flowing from the various canyon mouths.

Because it's a dry area, with a minimum of vegetation, one can easily walk up the open ridges to the summits. The canyon bottoms have water, but it's more difficult walking. The ridges are easier routes, but are waterless and hot in summer. The lower slopes have sagebrush, the middle slopes have a few pine trees, and towards the top only rocks.

Because Borah is the highest summit in Idaho, there's a well marked road, then a trail, leading to the summit. This is an easy one day hike from the end of the road on Cedar Creek.

The northeast side of the range has a few trails, as well as some 4WD roads extending into the canyons. These canyons can be reached via US Highway 22, leading out of Arco.

Mackay is the only town in the vicinity, so make it your gas, food and information stopping place. The ranger station in Mackay can provide the latest forest service maps and information concerning trails and 4WD roads. Summer and early fall is the best time to climb, with no special equipment needed.

**Map:**  Challis National Forest, Eastern Half, 1 : 125,000, from Mackay Ranger Station.

Borah Peak to the left, Leatherman to the right.

# Map 231-1, Borah, Lost River Range, Idaho, USA

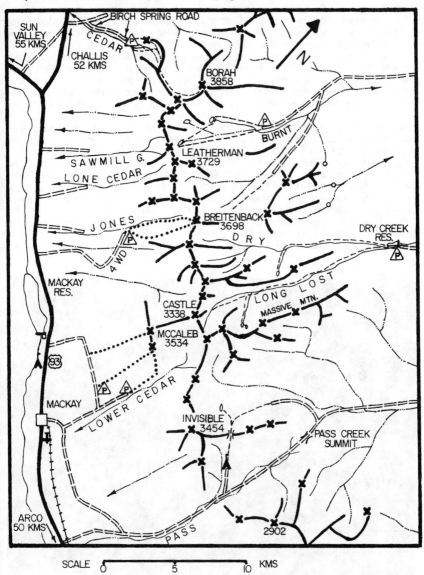

SCALE

## Diamond Peak, Lemhi Range, Idaho, USA

The Lemhi Range is one of several ranges running in a northwest to southeast direction, in south central Idaho. This mountain range is long and narrow and rather dry. At the mouths of most major canyons water is available, but most everywhere else it's nonexistent.

The highest summit in the Lemhi Range is Diamond Peak at 3719 meters. In the northern part of the mapped area, is the second highest peak, Mt. Bell, 3540 meters. Climbing in the Lemhi Range is likely to be lonely, as not many hikers or climbers make it to these mountains.

The easiest access route for climbing Diamond Peak, would be to drive up the Badger Creek Road, to the area near the Badger Mine. From the end of the road, one can route-find up a ridge or follow the creek bed—whichever seems easiest.

One could also drive up Pass Creek Canyon and reach the summit from the east—from Highway 28 and the Birch Creek Inn. From the end of the road, again route-find in a westerly direction to the summit. For either route mentioned, it's a one day hike.

The mountains are covered with sagebrush on the lower slopes, but the vegetation turns to pine forest further up. At all elevations, no matter what the vegetation, walking is easy—with or without a trail.

To climb Mt. Bell, use the approach road reaching Black and Basinger Creeks, then route-find to the summit. This is from the west and Highway 22. Mt. Bell can also be ascended from the east and Highway 28.

From the Badger Creek and Diamond Peak area, it's about 55 kms to Arco, Idaho, the closest town in the vicinity. To the north is Challis and Salmon, to the southeast is Idaho Falls, and to the east of the Lemhi Range is St. Anthony. One must buy supplies in one of these towns, as there's nothing else in between. Not many trails exist in the Lemhi Range, and only a few 4WD type roads reach the mountains from the two main highways.

For additional information about access roads, trails or routes, stop at the ranger stations in St. Anthony or Arco, or the Kaufman Guard Station (in summer only).

**Map:**   Challis or Targhee National Forests, 1 : 125,000, from any ranger station in the region.

The south face of Diamond Peak, with east ridge to the right.

## Map 232-1, Diamond, Lemhi Range, Idaho, USA

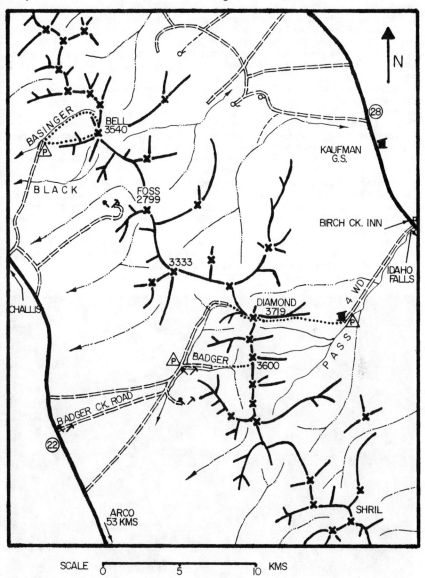

## Glacier National Park, Montana, USA

The northern-most Rockies in Montana and the USA, are included in the Glacier National Park, which borders on Canada's British Columbia and Alberta Provinces. The map shows a large part of the Glacier Park, and a small section of Waterton Lakes National Park of Canada.

These mountains are very similar to the rest of the Rocky Mountains throughout Montana and Canada. They're composed mostly of limestone and have been uplifted and folded. In recent geologic time they have been heavily glaciated. To this day, many smaller cirque glaciers remain, offering some interesting climbing, on ice, snow and rock.

Mt. Cleveland is the highest peak in the park at 3190 meters, with Mt. Jackson to the south, also over 3000 meters. Both offer some good climbs.

The "Going to the Sun Highway," the only road to cross the range within the park, is a good access road, but there are others—one being the highway from Babb to the Many Glacier Hotel area.

The two best ways to get to Mt. Cleveland are either from the Alberta side at the Waterton Lakes Park Headquarters (by boat or trail); or on the 4WD road-trail, beginning at Chief Mountain on U.S. Highway 17, at the U.S. Customs Station next to the international border. Take no less than 2 or 3 days of food, regardless of the approach route.

To climb Mt. Jackson hike up the trail following the St. Marys River, to Gunsight Lake, where is located a small aluminum hut (sleeps 6 persons). The normal route is then up the northeast ridge. Other climbs and normal routes include: Wilber—east face; Gould—west face; and Going to the Sun Peak, 2939 meters—west face.

For more detailed maps contact the ranger stations at West Glacier, Rising Sun—St. Mary's Lake, Lake McDonald, Swiftcurrent or Park Headquarters at Waterton Lakes.

Be sure and buy all supplies before entering the park. To the west are towns Whitefish and Kalispell; on the east are Browning, Babb and St. Mary, all in Montana; and on the north is Cardston, Alberta.

Most climbs here can be done on "all rock routes," but one should have an ice ax and crampons along, as well as a tent. Keep in mind that away from the highways, lodges, campgrounds, and gas stations, this is wild and rugged country.

**Map:** Glacier National Park, 1 : 125,000, from the USGS, or any park visitor center.

Looking north toward the Cleveland Peak area from Mt. Wilber.

# Map 233-1, Glacier National Pk., Montana, USA

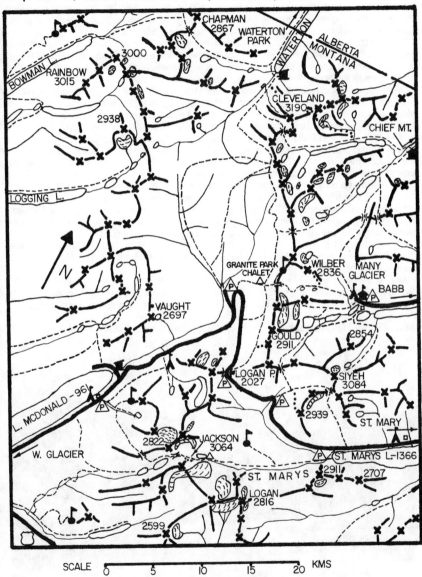

CHAPMAN 2867
WATERTON PARK
WATERTON
ALBERTA
MONTANA
BOWMAN
RAINBOW 3015
3000
2938
CLEVELAND 3190
CHIEF MT.
LOGGING L.
N
GRANITE PARK CHALET
WILBER 2836
MANY GLACIER
BABB
VAUGHT 2697
GOULD 2911
2854
LOGAN P. 2027
SIYEH 3084
L. McDONALD - 961
2939
ST. MARY
W. GLACIER
2822
JACKSON 3064
ST. MARYS L.-1366
ST. MARYS
2911
2707
LOGAN 2816
2599

SCALE 0   5   10   15   20   KMS

# Stimson, Glacier National Park, Mont., USA

This map covers a large area in northwest Montana. Nearly all the area to the north of US Highway 2 is part of Glacier National Park. It's here that some of the better climbs exist. Between Hungry Horse Reservior and Highway 2, and to the south of Highway 2, is a roadless region called the Great Bear Wilderness Area. This entire mountainous section is wild and makes for fine hiking, climbing, camping and fishing.

The highest peak on the map is Mt. Stimson, at 3104 meters. Another mountain, one having claim to be the toughest climb in the national park, is Mt. St. Nickolas, 2859 meters. And just to the south of Stanton Lake is Great Northern Peak with a fine glacier.

The normal route to Stimson begins at Nyack on Highway 2. Cross the Flathead R. by fording and proceed up Nyack Creek to a point just northwest of the peak. Bushwack up a ridge or a valley, whichever seems easiest, in the direction of the peak. After gaining the southwest ridge continue on to the summit. An easy climb most people can make.

On St. Nickolas, the authors' information comes from the *Climbers Guide to Glacier National Park*. The information on the approach to the mountain is totally unclear, so gather more information on the way in. Park at Essex Post Office and cross the Flathead River. Walk north to Park Creek, then follow it upstream to about 3 kms past the snowshoe cabin. Then head northwest over Chuch Butte and to the east base of this sharp and steep pyramid peak. The normal route is up to the Great Notch on the northeast ridge, then tough climbing to the summit on generally the same ridge (northeast). This climb is for experienced climbers with at least a rope for protection. A two day climb, maybe three.

One of the best climbs on this map outside Glacier Park is Great Northern, at 2653 meters. There are trails leading from the Stanton Lake area, both up the creek to the west, and to a ridge to the southwest, but this is not the easy way. Instead, drive southeast out of Martin on Highway 2 on the East Side Road of Hungry Horse Reservoir. About 13 kms southeast of Emery Creek boat landing area one comes to Hungry Horse Creek where a side raod makes an abrupt left turn. Park here and cross the creek and walk up the prominent ridges to the south of the creek. This leads to the summit of G. Northern. There's some bushwhacking at first, but the going gets easier further up.

July, August and September are the best months for climbing, but late summer is best for fording the Flathead on the way to Stimson. National Park ranger stations are good places to get maps and information, both at East and West Glacier. Buy food before arriving to this area. It's expensive in the mountains.

**Map:**   Glacier National Park, 1 : 125,000, USGS or from ranger stations.

From Stanton Lake looking towards Mt. Stimson to the east.

# Map 234-1, Stimson, Glacier N.P., Montana, USA

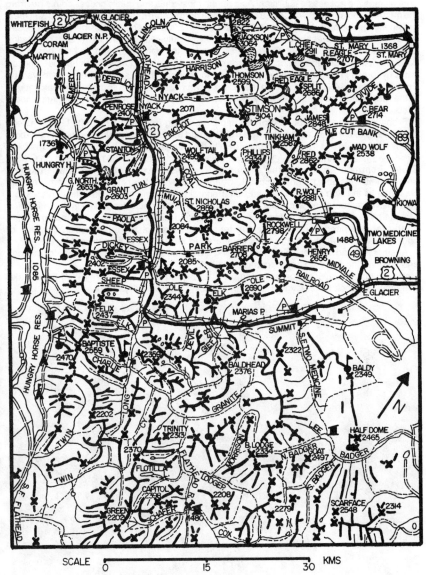

SCALE  0     15     30   KMS

## McDonald, Mission Range, Montana, USA

Located in northwestern Montana just south of Flathead Lake and west of the Bob Marshall Wilderness Area is another mountain range little known outside the immediate area. This is the Mission Range. And in the heart of this range is the Mission Mountains Primitive Area. Also, all areas to the west of the main divide are part of the Flathead Indian Reservation, a factor which complicates the access possibilities. As a result, most trails and public access points are from the eastern side and Highway 201, a road running north-south between Missoula and Kalispell.

The highest point in the area is McDonald Peak at 3008 meters. But this peak is in a closed area as of 1982. The reason is Grizzley Bears. It's the only peak with the right insect population to sustain a bear population. Therefore because of the danger to man and the bears own possible destruction, an area of 3 or 4 kms on either side of McDonald Peak has been put off limits by forestry people. However, if one were to go there, the best route would be to walk up Post Creek from McDonald Lake on the indian reservation, then turn south to the peak. Inquire at the ranger stations at either Seeley, Holland or Swan Lakes for up-to-date information about this situation.

Probably a better all around area for camping, hiking or climbing is in the Glacier Creek drainage. One can reach this basin by a road beyond the Lindbergh Lake Campground. About 5 kms up the road is a trail, but it drops down to the Glacier Creek. This is the longer walk, but has a better and shorter road. Or one can drive on the forest road 561 to its' end on Glacier Creek. From there a well-used trail takes one to Turquoise Lake. This lake lies between several fine summits including Panoramic, St. Charles (2537 meters), Glacier, Shoemaker and Daughter of the Sun (2675 meters). Each mountain has some good and difficult routes, but each has easy routes as well. One must keep in mind that below timberline in these Mission Mountains the vegetation is rather thick and difficult to bushwhack through. It is here and to the north that one needs to trail up to the tree line. There's a big difference in the type of undergrowth in the forest in this area compared to the ranges of southwest Montana.

Another fine and popular hiking and climbing area is around Gray Wolf Peak. Get to this peak and lake via the Beaver Creek drainage or Lindbergh Lake.

**Map:** Flathead National Forest (south) and 1 : 24,000 scale maps Gray Wolf Lake, Lake Marshall, Hemlock Lake, Cygnet Lake, Mt. Harding and St. Marys Lake.

McDonald Mtn. right, highest of the Mission Range summits (from Holland Lake).

# Map 235-1, McDonald, Misson Ra., Montana, USA

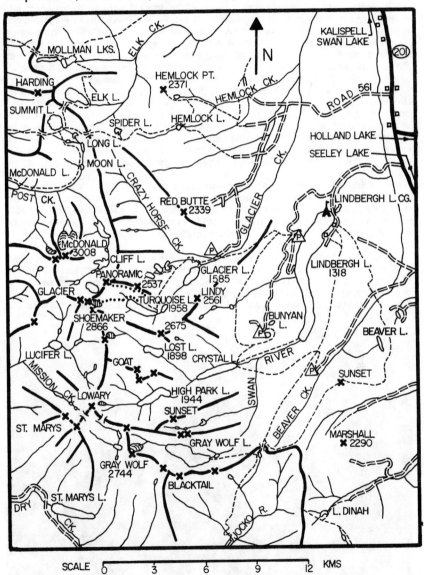

KALISPELL
SWAN LAKE
201

N

MOLLMAN LKS.
ELK CK.
HEMLOCK PT.
2371
HEMLOCK CK.
ROAD 561

HARDING
ELK L.
SUMMIT L.
SPIDER L.
HEMLOCK L.
HOLLAND LAKE
LONG L.
SEELEY LAKE
MOON L.
McDONALD L.
CRAZY HORSE CK.
POST CK.
RED BUTTE
2339
GLACIER CK.
LINDBERGH L. CG.

McDONALD
3008
CLIFF L.
P
PANORAMIC
2537
GLACIER L.
1585
LINDBERGH L.
1318
GLACIER
TURQUOISE L.
1958
LINDY
2561
SHOEMAKER
2866
2675
BUNYAN
L.
BEAVER L.
LOST L.
1898
CRYSTAL L.
P
LUCIFER L.
SWAN
RIVER
P
SUNSET
GOAT
MISSION CK.
LOWARY
HIGH PARK L.
1944
BEAVER CK.
ST. MARYS
SUNSET
MARSHALL
2290
GRAY WOLF L.
GRAY WOLF
2744
BLACKTAIL
ST. MARYS L.
DRY CK.
LOCKO R.
L. DINAH

SCALE  0    3    6    9    12   KMS

## Chinese Wall, Rocky Mts., Montana, USA

The mapped area here is in the Rocky Mts. of Montana not far south and east of Glacier National Park. It includes the northern half of the Bob Marshall Wilderness. There are a number of peaks just under the 3000 meter mark, so the summits are not high. However, this is one of the largest roadless areas in the continental USA. Hunting and backpacking are the most popular activities here, followed by fishing and climbing.

Keep in mind these mountains are an extension of the Rocky Mountains which run north into Canada, and are similar to those ranges in Banff and Jaspers Parks. Rocks are folded and ridges run north-south. The rock is predominatly limestone. The biggest attraction in the area is an imposing feature known as the Chinese Wall. This is simply a very long and rather straight ridge which drops steeply on the east side and gently on the west. It is about 20 kms long with an altitude of about 2600 meters. There are some routes up from the east, but not many.

Access to this region is most often from Gibson Reservoir, located about 35 kms west of Augusta. From the campground near the dam, there's a trail running past the lake and up the Sun River. Most people arrive at the wall via Moose Creek. One can also use Rock Creek to the north, or the South Fork of Sun River. Maps show a trail running from about Redhead Peak in the north to about Sphinx in the south on the east side of the wall. Camping is said to be prohibited within 1½ kms of the wall on the east slope. That's due to the popularity of the place. Roundtrip from Gibson Res. is about 100 kms. The wall could also be reached via Spotted Bear River or the Flathead River and the Meadow Creek Ranger Station, but these approaches are very long.

Here are some of the higher and better known peaks in the area and their routes of access. Sphinx Mountain is usually climbed from Moose Creek. Somehow gain access to the top of the wall, then walk along the crest south to the summit. Holland Peak at 2826 meters, is usually climbed via Holland Lake, located just off the map and south of Peak 2545. It appears an east ridge is the better way to the summit. Swan Peak, at 2821 meters, has a glaciated north face, so a south ridge route form Lion Creek is likely best.

For food and supplies, best to buy them in Augusta, Kalispell or some other larger town before arriving to this area. There are ranger stations at Goat Creek, Swan L., Gibson Res., South Fork of Sun River, and Holland Lake. Cabins shown on map are forest service maintenance cabins, and to be used in emergencies only.

**Map:** Bob Marshall Wilderness Area, 1 : 125,000?, National Forest Service and Choteau, 1 : 250,000, USGS.

Typical mountain scene in western part of map (Ptarmigan Peak).

# Map 236-1, Chinese Wall, Rocky Mts., Mont., USA

SCALE

0      15      30   KMS

## West Goat, Anaconda Range, Montana, USA

Still another interesting mountain range located in southwestern Montana is the Anaconda Range. It lies to the immediate southwest of Anaconda, one of the worlds' better known copper mining cities. Within this range are dozens of peaks over 3000 meters and many high country lakes, which makes fishing the number one sport. This map includes the higher northeastern part of the range. The higher portions of the Anaconda is part of the Anaconda-Pintler Wilderness Area.

About 1/3 of the area shown is private land, which includes the eastern part and Short and Haggin Peaks. About another third is part of the Deerlodge National Forest and the last third belongs to the Beaverhead National Forest. Nearly all the land near the main highways is private, while all the highland regions are public lands.

The highest peak in the Anaconda is West Goat Peak, at 3290 meters. This summit is part of a group of peaks clustered together on the southern slopes of the range, which are not set along the watershed divide. It's a fairly long hike to reach West Goat, as it lies near the center of the most remote part of the range. The shortest hike possible would be to drive up Meadow Creek, to where the road ends on Carpp Creek, then take the Carpp Lake trail to the higher basin, route-find over one pass, and down to the area of Warren Lake. From there an easy hike to the top although a bit of a complicated route. Less complicated routes of approach would be to drive up either Lamarche or Fishtrap Creeks, then walk up one of the trails along the West Forks of either creek to near Warren Lake, and to the summit. Which ever approach is used, it'll be at least a two day hike for the roundtrip. As an example of time and distance, the author (a fast hiker) walked from Lower Seymour to upper Seymour Lake, then to the top of Howe and return to Lower Seymour in 7 hours. Doing West Goat in one day by any one seems almost impossible.

One good point of access is the Lower Seymour Lake and Campground. There are no public access problems here and it's a good road to the lake. The basin's holding Storm and Twin Lakes are popular with good hiking and climbing possibilities nearby. Also good fishing. Remember too that this Southwestern part of Montana has generally better weather than does the northwest part of the state.

**Map:** Beaverhead, Deerlodge, and Bitterroot National Forest, and 1 : 24,000 maps Carp Ridge, Warren Park, Long Peak, Storm Lake, Mt. Evans, Lower Seymour Lake.

Mt. Howe left, and Mt. Evans to the right.

## Map 237-1, West Goat, Anaconda Ra., Mont., USA

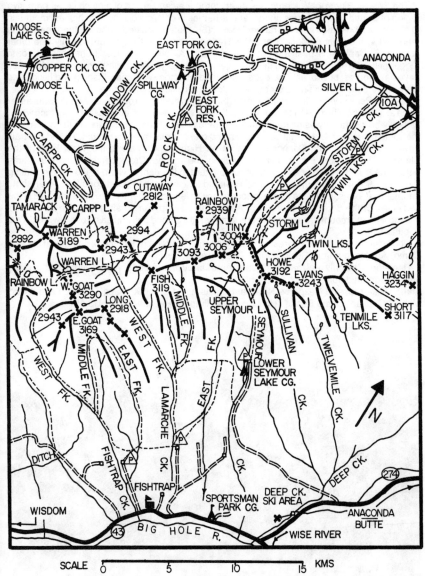

## Trapper, Bitterroot Mts., Montana, USA

The area included in this map is in the extreme southwestern corner of the state of Montana just south of Hamilton. The left hand side of the map is part of Idaho, but for this part of the Selway-Bitterroot Wilderness Area, one must approach from the Montana side and Highway 93.

The Selway-Bitterroot Wilderness is a very large area and is part of a much larger primitive region of Central Idaho. It goes under various names in different places. The highest mountain in all this vast unsettled land is Trapper Peak, 3094 meters, located in the southern part of the map and to the west of Conner and the Trapper Creek Job Corps Center. Only one other summit, El Capitan, is over the 3000 meter mark. All others are less in height, but not in ruggedness. All higher peaks on this map have some very difficult climbing routes. Most also have easy routes, but not all. There are some lakes, but they are small. Fishing and hiking and later in the season, hunting are popular outdoor activities in this range.

Trapper Peak is in full view from the main highway in the region of Conner and to about as far north as Darby, both in the Bitterroot Valley. It has a very steep and impressive north face which can only be climbed by using ropes and other equipment. But there is a trail to the summit via the south face which is a gentle slope reminding one of a plateau escarpment. To find this trail, drive or hitch hike from Conner southwest on Highway 473, along the West Fork of the Bitterroot River. About 8 or 9 kms southwest of the Trapper Creek center and about 3 kms before the Boulder Creek Campground turnoff, turn to the right or west, at the sign indicating the Trapper Peak road, then trail. This is an old logging road in good condition. After about another 8 or 9 kms, there is a large signboard on the left and several places to park. This is the beginning of the 8 km trail to the top. About half way up is a small spring, the only water available on the mountain, except in early summer. It's a good trail and easy to follow. And it's a popular hike.

Rock climbers might be interested in El Capitan, a Matterhorn type peak southwest of Lake Como. Approach it from Rock or Little Rock Creeks.

Hamilton is the only real town in the valley, but Darby has some services. Climbing and hiking here is from mid-July through September.

**Map:** Bitterroot and Nezperce National Forests and 1 : 24,000 maps Tenmile Lake, Ward Mtn, El Capitan, Como Peaks, Tin Cup Lake, Trapper Peak, from the USGS.

From the Bitterroot Valley. Trapper Peak left, and North Trapper right.

# Map 238-1, Trapper, Bitterroot Mts., Montana, USA

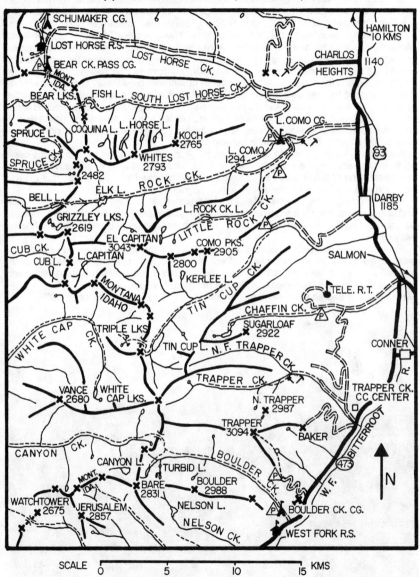

## Homer Youngs, Bitterroot Range, Montana, USA

This map includes parts of the Bitterroot Range which runs along the Montana-Idaho line, in an area not far north of Salmon, Idaho and south of Wisdom, Montana. It's in the southwestern corner of Montana. Most of the area of the map is in Montana, with just the extreme left hand side of the map showing Idaho.

One could enter this mountainous area from either Idaho or Montana, but most of the popular access routes seem to be from the Montana side, thus all attention here is given to that side of the line. The Beaverhead and Salmon National Forests are represented here.

The highest peak in this part of the range is Homer Youngs Peak at 3237 meters. It sits inside Montana by 3 or 4 kms, and wholly within the Beaverhead National Forest. Homer Youngs is a prominent peak that stands for the most part alone, being much higher than surrounding summits. It's an easy hike to the top. The normal way to climb Homer Youngs is like this: From Highway 278 and the small ranching community of Jackson, drive the 20 kms to Lower Miner Lake via a good and well-used gravel road. At the lake is a large campground with all facilities. One can drive any car or truck about 3 or 4 kms past the campground to where a locked gate is located. Just beyond the gate and before Kelley Creek is a trail which runs north, then west, to the vicinity of Heart Lake at the eastern base of the peak. From there climb to the ridge top and walk to the summit. There's water in several locations.

Another way would be to walk all the way to the Rock Island Lakes at the head of the basin. Many might want to camp and fish here. From the Rock Island Lakes it's an easy hike up the southwest ridge or the south face. This would be the best way for most people, but the east ridge route can be done in one day by almost anyone.

The second highest summit is believed to be Squaw Peak located not far from Twin Lakes and Campground. It too is a prominent peak standing alone and towering over its neighbors. It can be reached via Twin Lakes, or from the Big Swamp Creek side of the mountain. Another easy climb.

Since this area is in southwestern Montana (and central Idaho), one can expect good weather during the summer months, in direct contrast to regions in the northern part of the state. The drier climate is reflected in the vegetation. One can walk through the forest very easily, with or without trail—again unlike the more northerly regions.

**Map:** Beaverhead and Salmon National Forests and 1 : 24,000 maps from USGS.

Above the ranching town of Jackson, Homer Youngs Peak dominates.

Map 239-1, Homer Youngs, Bit., Ra., Mont., USA

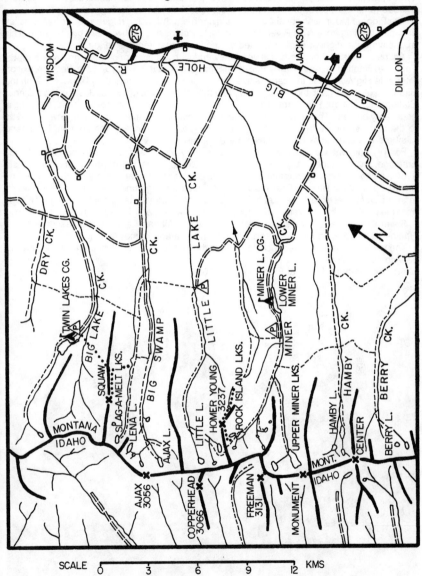

## Torrey, Pioneer Mts., Montana, USA

All of Montanas' higher peaks are located in the southwestern part of the state. One of these ranges is the Pioneer Mountains, just northwest of Dillon and southwest of Butte. It's not a large range, but has two summits at or near 3400 meters. The highest peak in the Pioneers is Tweedy, at exactly 3400 meters. However, the most noted mountain seems to be Torrey Peak, at 3398 meters. Apparently, most people believe Torrey to be the highest.

The Pioneer Mountains consist of two main north-south-tending ridges, divided by the valley and road running from Wise River on the north, to Polaris and Highway 278 on the south. This map covers the highest portion located on the eastern side of the range.

Access to this mapped region is very easy and with a minimum of dusty and rough roads. For those wanting to climb Torrey Peak, the Birch Creek road leading up from the Apex exit on Interstate Highway 15 is the better access route. Apex is 20 kms north of Dillon. Drive on the Birch Creek road past the Aspen and Dinner Station Campgrounds. Just beyond Dinner Station C.G. is about 1 km of rough road, then a gate. The gate is likely to be locked, so hiking is necessary beyond. The author walked about one hour beyond the gate, then bushwhacked up to the ridge to the north, then walked west along an easy route to the summit. For strong climbers this is an easy half day hike, for other most of a day.

For Tweedy, one would have to drive on past the Aspen Campground to the Willow Creek drainage, and at Gorge Creek, take the trail to the Gorge Lakes. From somewhere in that basin a route can be found to the summit. Or one could approach the peak from the north and west, by driving up the Wise River or Creek to the Mono Creek Campground where a trail begins which leads up David Creek to Torrey Lake. From just before Torrey Lake, turn left and climb Tweedy from the western slopes. Walking the ridge between Tweedy and Torrey is a difficult passage.

Several high peaks in the south, such as Baldy and Alturas 1 and 2 can be ascended from Rattlesnake Creek and Kelly Reservior, or from the area around Polaris.

The larger towns in the area include Butte to the northeast and Dillon, both of which are full service communities.

**Map:** Beaverhead National Forest, 1 : 125,000.

Foto shows the south face of Twiddy, from summit of Torrey Peak.

# Map 240-1, Torrey, Pioneer Mts., Montana, USA

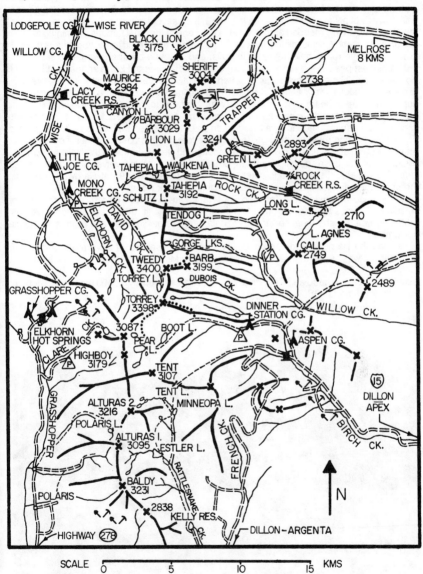

LODGEPOLE CG — WISE RIVER
WILLOW CG.
BLACK LION × 3175
MELROSE 8 KMS
SHERIFF × 3004
× 2738
WISE CK.
MAURICE × 2984
LACY CREEK R.S.
CANYON L.
CANYON CK.
TRAPPER CK.
BARBOUR × 3029
LION L.
× 3241
× 2893
GREEN L.
LITTLE JOE CG.
TAHEPIA
WAUKENA L.
ROCK CREEK R.S.
MONO CREEK CG.
TAHEPIA × 3192
ROCK CK.
LONG L.
SCHUTZ L.
ELKHORN CK.
TENDOG L.
× 2710
L. AGNES
DAVID CK.
GORGE LKS.
CALL × 2749
TWEEDY × 3400
BARB × 3199
TORREY L.
DUBOIS CK.
× 2489
GRASSHOPPER CG.
TORREY × 3398
DINNER STATION CG.
WILLOW CK.
ELKHORN HOT SPRINGS
× 3087
BOOT L.
ASPEN CG.
CLARK CK.
PEAR L.
HIGHBOY × 3179
TENT × 3107
TENT L.
15
DILLON APEX
GRASSHOPPER
ALTURAS 2. × 3216
MINNEOPA L.
POLARIS L.
ALTURAS 1. × 3095
ESTLER L.
FRENCH CK.
BIRCH CK.
BALDY × 3231
RATTLESNAKE CK.
N
POLARIS
× 2838
KELLY RES.
HIGHWAY 278
DILLON–ARGENTA

SCALE 0        5        10        15   KMS

## Jefferson, Tobacco Root Mts., Montana, USA

Another of the small and compact mountain ranges in southwestern Montana is the Tobacco Root Mountains, located southeast of Butte and directly west of Bozeman. There are two national forests involved in administering these lands; the Beaverhead in the southern half, and the Deerlodge in the northern half. The make-up of the geology is that of crystalline or metamorphic rocks of various kinds, including quartzite and granite. The area is criss-crossed with patches of private lands which have been in the past old mining towns and claims. Just a few kms south of this mapped area is Virginia City, one of the most famous old mining towns in the USA. As a result of this mining, the area is well endowed with old roads and miners trails. By now most of the roads have reverted to trails, and is now a backpackers paradise.

The highest peak in the range is Mt. Jefferson, 3232 meters. However, the best known is Hollow Top, 3205 meters, just south of Jefferson. Between these two peaks is an easy saddle to traverse, making it very easy to climb both mountains at the same time. The easiest route of approach seems to be from Harrison on the main highway, then via the small town of Pony. It's a paved road to Pony, then only about a 1½ or 2 kms drive on a good dirt road to where most cars must be parked. Then the walk begins on an old road, then trail, up to Hollow Top Lake. From this lake one must simply walk through the forest to the base of either mountain, then make the climb above timberline. This is a popular and well-used trail to the Hollow Top Lake.

One could also drive south up the South Boulder Creek, but this involves driving on about 25 kms of dirt roads. If this route is taken, exit Interstate Highway 90 at Cardwell, then pass through Jefferson and finally up the South Boulder Creek Road.

All the higher summits in the Tobacco Root Range are over 3000 meters, so there is a good selection of climbs to choose from. Most peaks have difficult routes, but all also have easy routes as well. For the most part these mountains make easy climbs and require no special equipment.

Besides the Harrison-Pony approach, one can also use one of several routes up from Sheridan, as well as two or three different routes from McAllister on the south-east side of the range.

**Map:**   Both Beaverhead and Deerlodge National Forests and 1 : 62,500 maps Waterloo and Harrison from the USGS.

Hollow Top Peak left, with Jefferson on the right.

# Map 241-1, Jefferson, Tob. Root Mts., Mont., USA

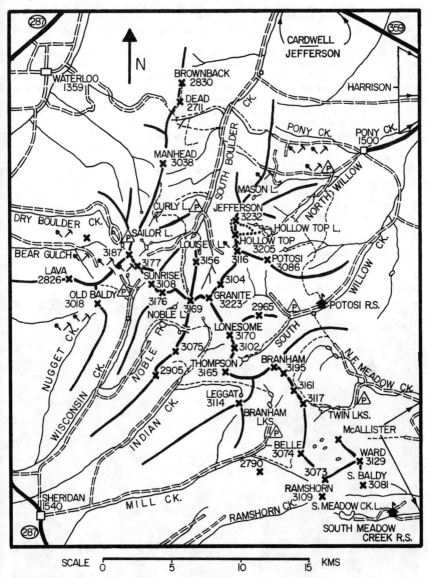

CARDWELL
JEFFERSON

HARRISON

N

BROWNBACK
2830

WATERLOO
1359

DEAD
2711

PONY CK.

PONY CK.

PONY
1500

MANHEAD
3038

MASON L.

P

SOUTH BOULDER CK.

NORTH WILLOW CK.

DRY BOULDER CK.

CURLY L.
P

JEFFERSON
3232

WILLOW CK.

HOLLOW TOP L.

SAILOR L.

LOUISE L.

HOLLOW TOP
3205

BEAR GULCH
3187

3177

3156

3116

POTOSI
3086

LAVA
2826

SUNRISE
3108

3104

OLD BALDY
3018

P

3176

GRANITE
3223

POTOSI R.S.

NOBLE L.
3169

2965

P

NUGGET CK.

WISCONSIN CK.

NOBLE FK.

3075

LONESOME
3170

3102

SOUTH

N.F. MEADOW CK.

INDIAN CK.

2905

THOMPSON
3165

BRANHAM
3195

3161

3117

P

LEGGAT
3114

BRANHAM
LKS.

TWIN LKS.

P

McALLISTER

BELLE
3074

WARD
3129

2790

3073

S. BALDY
3081

SHERIDAN
1540

MILL CK.

RAMSHORN
3109

S. MEADOW CK. L.

RAMSHORN CK.

SOUTH MEADOW
CREEK R.S.

SCALE  0          5          10          15   KMS

## Crazy Peak, Crazy Mountains, Montana, USA

Never heard of the Crazy Mountains? Few others have either, that's what's so good about them. Almost nobody goes there, so one can feel a little lonely at times. The Crazy Mountains are located north of Interstate Highway 90, and northwest of Big Timber, Montana. It's a small mountain range, but has a number of fine peaks around the 3400 meter level, including the highest in the range, Crazy Peak, 3418 meters. The peaks are high enough for several small, cirque glaciers to have developed near Twin Lakes. Travelers along Interstate 90, often go to the south and Yellowstone Park, or north to Glacier Park, so this small range is usually overlooked.

Access can be a problem, as all land surrounding the range is private. The only real, bonafide public access road is up the Big Timber Creek to the Half Moon Campground, both located on the east side of the range. As one gets close to the mountains, it's necessary to stop at a gate, right next to a ranch house. The driver of each vehicle must stop, open, then close the gate, but it's apparently not required to ask for permission to pass.

The normal route to Crazy Peak, is from the Half Moon Campground. One can walk on a good trail to the Blue Lake area, where a base camp could be set up, from which climbs to the surrounding peaks may be made. From Blue Lake one can easily climb Crazy Peak. Strong climbers however, could make the Crazy Peak hike in one long day from Half Moon Campground.

A second approach to Crazy Peak might be made from the ranch gate. With permission, one could walk from the gate up to the ridge to the south, then turn west and walk to the summit.

The big ridge to the south of Twin Lakes offers some very good ice, snow and rock climbing. The rock there is a mixture of granite, quartzite and limestone.

For additional information and maps on this eastern side of the range, see the ranger station in Big Timber, or for access to the western half, see the rangers at the Livington office. Big Timber is the very last settlement to buy food, and is 44 kms from the Half Moon Campground.

July through September are the very best months to climb, but in some years June and October are good as well.

**Map:**  Gallatin National Forest, Big Timber Ranger District, Northern Half, 1 : 62,500, from the Big Timber Ranger Station.

Small glaciers inside the cirque holding Twin Lakes.

# Map 242-1, Crazy, Crazy Mts., Montana, USA

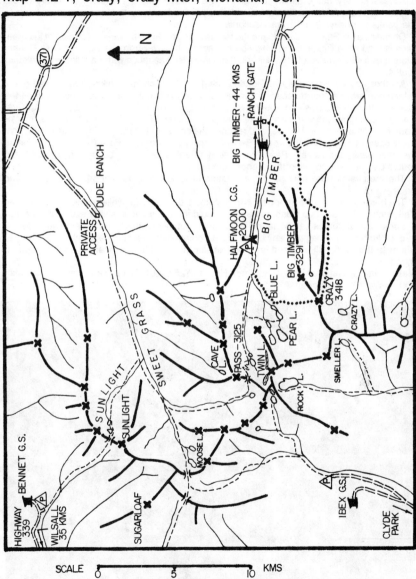

SCALE 0         5         10    KMS

## Gallatin Peak, Madison Range, Montana, USA

Gallatin Peak, at 3358 meters, is the highest summit in a group of mountains known as the Spanish Peaks Wilderness Area. This area is just north of Big Sky and southwest of Bozeman, Montana. The area is not large, but does have some interesting peaks and lakes in a wilderness setting.

Access is very easy, as the Gallatin River, which forms the eastern boundary of the wilderness area, flows next to the main highway. From Highway 191, one can gain access to the peaks from several different locations.

On the north is Spanish Creek, and the main access route to the western portion of the area. Next is the Indian Ridge route, which begins across the river from the Squaw Creek Ranger Station. A disadvantage of this trail—perhaps there isn't as much water available as on other routes.

Another way would be the Hell Roaring Creek Trail, which takes hikers to the heart of the wilderness area. A fourth access route is the Cascade Creek Trail. It connects with all the others in the area and is perhaps the most used of all trails. The next route begins at Karst Camp and reaches the summit of Table Mountain. The Deer Creek Trail begins across the river from the Wilma Summer Homes, and reaches the center of the range. The most southerly of the access trails begins to the west of Big Sky, and follows the North Fork of the Gallatin River to the Bear Basin and Gallatin Peak. With Gallatin Peak about in the center, any one of these routes can be used to climb this highest summit.

The mountains here consist of many different rock types, including granite, shists and gnisses.

The best place to do the shopping is in Bozeman, on the north, while on the south it's West Yellowstone. Big Sky is a plush, retirement-type community and is a very expensive place.

Some difficult routes can be found in this area, but all mountains have easy routes too. A strong climber could begin at any of the access points described above, climb any peak, and return to the road—all in one day. However, for many others an overnight stay is recommended.

**Map:**   Gallatin National Forest, Southern Half, 1 : 125,000, from ranger stations in Bozeman and     West Yellowstone.

Lone Peak rises to the west of church in the community of Big Sky.

# Map 243-1, Gallatin, Madison Range, Montana, USA

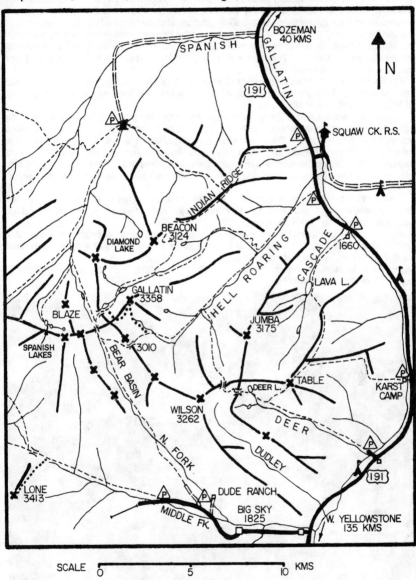

SCALE 0      5      10   KMS

## Mt. Hilgard, Madison Range, Montana, USA

Mt. Hilgard is the highest summit in a group of peaks known as the Madison Range of southern Montana. In this group of peaks, located just north of the Earthquake Lake National Memorial Site, are several summits over 3400 meters, with Hilgard the highest at 3450 meters.

These peaks are composed mostly of quartzite and other metamorphic rocks, with some good rock routes on the eastern side of the higher summits. This area has been glaciated and has many lakes, which makes fishing the number one recreational activity in the region.

Because of the 1959 earthquake, the southern portion of the range is heavily visited—that is, the Madison River Gorge. The main access route is the Beaver Creek Road, running north from the Beaver Creek Campground and Highway 287, and along Beaver Creek, to a summer ranger station and car park. The road is good enough for most cars. From that trailhead, one can reach most peaks in the area.

For Koch Peak and others to the north, drive up the Taylor Creek Road to a trail which heads southwest along South Fork of Taylor Creek. Look for this road and creek about 21 kms south of Big Sky, on Highway 191.

Access on the west side of the range is easy, as far as climbing goes, but all the land at the base of the mountains is private ranch and range land. If one can inquire at one of several ranches along the Madison River and Highway 287, and get permission to enter the area (along with information about the roads), this would present some easy routes. The ridges are sagebrush covered on the lower slopes, then sparsely covered with timber up high. Ridge tops are generally open and easy for hiking. However, water will be harder to find on the western side.

West Yellowstone or Ennis are the closest towns to the area. There are many dude ranches, resort motels, and gas stations, but these latter places are hardly the best for buying food. Do your shopping in the towns mentioned.

July through September is the normal climbing and hiking season, but sometimes June and October bring fine weather. This would be classed as a good weather area, which makes route-finding easy, under generally cloudless skys.

**Map:** Gallatin National Forest, Southern Half, 1 : 125,000, from the ranger stations at Bozeman or West Yellowstone.

Mid summer scene from the south face of Mt. Hilgard.

# Map 244-1, Hilgard, Madison Range, Montana, USA

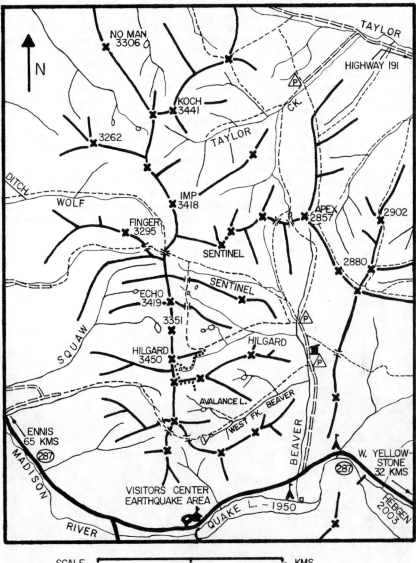

# Hyalite Peak, Gallatin Range, Montana, USA

Hyalite Peak is one of several peaks in an area south of Bozeman and east of the Spanish Peaks Wilderness Area. This group is known as the Hyalite Peaks. There aren't many steep mountains here to challenge the rock climber, but it's a wild area with little traffic, and is an interesting backpacking region.

The rock here is mostly volcanic lava, but the peaks are not volcanos. Geologically they are the same age, and were made by some of the same forces, as those which created many features of Yellowstone Park to the south.

Access to this area is good. The best and most popular route is the road heading south out of Bozemen, which follows Hyalite Creek to Hyalite Reservoir. There are campgrounds along the way and at the lake. Above the lake (to the south) a trail begins at the end of the road, then follows Hyalite Creek to Hyalite Peak, 3140 meters, and the heart of the group.

Another route is via Squaw Creek Road, which begins at the Squaw Creek Ranger Station, next to Highway 191, about 20 kms south of Bozeman. This road is good for any vehicle, and places one in a good position to reach the high country. A slightly better route from the west however, is via Swan Creek. This road goes as far as the Swan Creek Campground, and there a trail begins. This Swan Creek Road is the second best point of entry for climbing Hyalite Peak.

For many people, it would take 2 days to climb Hyalite Peak, from any route. However, a stronger climber or hiker could reach any peak and return in one long day, from any entry point.

As in all the mountains of Montana, July through September are the best months for climbing. Bozeman is the best place to buy food and supplies.

For those people traveling on public transportation, there's bus service from Bozeman to West Yellowstone, along Highway 191, but to nowhere else on the map. For people who are hitch hiking, use one of the western access routes. Highway 191 should be reasonably good for getting lifts. Once on side roads near your destination, nearly any passing vehicle will stop for a backpacker.

**Map:** Gallatin National Forest, Southern Half, 1 : 125,000, from any local ranger station, and the national forest visitor center in Bozeman.

Meadows and medium high mountains make the Hyalites good for hiking.

# Map 245-1, Hyalite, Gallatin Ra., Montana, USA

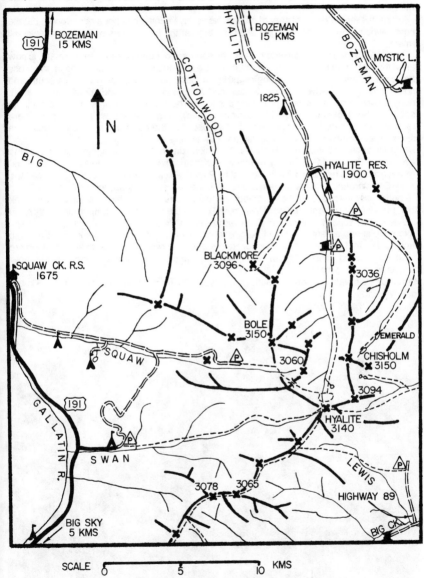

# Douglas, Absaroka Mountains, Montana, USA

The Absaroka Mountains run from about the southeast corner of Yellowstone National Park, northward to about Livingston, Montana, and Interstate 90. Covered on this map is the northern section, the part directly north of Yellowstone Park. Some of the higher peaks here include: Cowens, 3416 meters; Douglas, 3444 meters—which is the highest in this part of the range; and Needles, at 3325 meters. These mountains consist of various rocks—from volcanic lava to granite.

Part of this region has a history of mining. Nowadays mining has been abandoned, but the ghost towns of Independence and Lake City, both at the headwaters of Boulder Creek, still remain.

The area just north of Yellowstone Park (the southern or bottom portion of this map), is now part of the Absaroka Primitive Area, so that part is a wild and roadless region. The main access road is via Boulder Creek, which begins at Big Timber, and heads southwest, then south, and ends near the Box Canyon Ranger Station and workshop. From various points on this road, one can reach any of the high peaks on this map. The Boulder Creek Road is paved in its beginning, then higher up (where it's seen on the map), it is gravel—but well maintained. There are many forest service campgrounds on the road. For the out-of-state travelers, this is an unknown region, even though Yellowstone Park is very near.

Another access route, is via Highway 89, which runs between Livingston, Montana, and Yellowstone Park and Gardiner. This highway is the northern approach to Yellowstone Park. From Highway 89, one can drive to the east on Pine Creek to its end, where is located the Pine Creek Campground. This is not a good route if the higher peaks are to be climbed.

A better access route from the west would be to drive east from Highway 89, on the Mill Creek Road (number 476). Near the end of Mill Creek Road is the Snowbank Campground. This route provides good access to Pyramid, Crow and Wallace Peaks.

No special equipment is needed here, except for those intentionally seeking out a tough climb. Only a tent and good pair of boots are needed. The two best places to shop for food are Livingston and Big Timber. For forest service maps and other information, stop at the ranger stations in these two towns.

**Map:**  Gallatin National Forest, South Half, 1 : 125,000, from the ranger stations in Big Timber and Livingston.

The western slopes of Mt. Douglas, a huge, massive mountain.

# Map 246-1, Douglas, Absaroka Mts., Montana, USA

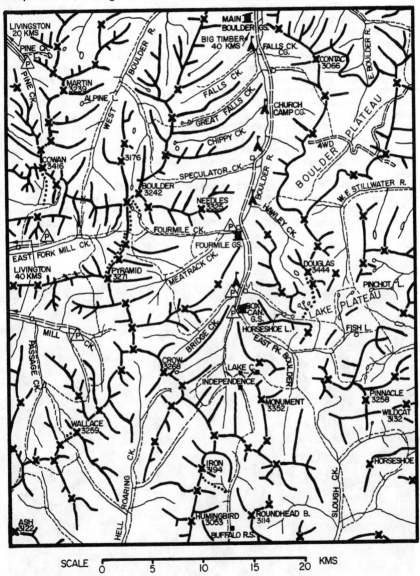

SCALE 0 5 10 15 20 KMS

## Granite Peak, Beartooth Mts., Montana, USA

Granite Peak, at 3902 meters, is the highest peak in Montana. It's located in the Beartooth Mountains, northeast of Yellowstone National Park, and west and south of Red Lodge, Montana. These mountains are made up mostly of granite, but also quartzite and other rocks.

Generally speaking, the Beartooths are not rugged as glaciated mountains go. For the most part, the area is merely a large plateau, with occasional canyons, created by glaciation during the last ice age. Often the north faces are steep and have ice patches, but the rest are gently sloping dome mountains.

The summit part of Granite Peak is steep and a challenging climb, at least for the beginner. No special equipment is necessary for the "tourist route," but it's an interesting climb none-the-less. The normal way to Granite Peak is from either East Rosebud Lake and Alpine, located about 23 kms southwest of Roscoe; or up the West Rosebud Creek to the Hydroelectric Station parking lot and past Mystic Lake. A good, well used trail connects these two areas. At the pass, a trail (a series of stone cairns) leads to the summit. There are three groups of stone walls, or enclosures, used as campsites, on this big flat plateau, each having water nearby (most of the time). Some people do the trip from East Rosebud in two days, but many people take three. A strong climber could do the climb from West Rosebud, in one very long day.

Another possible route, but which is longer, is from Clark Fork Campground, located on US Highway 212, east of Cooke City. A well used trail connects East Rosebud Lake with the Clark Fork Campground. One could head northwest to Granite Peak, from a point west of Rainbow Lake.

Best places to do the shopping would be Red Lodge, Columbus, or Cooke City, Montana. July, August and September are the best months to climb here, but sometimes June and October have fine weather. No special equipment is needed for the climb. For more information and forest service maps, see the forest ranger stations in Red Lodge or the one east of Cooke City.

**Map:** Custer National Forest, Beartooth Division, 1 : 125,000, from ranger stations at Red Lodge, Cooke City or Big Timber.

Granite Peak north face. Normal route is up the left hand skyline.

# Map 247-1, Granite, Beartooth Mts., Mont., USA

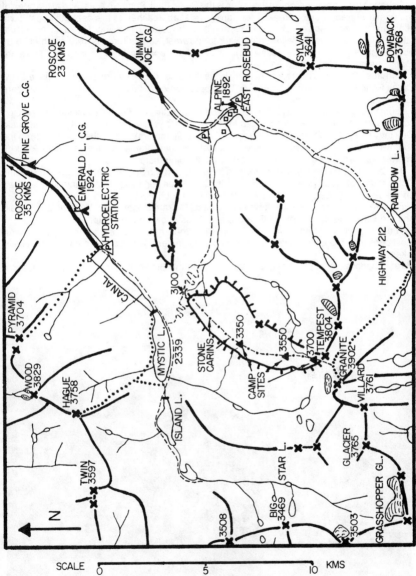

ROSCOE 23 KMS

JIMMY JOE C.G.

EAST ROSEBUD L.

SYLVAN 3641

BOWBACK 3768

PINE GROVE C.G.

ALPINE 1892

EMERALD L. C.G.

EMERALD L. 1924

ROSCOE 35 KMS

HYDROELECTRIC STATION

RAINBOW L.

HIGHWAY 212

CANAL

3100

PYRAMID 3704

MYSTIC L. 2339

STONE CAIRNS

3350

3550

3700

TEMPEST 3804

GRANITE 3902

VILLARD 3761

WOOD 3829

HAGUE 3758

ISLAND L.

CAMP SITES

GLACIER 3765

GRASSHOPPER GL.

TWIN 3597

STAR L.

BIG 3469

3508

3503

N

SCALE 0          5          10 KMS

## Cloud Peak, Big Horn Mts., Wyoming, USA

Cloud Peak, at 4017 meters, is the highest summit in the Big Horn Mountains of north central Wyoming. The Big Horn Mountains in many ways are similar to other ranges of the west, such as the Wind Rivers and Uintas. They are uplifted and dome-like, having various rock such as granite in the center, and others, like quartzite and sandstone, on the outer edges of the range.

Covering the higher portions of the range is the Cloud Peak Primitive Area, and at the heart of the primitive area is Cloud Peak. There are several approaches to this peak, the best is via Highway 16, Tensleep Lake, Helen Lake, and then the summit. Highway 16 is a national route taking a lot of tourists to Yellowstone Park to the west, so this route is very much used by out-of-staters (non-Wyoming residents). The road to Tensleep Lake is good and there are many campgrounds in the area.

Perhaps the second best route of entry is via the Clear Creek Guard Station, and the Clear Creek Road to the Northfork Trailhead. The upper portion of this road is rough, but with care most cars can negotiate it.

From this trailhead, a good path leads up North Clear Creek to Florence Lake and Pass. One could then follow the ridge over Bomber Mt. then down to yet another pass and up Cloud Peak. Or it may be best to go down to Mistymoon Lake (3120 meters) and up the mountain from the southwest, which is an easier route. For rock climbers the east face of Cloud Peak is impressive. One can do ice and snow or rock climbing there.

The best time to climb in the Big Horns is from July through September, but sometimes early October still has good weather. Food and supplies can be purchased in Worland and Tensleep on the western slopes, or in Buffalo to the east of Cloud Peak.

For forest service maps and information, contact the ranger stations at Worland and Buffalo and the Clear Creek and Tyrrell Guard Stations, as shown on the map.

The time needed to climb Cloud Peak from either route mentioned is one long day. However, most people do the hike in two days. No special equipment is needed if the normal routes are taken.

**Map:**  Bighorn National Forest, 1 : 125,000, from the Buffalo or Worland Ranger Stations.

In the distance is Fremont Peak (no foto of Cloud Peak) (see map 253).

# Map 248-1, Cloud, Big Horn Mts., Wyoming, USA

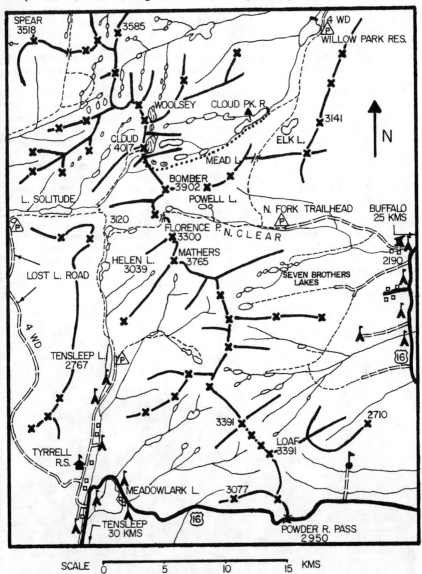

SPEAR
3518

3585

4 WD

WILLOW PARK RES.

WOOLSEY

CLOUD PK. R.

CLOUD
4017

3141

ELK L.

MEAD L.

BOMBER
3902

POWELL L.

N. FORK TRAILHEAD

BUFFALO
25 KMS

L. SOLITUDE

3120

FLORENCE P. N. CLEAR

2190

HELEN L.
3039

MATHERS
3765

LOST L. ROAD

SEVEN BROTHERS
LAKES

4 WD

TENSLEEP L.
2767

16

2710

3391

LOAF
3391

TYRRELL
R.S.

MEADOWLARK L.

3077

16

TENSLEEP
30 KMS

POWDER R. PASS
2950

N

SCALE    0      5      10      15   KMS

# Holms, Gallatin Range, Wyoming, USA

The area covered by this map includes the extreme northwest corner of the state of Wyoming and also the northwest corner of Yellowstone National Park. The boundaries of Montana and Wyoming and the national park are outlined. Virtually all peaks are within Yellowstone Park.

The highest summit on the map is Electric Peak at 3350 meters. It sits on the state line and is one of the more difficult of access of any peak on the map. The best way of approach is from very near the place called Golden Gate. This is where the highway begins to drop off the plateau and decends to Mammoth Hot Springs. At that point there is an old fire road following Glen Creek. Follow this road-trail to Cache Lake, or make a left hand turn near the end of the road and walk on the Sportsman Lake Trail along the Gardiner River until the southeast or southwest ridge is met, then walk to the summit. This will make a very long day hike for anyone. Most will want to climb it in 2 days.

The best known peak on the map is Mt. Holmes. It's a popular hike for park employees and travelers. One reason is that it has a small fire lookout station at the top and is manned from about June to September. Each person is now helicoptered in. But there is a fine and well used trail to the summit as well. Drive or hitch hike to the trailhead located on the Mammoth Hot Springs—Norris Junction Highway. It's just north of Beaver Lake and has a small parking place. The trail is well marked and is very flat until one reaches the mountain base. Along this trail one has an excellent chance to view wildlife such as elk, bear, deer and moose. The author also remembers more mosquitoes here than in any other place except in Alaska! There's one ranger cabin along the way but it's locked. One can get shelter in the summit building however, if it's occupied. Most people do this hike in one day, but it's a long one.

In the northwest corner of the map and park are two fairly high peaks running along the park boundary. They are Sheep Mt. and Bighorn Peak. The best way to reach either of these is to begin walking at the Specimen Creek Campground. The trail follows Specimen Creek to the summit of Sheep Mt. Maps also show a trail connecting Sheep with Bighorn Peak, but that hasn't been confirmed. But from this Specimen Creek Trail one can bushwhack up the southeast ridge of Bighorn.

**Map:** Yellowstone National Park, 1 : 250,000, from the USGS, or at visitor centers and park ranger stations in Y.N.P.

A surprise. On top of Mt. Holms, a fire lookout. But the hike is worth it.

# Map 249-1, Holms, Gallatin Range, Wyoming, USA

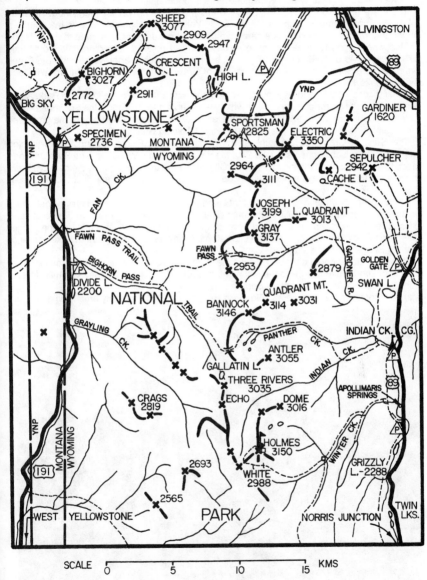

SCALE

0    5    10    15    KMS

# Trout Peak, Absaroka Mountains, Wyoming, USA

Trout Peak is the highest summit in an area lying just north of combined National Highway 14-16-20, connecting Cody, Wyoming, with Yellowstone National Park. With the exception of places near this major highway and the Sunlight Creek Road, this area is part of the North Absaroka Wilderness Area. These mountains have been made predominantly from basalt and lava rock, much the same as Yellowstone Park's mountains.

There are only two main access roads to this region, as previously mentioned. Highway 14-16-20, more commonly known as the Cody-Yellowstone Highway, follows the southern boundary. From this highway, one can drive about 3 kms up Big Creek road to a ranch and cabins, where a good trail leads north to the base of Dead Indian, 3724 meters, and Trout Peak, 3733 meters. As of 1983, there has not yet been public access approved for the Big Creek drainage. Use Sunlight Ck. routes such as Elk or Gravelbar Creeks, if climbing Trout or Dead Indian Peaks.

Other places where good trails begin are near the east entrance of Yellowstone Park. About 3 kms east of the entrance gate is a trail which heads up the North Fork of the Shoshone River. This trail is the one main entry point for the area along the east boundary of the park, and eventually joins the other access road—the one following Sunlight Creek.

The Sunlight Creek Road begins at the Sunlight Creek Picnic Grounds, on Wyoming Highway 296, which connects Cooke City, Montana with Cody, Wyoming. The Sunlight Road leads to the abandoned mining town of Lee City, and other mines further up the canyon. From the end of this road, one can cross the divide and enter Yellowstone Park via the Lamar River Trail.

There are many dude ranches and resorts along the Cody-Yellowstone Highway, but one is advised to shop in Cody, which is the only sizable town in the entire region. Both easy and difficult routes exist, so go equipped accordingly. Get additional information at the ranger stations in Cody, at the entry gate to Yellowstone, inside Yellowstone Park at Lake Lodge or Fishing Bridge, or at the Wapiti or Sunlight Ranger Stations.

Many facilities along the Cody-Yellowstone Highway, close down for the season just after the Labor Day weekend—that's the first week of September. The tourist season, therefore, is from late June to the first week of September.

**Map:**  Shoshone National Forest, Northern Half, 1 : 125,000, from any area ranger station.

Looking south on the road to Cooke City, we can see Trout and Dead Indian Peaks.

# Map 250-1, Trout, Absaroka Mts., Wyoming, USA

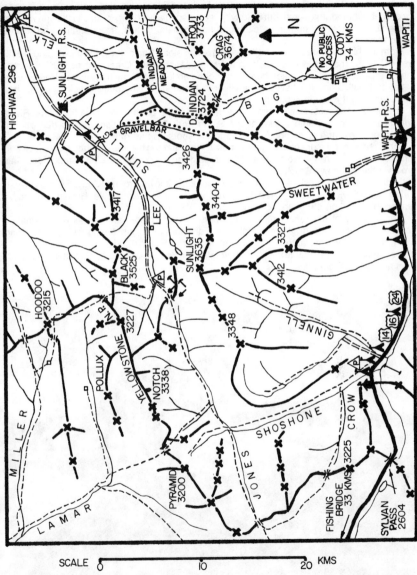

HIGHWAY 296

SUNLIGHT R.S.

ELK

D. INDIAN MEADOWS

TROUT 3733

CRAG 3674

N

NO PUBLIC ACCESS

CODY 34 KMS

WAPITI

BIG

WAPITI R.S.

D. INDIAN 3724

GRAVELBAR

D. INDIAN 3426

SUNLIGHT

3404

SWEETWATER

3417

LEE

3327

SUNLIGHT 3635

3342

BLACK 3525

3348

HOODOO 3215

YELLOWSTONE N.P.

3227

POLLUX

NOTCH 3338

GINNELL

14  16  24

CROW

SHOSHONE

MILLER

JONES

PYRAMID 3200

FISHING BRIDGE 33 KMS

3225

SYLVAN PASS 2604

LAMAR

SCALE  0        10        20  KMS

# Fortress Peak, Absaroka Mts., Wyoming, USA

Fortress Peak, at 3681 meters, is the highest summit in an area southeast of Yellowstone Park, southwest of Cody, Wyoming, and south of the US Highway 14-16-20. Getting into this region requires some long hikes, as this area bordering the eastern side of Yellowstone National Park, is one of the wildest mountain areas in the continental USA.

The best route of access is the national highway shown across the upper part of the map, which connects Fishing Bridge in Yellowstone Park and Cody, Wyoming. This highway is open for only about 7 months a year, but is heavily used, especially from mid-June to the first week of September. There are numerous campgrounds, motels, cabins, scout camps and resorts along this road.

From the highway are several trails leading south along Eagle, Kitty, Fishhawk, and Blackwater Creeks. The best way to reach Fortress, is via Blackwater Creek and the natural bridge, then the peak. To reach the southern peaks one can leave this main road near Yellowstone Lake, and walk along the Yellowstone River to Mountain or Thorofare Creeks, but this is a week-long trip if more than one peak is to be climbed.

Another access route (not shown on the map) is via the South Fork of the Shoshone River, southwest of Cody. Begin a hike at the South Fork Ranger Station. This is due east of Kingfisher Peak, and is the shortest route to the southern part of the region.

For those wanting more challenging climbs, try the peaks in the area of Chaos, Overlook and Ishawooa Peaks, which have some small snowfields on their north and east slopes. Reach this area via the Fishhawk Creek.

If coming from the east, stop and shop in the biggest town around, Cody. From the west, Yellowstone Park has some stores, but things there are very expensive. Hitching should be reasonably good on the main highway shown.

Stop in Cody at the ranger station, for more detailed maps, and the latest information concerning places outside the national park. For information concerning hiking or climbing within the park, enquire at the entry gate shown, or at Fishing Bridge.

**Map:**  Shoshone National Forest, Northern Half, or Yellowstone N.P., both at 1 : 125,000, from any local ranger station.

Fortress Mountain from the northeast. Its south face is more interesting.

## Map 251-1, Fortress, Absaroka Mts., Wyoming, USA

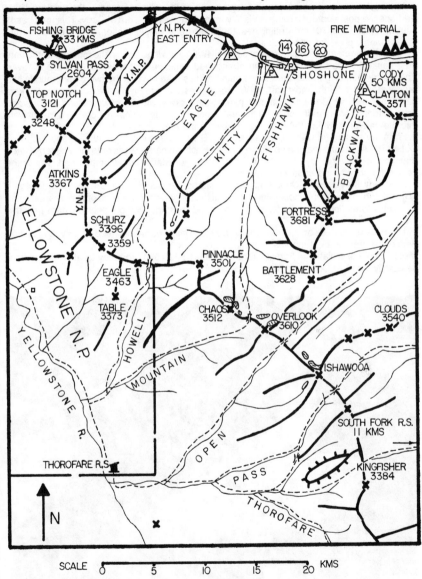

FISHING BRIDGE
33 KMS

Y.N.PK.
EAST ENTRY

FIRE MEMORIAL

14 16 20

SHOSHONE

CODY
50 KMS

SYLVAN PASS
2604

Y.N.P.

CLAYTON
3571

TOP NOTCH
3121

3248

EAGLE

KITTY

FISHHAWK

BLACKWATER

ATKINS
3367

Y.N.P.

SCHURZ
3396

3359

FORTRESS
3681

EAGLE
3463

PINNACLE
3501

BATTLEMENT
3628

TABLE
3373

CHAOS
3512

OVERLOOK
3610

CLOUDS
3540

YELLOWSTONE

N.P.

HOWELL

MOUNTAIN

ISHAWOOA

YELLOWSTONE R.

OPEN

SOUTH FORK R.S.
11 KMS

THOROFARE R.S.

PASS

KINGFISHER
3384

THOROFARE

N

SCALE    0    5    10    15    20    KMS

## Francs Peak, Absaroka Mts., Wyoming, USA

Francs Peak at 4006 meters, is the only 4000 meter mountain summit in the Absaroka Range of northwest Wyoming and southern Montana. Francs Peak is located in the South Absaroka Wilderness Area, southwest of Meeteetse and southeast of Yellowstone Park. This is a little known area, as most tourists head for the Tetons, the Wind Rivers or Yellowstone National Park. Neither are there many lakes in this area, so there aren't many fishermen either.

Access is rather poor, making this region one of the wildest areas in the western USA. Perhaps the best approach route is via Wyoming Highway 291, out of Cody. This road heads southwest for about 70 kms, ending near the South Fork Ranger Station. To this point the road is reasonably good for all vehicles.

From the Meeteetse area, there are several 4WD roads leading into the mountains, the very best being the road ending near the abandoned settlement of Kirwin on the Wood River. There's been mining in this area in the past and this road beyond the two campgrounds and ranger station is, for the most part, a 4WD road. (Best route to Francs Peak is to drive 2-3 kms past the Brown Mt. Campground, and park at the locked gate. Then walk along the old road open to foot or horse traffic only, 'till the first major canyon to the north. Look for a trail or walk into the canyon and find the trail, then follow as the map shows).

From the south and Dubois, are several 4WD type roads into the southern section. From Dubois, take the road leading up Horse Creek, which ultimately leads onto the Wiggens Creek drainage, and eventually to the Double Cabin Ranger Station and Campground. This is the best entry point to the southwestern part.

Use Cody, Meeteetse or Dubois as your last shopping place, and be sure and have a full tank of gas before entering the mountains. Check at the ranger stations in one of these same towns for more information about roads, trails, snow conditions and for more detailed maps than this one.

There are no glaciers or snowfields to speak of, so ice axes are not needed. July, August and September are the best months for hiking or climbing.

**Map:** Shoshone National Forest, Northern Half, 1 : 125,000, from any local ranger station, especially those at Cody and Meeteetse.

Looking north to the south ridge of Francs Peak.

# Map 252-1, Francs, Absaroka Mts., Wyoming, USA

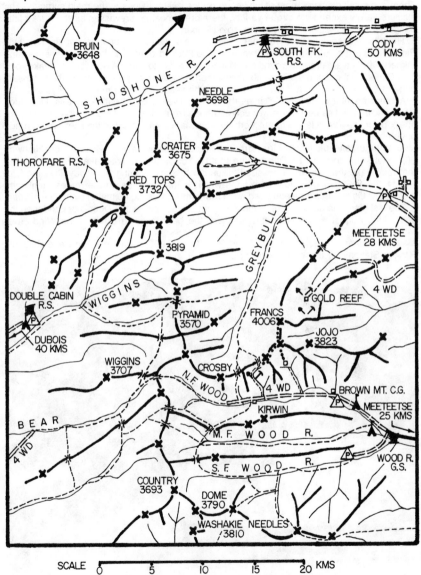

BRUIN
×3648

SHOSHONE R.

CODY
50 KMS

SOUTH FK.
R.S.

NEEDLE
3698

CRATER
3675

THOROFARE R.S.

RED TOPS
3732

MEETEETSE
28 KMS

3819

4 WD

WIGGINS

DOUBLE CABIN
R.S.

GREYBULL

GOLD REEF

DUBOIS
40 KMS

PYRAMID
3570

FRANCS
4006

JOJO
3823

WIGGINS
3707

N.F. WOOD

CROSBY

4 WD

BROWN MT. C.G.

BEAR

KIRWIN

MEETEETSE
25 KMS

4 WD

M. F. WOOD R.

S. F. WOOD R.

WOOD R.
G.S.

COUNTRY
3693

DOME
3790

WASHAKIE NEEDLES
3810

SCALE   0    5    10    15    20  KMS

## Gannett Peak, Wind River Mts., Wyoming, USA

Gannett Peak, 4208 meters, is the highest summit in the Wind River Mountains and in the state of Wyoming. The Wind Rivers are located in west central Wyoming, southeast of Yellowstone National Park.

In the area around Gannett Peak, the rock is almost entirely granite which makes for some very fine climbing. Not only is the rock good, but there's some ice and snow climbing as well. There are small glaciers, most of which are on the eastern sides of the main summits. The glaciers hardly exceed the cirque variety, therefore almost no crevasses exist. There's little danger on these glaciers, even for the solo climber.

The best access points are from the western side of the range, the most popular being via Pinedale and the Elkhart Park entrance. A good paved road runs between Pinedale and Elkhart, where a small campground and visitors center are located. A well used trail takes one past Seneca, Island and the Titcomb Lakes, thence to Dinwoody Pass and up the southeast ridge of Gannett. This is a snow route early in the season, and for most of the year.

Another popular route is via Daniel, the Green River Lakes, Knapsack Pass, Dinwoody Pass, and then the same as the previously mentioned route. For the climber properly equipped, one could make a west face attempt, perhaps from Mammoth Glacier on the southwestern side of Gannett.

Another route would be from the north and eastern side of the Wind Rivers. From Highway 26, about 6 kms southeast of Dubois, turn south to Torrey, then to Trail Lakes. From the end of that road, take the trail which passes Phillips Lake, later following Dinwoody Creek to Dinwoody Glacier, then the south east ridge which is the same as on the routes mentioned previously. Go into this area equipped with crampons and ice ax, no matter what time of year.

The last places to get food are at Pinedale on the west, and either Dubois or Lander on the east. July, August and early September are the best times to climb in the Wind River Mountains.

**Map:** Shoshone National Forest, South Half, 1 : 125,000, from the Elkhart and Pinedale Ranger Stations, or those at Lander or Dubois.

From around Jackson Peak looking north to east face of Gannett Peak.

# Map 253-1, Gannett, Wind River Mts., Wyo., USA

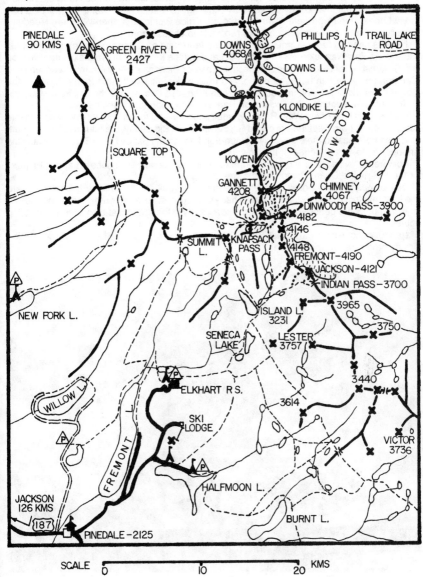

PINEDALE
90 KMS

GREEN RIVER L.
2427

DOWNS
4068

PHILLIPS L.

TRAIL LAKE
ROAD

DOWNS L.

KLONDIKE L.

SQUARE TOP

KOVEN

GANNETT
4208

DINWOODY

CHIMNEY
4067

DINWOODY PASS-3900
4182
4146

SUMMIT
L.

KNAPSACK
PASS

4148

FREMONT-4190

JACKSON-4121

INDIAN PASS-3700

NEW FORK L.

ISLAND L.
3231

3965

3750

SENECA
LAKE

LESTER
3757

3440

WILLOW L.

ELKHART R S.

SKI
LODGE

3614

VICTOR
3736

FREMONT

HALFMOON L.

JACKSON
126 KMS

187

PINEDALE-2125

BURNT L.

SCALE    0          10          20   KMS

# Wind River, Wind River Mts., Wyoming, USA

In the southern half of the Wind River Mountains the highest summit is Wind River Peak, at 4085 meters. Although this is the highest mountain around, it's not necessarily the most impressive or challenging to climb. The peaks surrounding Lonesome Lake, sometimes known as the "Cirque of the Towers," is one of the best climbing areas in the USA.

All of the region towards the center of the range is part of one wilderness area or another, which makes for some solitary backcountry climbing. To reach Wind River Peak, the best way is via Lander, the Popo Agie River Road to the Bruce Picnic area, then Worthem Meadows Reservoir. From the reservoir one has two trails to choose from.

If one is heading for the Cirque of the Towers (surrounding Lonesome Lake), then the best route is via Fort Washakie, 23 kms north of Lander. One km south of Washakie, turn west on the Dickenson Park Road, then to Moccasin Lake or Dickenson Park. From Dickenson Park Campground, one can begin on one of two trails which ultimately lead to the Cirque of the Towers. For those wanting to reach Hooker and Pyramid Peaks, take the trail from Moccasin Lake and Campground. The Dickenson Park Road is good for all vehicles.

On the west side of the Wind River Mountains are several roads (mostly 4WD) leading into the mountains from a settlement called Big Sandy. From Big Sandy, the main road leads south and then northeast to the Big Sandy Campground on the Big Sandy River. This is perhaps the shortest route to the Cirque of the Towers.

For forest service maps and more information, stop at the ranger stations at Lander, Pindale, or the Dutch Joe Guard Station on the way to Big Sandy Campground.

Best places to buy supplies are at Pindale or Lander. July, August and early September are the best months to climb. All the summits have easy routes, but also some difficult ones. Ice ax and crampons are generally not needed, except early in the season, and on a few north facing routes.

**Map:**  Shoshone National Forest, Southern Half, 1 : 125,000, from the Lander Ranger Station or any other area ranger station.

Lizard Head to the left, and still further left is Lonesome Lake.

# Map 254-1, Wind River, Wind R. Mts., Wyo., USA

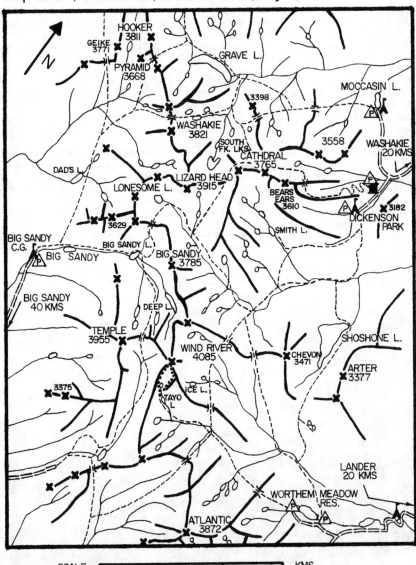

SCALE 0 5 10 15 KMS

# Grand Teton, Teton Range, Wyoming, USA

In the northwest corner of the state of Wyoming, and just south of Yellowstone National Park, is the Grand Teton National Park. The western border of the park runs along the crest of the Teton Range, which is small in square kms, but contains some of the most spectacular scenery and best climbing possibilities in the continental USA.

The mountains run along a fault line which gives the east face of the range great local relief, and an unobstructed rise from 2000 to 4200 meters. The highest peak is Grand Teton, 4197 meters. The higher portion of this peak, and many others in the range, is composed of granite.

Most people get to this area via Yellowstone Park on the north, or from Jackson on the south, which is the southern gateway to the national park. Little or no public transportation exists in the area. You've almost got to have your own car or hitch hike.

Most people begin climbing on the east side, from Jackson Hole, and usually from Lupine Meadows, Jenny Lake, or Leigh Lake. Big crowds are there in July and August.

The normal route to the Grand Teton is via Jenny Lake, Lupine Meadows, and the south col. Mt. Owens, the second highest in the range, 3946 meters, is ascended by nearly the same route. Mt. Moran is climbed from Leigh Lake, and from a trail heading north, then up the east face. There's no easy climbs on Moran, but the easiest route is on the east face and the Skillet Glacier. Crampons and ice ax are needed for most people.

If you don't like crowds or the requirements to have reservations for some campsites high in the mountains, then you might try the west side of the mountain which is not in the national park. Head for Driggs, Idaho, and make inquiries there as to some of the approach roads.

As mentioned, on some routes an ice ax and crampons are required, but for the most part, especially later in the season, only a good pair of boots are needed.

Jackson is a tourist town, but has large supermarkets and sporting goods stores. It's a good place to buy everything.

There's a forest ranger station in Jackson; the national park headquarters near Moose; and a small ranger station for climbers at Jenny Lake. These are the best places to get the latest information.

**Map:** Teton National Forest, 1 : 125,000, or Teton National Park, 1 : 62,500. Both maps and others can be found in Jackson, Moose, Jenny Lake, or Jackson Lake Lodge.

From left, South, Middle and Grand Teton Peaks. Snake River, foreground.

# Map 255-1, Grand Teton, Teton Ra., Wyo., USA

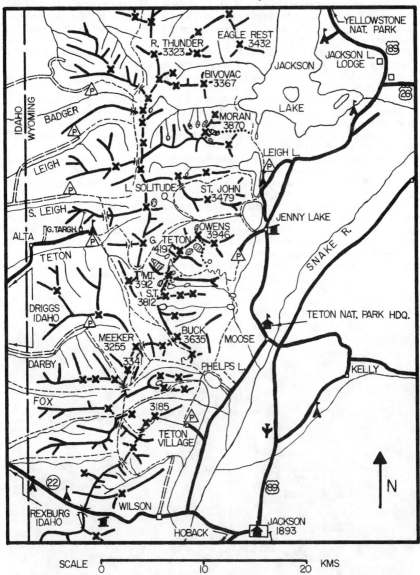

YELLOWSTONE NAT. PARK

JACKSON L. LODGE

R. THUNDER 3323

EAGLE REST 3432

BIVOVAC 3367

JACKSON

IDAHO
WYOMING

BADGER

MORAN 3870

LAKE

LEIGH L.

LEIGH

L. SOLITUDE

ST. JOHN 3479

S. LEIGH

JENNY LAKE

ALTA

G. TARGH.

OWENS 3946

SNAKE R.

TETON

G. TETON 4197

T. MT. 3912

S.T. 3812

DRIGGS IDAHO

TETON NAT. PARK HDQ.

BUCK 3635

MOOSE

DARBY

MEEKER 3255

3341

PHELPS L.

KELLY

FOX

3185

TETON VILLAGE

REXBURG IDAHO

WILSON

JACKSON 1893

HOBACK

N

SCALE    0        10        20    KMS

# Kings Peak, Uinta Mountains, Utah, USA

In the northeast corner of Utah lie the Unita Mountains, the only major mountain range in the USA running in an east-west direction as opposed to north-south. Within this range are at least five named peaks over 4000 meters, and around 2000 lakes, left over from the last ice age. Only the very largest lakes and highest peaks of the central portion of the Unitas are included here. A large part of this map shows the High Uintas Primitive Area.

The highest summit in Utah is Kings Peak, 4124 meters. Its south summit is 4119 meters. Probably the shortest route to Kings Peak is via Henry's Fork Creek and Campground, and Gunsight and Anderson Passes. Only the west face of Kings Peak has any difficult routes—all others are simply walk-ups.

The peak can also be approached from the Swift Creek Campground and Yellowstone Creek. It's about 40 kms from the campground to the top. A still longer route is via the Uinta River and the U Bar ranch (southeast of the peak) and is about a 50 km walk. It's a three day outing to climb Kings Peak, regardless of the route taken.

Gilbert is the second highest peak at 4098 meters. It's on the north slopes of the range, with the shortest approach route being from Henrys Fork Campground. The third highest summit in Utah and this range, is Emmons, 4097 meters. The easiest way to approach this mountain is via Yellowstone and Swift Creeks. It can also be reached from the U Bar Ranch and the Uinta River, which is north of Roosevelt and Neola.

Loveina and Wilson Peaks, 4030 and 3979 meters, can be reached from either Moon Lake, located on Lake Fork Creek, or East or West Forks of Blacks Forks Creek, or even from Yellowstone Creek. These two peaks are between 40 and 50 kms from the nearest roads, and will take at least 3 days on foot, maybe longer, to reach and climb either one.

To get to the north slopes, exit Interstate 80 in Wyoming at either Fort Bridger or Lyman, and proceed south to Robertson. From there go to either Henrys or Blacks Forks. On the south slopes, drive north from Duchesne and Altamont, to Yellowstone or Lake Fork Creeks. Ranger stations in Mountain View, Wyoming and Duchesne, Utah are open year round. Get more information and forest maps at these locations.

**Map:** Wasatch-Cache, or Ashley National Forests, both at 1 : 125,000, from ranger stations in Salt Lake, Ogden, Duchesne, Vernal or Mountain View Wyoming.

Kings Peak in upper left of foto. From Henrys Fork Basin.

## Map 256-1, Kings, Uinta Mountains, Utah, USA

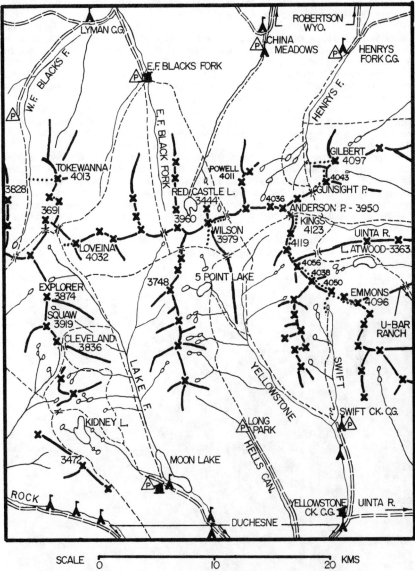

# Timpanogos, Wasatch Mountains, Utah, USA

In Utah's central Wasatch Mountains are some of the best and well known ski resorts in the country, some of the best climbing areas in the state, and many of the better developed trails in Utah.

The best known mountain in Utah and most popular to climb, is Mt. Timpanogos, or "Timp." At 3582 meters, it's the second highest peak in the Wasatch Mountains, next in height to Nebo, which is further south. Timp has the closest thing to a real glacier in the state, and about the only mountain hut (emergency type only) as well.

The most popular route up Timp, is via Provo Canyon to Aspen Grove, the Timp Trail to Emerald Lake and to the top via the glacier or northwest trail. Another route begins on the north side, at a place called Timpooneke, where is located a seasonal ranger station. It can also be climbed from the southwest face and Pleasant Grove City water tanks.

Up until about 1970, there was an annual "Timp Hike," which brought 5000 people to the top on one Saturday. That has been discontinued for obvious reasons. The mountain is now a small wilderness—the Timp Scenic Area.

To the north of Timp, and to the southeast of the Salt Lake Metropolitan area, is the second most popular hiking and rock climbing area in the state. These are the peaks and canyon walls in or near the Lone Peak Wilderness Area, and the Little Cottonwood Canyon area. The granite of Lone Peak and the canyon walls offer Utah's best rock climbing.

Further up the canyon are located Snowbird and Alta ski resorts. There are many trails in the vicinity including a couple which can be taken to the Brighton and Solitude ski areas. The road reaching Brighton is the one through Big Cottonwood Canyon. These two major canyons southeast of Salt Lake, can be reached best from the 7200 S. and the 9000 S. exits from Interstate Highway 15. Salt Lake City buses serve these two canyon resort areas in winter only. If you're on foot, it's easy to hitch a ride to either of these canyons, as there's traffic the year-round.

Forest ranger stations exist in Salt Lake, Pleasant Grove, Heber and Provo. Seasonal ranger stations exist in American Fork Canyon. All mountains can be climbed with no special equipment needed.

**Map:** Uinta National Forest, 1 : 125,000, from rangers stations at Provo and Pleasant Grove

Emerald Lake Hut and Timp Glacier. Summit is to the right, out of sight.

536

# Map 257-1, Timpanogos, Wasatch Mts., Utah, USA

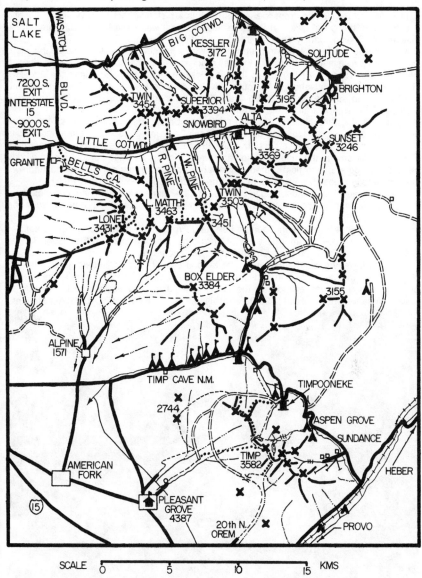

SALT LAKE

WASATCH BLVD.

BIG COTWD.

KESSLER 3172

SOLITUDE

7200 S. EXIT
INTERSTATE 15
9000 S. EXIT

TWIN 3454

SUPERIOR 3394

3195

BRIGHTON

SNOWBIRD

ALTA

LITTLE COTWD.

SUNSET 3246

GRANITE

BELLS C.A.

R. PINE

W. PINE

3369

MATTH 3463

TWIN 3503

LONE 3431

3451

BOX ELDER 3384

3155

ALPINE 1571

TIMP CAVE N.M.

TIMPOONEKE

2744

ASPEN GROVE

SUNDANCE

TIMP 3582

HEBER

AMERICAN FORK

15

PLEASANT GROVE 4387

20th N. OREM

PROVO

SCALE  0    5    10    15   KMS

## Mt. Nebo, Wasatch Mountains, Utah, USA

The high mountains running north and south through central and northern Utah are known as the Wasatch Mountains. Most of the population of Utah lives along the western front of the Wasatch. The highest summit in the range lies at the extreme southern end, that's Mt. Nebo, 3637 meters. What otherwise would be an unimpressive elevation, Nebo rises from 1498 meters, at the village of Mona, to the summit—a rise of over 2100 meters in "one step."

One reason for Nebo's presence in this book is a historical fact—it was one of several mountains in the Great Basin of Western America, that was used by the U.S. army for a Heliograph Station, dating back to the early 1880's.

Mt. Nebo is one very long and high ridge with a number of peaks. One of the more northerly summits is the highest, but the trail reaches only to the South Peak, which rises to 3621 meters. There are two trails to the top. Possibly the most used one is the Andrews Ridge route. To climb Nebo by this route, drive up Salt Creek east of Nephi. On the paved road is a sign stating the Mt. Nebo Trail. Walk or drive 1 km on a rough road to the trailhead. It's a good trail to the summit.

If you're on foot and hitch hiking, then the Willow Creek Trail is easiest to access. Drive south, then east, out of Mona and up Willow Creek Canyon. At the end of the rough road is the trail leading to the summit. On both trails, there's water at the beginning, but there may or may not be any up the mountain, so carry water. For the average person, it's an all day hike, but 4 hours for the fleet footed. There are good campsites on Willow and Andrews Creeks (another possible route is to use the Cedar Ridge—but without trail).

The old roads have undoubtedly changed in the Mona area with the completion of Interstate Highway 15, so it may be necessary to enquire locally about how to reach the Willow Creek Road.

There are ranger stations in Spanish Fork and Provo, both to the north, and a smaller one in Nephi. Up-to-date information about Nebo can best be found in the Nephi Ranger Station, but maps can be found in the other two locations.

No need for any special equipment, just a good pair of boots. Climbing season on Mt. Nebo is from mid-June through mid-October. The only public transportation in the area is bus service, with stops at most of the towns along Interstate Highway 15.

**Map:**   Uinta National Forest, 1 : 125,000, from Nephi, Spanish Fork or Provo Ranger Stations.

From the South Summit of Nebo, looking north along summit ridge.

# Map 258-1, Nebo, Wasatch Mountains, Utah, USA

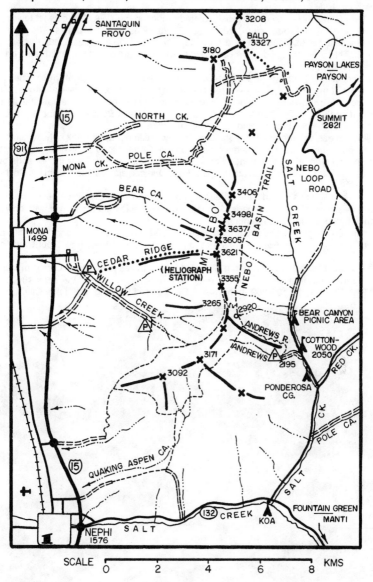

SCALE  0   2   4   6   8  KMS

# Ibapah Peak, Deep Creek Range, Utah, USA

Ibapah Peak, 3684 meters, is the highest point in the Deep Creek Range of western Utah. It lies near the Nevada-Utah line (very near the left hand border of the map), and is just east of the small Goshute Indian Reservation. Although the Deep Creek Range is surrounded by dry, flat and barren lands, it is an "oasis in the desert." These are the highest mountains in the continental USA *not* part of a national forest. The area is administered by the Bureau of Land Management (BLM).

The Deep Creeks are one of the most isolated ranges in the USA. The closest towns are Wendover and Ely, Nevada—both are about 150-200 kms from the peaks. They are the nearest places to get gasoline and food. One may get some food and gas in Ibapah, but don't count on it. This is an area of dying mining towns, and there are only a few Indians left on the reservation in Goshute.

The author climbed the high peaks from Dugway, Callao, and Indian Farm Creek. The route down was via Toms Creek and the 4WD road nearby. There's a good campsite at the end of the road on Indian Farm Creek, where good water is found. There's no trail in the area, but it's not hard to find one's way. The Toms Creek route was the easiest. By camping one night at the mountain base, the climb can be completed in one day.

Possibly the easiest and most straight forward way to climb Ibapah Peak only, would be to approach the mountain from the southwest and Granite Creek. Good campsites can be found in the higher canyon, along with water. From Granite Creek, one can find a trail-of-sorts over the pass separating Red Mountain and Ibapah Peak. One can also get there from the Goshute side.

If one doesn't like dusty roads, then the route from Wendover or Ely will be best. This route has the fewest kms of graveled roads. All roads shown on this map are gravel, with only the main ones being graded and maintained.

One can also approach the region via Highway 50-6 from the south and the Delta and Wheeler Peak area. From 50-6, there's a road passing Gandy, then on to Trout Creek and Callao.

Take a good vehicle and plenty of gasoline and food supplies to this area. On top of Ibapah there's the remains of an old US Army Heliograph Station, dating from the early 1880's.

**Map:**   Fish Springs, 1 : 100,000, from the USGS, Federal Building, Salt Lake City, Utah.

From summit of Ibapah, one can see the second highest peak, Haystack.

# Map 259-1, Ibapah, Deep Creek Ra., Utah, USA

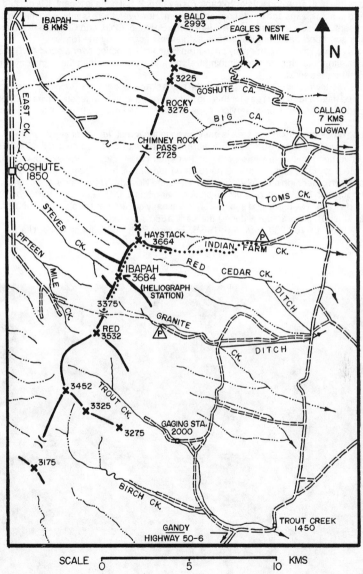

IBAPAH
8 KMS

BALD
2993

EAGLES NEST
MINE

N

3225

GOSHUTE CA.

ROCKY
3276

BIG    CA.

CALLAO
7 KMS
DUGWAY

EAST CK.

CHIMNEY ROCK
PASS
2725

GOSHUTE
1850

TOMS CK.

STEVES   CK.

HAYSTACK
3664

INDIAN FARM CK.

FIFTEEN

MILE   CK.

IBAPAH
3684
(HELIOGRAPH
STATION)

RED  CEDAR CK.

DITCH

3375

GRANITE

RED
3532

CK.

DITCH

3452

TROUT CK.

3325

3275

GAGING STA.
2000

3175

BIRCH  CK.

GANDY
HIGHWAY 50-6

TROUT CREEK
1450

SCALE  0        5        10   KMS

## Delano, Tushar Mountains, Utah, USA

Delano at 3711 meters, is the highest summit in a group of high peaks called the Tushar Mountains. This high area is located in south central Utah, just east of Beaver, which lies near Interstate Highway 15. On the east side of the Tushars lies Marysvale and Junction, both on US Highway 89. A good road connects Beaver with Junction, passing near the Mt. Holly ski resort.

Much of this high area consists of volcanic (or lava) rock, but none is recent. It is pocked with mines and mining claims and roads connecting them. However, there is little or no mining going on at present. These roads are most evident in the Belknap, Gold, and Copperbelt Mt. areas. Access is good and easy, but the area is extensively scarred by the roads.

With a 4WD vehicle one can easily drive from Beaver or Junction over a good 4WD road to Marysvale, stopping enroute and climbing Delano and Belknap both in the same day. Few if any difficult routes exist.

Of the three towns mentioned, Beaver is the biggest and best place to stock up on supplies. Be sure and have a full tank of gas for this trip. Beaver has a forest ranger station as well, for the latest road conditions and forest service maps. Circleville, 12 kms south of Junction, also has a ranger station.

Walking cross-country in this area is easy, even in the forest, as it's mostly open and with a minimum of undergrowth. Summers are warm and dry, with winters rather mild. The higher slopes have deep snows in winter, but good weather is the rule, not the exception.

Of interest to historians are the stone ruins on top of Belknap. They resemble the same things seen on other high summits in western Utah and Nevada. They appear to be remains of an old Heliograph Station, with a summit platform, and half a dozen stone shelters. They were likely used as a survey camp and station during the early government explorations of Utah and Nevada. Most of that was done during the early 1880's.

**Map:** Beaver, 1 : 100,000, from the USGS, Federal Building, Salt Lake City, Utah.

Looking at Belknap from the summit of Bald Mountain.

# Map 260-1, Delano, Tushar Mountains, Utah, USA

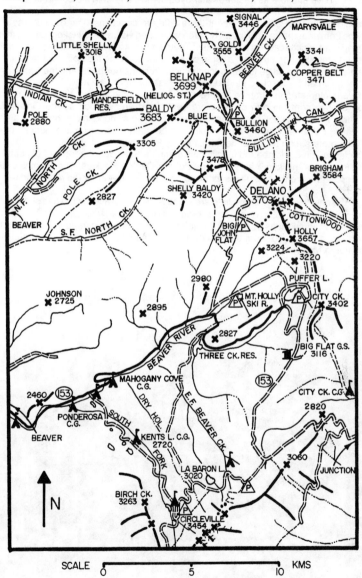

SIGNAL 3446
MARYSVALE
LITTLE SHELLY 3018
GOLD 3555
3341
COPPER BELT 3471
BELKNAP 3699
INDIAN CK.
MANDERFIELD RES.
(HELIOG. ST.)
BALDY 3683
BLUE L.
P
BULLION 3460
CAN.
POLE 2880
BULLION
3305
3478
BRIGHAM 3584
NORTH CK.
POLE CK.
N.F.
SHELLY BALDY 3420
DELANO 3709
2827
COTTONWOOD
BEAVER
S.F. NORTH CK.
BIG JOHN FLAT
P
HOLLY 3657
3224
3220
2980
PUFFER L.
JOHNSON 2725
2895
P
MT. HOLLY SKI R.
P
CITY CK. 3402
BEAVER RIVER
2827
THREE CK. RES.
BIG FLAT G.S. 3116
MAHOGANY COVE C.G.
153
CITY CK. C.G.
2460
153
DRY HOL.
E.F. BEAVER CK.
2820
PONDEROSA C.G.
SOUTH
BEAVER
KENTS L. C.G. 2720
FORK
3060
JUNCTION
LA BARON L. 3020
P
BIRCH CK. 3263
N
P
CIRCLEVILLE 3454

SCALE 0     5     10 KMS

## Mt. Peale, La Sal Mountains, Utah, USA

In southeastern Utah, near the border of Colorado, lies the La Sal Mountains. It's a small mountain range, rising sharply from the flat-lying Colorado Plateau. The highest mountain summit in the area is Mt. Peale, 3878 meters. In addition to Peale, there are about 7 other summits or peaks over 3700 meters. These Mountains are in the middle of a dry land, but the higher places have fine forests and three improved campsites within the boundaries of the La Sal National Forest.

One could climb Mt. Peale from about three different directions. The easiest way would probably be from near the La Sal Pass. This area is reached via La Sal Junction, La Sal, and the unimproved road which reaches La Sal Pass. There's no trail to the summit, but if one were to stop about 4 kms short of the pass, a route could be found to the top going about due north.

Another possibility would be to approach the peak from the northeast and the Dark Canyon Lake. That lake can be reached via the Geyser Pass, or from La Sal to the south.

If one were interested in climbing several peaks or spending several days in the region, it would be best to camp in one of the more centralized areas, such as the Oowah Lake Campground. From this spot, any of the high peaks can be climbed in one day. The areas of Geyser Pass or Warner Campground would also be good places to make climbs from Mt. Waas, 3759 meters, can be ascended most easily from the Miners Basin.

No special equipment is needed for climbing in the La Sals, only a good pair of boots. The weather situation is the same as for the rest of the Central Rockies. The months of June through September are the best times for climbing, with good weather the rule—bad weather the exception.

Moab is the only town in the immediate area, and is the best place to stop and shop for both food and information. There's a small forest ranger station located there, and that would be the place to get additional maps and the latest information on roads, campgrounds and trails.

**Map:** La Sal, 1 : 100,000, from the USGS, Federal Building, Salt Lake City, Utah. Or the visitor center in Moab.

It's one long summit ridge running from Peale to Tukuhnikivatz (distance).

# Map 261-1, Peale, La Sal Mountains, Utah, USA

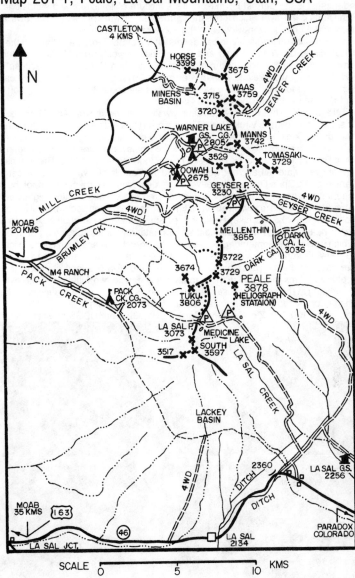

CASTLETON
4 KMS

N

HORSE
3399

3675

WAAS
3759

BEAVER CREEK

4WD

MINERS
BASIN

3715

3720

WARNER LAKE
GS. - C.G.
2805

MANNS
3742

3529

TOMASAKI
3729

OOWAH L.
2675

GEYSER P.
3230

GEYSER CREEK

4WD

MILL CREEK

MOAB
20 KMS

4WD

MELLENTHIN
3855

DARK
CA. L.
3036

BRUMLEY CK.

3722

DARK CA.

3674

3729

PEALE
3878
(HELIOGRAPH
STATAION)

4WD

PACK CREEK

M4 RANCH

PACK
CK. CG.
2073

TUKU.
3806

P

P

LA SAL P.
3073

MEDICINE
LAKE

LA SAL CREEK

3517

SOUTH
3597

LACKEY
BASIN

4WD

2360

LA SAL G.S.
2256

MOAB
35 KMS
163

46

DITCH

DITCH

PARADOX
COLORADO

LA SAL JCT.

LA SAL
2134

SCALE    0          5          10    KMS

## Zion Narrows, Zion National Park, Utah, USA

This map shows much of the eastern portion of Zion National Park and includes Zion Canyon. Zion is located in extreme southwestern Utah between St. George, Mt. Carmel Junction, and Cedar City. Here is one of Utahs' best canyon hikes, Zion Narrows.

The small geologic cross-section on the map shows the geology. Capping much of Zions' buttes and mesas, is the Carmel Formation. It's a mixture of limestone and sandstone. The Navajo Sandstone is the layer which forms the narrow canyon walls of the Zion Narrows. Below the Narrows and as the canyon widens, is the Kayenta Formation.

Access to Zion Canyon is easy. One can drive east out of St. George and through the small towns of Hurricane, La Verkin, Virgin and Springdale, or west, from Mt. Carmel Junction located on US Highway 89. The road running north into Zion Canyon gives access to the bottom end of the Narrows Hike and is open year-round. To reach the upper end of the canyon, and the starting point for the hike, drive east out of the park about 3 kms, then turn north on a gravel road for 29 kms to the Chamberlain Ranch.

The Zion Narrows Hike has no trail—you simply walk down the canyon. About one quarter of the time is spent walking in the Virgin River. There is a short paved trail up-canyon from Temple of Siva for about 1½ kms. Many people park at the end-of-road parking lot and walk upstream into the narrows, then return the same way. But for the whole adventure, the trip is begun at the Chamberlain Ranch. The first part is on a 4WD road, then the river bottom. The real narrows being 2 kms above a waterfall, and end not far above the Temple of Siva. The narrowest part is downstream from Big Spring to near the paved trail. Ideal footwear is a canvas boot, but most people use running shoes. The slippery, algae-covered rocks make walking slightly difficult. From Chamberlain's Ranch to Siva is about 20 kms. Occasional deep pools make it impossible for small children to make this hike. Residents of Springdale run car shuttle services.

Because of heavy spring runoff and cold waters, late June is the beginning of the hiking season, which runs to late September. Be aware of thunderstorms and flash floods in late July and August. Always consult park rangers at the visitor center about weather, road conditions, etc., before entering the canyon. Chamberlain's Ranch to Siva is a long day-hike. If you're doing the entire 20 kms hike, and want to really enjoy it, take two full days. Take extra dry clothing if camping in the canyon-these cold waters and shaded canyon reduce body temps. Overnighting is permitted in the Narrows, but not below Big Spring.

**Map:** Kanab, 1 : 100,000, Zion National Park, 1 : 31,680, from USGS or visitor center.

The Narrowest of The Narrows in the Zion Narrows. It's near hip deep in places.

# Map 262-1, Zion Narrows, Zion N.P., Utah, USA

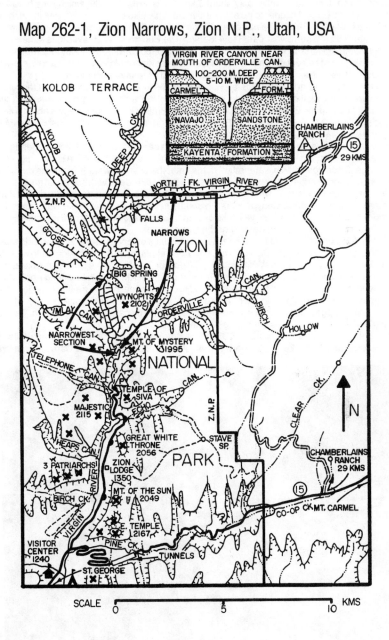

KOLOB TERRACE

VIRGIN RIVER CANYON NEAR
MOUTH OF ORDERVILLE CAN.
100-200 M. DEEP
5-10 M. WIDE
CARMEL FORM.
NAVAJO SANDSTONE
KAYENTA FORMATION

CHAMBERLAINS
RANCH
15
29 KMS

KOLOB CK.
DEEP CK.

NORTH FK. VIRGIN RIVER

Z.N.P.
FALLS
NARROWS
ZION
GOOSE CK.

BIG SPRING
WYNOPITS 2102
ORDERVILLE CAN.
BIRCH CAN.
HOLLOW
IMLAY CAN.
NARROWEST SECTION
MT. OF MYSTERY 1995
NATIONAL
TELEPHONE CAN.
TEMPLE OF SIVA
POND.
Z.N.P.
CLEAR CK.
N
MAJESTIC 2115
HEAPS CAN.
GREAT WHITE THRONE 2056
STAVE SP.
PARK
3 PATRIARCHS
ZION LODGE 1350
CHAMBERLAINS RANCH 29 KMS
VIRGIN RIVER
MT. OF THE SUN 2049
15
BIRCH CK.
CO-OP CK MT. CARMEL
VIRGIN
E. TEMPLE 2167
PINE CK.
VISITOR CENTER 1240
TUNNELS
ST. GEORGE

SCALE  0     5     10  KMS

## Paria River-Buckskin Gulch, Utah, USA

One of the best known Utah canyon hikes is the Paria River and its largest tributary, the Buckskin Gulch. One has to drive only about 3 kms off US Highway 89, which runs between Kanab, Utah and Page Arizona, to be at the trailhead. This hike is half in Utah, half in Arizona. End of hike is at Lee's Ferry. The narrows of Paria is about 8 kms long, and 7 or 8 meters wide the average, with the narrowest part 3 to 4 meters. The Buckskin Gulch averages 4 meters in width for 20 kms, with the narrowest part one meter. Depth of both is about 125 meters.

The geologic cross section shows the Navajo Sandstone making up the narrow canyon walls. Downstream the river cuts into the Kayenta and Moenave Formations.

Always start at the Paria River R.S. on Highway 89, 58 kms east of Kanab, to get the latest word on weather, additional maps and information on the water. Then drive 3 kms to the trailhead. If entering the Buckskin, use the House Rock Valley Road which begins about 8 kms west of the Paria R.S. on Highway 89. This road is rough, but most cars can make it to KM 0, about 6 kms from the highway.

There are no trails here, just walk in or along the stream. The Paria's flow depends on up-stream irrigation, but it's a flowing stream most of the year. The Buckskin is dry, with very few springs. Since you walk in water much of the time, the best footwear is a canvas boot, but many use a running shoe. The water in Paria is less than ankle deep with boy scout groups doing the hike regularly. If one is to walk from Whitehouse to Lees Ferry, a car shuttle is needed. There are people at Marble Canyon who run shuttle services. But one could walk down the Buckskin, up the Paria, then walk, hitch hike or bum a ride back to one's car on the House Rock Road. Buckskin is the more interesting of the two canyons.

The hike from Whitehouse to Lee's Ferry is about 3 days or longer, depending on side trips. Distance is 56 kms. If doing the Buckskin to Lee's Ferry expect about one day longer to walk 72 kms. If doing the Buckskin to the Whitehouse, plan on 2 or 3 days. For the Buckskin, take along a 10 meter long rope to make a safe descent in the rock jam at KM 24.2. Hike during April, May, June, September, October and November. Paria River water needs to be treated or boiled. July and August brings rain, flash flooding, and danger, especially to the Buckskin.

There are campgrounds at both ends of the hike, and many campsites in between. Take a backpakers' stove, as wood is becoming scarce.

**Map:** Utah Travel Council Map 5; USGS maps Smokey Mtn. (1 : 100,000), Paria (Utah), Paria Plateau and Lee's Ferry (Arizona) (1 : 62,500); or BLM map "Paria Canyon Primitive Area".

Best part of the Paria River Hike is the Buckskin Gulch seen here.

# Map 263-1, Paria River-Buckskin Gulch, Utah, USA

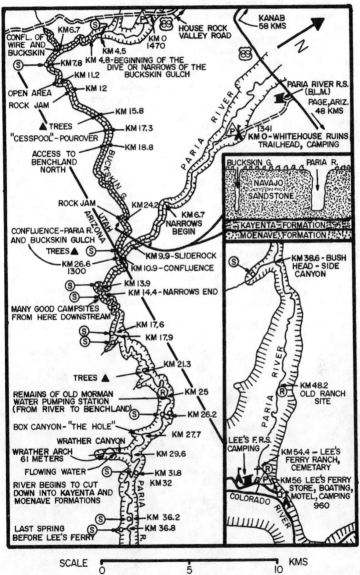

KANAB
58 KMS

HOUSE ROCK
VALLEY ROAD

KM 6.7

CONFL. OF
WIRE AND
BUCKSKIN

KM O
1470

KM 4.5

KM 4.8-BEGINNING OF THE
DIVE OR NARROWS OF THE
BUCKSKIN GULCH

KM 7.8

KM 11.2

KM 12

OPEN AREA
ROCK JAM

KM 15.8

KM 17.3

▲ TREES
"CESSPOOL"-POUROVER

KM 18.8

ACCESS TO
BENCHLAND
NORTH

PARIA RIVER

PARIA RIVER R.S.
(BL.M.)
PAGE,ARIZ.
48 KMS

1341
KM O-WHITEHOUSE RUINS
TRAILHEAD, CAMPING

ROCK JAM

KM 24.2

ARIZONA
UTAH

KM 6.7
NARROWS
BEGIN

BUCKSKIN G.          PARIA R.

NAVAJO
SANDSTONE

CONFLUENCE-PARIA R.
AND BUCKSKIN GULCH
TREES ▲

KM 9.9-SLIDEROCK

KAYENTA FORMATION
MOENAVE FORMATION

KM 26.6
1300

KM 10.9-CONFLUENCE

KM 13.9

KM 14.4-NARROWS END

KM 38.6 - BUSH
HEAD - SIDE
CANYON

MANY GOOD CAMPSITES
FROM HERE DOWNSTREAM

KM 17.6

KM 17.9

KM 21.3

PARIA    RIVER

TREES ▲

REMAINS OF OLD MORMAN
WATER PUMPING STATION
(FROM RIVER TO BENCHLAND)

KM 25

KM 26.2

KM 48.2
OLD RANCH
SITE

BOX CANYON-"THE HOLE"

KM 27.7

WRATHER CANYON

WRATHER ARCH
61 METERS

KM 29.6

LEE'S F.R.S.
CAMPING

FLOWING WATER

KM 31.8

KM 32

KM 54.4 - LEE'S
FERRY RANCH,
CEMETARY

RIVER BEGINS TO CUT
DOWN INTO KAYENTA AND
MOENAVE FORMATIONS

PARIA    R.

KM 56 LEE'S FERRY
STORE, BOATING,
MOTEL, CAMPING
960

COLORADO    RIVER

LAST SPRING
BEFORE LEE'S FERRY

KM 36.2

KM 36.8

SCALE
0          5          10    KMS

# Upper Escalante River, Utah, USA

This map covers the upper end of the Escalante River, located in extreme south-central Utah, not far north of the Arizona state line, and just east of Escalante.

The highest mesas and plateaus in the area are capped by Carmel Formation. Under that is Navajo Sandstone. This is exposed in the canyon walls between Escalante and Horse Canyon. In the lower Escalante River the Kayenta and Wingate Sandstones are exposed and form the steep and narrow canyons in that region.

Found in most canyons of the Upper Escalante River are ruins from the Fremont Indian Culture. They're from the same time as Anasazis (500 AD to 1250 AD), but lived and farmed in the canyon bottoms. Storage granaries are seen on cliffs.

Utah Highway 12, running between Panguitch, Escalante and on to Torrey, is the only road to this area. From Highway 12, the Pine Creek Road runs north of Escalante; the Burr Trail runs east of Boulder; and the Hole-in-the-Rock Road runs southeast from Escalante.

Not many trails here, almost all hiking is done in the canyon bottoms or in the stream itself. Because of the high altitude of the drainage, all the major canyons have year-round flowing streams. The walk through Death Hollow begins north of Escalante, and 3 or 4 kms east of Pine Creek Campground. The upper part is dry, but lower down it has a nice stream. At one point about 3 kms north of the Escalante River, is a large, deep hole. Swimming is required to cross it, with an air mattress or inner tube to float packs across. Most water in the Escalante River is ankle to knee deep. Another hike is from Escalante to Highway 12. Some park at Highway 12-Escalante River, and come out the Harris Wash. The Gulch, Horse Canyon and Deer Creek are other entry points. Calf Creek is a popular day hike, with ruins and pictographs. At the bottom of the map is 25 Mile Wash and the Egypt entry points, one of the most popular in the whole Escalante River. The road going to Pine Creek C.G. and the Hole-in-the-Rock Road are very good. All roads on the map are open to all cars most of the time. Do not hike without consulting the BLM office in Escalante for up-to-date conditions. Best footwear is canvas boots, but running shoes are often used.

The Death Hollow hike should be done from late June to mid-September, but hike other areas from late May on through October. With cold water, spring and fall are not the best times to hike here. The Death Hollow hike to Escalante is about 3 days. From Highway 12 to Escalante R. and up Harris, about 3 days with car shuttle. Many excellent campsites along creek bottoms. All streams have good water, but the Escalante River water, below Escalante, should be boiled or treated.

**Map:** BLM map "Hiking the Escalante River"; USGS map Escalante (1 : 100,000).

This is typical scenery from the upper part of the Escalante River.

# Map 264-1, Upper Escalante River, Utah, USA

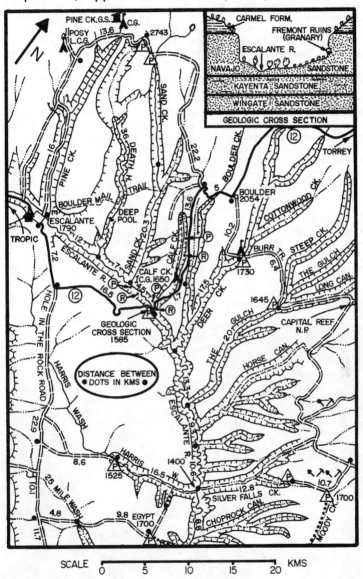

GEOLOGIC CROSS SECTION

CARMEL FORM.
FREMONT RUINS (GRANARY)
ESCALANTE R.
NAVAJO    SANDSTONE
KAYENTA SANDSTONE
WINGATE SANDSTONE

PINE CK. G.S.    C.G.
POSY L.C.G.    13.6    2743
N

SAND CK.
36 DEATH H.
TROPIC
BOULDER MAIL    TRAIL
22.2
BOULDER CK.
TORREY
5
BOULDER 2054
DEEP POOL
COTTONWOOD CK.
ESCALANTE 1790
SAND CK. 20.3
13.6
CALF CK.
10.2
STEEP CK.
BURR TR.
1730
THE GULCH
CALF CK. I.C.G. 1650
4.5
ESCALANTE R.
16.5
7.2
HOLE IN THE ROCK ROAD
12
R
R
DEER CK.
17.5
1.7
6.4
1645
CAPITAL REEF N.P.
THE GULCH 20.7
GEOLOGIC CROSS SECTION 1585
DISTANCE BETWEEN DOTS IN KMS
HORSE CAN.
LONG CAN.
13.3
HARRIS WASH
22.9
8.6
HARRIS 1525
ESCALANTE R. W. 10.6
9.3
1400
16.5
SILVER FALLS CK.
12.8
10.7
1700
25 MILE WASH
10.1
4.8
9.8    EGYPT 1700
8.8
CHOPROCK CAN.
MOODY CK.
11.7

SCALE    0    5    10    15    20    KMS

## Lower Escalante River, Utah, USA

Covered here is the lower or bottom end of the Escalante River, located in extreme southern Utah, very near the Arizona state line. It's between Bryce Canyon, Capital Reef N.P. and Glen Canyon N.R.A.

Most of the canyon walls here are made up of the Navajo Sandstone, as is the case in the Coyote Gulch. The geologic cross-section shows one arch and one of several huge undercuts. Further to the east and downstream, one can observe the Kayenta and Wingate Sandstones and Chinle Formations.

All parts of the Lower Escalante River can be reaced via the Hole-in-the-Rock Road. This road begins about 8 kms southeast of the town of Escalante and ends at the Hole-in-the-Rock Historical Marker. This is where the Mormon San Juan Mission Party cut a trail down through the cliff and eventually took wagons and livestock across the Colorado River. The last 5 kms of road is good, but next-to-last 5 kms is rough. Any car can make it—with care. One can also use the Burr Trail to reach Moody Creek. Always drive more cautiously when on side roads leading off the Hole-in-the-Rock Road.

Few trails here, just walk in the canyon bottoms. Water is always present in lower canyons, most of which can be used without treatment. But treat Escalante River water. Best footwear is high-topped canvas boots, but most use running shoes. You'll be in water perhaps 1/10 of the time, depending on the canyon. Water is ankle to knee deep. The most popular canyon for hikers is Coyote Gulch. Walk into this canyon where Hurricane Gulch crosses the road, or one could also walk in or out from 40 Mile Ridge or Red Well. Another popular hike is to park at Egypt, walk down the Escalante, then up 25 Mile Gulch and back to the car. Choprock, the Moodys and Stevens Canyons are interesting. There are many other entry points, most of which are shown on the map. Before hiking, always stop at the BLM and Glen Canyon N.R.A. office west of Escalante, for free maps and up-date information on roads and water.

Best time to visit the Lower Escalante River is in spring and fall. May, June, September and October are best times. Mid-summer is warm, but there's always a river to jump into. The author parked at the Hurricane Gulch Trailhead (on the Hole-in-the-Rock Road) walked down to the first arch, shot a roll of film, and returned in 5½ hours. Many do this hike to the Escalante River and maybe a side canyon or two, in two days, maybe three. Camp anywhere, but take climber's stove. Possibly mosquitoes in summer.

**Map:** BLM map "Hiking the Escalante River"; and USGS maps Smokey Mtn. and Escalante (1 : 100,000).

This is Jacob Hamblin Arch in Coyote Gulch, Lower Escalante River.

# Map 265-1, Lower Escalante River, Utah, USA

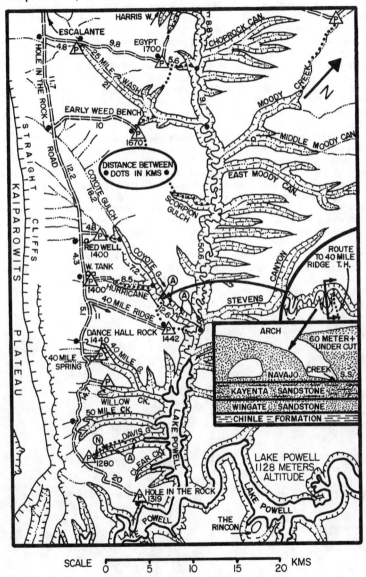

HARRIS W.

CHOPROCK CAN.

ESCALANTE

EGYPT 1700

8.8

MOODY CREEK

N

4.8 P 9.8

25 MILE WASH

HOLE IN THE ROCK

5.6

11.7

21

9

EARLY WEED BENCH

MIDDLE MOODY CAN.

ROAD

10

P 1670

STRAIGHT

KAIPAROWITS

CLIFFS

PLATEAU

12.2

COYOTE GULCH

18.2

DISTANCE BETWEEN DOTS IN KMS

EAST MOODY CAN.

SCORPION GULCH

4.8

RED WELL 1400

COYOTE G.

906

4.3

W. TANK

7.2

CANYON

ROUTE TO 40 MILE RIDGE T.H.

P 1400

8.5

HURRICANE

(A)

40 MILE RIDGE

12.6

(A)

STEVENS

5.1

11

DANCE HALL ROCK 1440

P 1442

ARCH

60 METER+ UNDER CUT

40 MILE

8

40 MILE SPRING

P

NAVAJO CREEK S.S.

LAKE POWELL

KAYENTA SANDSTONE

P

WILLOW CK.

WINGATE SANDSTONE

50 MILE CK.

CHINLE FORMATION

DAVIS G.

N

(A)

LAKE POWELL 1128 METERS ALTITUDE

P 1280

CLEAR CK.

20

HOLE IN THE ROCK

P 1319

LAKE POWELL

LAKE POWELL

THE RINCON

LAKE

SCALE 0    5    10    15    20 KMS

# Dark Canyon, Utah, USA

Dark Canyon is located directly west of the Abajo Mountains, and east of Hite Marina on Lake Powell, in southeastern Utah. It's also due north of Natural Bridges National Monument. The lower end of Dark Canyon is very deep with steep walls rising about 500 meters to the mesa tops. This part is similar to the Grand Canyon of Arizona, with a clear stream at the bottom. Some upper canyons have Anasazi ruins.

Near the Colorado River, now Lake Powell, one sees the Cedar Mesa Sandstone on top, then the Rico Formation, and below the mouth of Black Steer Canyon the Hermosa Group, made up mostly of limestone and shale.

Since the building of Glen Canyon Dam and creation of Lake Powell, some people arrive at the mouth of Dark Canyon by boat. Most however, prefer to hike into Dark Canyon Primitive Area. Most popular entry point is at the head of Woodenshoe Canyon. Reach this place by driving along Highway 95, then turn off to the Bridges N.M. One km from the junction, turn off on a dirt road and proceed through the Bears Ears to a parking place near the corral, as shown. One can reach the bottom end of Dark Canyon via Highway 95, not far from Hite. Turn northeast onto a dirt road just to the west of the White Canyon Bridge, and follow signs to Sundance Trail.

Most walking is done in the dry creek bed or along side the stream in Lower Dark Canyon. Other entry points are Black Steer, Youngs, Lean-to, and Trail Canyons. Many people park at the corral, walk down Woodenshoe, into Dark Canyon to the lower end, then retrace their steps 'till upper Dark, and exit at Peavine Canyon; this eliminates a car shuttle. The author did this trip down to Youngs Canyon, and return in 3 full days. It's 5 days for most people.

If the average hiker were to walk down Woodenshoe, to Lake Powell, then return and exit at Peavine, it would take very close to one week. A good and short hike for those with little time, would be to walk down the Sundance Trail. The lower part of Dark is the best part anyway. July and August heat turns most people off, so most hiking is done in Spring and Fall.

There are many campsites in the canyon, but not much water above Black Steer Canyon. The intermittent running water shown was what the author encountered after heavy September rains of 1982. Don't enter the upper parts of the canyon until consulting the rangers at Bridges N.M. or the Kane Gulch Ranger Station concerning the current availability of water. Running shoes or canvas "jungle" boots are recommended.

**Map:** USGS maps Hite Crossing and Blanding (1 : 100,000).

One of several pourover pools seen in Dark Canyon. Middle sections of canyon.

# Map 266-1, Dark Canyon, Utah, USA

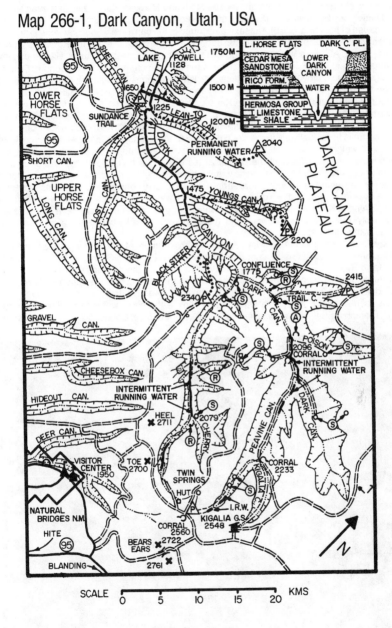

SCALE | 0 5 10 15 20 | KMS

# Grand Gulch, Utah, USA

Grand Gulch is located just south of Natural Bridges Monument in southeastern Utah. It's also just east of State Highway 263, formerly the old Mormon Hole-in-the-Rock Trail, and west of Highway 261 which runs between Bridges N.M. and Mexican Hat on the San Juan River. Grand Gulch has been made into a primitive area because of its scenic and primitive nature, and because of the hundreds of Anasazi ruins found in the canyon and side canyons. The little geologic cross-section on the map is of the upper part of the canyon where the Kane and Grand Gulches meet. All rocks seen are made of Cedar Mesa Sandstone. Ruins always occupy overhangs facing south. Farming was done in the 25-50 meter wide canyon bottom. Cottonwood, gamble oak, pinyon, juniper and sagebrush in bottoms. In Slickhorn drainage farming was on the mesa top. It's the best place in Utah to see and inspect Anasazi ruins.

Most people enter the canyon at the Kane Gulch Ranger Station after getting last minute information, then exit through Bullet Canyon. Others enter or exit at Collins Spring, while extra hardy people may enter in the upper canyon somewhere and exit via the Slickhorn Canyon.

No real trails here, just walk in the dry creek bed or along one side. Easy walking, mostly in sand. Light-weight leather boots, canvas "jungle" type boots and common running shoes are all adequate footwear. Contact the ranger at the Kane Gulch R.S. or at the visitor center, Natural Bridges N.M. for updates on the water situation. There is normally no running water in the canyon anywhere, only occasional springs. Always carry some water, and if encountering hikers ask of its whereabouts. You'll "go nuts" over the ruins, so take a camera and plenty of film. If parking at Kane Gulch and exiting at Bullet Canyon, one can usually get a ride back on the highway. Places where water is found in this and other nearby canyons are referred to as "seeps," rather than springs.

Most hikers do this trip in April, May and June, with a number of others doing it in September and October, July and August are hot. From Kane Gulch R.S. down Grand, up Bullet and back to the Kane Gulch R.S. is 2 long or 3 easy days. A week to 10 days if doing entire Grand Gulch and returning up Slickhorn. There are countless good campsites in the canyon. It's recommended at least on 3½ liter jug (1 US gallon) be taken, for water, which will allow hikers to camp in areas not near seeps. Also, carry water in your vehicle, there's no water on the rim or plateau.

**Map:**   Blanding, Bluff, Navajo Mtn. (1 : 100,000) or Utah Travel Council Map 1, Southeastern Utah.

This is but one of many Anasazi ruins seen in Grand Gulch.

# Map 267-1, Grand Gulch, Utah, USA

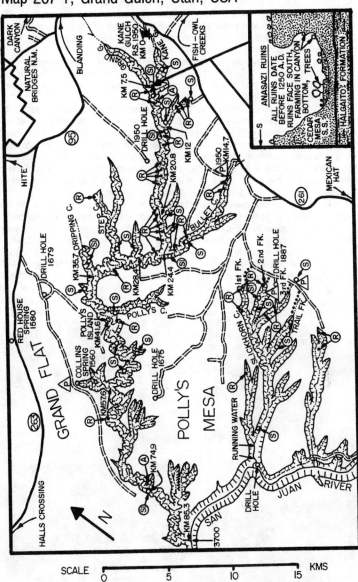

ANASAZI RUINS

ALL RUINS DATE
BEFORE 1250 A.D.
RUINS FACE SOUTH,
FARMING IN CANYON
BOTTOM, TREES

SCALE

0   5   10   15   KMS

## Fish and Owl Creeks, Utah, USA

This mapped area is located in the southeastern corner of Utah, south of the Abajo Mountains and north of the San Juan River. It's also sandwiched in between US Highway 163 and Highway 261. Fish Creek has several places with permanent running water. There are even small fish in one section. As the geologic cross section shows these streams have cut deep canyons into the Cedar Mesa Sandstone. The flat-topped plateau is known as Cedar Mesa and is about 1850 meters altitude. Canyons are 200 meters deep. This is both a primitive area and has ruins; second best place in Utah to see ruins. Ruins face south to catch the winter sun. Farming here was on mesa tops. Inhabitants left by 1250 AD.

Drive south from Utah Highway 95 (running between Blanding and Lake Powell) on Highway 261 from the area around Natural Bridges N.M. to a point about 3 kms south of the Kane Gulch Ranger Station. Then turn east and drive about 8 kms on a good dirt road to where the road ends at a drill hole and trailhead.

There are few trails in these canyons, but there's little need for them. Simply follow the dry stream beds or walk along the small streams. Most people hiking in this drainage walk down Fish and up Owl Creek. From the drill hole, where is located a trail register, walk north-northeast using a compass, to the rim overlooking the confluence of Fish Creek's two upper tributaries. At the rim, search for one of two or three routes down into the canyon. Once in the canyon the way is easy. Coming up from Owl is a trail beginning at about point 1585 meters. There are stone cairns along the way to the drill hole. Best hiking boots here are light-weight leather hiking boots, but jungle boots are also popular as are common running shoes.

July and August are too hot, making spring and fall ideal. Most people make the hike in spring—April, May or June, with others coming in September and October. The author did this hike in one long and tiresome day, but most people spend one night and sometimes two in the canyon. Round trip distance is about 25 kms. Running water as of October 1982, just after heavy September rains are as shown. Only bathers may pollute the water. It's good for drinking. Water isn't the problem here as in other canyons. Always consult the rangers at Kane Gulch Ranger Station before entering the canyons. Camping can be done at the trailhead or anywhere in the canyons, as good sites are abundant everywhere. Have a supply of water in your car, as there's none on the mesa.

**Map:**   Utah Travel Council Map 1—Southeastern Utah, and USGS map Bluff (1 : 100,000).

These Anasazi ruins are 500 meters from trailhead in Upper Fish Creek Canyon.

# Map 268-1, Fish and Owl Creeks, Utah, USA

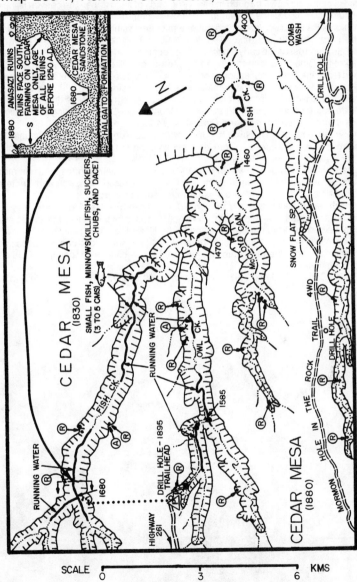

SCALE

0        3        6    KMS

# Grand Canyon, Arizona, USA

Included here is the most famous canyon in the world, the Grand Canyon of the Colorado, located in northern Arizona in the USA. This giant and most spectacular of all river-made features is now part of the Grand Canyon National Park.

The canyon has been made during the last couple of million years or so, by the waters of the Colorado River cutting down through the flat-lying beds of sandstone. The canyon is included here because it's a fine place to hike in a unique setting.

The National Park Service maintains but one main trail within the National Park boundary; this is the Bright Angel and Kaibab Trail (the Kaibab Trail begins at Yaki and goes to the bottom). This trail crosses the canyon with one end beginning at the North Rim, located south of Jacob Lake; the other end is at the South Rim, north of Williams and Flagstaff.

One can leave the South Rim at one of two points. These two trails connect near the bottom. At the bottom is a suspension bridge making the river crossing possible. Immediately to the north of the bridge is the Phantom Ranch and nearby a campground. Note the elevation—732 meters. The trail then runs to the northeast up Bright Angel Creek, passing two designated campsites, before reaching the North Rim, at about 2500 meters.

Another interesting place to hike is down into the canyon where the Havasupai Indian Reservation is located. There's a store and campground in that canyon—but the entry fee costs a fair amount of money these days.

Because of millions of people visiting the park each year, camping reservations must be made early for all campsites—at least during the busy season, June through September. During other times of the year, there's usually not much of a problem.

Best time of year to hike across the canyon is during the fall or the spring season, as summer temperatures at the bottom are very high. The South Rim is open the year round, but no attempt is made to clear snow from the road leading to the North Rim during winter.

At both the North or South Rims there are ranger stations where one can get maps and the latest information about the tails, camping, etc. It's best to do your shopping for food before reaching the canyon.

**Map:**  Grand Canyon National Park and Vicinity, 1 : 62,500, from North or South Rim visitor centers.

Grand Canyon, best known and most often visited canyon in the World.

## Map 269-1, Grand Canyon, Arizona, USA

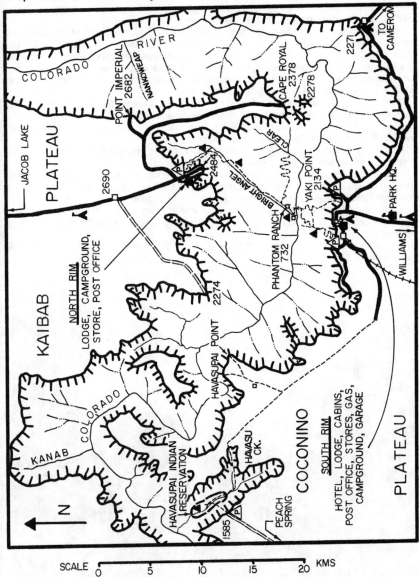

# Humphreys, San Francisco Mts., Arizona, USA

The highest mountain in the state of Arizona is Humphreys Peak, reaching 3862 meters elevation. Humphreys is located immediately north of Flagstaff and not far to the southeast of the Grand Canyon, in northern Arizona. Humphreys and other nearby peaks together form the San Francisco Mountains.

Humphreys Peak is a very old and highly eroded volcanic mountain which retains little or none of its original conal shape. There are several other more recent or newer cones in the area, namely Sunset Crater to the northeast.

Access is very easy to these mountains, especially to Humphreys and Mt. Agassis, the second highest peak in the group, at 3766 meters. The easiest and normal route is from Flagstaff and the Snow Bowl Ski Lodge. The lodge is located on the western slopes of Agassis, 24 kms from Flagstaff. From the lodge there are trails leading up to the top of the ski lift, the summit of Aggasis, and eventually to the summit of Humphreys. During most of the summer the ski lift is operating for those who prefer riding to hiking.

There's another route beginning near some water storage tanks (small reservoirs) to the southeast of the high peaks, but there's some private land and a maze of 4WD roads in the area, so finding the trail may be difficult. From those water reservoirs, the trail leads up over Fremont Pass and eventually to the top of Humphreys.

If you're planning any long hikes or overnight campouts, keep in mind there is no live water or streams on the mountain. This is typical of volcanic mountains.

When the ski lodge is open they serve meals and snacks, but it's best to buy your food in Flagstaff. If you'd like more information and maps of the San Francisco Mountains and the Coconino National Forest, stop at the ranger station in Flagstaff.

Humphreys is in a dry region, but heavy rains come at times in July and August, and heavy snows in winter. For warm weather hiking make the climb during the months of June through October.

**Map:**   Coconino National Forest, 1 : 125,000, or the USGS map Humphreys Peak, 1 : 24,000, from the Flagstaff Ranger Station.

Looking upslope at Mt. Agassis from the ski runs of the Snow Bowl.

# Map 270-1, Humphreys, S. Francisco Mts., Ariz., USA

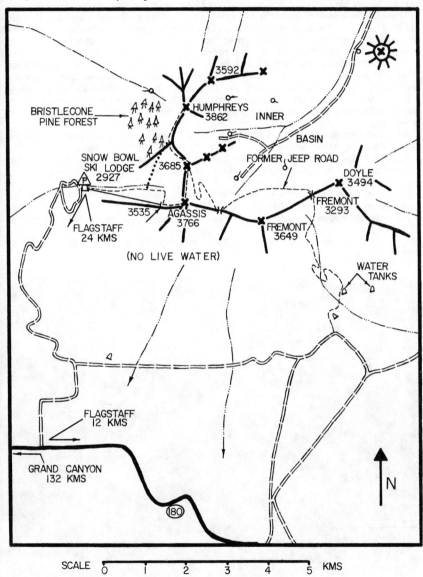

BRISTLECONE
PINE FOREST

3592

✗ HUMPHREYS
3862

INNER

BASIN

SNOW BOWL
SKI LODGE
2927

3685

FORMER JEEP ROAD

DOYLE
3494

3535    AGASSIS
3766

FREMONT
3293

FLAGSTAFF
24 KMS

FREMONT
3649

(NO LIVE WATER)

WATER
TANKS

FLAGSTAFF
12 KMS

GRAND CANYON
132 KMS

N

180

SCALE    0    1    2    3    4    5    KMS

## Truches, Sangre de Cristo Mts., N.M., USA

Truches Peak, at 3995 meters, is the 2nd highest peak in New Mexico, and is the highest in the Pecos Wilderness Area. Truches Peak is near the southern end of the Sangre de Cristo Range, which extends south from central Colorado. These mountains are folded and uplifted and composed of many rocks, from granite to sandstone and quartzite.

These peaks are typical of all the central and southern Rockies; mostly dome type summits, with old glacier cirques and some rugged north faces. Normally, most routes are walk-ups.

There are three ways of access to this highest area. One is from Santa Fe and the Ski Basin, but it's the longest. The second is from Jacks Creek and Campground, which is about 30 kms due north of Pecos, and on the Pecos River. This route is also long, but could be attractive to someone who is interested in a long backpacking trip.

The shortest and most used route is via Truches Village and Truches Creek. One can drive 10 or 11 kms southeast of Truches on a poor dirt road, which follows Truches Creek. There are many good camping sites along this creek. This same 4WD road continues to the national forest boundary, where a good trail begins and follows Quemado Creek to a large cirque basin, thence to Truches Peak. A strong climber can make this hike in one long day, but many do it on a weekend.

Road signs are sometimes confusing in this part of America. It has something to do with the Spanish ancestry of the people who are a majority in this part of New Mexico.

Truches Village has stores, gas stations, garages and a forest ranger station. Good weather is common, with late summer and December and January being the months of heaviest precipitation.

One must have his own car for transport; however, on weekends, hitch hiking can be good—especially if you put up a sign stating your destination.

For more information and maps of these areas see the ranger stations at Santa Fe, Penasco, or Truches.

**Map:** Santa Fe National Forest, 1 : 125,000, from ranger stations in Pecos, Santa Fe, or maybe Truches.

There are several high summits along this main ridge, one of which is Truches.

# Map 271-1, Truches, S. de Cristo Mts., N.M., USA

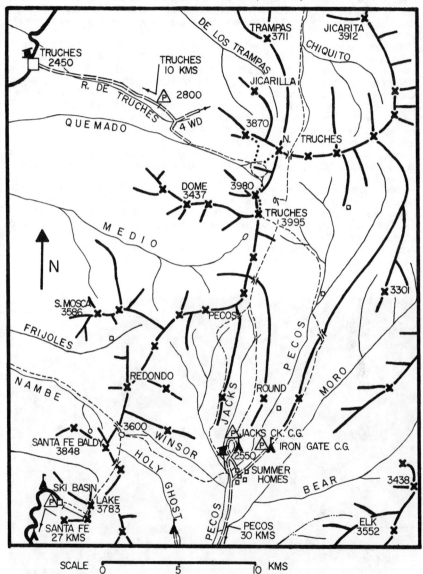

SCALE  0    5    10  KMS

## Wheeler, Sangre de Cristo Mts., N.M., USA

Wheeler Peak, at 4012 meters, is the highest peak in New Mexico. It's located towards the southern end of the Sangre de Cristo Range and just south of the Taos Ski Bowl. The peak and resort are both northeast of Taos, N.M.

By far the least complicated way of approach is via Taos and Taos ski resort. An all-national forest service route first heads northeast from Twining C.G. towards the Bull-of-the-Woods pasture, which is near the end of the road on the Red River; then it doubles back to the south, along the prominent ridge to Wheeler Peak. This is the longest route, but doesn't cross any private land.

The best and shortest route is one that crosses private land. One must inquire at the ski resort as to the present situation for public access along Lake Fork Creek. A good road can be taken about 2*3 the way to Williams Lake—if it's open to the public. From Williams Lake, at 3350 meters, one can climb Wheeler or a number of peaks which range up to 4000 meters. Also, there's some pretty good north face routes just south of Williams Lake. Timberline here is nearly the highest in the world, at about 3650-3700 meters. (The highest trees the author has seen are on the slopes of Iliniza in Ecuador, at about 4300 meters.)

Access on Lake Fork Creek is apparently not as much of a problem in winter as it is in summer, so winter climbing should be easy and fun.

Another way of approach is via Questa and the Red River, but it is much longer. If one is using the Williams Lake route, water is never a problem, but if the ridge route is taken, have a canteen full.

Good weather is never far away, but in July and August some heavy showers can be expected. In winter, December and January have more precipitation than other months.

For more information visit the forest ranger stations in either Questa or Taos. Forest service maps are also available at these two locations. Food and all supplies can be found at the ski village, or better still in Taos.

**Map:** Carson National Forest, 1 : 125,000, or the USGS map Wheeler Peak, 1 : 24,000, from the Taos or Questa Ranger Stations.

At the summit of Wheeler Peak, the author actually touched these Ptarmigans.

# Map 272-1, Wheeler, S. de Cristo Mts., N.M., USA

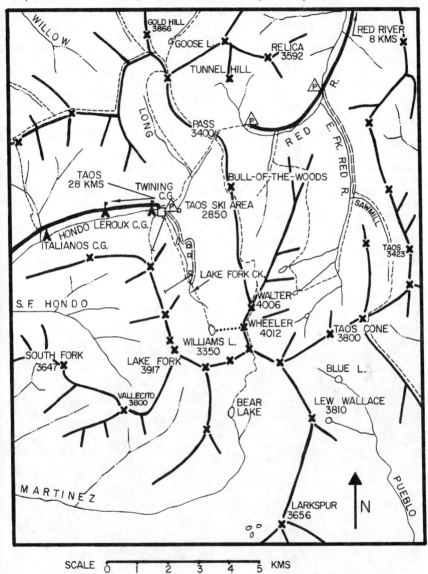

SCALE 0 1 2 3 4 5 KMS

# Windom, Needle Mountains, Colorado, USA

Included on this map are three of Colorado's 14'ers. This small group of high summits is known as the Needle Mountains, and is part of the greater San Juan Range in southwest Colorado. They lie about 40 kms northeast of Durango (which is the largest city in the region), and at the western edge of the Weminuche Wilderness Area. The highest peak is Windom, at 4295 meters, followed closely by Eolus, 4294 meters, and Sunlight, 4286 meters. Remember, a 14,000 foot mountain, of which Colorado has about 53, is equal to 4268 meters elevation.

The Needles are composed of different rock types. The western parts have Eolus Granite, while other places have slate, conglomerate and quartzite. These peaks are one of the more isolated groups of 14'ers in Colorado. To give an example of distance, it's a long one day hike from the trailhead at Purgatory Campground to the Chicago Basin. That's a distance of 26 kms. It's another day (or two) to climb the 3 summits, and a third day to return to Purgatory. The author did this trip in 2 very long days, but for most people it's a 3 day trip.

Once inside the Chicago Basin, Sunlight and Windom can best be climbed by walking from the two upper lakes to the basin between the peaks—then to either peak. Eolus can best be climbed from the lower part of the basin, and the southeast ridge.

The normal route to Chicago Basin can be shortened by taking the train running between Durango and Silverton, and getting off at Needleton.

A second route is via Lemon Reservoir (not shown), to the Transfer Park Campground, and the route past City Reservoir, to the Needle Creek Trail. The third possible route is via Vallecito Reservoir, and Vallecito Creek—then to Johnson Creek and Columbine Pass.

The months of July, August and September are the best times for climbing here, but the author has made two trips to Colorado at the beginning of October, and found fine weather. Each year brings different conditions.

For all three routes, it's recommended that you begin your journey in Durango. It's a good shopping place and there's an office of the San Juan National Forest located there where the latest information concerning roads, snow conditions, and trails can be found.

**Map:** San Juan National Forest, 1 : 125,000, or USGS map Columbine Pass, 1 : 24,000, from the Durango Ranger Station.

From summit of Eolus, Sunlight left, and Windom to the right.

## Map 273-1, Windom, Needle Mts., Colorado, USA

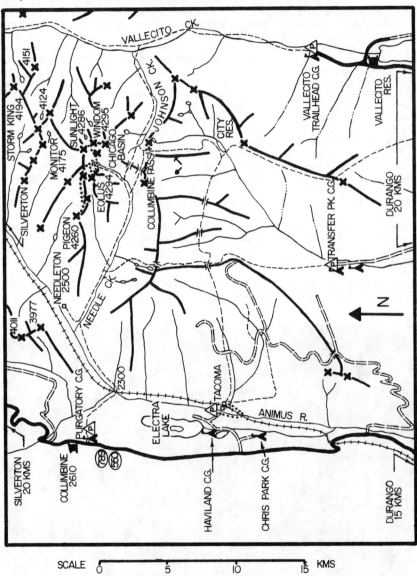

SCALE 0 5 10 15 KMS

# Mt. Wilson, San Miguel Mts., Colorado, USA

Included on this map are four of the 14'ers in Colorado, three of which—Mt. Wilson, 4343 meters; Wilson Peak, 4273; and El Diente, 4317 meters—are located in the San Miguel Mountains not far southwest of Telluride. The other is Sneffels, with an altitude of 4314 meters, which is in the extreme northwest section of the San Juan Mountains.

Sneffels can best be reached from the town of Ouray, situated on Highway 789-550. From Ouray drive southwest up Canyon Creek to Camp Bird—that's where the better road ends. From Camp Bird, there's a 4WD road heading in a northwesterly direction, eventually turning into a trail. Take this trail to Blue Lakes Pass, and climb Sneffels from the south ridge. It can also be ascended from an east pass or col, as shown on the map—both routes are easy, but each involves some scrambling. Sneffels could also be climbed via Telluride, on the other side of the mountain, but this is a much longer hike.

To reach the other three 14'ers located to the southwest, drive to the Lizard Head Pass, at 3116 meters altitude. From the pass one can walk cross-country to find the Lizard Head Trail (which begins lower down at Trout Lake). Follow this trail to a point just south of Wilson Peak. From there one can climb all three of these higher summits. There are no real trails as such to these summits, but as climbing 14'ers becomes more popular in the state of Colorado, the normal routes are slowly becoming trails.

This same area can be reached also from near the Burro Bridge Campground, and the Navajo Lake Trail, which follows the upper Dolores River. Still another route possibility is from the north. At a junction called Vanadium, an old mining road heads due south up Big Bear Creek, and ends near Wilson Peak and the Silver Pick Mill. There are several of these old roads, and even more old mines in the area, so keep your direction in mind rather than one particular road.

The main towns in the area are Silverton, Ouray, and Telluride. All three have stores and gas stations. The only public transportation in the area is bus service on Highway 789-550, but hitching is generally good, even on side roads. For additional information and forest service maps of the area, stop at the ranger stations at Montrose or Delta, both of which are located to the north.

**Map:** Uncompahgre National Forest, 1 : 125,000, or USGS maps Mt. Wilson, Dolores Peak, or Mt. Sneffels, all 1 : 24,000, from Montrose, Delta, or Durango Ranger Station.

An old miners cabin is near the base of Sneffels, seen to the upper right.

# Map 274-1, Wilson, S. Miguel Mts., Colo., USA

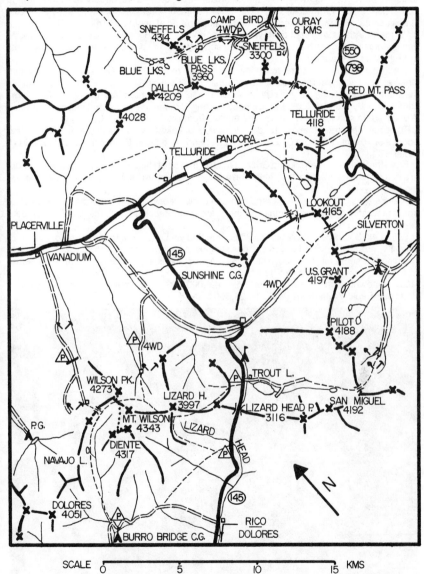

SNEFFELS 4314
CAMP BIRD 4WD
OURAY 8 KMS
SNEFFELS 3300
550
798
BLUE LKS. PASS 3960
BLUE LKS.
DALLAS 4209
RED MT. PASS
4028
TELLURIDE 4118
PANDORA
TELLURIDE
LOOKOUT 4165
SILVERTON
PLACERVILLE
VANADIUM
145
SUNSHINE C.G.
4WD
U.S. GRANT 4197
PILOT 4188
P 4WD
P
WILSON PK. 4273
LIZARD H. 3997
P TROUT L.
LIZARD HEAD P. 3116
SAN MIGUEL 4192
MT. WILSON 4343
LIZARD
P.G.
DIENTE 4317
HEAD
NAVAJO L.
P
DOLORES 4051
145
P
RICO
BURRO BRIDGE C.G.
DOLORES
N

SCALE  0        5        10        15   KMS

## Uncompahgre, San Juan Mts., Colorado, USA

Included on this map are five of Colorado's 14'ers. They include: Uncompahgre, 4362 meters; Wetterhorn, 4273; Handies, 4283; Redcloud, 4279; and Sunshine, 4268 meters.

Uncompahgre is the most famous of the group and the highest—it's the 6th highest in Colorado. Getting to Uncompahgre and the surrounding region is easy. Lake City can be reached via a good highway from the Gunnison area, or on a secondary road through the Baxterville region. From Lake City drive west up Henson Creek about 8 kms to where Nellie Creek comes in. At that junction is located a campground at about 2850 meters. From there, a 4WD road winds its way up the canyon to the north for about 5 kms. At that point a trail begins and eventually reaches the summit from the south side of the peak. The summit is only 3 kms from the end of the road.

Wetterhorn is usually climbed by itself. It is best reached from Henson and Matterhorn Creeks. The section at the base of the mountain is without a trail, but it's easy to make it up to the south ridge from the canyon bottom. As one nears the summit, a trail emerges. The summit pitch is slightly more difficult, but still easy. Strong climbers can do both Uncompahgre and Wetterhorn in one long day, as did the author, from the Nellie Creek Campground.

To reach the three other 14'ers, drive south out of Lake City, past Mill Creek Campground about 9 or 10 kms, to where Grizzly Gulch, Lake Fork, and Silver Creeks meet. That's at 3170 meters.

From that point one can hike up Grizzly Gulch to the top of Handies, or continue up Lake Fork to a point on the west side of the peak, then walk past a pond, and finally up the south side of the mountain.

There's a trail up Silver Creek, and one can climb Redcloud from a northerly approach or from the west. Sunshine is normally climbed along with Redcloud, with the final summit route being from the north.

With a 4WD vehicle, this region could be reached via Ouray, but that's not recommended. Lake City has several small stores and gas stations, but for better varieties do your shopping in Gunnison or some larger place. There are ranger stations in both Gunnison and Del Norte, where forest service maps can be found.

**Map:** Uncompahgre National Forest 1 : 125,000, or USGS maps Uncompahgre Peak, Redcloud Peak, Wetterhorn Peak, 1 : 24,000.

A bright, sunny October morning on the eastern slopes of Uncompahghre.

# Map 275-1, Uncompahgre, S. Juan Mts., Colo., USA

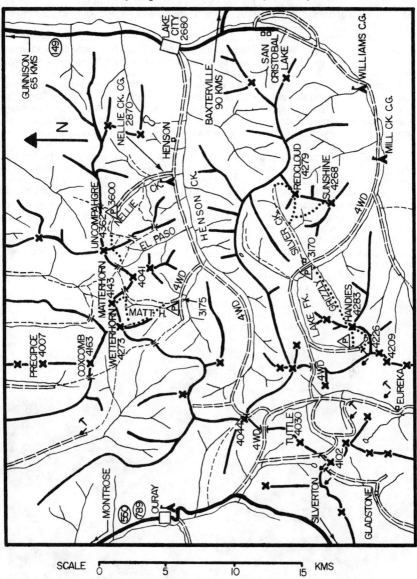

# San Luis, San Juan Mts., Colorado, USA

The 50th ranking peak in the state of Colorado is San Luis, listed at 4272 meters. At present this is the only 14'er on this map. However, before some of the more recent surveys were taken, another peak on this map was listed as one of the 53 highest in the state. That peak is Stewart, now set at 4263 meters elevation.

San Luis is one of the more isolated of the 14'ers in Colorado. There are some very rough 4WD roads surrounding the peak, but they are very much for 4WD vehicles. There are no sizeable towns or cities in the immediate vicinity; however, there is the small mining community of Creede.

Perhaps the most normal route of approach is via Gunnison, Powderhorn, and to the ranching area known as Cathedral. From there follow the 4WD road up Spring Creek to where the road ends, or where your vehicle must stop; then continue up the trail, to a point west of the peak. Any place on the western face can be used for the ascent.

A second route of approach is from the northeast and the Upper Dome Reservoir, located between Gunnison and Saguachi. From near the end of the road, at either Natrus, Stewart or Cochetopa Creeks, one can walk west and climb either Stewart, Baldy Alto, or San Luis Peak. Stewart Creek seems the more normal route or trail from that side of the mountain. There appears to be no problem in crossing private land on this route, as is the case on some other high peaks of Colorado.

A third approach route, and one used by the author, is the one on the south, from the direction of Creede. This involves taking the newly built Bachelor Road, first west and then north, out of Creede. Any vehicle can make this trip, at least to the old Equity Mine. Some people might want to park their cars at the mine or the beaver ponds (marked 3350 meters). This 4WD road gradually fades away into a trail. Then the trail heads in an easterly direction, crossing one pass before the south ridge of San Luis is reached. This ridge is used to gain the summit—an easy one day walk from the mine.

There are ranger stations in Creede and Gunnison. These stations have information centers and the people there are helpful in describing routes and roads. One can also buy good forest service maps.

**Map:**  Gunnison or Rio Grande National Forest 1 : 125,000, or USGS map Creede, 1 : 62,500, from the ranger stations in Gunnison or Creede.

San Luis Mountain, an uninspiring peak, but it's over 4268 meters.

# Map 276-1, San Luis, San Juan Mts., Colo., USA

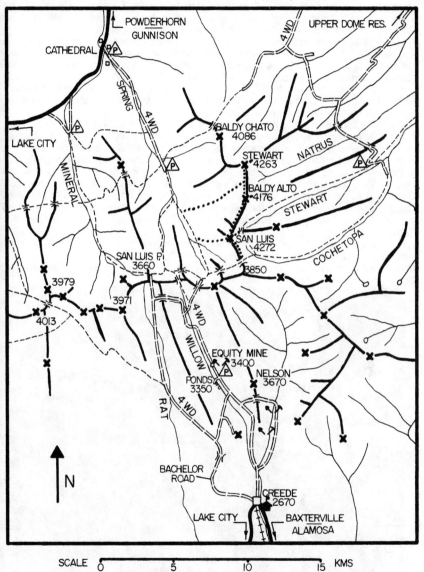

POWDERHORN
GUNNISON

CATHEDRAL

UPPER DOME RES.

4 WD

BALDY CHATO
4086

SPRING

4 WD

LAKE CITY

STEWART
4263

NATRUS

BALDY ALTO
4176

STEWART

MINERAL

SAN LUIS
4272

COCHETOPA

SAN LUIS P.
3660

3850

3979

3971

4013

4 WD

WILLOW

EQUITY MINE
3400

NELSON
3670

PONDS
3350

RAT

4 WD

BACHELOR
ROAD

CREEDE
2670

LAKE CITY

BAXTERVILLE
ALAMOSA

N

SCALE  0          5          10          15   KMS

# Castle, Elk Mountains, Colorado, USA

In the area just south and southwest of Aspen—possibly Colorado's most famous ski resort—lies six of the state's 14'ers. These six summits form the high portion of the Elk Mountains. None of Aspen's ski runs approach the really high peaks—but are confined to the lower slopes above town.

The six mountains are: Castle, the highest at 4349 meters; then South Maroon Bell, 4316; followed by Capital Peak, 4308; Snowmass Mountain, 4296; Pyramid, 4275; and North Maroon Bell, 4272 meters. All these summits are within the boundaries of the White River National Forest, and the Maroon Bell—Snowmass Wilderness Area.

This high region can be approached from three main directions: from Aspen and the north and east; from the west, via Carbondale and Marble; and from the south, via Gunnison, Crested Butte and Gothic. All the 14'ers can be climbed from the Aspen area—which is the recommended route of approach.

For Castle Peak, drive south out of Aspen along Castle Creek, to the end of the paved road—about 20 kms. Then walk up a 4WD road to or near an old mine just east of the peak, then take a route up the north ridge or east face.

The three central peaks of the Maroon Bells and Pyramid can best be reached on the surfaced road running southwest out of Aspen. This road runs along Maroon Creek where there are three established campgrounds. To climb the Maroon Bells, walk up the trail beyond Maroon Lake Campground, past Crater Lake, and to a point just east of South Maroon, then up to the south ridge to the summit. North Maroon can also be climbed this way, or from the north—near Crater Lake, or on two other trail routes which begin at, or near, the Snowmass Creek Campground. Capital and Snowmass Peaks can be climbed from the Snowmass Creek Campground, or from the ranch at the end of the road. These last two can also be climbed from the old mining town of Marble. The Maroon Bells and Pyramid can also be ascended from Gothic.

Gunnison, Aspen, and Crested Butte all have shopping centers and forest ranger stations, where the latest information can be found.

**Map:** White River National Forest, 1 : 125,000, or USGS maps Hayden Peak, Maroon Bells, Capital Peak, Snowmass Mtn. 1 : 24,000.

The north face of Pyramid Peak, one of the most rugged summits in Colorado.

# Map 277-1, Castle, Elk Mts., Colorado, USA

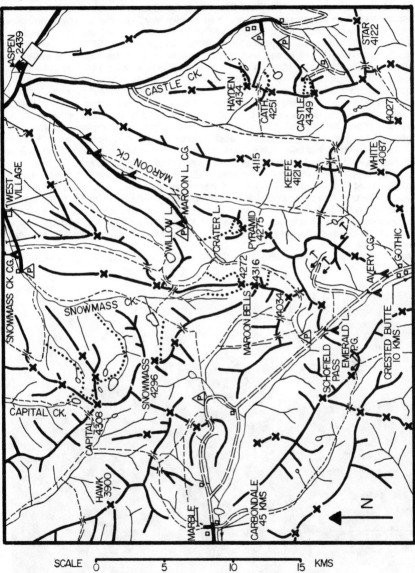

ASPEN 2439
STAR 4122
CASTLE CK.
HAYDEN 4134
CATH. 4251
CASTLE 4349
4027
MAROON CK.
MAROON L. CG.
4115
KEEFE 4121
WHITE 4087
WEST VILLAGE
WILLOW L.
CRATER L.
PYRAMID 4275
AVERY CG.
GOTHIC
SNOWMASS CK CG.
SNOWMASS CK.
MAROON BELLS 4272
4316
4034
SCHOFIELD PASS
EMERALD L. P.G.
CRESTED BUTTE 10 KMS
CAPITAL CK.
SNOWMASS 4296
CAPITAL 4308
HAWK 3900
MARBLE
CARBONDALE 45 KMS
N

SCALE  0     5     10     15   KMS

# Holy Cross, Sawatch Mts., Colorado, USA

The map on the opposite page contains only one of Colorado's 14'ers; that is, peaks over 14,000 feet or 4268 meters. This summit is Mount of the Holy Cross, at 4269 meters, tentatively ranked at number "52" in the state. Holy Cross is at the extreme northern end of the Sawatch Range in the heart of Colorado.

Getting to Holy Cross is quite easy. If you're coming from the south and the Leadville side, take Highway 24 north over Tennessee Pass, to a dirt road about 3 kms north of Gilman. If you approach the area from Interstate 70, get off where Highway 24 intersects, a place previously known as Dowde Junction—then drive south about 7 kms to the dirt road just mentioned.

Drive to the Halfmoon Campground (on a terrible road), situated at 3200 meters. From there one has a choice of two trails, and two possible routes to the mountain. The normal route to the top of Holy Cross is via the Halfmoon Pass, at about 3536 meters, then down to Cross Creek, and finally up the north ridge to the summit—a very easy climb; but on the return trip hikers must again walk from Cross Creek, back up to the pass. This can be difficult for some. At Cross Creek is located an old cabin with a dirt floor, which can be used as an emergency shelter.

Holy Cross became famous, because on its east face is a configuration in the shape of a cross. It's some kind of a sill and dike and when filled with snow, gives the appearance of a cross. This can be viewed best from the east, and from another peak named Notch Mountain. In the "notch" itself, has been built a small chapel, which is seen in many fotos. To reach this chapel, take the Notch Mountain Trail south from Halfmoon Campground.

The second highest mountain in the area is Mt. Jackson, 4164 meters. It can be reached from the Gold Park Campground area, but this is the longest route. The shortest one is via the Cross Creek trail to a point about due east of Jackson, then simply route-find to the summit.

Leadville is the closest town to the area of Holy Cross—therefore, the logical place to do the last minute shopping. If one is coming from I-70, then perhaps one should stop in Glenwood Springs to the west, or Denver to the east. Leadville has a ranger station, where forest service maps can be bought.

**Map:**   White River National Forest, 1 : 125,000, or USGS map Mt. of the Holy Cross, 1 : 24,000.

Holy Cross from Halfmoon Pass. Normal route is north ridge to the right.

# Map 278-1, Holy Cross, Sawatch Mts., Colo., USA

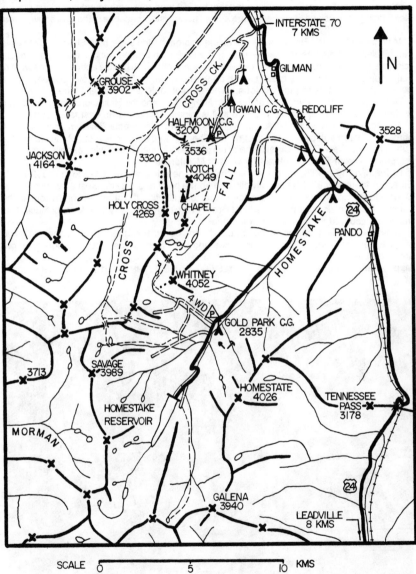

INTERSTATE 70
7 KMS

GILMAN

REDCLIFF

3528

GROUSE
3902

CROSS CK.

TIGWAN C.G.

HALFMOON C.G.
3200

JACKSON
4164

3320

3536

NOTCH
4049

FALL

HOLY CROSS
4269

CHAPEL

HOMESTAKE

24

PANDO

CROSS

WHITNEY
4052

4 WD

GOLD PARK C.G.
2835

3713

SAVAGE
3989

HOMESTATE
4026

TENNESSEE
PASS
3178

HOMESTAKE
RESERVOIR

MORMAN

24

GALENA
3940

LEADVILLE
8 KMS

N

SCALE   0        5        10   KMS

## Mt. Elbert, Sawatch Mountains, Colorado, USA

Mts. Elbert and Massive are the 1st and 2nd highest peaks in Colorado, at 4400 and 4397 meters, respectively. Because they're so near each other, they're normally climbed together—but not on the same day. These two summits are located in the northern part of the Sawatch Mountains, southwest of Leadville, east of Aspen, and northwest of Buena Vista.

As with the rest of the Sawatch, these peaks are rounded and dome-like, and make for easy climbs or hikes. The rock is mostly quartzite, but differing rocks are found in various places. North facing cirques and snow basins are almost non-existent because of the light snowpack in winter.

Most people use the Halfmoon Creek as the approach, and since both Elbert and Massive can be climbed from one campsite—usually the Halfmoon Campground is used. Both mountains are normally climbed by using the Main Range Trail, which begins about 1½ kms west of Halfmoon Campground. By turning south on the Main Range Trail to a point due east of the peak, the summit trail to Elbert is found. This normal route is up the east face.

By turning north at the junction of the Main Range Trail and the Halfmoon Creek Road, and walking for 4 or 5 kms, the Mt. Massive trail is joined. This too is an east face route.

Another easy way to Elbert, is via Highway 82, which connects Balltown and Aspen. A sometimes-used trail begins just east of the Elbert Lodge, and leads most of the way to the summit, along Black Cloud Creek. One could also climb Elbert from Twin Lakes, southeast of the peak, or from Echo Creek not far west of Monitor Rock.

La Plata, rising to 4372 meters, is the 5th highest peak in the state. It lies to the south of Mt. Elbert and Highway 82. It's normally climbed from a point about 2 kms west of Monitor Rock. One needs to cross the small stream, then climb to, and follow the prominent north ridge to the summit. One can also use the trail almost directly across the highway from Monitor Rock. This trail leads south to the basin east of the peak.

Leadville is the largest town in the area, so it's the best place Zto shop. Also, one might find small stores at Malta, Balltown, Twin Lakes and the Elbert Lodge. There's a forest ranger station in Leadville.

**Map:** San Isabel National Forest, 1 : 125,000, or USGS Mt. Elbert and Mt. Massive, 1 : 24,000.

You'll see this old miners cabin if using the Black Cloud Canyon route.

# Map 279-1, Elbert, Sawatch Mts., Colorado, USA

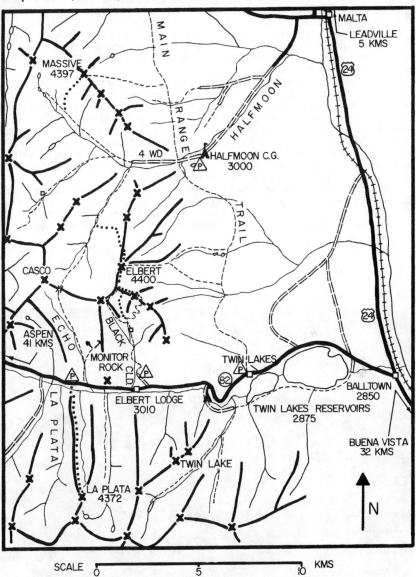

## Mt. Harvard, Sawatch Mountains, Colorado, USA

Within Colorado's central Sawatch Mountains is a high area generally known as the "Collegiate Range." The reason for this name is that many of the highest peaks have been named after eastern colleges and universities. Among these peaks is the third highest mountain in Colorado, Mt. Harvard, at 4396 meters.

These rounded and mostly smooth summits consist of various rock types, but are mostly quartzite. There are no glaciers in the entire region, and hardly any perpetual snowbanks, even in the north face cirques.

This map shows 7 of Colorado's 14'ers—that is, peaks over 14,000 feet, of which there are 53 in the state. These include: Huron, Missouri, Belford, Oxford, Harvard, Columbia, and Yale. All are reasonably easy to get to, and all are easy to climb. There's hardly a difficult route in the entire area shown on this map.

Huron, Missouri, Belford and Oxford are normally climbed from the road running alongside Clear Creek. This road begins at Highway 24, and heads west to the old mining town of Winfield. Huron is usually climbed from the Lake Fork Creek Trail, while the remaining three can all be easily scaled via the Missouri Gulch Trail, which begins at the Vickburg Trailhead.

Mts. Harvard and Columbia are most often climbed together and usually from Frenchman Creek and the small community of Riverside. Another popular route to Harvard is the trail which runs up the valley next to Pine Creek. It's also possible to begin a hike at the end of the road on North Cottonwood Creek. A trail goes to just beyond Bear Lake where a camp could be set up. Both Columbia and Harvard could be climbed from Bear Lake.

Yale is usually climbed from somewhere along Middle Cottonwood Creek. A good road leads up and over Cottonwood Pass, running south of Mt. Yale. One can climb from the Collegiate Campground, just east of Dennys Gulch. Yale is usually climbed in one day, as are Harvard and Columbia (for fit climbers), and for really strong hikers, Missouri, Belford and Oxford, all in one day as well.

Private land ownership is almost no problem in this area, but it does exist near Highway 24, the link between Leadville and Buena Vista.

For further information and forest service maps stop at the ranger stations in Leadville and Salida.

**Map:** San Isabel National Forest, 1 : 125,000, or USGS map Mt. Harvard, 1 : 24,000.

From the summit of Oxford looking west to the top of Belford.

# Map 280-1, Harvard, Sawatch Mts., Colorado, USA

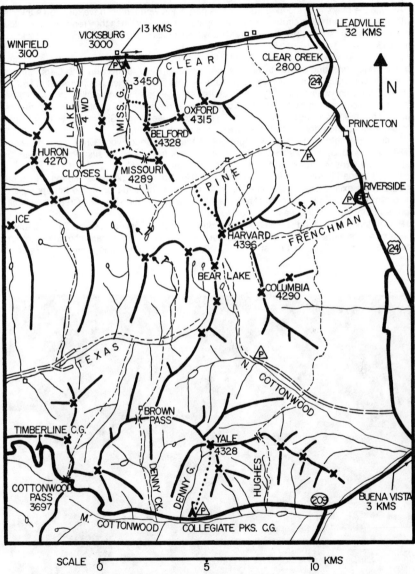

# Antero, Sawatch Mountains, Colorado, USA

The southern Sawatch Mountains has 4 of Colorado's 14'ers, with Princeton, 4328 meters; Antero, 4350; Tabequache, 4316; and Shavano, 4338 meters, from north to south. The good thing about climbing in this part of the Sawatch is that the area has little private land surrounding the peaks and forests, therefore access is no problem. Virtually all the forested lands here are part of the San Isabel National Forest.

As with the majority of the mountains in this part of the world, most have rounded summits, with only a few north face cirques. The west winds are very dry when they reach the Sawatch, making the yearly snowfall too light to create any snowfields or glaciers. All summits in this area are walk-ups.

For those interested in Shavano and Tabequache, the best approach is from Poncha Springs, Maysville and the North Fork of the Arkansas River to the Shavano Campground. From this campground one can walk due north and up a ridge which lies just west of McCoy Creek. Or one can walk up McCoy Creek, on its east side (to avoid some cliffs and waterfalls). This route is being used a lot now, and is getting better developed by climbers as time passes. Another route is to walk up the road about 2½ kms (to the west) from Shavano C.G. to Jennings Creek, then up the ridge on the east side of the creek.

To climb Princeton, one can drive from Buena Vista, up Cottonwood Creek to Cottonwood Lake Campground, then walk south to the peak. Also, from its south side, Princeton can be climbed, via Grouse Creek, located just east of Alpine.

There's a road leading up from Mt. Princeton Hot Springs to near the summit, but some private lands exist there, so one is advised to inquire of this situation at the hot springs.

To climb Antero Peak, the normal route is via Chalk Creek, then Baldwin Creek, and finally up the mountain from the west and northwest.

Plan to stock up on food supplies at either Buena Vista or Poncha Springs. To climb any of these peaks is a one day climb. Tabequache and Shavano are normally climbed together.

**Map:** San Isabel National Forest, 1 : 125,000, or USGS map Poncho Springs, 1 : 24,000.

Mining equipment from the 1800's still lies about at the mine south of Shavano.

# Map 281-1, Antero, Sawatch Mts., Colorado, USA

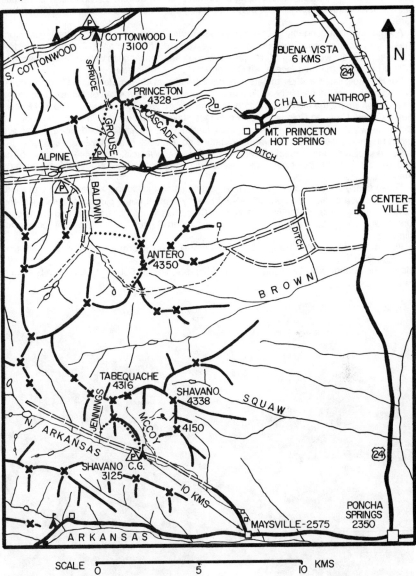

# Crestone, Sangre de Cristo Mts. Colorado, USA

The Crestone Peaks area includes Humbolt, Kit Carson, Crestone Needle, and Crestone Peak. These are all 14'ers, with Crestone Peak ranking 7th in the state of Colorado at 4357 meters. This area is northeast of Alamosa, east of Moffat and Crestone, and southwest of Westcliff, and is near the center of the north-south running Sangre de Cristo Mountains. These peaks are among the most challenging of all the 14'ers in Colorado. The rock is of various kinds, but Kit Carson Peak is made of very solid aggregate or conglomerate, something rather rare.

Accessibility is reasonably good—with access routes mostly on national forest lands. From the west, one can drive to Crestone and at the post office turn east; then up Crestone Creek to a trailhead, where a well used trail crosses a low ridge and descends to Willow Creek; thence to Willow Lake and the east face of Kit Carson Peak, at 4299 meters.

For Humbolt, listed at 4291 meters, Crestone Needle, at 4326 meters, and Crestone Peak, an approach from the east is best. One must drive south from Westcliff on Colfax Lane, to the intersection where the old Becks School is located, then west to a trailhead. The trail follows South Colony Creek to Colony Lakes. From these lakes, often used as a campsite, one can climb the two Crestones and Humbolt. The Crestones are usually climbed together, and are ranked high in difficulty, as Colorado mountains go. Humbolt is an easy walk-up.

Some supplies can be bought in Moffat, Crestone and Westcliff, but these are small towns and one is advised to seek out larger places (with supermarkets—for buying food) such as Alamosa.

These peaks contain some good climbs, but by using the "tourist routes," one can climb without the use of extra equipment. A very healthy climber could climb the Crestones and Humbolt in one day from Colony Lake, or both Crestones in one day from the end of the road. Only a tent and good boots are needed. July through September are the best months for climbing.

Visit the Alamosa Forest Ranger Station for more current information concerning trails and access roads.

**Map:**  Rio Grande and San Isabel National Forests, 1 : 125,000, or USGS map Crestone Peak, 1 : 24,000.

The northeast face of Kit Carson Peak as seen from just above Willow Lake.

# Map 282-1, Crestone, S. de Cristo Mts., Colo., USA

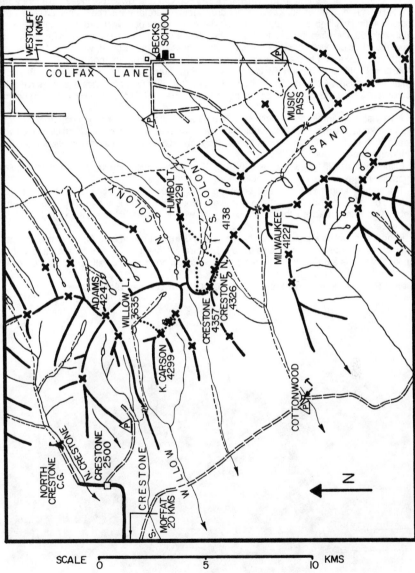

SCALE  0          5          10  KMS

# Blanca, Sangre de Cristo Mts., Colorado, USA

Mt. Blanca at 4373 meters, is the 4th highest summit in Colorado and is the highest peak in the Sangre de Cristo Range, which runs south from central Colorado into northern New Mexico. Blanca is just north of Fort Garland and northeast of Alamosa. Access is easy to this mountain massif.

There are routes leading north from Blanca and Fort Garland towns, but these are entirely on private land (which dates back several hundred years), therefore won't be discussed here. For those wanting to climb Blanca only, the best way is from the southwest. From the Sand Dunes Highway 150, there's a carroad for 3 or 4 kms, then a very poor 4WD road to as far as Como Lake (which is private property—but with public access). Then a good, well used trail, leads past Crater Lake and to the summit. There's another route from the north, via Gardner and Huerfano Creek and Canyon. By using this northern route, one can climb Blanca by its east ridge and Lindsey, 4281 meters, by its west ridge. The north face of Blanca has some difficult routes. Little Bear, 4279 meters, can be climbed from the trail just above Como Lake, as shown on the map.

A very strong climber could climb both Blanca and Little Bear in one long day from the car park marked 2600 meters. Most people, however, camp above Como Lake, and climb the two peaks from there—one day for each peak. It's a one day climb for Lindsey or Blanca on the Huerfano Creek route.

Ellingwood, at 4281 meters, is over the 14,000 foot level, but is generally considered to be a subsidiary peak of Blanca. That could change in the future.

The timberline in the Blanca area is high, around 3600 meters. Since most of the moisture laden clouds come from the west and northwest, most of the water is already taken out of them before this area is reached; therefore it's very dry, with good weather the rule and bad weather the exception.

Food and supplies should be purchased in Fort Garland or Alamosa. Alamosa is a college town and the largest in the San Luis Valley. The nearest forest ranger station is located there, making Alamosa a good place to get the latest information on roads, trails and public access, and buy forest service maps.

**Map:** Rio Grande National Forest, 1 : 125,000, or USGS map Blanca Peak, 1 : 24,000.

From the summit of Blanca, we see Mts. Linsey right, Iron Nipple left.

## Map 283-1, Blanca, S. de Cristo Mts., Colorado, USA

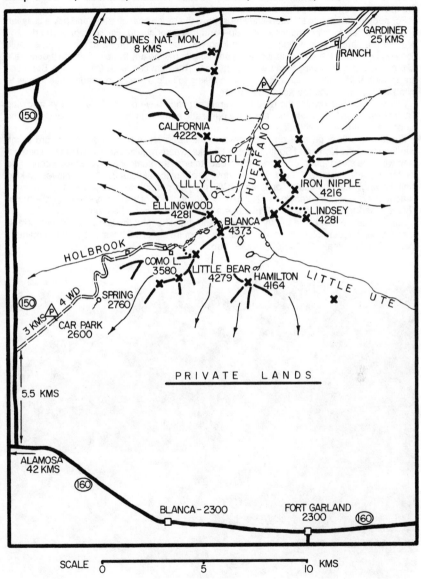

## Culebra, Sangre de Cristo Mts., Colorado, USA

Culebra Peak, 4282 meters, is located east of San Luis and Chama in south central Colorado. It's the most southerly of Colorado's 14'ers, and is in the southern part of the Sangre de Cristo Mountains. The rock is composed mostly of quartzite.

Culebra Peak is one of the most difficult of access of any mountain in Colorado. There are roads to within a short distance of the top, but it's all on private land, at least as of 1978, when the entire western part of the range belonged to the Taylor Ranch.

For people driving into the area, they must pass the ranch headquarters and pay a daily fee and another fee for climbing the mountain—and that's not cheap. For someone who doesn't want to pay, but who is willing to walk a long way (perhaps a long 2-day hike), one could possibly *walk* over the area without losing anything or having any trouble. But one would want to park his car a long way from the property line. The local people at Chama and San Luis, aren't fond of Mr. Taylor, so would surely be willing to help out with good advice as to how to climb without involving the absentee owner.

Since Taylor has owned the ranch, several shootings have taken place (always involving Taylor—who has been on both ends of the gun), and some cars have been impounded, so be careful as to the entry situation.

If one has official permission, then drive to the large stone gate and cattle guard at the confluence of the North and South Culebra Creeks, where regular cars would best be parked; then walk the steep, but pretty good 4WD road, to near the summit and hike cross-country to the top. If a 4WD vehicle is used, one can drive to about the 3600 or 3700 meter level, making the hike very short and easy. If one has a 4WD, then it's possible to drive due east of the ranch headquarters to a place known as "The 4-Way" (the location of the sign is shown on the map). This is a shorter route. The ranch managers can put you on the best driving route.

San Luis is the last place to buy groceries and gasoline, and the last place where garage services can be found. It's also the best place to enquire about the latest entry requirements.

**Map:** Culebra Peak, 1 : 24,000, USGS map.

At "The 4 Way" road junction. Summit of Culebra is just over the hill.

# Map 284-1, Culebra, S. de Cristo Mts., Colo., USA

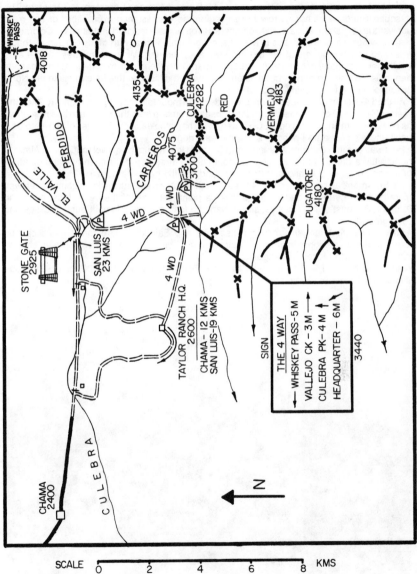

SCALE 0 2 4 6 8 KMS

## Lincoln, North Mesquito Range, Colorado, USA

To the east of Leadville and Climax, two of Colorado's high altitude lead and zinc mining towns, lies the North Mesquito Range and five of the state's 14,000 foot—4268 meter—summits (Mt. Cameron is 4341 meters, but is apparently considered a subsidiary peak of Mt. Lincoln and not regarded as one of the 14'ers).

Here are the 14'ers, from north to south: Quandary, 4345 meters; Lincoln, 4355, and the highest in this immediate area; Democrat, 4311; Bross, 4320; and Sherman, 4279 meters. The Mesquito Range is rather narrow in this region, so the distance from either of two main highways is very short, at least when compared to other more isolated mountains in Colorado.

As previously mentioned, this is a lead and zinc mining area, with many old mines, roads, mills, and other remnants of the old mining era still around. Mining continues today—as a result, there are many used as well as unused roads in the region. In fact, there are more roads than trails—which are almost not-existent. It would be difficult at this time to make the North Mesquito Range into a primitive area.

All the 14'ers can be climbed from either side of the mountain range, from Highway 91 on the west, or Highway 9 on the east. Quandary is usually climbed from the Blue Lake basin, south of the peak, or from an eastern ridge. Quandary is perhaps the easiest of access of all 14'ers-as a result, there's now a trail-of-sorts along the east ridge.

Best way to climb Democrat, Lincoln and Bross, is to drive up the gravel road above Alma, to the Kite Lake Campground, located just south of the three peaks. From the campground, all three can be climbed in one day (for the fit and healthy people at least).

Mt. Sherman can be climbed from the east, southeast or west, but the least complicated way might be from Leadville and up the road to a point just west of the peak. Most people in Colorado live east of the Rockies, so for them the fastest way up is via Fourmile Creek and Campground.

There are forest ranger stations in Leadville and Fairplay where forest maps can be purchased and additional information gathered, as there are three national forests sharing parts of the North Mesquito Range.

**Map:** San Isabel, Pike, or Arapaho National Forest maps, 1 : 125,000, or USGS maps Climax, Mt. Sherman, Alma, and Breckenridge, all 1 : 24,000.

Looking south from the summit of Quandary towards Lincoln, Democrat and Bross.

# Map 285-1, Lincoln, N. Mesquito Ra., Colorado, USA

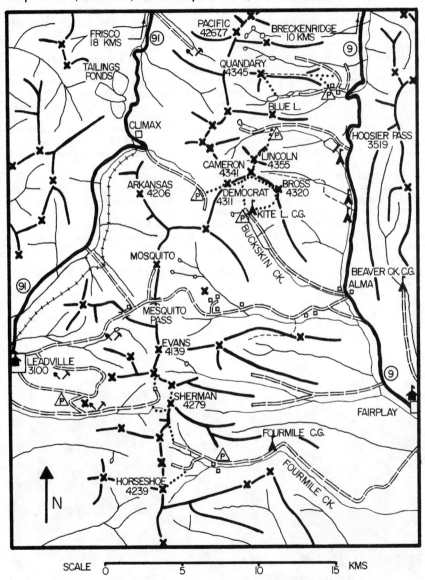

# Grays Peak, Front Range, Colorado, USA

In the region just east of Loveland Pass, and at the southern end of the Front Range, are four more of Colorado's 14'ers, or peaks over 14,000 feet (4268 meters). These peaks are in a small area with good accessibility—in fact, one road (the highest in North America), winds its way to very near the summit of Mt. Evans.

The high peaks include Mt. Evans, 4349 meters, and nearby to the southwest, Bierstadt with an altitude of 4287 meters. Further to the west and near Loveland Pass are the other two, the highest of which is Grays Peak, 4351 meters, and just one km north, Torreys Peak, 4350 meters. Evans and Bierstadt are on or near the boundaries of the Arapaho and Pike National forests, while Grays and Torreys are within the Arapaho Forest.

Access to these summits is easy, especially Mt. Evans, where a good surfaced road ends near the top at a research station. Fortunately, there are other routes to this mountain, of which the route from Guanella Pass is one. Most Coloradoans doing the 14'ers trip, also climb Bierstadt at the same time. It can be, and usually is, climbed from Evans.

The normal approach to Grays and Torreys is from the north and northeast. From Interstate 70, take the Bakersville exit (Bakersville has a gas station, bar and several homes—no more), and drive up the very rough road into Stevens Gulch. Even though this is a very poor road fit only for 4WD's, most cars can make the journey—with lots of care. Nowadays, the end of the road is the Stevens Mine. An older track leads further up the canyon, but it's now blocked off and used as a trail only.

A good trail leads to the summit of Grays Peak, a distance of 4 or 5 kms from the trailhead. One can then walk along the ridge north, to the summit of Torreys. Usually everyone climbs both peaks during the same hike. In the vicinity of Stevens Mine, there are many good places to make camp, with a good water supply nearby.

The towns in the area are small, the largest being Idaho Springs. Some shopping can be done there, but it's recommended that the shopping be done elsewhere, before reaching the area. If forest service or topographic maps are wanted, one should stop at the ranger station in Idaho Springs.

**Map:**  Arapaho National Forest, 1 : 125,000, or USGS maps Mt. Evans and Grays Peak, 1 : 24,000.

Looking south from Torres at Greys Peak. Trail is on left of mountain.

# Map 286-1, Grays, Front Range, Colorado, USA

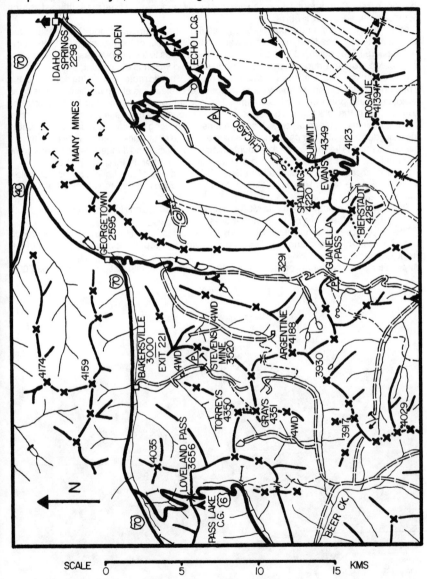

IDAHO SPRINGS 2298

GOLDEN

ECHO L. C.G.

ROSALIE 4194

MANY MINES

CHICAGO

SUMMIT L.

EVANS 4349

4123

SPALDING 4220

GEORGETOWN 2595

GUANELLA PASS

BIERSTADT 4287

3291

BAKERSVILLE 3000
EXIT 221
4WD

STEVENS MINE 3520
4WD

ARGENTINE 4188

3930

4174

4159

TORREYS 4350

GRAYS 4351
4WD

3917

4029

4035

LOVELAND PASS 3656

N

PASS LAKE C.G. 6

BEER CK.

SCALE  0    5    10    15   KMS

## Longs, Rocky Mt. National Park, Colorado, USA

Included on this map is part of the Rocky Mountain National Park, located in north central Colorado in the northern sections of the Front Range. This national park is west of Fort Collins and Greeley. Within the park boundaries is one of the state's 14'ers, Longs Peak, 4345 meters.

The mountain is easy of access. Estes Park, north of the peak, can be reached via Loveland or Longmont, both located to the east. From Estes Park, one can drive south on Highway 7 to the Longs Peak Campground. One can also get to this campground from the southeast and the Boulder area, again via Highway 7.

At the trailhead is found a campground, parking lot and ranger station. This easiest and normal route to Longs Peak heads due west up the shoulder of the mountain to a fork of the trail. One trail goes down to Chasm Lake and gives access to the famous east face. The other trail curves around a ridge, then enters a boulder field which is almost flat.

On the boulder field, one has a choice of two routes. The old route went up the north face, but it has one steep section. Formerly there was a steel cable at the steep place, but it has been removed, making it a more difficult climb. The normal route today, is one leading from the boulder field to the rock hut and pass, located on the northwest ridge at 4000 meters. From that small shelter, the route (marked with paint) heads south along the west face of the peak. Later, the trail goes up to another pass and turns east along the south face, then straight up to the flat summit. If there is fresh snow on the mountain it can be difficult and dangerous, as there's some smooth rock faces to cross. This is a one day climb from Longs Peak Campground.

Another access route would be from Estes Park, and one of two trailheads located below Bear Lake, to the north of the peak. One route or trail follows Boulder Brook—the other, Glacier Gulch.

One could also reach the peak via Mt. Meeker, 4241 meters, and Hunters Creek, to the south of the peak, but there are no trails in that area.

The only place on the map in which to buy food is Estes Park. However, it's recommended that climbers buy all food and supplies before leaving the populated areas to the east of the Front Range.

**Map:**   Roosevelt National Forest, 1 : 125,000, or Rocky Mountain National Park, 1 : 62,500.

Substituting for Longs Peak foto is La Plata Peak and its north ridges (Map 279).

## Map 287-1, Longs, Rocky Mt. N.P., Colorado, USA

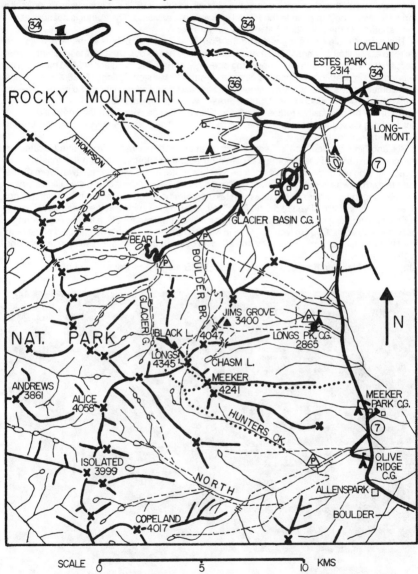

ROCKY MOUNTAIN

LOVELAND

ESTES PARK
2314

LONG-MONT

THOMPSON

GLACIER BASIN C.G.

BEAR L.

BOULDER BR.

GLACIER G.

JIMS GROVE
3400

LONGS PK. C.G.
2865

BLACK L. 4047

NAT. PARK

LONGS
4345

CHASM L.

ANDREWS
3861

MEEKER
4241

MEEKER
PARK C.G.

ALICE
4058

HUNTERS CK.

OLIVE
RIDGE
C.G.

ISOLATED
3999

NORTH

ALLENSPARK

BOULDER

COPELAND
4017

N

SCALE   0          5          10   KMS

## Pikes Peak, Pikes Pk. Massif, Colorado, USA

Pikes Peak, 4302 meters, is one of Colorado's 14'ers and probably the most famous mountain in the state, if not in the nation. If it weren't for these facts, the mountain would not be here in this book—as there's a road and cog railway to the summit. That road is a toll road with no overnight parking. There's also a restaurant on top. But the mountain is saved by the fact there are several ways in which to walk to the top via trails.

Each summer there's a road race to the summit, but the road is not open year-round to the top. However, one can drive to the Pikes Peak ski area any time. The author is not sure about the schedule of the train, but that's unimportant here.

The normal route to the top is called the Barr Trail. This trail begins at the terminal of the railroad at Manitou Springs, 2000 meters altitude, and heads due west up the mountain. Most people do the climb in two days, spending one night at Barr Camp, at about 3000 meters. The second day is used to complete the climb and return to Manitou Springs. At 3600 meters is a small emergency shelter. Only the more fit individuals should attempt the climb in one day—as the vertical rise of this climb is 2300 meters—a workout for anyone!

There are other possible routes for a good hike. It could be done from the end of a dirt road not far from Cascade, then up to where it meets Barr Trail; or up Severy Creek and to Barr Camp—thence to the top.

Still another way would be to begin the climb at or near the Crags Campground located on the northwest side of the mountain. There's no actual trail to the top from this location, but route—finding is not difficult. Still another possible route, if you want to get away from all the people and crowds, would be to walk (without trail) up Beaver Creek from the Gillette area.

One thing to remember is that one must take a water bottle on the mountain, as water is not available everywhere. If you're on the Barr Trail, it can be very warm at the lower elevations.

One can get additional information and maps at the forest ranger office in Colorado Springs, or better still, at the Cog Railway terminal in Manitou Springs. There's no camping place near the RR terminal, but one can usually find a hiding place in the trees or brush for a tent for one night.

**Map:**   Pike National Forest, 1 : 125,000, or USGS map Pikes Peak, 1 : 24,000.

Here is an emergency shelter half way between Barr Camp and summit of Pikes.

# Map 288-1, Pikes, Pikes Pk. Massif, Colorado, USA

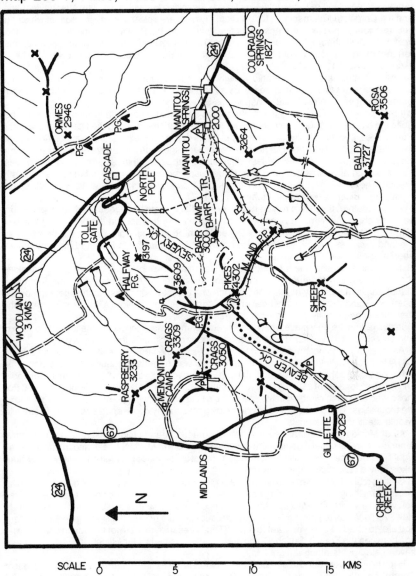

SCALE

0   5   10   15   KMS

# Chapter 7 Mexico, Central America, Caribbean

There are 24 maps in this section which covers Mexico, Central America, and the Caribbean. The individual countries or islands discussed here are Mexico, Guatemala, Costa Rica, Panama, Jamaica, Haiti, Dominican Republic, Puerto Rico, Guadeloupe, Dominica, Martinique, St. Vincent, and Trinidad.

About half of the upland areas included on these maps are folded mountains. They are the ranges on the island of Hispanola—Haiti and Dominican Republic, the Blue Mts. on Jamaica, and the Cordillera Talamanca in Costa Rica. The rest are volcanic in origin, most of which are volcanic cones and still active or semi-active. Aside from the Pacific area, this region has more volcanic activity than any other in the world. The author had the good fortune (almost misfortune) of being camped right near the summit of La Soufriere on St. Vincent Island, when it erupted on April 13, 1979.

The two main areas of volcanic activity are from southern Mexico, southeast through Guatemala, to Irazu near San Jose in Costa Rica; and the Lesser Antilles or Windward Islands of the Caribbean. (West Indies—W.I. in this book).

Many people would classify this entire region as being part of Latin America, but this is not quite the case. The language spoken in Mexico, Central America, and the Islands of Cuba and Puerto Rico, and the Dominican Republic is Spanish. But, Jamaica, Dominica, St. Vincent and Trinidad are populated by blacks (former slaves) and speak an African dialect along with some English (Trinidad is about 40% East Indian, along with some Chinese). The two French West Indies islands of Guadeloupe and Martinique, also have black people, but they speak mostly French. The Nederlands has several islands in the Caribbean as well, and those people speak mostly an African dialect and Dutch.

As for weather, this entire region has a very similar climate throughout, with the wet and dry seasons about the same from one place to another. For this section the best time to hike or climb is in the months of November or December through about April. During this time of year, the land becomes very brown in Mexico south to Nicaragua. Costa Rica and Panama have a shorter dry season.

The Caribbean also has a dry season in December through April, but generally speaking these places are a bit greener than in Mexico and northern C.A. An interesting thing about the Caribbean is that on any of the small islands one can see both green lush vegetation on the east side—and a brown almost desert-like landscape on the west side. This indicates the moisture is perpetually coming from the east.

In this region the only place where one needs crampons and ice ax are the tops of Popo, Ixty and Orizaba, all in Mexico. There's not one good rock climb in the whole area.

As for crimes against travelers, the worst places are the large cities of Mexico and Panama City. These crimes involve someone grabbing your watch, camera, shoulder bag or small pack; either on the street or at bus or train stations. This is very similar to what goes on in Columbia and Peru; so for a list of security measures, see the chapter introduction for South America. For those who are going climbing in Mexico, there's little need for worry—except when traveling to the mountains. The Caribbean seems to enjoy a reasonably good reputation when it comes to people stealing from tourists.

All of Mexico and Central America has good and cheap public transportation. In Central America, travel is usually done in the daytime hours, but in Mexico, buses and trucks travel all night. The Caribbean is similar to C. America, in that the islands are small and getting anywhere takes only a few hours during the day.

Getting to the Caribbean Islands can be done by cruise ship, but you'll not have time to hike or climb anything. There's no ferry boat system in the islands so count boat travel out—unless you've got a yacht. The only sensible way to see the Caribbean is to island-hop using aircraft. However, one has to plan a trip carefully, because there's not always flights going from where you are, to other islands you want to reach. That's because there's not that much communication between the French, British, Dutch and American islands. Many flights, however, do have several stop-overs along a flight line.

Hitch hiking is very good in Mexico (called dado), fair in Panama, and a little slow in the rest of Central America. It's slow in the French West Indies and most of the Lesser Antilles, but good on Trinidad—they have lots of oil. In Mexico and Central America, food and hotels are cheap, but these same things are about twice or 3 times as expensive in the Caribbean. The French W.I. are the most expensive.

Foto was taken from near La Hoya, looking at the south and western slopes of Ixty (Map 294).

Volcan Colima, just south of Nevado Colima, is an active volcano (Map 291).

## Encantada, Sierra S. Pedro, Baja, Mexico

The mountains on this map are located in the northern end of Baja California, in northwest Mexico. Few people know of this range called the Sierra San Pedro Martir, or it's highest peak, called Cerro de la Encantada, 3095 meters, on most Mexican maps. It seems that most people who venture out that way are North Americans and they usually call it Picacho del Diablo (Devil). Some even call it La Providencia. Regardless of the name, it's the highest mountain in Baja, and because of the granite rock making up the range, it has some very good and difficult routes.

More exactly, Encantada is located directly west of the gulf resort town of San Felipe, and southeast of Ensenada. There's three possible routes of access. The normal route is from the east side of the range, either from Highway 3 to the north, or directly from San Felipe on an all-dirt road. Highway 3 is paved, but there's still some dusty roads from there to the trailhead (T.H.) at 610 meters. Since this is the dry side of the range, there's no water except in the major canyons, so it's likely someone on foot would have a hard time reaching the mountain (although there are daily buses running from San Felipe to Ensenada along Highway 3). The other approach is from the west and the west coast Highway 1. This road ends at the Observatorio Astronomico Nacional, not far to the northwest of Encantada. This will be a good road, but may or may not have bus service. So no matter which way you approach the mountain, you've almost got to have a car.

Again, the normal route is to drive to Santa Clara, then west to the trailhead. From there, a trail leads to the Cañon Del Diablo. This trail leads about 22 kms up the canyon to three campsites called Smatko Camp (1790 meters), Campo Nocho (1920) and Cedaroak Camp (2010). There's a waterfall and pool at 675 meters, which is no problem to climbers, but stops the casual hiker. The normal route then leads up from Campo Nocho in a wash or gully directly to the summit. Still another possibility is to use Providencia Canyon which makes for an east face route. It's also been climbed from Teledo and Diablito Canyons.

Hiking on the west or plateau side of the range is perhaps more enjoyable because of the meadows, and Lodgepole Pine and White Fir forests there, but climbing Encantada from the observatory is difficult because one has to drop down into Diablo Canyon before climbing the peak. Fall and spring would likely be the better times to climb here, since the summers are hot and winters are wet, with some snow. Buy food in Mexicali, Ensenada or San Felipe. Better count on about 3 to 5 days for the climb, with your own vehicle.

**Map:** San Felipe and Lazaro Cardenas, 1 : 250,000, from the Direccion General De Geografia Del Territorio Nacional, Mexico. Buy at Detenal, Balderas 71, Mexico City.

The Mexican National Observatory with Encantada in the background.

# Map 289-2, Encantada, S. San Pedro, Baja, Mexico

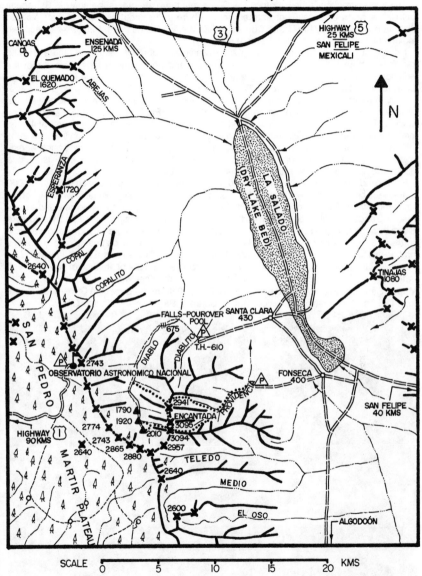

CANOAS

ENSENADA
125 KMS

HIGHWAY 5
25 KMS
SAN FELIPE
MEXICALI

EL QUEMADO
1620

ABEJAS

ESPERANZA

1720

N

COPAL

COPALITO

LA SALADO
(DRY LAKE BED)

2640

TINAJAS
1080

SAN PEDRO

FALLS-POUROVER
POOL
675

DIABLO

DIABLITO

SANTA CLARA
430

T.H.-610

P

2743
OBSERVATORIO ASTRONOMICO NACIONAL

FONSECA
400

PROVIDENCIA

P

2941

SAN FELIPE
40 KMS

ENCANTADA
1790
1920
3095

2774

2010
3094

HIGHWAY 1
90 KMS

2743
2865
2957

2640
2880
TELEDO

2640

MEDIO

MARTIR PLATEAU

2600

EL OSO

ALGODOÓN

SCALE  0      5      10      15      20   KMS

## Barranca Del Cobre, Sierra Tarahumara, Mexico

The setting for this map is in the northwest section of Mexico in the state of Chihuahua. The mountain range is called the Sierra Tarahumara, but it's not so much of a mountain range as it is a high plateau with high escarpments and deep canyons. The most famous canyon or barranca, is the Barranca Del Cobre, or Copper Canyon. The more exact location of this particular canyon is southwest of Chihuahua, the capital city of Chihuahua state.

The main attraction is the Barranca Del Cobre, but there are others, namely the Barrancas Del Urique and Batopilas. There are similarities here to the great canyons of the Colorado Plateau and especially the Grand Canyon in Arizona, USA. The factor that makes these two regions similar are the flat-lying beds of rock.

Not only are the physical features of the Barranca Del Cobre interesting, but there are also the Tarahumara Indians, who live in the canyons and on the mesa tops. Because of the isolation of the canyons, these indians are still living much the same as they always have. Civilization is just now reaching the Tarahumaras.

Only in recent years has this country been known to outsiders. But in the mid 1950's the railway was completed which ran from Chihuahua to the Pacific Coast and to the city of Los Mochis. There is also now a maze of dirt and gravel roads onto the mesas and plateaus, made by ranchers and lumbermen over the years. But by far the most commonly used means of transport for tourists getting into the barranca country is the train, which runs once-weekly from Chinuahua to Los Mochis. The most famous stop for the train tourists is El Divisadero, a station located right on the edge of the Barranca Del Cobre.

For hikers, this is one of the finest hiking areas in Mexico. The author used the 1 : 250,000 scale maps below in creating this one, but there are larger scale maps available which will show many more trails. Starting or ending points for hikes would be just north of Pitorreal and a point east of Guagua Chique, both locations marked by the parking sign. This route would take hikers through Cobre, and many indian villages. One could also begin at Urique and walk in a northerly direction on one of many trails to reach the Cobre. It might be best to stop in Creel, a lumber-mill town, and get information about the canyons before entering. Buy supplies at Los Mochis, Chihuahua or no later than Creel. Hiking can be done about anytime of year, but high water might cause fording problems in the June to September wet season.

**Map:**  San Juanito and Ciudad Obregon, 1 : 250,000, from the Direccion General De Geografia Del Territorio Nacional Mexico. Buy at Detenal, Balderas 71, Mexico City.

The rugged canyon of the Barranca del Cobre is similar to the Grand Canyon.

# Map 290-3, Barranca Del Cobre, S. Tara., Mexico

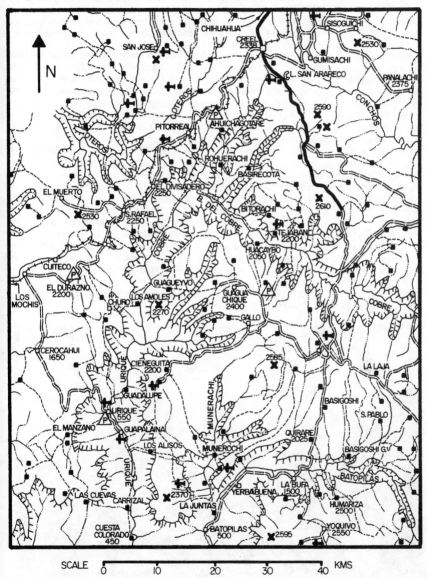

# Colima, Cordillera Anahuac, Mexico

Featured on this map is one large mountain but with two high summits. The highest is known as Nevado de Colima, at an altitude of 4240 meters (on some maps it is listed as high as 4450 meters). The name nevado means snow mountain or range in spanish. At times snow does fall on the high peak, thus the name. This nevado is a hugh hulk of a mountain, and on top is an old volcanic crater with some erosion. It still retains its conal shape. The other peak is known as Volcan de Colima, at 3820 meters. This is a new cone, without vegetation. When the author visited the summit it was emitting large amounts of smoke, but there was no trembling or explosions. The summit area was very warm with choking gases coming from vents inside the crater. Most would classify it as an active volcano.

This was the authors experience. He started the trip at the terminal de buses in Guadalajara. He took a bus bound for Colima, a city southwest of the mountain. After getting off and getting information in Atenquique, he walked up the road towards El Paso Radon, but didn't get far the first day. He camped just above the finca at 1540 meters. There was no water here (only at the farm or finca); he carried it from Atenquique on the main highway. The next morning he walked all the way to the top of Volcan de Colima and back to camp. That was about 12 hours—very long walk! The third morning he returned to Atenquique and found a bus back to Guadalajara.

The second day was far too long, so it's recommended that if planning to walk all the way to either peak, get an early start and camp higher on the mountain. That would make the second day much shorter, but would also extend the trip to a third day. On this route, don't plan on finding water beyond the finca. That's a big problem on a walking trip. However, if you can speak spanish and can communicate, talk to people at the pulp and lumber mill at Atenquique, and they can surely arrange for a lift to the mountain. Trucks passed the authors camp both mornings at about 5 am. This would eliminate a lot of walking and carrying of water. One can also drive most vehicles to the refugio at the Radon Pass, where 4 to 6 people can sleep on the floor. A bushwhacking route can be found to the summit of the nevado, but the normal route there is up the steep road to the Miroondas just west of the summit cone. On weekends surely rides can be found to either peak. Regardless, plan on 3 days of food and lots of water. Once on either cone the climbing is easy, but take a tent for sleeping and rugged boots. Dry season; October to March.

**Map:**  Colima, 1 : 250,000, from the Direccion General De Geografia Del Territorio Nacional Mexico. Buy at Detenal, Balderas 71, Mexico City.

Snow sometimes falls on the top of Nevada Colima.

## Map 291-1, Colima, Sierra Madre, Mexico

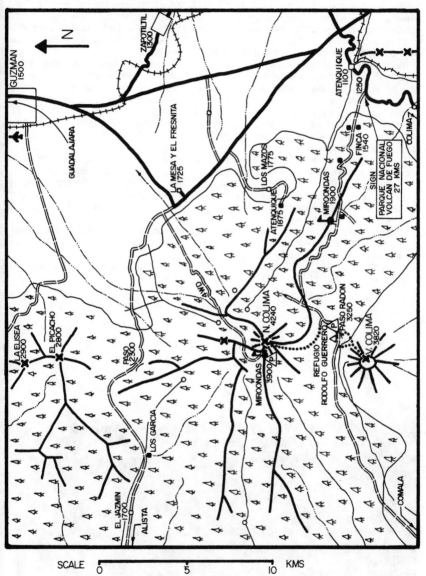

N

GUZMAN 1500

ZAPOTILTIL 1300

ATENQUIQUE 1100

1250

COLIMA 7

GUADALAJARA

LA MESA Y EL FRESNITA 1725

LOS MAZOS 1775

ATENQUIQUE 1875

MIROONDAS 1900

FINCA 1540

SIGN

PARQUE NACIONAL
VOLCAN DE FUEGO
27 KMS

LA ELISEA 2900

EL PICACHO 2800

PASO 2300

WIND

N. COLIMA 4240

PASO RADON 3250

N. COLIMA 3820

MIROONDAS 3900

REFUGIO
RODOLFO GUERRERO

LOS GARCIA

EL JAZMIN 1700

ALISTA

COMALA

SCALE 0          5          10   KMS

## Paracutin, Sierra Madre, Mexico

Included in this book are many mountains, some of which are not high or difficult to climb, but are interesting for other reasons. On this map is just such a mountain. This is the Volcan Paracutin at about 2744 meters, located in the state of Michoacan, in southwest Mexico. Large towns or cities in the area are Uruapan to the southeast and Zamora to the northeast.

A couple of things make this volcano interesting. First, it's a new or "young" mountain. This is the one which erupted in a farmer's corn field in 1943. As the story goes, the man was in his field plowing. He looked behind and saw a crack develop and lava, steam and gases began to flow out. Over a period of weeks the hill grew into a mountain. The lava spread out covering valuable farmland and finally a small village named San Juan. At the end of the activity, a small cinder cone developed, which is now the highest point of the area.

The second thing of interest is the San Juan Church. The lava surrounded the village finally engulfing it, and the only thing standing today is that church, which rises out of the lava near the edge of the flow. The lava covering the village is from 3 to 5 meters deep. Today the mountain is quiet, but still steaming, and the church of San Juan has become a bit of a tourist attraction.

To arrive at the area, most people drive on Highway 15 that connects Zamora with Morelia. At the junction of Highways 15 and 37—at Carapan, turn south on Highway 37 in the direction of Uruapan. About halfway between Paracho and Uruapan, take the road to Los Reyes, stopping at the village of Angahuan.

From Angahuan, there's an old road or trail leading to the south, then southwest to the north end of the lava flow. It's easy to find the church standing out of the lava. It reminds one of the Cagsawa Church and ruins on the southeast side of Volcon Mayon in The Philippines. Many routes can be taken to the top of the cinder cone of Paracutin, but there is a trail to the west of the lava, which is the easiest route. It's a long one day hike to see the church, climb the mountain, and return to Angahuan.

Food and water can be found in Angahuan, as well as people who act as guides. However, any person in this village will be helpful in putting you on the right trail. Hitch hiking into the area is fairly easy, but traffic is light.

**Map:** Colima, E13-3, 1 : 250,000, from the Direccion General De Geografia Del Territorio Nacional Mexico. Buy at DETENAL, Balderas 71, Mexico City.

Lava has engulfed the village of San Juan, leaving the church above the flows.

# Map 292-1, Paracutin, Sierra Madre, Mexico

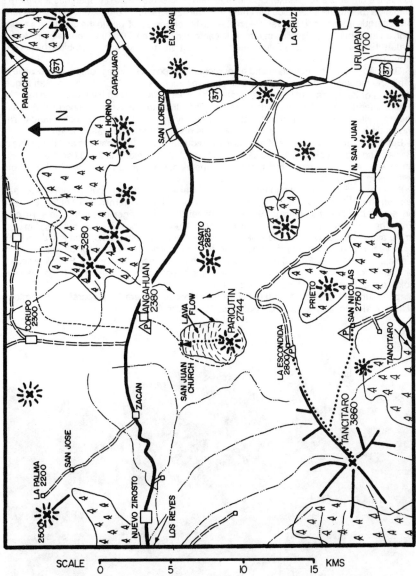

SCALE 0 5 10 15 KMS

# Toluca, Cordillera Anahuac, Mexico

Toluca is the high prominent peak seen to the south and southwest of the large city of Toluca, which is to the west of Mexico City about 50 kms. Nevado Toluca rises to an altitute of 4704 meters (4690 on some maps), placing it as the 4th highest mountain in Mexico. It too is an old and eroded volcano, but it still retains a conal shape, and has a large crater at the summit. Inside the crater is a large lake. On the mountain are several radio-TV antennas and there's actually a road to the lake inside the crater at about 4200 meters. Fortunately, the road beyond the albergue is steep and few vehicles make it to the crater lake. Despite the fact there's a road high on the mountain, it is a fine mountain to camp and climb on. Of all the mountains in Mexico featured in this book, Nevado Toluca seems to have more running water available to hikers and campers.

The map shows the mountain and all or most of the possible hiking routes. It's possible to climb the mountain from the east, and small towns such as San Pedro Tlanisco, San Miguel Balderas or Zaragoza, but using these routes involves a two day climb for sure. The map the author used to make this one didn't show any trail from the above mentioned villages, but there's trails all over these mountains, used mostly by wood cutters and shepherds. The mountain is covered with a pine forest, which is open and easy to walk through.

But the recommended route of access to the mountain is via the west side and the village of Raices and the refugio or albergue located at about 3810 meters. In 1983 construction was underway near the campground as shown on the map, which means there will likely be more refugios in the future.

If you're on foot, hitch hike in the direction of Raices or Sultepec, but get out at the road leading to the albergue. If taking a bus, and you're at the bus terminal in Toulca, take the once-ever-half-hour bus towards Sultepec, and tell them you're going to just beyond Raices. From the main highway you may or may not get a lift further up the mountain, but the 5 km walk to the albergue is enjoyable. The albergue is a regular hotel, with rooms, food and drinks. It's open year-round, and of course is busiest on weekends. It holds perhaps 100 people. One can also camp in the area. From the albergue to summit is an easy half day hike. Snowline shown on map is for the wet season, so ice climbing gear is not normally needed. But of course it is cold on top. Buy food in Toluca or even Raices.

**Map:** Ciudad De Mexico, 1 : 250,000, from the Direccion General De Geografia Del Territorio Nacional Mexico. Buy at Detenal, Balderas 71, Mexico City.

Toluca from the Albergue located on the mountains west side at 3810 meters.

# Map 293-1, Toluca, Cordillera Anahuac, Mexico

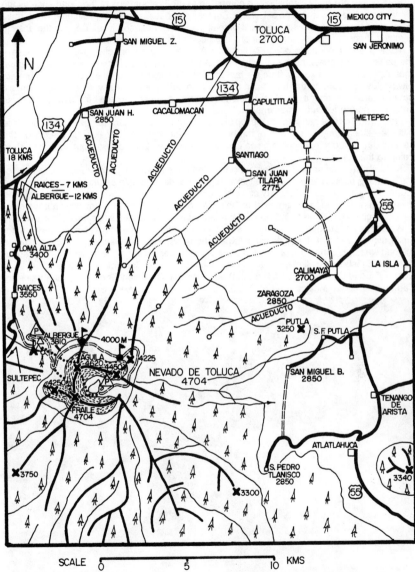

N

TOLUCA 2700

MEXICO CITY →

15

15

SAN JERONIMO

SAN MIGUEL Z.

134

CAPULTITLAN

METEPEC

134

SAN JUAN H. 2850

CACALOMACAN

TOLUCA 18 KMS

ACUEDUCTO

ACUEDUCTO

ACUEDUCTO

ACUEDUCTO

SANTIAGO

RAICES – 7 KMS
ALBERGUE – 12 KMS

SAN JUAN TILAPA 2775

ACUEDUCTO

55

LOMA ALTA 3400

CALIMAYA 2700

LA ISLA

RAICES 3550

ZARAGOZA 2850

ACUEDUCTO

ALBERGUE 3810

4000 M

PUTLA 3250

S. F. PUTLA

SULTEPEC

AGUILA 4620·4450

4225

4250

NEVADO DE TOLUCA 4704

SAN MIGUEL B. 2850

FRAILE 4704

TENANGO DE ARISTA

ATLATLAHUCA

3750

3300

S. PEDRO TLANISCO 2850

3340

55

SCALE    0          5          10    KMS

## Popocatepetl, Cordillera Anahuac, Mexico

The most famous mountain in all of Mexico is one of two high volcanos rising to the southeast of Mexico City. The highest and best known of the two is Popocatepetl, 5452 meters, while its sister peak to the north is Ixaccihuatl, is at 5286 meters. Both of these summits can be seen from Mexico City on clear days. Both peaks are crowned with snow and ice that form small glaciers at the higher elevations. There are few crevasses to be found.

Both peaks are easy climbs, when compared to other mountains of the world such as the Himalayas, Andes, or the Alps of Europe. But they do possess some high altitude, which must be of concern to people who live most of their lives at or near sea level. Despite the ease of climbing them, an ice ax and crampons are needed for a safe ascent.

To climb either mountain, one must first go to Amecameca, a small city at the western base of the peaks. Many buses pass that way. From Amecameca, there is no public transport to the mountain, but on weekends there's a fair amount of traffic going up the mountain. There are always tourists from north America on this road, so getting a lift is easy. At Tlamaca there's a small hotel and climber's hut. Some food can be purchased at Tlamaca but it's best to do your shopping before leaving Amecameca.

From Tlamaca one can climb to the top of Popo in one day, but many people—because of the altitude—sleep one night in one of the huts on the mountain, and make it to the top on the second day. If you're coming from sea level it's wise to sleep one or two nights up high before going to the summit.

To climb Ixty, one should turn left or north at the Paso de Cortez, and proceed to the end of the road and parking area called La Hoya. Higher on the mountain are three small huts close together where one can sleep. Ixty can also be climbed in one day, but again the high altitude makes it a two day trip for many. Ixty is the longer of the two climbs and involves a traverse of several high points along a high ridge. (More huts have been added since the author's visit).

Water can be found at Tlamaca and at or near the huts on either mountain. All the huts are small, sleeping about 4-6 people each. Expect them to be full on weekends, especially in times of good weather. June through September are the wettest months, December through about April the driest. Many climbers are on the peaks during the Christmas Holidays.

**Map:**  Ciudad De Mexico, E14-2, 1 : 250,000, from the Direccion General De Geografia Del Territorio Nacional Mexico. Buy at DETENAL, Balderas 71, Mexico City.

Looking at Popo located to the south of Ixty, where foto was taken.

# Map 294-1, Popocatepetl, Cord. Anahuac, Mexico

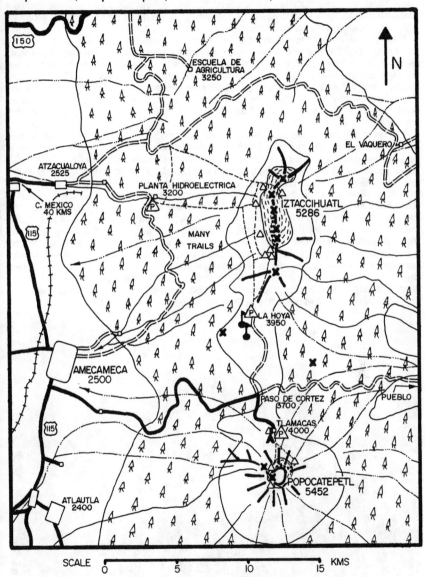

## La Malinche, Cordillera Anahuac, Mexico

For visitors to Mexico who would like an interesting hike, but one which lacks the higher altitudes of Orizaba, Popo and Ixty, this might be a good mountain to try. It's called La Malinche, rising to 4431 meters. The location is between Orizaba and the twin summits of Popo and Ixty, and just to the northeast of one of Mexicos largest cities, Puebla. It's surrounded on all sides by major highways, so transport is fast and easy. Once on the mountain, one finds a beautiful pine forest from about 3000 on up to about 4000 meters. It's a fine mountain for camping, except for the lack of water on the standard routes.

There are several routes one might use to reach the summit. With several water pipelines (acueductos) on the east side of the mountain which supplys a number of towns with drinking water, it's reasonable to assume one might walk up these pipelines to the east face, however from the springs to top it might be steep. Another possible route is to drive from Pueblo to San Isidro. The map the author used (scale 1 : 250,000) didn't show a trail, but it's likely one is there. From the small city of Amozoc, to the south of the mountain, there's a road to a place called Axaltenco, at 3200 meters. There must be a trail to the summit from there, but it's not confirmed.

This is the ruta normal and the one used by the author. Proceed to Huamantla and the west end of town on the main highway. There's a Pemex station at the junction where the road to Altamira begins. At that point one can see a sign, "Camino Rural—Altamira 8 kms". From that same place one can ride a small collectivo, or bus-taxi, the 3 kms to Matamoros. One leaves every half hour or so. From Matamoros, walk or maybe get a lift to the high farming community of Altamira. Turn left at the church and walk to the end of the road for most vehicles, which is at the school. From there it's first a 4WD road, then a well-used trail to the top. There are fine camping places at 3800-4000 meters, but no water. The author went up this route, then followed a very-well-used trail down to the old refugio (now in ruins), but isn't exactly sure about the road leading to that point. Make enquiries about using this "old refugio" route. If using the Altamira route, do all your shopping in Huamantla, or surely not later than Matamoros. Also be sure and get water in Matamoros, as do the people in Altamira, with the use of donkeys. Hitch hike or take a bus to Huamantla. The dry season is from October through March.

**Map:** Ciudad De Mexico and Veracruz, 1 : 250,000, from the Direccion General De Geografia Del Territorio Nacional Mexico. Buy at Detenal, Balderas 71, Mexico City.

La Malinches summit rises far above the pines on the north slopes.

# Map 295-1, La Malinche, Cord. Anahuac, Mexico

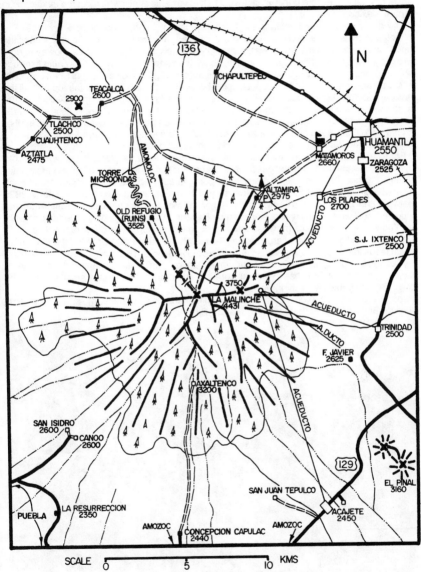

N

136

CHAPULTEPEC

TEACALCA
2600

2900 ✕

TLACHCO
2500

CUAUHTENCO

AZTATLA
2475

AMONOLOC

TORRE
MICROONDAS

OLD REFUGIO
(RUINS)
3525

HUAMANTLA
2550

MATAMOROS
2660

ZARAGOZA
2525

ALTAMIRA
2975

LOS PILARES
2700

S.J. IXTENCO
2500

ACUEDUCTO

3750 ✕

✕ LA MALINCHE
4431

ACUEDUCTO

A. DUCTO

TRINIDAD
2500

F. JAVIER
2625

CAXALTENCO
3200

ACUEDUCTO

SAN ISIDRO
2600

CANOO
2600

129

EL PINAL
3160

SAN JUAN TEPULCO

ACAJETE
2450

PUEBLA

LA RESURRECCION
2350

AMOZOC

CONCEPCION CAPULAC
2440

AMOZOC

SCALE   0        5        10   KMS

## Cofre De Perote, Cordillera Anahuac, Mexico

Of all the mountains of Mexico covered in this book, this one is likely the least interesting. However, this old and very eroded volcano has some unique aspects which make it an enjoyable hike or climb. This mountain called Cerro Cofre De Perote, at 4282 meters, is located directly north of Mexicos highest mountain, Orizaba, and due west of Veracruz and the much closer city Jalapa. Perote is in the east-west belt of volcanic cones which dot the landscape in central Mexico.

The name cofre means coffin in english, which is the way the summit rock appears. The mountain itself is a large and rounded mound with few canyons (except on the east side of the mountain where it drops to low elevations rapidly) and few interesting features. However, right on top is a huge rock, rising about 40 meters above the surface. This is the black coffin-like-rock which gives the mountain it's name. But, what could be a good rock climb has been ruined by T.V. and radio antennas right on top. Despite the fact that there is a road to the top with all the metal apparatus, this is a good hike. There are many roads on the mountain, especially on the northern half, where is located many farms or fincas and ranchos. There's also many trails going in all directions, and in places, native forests which have been used in a small lumber industry. On the lower slopes just above Perote town, is a fine pine forest, while further up it's more like a rain forest. It's easy to walk through however.

For hikers, this is the recommended route. Walk from the central plaza in downtown Perote toward the mountain. A dirt road passes a garbage dump, then turns left up the mountain, later turning into a trail. Take one of many trails going directly up the slope. There are springs somewhere high on the mountain because you'll hear water gushing from a pipe at 2825 meters. Otherwise the only places to find water on the mountain are at ranchos. Take water and a lunch. You'll pass a fairly well used road near Rancho Nuevo, then find trails heading straight up. You'll pass potato fields (harvest time is around Christmas), the highest of which is about 3550 meters. Higher up one can walk easily through the puno grass or along the 4WD road which leads to the top and the homes of workers staying there. This is an all day hike, with the dry season being from about October through March, but can be climbed anytime. Perote town is on a busy highway and has two small hotels, a supermarket, and many small stores. Nice town. Get to Perote by hitching or bus.

**Map:**   Veracruz, 1 : 250,000, from the Direccion General De Geografia Del Territorio Nacional Mexico. Buy at Detenal, Balderas 71, Mexico City.

Cofre de Perote is seen from the main plaza in Perote.

# Map 296-1, Cofre de Perote, Cord. Anahuac, Mexico

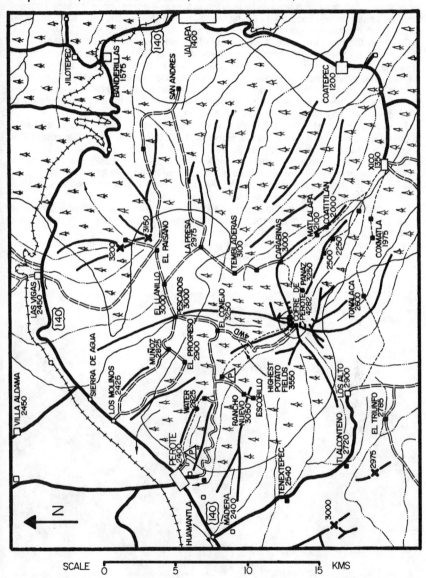

SCALE 0 5 10 15 KMS

## Orizaba, Cordillera Anahuac, Mexico

The highest mountain in Mexico and the third highest in North America, is the volcano Orizaba, reaching 5760 meters. Its location is just north of the city of Orizaba, and east of Puebla and Mexico City. It sits on the boundary of the states of Vera Cruz and Puebla and is not far from the Gulf of Mexico.

Orizaba is an eroded volcano that still retains most of its symmetrical shape. The summit is heavily glaciated, but these glaciers have few crevasses—certainly none to cause concern, even for a solo climber. Because it's the highest summit in Mexico, one can find many people climbing the mountain on good roads and trails and well used routes.

Reaching the mountain is relatively simple. The normal route is via the small town of Tlachichuca on the road reaching the northern slopes and the two huts not far from the snowline. Tlachichuca can be reached by public bus or by hitch hiking from the main road, Highway 140, which runs from Acatzingo to Zacatepec and Jalapa. Beyond Tlachichuca, the road is poor and steep in places, and is for the most part a 4WD road—at least the upper portion. If you're there on weekends it should be easy to get a lift all the way to the huts, but on other days, one may have to walk from Tlachichuca.

Tlachichuca is a small town, but there is at least one gasoline station, and several small shops where all food can be purchased. However, for better variety it might be best to food shop in larger towns before reaching this area.

If one has his own vehicle, the climb can be made in one day from Tlachichuca, but if you end up walking all that way, it'll take two long days. Most people spend one night in the huts or camp nearby, then climb to the summit the next day. As the elevation is fairly high, people who live at or near sea level sometimes have problems with altitude.

Ice ax and crampons are needed as well as warm clothing, but it's not a difficult or dangerous climb. December through April are the dry months, with summertime bringing heavy rains and snow to the mountain. (May through October).

**Map:** Veracruz, E14-3, 1 : 250,000, from the Direccion General De Geografia Del Territorio Nacional Mexico. Buy at DETENAL, Balderas 71, Mexico City.

Summit of Orizaba is seen above the refugios on the north slopes.

# Map 297-1, Orizaba, Cordillera Anahuac, Mexico

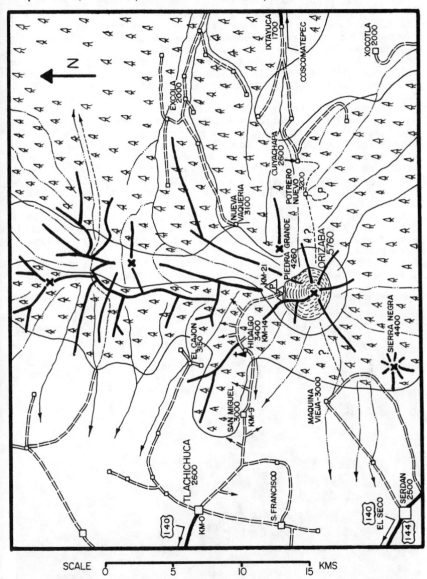

# Tajumulco, Sierra Madre, Guatemala

This is the first of two maps which cover most of the high peaks in Guatemala. The highest peak on this map and in Guatemala, is Tajumulco, rising to 4220 meters. It's location is west of Quezaltenango and northwest of the twin cities of San Marcos and San Pedro. Tajumulco, like all other high peaks in Guatemala, is a volcano, but with some erosion and for a long time dead.

The next highest peak on this map is one that overlooks Quezaltenango. This is Santa Maria and it rises to 3789 meters. It retains its conal shape. All other high summits in this area are either non-volcanic or have lost all or most of their symmetrical appearance.

Getting into this region is easy. There are many buses leaving Guatemala City each day for Quezaltenango, some of which run on to San Marcos. There's only one bus terminal between these twin cities and that is in San Pedro. From that bus station, one can find several buses each day heading in the direction of Tacana. Take one of these, or a truck making the same run. Tell the driver you're heading for Tajumulco and to let you off near the very small village of Tuchan.

From a point on the road just below Tuchan, at about 2990 meters, many trails head up and to the southwest. The lower slopes are farmed, the higher ones covered with a wonderful pine forest. Take any one of many trails going up a prominent ridge. Eventually it's only one trail, leading to Los Romero. At the pass, about 3655 meters, turn right and continue up the same ridge to the summit. There's a trail all the way, and one can even do this climb in the clouds and rain as the author did. There's no running water above the road, but around Tuchan, they actually have piped water. This is a short hike of 3 or 4 hours from the road to the summit. The author made the climb from San Pedro in one day, riding a bus up and a truck down. Buy all food in San Pedro or Marcos.

For Santa Maria, take a bus or truck from the main bus terminal in Quezaltenango heading for the village of Pinal. Once there ask the local people to direct you to the trail leading to the northwest side of the volcano. Maps indicate lava with no vegetation on the southwestern slopes. Best time to climb here is in the months of November through about March.

**Map:** Quezaltenango, ND-15-7, and Cuilco, ND-15-3, both 1 : 250,000, also available in 1 : 50,000, from Servicio Cartografia Militar, Av. Las Americas 5-76, Zona 13, Guatemala City.

This is the east ridge of Tajamulco in the clouds and near treeline.

## Map 298-1, Tajumulco, Sierra Madre, Guatemala

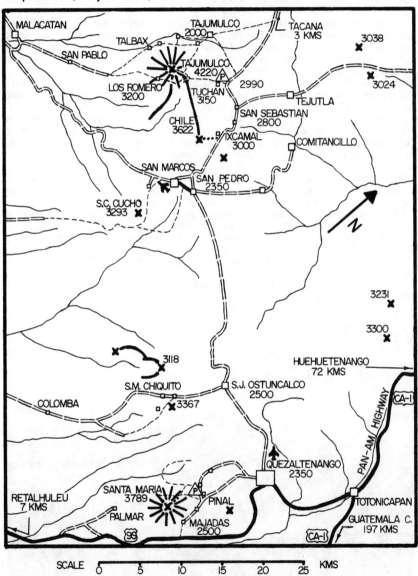

MALACATAN

TALBAX

SAN PABLO

TAJUMULCO
2000

TACANA
3 KMS

3038

3024

TAJUMULCO
4220  P

2990

LOS ROMERO
3200

TUCHAN
3150

TEJUTLA

SAN SEBASTIAN
2800

CHILE
3622

IXCAMAL
3000

COMITANCILLO

SAN MARCOS

SAN PEDRO
2350

S.C. CUCHO
3293

N

3231

3300

3118

HUEHUETENANGO
72 KMS

S.M. CHIQUITO

S.J. OSTUNCALCO
2500

CA-1

COLOMBA

3367

PAN-AM. HIGHWAY

QUEZALTENANGO
2350

RETALHULEU
7 KMS

SANTA MARIA
3789    P

PINAL

TOTONICAPAN

PALMAR

MAJADAS
2500

CA-1

GUATEMALA C.
197 KMS

9S

SCALE    0    5    10    15    20    25    KMS

## Acatenango, Sierra Madre, Guatemala

This is the second map of Guatemala covering the high peaks of the Sierra Madra. This mountain range runs the length of Guatemala in a northwest to southeast fashion, with all the higher summits volcanos. Many are conal shaped and several are still active, including Fuego.

The highest peak on this map is Acatenango at 3976 meters. This peak is actually the twin summit of Fuego, a bit lower at 3763 meters. Both are considered active, but only Fuego is still emitting smoke and fumes from its summit.

To climb either or both of these peaks, one has a choice of two routes. The easiest way is actually a trail, but getting to it may be difficult. This trail begins about 2 kms east of Solidad and winds up the north slopes of Acatenango. From the top one can walk down to the saddle and up again to the top of Fuego. If one were to do that, it would be best to come off the mountain via the other route, that being from Alotenango.

The main problem with the Solidad route is that there's not much traffic on that road and it may take time to get a ride. It's a 15 km walk from San Miguel Duenas to the trailhead. However, there are many buses at all hours going to as far as Alotenango from the bus terminal in Antigua. From the river bridge just below Alotenango, take the trial going in the direction of the mountain, which begins about 100 meters beyond that bridge. It's a well used path leading to farms higher up. Head in the direction of the lava and the deep gully between the two summits. At the gully, one must cross to reach the open slopes on the other side. Crossing that gully is difficult.

To climb Volcan Agua, take a bus or truck from the Antigua bus terminal going to Santa Maria de Jesus. Just before reaching that village, there's a road going about halfway up. From the road's end, there's a trail to the top. This is an easy one day hike from Antigua.

Near Lago de Atitlan are several volcanos rising from the lake shores. This is the most fotogenic scene in Guatemala. The highest peak here is Atitlan, at 3537 meters. Its twin is Toliman, 3158 meters. To climb these peaks, take a bus from Panajachel to near the town of San Lucas Toliman. Start hiking near the finca or farm known as Santa Alicia. Climb San Pedro, 2995 meters, from the village by the same name. The dry season is best for climbing, usually from November to March.

**Map:** Guatemala, ND-15-8, 1 : 250,000, all from Servicio Cartografia Militar, Av. Las Americas 5-76, Zona 13, Guatemala City.

Looking south from the upper slopes of Fuego at Volcan Agua.

# Map 299-1, Acatenango, Sierra Madre, Guatemala

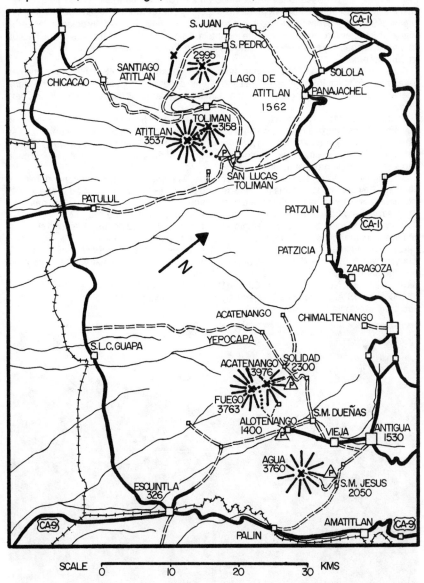

# Chirripo, Cordillera Talamanca, Costa Rica

The Central American country of Costa Rica is famous for its active volcanos, but none of these make the highest summit in the country. That distinction belongs to Cerro Chirripo rising through the clouds to 3819 meters. This summit is part of the Cordillera Talamanca running northwest to southeast, in the southeastern portion of Costa Rica. The rocks here are mostly metamorphic, as opposed to lava rock found on the volcanos near San Jose.

The climb of Chirripo is always made from the city of San Isidro, located southeast of the capital of San Jose. From San Isidro, there are usually two small buses daily going as far as the village of San Gerardo, at the base of the mountain. This distance of 19 kms can also be hitched very easily, especially on weekends in the dry season. For walkers, it's about a 5 or 6 hour walk to San Gerardo.

Because Chirripo is part of a national park, there's a park office in San Gerardo. One can always get the latest information on trail and refugio conditions from someone working there. There's also an office in San Jose, which has information about all the national parks in Costa Rica.

Chirripo is normally climbed in 2 days, but a very fast and fit hiker could do it in one very long day. From San Gerardos church, walk up the road to the northeast, crossing 2 streams. Less than 1 km past the second bridge, find your own way up the ridge running east-west. There's not one, but many cow trails, zigzagging up the slope. At the top of the ridge is the very good and well used trail to the summit.

Since the trail is always on the ridge, water can be a problem with the high temperatures and humidity. Be sure and take some from the second bridge, as the spring, located at about 2525 meters, may be dry in the months of December through March (the dry season). One passes a small stream at about 3125 meters, the first real water supply on the route.

At about 3310 meters, is the first refugio—which sleeps about 10 people. A second shelter a bit further up the trail at 3475 meters, can sleep perhaps 20 people.

Keep in mind these mountains are probably the wettest places in Central America, so have rain gear with you even in the dry season. Food can be found in all the small villages enroute to the mountain, but San Isidro has better selections.

**Map:**   San Jose, NC-17-9, 1 : 250,000, and Durika, 3544-III and San Isidro, 3444-II, both at 1 : 50,000, from US Army Defence Mapping Agency (Joint Operations Graphic), or the Instituto Geografia de Costa Rica, San Jose.

This is the highest chain lake just west of Chirripos summit.

# Map 300-1, Chirripo, Cord. Talamanca, Costa Rica

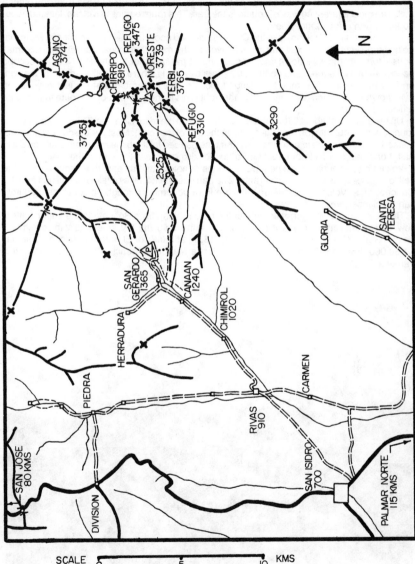

## Volcan Baru (Chiriqui), Panama

In the extreme western end of Panama, just north of the cities of David and La Concepcion, lies the highest mountain in that country, Volcan Baru, at 3474 meters.

Sometimes called Volcan de Chiriqui—after the name of the state in which it is located—this mountain is an old and highly eroded volcano. Only slightly resembling a volcano at this time, the mountain has deep canyons or quebradas and mature rain forests on its slopes.

There are two routes in which to reach the summit of Volcan Baru, one is a road, the other a trail. The most interesting way of course is the trail. This route begins at Volcan, located about 30 kms north of La Concepcion.

From the center of Volcan, take the Cerro Punta road about 3 kms to the northeast. From that point a road leads to the right and into a canyon on the mountain's west side. Just past a small house, turn left and walk down into the canyon and past another farmhouse. Near the second house or hut, is a spring, and about 300 meters beyond is where the trail leads off to the right and up the mountain. It may be difficult to locate, but remember that it's just beyond the overgrown road, which also leads off to the right. This is the only part of the route that may be difficult to locate.

Up the trail and at about 2400 meters, is a spring and place for camping. This is the only water found on the mountain (beyond the spring at the end of the road). Most people do not camp, but instead make the climb in one long day. The time needed to climb the mountain could be cut in half if one had a vehicle or could hire a taxi for riding to near the end of the road.

Volcan has a couple of inexpensive pensions or hotels, and at least three small stores that sell food, as well as several restaurants. One can easily hitch hike or take a small bus from La Concepcion to Volcan. The drier months are from December through April, but the mountain can be climbed any time.

The author has little information about the road running from Boquete to the summit. It's a new road and not on any maps. It's used to service the radio and T.V. antennas at the summit.

**Map:**   Golfito (Costa Rica-Panama), NC-17-13, 1 : 250,000, or El Hato Del Volcan, Panama, 1 : 50,000, 3642-11. From the US Army Defence Mapping Agency, Washington D.C., and Panama City(?).

Volcan Baru is seen piercing the clouds as it rises above the village of Volcan.

Map 301-1, Baru (Chiriqui), Panama

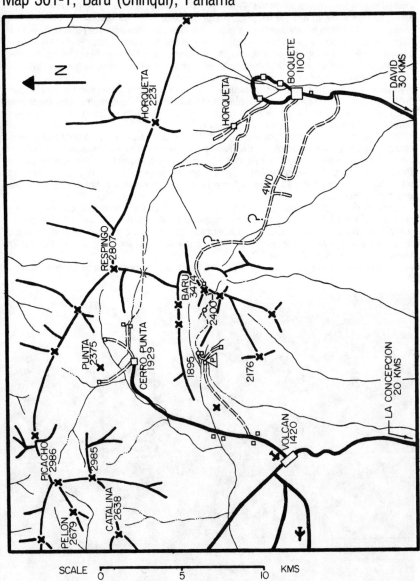

SCALE 0       5       10    KMS

## Blue Peak, Blue Mts., Jamaica, West Indies

Near the eastern end of Jamaica lies the Blue Mountains, an uplifted area of the same age and of the same tectonics as the mountains of Haiti and Dominican Republic. The higher portions of these mountains have virgin rain forests, mostly on the eastern and northeastern sides which receive the most rainfall. The highest peak is Blue Mountain Peak at 2257 meters. This summit is the culmination of the "Grand Ridge" of the Blue Mountains. A number of other peaks can be found at or near the 2000 meter elevation mark as well.

Access to this area is very easy as it's only a few kms from the capital city of Kingston. From Kingston, a bus can be taken from the station at Papine, to Mavis Banks. From Mavis Banks one can walk on a good trail or "bridle path" to a place called Whitfield Hall, at 1219 meters altitude. Whitfield Hall is a small hostel or hotel, something like the huts in the Alps. Whitfield Hall has cooking facilities, but no food—bring it yourself.

At Whitfield Hall, the trail to the top begins. There are two small forest service huts enroute, but you'll have to inquire as to their condition at Whitfield Hall, if an overnight stay is anticipated. From Whitfield Hall to the top and return is an easy one day hike. Don't forget a bottle of water—the heat and humidity are terrible.

There's another way to the top, and that's through Elevan Mile (which is on the coast-road east of Kingston), Ramble, Hagley Gap. From Hagley Gap there's a 4WD road to Whitfield Hall, but it's for Land Rovers only. There's also a poor road from Mavis Banks to Hagley Gap, as shown on the map. The simplest way for most people seems to be to take public transport to Mavis Banks, and walk the 11 kms to Whitfield Hall. This means the entire trip from Kingston would take two days.

Excellent maps of the Blue Mountains can be found at the Lands and Survey office in Kingston. Additional information can be obtained at the tourist offices at the airport or downtown Kingston. This climb can be made at any time, but the dry season is from the end of November through April. The dry period here is the same as for Central America and the northern parts of South America.

**Map:** Kingston, sheet L, 1 : 50,000, from the Lands and Survey of Jamaica, Kingston.

Looking northeast from Jamaicas capital of Kingston to the Blue Mountains.

# Map 302-2, Blue, Blue Mts., Jamaica, West Indies

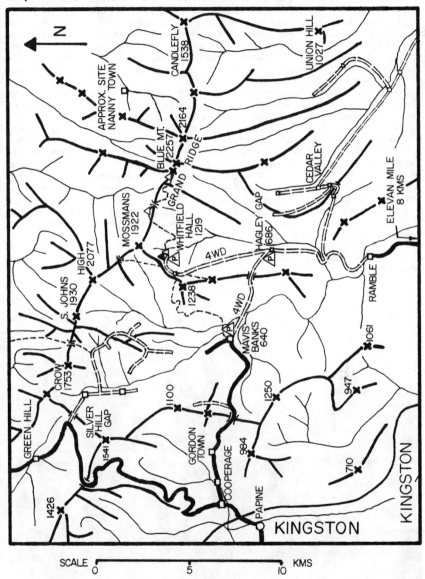

SCALE  0       5       10   KMS

## La Sella, Haiti, West Indies

In the Caribbean or West Indies, the highest mountains are concentrated on the island of Hispanola. This island is the second largest in the Caribbean, next to Cuba. On the eastern half of Hispanola is the Dominican Republic, while the western portion is the Republic of Haiti. Next to Pico Duarte and the surrounding mountains in the Dominican Republic, the highest peak on the island is in Haiti. This is La Sella, at 2674 meters. La Sella is located southeast of the capital city of Port au Prince, and not far from the border of Dominican Republic.

The author approached this area from Port au Prince, Petionville, Kenscoff and to the mountains south of Furcy. This is the wrong approach route, unless it's a trek through some high and isolated villages you want. The very best way in reaching La Sella is to take a bus, called "Tap Taps" in Haiti, from Port au Prince to Ganthier and Fond Verrettes. There should be no problem getting to Fond Verrettes, but beyond this village there's very little traffic. However, it may be best to start walking from there anyway.

From Fond Verrettes, at 800 meters elevation, there's one main trail heading in a southwesterly direction to the forest roads, as shown on the map. There are many trails in the mountains, so a little knowledge of French comes in handy, when trying to stay on the right path. From the end of one of these roads, one must walk cross-country to the west to reach the highest peak.

Topographic maps show a telepherique on the mountain, beginning somewhere north of Chambon. This is most likely a carrier of aluminum or Bauxite ore, and couldn't be of value to a climber, except that it could be used to help locate the route to the higher mountains from the town of Chambon. Keep in mind, the northern slopes are much steeper than the more gently sloping southern approaches. Also keep in mind that public transportation in Haiti is not as good as some might wish. Communication is a big problem, even for those speakling French.

The best time of year to climb in this region is from December through April. Food should be bought in the larger towns, preferably at Port au Prince. For information concerning buses, contact the tourist office in the capital.

**Map:** Port-Au-Prince (5771), Fond Parisien (5871), Belle-Anse (5770), and Grand Gosier (5870), all 1 : 100,000, from the Service de Geodesie et de Cartographis et les Forces Armees d'Haiti, Port Au Prince.

Foto taken to the west of La Sella, showing fields on mountain slopes.

# Map 303-1, La Sella, Haiti, West Indies

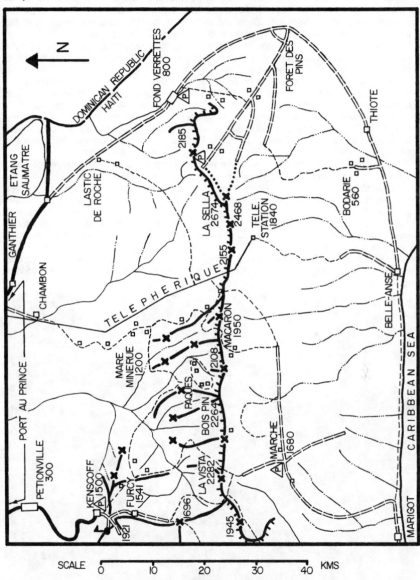

N

DOMINICAN REPUBLIC
HAITI

FOND VERRETTES 800

FORET DES PINS

THIOTE

ETANG SAUMATRE

LASTIC DE ROCHE

2185

LA SELLA 2674

2468

TELE. STATION 1840

BODARIE 560

GANTHIER

2155

CHAMBON

T E L E P H E R I Q U E

MACARON 1950

BELLE-ANSE

PORT AU PRINCE

MARE MINERUE 1200

PAQUES

2108

C A R I B B E A N   S E A

PETIONVILLE 300

BOIS PIN 2264

MARCHE 1680

KENSCOFF 1500

FURO 1541

LA VISTA 2282

1696

1921

1945

MARIGOT

SCALE   0        10        20        30        40   KMS

# Duarte, Cord. Central, Dominican Republic, W.I.

Pico Duarte, at 3087 meters, is the highest mountain in the Dominican Republic, on the island of Hispanola, and in the entire Caribbean. Pico Duarte is part of the Cordillera Central, which is a folded and uplifted range, located near the center of the country. The Cordillera Central is the dominating mountain range on the island.

Getting to this region is fairly easy. The journey will likely start in the capital city of Santo Domingo. From the capital, take one of many buses heading in the direction of La Vega (not far south of the large city of Santiago). On this main highway, hitch hiking is reasonably good, but buses are cheap. Standing on the roadside is a hot and sweaty situation.

At La Vega, another bus will have to be taken for the next part of the trip, that being to the mountain resort town of Jarabacoa, situated at 529 meters. This area is cooler than the rest of the country, so many "summer homes" are being built.

From Jarabacoa, there seems to be no public transport in the direction of Manabao, but hitching on this rather lonely section of paved road is easy. Beyond Manabao, the road becomes rougher and less used, and one will surely have to walk the rest of the way.

Between Manabao (at 900 meters) and the beginning of the trail at Casa Tablone, are several small villages, all with small shops or stores, where some food can be found. A very poor road exists between La Cienega and Casa Tablone, where is located a work crew hut and gate, which is the entrance to the Parque Nacional J. Armanda Bermundez.

Upon arrival at Casa Tablone, the author was told that permission was needed in order to go beyond that gate. After a long "begging" session, the author was allowed to go up the mountain. He eventually climbed Rucilla—but went no further, as time was short, and he was not allowed to stay overnight. Get permission in Santo Domingo for the hike, at the national park headquarters.

It's a hot climb, so have water. There's a crude bush shelter at about 2650 meters, as well as a small spring, then a trail goes to the top of the twin summits of Duarte. This is a two day hike from Casa Tablone.

**Map:** Santiago(NE-19-1), San Juan(NE-19-5), and Santo Domingo (#?), all 1 : 250,000, and Lamedero(5973-II), and Monabao(6073-III), both 1 : 50,000, from the US Army Defence Mapping Agency, Washington D.C., and Santo Domingo(?).

The upper slopes of Duarte are covered with a fine pine forest.

# Map 304-1, Duarte, Cord. Central, Dominican R., W.I.

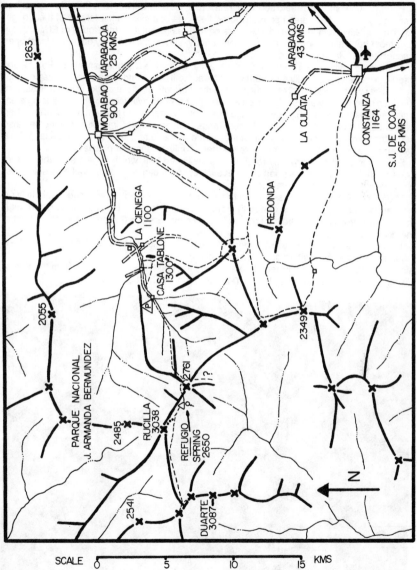

JARABACOA 25 KMS

MONABAO 900

JARABACOA 43 KMS

LA CULATA

CONSTANZA 1164

S.J. DE OCOA 65 KMS

1263

REDONDA

LA CIENEGA 1100

CASA TABLONE 1300

2055

2349

2761

PARQUE NACIONAL J. ARMANDA BERMUNDEZ

RUCILLA 3038

2485

REFUGIO SPRING 2650

2541

DUARTE 3087

N

SCALE 0        5        10        15   KMS

# El Toro, Sierra de Luquillo, Puerto Rico, W.I.

El Toro, 1074 meters, is the highest summit in the Sierra de Luquillo, located in eastern Puerto Rico. To most this small, compact mountain range is known as El Yunque, same as the second highest peak, at 1065 meters. Tourists and natives alike come here to see and hike in the tropical rain forest. It's one of the few places on the island of Puerto Rico where one can escape from the tropical heat.

Perhaps more should be said about the rain forest. It's different than any other the author has personally seen. There aren't so many large trees, as one sees in the forests of the Congo, Amazon or New Guinea; instead, there are palm trees (at least on the slopes of El Yunque.). Like most tropical rain forests, it has a high canopy, under which is fairly open—at least open enough to walk through.

Most of the trails shown on this map are maintained by the Caribbean National Forest, and used extensively, especially those between the summit of El Yunque and the visitors center.

The best way to reach El Toro, which is the most remote of all the peaks in the area, is from the main road—Highway 191. Begin on a trail not far from an aviary and workers housing area. This trail (for the most part) follows a ridge in a westerly direction to the summit of El Toro, then descends, and ends at some kind of forest ranger station, called Cienega Alta. One can also begin the hike at km 20 on the south slopes of the range, 5 or 6 kms up from Florida. Take a canteen of water on this hike, as there's water in only a couple of places.

El Yunque can be reached by road or by a well used trail, which begins near the visitors center. On this path there is good water available. Many people use this trail on week-ends, which is only about a 3 km walk to the top.

There is no scheduled bus service to this area, but hitch hiking is very good, especially on weekends. The dry season is generally from December to April, but with the constant high humidity and tropical heat, the time of year for a hike matters little (except fotography is best in the dry season).

The last place to buy food is in Mameyes, located on National Highway 3 to the north. Make inquiries at the forest visitors center as to trails, etc.

**Map:**   Caribbean National Forest, Luquillo Experimental Forest, 1 : 30,000, from the Forest Visitor Center, or Puerto Rico, 1 : 120,000, from the USGS, San Juan(?).

A small but pure, clear stream of water runs down the slopes of El Junque.

# Map 305-1, El Toro, Sierra Luquillo, P. Rico, W.I.

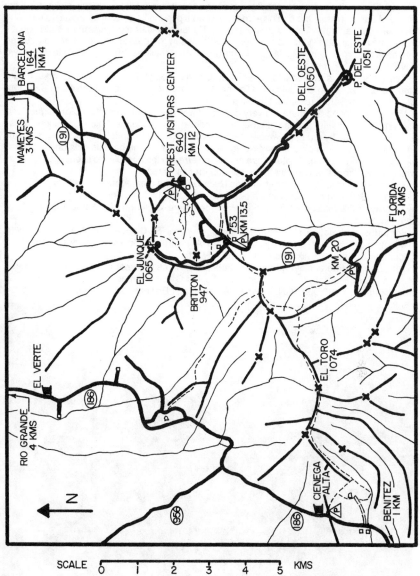

BARCELONA 164 KM 4

MAMEYES 3 KMS

(191)

P. DEL OESTE 1050

P. DEL ESTE 1051

FOREST VISITORS CENTER

640 KM 12

P

753 KM 13.5

P

FLORIDA 3 KMS

EL JUNQUE 1065

BRITTON 947

(191)

KM 20

P

EL VERTE

(186)

EL TORO 1074

RIO GRANDE 4 KMS

P

N

CIENEGA ALTA

P

BENITEZ 1 KM

(956)

(186)

SCALE 0 1 2 3 4 5 KMS

# La Soufriere, Guadeloupe, French West Indies

La Soufriere, 1467 meters, is located on the French West Indies Island of Guadeloupe. As are all the mountains in the Lesser Antilles, it too is a volcano, and very much active. The mountain changes every few years, as a result of new eruptions.

There is a good paved road from the city of Basse Terre, to the base of the cone, where several trails begin. From the end of that road and parking lot, it's only about an hour's hike to the top. This is also one of the popular places to begin a longer hike along the backbone of the island of Basse Terre. One can hike from Soufrieres parking lot or from Matouba, to the north and come out at either Vernou or Montebello. By taking either the Merwart or Victor Huges trails, one can climb several of the highest volcanos in the Lesser Antilles. For the average person, it takes one very long day, to do this north-south traverse, but many people do it in two days.

Public transport is available to as far as St. Claude, Montebello and Vernou. One can auto stop, but that's slow on Guadeloupe! Distances are short however, so one can easily walk from Basse Terre to Soufriere—about 10 kms.

Most trails around Soufriere are very good and well used; however, the Victor Hugues and Merwart trails are little used and in rougher condition. For the longer hikes, one should wear boots not affected by mud and water—as there will be plenty around. If overnighting, an extra set of dry clothing in a plastic sack would be good, as on the higher summits one is always exposed to wet and cold. Pointe a Pitre or Basse Terre are the best places to buy food (most of which comes from France), but it's not cheap on this island.

There are two refuges, one near Grande Decouverte, the other Ajoupa Maynac, near Morne Incapable. Both can be used, but it's best to get the latest information on their condition and availability at the Maison Forestiere in Matouba before venturing out. It's best to hike from south to north.

For further information, stop at the Maison du Volcan in St. Claude or the Maison Forestiere in Matouba, or the tourist office in Pointe-a-Pitre. As in all the Caribbean, the dry season is from December to April, but hiking can be done any time.

**Map:** See the free booklet with maps, **Walks and Hikes (Promenades & Randommees),** from the Parc Natural de Guadeloupe and Tourist Office of Guadeloupe, Point a Pitre. Or Guadeloupe, 1 : 100,000, IGN, Service des Ventes et Editions, 107, Rue La Boetie, 75008 Paris.

The ridge-top trail which runs from La Soufriere to Vernou.

Map 306-1, Soufriere, Guadeloupe, French W.I.

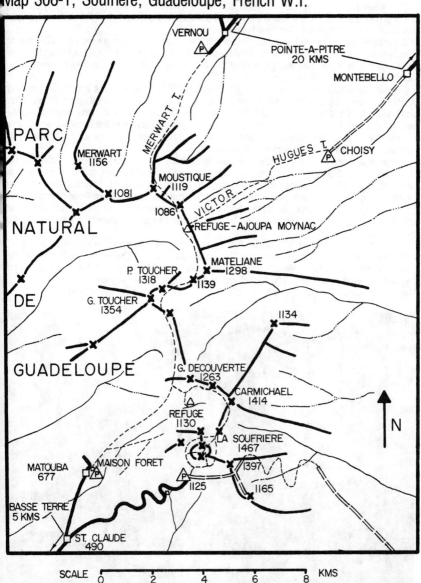

VERNOU

POINTE-A-PITRE
20 KMS

MONTEBELLO

PARC

MERWART
1156

MERWART T.

CHOISY
HUGUES T.

MOUSTIQUE
1119

1081

1086

VICTOR

NATURAL

REFUGE-AJOUPA MOYNAC

MATELIANE
1298

P. TOUCHER
1318

1139

G. TOUCHER
1354

DE

1134

GUADELOUPE

G. DECOUVERTE
1263

CARMICHAEL
1414

N

REFUGE
1130

LA SOUFRIERE
1467

MATOUBA
677

MAISON FORET

1397

1125

1165

BASSE TERRE
5 KMS

ST. CLAUDE
490

SCALE    0    2    4    6    8    KMS

## Diabloting, Dominica, West Indies

Morne Diabloting, at 1447 meters, is the highest summit on the island of Dominica in the Caribbean, and is located in the wildest and least developed part of the island. More exactly, its location is about 20 kms due north of Roseau, the capital—and about 10 kms from the important town of Portsmouth, which is on the northwest coast.

The mountain originated as a volcano (as did the whole of the island), but is highly eroded, and has no resemblance to a volcano now. The area has a great deal of virgin rain forest, one of few such places left in the Caribbean today.

Before doing any climbing one must first reach the Syndicate Estate. It's located at the end of a ridge-top road, about 6 or 7 kms from the main west coast highway, running between Roseau and Portsmouth. If you're walking this road, have a canteen full of water, as there's none to be found until arriving at the estate.

There's no permanent residence at the Syndicate Estate, which is a grapefruit growing plantation. The people working there live on the coast and are transported up each day. With luck one can get a lift with the workers. The author was there in 1979, and at that time the estate was being broken up and sold. The future may see great changes in the area, as one of the prospective buyers was a church group that wanted to build a summer camp. If and when this happens, the road will be improved as well as trails.

The author found a trail, as shown on the map, which leads *toward* the top of Diabloting. However, about 2/3 of the way up, that trail gradually petered out and the summit was not reached. This may or may not be the correct route. It's possible to use this trail, but higher on the mountain, one will be required to "bushwhack" the last km or two. Even if one doesn't reach the top, it's well worth the hike as it's through one of the best rain forests in the Caribbean. At the beginning of the trail, the trees are so large and the canopy so thick, it's difficult to take fotos—even at mid-day.

The Syndicate Estate, at 625 meters, is a wonderful place to spend a few days, if getting away from the tropical heat is desired. The dry season is from December to April, with the grapefruit harvest time in March and April. The island of Dominica is the greenest, least developed, least expensive, and friendliest of all the Caribbean islands.

**Map:**  Dominica, Sheets 1 and 2, 1 : 25,000, from Lands and Survey, Roseau.

At the edge of the tropical rainforest near the Syndicate Estate.

# Map 307-1, Diabloting, Dominica, West Indies

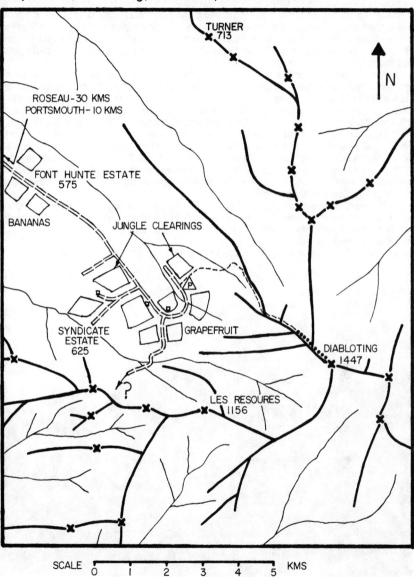

TURNER
713

N

ROSEAU-30 KMS
PORTSMOUTH- 10 KMS

FONT HUNTE ESTATE
575

BANANAS

JUNGLE CLEARINGS

P

SYNDICATE
ESTATE
625

GRAPEFRUIT

DIABLOTING
1447

?

LES RESOURES
1156

SCALE   0   1   2   3   4   5   KMS

## Trois Pitons, Dominica, West Indies

On the Lesser Antilles island of Dominica, and just east of the capital "town" of Roseau, lies the Morne Trois Pitons National Park. In this part are several old and eroded volcanic cones, with Trois Pitons, 1387 meters, the highest. Because it's a national park, several good trails have been made, but these are not to any mountain summits—merely to natural features such as Boiling Lake. Dominca, formerly French owned—then British, is now independent.

The information given to the author concerning routes to Trois Pitons, is that there is a good trail to the top, but its exact location was not pinpointed. One report said it began behind the police station at Ponte Casse—but the policeman there didn't know of it. Others said it began about 2 kms to the east of Ponte Casse. For sure, there is in the area somewhere, a pretty good trail to the top of Trois Pitons.

For Micotin, which is perhaps the most challenging climb in the area, one should walk along the 4WD road which connects Laudat with Freshwater Lake, to a large gully next to a sign stating the national park boundary. Going up the gully is easy—but slippery. Where the gully peters out, about 140 meters from the summit, it's "bushwhacking" on to the top. People informed the author of trails on the southwest side of Micotin, but he didn't find any.

There's no public transport to Laudat, but the walk from Roseau is enjoyable. It's very likely you'll get a lift part way on that steep, but paved road. Ponte Casse lies on the main road connecting the capital with the "national airport" at Melville Hall. Plenty of buses pass that way.

The dry season is from December to about April. Footwear should be the type which is unaffected by mud and water, for the muddy trails of the national park. Long pants are best if one is to "bushwhack" up any mountains.

There's a small store in Laudat, but Roseau has much better variety. There's a fine campsite just above Laudat, near a stream and meadow. In Roseau there's the national park headquarters, where additional information can be obtained. By the time you get there, they may have some good maps printed.

**Map:**   Dominica, Sheets 2 and 3, 1 : 25,000, from Lands and Survey, Roseau.

Micotin as seen from the village of Laudat.

# Map 308-1, Trois Pitons, Dominica, West Indies

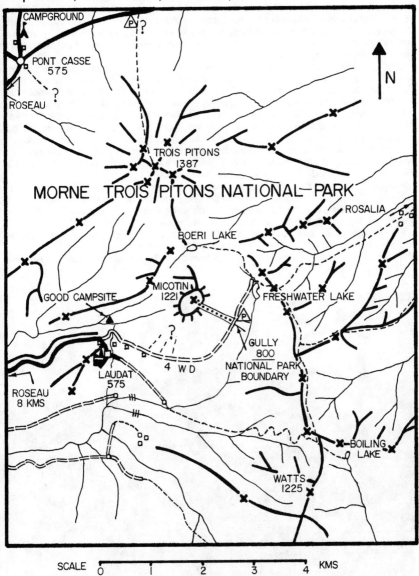

CAMPGROUND

P ?

PONT CASSE
575

ROSEAU
?

N

TROIS PITONS
1387

MORNE TROIS PITONS NATIONAL PARK

ROSALIA

BOERI LAKE

GOOD CAMPSITE

MICOTIN
1221

FRESHWATER LAKE

P

?

GULLY
800

4 W D

NATIONAL PARK
BOUNDARY

LAUDAT
575

ROSEAU
8 KMS

BOILING
LAKE

WATTS
1225

SCALE  0    1    2    3    4  KMS

# Mt. Pelée, Martinique, French West Indies

Mt. Pelée at 1397 meters, is the highest summit on the island of Martinique in the French West Indies. Pelee is considered an active volcano, but hasn't had a big eruption since May 2, 1902, when it sent a superheated cloud down its southwest slope to annihilate the city of St. Pierre, killing more than 30,000 people. Only a condemned murderer in a protected jail cell survived the holocaust.

Today Pelee can be climbed in half a day from the parking lot next to the old Aileron Refuge, at the end of the road. This shelter is in ruins, but can offer some protection from the elements. On the summit, there are two small huts: one is some kind of volcano observatory which is always locked and can't be used by hikers; the other is a hikers shelter and dilapidated to a point of giving no protection at all.

Getting to the mountain is fairly easy. One can take publicos (regular cars which carry several passengers and operate along a route, the same as buses), as far as St. Pierre—where many ruins and a museum can be seen. Other publicos go on Le Morne Rouge. Publicos can also be taken direct from Fort-du-France along Highway N-3 to Le Morne Rouge.

From Le Morne Rouge, it's about 6 kms to the parking lot at the base of the peak. One may have to walk from Le Morne Rouge, as public transport is minimal from there on, but that distance is short. Auto stopping is very poor in Martinique, but that's another possible way.

There are other trails to the summit leading from both Le Precheur, on the west coast, and from Macouba, on the north, but the author is unfamiliar with those trails. An educated guess is that they are little used—therefore probably overgrown.

From the parking lot it's a cool hike, the area being in constant clouds. The summit's even cooler, so a lite jacket should be taken. The dry season is from December to April. The trail is good, so no special equipment is needed. There's a restaurant about one km down from the parking lot, but one should buy food in Le Morne Rouge.

Further information can be found in the tourist office in Fort-du-France. Some special bookshops there sell good topographic maps of Pelée and the island.

**Map:**   Fort de France-St. Pierre, 1 : 50,000, from the IGN, Service des Ventes et Editions, 107, Rue La Boetie, 75008 Paris.

Below the deadly slopes of Volcan Pelee is St. Pierre.

# Map 309-1, Pelée, Martinique, French W. Indies

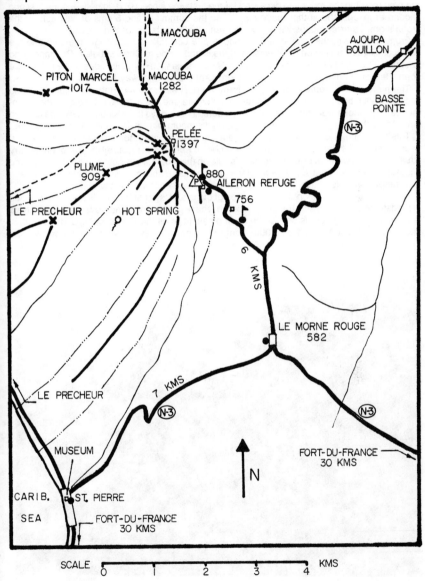

MACOUBA

AJOUPA
BOUILLON

PITON MARCEL
1017

MACOUBA
1282

BASSE
POINTE

N-3

PELÉE
1397

PLUME
909

880
P
AILERON REFUGE

756

LE PRECHEUR

HOT SPRING

6 KMS

LE MORNE ROUGE
582

LE PRECHEUR

7 KMS

N-3

N-3

MUSEUM

FORT-DU-FRANCE
30 KMS

N

CARIB.

ST. PIERRE

SEA

FORT-DU-FRANCE
30 KMS

SCALE

0    1    2    3    4    KMS

# Soufriere, St. Vincent, West Indies

The Soufriere Volcano on the northern end of St. Vincent Island in the Caribbean, is one of the most active volcanos in the world. The summit is at 1219 meters, while the lake within its crater is about 670 meters. Due to a lack of population, an exciting history, and good footpaths on the mountain, this climb is one of the best in all the Caribbean.

The author had the privilege of being camped at Jacobs Well the night of April 12, 1979. Early the next morning the mountain exploded for the first time since 1970. In between the first and second eruptions, the author made his way to the summit to find 5 cms of new ash on the crater's rim. Later eruptions were viewed from a safer distance at Kingstown.

From Kingstown, the capital of St. Vincent, one can take a bus to Georgetown and the Rabacca Dry River Bed on the east side of the island; or go to Chateaubelair, Richmond and Lashum, all located on the western side. These two areas, on opposite sides of the island, are connected by a good trail, with the Soufriere Crater about halfway between.

The more normal route seems to be from the east side, via the Rabacca Plantation and Jacobs Well. If one has the money to rent a car or hire one, it's a half-day hike from the end of the road. For those wanting to traverse the mountain, two days from Kingstown will be enough time. About the only year-round water supply on the mountain is at Jacobs Well, at 488 meters.

This mountain is easy to climb so no special equipment is needed except for a tent (if overnighting). The drier season is from December to April, the same as all the Caribbean. Carry a full canteen of water at all times as there's little on the mountain. Kingstown has the most and biggest shops, so that's the best place to buy food and supplies. Chateaubelair and Georgetown are also large towns, with a market place each and many shops.

For additional information and good maps of the island, stop at the Lands and Survey office in Kingstown. There are also travel agencies that have guides and Land Rovers available. Next to Dominica, St. Vincent is one of the most pleasant of all the Caribbean islands to visit.
**Map:** St. Vincent North, 1 : 25,000, from Lands and Survey Department, Kingstown, St. Vincent.

Foto shows author on Soufrierre just after the first eruption of May, 1979.

# Map 310-1, Soufriere, St. Vincent, West Indies

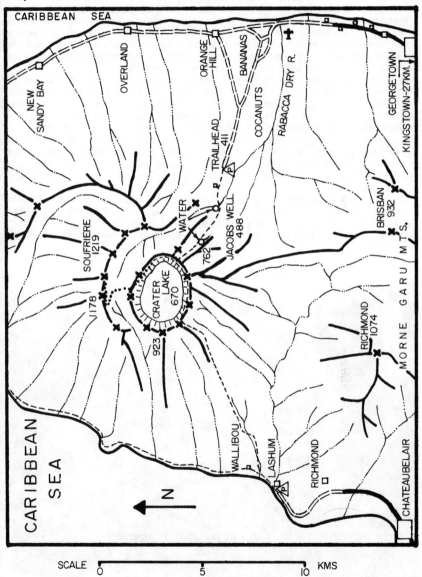

CARIBBEAN SEA

NEW SANDY BAY

OVERLAND

ORANGE HILL

BANANAS

COCANUTS

RABACCA DRY R.

GEORGETOWN

KINGSTOWN–27 KM.

TRAILHEAD 411

WATER

JACOBS WELL 488

762

SOUFRIERE 1219

1178

CRATER LAKE 670

923

BRISBAN 932

RICHMOND 1074

MORNE GARU MTS.

WALLIBOU

LASHUM

RICHMOND

CHATEAUBELAIR

CARIBBEAN SEA

N

SCALE 0        5        10    KMS

# Cerro Aripo, Blue Mts., Trinidad, West Indies

The highest mountain on Trinidad is El Cerro del Aripo, 941 meters elevation. It's located in the central part of the Blue (Bleu) Mountains, northeast of Arima and to the southeast of Blanchisseuse. The altitude of this mountain and others in the area is not high, nor are they rugged, nor are there any well developed trails in the area; but there are places of solitude and remnants of virgin rain forest which make an outing to the area interesting.

If a person had his own vehicle, the trip to Cerro Aripo could take one day from Port of Spain, as the Lalaja South Road is good up to the point marked "440 meters" on the map. But if one is taking public transport or hitch hiking, one should plan on an overnight stay somewhere on the mountain. Regular buses can be taken, running from Arima to Blanchisseuse several times each day. Get off at the Lalaja South Road and walk from there.

A good trail exists, going over a pass (600 meters) between Brasso Seco village and the old plantation house at 440 meters. From the 600 meter pass, merely walk east along the crest of the ridge until the highest point is reached. It's not much of a trail—that is, it's never been made into a regular path, but because it's on the ridge top, and because it's virgin rain forest, it's not too difficult to negotiate. Don't forget to take a supply of water for this ridge-top walk.

As with other Caribbean islands, the dry season is from December to April, but the climb can be made at any time of year. Even in the wet season, it shouldn't be too muddy or extra difficult. High topped boots and long pants should be worn, as the ridge top has some brush in places. All food should be purchased in either Arima or Blanchisseuse, or as a last resort, Brasso Seco.

For good topographic maps of the area, contact the Lands and Survey office in Port of Spain. There's also bound to be a surveyor or geologist around that office who can help in planning a trip, as well as point out other hikes and climbs in the Blue Mountains.

**Map:**    Sheets 14 and 15, 1 : 25,000        from the Lands and Survey Department, Port of Spain.

Seen here on the Lalaja Road near Aripo, is a pile of cocoa pods.

# Map 311-1, Aripo, Blue Mts., Trinidad, W.I.

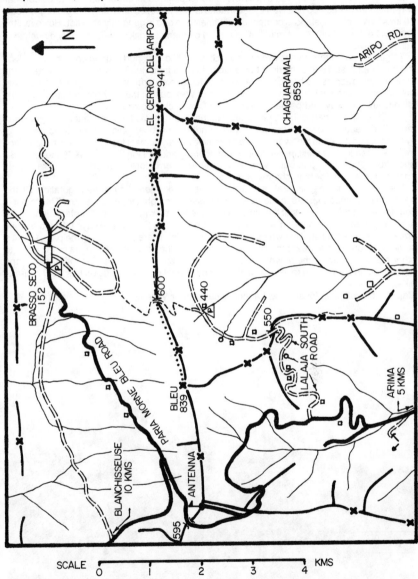

N

EL CERRO DEL ARIPO
941

ARIPO RD.

CHAGUARAMAL
859

BRASSO SECO
152

PARIA MORNE BLEU ROAD

BLANCHISSEUSE
10 KMS

ANTENNA
595

BLEU
839

600

440

550

LALAJA SOUTH ROAD

ARIMA
5 KMS

SCALE 0 1 2 3 4 KMS

## Christoffel, Curacao, Dutch West Indes

Included on this map is the shortest or smallest mountain in this entire book, but the hike involved was one of the more interesting hikes the author has made. This mountain is known as Christoffel and rises to 370 meters. It's on the island of Curacao, which is part of the Dutch Antilles or West Indes. It's located north of the Venezuelan coast about 100 kms, and about half way between Maracaibo and Caracas. Curacao is only about 65 kms long and averages about 10 kms in width. The island is composed of Limestone and is generally very flat. However, the top most part of Christoffel is made of somekind of quartzite rock. This is the only mountain or hill on the island.

To get to Christoffel one has two choices. Since public transport is good on Curacao, taking the bus is easiest. To find the right bus go to the Ortobanda Bus Terminal in Willemstad—the capital. This is across the harbor or inlet from the famous waterfront and swinging bridge. There are buses leaving each hour for the small town of Westpunt at the very northwestern tip of the island. Another way and perhaps even faster is to hitch hike or auto stop.

Mt. Christoffel is part of the Christoffel National Park, a small but very interesting piece of land. The headquarters for the park is at Landhuis Savonet, about 40 kms northwest of Willemstad on the main highway. Before heading that way contact the tourist information office in Willemstad for the latest information about opening and closing times. In 1978 the park was open from 8 am 'till 3 pm, but it was necessary to enter before 12 noon. The entire park is enclosed in a 2 meter high chain-link fence.

The thing that makes this peak, and especially the park, interesting, is the vegetation. On the trail from park headquarters to the peak, one passes through a forest of cactus. This forest is composed entirely of cactus of the largest variety, some of which are 5 or 6 meters high. There are many roads in the area so when walking from Landuis Savonet, always follow the white arrows along the main trail known as Voetpad Christoffel. There's no water in the park, so have some with you. As one nears the summit of Christoffel the vegetation changes from cactus to other types of trees, some of which are draped in moss. The peak itself is rather steep and rugged, but there's a path to the summit. Any kind of boot or shoe will do on this easy half-day hike.

**Map:**   Christoffel National Park, Landhuis Savonet or Willemstad.

One must walk through this forest of cactus to reach Mt. Christoffel.

## Map 312-1, Christoffel, Curacao, Dutch W.I.

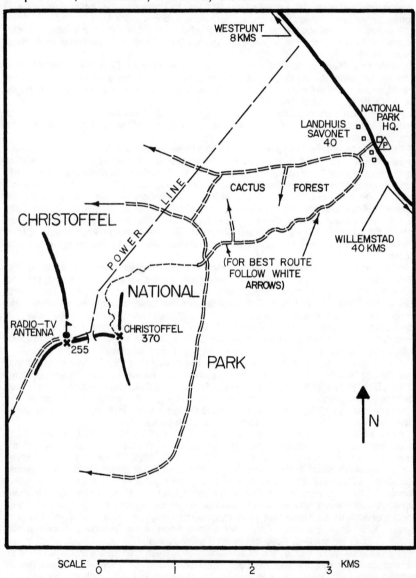

WESTPUNT
8 KMS

NATIONAL
PARK
HQ.

LANDHUIS
SAVONET
40

CACTUS    FOREST

CHRISTOFFEL

WILLEMSTAD
40 KMS

(FOR BEST ROUTE
FOLLOW WHITE
ARROWS)

NATIONAL

POWER LINE

RADIO–TV
ANTENNA
255    CHRISTOFFEL
370

PARK

N

SCALE   0        1        2        3   KMS

# Chapter 8 South America

This chapter on South America includes 65 maps, beginning with the Santa Marta region in Colombia and ending with the Darwin Range in Tierra de Fuego. One nice thing about traveling on this continent is that there is really one common language—Spanish. The people in Brazil speak Portuguese, but there are no mountains there anyway.

If one were to look at a map of South America which showed the highest peaks, one would be looking mostly at volcanos. A great many of the high mountains on the continent are volcanic cones, or are built of volcanic lavas laid down long ago and eroded.

The areas of most volcanic activity are in southern Colombia and north central Ecuador, southwest Peru, western Bolivia, and along the frontier of Chile and Argentina down to about Puerto Montt.

Folded or uplifted mountains are those in Venezuela, northern Colombia, most of Peru—from the Cordillera Blanca to Lake Titicaca. In Bolivia, the Cordillera Real east of La Paz is folded, as are those in the extreme south of Chile-Argentina. Many of these mountain ranges have granitic type rock at the core.

Weather-wise, most of South America is in the topics, but when you're in the high mountains and half frozen, it seems otherwise. Only the southern third of the continent is south of the Tropic of Capricorn.

The Andes Mountains can be broken down into three generalized climatic regions. Two are in the tropical regions, which include all the mountains from Colombia south to the area of northern Argentina. From about the border of Peru—Ecuador north and including all of the northern part of the continent, the dry season is from November or December, through about April. South of that border, down to and including all the Cordillera Real in Bolivia, the dry season begins in May and ends about the first part of September. South of where Bolivia, Chile and Argentina meet is under the influence of the middle latitude cyclonic storms. However, most of the activity is from central Chile on the south. The driest place in South America is from the Peru-Ecuador border south along the coast to central Chile. This in known as the Atacama Desert.

In the tropical Andes, the permanent snowline or where the glaciers end, is at about 4600 to 4800 meters elevation. This is generally the case for the mountains of Venezuela and Colombia, south to the Cordillera Real in Bolivia. In the volcanic and dry regions of southwest Peru and south along the Chile-Argentine border to central Chile, is the highest snowline in the world. In some areas, permanent snow is near the 6000 meter level. However, throughout all of these areas mentioned, snow does fall (though very seldom!) down to below 4000 meters, but doesn't stay long on the ground. From central Chile south, the snowline ranges from about 5000 meters down to where several glaciers in Tierra del Fuego empty into the sea.

Difficulties in climbing range from the "best in the world" in Peru's Cordilleras Blanca, Huayhuash, Vilcanote, and Vilcabamba; to some of the easiest on the volcanos of Peru, Bolivia, Chile and Argentina. The mountains of Ecuador and Colombia are generally very easy for experienced climbers. Some of the best rock climbing in the world is in Patagonia.

In each country of South America, the Instituto Geografico Militar (IGM), publishes maps of their own country. These maps can be found in each capital city.

As of 1980, the most expensive countries in S.A., were in this order; Argentina, Brazil, and Venzuela, with Colombia and Chile about equal. The poorest countries and the cheapest for travelers, are Bolivia, Peru and Ecuador (in 1982 Chile was most expensive).

If you're going to South America, whether it be for a short visit or long, pay attention to this last part. The crimes against travelers or tourists are the highest in the world in parts of this continent. Peru is the worst, with Colombia close behind (all other countries appear about equal)! Virtually every traveler who has visited these two regions has had some kind of encounter with thieves. These encounters range from having something taken from a pocket of a pack, to an entire backpack stolen. A high proportion of the "grabbing" comes at bus terminals and train stations. Keep this in mind as you travel.

To save what might be the "trip of a lifetime," take these precautions: replace straps of camera, camera bags, and shoulder bags, with small chains; carry money and passports in neck pouch or belt; carry a one meter long chain and padlock to secure pack onto bus or truck, or at bus or train terminals; make your watch band tight, and extend your shirt sleeve on your watch arm; don't hang clothes on hotel clothes lines; don't carry valuables in pack pockets; and don't carry a wallet (leave it home). If you make these changes and change some old habits, it's likely you'll have a good trip.

The author found Chiquian, gateway to Yerupaja, the nicest pueblo in Peru. (Map 333).

South of Illampu, is Cherroco, left, and Chachacumani, right (Map 352).

# Pico Bolivar, Andes Mountains, Venezuela

The highest mountain in Venezuela is Pico Bolivar at 5007 meters. This mountain is located just to the southeast of the tourist city of Merida, in western Venezuela. It is the only summit in Venezuela to surpass 5000 meters.

Getting to Pico Bolivar can be very easy. There's a lift or teleferico from the southeastern edge of Merida to the top of Pico Espejoe, 4765 meters. On the mountain are four different way stations of the teleferico, the highest of which requires a doctor or medical aid be present at all times while the lift is in operation. The problem of course, is the rapid rise in elevation. Bottled oxygen is a common sight inside the upper terminal.

From the end of the teleferico, to the top of Bolivar, is a short but steep climb, up a snow couloir. Most people rope up for the route, but a confident climber can do it solo or without rope. Just behind the top lift terminal is the Refugio Timoncito for those who prefer to spend one night or more on the mountain.

In times past, climbers who were members of the Club Andino de Merida were given free passes on the teleferico, and with luck were allowed to sleep on the floor of the upper terminal. Fortunately, for "real climbers," there's a trail from Merida and the lower terminal, to the top of Bolivar, as shown on the map. Another alternate route to the peak is the one via the La Vega area. This is a more difficult route, so expect a good climb.

There is some interesting rock climbing to the west side of Bolivar, on Leon and Torro. Also, to the east are other glaciated summits, namely Humbolt, Bonplano and Concha. These peaks can be reached from Merida, either on the lift or by trail, or from the road which leaves the main highway near Tabay. Trails passing El Paramito, La Mucuy and the Refugio La Coromoto, ultimately pass another Refugio, La Corona. Since this highest part of the Venezuelan Andes is part of the Parque Nacional Simon Bolivar, the trails are well used and maintained.

Inquire at the tourist office in Merida as to the use of the refugios and other pertinent information. Do all your shopping in Merida as well. The dry season is from December through about March—maybe into April. There are plenty of buses going to Merida from San Christobal or Caracus. Hitch hiking (called "La Cola" in Venezuela) is very good to this area.

**Map:**  Andes Centrales de Venezuela—Mapa Alpinistico y Turistico, from the Parque Nacional de Sierra Nevada, Merida.

A good look at the summit of Pico Bolivar from Torre.

# Map 313-1, Bolivar, Andes Mts., Venezuela

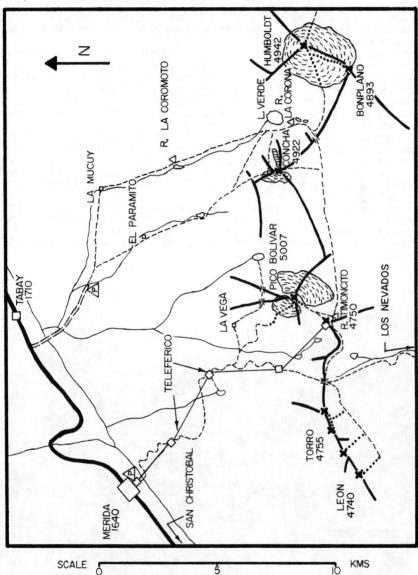

SCALE | 0      5      10 | KMS

## C. Colon, Sierra Nevada de Santa Marta, Colombia

The massif or mountain range known as the Sierra Nevada de Santa Marta is located in the extreme north of Colombia, between Santa Marta on the coast and Valledupar, to the southeast of the range. These mountains are high and wild and one of the few remaining places in Colombia where native Indians or "Indios" are found. The highest summits are Cristobal Colon and Simon Bolivar, but the former is usually shown as the highest summit in Colombia, at 5776 meters.

When the author was there, he had bad information and ended up taking a jeep (bus) to Pueblo Bello, then walking from there. He wandered for four days and didn't even get close—but it was an adventure.

The only real approach route is from Valledupar, on a 4WD road to the northwest and to the village of Sacaracungue. This is about 60 kms in a rugged area. One may have to look around Valledupar for several days to find a jeep or 4WD going that way. It may be best to start walking and hope to stop someone on the way. If you can get a ride to Sacaracungua, then it should be 3 or 4 days climbing to the top and back to Valledupar, as the population on this route is small and traffic minimal. To be assured of success, take a week's supply of food. The normal route to Colon and Bolivar, is from the south and Laguna Raider.

There's a good path to Meollach, but from there it's sheep country, with only scattered trails. One has to walk upstream to the west where, higher up various routes can be found. With these mountains so near the coast and the area being so humid, expect rain showers every day—even in the dry season. Rain equipment for both climber and pack are the most important items one will need. A good tent is next. Also, one will need an ice ax and crampons for the very top portions of the higher summits.

Valledupar is the only large town in the area. It's a good place to buy all food and supplies for the trip. December through March is the dry season. (The latest rumors are that climbers and hikers must pay some kind of fee to the Indians for entering this region.)

**Map:** Planchas (sheets) 19, 20, 26, 27, 1 : 100,000, from the Instituto Geografico—Agustin Codazzi, Bogata.

The author took the wrong route and ended up here at Durimeina.

# Map 314-1, C. Colon, S.N. de St. Marta, Colombia

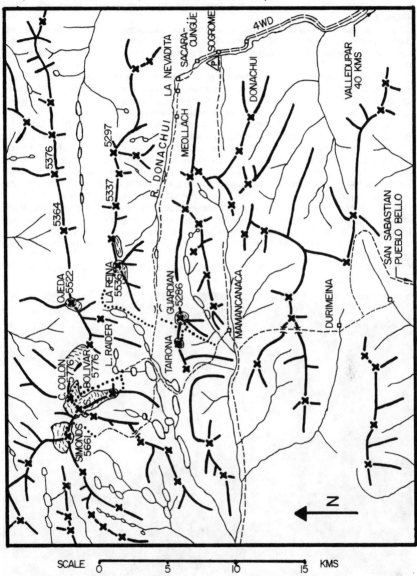

SCALE 0   5   10   15   KMS

# Ritacuba Blanco, S. Nevada Cocuy, Colombia

Located in eastern Colombia and in the Cordillera Oriental, is a small and compact mountain range known as the Sierra Nevada del Cocuy. These mountains are different from many other ranges in Colombia in that they are not volcanic in origin, but consist of metamorphic rock and granite. The highest summit is known as Ritacuba Blanco at 5493 meters.

The higher summits are all snow capped, with the snow line generally at about 4700 or 4800 meters. Glaciers are not large, but some fairly large crevasses do exist, especially around Ritacuba Blanco and Negro.

Most people reach this area via Bogota and by night bus (about a 14 hour ride). The best place to begin walking is from the village of Guican—the last bus stop. In Guican are located 3 small hotels, several restaurants and many stores, where all food needed for climbing can be found.

From Guican, one can approach either the northern or southern sections of the range. From Guican walk uphill on Calle 6 to a trail which eventually joins the road just above a small country school. About 200 meters beyond that point another trail begins on the left, and continues northeast to the area of Ritacuba and the Laguna Grande de Las Verdes.

One may wish to continue following the road and end up at the hacienda called La Esperanza, at the road's end. This is the best way to reach the southern portion of Cocuy.

To give an example of time and distance, the author left Guican in the early morning, walked to a base camp near the lake west of Ritacuba Negro, and climbed Ritacuba Norte in the afternoon. Next morning Blanco was climbed, then a long walk was made to the area of La Esperanza for a second camp. The third day was spent hiking up to Laguna Grande and returning to Guican for lunch. Later that same afternoon he took a bus back to Bogota.

A small party of strong climbers (or solo climber) could leave Guican, climb in the northern sections, then walk and climb south along the western edge of the glaciers to the last high peak in the south, Pan de Azucar, then return to Guican, all in about one week's time.

The dry months are December through March. Crampons and ice ax are definitely needed for safe climbing.

**Map:** Planchas (sheets) 137 and 153, 1 : 100,000, from the Instituto Geografico—Agustin Codazzi, Bogata.

From what is marked Ritacuba North, looking at Ritacuba Negro.

# Map 315-1, Ritacuba Blanco, S.N. Cocuy, Columbia

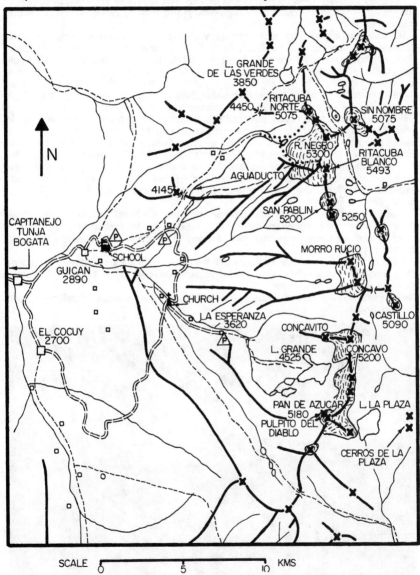

L. GRANDE
DE LAS VERDES
3850

4450

RITACUBA
NORTE
5075

SIN NOMBRE
5075

N

R. NEGRO
5300

RITACUBA
BLANCO
5493

AGUADUCTO

4145

SAN PABLIN
5200          5250

CAPITANEJO
TUNJA
BOGATA

MORRO RUCIO

SCHOOL

GUICAN
2890

CHURCH

CASTILLO
5090

LA ESPERANZA
3620

CONCAVITO

EL COCUY
2700

L. GRANDE
4525

CONCAVO
5200

PAN DE AZUCAR
5180

L. LA PLAZA

PULPITO DEL
DIABLO

CERROS DE LA
PLAZA

SCALE  0          5          10   KMS

## Nevado El Ruiz, Cordillera Central, Colombia

Near the center of Colombia in the Cordillera Central, is a group of volcanic peaks—most of which are high enough to have glaciers at their summits. The highest peak is Nevado El Ruiz at about 5335 meters, followed closely by Tolima at about 5215 meters. These mountains are south and east of Manizales and north of Ibague.

Generally speaking, the snowline comes down to about 4700 or 4800 meters. Besides Ruiz and Tolima, Nevado Santa Isabel has a large enough glacier to require the use of an ice ax and crampons.

The area is not large and the access is easy, at least to Ruiz. To give an example of time and distance, the author boarded the weekly 9 a.m. Sunday bus which leaves the main square in Manizales bound for the refugio on Ruiz. Around mid-day he climbed Ruiz, then walked south along the road as shown. Because of bad weather, the only other peak attempted was Tolima, on the morning of the third day. On the morning of the fourth day, he took an hourly bus from Junta and rode the 16 kms to Ibague. Remember, there are weekend buses only to the refugio on Ruiz, and the road to L. Otun is used exclusively by a few hacienda owners.

Ruiz, via the west face, is very easy and safe to climb—with only one or two crevasses to cross. There are however other much more challenging routes on the mountain. El Cisne is a walkup along the north ridge, which seldom has snow. Santa Isabel can be climbed from the north or westerly routes as well as from Laguna de Otun. El Quindio is generally climbed from the pass marked 4410 meters on the map. Tolima, the newest and most symmetrical of the volcanos, can be approached via the northwest ridge (which has large crevasses), or a route on the west face. According to Luis Fernando Toro of Manizales, the easiest route on Tolima is the southeast face.

In times of good weather, which can be expected in the months of December through about March, it's possible for a strong and determined climber, to do a trip similar to that of the author, but climbing all the five major summits along the way, in about one week. The route from north to south is recommended.

Along this route the way is easy fo find with the exception of the area between Laguna de Otun, across the two lava flows and over two passes marked 4410 and 4205 meters. Take a compass as standard equipment.

**Map:** Planchas (sheets) 206, 225, 244, 1 : 100,000, from the Instituto Geografico—Agustin Codazzi, Bogata.

This is the Refugio, located on the western side of Ruiz, just below the glacier.

## Map 316-1, Ruiz, Cordillera Central, Columbia

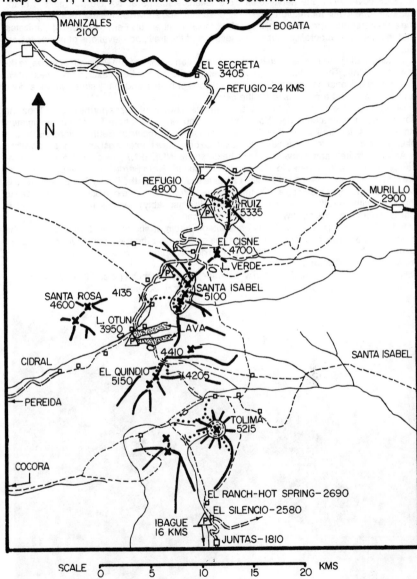

MANIZALES
2100

BOGATA

EL SECRETA
3405

REFUGIO-24 KMS

N

REFUGIO
4800

RUIZ
5335

MURILLO
2900

EL CISNE
4700

L. VERDE

SANTA ROSA
4600

4135

SANTA ISABEL
5100

L. OTUN
3950

LAVA

SANTA ISABEL

CIDRAL

4410

EL QUINDIO
5150

4205

PEREIDA

TOLIMA
5215

COCORA

EL RANCH-HOT SPRING-2690

EL SILENCIO-2580

IBAGUE
16 KMS

JUNTAS-1810

SCALE 0 5 10 15 20 KMS

# Mayor, Nevado Huila, Cord. Central, Colombia

Located in the southwestern part of Colombia and at the southern end of the Cordillera Central, is the Sierra Nevado de Huila, with the highest peak, Pico Mayor, about 5365 meters. This mountain is at the center of a triangle formed by the cities of Popayan, Cali and Neiva.

Good maps of this region are lacking. The ones that are available are only half complete, due to cloud cover when the aerial fotos were taken. Also, the author did not make it to the summit—due to misinformation. The route described and shown on the map is a composite of the author's personal information, that of Colombian climber Luis Fernando Toro of Manizales, and the Institute Geografico maps. The location of the trail and elevations of campsites are approximate.

Getting to the mountain is relatively easy. Buses can be taken from Popayan or Neiva, to the town of La Plata. Then another bus must be taken to the town of Belalcazar, sometimes known as Paez. Belalcazar has one or two small pensions or hotels, and many stores where all food and supplies can be purchased for the climb.

Beyond Belalcazar, traffic is thinner, but still usually two small buses ply the road to Toez and sometimes to Irlanda each day. You'll likely be required to walk from Toez, at approximately Km 20. The actual trail begins near Km 44, at the hacienda known as Berdun. Irlanda is the last place in which to buy food—as beyond this village only a few homes exist and almost no traffic.

At Km 42 there's some kind of building belonging to INDERENA, the government organization protecting national parks in which Huila is included. From Berdun a trail leads up through the rain forest in the direction of the first camping site, known as the Polish Camp. This camp is on the Paramo, or grasslands above the treeline, so from there one can usually find the way to the peaks with little difficulty—assuming visibility is reasonably good. The normal base camp is Camp Piedras, on the northwest side of the ice cap.

From Toez, where your walk will undoubtedly begin, it should take 5 or 6 days for the round-trip. For Huila and for all the mountains of Colombia the best months for climbing are December through about March. However, rain gear should always be part of your equipment, as well as crampons and ice ax.

**Map:** Maps are poor—half covered with clouds, but see Plancha (sheet) 321-IV-B and D, 1 : 25,000, from the Instituto Geografico—Agustin Codazzi, Bogata.

In the distance is N. Huila, from the road just below Toez.

# Map 317-1, Mayor, Nevado Huila, Colombia

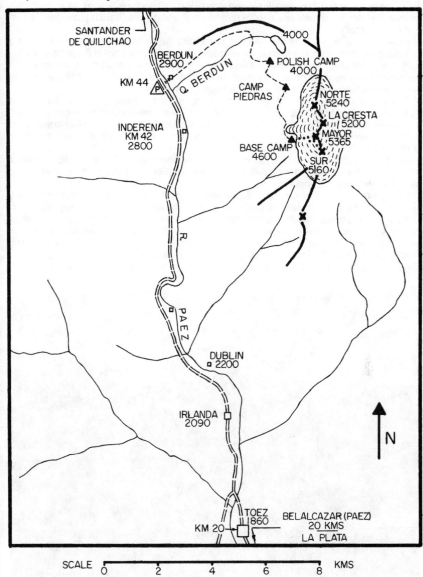

# Volcan Purace, Cordillera Central, Colombia

In the southwest part of Colombia, and in the extreme southern end of the Cordillera Central, is located a number of volcanos, some of which are still active. This band of volcanic activity is an extension of those volcanos that are so prominent just to the south, in Ecuador. In this section, between Pasto and Popayan, the highest and best known mountain is Volcan de Purace, reaching a height of 4756 meters.

For many years this mountain has been active and has become famous as a result. It is located directly east of Popayan, a tourist center itself, and on clear days is highly visible from that city's center.

Because of its activity and its nearness to this population center Purace has become a national park. The mountains shown on this map include only about half of the national park.

Purace is not a high mountain and it doesn't even have permanent snow on its summit, but because it's very near the main north-south tourist route and the Pan American Highway, it has become a popular climb with native and foreign tourists alike.

Reaching Pilimbala and the beginning of the trail to Purace's summit, is very easy. From Popayan there are buses leaving and passing near the mountain every hour, most of which travel to the town of La Plata, on the mountain's eastern slopes. Ask the bus driver to stop at the intersection known as Cruz Mina. From there one will have to walk the 2 kms or so to the resort of Pilimbala.

Pilimbala is not a village, but a small tourist resort, with hot springs. There are cabins, hotel, a restaurant and a building housing national park people. For additional information about the hike, ask someone at Pilimbala.

The beginning of the trail is obscure for the first 400 or 500 meters. Hikers must simply walk up through some cow pastures and past one small farmhouse. As of 1980, one was required to climb over 4 or 5 fences before the two-meter-wide trail was reached. That should change as time goes on. Also in 1980, there were two buildings of some kind under construction at 3760 and 4060 meters. The trail is very good all the way to the summit and is an easy one day climb even from Popayan. Buy your food before reaching Pilimbala.

**Map:** See simple map of Parque National Purace, from Tourist Office, Popayan.

From about Cruz Mina we see the summit of Volcan Purace.

# Map 318-1, Purace, Cordillera Central, Colombia

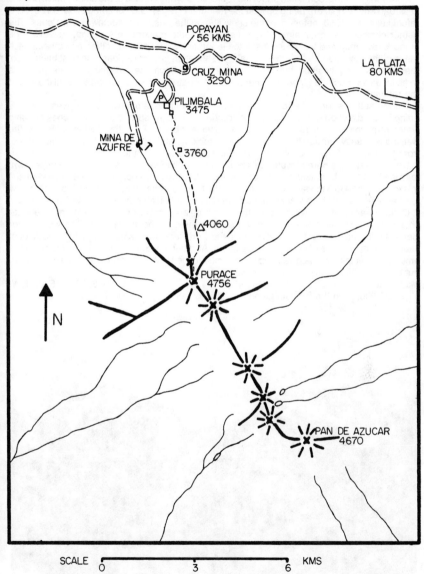

POPAYAN
56 KMS

LA PLATA
80 KMS

CRUZ MINA
3290

PILIMBALA
3475

MINA DE
AZUFRE

3760

△4060

PURACE
4756

N

PAN DE AZUCAR
4670

SCALE 0          3          6    KMS

## Cayambe, Cordillera Real, Ecuador

The third highest summit in Ecuador is Cayambe rising to 5840 meters. Cayambe is located 18 kms east of Cayambe town, which in turn is about 86 kms to the northeast of Quito, Ecuadors capital city. Because of its easterly position and being so near the Amazon Basin, Cayambe receives heavy precipitation, resulting in a large glacier ice cap.

There will be some confusion about the routes to Cayambe since at the time of this writing, a new road and refugio are being built on the mountain (1981). Due for completion in 1981, is a refugio at about 4660 meters near the snow line on the western or southwestern slopes. The author climbed the mountain in 1972, using the route marked on the map. However, the author's own map and that of the Instituto Geografico Militar seem to differ, and other sketch maps of the new road and hut do not make the situation any more clear. The best thing to do, therefore, is to inquire about the new route in the city of Cayambe. One thing for sure, the route to as far as the Hacienda Monjas is the ruta normal (late word is that a road goes all the way to the refugio).

On the author's climb, he found many homes of Indians, along with many livestock trails going in the direction of the mountain. Also, there are many small canals or ditches bringing water from the mountain to the pastures in the valleys below. From the Hacienda Monjas, the walking was easy through the "puno" grass. It took the author 3 days for the climb round-trip, from the town of Cayambe, where he had purchased food for the trip.

Up until 1980, one normal route was via the town of Olmedo, 10 kms north of Cayambe town, then the Hacienda La Chimba, La Dormida, and to the peak via a northerly route. Reports insist this route takes 4 to 5 days—a bit longer than the Monjas route. With the completion of the new road and refugio, it'll be a weekend trip from Quito—at least for those with 4WD machines.

On the peak itself, one will need all the normal ice and snow climbing equipment. The route shown is heavily crevassed, but finding a route through should be easy. The weather for Cayambe is similar to that of other peaks in the Cordillera Real, in that June, July and August seem to be the months of heaviest precipitation. All other months are about the same as for the amount of precipitation received. From Cayambe to the H. Monjas there is no public transport, but getting rides is easy, at least part way.

**Map:** See maps 3994-11-SW and SE, 4094-111-SW, 4093-IV-NW, and 3993-1-NE and NW, all 1 : 25,000, from the Instituto Geografia Militar, Quito.

Cayambe is sometimes visible in the early morning (southwest slope).

Map 319-1, Cayambe, Cordillera Real, Ecuador

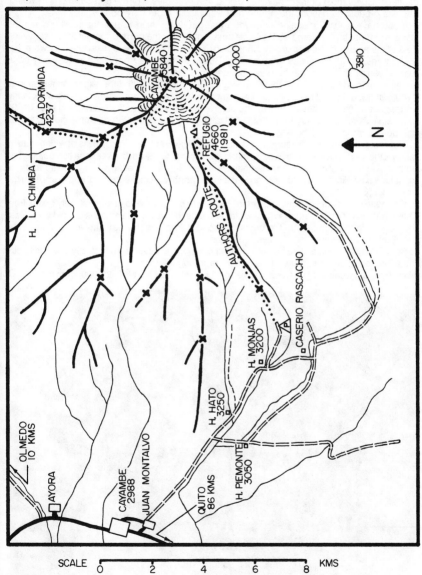

CAYAMBE 5840

LA DORMIDA 4237

H. LA CHIMBA

4000

3810

REFUGIO 4660 (1981)

AUTHORS' ROUTE

CASERIO RASCACHO

H. MONJAS 3200

H. HATO 3250

H. PIEMONTE 3050

OLMEDO 10 KMS

AYORA

CAYAMBE 2988

JUAN MONTALVO

QUITO 86 KMS

N

SCALE    0    2    4    6    8    KMS

## Antisana, Cordillera Real, Ecuador

The fourth highest mountain in Ecuador is Antisana at 5753 meters. This mountain is a volcano, but it's inactive and greatly eroded. Antisana is extensively glaciated and is said to have the largest snow and ice mass in the country.

There are two ways to reach the mountain. The usual way is via Pintag and the Hacienda Antisana. But keep in mind this way is the normal route for the people living and working in the capital of Quito, most of them have access to 4WD vehicles. For the person who is traveling, and using public transport, the northern or Papallacta route may be best.

If you have a 4WD machine then you must get permission to use the road beyond the Hacienda Pinantura, located about 8 kms past Pintag. For the permit, contact the Associacion de Andinismo de Pinchincha or any other "club andino" in Quito. If you're on foot, be aware that public transport goes only as far as Pintag. Buses arrive there from Quito about every hour. Also, if you're on foot, a permit is not needed for the trip.

The road from Pintag is rough all the way to the H. Antisana and the experiment station at 4180 meters, but small trucks make it all right. From the experiment station simply walk to the northeast and make a base camp in one of several locations near the snowline at about 4600 meters. Walking all the way from Pintag will take 4 or 5 days (round-trip), but some short rides can be expected along the way.

The route to the summit requires passing some large crevasses regardless of which route is taken. One guidebook says to head southeast and climb to the col between the two peaks. The author tried this route, but was turned back on five different probes. Probably a safer route, at least for a solo climber, would be to go to the left or north, and make the final approach from the north face.

For those using public transport, get to Papallacta by taking one of several daily buses from Quito, but get off at the Luguna Papallacta, and take the trail which crosses the old lava. Near the second lake route-find up the grassy slope to the south. The way shown is the author's. using this route takes about 3 days round-trip.

Both Pintag and Papallacta have a hotel or pension, and several small stores in which to buy food. Wettest months in the C. Real are June through August.

**Map:** Pintag, Papallacta, La Cocha, Antisana, Lago Micacocha, all 1 : 25,000, from the IGM, Quit

This is the crevasse scarred western side of Antisana.

## Map 320-1, Antisana, Cord. Real, Ecuador

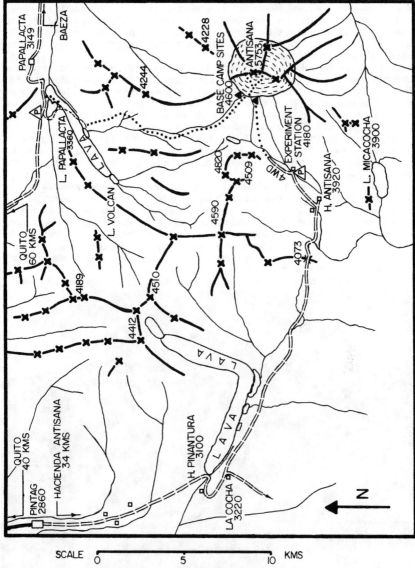

## Tungurahua, Cordillera Real, Ecuador

Of the eight mountains in Ecuador included in this book, the one with the lowest elevation and the smallest amount of ice and snow at the summit, is Tungurahua with an altitude of 5087 meters.

Tungurahua is considered an active volcano because of the strong smell of sulfur coming from fumerals at the crater rim. It's one of the most symmetrical cones in Ecuador. Only at the very summit does one encounter ice and snow and small glaciers. This mountain is definitely a walk-up, but there are some difficult and challenging routes on the upper east face, where is located a small ice fall. Using the normal route, climbers can generally get by without crampons and ice ax, but there is a slope at the very summit where this equipment could come in handy for some people. June, July and August seem to have the most rain, with all other months about equal in the amount of precipitation.

Getting to Tungurahua is easiest of all the mountains in Ecuador. There are many buses each day using the road between Rio Bamba and Banos, and between Ambato and Banos. From the center of Banos, walk about 2 kms west on the main highway to where the police control is located (as of 1980 this was abandoned but may be used periodically). From the police control, a dirt road veers to the southeast, and about 100 meters away is a tall sign pointing out the trail and mentioning the refugio on the mountain.

From that narrow dirt road the trail begins and eventually ends at the summit. It generally follows the prominent east-northeast ridge, so it's very important to have a water bottle full when beginning. The relatively low elevation makes it a hot and exhausting climb up to the refugio.

At about 2475 meters, in an area heavily farmed, is a house whose owner collects a fee from everyone carrying a pack up the mountain. This is said to be a charge for using the refugio. If it's a day climb only, no fee is charged. Above about 2600 meters, remember to follow the red painted trees or fence posts, as that marks the right trail to the shelter. Just at treeline is located the Refugio Nicolas Martinez, at 3835 meters. It has a stove with fuel, and can sleep 10 to 15 people. Above the hut the trail zigzags up the same ridge to the summit crater.

In the valley, the town of Banos is a fine place to spend some time. Banos has many inexpensive hotels and hot thermal springs.

**Map:**  The yet-to-be-completed map is NIV-II, 3989-III, 1 : 50,000, from the IGM, Quito.

The summit of Tungurahua from the Refugio Nicolas Martinez, at 3835 meters.

## Map 321-1, Tungurahua, Cord. Real, Ecuador

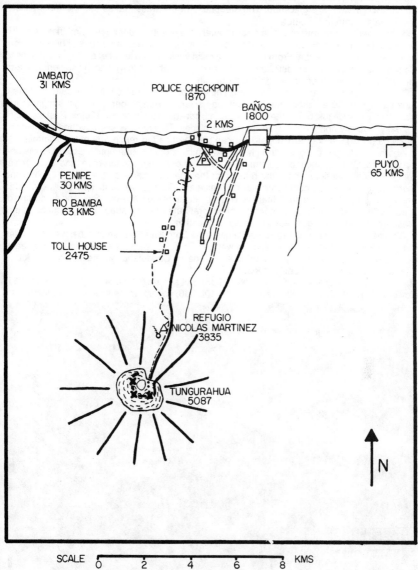

AMBATO
31 KMS

POLICE CHECKPOINT
1870

BAÑOS
1800

2 KMS

PUYO
65 KMS

PENIPE
30 KMS

RIO BAMBA
63 KMS

TOLL HOUSE
2475

REFUGIO
NICOLAS MARTINEZ
3835

TUNGURAHUA
5087

N

SCALE   0    2    4    6    8   KMS

## El Altar, Cordillera Real, Ecuador

If one were to choose the most spectacular, impressive and challenging mountain in Ecuador, it would have to be El Altar. This mountain's highest peak, Obispo, is 5465 meters (various other altitudes are sometimes used). This is the remains of an old volcano which blew its top some time in the distant past. Today there remains the circular crater rim with the western section removed, and inside, a lake by the name of Laguna Amarillo. All areas above about 4700 meters are glaciated. The steepness of the walls makes this the most difficult mountain to climb in Ecuador.

There are two main routes of approach to Altar. The one the author used, and the one which seems to be the normal route, is from Penipe. Penipe can be reached by bus or hitching, from either Banos or Rio Bamba. From Penipe one must walk (or with luck get a ride), the 10 kms to Candelaria. About 1½ kms past Candelaria turn to the northeast ½ a km to the hacienda. There the trail begins which ends next to the mountain.

This is a very good and well used path. The only place the trail is hard to locate is where it runs through pastures about one km past the hacienda. Remember that it goes high on the west-facing hillside just below the small waterfall, but above the cultivated fields. Past that point it's easy to follow and there's water at various places. This route is used by those wanting to climb peaks on the northern slopes, but can also be used to reach any of the summits.

Another route and the one normally used when climbers are attempting Obispo, is the one via Quimag, Chanag and the Hacienda Sali. The author did not use this route and is unfamiliar with the middle sections; that's the reason for the question marks on the map. Keep in mind there are no good maps of the area east of Penipe and Quimag, so locations of trails and roads are approximate only. For sure, there is a road to as far as the Hacienda Sali, and some kind of a trail to the "vaqueria", which consists of several huts used by shepherds pasturing cattle. Make inquiries as you get near the areas in question.

Weather-wise, Altar, as with all the summits in the Cordillera Real, seems to have an endless rainy season, but June—August are the wettest. For food buying, Penipe and Quimag each have several small stores, and there's even one in Candelaria, where the author found adequate, but poor selections of food.

**Map:** IGM maps are not-yet-completed (1983), but see magazine **Andinismo,** Volumen I, Noviembre 1979. The Chimborazo map, 1 : 100,000, covers areas west of Candelaria.

Altar from the west. It's a giant crater, with this (western) side blown out.

# Map 322-1, Altar, Cordillera Real, Ecuador

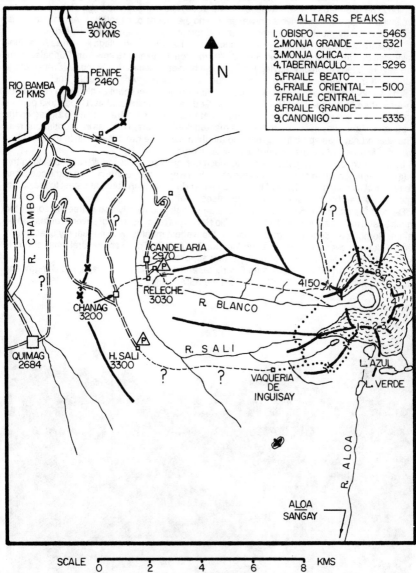

ALTARS PEAKS

1. OBISPO ————— 5465
2. MONJA GRANDE ——— 5321
3. MONJA CHICA ————
4. TABERNACULO ——— 5296
5. FRAILE BEATO————
6. FRAILE ORIENTAL——— 5100
7. FRAILE CENTRAL ———
8. FRAILE GRANDE————
9. CANONIGO ———— 5335

N

BAÑOS
30 KMS

PENIPE
2460

RIO BAMBA
21 KMS

R. CHAMBO

?

?

CANDELARIA
2970
P

RELECHE
3030

R. BLANCO

CHANAG
3200

P

QUIMAG
2684

H. SALI
3300

R. SALI

?          ?

VAQUERIA
DE
INGUISAY

4150

9 8
7 6 5
4
1 2 3

L. AZUL

L. VERDE

?

R. ALOA

ALOA
SANGAY

SCALE  0    2    4    6    8    KMS

## Sangay, Cordillera Real, Ecuador

Of all the high mountains in Ecuador, the live and very active volcano known as Sangay, is the most isolated and most difficult to reach. The elevation of Sangay is generally placed at 5230 meters, but during the late 1970's and early '80's, activity has undoubtedly changed that by a few meters.

One of the major obstacles to climbing Sangay, is that there are no real good maps of the region. The two maps that are available of the area, Rio Sangay and Lago Tinguichaca, are preliminary maps showing rivers and lakes, but no elevations or vegetation. Another factor is, the area is pretty much surrounded by natural forests and is all but uninhabited.

There are two access routes, both beginning at the hacienda and village known as Aloa. Aloa is located 38 kms southeast of Rio Bamba, 20 kms from Licto and 15 kms from Pungala. There are several buses each day leaving Rio Bamba which end their runs at Pungala. From there to Aloa, one must walk, hitch hike, or get a ride on a hacienda vehicle or milk truck.

The author's experience went like this. The first morning was spent getting from Rio Bamba to Aloa, then he crossed the Rio Aloa and walked east on a very bad 4WD road to a pasture area above which is a stream and a series of waterfalls. There the trail begins to zigzag up the mountain. Camp was set up near the pass marked 4065 meters. This was in a continuous rain. The second day was spent in the tent and the third day hope ran out—again in the rain. This was the first part of August, one of the rainier months.

In times of good visibility, there's not so much of a problem. One should continue along this trail to a hacienda cabin or shelter located about half way to the mountain. This same cabin can be reached by taking a trail from Aloa to the Hacienda Eten, then south and east to the cabin. The route taken by the author is the most used one.

Beyond the cabin no trails exist, but the area is high and mostly above treeline so not too much bushwhacking is involved. Once the Rio Sangay is reached, one of several routes can be taken. Remember, June through August are the wettest months, with no real dry season any time. Take rain gear and compass and food for 7 or 8 days. There are several small shops in Aloa, but Rio Bamba is the best place to buy supplies.

**Map:** See the 1 : 50,000 scale map Guamote, and two preliminary maps, Rio Sangay and Lago Tinguichaca, both 1 : 50,000 all from the IGM, Quito.

This is the hacienda and village of Aloa, to the northwest of Sangay.

# Map 323-1, Sangay, Cordillera Real, Ecuador

N

SANGAY
5230

R. SANGAY

H. CABIN

HUAMBOYA

4065

ALOA
3173

CANAL

MELÁN

CANAL

H. ETEN

RIO BAMBA – 38 KMS
PUNGALA – 15 KMS
LICTO – 20 KMS
R. ALOA

SCALE  0        5        10  KMS

## Cotopaxi, Cordillera Real, Ecuador

After Chimborazo, the highest mountain in Ecuador is Cotopaxi, with an altitude of 5897 meters. Like all summits in Ecuador over about 5000 meters, Cotopaxi is snow capped and has some sizeable glaciers. This mountain's glaciers are big enough to have crevasses, but the "ruta normal" is a fairly safe climb, even for solo climbers. The normal route bypasses most of the heavily crevassed areas.

Cotopaxi is located about 80 kms south of the capital city of Quito, in central Ecuador, and about 20 kms east of the Pan American Highway. This makes access to the mountain simple. Buses can be taken from anywhere on the Pan American Highway to the junction west of Cotopaxi, as shown on the map. From there a good dirt road heads northeast in the direction of Laguna de Limpiopungu and the Cotopaxi Turnoff. There's usually enough traffic on this section of road to get a fast lift with the thumb.

From the Cotopaxi Turnoff to the old refugio is about 8 kms. This old refugio is useless as a shelter, but the new refugio, known simply as Refugio del Cotopaxi, is well equipped with beds, stove, cooking facilities, and a watchman. Payment is required for the use of this hut.

Most people spend a night in the new refugio before making the summit climb on the second day. With one's own vehicle, it can be climbed in two short days or one long day from Quito. Needless to say, an ice ax and crampons are required. If you're planning to use the refugio for sleeping, it might be best to do the climb during the week, as on weekends it can be crowded. Cotopaxi is perhaps the most climbed mountain in Ecuador. Everyone is welcome to use the cooking facilities at the refugio, but there's no food available there.

If you're coming out of Quito, buy your food there. However, any small store on the highway has the kinds of food that are needed for this short climb.

The Andes of Ecuador are moist mountains for the entire year, but for Cotopaxi which is centrally located in the highlands, June and July are generally the driest months. If additional maps are desired, contact the Instituto Geografico Militar in Quito. English language guidebooks are also available in Quito.

**Map:**   Sincholagua and Cotopaxi, both 1 : 50,000, from the IGM, Quito.

The normal route to the summit of Cotopaxi goes below this large outcrop.

## Map 324-1, Cotopaxi, Cordillera Real, Ecuador

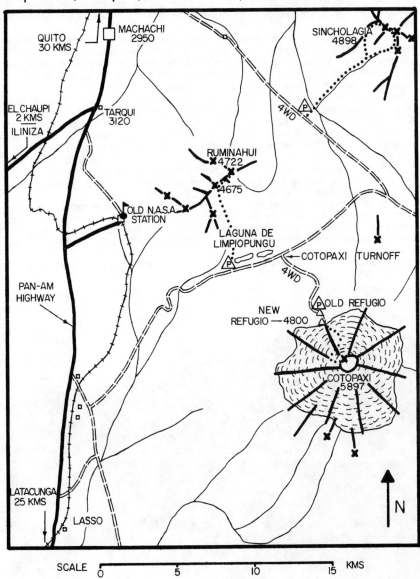

QUITO
30 KMS

MACHACHI
2950

SINCHOLAGUA
4898

EL CHAUPI
2 KMS
ILINIZA

TARQUI
3120

4WD

RUMINAHUI
4722

4675

OLD N.A.S.A.
STATION

LAGUNA DE
LIMPIOPUNGU

← COTOPAXI TURNOFF

PAN-AM
HIGHWAY

4WD

OLD REFUGIO

NEW
REFUGIO — 4800

COTOPAXI
5897

LATACUNGA
25 KMS

LASSO

N

SCALE

0     5     10     15     KMS

# Iliniza Sur, Cordillera Occidental, Ecuador

Less than a one hour drive south of Quito stands the twin summits of Iliniza. The highest of the two is Iliniza Sur reaching to 5305 meters. Iliniza Norte is 5116 meters. This mountain is an old volcano, with more erosion than most of Ecuador's mountains.

The snowline on Iliniza is around 4900 meters. Iliniza Sur is capped with a glacier and has many small, but steep ice falls. Iliniza North has no glaciers, but does have some permanent snow. Normally, the north peak is a rock scramble, while the south peak is a snow and ice climb.

Getting to Iliniza is perhaps easier than to any other big mountain in Ecuador. The distance from Quito is only about 40 airline kms, and there's a road to near the refugio. From a point 6 kms south of the city of Machachi, called Jambeli Bridge, drive or hitch hike southwest to the village of El Chaupi. There's not much at this village except two small stores, but that's where the author bought all the food he used on the mountain.

From El Chaupi, take the dirt road west past the church about 3 kms, where another road turns south and enters the large grove of pine trees. Amongst these pine trees is the Hacienda El Refugio. From this hacienda, continue up the road to the southwest. One can see the road higher on the mountain as it switchbacks up a prominent ridge. Most vehicles can be driven to an altitude of about 4300 meters, then it's a 4WD road to where the trail begins. It's about a one hour walk from the end of the road to the Refugio Nuevos Horizontes, at 4775 meters. This shelter is large enough to sleep 25 or 30 people, but has no beds or stoves. It's also free! (As one walks along the 4WD portion of the road to the refugio, small trees can be seen at about 4300 meters—the highest the author has seen in Ecuador).

Don't underestimate these two peaks. The rhime build-up on the eastern slopes of Iliniza Sur was the worst the author has seen, making climbing both difficult and dangerous. There is no walk-up route on Iliniza Sur, which compares with some of Altars Peaks in difficulty. Iliniza Norte is an easier climb. If you've got a vehicle, it's a one day climb from Quito, but many people spend a night on the mountain.

The weather patterns on Iliniza is the same as for Quito, with the two driest months being June and July.

**Map:** Machachi, 1 : 100,000, from the Instituto Geografico Malitar, Quito.

The Refugio Nuevos Horizontes on the north side of Iliniza Sur.

# Map 325-1, Iliniza, Cord. Occidental, Ecuador

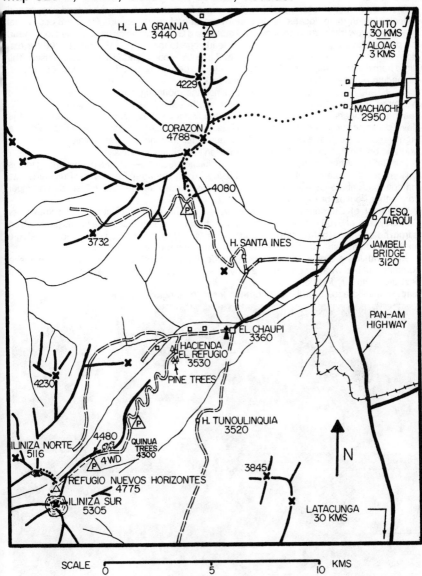

H. LA GRANJA
3440

QUITO
30 KMS
ALOAG
3 KMS

4229

MACHACHI
2950

CORAZON
4788

4080

ESQ.
TARQUI

H. SANTA INES

3732

JAMBELI
BRIDGE
3120

EL CHAUPI
3360

PAN-AM
HIGHWAY

HACIENDA
EL REFUGIO
3530

PINE TREES

4230

H. TUNOULINQUIA
3520

4480

QUINUA
TREES
4300

ILINIZA NORTE
5116

4 WD

N

REFUGIO NUEVOS HORIZONTES
4775

3845

ILINIZA SUR
5305

LATACUNGA
30 KMS

SCALE    0          5          10   KMS

# Chimborazo, Cordillera Occidental, Ecuador

The highest mountain in Ecuador and one of the most famous summits in South America, is Chimborazo at 6310 meters.

Chimborazo is a volcano which has not shown activity in recorded history. Because of its elevation and location (in wet and humid Ecuador), it possesses a large ice cap with many glaciers.

There are now two "ruta normals" to the summit. First, there's the time-honored Pogyos and Refugio Fabian route, located on the northwest side of the mountain. There are occasional buses and a few trucks running between Ambato and Guaranda which can be taken to, or near, the pass called Pogyos. From there a trail leads one to the Refugio Fabian at 4700 meters. However, this hut is in very poor condition and a tent is recommended if this route is used. The climb from the hut to the summit takes one very long day. Climbing this route takes 2 or 3 days, depending on one's physical condition and luck in getting a ride to the area.

As of 1980, to celebrate the 100 years since the mountain was first climbed by Edward Whymper, a new hut was constructed on the southwest slopes at 4900 meters. This refugio bearing Whympers name, is on the route of the first ascent. By using this second route the elevation gained between hut and summit is less than on the northwest route, but it's said to be slightly more difficult and dangerous. One must pass through a crevasse field on this route, whereas on the Fabian route, the author doesn't recall any crevasses.

The Refugio Whymper has beds, stoves and kitchen facilities—all for a price. Getting to this hut may be a bit more difficult, as the traffic using the road between Pogyos and Pulingui is less than on the Ambato-Guaranda road. As a last resort one can walk to the Refugio Whymper from either Pogyos or Pulingui.

Northeast of Chimborazo is another very old and eroded volcanic peak known as Carihuayrazo, at 5106 meters. The map shows the normal approach route to this peak, which is from near Pogyos, or from the east and Mocha. One map seen by the author shows a refugio on the southeast side of this mountain, but that has not been confirmed.

June and July are generally considered to be the best months for climbing either of these summits, but bad weather can come at any time. The cities of Rio Bamba and Ambato are the best places to buy food and supplies.

**Map:** Chimborazo, 1 : 100,000, from the Instituto Geografico Militar, Quito.

This is the old Refugio Fabian as it was in 1972 (It's unuseable today).

# Map 326-1, Chimborazo, Cord. Occidental, Ecuador

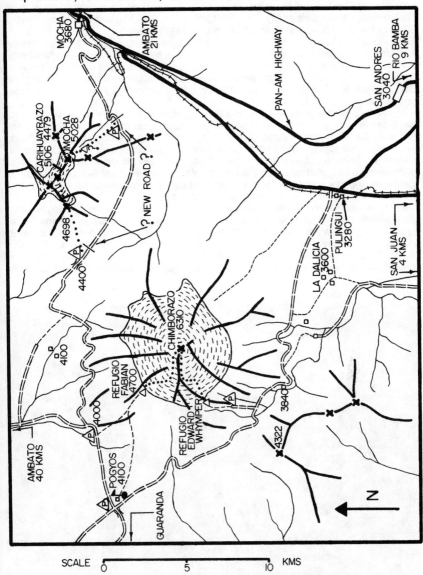

# Volcan Wolf, Galapagos Islands, Ecuador

The Galapagos Islands, or the Archipelago de Colon, as it's known in Ecuador, lies 1000 kms due west of Guayaquil on the equator. The islands are all volcanic in origin, with the older and more eroded ones in the east and the newer volcanos to the west and northwest. The volcano on Pinta is the most active, but several others are considered semi-active.

The higher mountains are mostly on the largest island, Isabela. This island makes up about half of the total land area of the group, and has 5 volcanos. The highest peak is Volcon Wolf, 1707 meters. Cerro Azul is nearly as high at 1689 meters. The third highest summit is on the island of Fernandina, and is called La Cumbre, at 1494 meters.

Getting to the Galapagos Islands isn't too difficult, but getting around from one island to another is. Apparently there are two ships or boats sailing between Guayaquil and the islands. These ships, carrying passengers and cargo, make the rounds to the different islands—to deliver goods and pick up products (such as cattle). Presumably they stop at the 5 main ports: Baquerizo, on San Cristobal; Seymour, on Baltra; Villamil, on Isabela; Flores, on Santa Maria; and Puerto Ayora, on Santa Cruz.

In just the past few years with the increase in tourism, airlines have established several flights a week to service the island of Baltra. Most tourists end up on Santa Cruz after the flight, and at the Darwin Research Station. It's at the port (near the research station) called Puerto Ayora, that boats taking tourists out to the different islands dock. Some are very expensive, while other "fishing type boats" are cheaper. The bay at P. Ayora is known as Academy Bay.

The island of San Cristobal seems to have most of the government offices, as well as the only real live water on the islands. In the past there have been penal colonies on San Cristobal, and at Alemania on Isabela—but the latter was closed in 1958.

Once in the islands one can live relatively inexpensively, especially if you're willing to camp. Most food should be brought from the mainland, but if you're on San Cristobal or Santa Maria, fruits and vegetables are abundant and cheap. Baltra and Santa Cruz are very expensive, because of the many tourists.

**Map:**  Plans are to make 1 : 25,000, 50,000, and 100,000, scale maps of the Galapagos Islands, but now the best maps are in the book, **Galapagos Guide** (English) (see in rear of this book).

From Isla Fernandina looking at Volcan Darwin on Isla Isabela.

Map 327-3, Wolf, Galapagos Islands, Ecuador

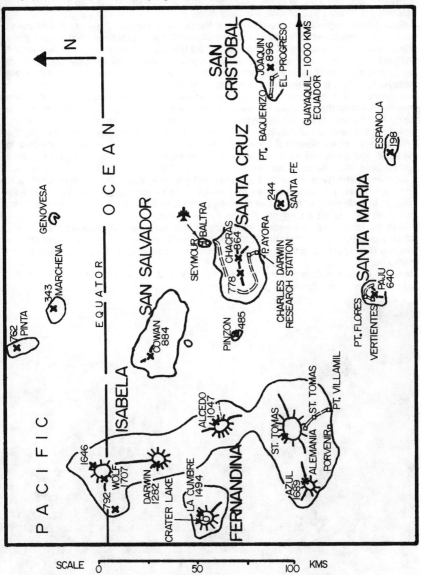

# Champara, Cordillera Blanca, Peru

Included on this map is the Cordilleras Rosco and the extreme northern end of the Cordillera Blanca. "Rosco" is the name more commonly known is climbing circles, but that used on the IGM maps in Peru is "Pacra." Regardless of the name, this small group of peaks is the most northerly of Peru's snow-capped summits.

Many people would classify Rosco as part of the Cordillera Blanca, but there is a lengthy gap between Rosco and the Champara Group. Both groups included on this map are made up of essentially the same type of rock, mostly granite.

Getting to this region is very easy, at least to the Champara Group. There are several buses each day running between Huaras, the center of government and activity along the Cordillera Blanca, and the coastal city of Chimbote. Get off the bus at Yuramarca, then wait for still another bus or truck heading in the direction of Corongo—if the Rosco is your destination. From Corongo take the trail to Aco and Cusca, then up the quebrada (or canyon), to the area of the Laguna Rutu. This is where most base camps are set up.

Since the 1970 earthquake, the route to the Champara Peaks has been altered a bit. At one time the trail along the aquaducto above Santa Rosa was used to reach the lakes and basin to the north of Champara, but the quake broke the aquaducto leaving that trail high, dry and hot. Now it's best to walk or catch a ride to a place called Ranhuas. From there a trail winds up the mountain to some shepherd huts called Tayabamba. Then another trail leads over the pass to the south and down into the upper lakes basin. Apparently, this is the route used to drive grazing animals to the high pastures.

Another possibility is to go to the Hacienda Mirasanta, and follow another aquaducto upstream. However, the author was told there's a 450 meter long tunnel one must walk through, in knee deep water, before reaching the high basin. Actually, the route from Santa Rosa isn't bad, but it's a long, hot climb to the first water.

From Yuramarca, better plan on at least 4 or 5 days to reach either Champara or Rosco, do a climb, and return. As usual, the dry months are May to September. And the best places to buy food are Huaraz and Chimbote. Also, be prepared for some difficult climbing with ice ax and crampons.

**Map:** Pallasca and Corongo, 1 : 100,000, from the Instituto Geografico Militar, 1190 Av. Aramburu, San Isidro (barrio), Lima.

The snows of Champara can just be seen from the region of the tunnel near Santa R.

# Map 328-1, Champara, Cordillera Blanca, Peru

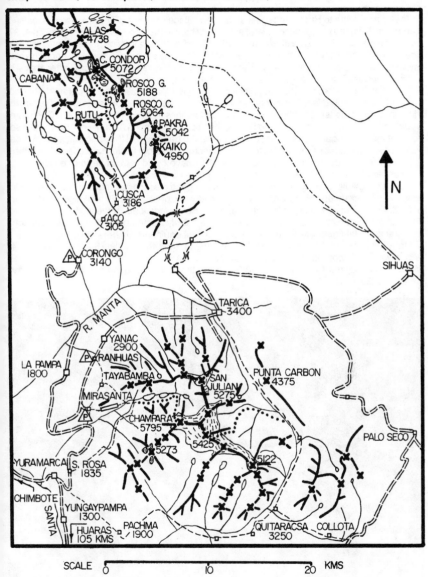

N

ALAS
4738

C. CONDOR
5072

CABANA

ROSCO G.
5188

ROSCO C.
5064

L. RUTU

PAKRA
5042

KAIKO
4950

CUSCA
3186

ACO
3105

CORONGO
3140

SIHUAS

R. MANTA

TARICA
3400

YANAC
2900

PARANHUAS

LA PAMPA
1800

TAYABAMBA

PUNTA CARBON
4375

MIRASANTA

SAN
JULIAN
5275

CHAMPARA
5795

5425

PALO SECO

5273

5122

YURAMARCA

S. ROSA
1835

CHIMBOTE

YUNGAYPAMPA
1300

PACHMA
1900

QUITARACSA
3250

COLLOTA

SANTA

HUARAS
105 KMS

SCALE    0            10           20    KMS

## Huandoy, Cordillera Blanca, Peru

This is the second in the series of maps covering the Cordillera Blanca. Well known areas and mountains included on this map are Canon de Pato, Alpamayo, Huandoy, and Lakes Llanganuco and Peron, and the new village of Yungay.

The highest mountain in this section in Huandoy, 6395 meters. If it weren't for the presence of Huascaran, just south of the Llanganuco Lakes, Huandoy would undoubtedly be much better known.

The normal route to Huandoy begins at the new village of Yungay. There are trucks leaving Yungay daily for the Llanganuco Lakes, and sometimes to the pass just beyond, marked 4737 meters on the map. There are also many tourists heading that way which makes it easy to get a ride; if you're alone or if your group is small. Not far from the upper lake, turn left, or northwest, and walk up the slope, as shown. The difficult part is in reaching the col, after that it's straight-forward. Plan on a 4 or 5 day outing from Yungay.

Probably the best known mountain included here is Alpamaya. This is a pyramid-shaped peak, with steep fluted faces and knife-edged ridges—a good prize for any climber. Getting to Alpamayo is a more lengthy hike than to most other peaks in the Cordillera Blanca. One route would be to begin at Caraz, walking to Banos, then up the Quebrada Alpamayo. One could also begin at the Hacienda Colcas, or at Los Cedros, at the beginning of the spectacular Canon de Pato, a canyon perhaps unrivaled in the world. Once in the upper basin, the western face, then the south ridge is the normal route. Climbing Alpamayo could take close to one week.

Most climbers and trekkers visiting the region make Huaraz their headquarters. Huaraz is at a relatively high elevation for acclimatizing, and is a good place to buy maps and books and to visit with other climbers. Huaraz has cheap, as well as expensive hotels, and a good selection of food. For information, stop at the 5th floor of the Hotel Barcelona, or the tourist office, or the office of the Huascaran National Park. May through early September is the climbing season. Mountains on this map are for experienced and well equipped climbers only.

Many trekkers walk from Yungay, to the Llanganuco lakes, then circling the Huandoy Massif, and down the Quebrada Santa Cruz to Caraz.

**Map:** Corongo and Carhuas, 1 : 100,000, from the Instituto Geografico Militar, 1190 Av. Aramburu, San Isidro (barrio), Lima.

One of many fluted peaks seen just above Huaraz. This is Chinchey (Map 331).

# Map 329-1, Huandoy, Cordillera Blanca, Peru

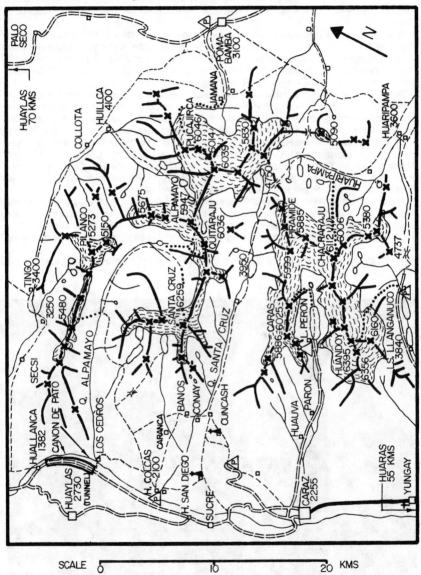

SCALE 0        10        20   KMS

## Huascaran, Cordillera Blanca, Peru

This third map in the series of five covering the Cordillera Blanca, includes the central region of the range. Included here is the highest summit in all of Peru, Huascaran, 6768 meters. It has twin summits with the south peak being the highest. The north peak is 6654 meters. Huascaran is composed of the same type of rock as the rest of the range, mainly metamorphic and granite.

Despite its elevation, Huascaran is one of the easier mountains to climb in the entire cordillera. However, it does have many crevasses which make it an interesting but hazardous climb.

The normal route to the summit is from the west face and the villages of Mancos and Musho. There are many buses on the main road running up and down the Rio Santa Valley, so it's easy to reach Mancos. Hitching is also very good. From Mancos you'll likely have to go on foot to Musho, then it's a well-beaten path the rest of the way to base camp at about 4600 meters. Anyone in Musho can direct you to the right trail.

Because of the altitude, it's necessary to make at least one camp on snow—for some groups it must be done with two snow camps. From Mancos it's about 4 or 5 days to the top and return. Last minute supplies can be found in Mancos or Musho, but it's best to stock up before leaving Huaraz. With so many groups on the mountain there's a well beaten path in the snow to the top.

Other high peaks include Hualcan, 6125 meters. This is considered an easy climb, but there is the threat of crevasses. It is usually climbed from the Hacienda Copa Chica, located north of Marcara. One will likely have to walk from the main highway to the top. Cerro Copa at the southeastern end of the same snow mass, has an altitude of 6188 meters. It too can be climbed from the village of Marcara and the Hacienda Copa Grande.

The city of Huaraz is not far south of the area covered by this map; that's the place to buy your supplies, get information from other climbers at the Hotel Barcelona, and maps at the Huascaran National Park office or tourist office. Huaraz has lots of cheap hotels and good food. Make your visit to these mountains in May through the beginning of September for the best climbing weather.

**Map:** Carhuaz and Huari, 1 : 100,000, from the IGM, 1190, Av. Aramburu, San Isidro (barrio), Lima.

Musho is the jumping off point for the trail up to Huascaran.

## Map 330-1, Huascaran, Cordillera Blanca, Peru

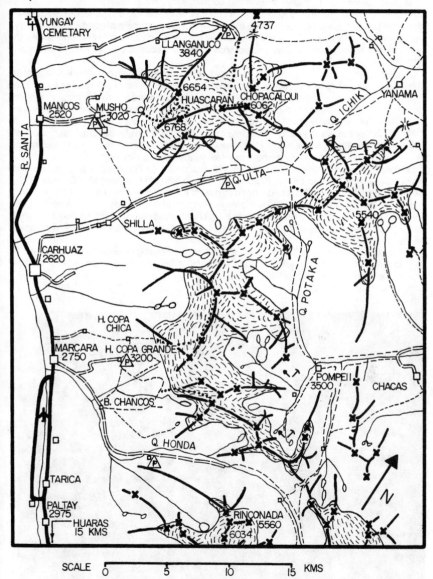

YUNGAY CEMETARY

4737

LLANGANUCO
3840

6654

CHOPACALQUI
6062

Q. ICHIK

YANAMA

MANCOS
2520

MUSHO
3020

HUASCARAN

6768

R. SANTA

Q. ULTA

5540

SHILLA

CARHUAZ
2620

Q. POTAKA

H. COPA
CHICA

MARCARA
2750

H. COPA GRANDE
3200

POMPEII
3500

CHACAS

B. CHANCOS

Q. HONDA

TARICA

PALTAY
2975

HUARAS
15 KMS

RINCONADA
5560

6034

N

SCALE    0        5        10        15    KMS

## Huantsan, Cordillera Blanca, Peru

This map, showing the city of Huaraz and the mountains to the east, is the 4th in the series of 5 which covers the Cordillera Blanca. At this point, the Rio Santa Valley is more open than it is to the north. One can walk directly from downtown Huaraz to most of the high mountain peaks on the map—however, there's a maze of roads, trails, farms, fields and scattered huts one must pass before reaching the canyons or quebradas.

Most climbing is done during June, July and August, when the sun is in the northern sky, and when little rain or snow is received. It's also possible to have long spells of good weather in May and September. The rest of the year is very wet. Remember, with the sun to the north, the north facing slopes have the more consolidated snow, while the south faces have more powdery, light snow.

On the map are drawn the more important roads and trails, along with probably the easiest or at least the earliest routes up some of the more prominent peaks in the Huaraz area. The summits here are only slightly lower than peaks to the north near Peru's highest mountain Huascaran, but are still just as rugged and present some peaks as difficult as any in this range or in the world. Generally speaking, access is very good and easy to these mountains.

Many climbers make their way from Lima to the Cordillera Blanca aboard buses, most of which make the 8 hour run at night. These buses use the Pativilca route. One can also reach Huaraz from Casma or Chimbote, both located on the coastal highway.

Some of the more prominent peaks include: Huantsan, 6395 meters, the highest in the region; Cashan, 5723 and Urusa, 5735—both to the south of Huantsan; also Cayesh, 5721 meters, one of the most difficult and jagged pyramids in the range; Ranrapallca, 6162 meters, one of the most dominant peaks overlooking Huaraz; and Chinchey (Rurichichay), 6309 meters. All these summits are for experienced and well equipped climbers. (Beware of many conflicting names and elevations in this section of the range; as a result the various maps used by the author.)

All the author's food came from Huaraz, which has good enough selections for any climb. If it's additional information you want, contact the tourist office, or find other climbers on the 5th floor of the Hotel Barcelona.

**Map:**  Huari and Recuay, 1 : 100,000, from the IGM, 1190, Av. Aramburu, San Isidro (barrio), Lima.

Foto taken just north of Catac, showing peaks southeast of Huaraz.

# Map 331-1, Huantsan, Cordillera Blanca, Peru

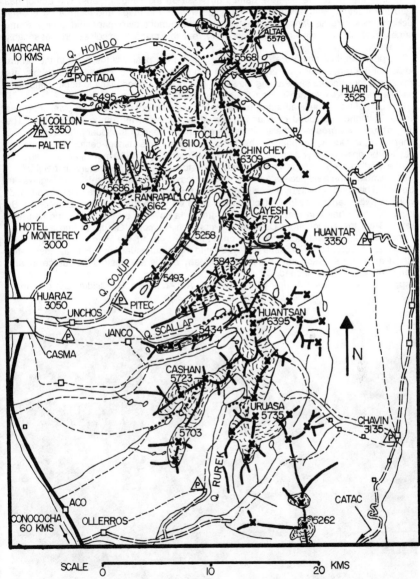

SCALE 0       10       20   KMS

## Pongos, Cordillera Blanca, Peru

This is the last of 5 maps covering the Cordillera Blanca of north central Peru. This map is the most southerly of the five, and includes the most southerly peak in the range, Rajo Cutac, at 5355 meters. The loftiest peak on the map is the highest of a cluster known as the Pongos Group. It is shown on the IGM maps as Murrorajo, 5688 meters.

One problem the author has had in creating this map, and all the maps of the Cordillera Blanca, is that there are different names of peaks on the various maps. The author has used the Instituto Geografico Militar maps, as well as the maps and information in John Ricker's book, "Yuraq Janka." Also used were the author's own maps and diaries. Some names may be different and elevations vary, but the maps themselves are reasonably accurate.

The peaks in this region are not nearly as high as the peaks to the north in the central portion of the range, nor are they as rugged and difficult to climb. For this reason they are well suited for climbers still learning the skills. This is also a good place to begin climbing in the Blanca in order to acclimatize for higher peaks.

This part of the range is attractive to people interested in botany. The rare plant known as "Puya Raimondi," is found here and in few other places in the range and in Peru. The author found two groups of these plants. One is at the head of the Quebrada Qeshqe, the other is in the Quebrada Ingenio. This latter group is near a visitors center, which may or may not be open when you arrive. Both groups are at 4200 to 4300 meters altitude, and are on the north facing slopes. These plants grow to about 8 to 10 meters in height.

For climbing, the best access route is the road leaving the main Lima-Huaraz Highway at Km 159. This road is used by trucks bringing ore from several mines, the most important of which is Mina Santon. It's not difficult to get rides on these trucks, either up or down. By using this road one can reach the heart of the area covered by this map. One can also walk, as did the author, from Catac to the northern Raimondi Group, in one easy day.

Food can be bought at Catac, the only town shown on the map. This is the least populated section of the Rio Santa Valley. Best to make headquarters in Huaraz, then catch one of many buses each day to this region. Many climbs are easy here, but ice ax and crampons will still be needed.

**Map:**  Recuay, 1 : 100,000, from the IGM 1190, Av. Aramburu, San Isidro (barrio), Lima.

These are Puyo Raimondi located just west of the Pongos Group.

# Map 332-1, Pongos, Cordillera Blanca, Peru

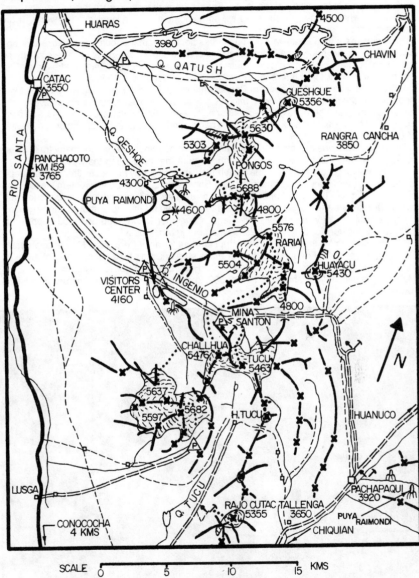

## Yerupaja, Cordillera Huayhuash, Peru

One of the most spectacular peaks in South America, and in the world for that matter, is Yerupaja, 6617 meters. This peak dominates the skyline of the Cordillera Huayhuash, a compact but towering mountain range, located just to the southeast of the Cordillera Blanca in west central Peru.

The physical makeup of the range is similar to that of the Cordillera Blanca, consisting of rock such as granite at the center of the range. For climbers, there's no such thing as a "walk-up" route in the whole range—these peaks are some of the most challenging in the world. There are seven peaks over 6000 meters.

In recent years the Cordillera Huayhuash has become rather popular among trekkers and climbers. There are many small companies or individuals, who take groups of hikers into these mountains, usually making a circular route around the range. For climbers and trekkers alike, the beginning point for entering the Huayhuash is almost always Chiquian.

Chiquian is located 32 kms east of Conococha, which is on the main highway linking Lima and Huaraz. Chiquian is a quiet town, with many small shops, at least three inexpensive hotels, and a daily market. There are daily—or rather nightly—buses, going there from Lima, and daily trucks linking it to Huaraz. It's also possible to begin a trek at the town of Cajatambo, southwest of the range.

From Chiquian, one can start by taking a trail to the southeast. There are many trails in the region, so sometimes it's necessary to inquire about the route along the way.

The normal base for climbers in the Huayhuash and especially for those climbing Yerupaja, is the area around Lugunas Jahuacocha and Solteracocha, on the northwestern slopes. For most, this is a two day hike from Chiquian. For trekkers, the normal thing to do is to walk completely around the range, taking about 10 to 12 days for the trip. Although many groups bring food all the way from their native land, the author found adequate food supplies in Chiquian. However, for better selections, shop in Lima or Huaraz.

The dry season for the Huayhuash is the same as for all of Peru, from May through early September. For further information and³or maps stop in Lima at the national tourist office or Instituto Geografico Militar; or in Huaraz at the Hotel Barcelona or tourist office.

**Map:** Chiquian and Yanahuanca, 1 : 100,000, from the IGM, 1190 Av. Aramburu, San Isidro (barrio), Lima.

Yerupaja as seen from near Lago Solterococha. Yerupaja Chico, left.

# Map 333-1, Yerupaja, Cord. Huayhuash, Peru

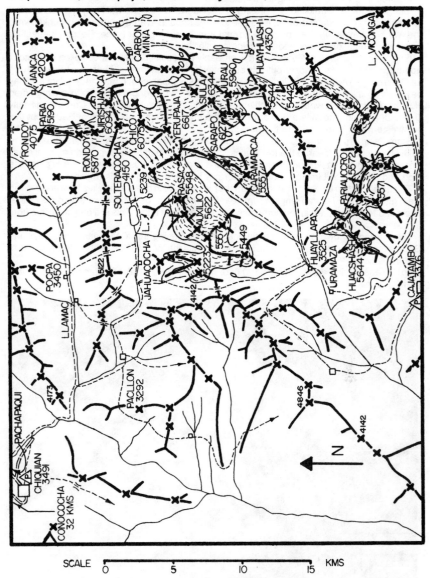

SCALE 0    5    10    15  KMS

## Santa Rosa, Cordillera Raura, Peru

Just to the south of the Cordillera Huayhuash, is another group of peaks known as the Cordillera Raura. Some people would classify them as part of the Huayhuash, but officially they are listed as a separate mountain range. The highest peak in this group is Santa Rosa, 5706 meters. Like the neighboring ranges to the north, this peak and the entire group, are glaciated and steep and very challenging for climbers.

One advantage of trekking or climbing in the Raura, is that one will likely not see or meet other climbers or trekking groups. It's close to some populated areas, but is simply unknown to the average traveler in Peru or to the normal armchair climber at home. Despite the fact it's unknown, it has some very good climbing possibilities.

Getting to the village of Oyon, which is probably the easiest and least complicated route of approach to the peaks, is not so difficult, but it may be time consuming. There are buses leaving for Oyon daily—or nightly, but finding these small bus companies in Lima can be difficult. It may be easier to take any bus and go 149 kms north of Lima along the coast, to a city named Huacho. From there it would be much easier to find a bus or truck to Sayan, Churin and finally Oyon. One could also take a bus or truck to the town of Cajatambo, west of Raura, but this involves a much longer hike to the peaks.

From Oyon, trucks or 4WD's can be found going to the many mines and haciendas in the valley to the north, closer to the mountains. One can find lodging in Oyon, and several small stores where most basic food items can be found. However, in this case it's better to purchase food and supplies in Lima or another larger city before arriving in this region.

The easiest route up Santa Rosa is from the high mountain basin which lies between the two main groups of the Raura Range. From near the end of the road, climb south into the glacier basin and to the summit via the north face or on an easterly ridge. This is a one day climb from the basin.

Other routes shown are approximations, made by using the IGM maps. These Instituto Geografico Militar maps can be found in Lima. Contact the tourist office for the latest address of that institution.

**Map:** Yanahuanca and Oyon, 1 : 100,000, from the IGM, 1190 Av. Aramburu, San Isidro (barrio), Lima.

From the Mina Raura at 4800 meters. Looking at the north side of Santa Rosa.

# Map 334-1, Santa Rosa, Cordillera Raura, Peru

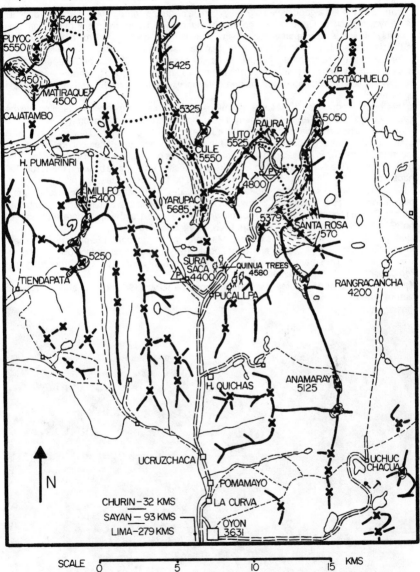

PUYOC 5550
5442
5450
MATIRAQUE 4500
CAJATAMBO
H. PUMARINRI
MILLPO 5400
5250
TIENDAPATA
5425
5325
CULE 5550
YARUPAC 5685
SURA SACA P. 4400
RAURA
LUTO 5525
P. 4800
5379
SANTA ROSA 570
5050
PORTACHUELO
QUINUA TREES 4580
PUCALLPA
RANGRACANCHA 4200
H. QUICHAS
ANAMARAY 5125
UCRUZCHACA
UCHUC CHACUA
POMAMAYO
LA CURVA
OYON 3631

N

CHURIN – 32 KMS
SAYAN – 93 KMS
LIMA – 279 KMS

SCALE  0    5    10    15    KMS

## Raujunte, Cordillera La Viuda, Peru

In central Peru, not far east of Lima, is a mountainous region with snow-capped peaks known as the Cordillera La Viuda. Even though they're close to Lima, they are virtually unknown in mountaineering circles. This makes the area an interesting place to visit for climbing or trekking, because it's likely that the people in the small villages have never before seen foreign travelers.

From Lima there's a good paved highway running northeast through Matucana, Morococha, La Oroya, and on to Cerro de Pasco and*or Huancayo. There are many bus companies traveling this line, so transport is no problem. From various towns on this main highway, such as Chicla, Casapalca or Morococha, entry can be made to all or most of the summits.

For traveling the secondary roads, trucks can be found. From Chosica or Casapalca trucks move to mining areas and haciendas in the northern sections. The road to Ondores is the main means of access to Marcapomacocha, the only real village in the region away from the main highway.

This region is populated in the lower elevations, and has many livestock trails leading into the higher valleys. It's also an area of many lakes, the result of past glaciation.

The highest peak on this map is Raujunte, estimated to be 5650 meters. The author has put a route on the mountain, from the west and the main junction, sometimes called Curves. No accurate information is available for the best route up this peak, or any other in the region. The routes shown to the summits of various peaks are guesses only, made by using the 1:100,000 maps from the IGM in Lima. They may or may not be the best routes.

Being so close to Lima, the capital is naturally the best place to buy food and obtain information about the mountains, buses, etc. Also, the best maps available can be purchased in Lima. Contact first the tourist office downtown or at the airport for the up-to-date addresses of the IGM, the South American Explorers Club, or various club andinos.

As with all mountainous regions of Peru, May through the first part of September is the best time to climb. For all higher summits, over about 5100 meters, snow and ice climbing equipment is needed. These are fairly rugged mountains, but not as difficult as in other ranges in Peru, such as in the Huayhuash.

**Map:** Matucana and Ondores, 1 : 100,000, from the IGM, 1190 Av. Aramburu, San Isidro (barrio), Lima.

The tren station at the tunnel is Galeria, the highest Railway point in the world.

## Map 335-2, Raujunte, Cord. La Viuda, Peru

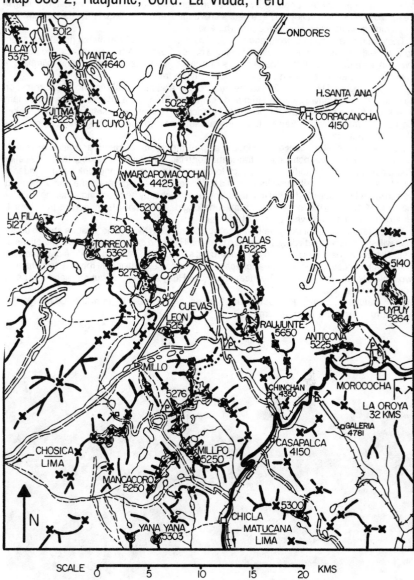

ALCAY 5375
5012
YANTAC 4640
JITMA 5225
H. CUYO
5025
ONDORES
H.SANTA ANA
H. CORPACANCHA 4150
MARCAPOMACOCHA 4425
LA FILA 5127
5200
5208
TORREON 5362
5275
CALLAS 5225
5140
PUYPUY 5264
CUEVAS
LEON 5215
RAUJUNTE 5650
ANTICONA 5225
P
MILLO
5276
P
CHINCHAN 4350
MOROCOCHA
LA OROYA 32 KMS
GALERIA 4781
CHOSICA LIMA
MILLPO 5250
CASAPALCA 4150
MANCACORO 5250
N
5300
CHICLA
YANA YANA 5303
MATUCANA LIMA

SCALE   0   5   10   15   20   KMS

## Tunshu, Cordillera Central, Peru

In the area due east of Lima, Peru's capital city, stands a group of snow capped peaks known as the Cordillera Central. The highest summit in the group is Tunshu, at 5730 meters. This peak stands alone, just east of the main ridge where most of the high summits lie. Within this section of the Cordillera Central, are many peaks with altitudes of 5400 or 5500 meters, and several others in the 5600 meter range. They have been glaciated much more in the past, resulting in many lakes in the high valleys. These peaks are rugged, and most require the use of snow and ice climbing equipment, plus someone who knows how to use it.

The mountains around Cuzco, and the Cordillera Blanca and Huayhuash get all the attention, while these mountains are almost unknown. For those seeking new routes and possibly even unclimbed peaks, this is the area. It's one place you'll likely not meet other climbers or trekkers. In other words, it's not a part of the "gringo trail"!

There is one 4WD road leading to the heart of the area, but you'll find no public transport beyond the main highway linking Lima and Huancayo. From Lima, of course, there are many buses and trucks on that paved highway to Huancayo. To visit the western part of this region, stop at the small village of San Mateo, and walk southeast to some mining areas along some old roads, then trails.

To reach the eastern section or slopes, stop at the village of Huari, and hitch or walk to Huay-Huay and Suitucancha, then a trail to the north face of Tunshu. Or stop at the place called Pachacayo, and take another bus or truck to Canchaylla; at that village look for other rides to the Hacienda Cochas. After that there's little traffic so it'll be a long walk to the end of the road, as shown. All of these roads lead to mines, some of which may be operating. Walking from the Hacienda Cochas to the roads-end will take one long day. One can also ride a bus from Lima to Huarochiri, in the southwest corner of the map.

Your starting point will likely be Lima, so buy all supplies there. The villages shown on the map will stock basic foods only. Huancayo is a small city and has very good food selections as well. The author began his trip into the Tunshu area from Huancayo. He took the daily morning tren from Huancayo, stopped at Panchacayo, and ended up walking all the way to Tunshu in two days. He later left by way of Suitucancha, Huay Huay and Huari. Four days and one peak, from the railway line.

**Map:** Matucana, Oroya, Huarochiri and Yauyos, all 1 : 100,000, from the IGM, 1190 Av. Aramburu, San Isidro (barrio), Lima.

We see Tunshu and its east ridge from the valley east of the peak.

## Map 336-1, Tunshu, Cordillera Central, Peru

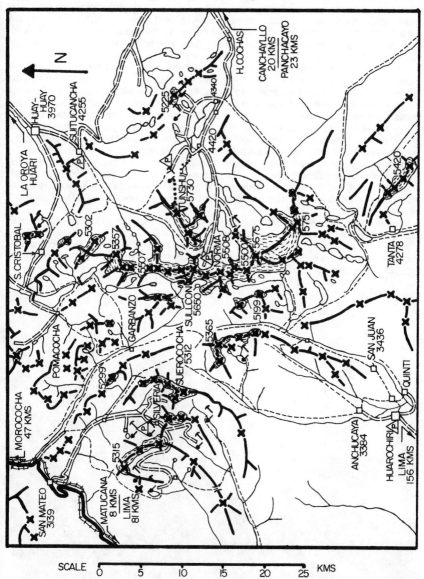

SCALE  0  5  10  15  20  25  KMS

## Ticlla, Cordillera Central, Peru

Included on this map is the second of two parts of the Cordillera Central located in central Peru. This section is directly east of Lima and west of Huancayo. Even though this mountain range is relatively near high population centers, it is still very isolated, with no paved highways shown on the map.

The highest peak in this southern section of the Cordillera Central is Nevado Ticlla, rising to 5897 meters. This summit is located in about the center of the high peaks on the map. The easiest route of approach to Ticlla is probably via Asia (on the main coastal highway south of Lima), Coayllo, Omas and finally the village of Ayaviri, at the end of the road. From Ayaviri, there are trails on both sides of the river leading east, then northeast, to a large lake named Huascacocha.

Another approach to this peak is from the south and the coastal town of Canete. From Canete, a road leads to the town of Yauyos, located about half-way between the coast and Huancayo. From Yauyos, the same road continues to near the village of Miraflores, east of Ticlla. This eastern approach seems to have more trails, shepherds and livestock than the western slopes, the presence of which may be advantageous in reaching the high peaks.

Whichever route is taken, take any bus running along the coastal highway south of Lima, and stop at Asia or Canete. From either of these places, trucks or buses can be found going to the upper valleys. (Later information tells of daily buses running from Lima to the town of Yauyos).

Perhaps the easiest way of approach to this group is the one used by the author in 1982. He took the three-or-four-times-weekly-bus from Huancayo to Tomas, Tinco Miraflores and which stops in Yauyos, but got off at T. Miraflores. From there he walked to the terraced village of Miraflores, then west to Ticlla. One can climb Ticlla and return to Huancayo, all in about 4 to 5 days.

Villages on the map are small, but each has several small shops for all the basic foods. Best to buy supplies in Lima or Huancayo though.

Peaks over about 5400 meters are for experienced and well equipped climbers—peaks under 5400 meters are generally safe to solo climb. Almost no other climbers or trekkers in this area. Check out the canyon below Tomas.

**Map:** Huarochiro and Yauyos, 1 : 100,000, from the IGM, 1190 Av. Aramburu, San Isidro (barrio), Lima.

The south ridge of Ticlla seems relatively easy (left).

# Map 337-1, Ticlla, Cordillera Central, Peru

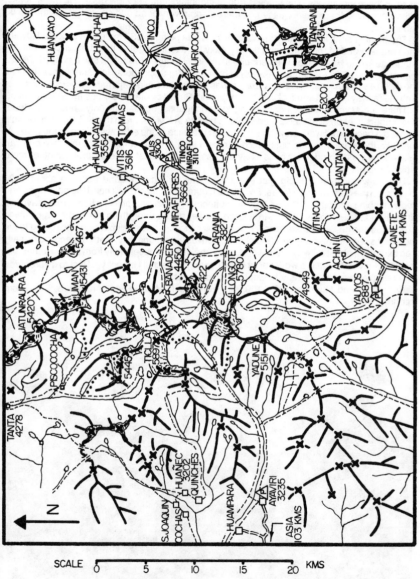

SCALE  0    5    10    15    20  KMS

## Jallacate, Cord. Huaytapallana, Peru

For someone interested in out-of-the-way places where few mountaineers dare venture one might try the Cordillera Huaytapallana. This small compact mountain range is located directly east of the city of Huancayo and the Mantaro Valley in central Peru. There are many tourists visiting Huancayo, especially on Sundays to see the weekly market, but few have ever heard of or seen these mountains. The same is true of mountaineers. Very few make it to these peaks, although getting there is very easy and there's some very good and challenging climbs to be found.

The highest peak in the Huaytapallana is Jallacata rising to 557 meters. It's located toward the southern end of the range and is very easy to reach. To get to it and other peaks in this range, go first to Huancayo. Then enquire at the local tourist information office about the exact location of the office (or departure-area) of buses and/or trucks going to Pariahuanca. In 1982 the daily bus or truck going to Pariahuanca was located on Calla Cajamarca where it intersects with the railway line just south of the railway station. But these places change from time to time.

There are several vehicles daily going to Pariahuanca, but usually only one takes a lot of passengers. Get off at the pass marked 4575 meters at KM 29. From there it's a two hour walk with a big pack to old work crew huts located at the base of the southwest face of the peak. At that lake there are 4 usable huts which can be a kind of base camp. From this lake one can ascend the western ridge which is likely the easiest and safest route, or pick out other more difficult routes.

The Huaytapallana has big glaciers and crevasses which extend down to about 4800 meters, on the drier western faces. For all the higher summits one will need the normal ice and snow climbing equipment. Before leaving Huancayo have all supplies on hand. Huancayo is a city with good selections of food in a large market place. Everything needed for a climbing expedition can be found there, and it's a good place to visit and acclimatize before going to the mountains. There are many hotels to choose from as it's a tourist city. Get to Huancayo by daily tren over the highest railway in the world, or by one of many buses daily from Lima. Remember that the Huaytapallana is a wetter area than the ranges west of Huancayo. Best to go prepared with raingear even in the May to September dry season.

**Map:** Jauja and Huancayo, 1 : 100,000, from the IGM, 1190 Av. Aramburu, San Isidro (barrio), Lima.

The highest peaks of the Cord. Huaytapallana, from the west side.

# Map 338-1, Jallacata, Cord. Huaytapallana, Peru

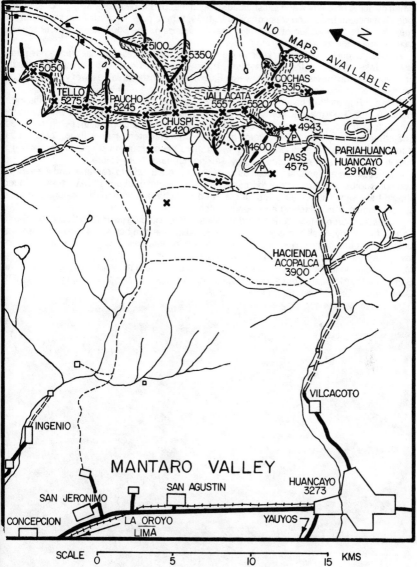

# Pumasillo, Cordillera Vilcabamba, Peru

The map here includes the central portion of the Cordillera Vilcabamba. The highest summit is actually Lasunayoc, at about 6100 meters, but more famous is Pumasillo, 6070 meters.

Before anything is said about the area, it must be made clear that good maps of this mountain range are lacking. The map used by the author is called "Carta de La Region Norte del Cuzco," put out by the IGM in Lima. Most climbers consider it to have many inaccuracies. However, the author used it when he visited the area between Santa Teresa and the Puerto Yanama and when climbing on the Nevado Quishua, and found that part to be reasonably good. That map does not include trails, and was compiled in 1959. Where question marks are shown on this map, it means the location of the trail or road is uncertain. The 5000 meter contour line was used to mark the snowline.

As one travels in this region, keep in mind that all major canyons or quebradas have trails used to take livestock to the high pastures. The lower valleys are all tropical, meaning that the first day or two on the trail will be very warm. Farmers living in these same lower valleys near the railway line, grow tropical fruits for their livelihood.

To reach Pumasillo or Lasunayoc there are two possible approach routes, both originating at Santa Teresa. Take the train from Cuzco (past Machu Pichu) to Santa Teresa, then walk up the major canyon above Huadquiña. There must be a trail in that canyon, but that is unconfirmed. The other way would be to find a truck going to Punta Carretera, then walk to Colcapampa, Yanama and to a place called Paccha. From there each group must find its own way. It's possible to find a route to Lasunayoc by walking northeast from Totura.

If the southern or Yanama route is used, plan on about 3 days to Yanama, and if a serious attempt is to be made on any of the major summits, a total of about 10 days supply of food should be taken. These peaks are all glaciated and challenging and require snow and ice climbing equipment. Climbing experience helps too.

It's best of course to have all food and supplies before boarding the train in Cuzco, but Santa Teresa has many small shops with basic foods. Also, one can buy some food and meals at Colcapampa and Totura, and possibly at Lucma and Retamayoc. Chaullay is also a larger town. May through the beginning of September is the dry season.

**Map:**   Carta de la Region Norte del Cusco, 1 : 200,000, from the IGM, 1190 Av. Aramburu, San Isidro (barrio), Lima, or Landstat Foto 2190-14131(I-10), from the IGM, Lima, or EROS Data Center, Sioux Falls, South Dakota, USA.

From the slopes of Quishua, looking towards Lasunayoc, left and Pumasillo, right.

## Map 339-1, Pumasillo, Cord, Vilcabamba, Peru

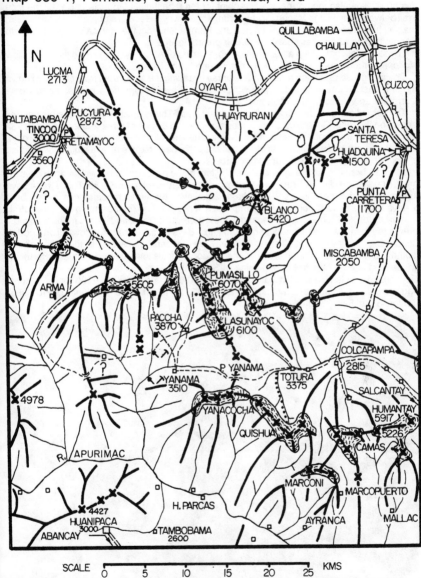

SCALE 0 5 10 15 20 25 KMS

## Salcantay, Cordillera Vilcabamba, Peru

The peaks included on this map are some of the highest in the Cordillera Vilcabamba. The Vilcabamba Range lies to the northwest of Cuzco in west central Peru. The highest summit on this map and in the entire Vilcabamba, is Salcantay, 6271 meters.

Reaching Salcantay is easy with three main ways of approach. The route most commonly used is the one beginning at Km 88 on the railway line running between Cuzco and Machu Picchu. This is also the normal starting point for the thousands of tourists who walk the Inca Trail between Km 88 and Machu Picchu. From Km 88, which is only a stopping point on the line, the trail heads south, past Huayllabamba and Pampacahuana, then over a pass and down to Sanay; thence to another possible starting point, Mollepata.

To reach Mollepata, take a bus or truck from Cuzco or Abancay, to the road junction below Mollepata, then either walk or catch another ride to the village.

One could also reach the region of Salcantay by taking the same train from Cuzco on down the line past Machu Picchu to the town of Santa Teresa. From there hike south to Punta Carretera and Colcapampa, then east.

The normal route up Salcantay is the northeast ridge. This is reached via the eastern pass as shown on the map. Once again, this can be approached by one of three routes, but the Km 88 route is by far the shortest and easiest. An experienced climber could probably do the ridge solo, but it's not an easy climb. All other routes up this peak require all available snow and ice climbing equipment, and experienced climbers.

The walk from Km 88 to a base camp at the foot of the northeast ridge, will take 1½ days for most. The summit climb will be one day, then another day to return to Km 88. That's 3 or 4 days for fit climbers with good luck and fair weather. However, the author recommends taking about 5 days supply of food for this trip, and much more if other routes are to be attempted. Humantay, at 5917 meters, is the second highest peak on the map, and it too is a difficult climb.

If it's the Inca Trail you want, plan on from 2 to 4 days to make the hike. Buy all your food in Cuzco. Big towns are Santa Teresa, Aguas Calientes, and Mollepata. In the valley above (south) Santa Teresa, families are now offering some meals to trekkers. As usual in Peru, the dry season is from May to the beginning of September.

**Map:** Carta de la Region Norte del Cusco, 1 : 200,000, from the IGM, 1190 Av. Aramburu, San Isidro (barrio), Lima, or Landstat Foto 2190-14131(I-10), from the IGM, Lima, or Eros Data Center, Sioux Falls, South Dakota, USA.

The second highest peak in the Salcantay Group is Humantay, from the northeast.

# Map 340-1, Salcantay, Cord, Vilcabamba, Peru

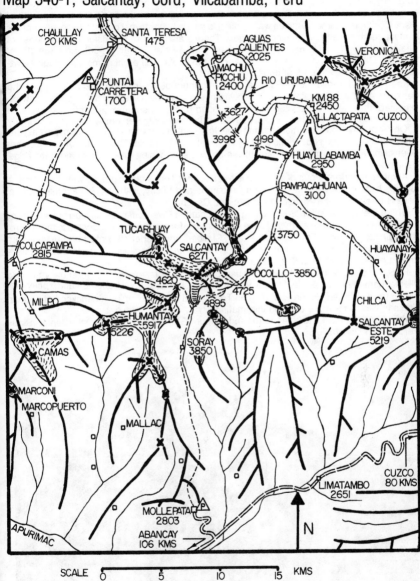

CHAULLAY 20 KMS
SANTA TERESA 1475
AGUAS CALIENTES 2025
VERONICA
MACHU PICCHU 2400
RIO URUBAMBA
PUNTA CARRETERA 1700
KM 88 2450
LLACTAPATA
CUZCO
3627
3998
4198
HUAYLLABAMBA 2950
PAMPACAHUANA 3100
TUCARHUAY
3750
HUAYANAY
COLCAPAMPA 2815
SALCANTAY 6271
OCOLLO - 3850
4620
4725
CHILCA
MILPO
4895
SALCANTAY ESTE 5219
HUMANTAY 5917
5226
SORAY 3850
CAMAS
MARCONI
MARCOPUERTO
MALLAC
CUZCO 80 KMS
LIMATAMBO 2651
N
APURIMAC
MOLLEPATA 2803
ABANCAY 106 KMS
SCALE    0    5    10    15    KMS

## Huaycay Huilque, Cord. Urubamba, Peru

This map shows the Cordillera Urubamba, located north of Cuzco and east of Manchu Picchu in the southeastern Andes Mountains of Peru. Some climbers may not recognize some of the names on these peaks. The author uses his own maps and experience, maps from "Le Ande", by Mario Fantin, the Tambo Treks map, "Ollantaytambo-Amparaes", and Landstat Foto 2190-14131 (I-10) in creating this map. The highest peak here is Huaycay Huilque, sometimes spelled Waqaywillka, and sometimes known as Veronica. In the small pueblo of Pisca Cocha, the name Veronica was applied to the peak northwest of that village, and not the highest summit they call Huaycay Huilque. There's also a lot of confusion on the names of peaks just north of Urubamba. Locals call it Media Luna (Half Moon), and sometimes Chiccon. Other maps, especially in "Le Ande", have totally different names, although elevations given here are from that book.

Keep in mind, these mountains are on the boundry between the Amazon Basin and the Peruvian Altiplano; therefore, during the rainy season, heavy amounts of precip can be expected: thus heavily glaciated and very rugged peaks. These climbs are for experienced and well equiped "Andinistas." The dry season is from May into September. The rock is largely

One report indicated the most normal route to the top of Huaycay Huilque if from the east and Abra Malaga, but the south ridge looks good, or at least possible. The summit of Veronica has been climbed from Pisca Cocha and the south face and then by walking west along the ridge, as shown.

Another important group of summits is Media Luna. This is one big ridge with many peaks. Groups have made ascents from both Urubamba and Yucay, with possibly another route of access being from the Hacienda Huaran and Cancha.

There are several other groups along the Urubamba River, but none so high or majestic as those mentioned. However, there is one more group of some importance located to the north of the main range. This is The Gruppo Terijuay. Climbers have penetrated into this area from Abra Malaga (possibly the best route) and from the road running from Amparaes to Colca. Little is known of these peaks but they make good climbs.

Reach the Rio Vilcanota Valley by bus from Cuzco or take one of several daily trens to Ollantaybambo or Chilca. Best to buy food in Cuzco, but Ollantay, Urubamba and Yucay are bigger towns. Contact R. Randall, Tambo Treks, at El Albergue; or T. Hendrickson of Andean Treks in Cuzco for more detailed information.

**Map:** Landstat Foto 2190-14131 (I-10), from the IGM, Lima, or EROS Data Center, Sioux Falls, South Dakota, USA.

From just north of Ollantaytambo, we have a good look at Huaycay Huilque, right.

# Map 341-1, Huaycay Huilque, Cord. Urubamba, Peru

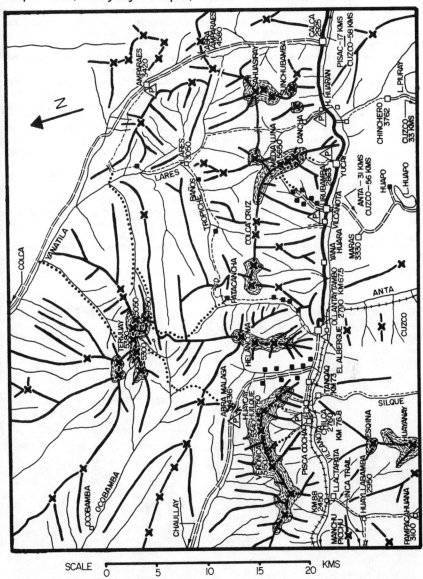

SCALE

0    5    10    15    20    KMS

# Ausangate, Cordillera Vilcanota, Peru

In the region southeast of Cuzco lie the Cordillera Vilcanota and some of the most rugged and spectacular peaks in Peru. The highest and most visible peak of all is Ausangate, at 6372 meters.

The Cordillera Vilcanota is easy to reach. There are several ways of approaching this range, but by far the easiest route is via Cuzco, Urcos then along the road passing through Ocongate, and ending at the Amazon city of Maldonado. From along this road, one of many trails can be taken to any region of the Vilcanota. The valley above Ocongate, the largest town on this map, is highly populated with small settlements and trails everywhere. There are shepherd huts in every valley up to about 4300 meters, with about 3 snarling dogs to each hut!

In recent years many trekkers have reached this area along with climbers. A popular trekking route is via Ocongate, Chillca, and Pitumarca, passing very near Ausangate.

To reach Ausangate and the normal climbing route up the south face, one should first find a truck in Cuzco heading for Maldanado. It's sometimes easier to take one of many buses to Urcos, then wait at the police checkpoint in Urcos for these trucks. All traffic must stop at that point. Get off the truck at either Yanama or the Hacienda Tinqui, about 5 and 9 kms further along the road above Ocongate. The author used the Yanama route to the lakes south and west of Ausangate. This is likely the easiest trail to follow. He actually walked from Ocongate to the highest lake in about 8 long hours. Other books indicate the trail from Tinqui and Upis is the normal route. It's about the same distance either way.

The south face of Ausangate is one continuous icefall, with literally hundreds of crevasses to negotiate. If you're following the tracks of someone else, it may take only one day to reach the summit from a high base camp, but one should plan on at least one night's bivouac on the face. It has apparently been climbed solo, but that's not recommended. Ausangate and the peaks in that area are for experienced and well equipped climbers only. For less experienced climbers, try the peaks just north of Laguna Sibinacocha, or north of the Maldonado road.

All supplies should be purchased in Cuzco, but many supplies can be found in several shops in Yanama. Climbing season is from May to early September.

**Map:**   Ocongate, 1 : 100,000, from the IGM, 1190 Av. Aramburu, San Isidro (barrio), Lima.

From about Labramarca, Ausangate stands tall and dominates the sky.

# Map 342-1, Ausangate, Cord. Vilcanota, Peru

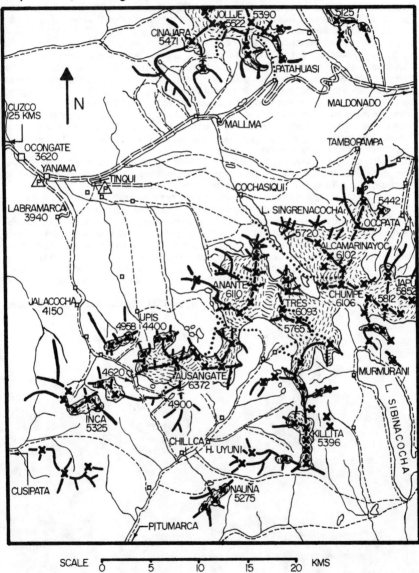

JOLLJE 5522 5390

CINAJARA 5471

PATAHUASI

5125

CUZCO 125 KMS

N

MALLMA

MALDONADO

OCONGATE 3620

YANAMA

TINQUI

TAMBOPAMPA

COCHASIQUI

LABRAMARCA 3940

L. SINGRENACOCHA 5720

5442 OCCPATA

ALCAMARINAYOC 6102

JALACOCHA 4150

ANANTE 6110

TRES 6093

CHUMPE 6106

5812 JAPU 5852

UPIS 4958 4400

5765

MURMURANI

4620

AUSANGATE 6372

4900

INCA 5325

CHILLCA

H. UYUNI

KILLITA 5396

L. SIBINACOCHA

CUSIPATA

NAUNA 5275

PITUMARCA

SCALE 0    5    10    15    20    KMS

## Cunurana, Cordillera La Raya, Peru

The map here includes the higher portions of the Cordillera La Raya which lies about half way between Cuzco and Juliaca and near the main highway and railway linking these two important cities. The La Raya is not one massive mountain range, but a series of small groups of peaks, all of which are within easy reach of the main highway and railway previously mentioned. The highest peak is Yana Cuchilla at 5472 meters. Next is Chinchina at 5463, and Cunurana at 5420 meters. This latter peak is the most famous of any in the cordillera and is an important landmark for travelers making the trip from Juliaca and Puno to Cuzco. It's the snow capped peak behind the town of Santa Rosa. All of these higher summits are glaciated, but mostly on the southern slopes. There are no really large snowfields anywhere.

Because there are no really high and difficult peaks to climb here, it's a good place for simple trekking or for the beginning or intermediate climber. There are of course difficult routes on all peaks, but not to the extent one finds on most of the well known ranges in Peru. This is a good area for regular tourists to stop and get a closer look at the altiplano of Peru.

There are many buses on this route all running from Juliaca to Cuzco. Occasionally one can find a through bus from Arequipa, Puno or La Paz Bolivia. One can also pass through the area by tren. Tren service begins at Cuzco to the north, and Juliaca on the south, with connecting lines coming in from Puno and Arequipa.

One should buy and have all or most of the food needed for any climb in the region before entering the mapped area. But if one is to stop at Santa Rosa everything needed can be purchased there. There's also one hotel or residencial in Santa Rosa.

Shown are some of the normal routes on the three highest summits. For Cunurana one can hike from the town of Santa Rosa, into the basin southeast of the peak and circle around to the backside to acsend by an all rock route; or one can pass between Cerro Negro and Cunurana, and make it an ice-and-snow climb up the south face. For Yana Chuchilla, stop at the La Raya Pass and walk to the northwest 3 or 4 kms, then use the trail running to the pass north of the main peak and make the final acsent from the north ridge. Keep in mind that north faces are generally all rock routes, whereas for south faces snow and ice equipment are needed. Remember too that the dry season is from May through September—with hardly a cloud in the sky during this time.

**Map:**   Ayaviri, Nunoa, Sicuani, all 1 : 100,000, from the IGM, 1190 Av. Aramburu, San Isidro (barrio), Lima.

One can climb Cunurana from the town of Santa Rosa, as pictured here.

# Map 343-1, Cunurana, Cordillera La Raya, Peru

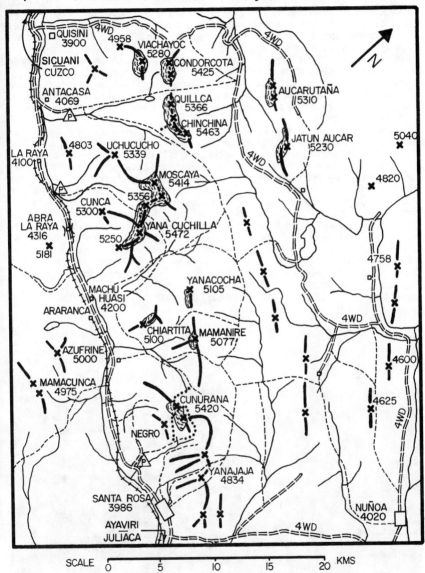

QUISINI 3900
4958
VIACHAYOC 5280
SICUANI CUZCO
CONDORCOTA 5425
AUCARUTAÑA 5310
ANTACASA 4069
QUILLCA 5366
CHINCHINA 5463
JATUN AUCAR 5230
5040
4803
UCHUCUCHO 5339
LA RAYA 4100
MOSCAYA 5414
4820
5356
CUNCA 5300
ABRA LA RAYA 4316
YANA CUCHILLA 5472
5181
5250
4758
YANACOCHA 5105
MACHU HUASI 4200
ARARANCA
4WD
CHIARTITA 5100
MAMANIRE 5077
AZUFRINE 5000
4600
MAMACUNCA 4975
4625
CUNURANA 5420
NEGRO
YANAJAJA 4834
SANTA ROSA 3986
NUÑOA 4020
AYAVIRI
JULIACA
4WD

SCALE   0    5    10    15    20   KMS

## Schio, Cordillera Carabaya, Peru

The area covered by this map is an isolated section of the Andes and completely unknown to the outside world. There have been groups into these peaks, but because of the lack of maps, long distances, and poor accessibility, you'll not find other trekkers or climbers around. The author was trying to get to Macusani, and climb something north of there, but had bad luck with finding a truck, so he ended up walking from Rosario to the Mina Quenamari and then climbing Cerro Quenamari, 5294 meters. A very easy climb. From that vantage point looking due north, he could see a rather isolated and very prominent group of high summits. The name comes from M. Fantins book, "Le Ande", and may very well be wrong. The elevations are estimates made by the author, and could be very far off the mark. None-the-less, these summits around the peak called here "Schio", are very rugged and present a challenge to any climber. These are folded and uplifted mountains, so count on the rock being largely metamorphic.

This map has been created by the author by using one map, Macusani, and one Landstat foto (see below). The Schio group lies just north of 14° north, and the mapped region, therefore, there's not much detail on that part of the map. Information on roads in this section come from a national highway map.

The best way to reach the valley around Macusani, which is by far the more important town in the region, is to proceed to the large market city of Juliaca, just north of Lake Titicaca. That seems to be the place where all transport trucks going to Macusani begin. Inquire at the north end of town as to the exact location where Macusani-bound trucks park. There's one or two trucks weekly going that way. The truck route passes through Ayaviri, another possible boarding place, then proceeds to Asillo, San Anton, the Hacienda Rosario, and finally to Macusani, perhaps a 12 hour day, or longer. Macusani should be your base, unless you're climbing something to the east on this map. In that case take the road leading to the town of Coasa (it also passes Ajoyani). Macusani is a rather large village at the bottom of a large, dry valley, where plenty of food and supplies can be found. It's not certain, but it's likely there's also a hotel or some place to sleep there as well. However, best to stock up well on supples in Juliaca, and be prepared for a long, cold, dusty, truck-top ride. From Macusani, plan on 4 or 5 days to climb Schio, maybe longer. The dry season in Peru lasts from about May through September. From Macusani, plan on 4 or 5 days to climb Schio, maybe longer.

**Map:**   Macusani, 1 : 100,000, and Landstat foto 2170-14030 (K-11), both from the IGM, 1190 Av. Aramburu, San Isidro (barrio), Lima.

From Quenamari looking northeast at Schio, left and Macusani in valley (left).

# Map 344-1, Schio, Cordillera Carabaya, Peru

SCALE  0    5    10    15   KMS

## Aricoma, Cordillera Carabaya, Peru

The peaks on this map are more than likely unknown to climbers and people living outside these valleys. The author isn't even sure of the name of the range or cordillera, though it appears to be the Carabaya. But it also could be the Cord. Aricoma. This is not a large range nor are the summits very high, at least by Peruvian standards. The highest peak is Aricoma, at about 5350 meters. However, the very good map of the area does not show exact elevation, with only one exception. So all the higher summits are about all the same height. Ipante is about 5225 meters, as are two peaks of the Nevado Pinquiyumi Orjo. Jalahuana is another interesting peak just southeast of a large glacier.

The author has not been to this mapped area, but has seen the snow summits from the north around Macusani and the northern Carabaya, and from the south and Cerro Ananea in the Cord. Apolobamba. Count on these peaks being fairly easy climbs, as snow climbs in Peru go. Remember, nearly all the higher nevados in Peru are for experienced climbers, with proper snow climbing equipment.

This section of the Carabaya is on the northeastern side of the Andes, not far from the Amazon Basin. Therefore, lots of precipitation in the wet months which extend from about late September through April and sometimes into May. This section is also about due north of Lake Titicaca, but quite a long way. On your map of Peru, find the towns of Crucero, Patambuco, and Limbani. These peaks are in the center of this triangle.

The best likely place to look for trucks going into these mountains is in Juliaca (there are no buses). Juliaca is the main market town or city in the mountains of south Peru. Trucks begin here to reach such places as Macusani, Ananea, Sandia, and Cojata, so it's likely they begin here for trips to Crecero, Limbani and Patambuco. The likely route is through Ayaviri, Asillo and San Anton, but some could reach the area by way of the road reaching Sandia and Ananea. Which ever route is ultimately taken, find a truck going to Limbani or Para (Phara), and get off in the region of Lago Aricoma. It's also possible to catch trucks in Ayaviri.

This is a grazing area for livestock; llamas, alpacas, cattle and sheep. There are hundreds of trails and small homes or shepherd huts in the valleys. There are some mines, but not in the immediate area. If any easy route is found up Aricoma, it's possible to climb it in one day from the road, but it may take two days to reach the mountains. Buy all food in Juliaca or Ayaviri, but limited supplies are found in towns enroute.

**Map:**  Limbani, 1 : 100,000, from the IGM, 1190 Av. Aramburu, San Isidro (barrio), Lima.

Substituting for Aricoma is a foto of N. Ananea from the south (Map 346).

# Map 345-3, Aricoma, Cordillera Carabaya, Peru

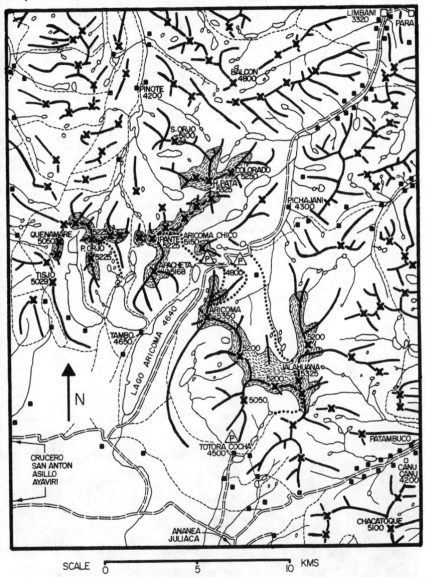

LIMBANI
3320
PARA
BALCON
4800
PINOTE
4200
S.ORJO
5100
COLORADO
5250
H.PATA
5325
PICHAJANI
4300
QUENAMARE
5050
PANTE
5225
ARICOMA CHICO
5150
P.ORJO
5225
PACHETA
5168
4800
TISJO
5029
ARICOMA
5350
TAMBO
4650
5200
5200
JALAHUANA
5325
5200
LAGO ARICOMA 4640
N
5050
TOTORA COCHA
4500
PATAMBUCO
CRUCERO
SAN ANTON
ASILLO
AYAVIRI
CANU
CANU
4200
CHACATOQUE
5100
ANANEA
JULIACA

SCALE 0        5        10 KMS

# Chaupi Orco, Cord. Apolobamba, Peru

The mountains on this map are known as the Cordillera Apolobamba, and lie mostly in Peru in this, the northern part of that range. The southeastern part of the Apolobamba lies entirely in Bolivia. This region is mapped by the IGM of Peru, at least their side of the frontier, but those maps are classified, and are not allowed to be seen or purchased by the public. Therefore, this map has been made from a map in "Le Ande", by Fantin, with the use of a Landstat Foto, and the authors' own map and notes from his experience there.

This is the authors' experience. He took an early (9 am) truck from Juliaca bound for Sandia and got off after dark at Pampilla Cruz. Camped. Early morning walked to and through Ananea and Mina Poto and past Laguna Parinani to east canyon of Nev. Ananea. Attempted an east face route up Ananea, then later to Paso Sina, and on the road to house at 4630. Another day was spent climbing Peak 5630 meters, then back to house 4630, and on the road towards Cojata. No traffic. From Ananea to Cojata was 3½ days, walking all the way. Later in the 5th day, a truck was taken to Juliaca, arriving about midnight. From Juliaca to Juliaca, 5 long days.

Remember, all trucks leaving for this area begin at the large market town of Juliaca. Ask in Juliaca where the parking place is for trucks leaving for Sandia or Cojata. Buy all your food and supplies in Juliaca, as everything is available there, although there are a number of small stores in both Ananea and Cojata where basic supplies can be found. There is likely not a hotel in either of these small towns, but if you know spanish, a place for sleeping can surely be found. The Ananea region has lots of mines while Cojata is a cattle, llama and alpaca raising valley. There are many llama and alpaca trails throughout this entire mapped area, with an occasional indian hut here and there, mostly in the lower valleys. The region is elevated very high and has night time temps of about -5 to -10 C in the dry season (from May to mid-September). Sometimes the lower valleys are colder than near the glaciers.

The routes shown on the map to various peaks are those taken by several different Italian groups in the past and those of the author. Snowline here is about 4800 meters, but snow falls down to about 4000 meters, then melts quickly. Full expedition and snow climbing equipment is needed as the peaks are heavily glaciated. These are folded mountains and are similar in appearence and difficulty of climbing to the Cord Real of Bolivia. Climbing season, from mid-May to mid-September.

**Map:** IGM maps if possible, maps from "Le Ande", Departamento de Puno map, 1 : 670,000 (IGM), or Landstat Foto 2223-13554, from IGM Lima, or Eros Data Center, Sioux Falls, South Dakota, USA

The northern side of Chaupi Orco, as seen from the east end of Ananea.

## Map 346-1, Chaupi Orco, Cord. Apolobamba, Peru

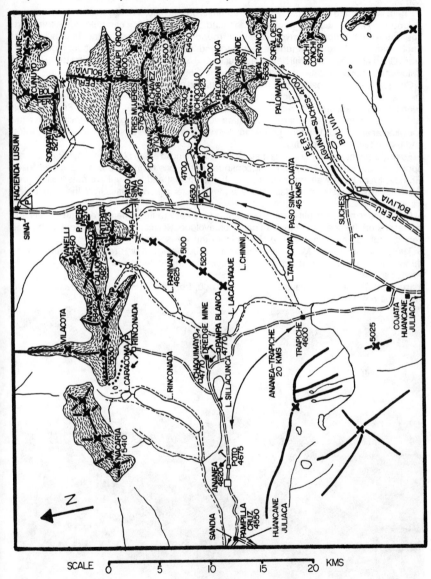

SCALE

0  5  10  15  20  KMS

# Coropuna, Cordillera Chila, Peru

Some of Peru's highest, yet some of the most easily climbed mountains, lie in the southwest part of the country in the region of Arequipa, Peru's second largest city. This is an area dotted with volcanos, some new like El Misti; some very old and eroded, like Solimani.

Because of their location in the central part of the Atacama Desert, these mountains have very little snowfall. However, all the peaks above about 5200 or 5300 meters, are capped with permanent snow.

There is one route of approach to all the summits on this map. Most people begin the journey in Arequipa, where buses or trucks can be found. The tourist office can help locate transport. The route is through the river valley surrounding Aplao, then to the high village of Chuquibamba, where is located the last hotel and last decent place to shop for food or fuel. From Chuquibamba, there will be several trucks and at least one bus daily, going to the town of Cotahuasi. There's a daily bus from Arequipa to Cotahuasi, but it departs at 3 a.m.!

Coropuna is the highest mountain in the region, and one of the highest in Peru, at about 6400 meters. Ask the driver of the vehicle to let you out near a lake named Pallacocha. It can't be seen from the road, but that area is the closest the road comes to the mountain. From near the lake, head for the right-hand or south summit. There are many good campsites near the snowline at about 5200 meters, or near the last water at 4900 meters. From the lake to the top and return takes one long day.

For the other high summit on this map, Solimani—rising to about 6093 meters, take the same approach route as to Coropuna, but continue on the bus or truck to a place called Visca Grande. From there walk cross-country to the southwest and to shepherd huts called Sora. From there, walk up the north face to the summit. Better plan on 3 days from the road for this climb.

Coropuna is high, has big glaciers, but some very easy routes. There are some icefalls and crevasses on the peak, but they can easily be avoided. Solimani is a jagged peak with some very difficult routes. The snowline shown is for the wet season.

The dry season is from May through September, but being in a dry area, climbs can be made throughout the year. For further information contact the tourist office or the club andino, in Arequipa.

**Map:** Cotahuasi and Chuquibamba, 1 : 100,000, from the IGM, 1190 Av. Aramburu, San Isidro (barrio), Lima.

The western slopes of Coropuna as seen from Laguna Pallococha.

# Map 347-1, Coropuna, Cordillera Chila, Peru

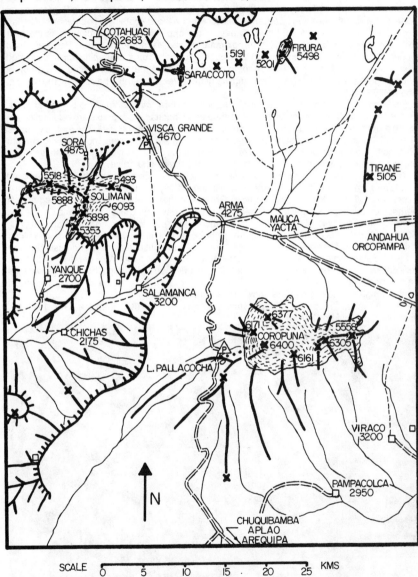

SCALE

0  5  10  15  20  25   KMS

# Rio Colca Canyon, Cordillera Chila, Peru

Included on this map is the western half of the Cordillera Chila and one of the most interesting canyons in Peru. This is the Canyon of the Rio Colca, which has it's beginnings on the high divide separating the Amazon River basin and the Atacoma Desert. The Rio Colca runs just to the south of the Cord. Chila and north of the Cord. Ampato, and passes the major village of Chivay. This canyon is interesting because one can be as low as 2200 meters at the bridge over the river between Tapay and Cabana Conde, and climb to 5432 meters on Sepregina just a few kms away. It has a number of small and isolated villages containing populations of indian and mixed-indian blood. Also, above Tapay on the opposite wall of the canyon, is the best example of a geologic feature known as columnar jointing, the author has seen. Between about December and June, one can buy and eat a cactus fruit called tuna, stemming from a cultivated cactus. And just off this map (see Ampato map) and above the Mina Madrigal, is a group of unusual plants called Puya Raymondi and the highest trees the author has seen in the world at about 4575 meters.

For climbers, the highest summit is Chila, 5665 meters, with Casiri close behind at 5631. These peaks can both be scaled from Andahua and Chachas. Both peaks are relatively easy as big mountains go in Peru, but expect some more difficult routes as well. The rock is volcanic in orgin, but the higher mountains which have very small glaciers, no longer resemble volcanos. There are many trails in this region, both in the canyon and on the mountains which are used by indians with herds of llamas, alpacas, sheep and cattle.

There are two ways of reaching this area. The easiest of access is from Chivay (see Ampato map), and the more difficult, via Andahua. Reach Chivay from Arequipa, on one of several buses daily, or hitch hike (or pay) on trucks. Get to Andahua by one daily bus from Arequipa, or perhaps on mining company truck. There is one bus a day from Chivay to Cabana Conde and another from Chivay to Mina Madrigal (see Ampato map). A long hike from M. Madrigal or C. Conde to Andahua is recommended, perhaps doing a climb in between. About 5 days walking from C. Conde to Andahua. Known bridges are as shown, but inquire of river crossings along the way. Some rain or snow can be expected from October to about April or May, but this is a very dry area. All higher valleys have water. Best to buy food in Arequipa, but all larger villages on the roads have stores. Chivay has a small hotel (basic). Take an ice ax and crampons, if climbing higher peaks. Snowline shown is for wet season.

**Map:** Huambo, Orcopampa, Chivay, and Cailloma, 1 : 100,000, from the IGM, 1190 Av. Aramburu, San Isidro (barrio), Lima.

The bridge in the Rio Colca Canyon between Malata and Cabana Conde.

# Map 348-1, Rio Colca Canyon, Cord. Chila, Peru

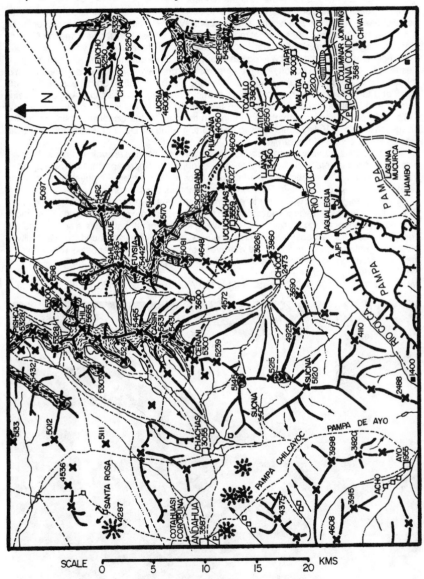

SCALE  0   5   10   15   20   KMS

## Ampato, Cordillera Ampato, Peru

In southwest Peru, in the area not far north of Arequipa, stands a number of snowcapped peaks, the highest of which is Ampato, at 6360 meters. Other peaks included in the Cordillera Ampato are Sabancaya, Hualca Hualca, Ananto and Huarancante. This range is south of the Colca River. To the north of the Colca is the Cordillera Chila, with a number of peaks in the 5500 meter range. Surihuiri, 5556 meters, is the highest.

All the peaks of the Cordillera Ampato are volcanic in origin, with Ampato still retaining the conal shape, and Sabancaya having a fairly recent lava flow. This entire region is dry, being on the edge of the Atacama Desert. What moisture does fall, comes from the east and the Amazon Basin during the months of October through about April. The rest of the year is cloud-free.

Climbing Ampato is easy but will require about 5 days. The author took a bus from Arequipa destined for Chivay, and got off near the Lluta road. From there it was a two day walk south of the lava flow to the base of the mountain. After the climb, he walked south, across the Lluta road, and to the village of Huanca, where a truck was taken to Arequipa. Ampata, Hualca Hualca and Sabacaya, can all be climbed from any of the towns in the Colca River Valley.

To climb peaks in the northerly mountains on the map, in the Cordillera Chila, any of the villages in the Colca Valley could be used as a starting point, but Lari and Mina Madrigal are the closest to the center of the range.

The Cord. Chila is a very old and eroded volcanic group, but none are volcanos now. Mismi is an easy and accessible peak, from Coporaque. Surihuiri and Sepregina can both be ascended from Mina Madrigal. Just above M. Madrigal are trees at 4575 meters—highest the author has seen, and about a dozen Puya Raymondi plants across the canyon.

All of the larger villages will have stores, small restaurants, and possibly a hotel or pension. Chivay is the largest and best known town in the valley, with several buses and many trucks running to Arequipa each day. As you're climbing keep in mind that water is scarce and the country is open. It's very easy walking cross-country, but plan your trip around the availability of water. The entire area is criss-crossed with livestock trails. All the higher peaks will require an ice ax and crampons. The snowline shown on the maps is for the wet season. There is much less snow during the dry season.

**Map:**   Chivay, 1 : 100,000, from the IGM, 1190 Av. Aramburu, San Isidro (barrio), Lima.

Looking at the east face of Ampato from a camp at the edge of the "lava".

# Map 349-1, Ampato, Cordillera Ampato, Peru

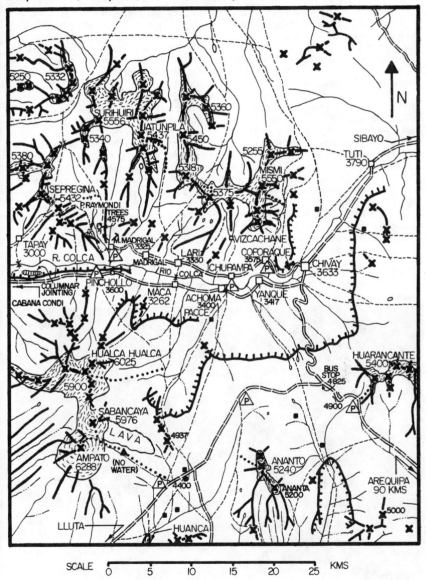

# Chachani, Cordillera Volcanica, Peru

In southern Peru, located about halfway between the coast and Lake Titicaca, is the countries second largest city, Arequipa. It sits at an elevation of 2306 meters along the edge of a belt of volcanos sometimes known as the Cordillera Volcanica. From the city's central plaza one can view three of the volcanos in this range.

The highest of the three is Chachani, at 6057 meters (there are Inca ruins at or near the summit). It is directly north of the city and consists of three groups of peaks. Getting to Chachani is fairly easy. Take a bus or truck from Arequipa going in the direction of Chivay. At a point about 47 kms from Arequipa is a 4WD road veering to the left or west, which heads toward the highest peaks. This road ends after about 9 kms, then a trail leads to a pass. From the pass one must go down a bit, then up to the final summit. Another route would be to start from a place called Cabreria. From there walk straight towards the mountain. There is no water on either route, except up high near the snow, so take plenty. Chachani, as well as El Misti and Pichu Pichu, can be climbed in 2 days each from Arequipa.

The most famous mountain of the three is El Misti, 5822 meters. It is the youngest of perhaps any volcano in Peru and is a perfect cone. It's been a few years since the last eruption, but it's still considered active. Take a bus or truck to the village of Chihuata (take a city bus to Banos de Jesus—the police checkpoint, and get another bus or truck from there).

From Chihuata, walk along the llama trails to the northeast or the back side of the mountain, where there are some stone corrals known as Monte Blanco, at about 4100 meters. A climber's trail reaches the summit from there. Monte Blanco can also be reached by the 60 km road past Cabreria and to the new dam and lake called Aguada Blanca (its position is also approximate on the map). From there one can easily find the way to the region of Monte Blanco. No water on this northern route either!

For Pichu Pichu, 5510 meters, the oldest and most eroded of the three mountains, take a bus or truck in the direction of Puno, and get off just before reaching Lago Salinas. From there simply walk toward the mountain. No water here either except for snow up high (Inca ruins have been reported at the summit of Pichu Pichu).

Make Arequipa your headquarters when climbing in this region. It has plenty of cheap hotels, a tourist office, and a small club andino.

**Map:** Characato and Arequipa, 1 : 100,000, from the IGM, 1190 Av. Aramburu, San Isidro (barrio), Lima.

The eastern side of the Chachani Group, photographed from KM 47 and Kutypampa.

# Map 350-1, Chachani, Cordillera Volcanica, Peru

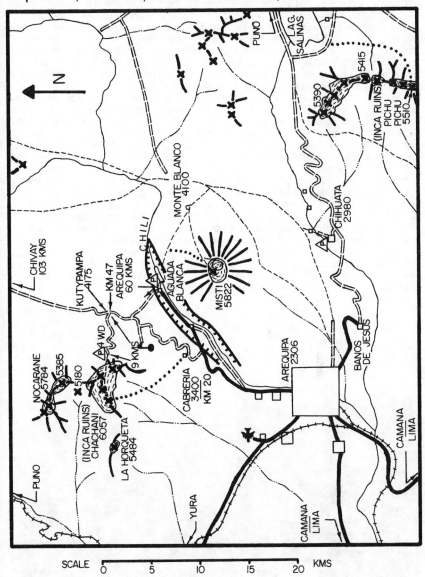

N

PUNO
LAG. SALINAS
5415
5390
(INCA RUINS)
PICHU PICHU 5510
CHIHUATA 2980
MONTE BLANCO 4100
CHILI
KUTYPAMPA 4175
KM 47 AREQUIPA 60 KMS
AGUADA BLANCA
MISTI 5822
CHIVAY 103 KMS
4 WD
9 KMS
NOCARANE 5784
5385
5180
AREQUIPA 2306
BAÑOS DE JESUS
CABRERIA 3400 KM 20
(INCA RUINS) CHACHANI 6057
LA HORQUETA 5484
CAMANA LIMA
PUNO
YURA
CAMANA LIMA

SCALE 0 5 10 15 20 KMS

## Southern Cordillera Apolobamba, Bolivia

The mountains on this map include the southern end of the Cordillera Apolobamba. All the mountains here are in Bolivia, just across the frontier from Peru. The location is just north of Lago Titicaca. The Apolobamba lies on the edge of the Altiplano or high plain on which Titicaca lies, while the northeast side of the range drops of rather steeply to the Amazon Basin.

There are virtually no maps of this region. Peru has them of their side of the border, but you can't buy them, and they wouldn't help much in this part anyway. And Bolivia has not as yet (1983) properly surveyed the area. This map was made by using provincial and national highway maps of both Peru and Bolivia, and the Landstat (satellite) foto which lies just north of the one covering Lago Titicaca. So don't expect his map to be entirely accurate. Most stream valleys and the larger lakes are in their proper places, but roads and high altitude peaks and ridges are possibly out of place. None-the-less, this sketch map should help a great deal in getting around an area all but unknown to mountaineers.

The author climbed in two areas in the northern Apolobamba, and viewed these peaks on the last two days of that trip from the town of Cojata and the road leading to it. These are nevados or snow peaks, and the highest summit in each major group of peaks is estimated to be about 5500 meters in altitude. The appearance and makeup of these peaks is similar to those high summits in the Cord. Real in the La Paz Bolivia area. The difficulty of climbing is rated about average when comparing them to other high peaks in Peru and Bolivia. The dry season is from May to mid-September.

Access can be a problem. Since it's in Bolivia, one would think the approach is from Bolivia, but it's likely to be eiser from the Peru side. If in Bolivia one would have to look for transport to the north shore of Titicaca, then from Pto. Acosta north, and to the lonely outposts of Ulla Ulla or Suches. There are likely very few trucks on the road to Ulla Ulla and beyond.

So it's recommended that the Peru side be used. Begin in Juliaca, a large market town, and look for the 2 or 3 times-weekly truck heading for Cojata, a llama and alpaca raising area. One could begin walking from there to the mountains, but it's best to check with the police first. It is a border! With a visa to Bolivia, there should be no trouble—even if you should meet a policeman.

**Map:**  Landstat foto 2223-13554, from the IGM, Lima, or from Eros Data Center, Sioux Falls, South Dakota, USA., and national highway maps of Bolivia and Peru.

From the village of Cojata looking east to the southern end of the Apolobamba.

# Map 351-2, Southern Cord. Apolobamba, Bolivia

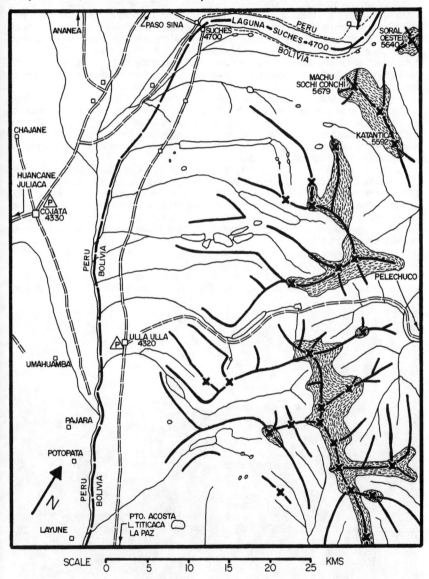

ANANEA

PASO SINA

LAGUNA — SUCHES • 4700  PERU

SUCHES
4700

BOLIVIA

SORAL
OESTE
5640

MACHU
SOCHI CONCHI
5679

KATANTICA
5592

CHAJANE

HUANCANE
JULIACA

P
COJATA
4330

PERU
BOLIVIA

PELECHUCO

ULLA ULLA
4320

UMAHUAMBA

PAJARA

POTOPATA

N

PERU
BOLIVIA

LAYUNE

PTO. ACOSTA
L. TITICACA
LA PAZ

SCALE    0    5    10    15    20    25    KMS

## Ancohuma, Cordillera Real, Bolivia

This map is the first in a series of 4 maps which covers the Cordillera Real of Bolivia. Will the reader please recognize that the region north of peak Chachacumani and Achacachi, or 16 degrees south, is unmapped by the IGM of Bolivia. The map here is a compilation of several sources: those in books *Le Ande*, and the *American Alpine Journal—1979*; Alain Mesiles map; and the author's personal data which he gathered when he climbed Chachacumani and Chearoco, and reconnoitered and southern parts of Ancohuma. Mistakes will surely be found, but the author feels this is the best map available for showing access routes as well as peaks.

The highest summit in this region is Ancohuma, at about 6427 meters, followed closely by Illampu, at 6362 meters. Many secondary summits near these two giants are also over 6000 meters; as well as Chearoco, 6127, and Chachacumani, at 6094 meters.

It seems that the most normal route to Ancohuma and Illampu is via Sorata, Ancoma, and the place called Cuco or Cooco. Base camp is usually made at one of the lakes shown on the map, then routes from the east and northeast are used for these climbs.

There are lots of buses and trucks going as far as Sorata. From Sorata—and with luck, you may find a truck going as far as Ancoma. You'll likely have to walk from Ancoma. All supplies for this trip can be found in Sorata, but of course La Paz has better variety. If you walk from Ancoma, you'll need at least one week's food, depending on your fitness and climbing abilities. Neither of these climbs is a walk-up. The north and northwest approach to Illampu and the south approach to Ancohuma look possible.

The author set up a camp at the lake at the bottom of the ice fall near Chearoco and Chachacumani, then on Day 2 climbed Chearoco via the southwest ridge. Day 3 was used to climb Chachacumani via a western route. Each was a one day climb from camp at 4800 meters. It is best to camp a bit higher through, at about 5150 meters. Getting to these two peaks and others nearby, will require more than a day's walk from either Achacachi, Huarina, or Peñas. If you're lucky enough to have a vehicle—it better be a 4WD, as the roads west of these mountains are just terrible!

The tourist office in La Paz can help in locating buses or trucks traveling to this area. Climb in Bolivia during May through early September.

**Map:** Cordillera Real—Bolivia, Illampu–Ancohuma Group, American Alpine Journal-1979, or Cordillera Real de Los Andes—Bolivia, 1 : 125,000, by Alain Mesili, TAWA: Casilla (P.O. Box) 8662, La Paz.

From somewhere above Tacamarca, we see the summit of Ancohuma, to the northeast.

# Map 352-1, Ancohuma, Cordillera Real, Bolivia

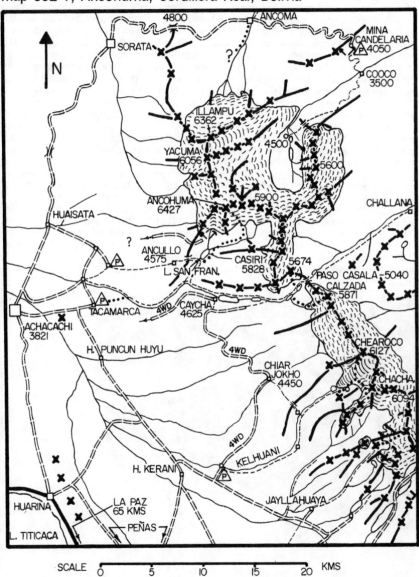

N

ANCOMA
4800
SORATA
MINA
CANDELARIA
P 4050
COOCO
3500
ILLAMPU
6362
YACUMA
6056
4500
5600
ANCOHUMA
6427
5900
CHALLANA
HUAISATA
?
ANCULLO
4575
CASIRI
5828
5674
PASO CASALA 5040
CALZADA
5871
L. SAN FRAN.
P
TACAMARCA
4WD
CAYCHA
4625
ACHACACHI
3821
H. PUNCUN HUYU
4WD
CHEAROCO
6127
CHIAR
JOKHO
4450
CHACHA
6094
4WD
KELHUANI
H. KERANI
P
HUARINA
LA PAZ
65 KMS
JAYLLAHUAYA
L. TITICACA
PEÑAS

SCALE
0      5      10      15      20    KMS

## Condoriri, Cordillera Real, Bolivia

This map is the second in the series of 4 covering Bolivias Cordillera Real. This map covers the area between just north of Huayna Potosi and 16 degrees south. The line formed by the 16 degrees south parallel is the northern limit of good maps of the Cordillera Real. North of that line the IGM of Bolivia has not yet finished surveying.

The highest summit on this map is Condoriri, listed at 5648 meters. However, there are many other peaks over 5500 meters, so Condoriri is only slightly above the rest. For residents of La Paz—both locals and foreign diplomats and businessmen—this is one of the more popular climbs in the Real, because of the ease of access. Most of them have their own vehicles.

Getting to Condoriri is easy—if you have a vehicle. Drive from La Paz towards Chacaltaya ski resort, then to Milluni and left to Tuni. Tuni can also be reached via the paved highway leading northwest out of La Paz, then 20 kms to a turn-off road leading to Tuni. If you're using public transport, inquire at the tourist office as to the whereabouts of the area where trucks load up every day taking cargo and passengers to Tuni and the twice daily buses to Milluni.

From Tuni, walk or drive on the road past Laguna Tuni to the northeast. This follows a small canal. At roads-end, walk up the valley to just beyond the largest lake, then turn left and climb steep slopes, eventually reaching and climbing a prominent south ridge. Condoriri can also be climbed via the Mina Palcoco, but this is a more difficult climb, and there is almost no traffic going in that direction. If one were to use the Palcoco route, it would likely mean walking from the paved highway 30 kms to the mine.

To climb other peaks further north, such as Yankho Huyo, 5512 meters, one should use the road from Peñas to the Mina Navidad, about 32 kms. That's one long day on foot. There's no public transport to this mine or the Mina Santa Rosa, which is now abandoned.

Condoriri is normally climbed on one weekend (2 days), but a strong climber could do it in one day, with vehicle, from La Paz. For other peaks, and by taking trucks and walking, plan on 3 to 5 days if only one peak is to be climbed. Peñas and Huarina are the only places on the map where food can be purchased. In the months of May through early September, the snow is good and hard. The rock is metamorphic and granite on most peaks.

**Map:** Lago Khara Khota, Peñas, Zongo and Milluni, all 1 : 50,000, from the IGM, Av. Saavedra, La Paz.

One of the best climbs in Bolivia is Condoriri, from its south face.

# Map 353-1, Condoriri, Cordillera Real, Bolivia

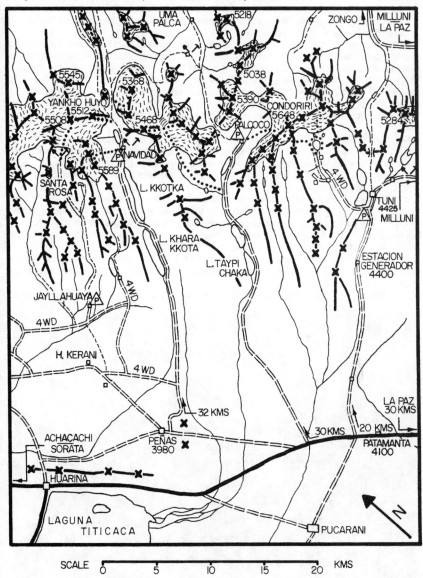

UMA PALCA

5218

ZONGO

MILLUNI LA PAZ

5545

5368

5038

YANKHO HUYO 5512

5508

5468

5390

CONDORIRI 5648

5284

PALOCO P

NAVIDAD

5589

SANTA ROSA

L. KKOTKA

4 WD

4 WD

TUNI 4425 P MILLUNI

L. KHARA KKOTA

L. TAYPI CHAKA

ESTACION GENERADOR 4400

JAYLLAHUAYA

4 WD

4WD

H. KERANI

4 WD

LA PAZ 30 KMS

32 KMS

ACHACACHI SORATA

PEÑAS 3980

30 KMS

20 KMS

PATAMANTA 4100

HUARINA

N

LAGUNA TITICACA

PUCARANI

SCALE    0    5    10    15    20    KMS

## Huayna Potosi, Cordillera Real, Bolivia

Included on this map is La Paz, the highest capital city in the world, and the central portions of the Cordillera Real. This is the third in the series of 4 maps covering this mountain range. The highest peak in the area is Huayna Potosi, at 6088 meters. Of interest to skiers, the Chacaltaya ski resort has a refugio at 5180 meters, with the ski lift reaching to about 5300 meters, highest in the world.

Huayna Potosi is perhaps the most climbed mountain in Bolivia. The reason is obvious, it's so near to La Paz. It's also right at 20,000 feet, which makes it inviting for climbers accustomed to using that "system" of measurement.

With one's own vehicle, it's a two hour drive from downtown La Paz, to Laguna Zongo, at the southeastern base of the mountain. From that small lake, one can walk on a trail which follows a small canal running beneath the glaciers. At a point below the east ridge, leave the trail and head up. The route is fairly easy, but there are some crevasses. Near the summit the route steepens, but in the months of May through early September, the snow is very hard, making the climb both easy and interesting. A very strong climber, with his own vehicle, could do the climb from La Paz in one long day. However, most people camp on the mountain, making it a two day affair.

For those using public transport, the best and surest way of arriving at the area is to contact the Bolivian Power Company (Canadian owned), about getting a ride to the power plant complex at or near Laguna Zongo. They have trucks going that way about every day. If you're alone or you have a small group, they'll likely help you get there. There are twice daily buses from La Paz to Milluni.

If that doesn't work, go to the tourist office in La Paz and get directions to the area where trucks load up taking passengers and cargo to the mines in the area of Milluni. For climbs further to the southeast, there's heavy traffic over the pass known as Cumbre.

The route symbol shows some of the normal routes up other mountains on the map. Half the mountains on this map can be climbed from the Milluni area.

Buy all food and supplies before leaving La Paz, as there are almost no other places where food can be found. The snowline is about 4800 meters, making snow and ice equipment necessary on most peaks.

**Map:** Milluni, La Paz(Norte), Chojlla, and Palca, all 1 : 50,000, from the IGM, Av. Saavedra, La Paz.

Huayna Potosi seen from a point just below Chacaltaya ski resort.

734

# Map 354-1, Huayna Potosi, Cord. Real, Bolivia

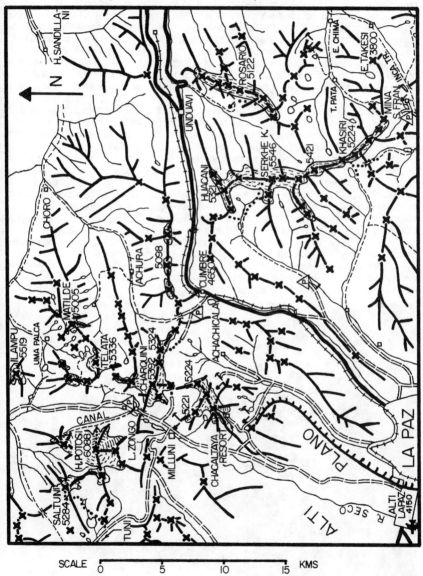

SCALE 0 5 10 15 KMS

## Illimani, Cordillera Real, Bolivia

Included on this map is the southern section of the Cordillera Real. It's the fourth in a series of 4 maps covering this mountain range. The highest mountain on the map is Illimani, 6402 meters. The second most important summit is Mururata, with its highest peak set at 5868 meters. (The large area shown as snow, east of Mururata is not glaciation, but instead is the normal snow line during the rainy season. The IGM maps are misleading.)

Illimani is by far the most famous mountain in Bolivia. Those familiar with La Paz know that it's this peak that dominates the southeastern skyline on clear days. Illimani can be reached by taking the daily bus or one of several trucks going from La Paz to the Bolsa Negra mining area. The downtown tourist office can direct you to the location of the bus departure area. One could also take a city bus to the southern part of La Paz to the police checkpost, then wait for vehicles heading in that direction; or with luck catch one going to Urania, south of the peak. If a Bolsa Negra vehicle is taken, get off at the junction shown on the map, and walk to the southwest face.

Once near the mountain look for the prominent ridge in the center of the southwest face. In 1972, there was an old building at the base of that ridge, which is at the beginning of a trail-of-sorts. For most climbers, it's best to make camp on the ridge, then reach the summit on the second day. It's an easy and safe climb, with almost no crevasses.

To climb Mururata, take a bus going to Bolsa Negra or Palca, and get off at Huancapampa and walk; or find a truck going all the way to the San Francisco Mine (in 1980 that was about twice a week). Whether you get a ride, or walk from Huancapampa, stop before reaching the San Francisco Mine, and turn east. There's an old road leading to a mine, then a trail leading to still another mine not far from snow line on the western slopes. From a camp at snow line, the author made the ascent in less than 2 hours. With one's own vehicle, a strong climber could do this climb in one long day from La Paz. This is the easiest big mountain in Bolivia.

Of the villages on the map, only Palca, Huancapampa and Bolsa Negra have food shops. Best to buy everything in La Paz. All peaks over about 4800 meters are snow capped. The dry season is from May to early September. Trekkers should check out the Inca Trail, between M. San Francisco and Takesi (note the proposed ski resort on Mururata).

**Map:** Chojlla, Palca, Chulumani, and Lambate, all 1 : 50,000, from IGM, Av. Saavedra, La Paz.

Illimani as seen from the summit of Mururata.

# Map 355-1, Illimani, Cord. Real, Bolivia

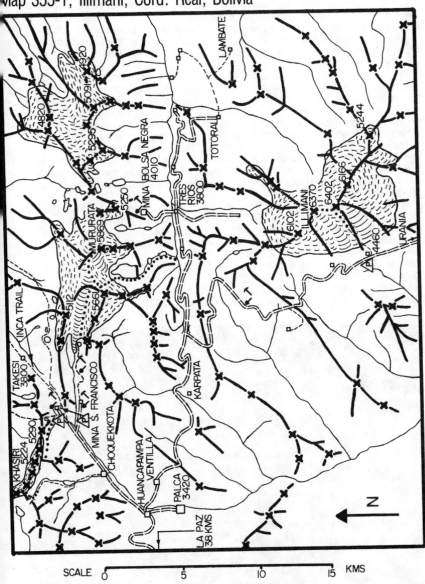

SCALE
0        5        10        15    KMS

## Gigante, Cord. Quimsa (Tres) Cruz, Bolivia

This map covers the central and highest portion of the Quimsa Cruz, a small and compact mountain range due north of Oruro and southeast of La Paz in north west Bolivia. Lots of confusion about names of peaks on mountaineering maps and those maps put out by the IGM in La Paz. First of all the name. "Quimsa" in Quechua means three or tres. On most Bolivian maps this range is called Tres Cruzes. It appears that most mountaineers know it as the Quimsa Cruz. Names of several peaks don't correlate either. But regardless of names this range has a number of fine peaks which can challenge any climber. Keep in mind the snow line shown is for the wet season. During the dry season, when you will likely be there, there will be less snow than shown.

To reach the Quimsa Cruz take a bus out of La Paz or Oruro and proceed to the small village of Panduro, located on the main highway which links the capital with Oruro. At Panduro one can find either a bus or, more likely a truck, going to this mountain region. By asking a lot of questions in La Paz, it's likely one can find a daily bus running direct to Caxata and beyond. Anyway there are trucks going to the areas of the Mina Caracoles and/or Viloco, which will put a climber within easy walking distance of about all the important peaks.

The highest summit is Gigante at 5748 meters. This and other high summits are glaciated and require all the normal ice and snow climbing equipment. There is a trail leading to an old mine on the western slopes of Gigante. Also the western slopes are much drier with the snow line at about 5000 to 5200 meters, whereas the eastern slopes have a snow line of about 4800 or 5000 meters.

Many peaks here are especially good for rock climbers. There are literally thousands of unclimbed rock summits, most of which are in the northern parts of the range.

One should buy all food in Oruro or La Paz for best selections, but some food can be bought at Caxata, Viloco, the estancia Rancho Pata and at the Mina Caracoles. From La Paz, into the range, and climbing say two peaks, and return to La Paz will take a week to 10 days. Expect to find bad roads, slow trucks, and lots of sun and good weather from May to September in the Quimsa Cruz.

**Map:** Mina Caracoles, Araca, Estancia Choquetanga, Chico Yaco, Cairoma, all 1 : 50,000, or La Paz, Cochabamba, map SE-19-4 and SE-19-7, all 1 : 250,000, from IGM, Ave. Saavedra, La Paz.

Gigante Grande, the highest peak in the Quimsa (Tres) Cruz.

# Map 356-3, Gigante, Cord.Quim.(Tres) Cruz, Bol.

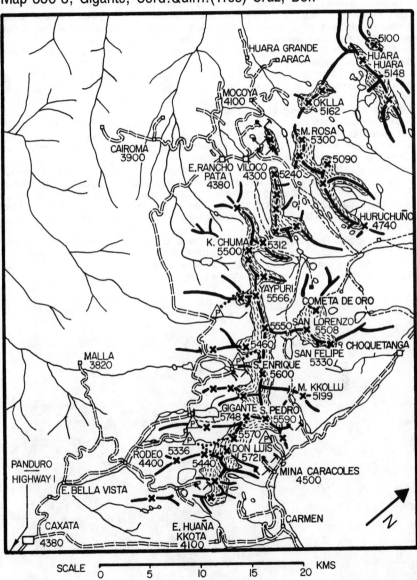

HUARA GRANDE
ARACA
5100
HUARA HUARA
5148
MOCOYA 4100
OKLLA 5162
M. ROSA 5300
5090
CAIROMA 3900
E.RANCHO PATA 4380
VILOCO 4300
5240
HURUCHUÑO 4740
K. CHUMA 5500
5312
YAYPURI 5566
COMETA DE ORO
5550
SAN LORENZO 5508
CHOQUETANGA
5460
SAN FELIPE 5330
MALLA 3820
S. ENRIQUE 5600
M. KKOLLU 5199
GIGANTE 5748
S. PEDRO 5590
5570
PANDURO
HIGHWAY I
RODEO 4400
5336
DON LUIS 5721
5440
MINA CARACOLES 4500
E. BELLA VISTA
CARMEN
N
CAXATA 4380
E. HUAÑA KKOTA 4100

SCALE    0    5    10    15    20    KMS

# Sajama, Cordillera Occidental, Bolivia

In western Bolivia, near the Chilean frontier, stands the highest mountain in the country, Sajama, at about 6520 meters. Not far to the west of Sajama, and lying on the border, are two more symmetrically shaped volcanic cones over 6000 meters. They are Pomerape, 6240, and Parinacota at 6330 meters. These last two mountains are now part of a national park in Chile.

To the southwest of Sajama about 50 kms, stand three more high peaks, two of which are over 6000 meters. Guallatiri is 6060 meters, and Acotango rises to 6050 meters. A 6th major summit included on this map is Tacora, 5988 meters. This is the famous volcano which forms part of the northeastern skyline of both Tacna in Peru, and Arica in Chile.

All mountains on this map are volcanic in origin—some are new, some are old. All mountains shown are over 5000 meters.

The mountains in this area are not difficult to climb. Sajama is probably the most challenging peak, because of its elevation and resultant ice cap. Difficulties lie in access to the region and the scarcity of water.

On the Bolivian side of the border, the streams shown are generally flowing the year-round. This eastern section receives much more rainfall than the Chilean side. In Bolivia, many llamas and alpacas can be seen pasturing, and the villages are generally occupied. On the Chilean side it's a barren wasteland with only an occasional mining operation to break the monotonous scenery. Streams that do flow are likely to be salty.

It's best to approach the area from the Bolivian side. In 1972, the author hitch hiked from La Paz to Oruro, then rode west on trucks to Turco, Chachacomani and Lugunas. That took two days. The climb took two more days, then one long day to return to La Paz via Tameripi. At that time about three trucks a week made this trip. From the Rio Sajama Valley, 5 of the 6 highest peaks on the map can be climbed. Of the villages, only Sajama had a store to buy food, and Lagunas a school.

To climb Tacora, one would be required to take the weekly train from either La Paz or Arica in northern Chile. Check to see if you'll be permitted to ride one of the many freight trains using the line. These peaks can be climbed any time, but snow does fall from October through April.
**Map:**   Arica, 1 : 500,000, from the IGM, 384 O'Higgins, Santiago.

Sajama from the south near Lagunas. Llamas and Alpacas grazing.

# Map 357-1, Sajama, Cord. Occidental, Bolivia

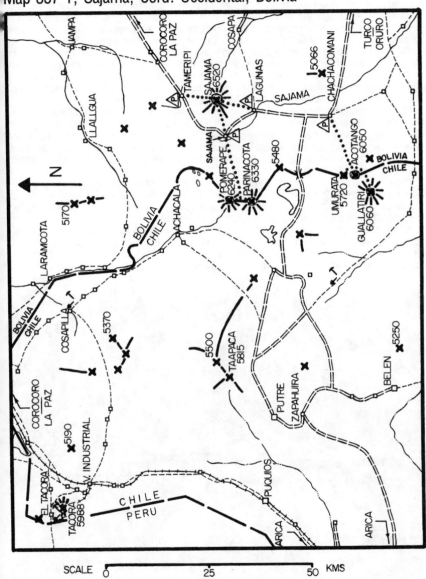

SCALE 0      25      50   KMS

# Aucanquilcha, Cordillera Occidental, Chile

The area covered by this map is the region north and east of Calama and Chuquicamata, two important copper mining towns in northern Chile's Atacama Desert. Of the dozens of volcanic mountains on the map, three are over 6000 meters. However, there are dozens more *near* 6000 meters. All peaks shown on the map are over 5000 meters.

The actual ascent of any one peak is hardly a problem—it's easy climbing. There are no glaciers, and only a few snow fields at the summits of the highest peaks. The problems that one does encounter though, are limited transportation, poor accessibility, and the lack of water.

As for water, the only flowing stream is the Rio Loa, which is the source of water for Calama and the mines. There are hot springs and geysers at Tatio, but that water is undrinkable. The further east one goes, the more precipitation and grass one finds, but this entire region is desert. The lakes shown are of salt water. What this all means is, you'll have to carry water from a railway station or Calama, and plan to camp very high on the peaks and melt snow. Permanent snow is usually above 5500 meters, but when stormy weather comes, it snows down to as low as about 4000 meters. Plan on carrying lots of water!

The only reliable means of transport is the train running from Antofagasta and Calama, to the border town of Ollague, then to Uyuni and terminating in La Paz, Bolivia. In 1980, there was a once-a-week scheduled passenger train running each way on the line. However, there are periodic unscheduled runs and freight trains which can be boarded with permission. Stops are made at the stations shown on the map, all of which have water. Ollague has a hotel and bar and two very small stores.

There are roads leading to mines very near the summits of Aucanquilcha and Ollague. The author rode to the sulfur mine, near the summit of Ollague. That trip lacked exercise, but not excitement. The mine near the summit of Aucanquilcha is the highest in the world (5800 meters). The old tram on this mountain is now unuseable.

To climb either San Pedro, 6154 meters, or San Pablo, 6118 meters, stop at San Pedro station and walk from there. To climb other mountains away from the railway you'll have to walk or hire a vehicle. Get road and traffic reports at Calama's tourist office.

**Map:** Zapaleri and Calama, 1 : 500,000, from the IGM, 384 O'Higgins, Santiago.

The railway depot of Buenaventure, and Volcan Ollague, with summit mine at 5600 meters

# Map 358-1, Aucanquilcha, Cord. Occidental, Chile

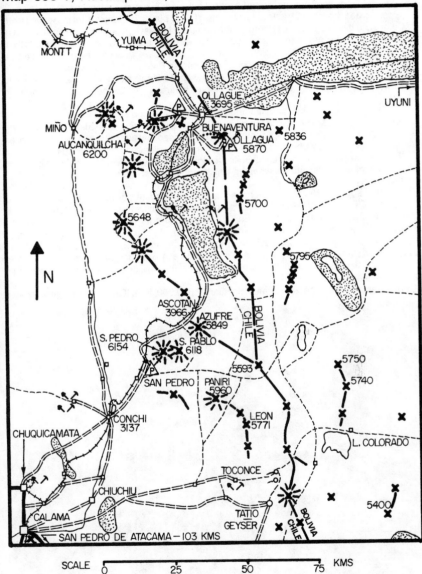

MONTT

YUMA

BOLIVIA CHILE

UYUNI

OLLAGUE 3695

MIÑO

P

BUENAVENTURA

5836

AUCANQUILCHA 6200

OLLAGUA 5870

P

5700

5648

5795

N

ASCOTAN 3966

AZUFRE 5849

BOLIVIA CHILE

S. PEDRO 6154

S. PABLO 6118

5593

5750

5740

SAN PEDRO

PANIRI 5960

LEON 5771

CHUQUICAMATA

CONCHI 3137

L. COLORADO

P

TOCONCE

CHIUCHIU

CALAMA

TATIO GEYSER

BOLIVIA CHILE

5400

SAN PEDRO DE ATACAMA — 103 KMS

SCALE  0   25   50   75   KMS

# Licancabur, Andes Mts., Chile-Bolivia

The area included on this map is the mountainous region where Chile, Bolivia and Argentina meet. It's southeast of Calama and Chuquicamata in Chile, and to the west of Salta in northwest Argentina.

This is the Atacama Desert—high, dry and cool. It's a region of volcanism, with all the higher summits volcanic cones. Every peak marked on the map is over 5000 meters. The problems climbers confront here are aridity and access, not mountaineering difficulties.

Access is best from the Chilean side. One must take a bus, or hitch hike from the mining town of Calama, to the village of San Pedro de Atacama, the largest settlement in the area. It's easy to get lifts, as there are many tourists going that way these days, as well as mining trucks. There's traffic—but not much—going south to Toconao, Peine, and Tilomonte. There's also a limited number of trucks crossing the cordillera from San Pedro and Toconao, to Cauchari and on to Salta. If you're going south from San Pedro, wait at the police control on the central plaza, as all vehicles must check with the police before departing. (1892—bus service, Calama to Salta).

This is a high, cool desert with little rain or snow. There's no running water in the region, except at the four oases shown on the map. All lakes shown contain salt water. One must carry water up to high camps, then melt snow. It's recommended that two days supply be carried, as it will take about that much time to walk from one of the villages to a high camp near snow.

There are no glaciers in the area, despite the high altitude. Only a few snow fields exist above about 5500 meters. With stormy weather, which rarely comes, snow falls down to about 4000 meters—but melts quickly.

Food and supplies should be purchased in Calama, a small city with plenty of shops and cheap hotels. Because of the world famous museum of Father Le Paige in San Pedro, there are several small hotels and shops there. Each of the other villages have at least one food shop.

Licancabur is 5921 meters, with Inca ruins on the summit. The author did this climb in 3 days from San Pedro, getting a ride down from the mountain on a truck leaving the Purico Mine, heading for Calama. Without rides, that's normally a 4 or 5 day hike. About every other mountain on this map will take at least that much time; that is, if one is walking all the way from the last settlement.

**Map:**  Calama, Antofagasta, Zapaleri, Socaire, 1 : 500,000, from IGM, 384 O'Higgins, Santiago.

Lincancabur from the south. It has pre-Columbian ruins on the summit.

# Map 359-1, Licancabur, Andes Mts., Chile-Bolivia

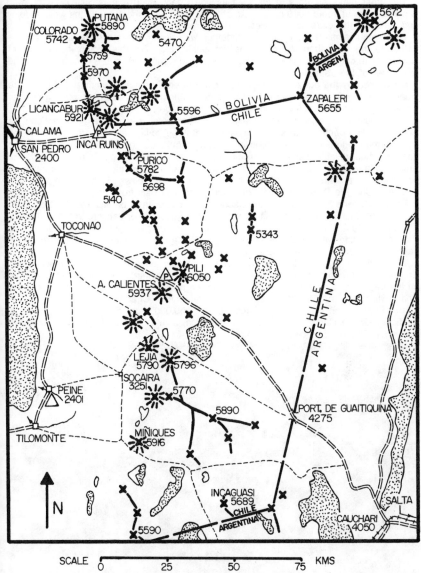

PUTANA 5890
COLORADO 5742
5470
5672
5759
5970
BOLIVIA ARGEN.
LICANCABUR 5921
5596
BOLIVIA
CHILE
ZAPALERI 5655
CALAMA
SAN PEDRO 2400
INCA RUINS
P
PURICO 5782
5698
5140
TOCONAO
5343
PILI 6050
P
A. CALIENTES 5937
CHILE
ARGENTINA
LEJIA 5790
5796
SOCAIRA 3251
5770
PEINE 2401
5890
PORT. DE GUAITIQUINA 4275
TILOMONTE
MIÑIQUES 5916
N
INCAGUASI 5689
CHILE
SALTA
ARGENTINA
CAUCHARI 4050
5590

SCALE 0    25    50    75    KMS

# Libertador, Nevado de Cachi, Argentina

Included on this map are 4 ranges or nevados all of which have peaks over 6000 meters. The highest peak on the map is El Libertador, at 6720 meters. This summit, perhaps one of the top 5 or 6 highest peaks in South America, is part of the Nevado de Cachi. Other summits included in this range are: Cerro Palermo, 6350 meters; Quemado, 6120; and Cienaga, 6030 meters.

The other major summits in the area include Chani, 6200 meters; Queva, 6130; and Nevado Acay, at about 6000 meters. All of these mountain ranges are to the west of Jujuy and Salta, in the extreme northwest part of Argentina.

These mountains are relatively close together, with similar climates. Only Queva, which is further to the west than the others, is noticeably drier. For this region the months of November through March (the Southern Hemisphere summer), is the rainy season. The remainder of the year is very dry.

Maps used by the author showed some glaciers on the higher summits, but these are small and insignificant. All peaks can be climbed without crampons or ice ax; however, an ice ax could be used to good advantage on Libertador.

All 4 mountains are easy to reach, especially when compared to other regions along the Chile-Argentina frontier. Perhaps the most difficult to get to is Queva. There's a road to the north of the mountain, from the direction of San Antonio, but there's almost no traffic. The best and most reliable way is to take the weekly train from Salta going in the direction of Antofagasta in Chile, and get off at the Olacapato Station. From there make your own way south to the mountain—a three day climb for most. Bad news! Tren service from Antofagasta Chile, to Salta ended in 1981. But still traffic exists from Salta to San Antonio.

To climb Libertador or others in the Cachi, take a bus or truck or hitch hike from Salta, to the town of Cachi. From Cachi simply walk up the quebrada or canyon, to the northwest. The best route is shown on the map. For Cienaga or Quemado, get off the bus or truck at Pueblo Viejo and walk up the Rio Las Conchas. The climb of Libertador will take 4 or 5 days from Cachi, for most people.

To reach Acay, get off the train at Muñano, or stop along the road at a place called Encrucijada. The normal route begins at Encrucijada, then heads southwest. For Chañi, get off the train or bus at Leon, then walk west to the peak. Acay will take 2 or 3 days, while Chañi will take 4 or 5 (Inca ruins are at the summit of Chañi).

**Map:** Socaire and Nevado San Francisco, 1 : 500,000, from the IGM, 384 O'Higgins, Santiago. Or the Carta Vial de Zona—Catamarca, Jujuy, Salta and Tucuman, from the Automovil Club Argentino, Buenas Aires.

Foto taken at a home at the Ovejeria, just southeast of Chañi.

# Map 360-1, Libertador, N. de Cachi, Argentina

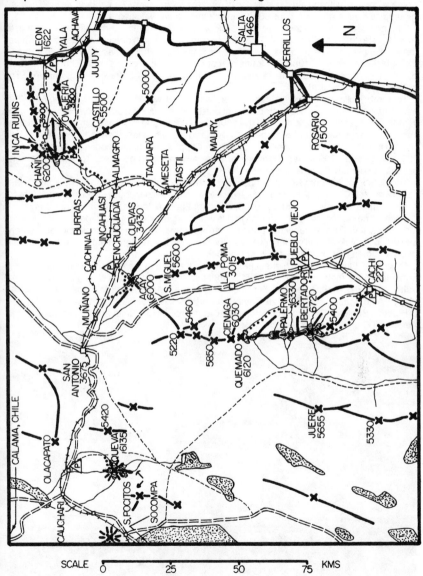

SCALE
0    25    50    75    KMS

# Llullaillaco, Andes Mts., Chile-Argentina

The highest peak included on this map is perhaps 4th or 5th highest in South America. This is Llullaillaco, with an elevation set at 6723 meters. Llullaillaco is claimed by some people to be the highest volcano in the world. However, Ojos del Salado, on the next map south, is slightly higher. For sure, both peaks are volcanos and both retain a conical shape.

Llullaillaco is in that part of the Atacama Desert that is widest; therefore, it is very dry. This dryness coupled with the almost absence of roads or railways, makes climbing very difficult. All mountains on the map are over 5000 meters, and all are volcanic.

The only real access to this region is via the weekly train running from Salta in Argentina, to Antofagasta on the north coast of Chile. Trains coming from both directions meet at Socompa, the frontier post (where customs and police are located), exchange passengers, and return to their places of origin. In 1980, the trains met at Socompa at about noon on Thursdays. (Bad news for climbers—in 1981 tren service from Antofagasta to Salta was discontinued. Try getting on a freight tren).

To climb Llullaillaco, stop at the frontier, with a full week's supply of food (within the boundaries of this map, there is probably not one store for buying food!). From Socompa, walk to the southwest past the remains of the 1000 dead cattle, and to a pass. On the other side is Laguna Tecar, a salt lake. From there it's over two more passes, then to the west up a "V" shaped canyon, and into an upper basin. The final approach is up the northeast face. At about 6250, 6500 and 6700 meters, remains of Inca dwellings can be seen. To locate the right passes, a compass is recommended.

The author took 4½ days for this trip, but for some it could easily be 6 or 7. The author's last camp was at 4700 meters, behind a large rock for wind protection, but it is recommended that a higher camp be made. At that elevation, climbing 2000 meters in one day is not easy.

There is no running water or springs in this entire region, except at Quebrada del Agua, on the railway line. Therefore, water must be carried from Socompa and snow melted. Recent snows would make things easier, otherwise the snowline is very high. What little snow does fall, usually comes in winter, May through October.

Other than Llullaillaco, the highest peaks on this map are to the north of Socompa, namely: Socompa, 6031 meters; and Pular at 6225 meters. The several roads shown have almost no traffic, as the railway handles it all. Find Inca ruins on top of Aracar, Antofalla and Tebenquicho.

**Map:** Antofagasta, Nevado San Francisco and Socaire, 1 ; 500,000, from the IGM, 384 O'Higgins, Santigo. Or Carta Vial de Zona—Catamarca, Jujuy, Salta and Tucuman, from the Automovil Club Argentino, Buenas Aires.

Arriving at the base of Llullaillaco from the northeast.

# Map 361-1, Llullaillaco, Andes Mts., Chile-Argen.

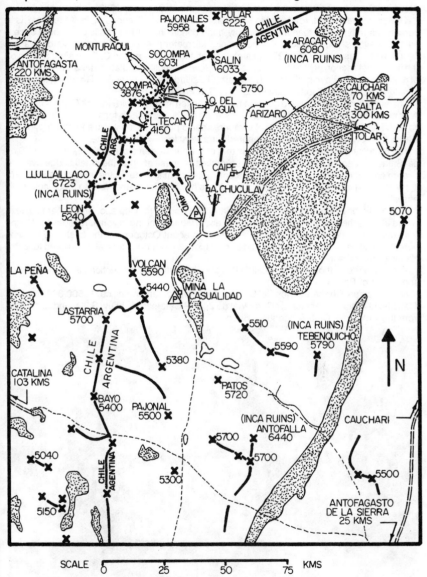

PAJONALES 5958
PULAR 6225
CHILE
AGENTINA
ARACAR 6080
(INCA RUINS)
MONTURAQUI
SOCOMPA 6031
SALIN 6033
ANTOFAGASTA 220 KMS
SOCOMPA 3876
P
5750
Q. DEL AGUA
CAUCHARI 70 KMS
SALTA 300 KMS
L. TECAR 4150
ARIZARO
TOLAR
CHILE ARG.
LLULLAILLACO 6723 (INCA RUINS)
CAIPE
A. CHUCULAV
5070
LEON 5240
4WD
P
VOLCAN 5590
LA PEÑA
5440
MINA LA CASUALIDAD
P
LASTARRIA 5700
CHILE ARGENTINA
5510
(INCA RUINS)
TEBENQUICHO 5790
5590
N
CATALINA 103 KMS
5380
BAYO 5400
PAJONAL 5500
PATOS 5720
(INCA RUINS)
ANTOFALLA 6440
CAUCHARI
5040
CHILE ARGENTINA
5700
5700
5500
5300
5150
ANTOFAGASTO DE LA SIERRA 25 KMS

SCALE 0    25    50    75    KMS

## Ojos del Salado, Andes Mts. Chile-Argentina

The highest mountain in Chile or on its border, is Ojos del Salado, 6880 meters. This old and eroded volcanic peak is due east of both Copiapo and Chañaral, Chile. It is generally considered to be the second highest summit in the western hemisphere.

This map shows more 6000 meter peaks than any other, outside the Himalayan region. The area surrounding the Paso de San Francisco is very dry, but is near the southern limits of the Atacama Desert. Inca ruins are found at the summit of Copiapo, 6080 meters.

The main east-west road, linking Copiapo, Chile, with Tinogasta, in Argentina, is a sometimes-maintained road in reasonably good condition, but has traffic only about once a week, caravan style. The author remembers a kilometer post east of Laguna Verde reading "270 kms to Copiapo." That's 270 kms of uninhabited country on the Chilean side. Shown on the northwest section of this map are two mining towns, whose population depends on the price of metals or minerals mined there. These are El Salvador and Potrerillos. Reaching these two mining camps is likely to be easier than the San Francisco Pass.

The author was lucky to have gotten a ride with government people who left Copiapo, went to Argentina, then returned 11 days later (he stayed on the mountains for 11 days). No one else could be so lucky! A serious group of climbers should plan to rent a vehicle for this trip, or buy lots of food and supplies and be prepared for a very long wait for a ride.

The route symbol shown on the map is that of the author's solo climb of Incahuasi and Ojos del Salado in January of 1973. After that climb, camp was set up at the small bridge over the stream east of Laguna Verde. This is the only good running water in the immediate area. For the rest of that trip, snow was melted. Climbing is never difficult, and walking cross-country is easy.

Obviously, one should buy all supplies in either Tinogasta, Copiapo, or Chañaral. These would also be the logical locations to inquire about vehicles going in your direction, or of hiring transportation. The winter months of May through about October are the best time to climb here. It would be colder, but there would also be more snow around for water. No need for snow climbing equipment.

The maps the author used in creating this one, left nothing but questions as to the location and height of Bonete and Pissis.

**Map:**   Copiapo, Chañaral, Ojos Del Salado, and Nevado San Francisco, 1 : 500,000, from the IGM, 384 O'Higgins, Santigo. Or Carta Vial de Zona—Catamarca, Jujuy, Salta, and Tucuman, from the Automovil Club Aregentino, Buenas Aires.

Incahuasi sits in the middle of the Atacama Desert, thus very little snow.

# Map 362-1, Ojos del Salado, Andes Mts., Ch.-Argen.

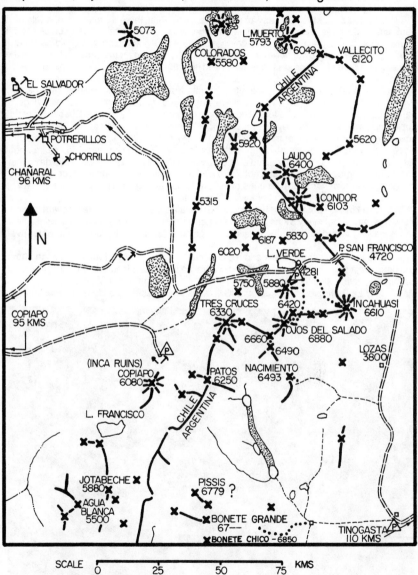

SCALE

0    25    50    75    KMS

## Belgrano, Nevado de Famatina, Argentina

In northwest Argentina and to the west of La Rioja, and southwest of Catamarca stands one of the highest of the "interior" ranges in Argentina. This is the Nevado de Famatina. The highest summit is General Belgrano, listed on various maps from 6250 to 6450 meters. The authors altimeter indicated something closer to 6100 meters however. Whatever the altitude, they are high mountains which rise from the small city of Chilecito at 1074 meters.

Climbing these peaks is very easy for several reasons. First, there's a road from the village of Famatina to Corrales and on to the Mina (or mine) Mejicana. This mine has been closed for many years, but is presently (1982) being reactivated. Still standing is the old cablecarril running from the mine to the railway at Chilecito. Another reason for the ease of climbing is the dry climate. There are some small glaciers at and near the summit, but there's no need for even an ice ax.

There are many daily buses running to Chilecito from locations to the southeast, namely Patquia and La Rioja. From Chilecito there are several buses each day to the village of Famatina, where is located one tourist hotel and a hospedeja run by Antonio Chabis. From this apple and grape growing valley one must walk or hitch hike up the road to Corrales, about 22 kms. There's a fair amount of traffic on this part of the route. Corrales is work-crew camp for those improving the road to the mines in the mountains. Stop at Corrales and inquire about vehicles going up. The author walked all the way from Famatina to the mine in two days, then on the third, climbed Belgrano, and got a ride all the way back to Famatina. Three days round trip. With luck from rides, or with ones own vehicle, it's an easy two day climb. However, a slower ascent is recommended because of the altitude.

There are km sign posts along the road from Corrales to the mine. There's several springs along this road about every 5 kms or so. The water in the Rio Amarillo (yellow) is undrinkable. If one is walking this road at the lower levels, it's going to be warm, so carry some water at all times.

Chilecito has many small hotels and residencials and many shops. Famatina has the hotel and hospedeja and also many small stores. Famatina is the last place to buy food. This area is always dry, with a slightly wetter period in December through about March.

**Map:** Any La Rioja provincial map, but IGM maps unavailable—too close to Chile frontier.

Foto taken from La Cueva Perez. Looking at the first ridge above Mina Mejicana.

## Map 363-1, Belgrano, Nevado de Famatina, Argen.

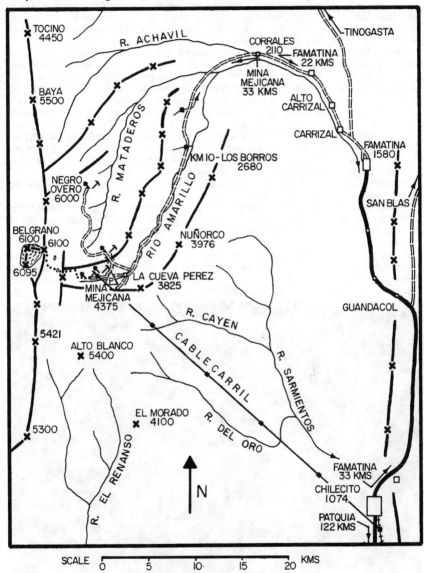

# Olivares, Andes Mts., Chile-Argentina

Included on this map is the region not far north of Santiago, Chile and Mendoza, Argentina. Included are three peaks over 6000 meters. The highest is El Toro, set at about 6380 meters. Next comes Las Tortolas, at 6332 meters, and finally the peak most famous of the three, Olivares, 6252 meters. Inca ruins are found at the summits of Toro, Tortolas and Doña Ana.

This region lies between the Atacama Desert, to the north, and the Mediterranean climatic area to the south. The area is dry, but not to the same degree that one sees in the area of Ojos del Salado further to the north. These mountains receive enough winter snow to form streams and block roads at higher elevations. There's also more water for heavier concentrations of people, as one can see in the valley between La Serena and Vicuña.

Accessibility to the Cordillera de Los Andes gets better and easier the further south you go, in both Chile and Argentina. Further south and with more water, there's more farming and grazing; therefore, more access roads to the heart of the mountains. The main access road for this area is the one running from La Serena, Vicuña and over the Paso de La Agua Negra, and down to Iglesia and San Juan in western Argentina. There's not a lot of traffic on this road, but it does exist-except in winter. There is no bus service over the pass—only trucks and private cars make the crossing.

Olivares can be climbed from the Argentine side and Iglesia. From Las Flores, just north of Iglesia, it's 86 kms to the pass of Agua Negra. Without a ride, that's 3 days walking for most. From the road junction just east of Colorado (Chile), it's 92 kms to the same pass. Once at the mountain, either a northeasterly or a southwesterly approach seems best.

For Tortolas, proceed to Vicuña by bus, then look for vehicles going to La Toroya or to the big mining area around Aguas Del Volcan.

To reach Toro, the Chilean side is best for the approach. From Vallenar, one would have to find a ride to the southeast to the places called El Transito, then to Los Chacayes—the end of the road. From that point it would be about a two day walk to a base camp on the western side of the mountain.

Best to buy all food and supplies in either San Juan or La Serena. Take snow climbing equipment, though it may not be needed. Climb here in months of December to March.

**Map:** La Serena, 1 : 500,000, from the IGM, 384 O'Higgins, Santiago. Or San Juan Province, by the Automovil Club Argentino, Buenas Aires.

The eastern side of Mercedario, as seen from just above the refugio (Map 365).

# Map 364-3, Olivares, Andes Mts., Chile-Argentina

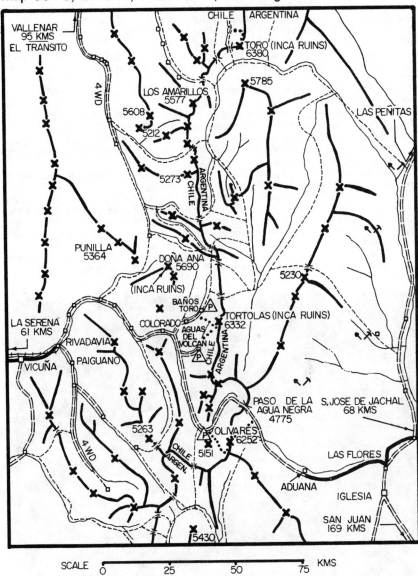

CHILE    ARGENTINA

VALLENAR
95 KMS
EL TRANSITO

4 WD

TORO (INCA RUINS)
6380

5785

LOS AMARILLOS
5577

5608

5212

LAS PEÑITAS

5273

CHILE

ARGENTINA

PUNILLA
5364

DOÑA ANA
5690

(INCA RUINS)

5230

LA SERENA
61 KMS

BAÑOS
TORO    P

COLORADO

TORTOLAS (INCA RUINS)
6332

RIVADAVIA

AGUAS
DEL
VOLCAN

CHILE

ARGENTINA

VICUÑA

PAIGUANO

PASO   DE LA
AGUA NEGRA
4775

S. JOSE DE JACHAL
68 KMS

5263

4 WD

OLIVARES
6252

CHILE
ARGEN.

5151

LAS FLORES

ADUANA

IGLESIA

5430

SAN JUAN
169 KMS

SCALE
0       25       50       75    KMS

## Aconcagua, Andes Mountains, Argentina

The highest summit in South America and in the Western Hemisphere is Aconcagua, with an altitude of 6959 meters. Besides Aconcagua, Mercedario at 6770 meters, the 3rd or 4th highest mountain in the hemisphere, is also on this map.

Despite its elevation, Aconcagua is climbed about as much as any mountain in South America. It also has killed as many climbers as any mountain in the world. The main problem seems to be the climb is too easy—that is, there's a trail to the summit and several refugios enroute. These factors encourage unacclimatized climbers to move too fast.

The author did the climb in 5 days from Puenta del Inca. Most people do it in 7 or 8 days. All his food and fuel was purchased in Puenta del Inca.

The trail to the peak begins about 5 kms west of Puenta del Inca, the first part being a dirt road. Perhaps the biggest danger on the mountain is the crossing of one stream at a point known as Confluencia.

The first two huts or refugios are very small and almost useless, but at about 4000 meters is the new Refugio Plaza de Mulas. This is a guarded hut, with several rooms, including indoor plumbing. The old Refugio Plaza de Mulas is at about 4230 meters. Next, is the Refugio Antarctica, at 5400 meters. It's very small and in bad condition, and most climbers bypass it in order to use one of the three Berlin Refugios located at 5900 meters. The Refugio Independencia at 6500 meters is seldom used. During the period of Christmas through March, no crampons or ice ax are needed.

For Mercedario, take one of several daily buses running from San Juan to Barreal. Stop at the army camp and see about traffic going to the mountain. They are usually happy to send troops and mules to the mountains on manuvers, so they likely will help with transport to the mountain. Or one can walk and hitch hikd to the place called Los Molles. Crossing the river near C. Amarillo is the most difficult part of the climb. From Los Molles it's about two days to a base camp at 5200 or 5500 meters. Ascent is up the northeast ridge. Easy hike—but take ice ax and crampons. It's about 8 days from Barreal if walking—about 4 days with rides both ways.

**Map:** San Felipe, 1 : 500,000, from the IGM, 384 O'Higgins, Santiago, or province maps of San Juan and Mendoza, from the Automovil Club Argentino, Buenas Aires.

Foto shows the trail to the summit of Aconcagua, from near R. Independencia.

# Map 365-1, Aconcagua, Andes Mts., Argentina

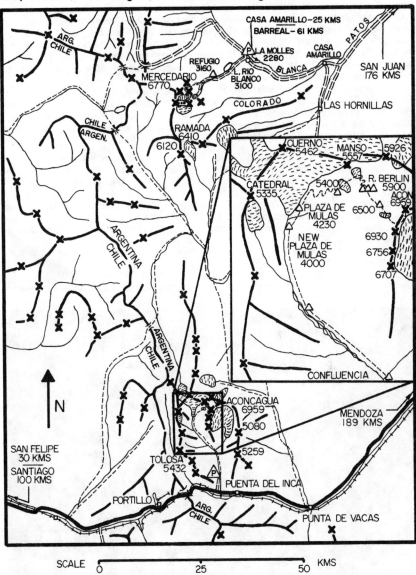

CASA AMARILLO—25 KMS
BARREAL—61 KMS

P. LA MOLLES
2280

REFUGIO
3160

MERCEDARIO
6770

L. RIO
BLANCO
3100

CASA
AMARILLO

BLANCA

SAN JUAN
176 KMS

COLORADO

LAS HORNILLAS

RAMADA
6410

6120

CUERNO
5462

MANSO
5557

5926

CATEDRAL
5335

5400

R. BERLIN
5900

ACON
6959

PLAZA DE
MULAS
4230

6500

NEW
PLAZA DE
MULAS
4000

6930

6756

6707

ARGENTINA
CHILE

ARG.
CHILE

CHILE
ARGEN.

ARGENTINA
CHILE

N

CONFLUENCIA

ACONCAGUA
6959

5080

5259

MENDOZA
189 KMS

SAN FELIPE
30 KMS

SANTIAGO
100 KMS

TOLOSA
5432

P

PUENTA DEL INCA

PORTILLO

ARG.
CHILE

PUNTA DE VACAS

SCALE   0          25          50   KMS

# Tupungato, Andes Mts., Chile-Argentina

This map covers the region east of Santiago and south of Aconcagua and includes the international highway running between Santiago and San Felipe, Chile, and Mendoza, Argentina. At the bottom of the map is El Volcan, a resort town, and the Volcano San Jose.

The highest peak on this map is Tupungato, at 6550 meters. This volcano lies very near the center of the map, and can be approached from three different directions. The distance and the length of time needed for this climb is about the same from any of the three approaches.

Chilean climbers normally drive or take a bus to a place called Cuayacan, then drive, hitch hike or walk northeast to the end of the road at Los Maitenes. From there they walk or hire mules, for the 3 or 4 day trip to the northern slopes of the mountain. The climb is then usually made up the north ridge. In late summer this route can be climbed without crampons or ice ax, but it's recommended this equipment is taken. The climb is normally done in one week to 10 days, depending on the climber's fitness.

For Argentine climbers the ruta normal is from the small village and military camp of Tupungato. This takes about one week for the trip. Contact the Army at Tupungato for the free use of mules and information. The author tried the route from Punta de Vacas, but couldn't cross the river. One must have mules if using this norther route. Another route possibility is from Tunuyan and Manzano Historico, to the Refugio Real de La Cruz, then north.

A popular climb for Chileans is Volcan San Jose. Take one of several daily buses running from Santiago to El Volcan, then hitch hike or walk up the canyon to the Refugio San Jose located on the west face of the peak. Route find above the refugio (no need for ice ax or crampons).

Another peak of interest is Marmolejo, 6110 meters. Make this climb from the Embolsa del Yeso. Pabellon and Piuquenes, 6152 and 6017 meters, are normally climbed from Yeso as well. Juncal, 6110 meters, is usually climbed from the north and from near the Portillo Ski Resort. Plomo, 6050 meters has Inca ruins near the summit.

Climbing is done between Christmas time and the end of March. Take ice ax and crampons for all higher peaks.

**Map:** Santiago, Volcan Tupungato, and San Felipe, 1 : 500,000, from the IGM, 384 O'Higgins, Santiago. Or the Province of Mendoza map from the Automovil Club Argentino, Buenas Aires.

Only the shoulder of Tupungato is visable from just north of R. Real de la Cruz.

## Map 366-1, Tupungato, Andes Mts., Chile-Argen.

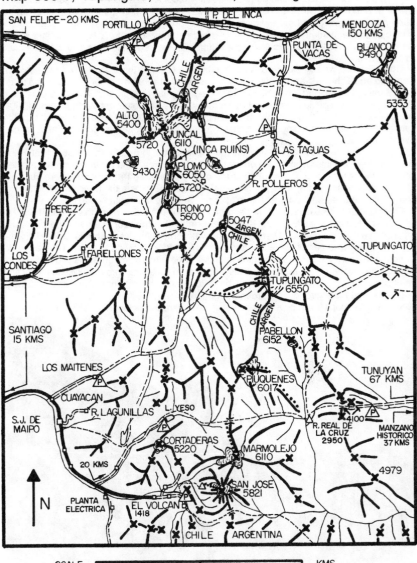

SAN FELIPE—20 KMS    PORTILLO    P. DEL INCA    MENDOZA 150 KMS

PUNTA DE VACAS    BLANCO 5490

CHILE    ARGEN.    5353

ALTO 5400    5720    JUNCAL 6110    (INCA RUINS)    LAS TAGUAS

5430    PLOMO 6050    5720    R. POLLEROS

P.PEREZ    TRONCO 5600    5047 ARGEN. CHILE    TUPUNGATO

LOS CONDES    FARELLONES    TUPUNGATO 6550

SANTIAGO 15 KMS    CHILE ARGEN. PABELLON 6152

LOS MAITENES    TUNUYAN 67 KMS

CUAYACAN    PIUQUENES 6017

S.J. DE MAIPO    R. LAGUNILLAS    L. YESO    R. REAL DE LA CRUZ 2950    MANZANO HISTORICO 37 KMS

CORTADERAS 5220    MARMOLEJO 6110    4100    4979

20 KMS    SAN JOSE 5821

N    PLANTA ELECTRICA    EL VOLCAN 1418

CHILE    ARGENTINA

SCALE  0    25    50  KMS

# Rano Aroi, Rapa Nui (Easter Island), Chile

Rapa Nui, Easter Island or Isla de Pascua all refer to the same island located about 3500 kms due west of central Chile. The people there are Polynesian—therefore the name Rapa Nui. This sub-tropical island belonging to Chile, is built up entirely of volcanic lavas, and has at least 14 volcanic cones. None are very high, the highest being Rano Aroi at 506 meters. There's no running water on the island and no native trees (except small scrubby specimens inside the crater of Rano Kau). The island is about 12 by 22 kms. It's simply a dot in the Pacific, but the ruins here are among the best and most fascinating of any in the world. The story of the people who carved the statues, or moai, is one of the great mysteries of our time. Readers should consult Thor Heyerdahl's books *Aku Aku* and *Kon Tiki,* and Peggy Mann's *Easter Island—Land of Mysteries.*

There are two weekly flights to Rapa Nui by Lan-Chile to the island which run between Santiago and Tahiti. It's an expensive flight, costing about $US 1000 for the round trip ticket from Santiago. Most food is brought by the twice-yearly navy supply ship, but some is airlifted. There are a couple of big tourist hotels, plus many family run hotels or boarding houses, all at Hanga Roa. There's never a problem to find a place to sleep, but the prices are very high. One can cut expenses by bringing food for the trip from Santiago, and by camping and walking everywhere.

The important archeological sites are as follows: first the main statue quarry at Rano Raraku—the most interesting place on the island. Next is Ana Kena where Heyerdahl erected some of the fallen statues. Puna Pau is the quarry where the red top-knots were cut. And Orongo, very near the only town on the island, Hanga Roa, where the birdman cult left ruins. Many fallen statues and ahus (statue platforms) lie along the south coast.

There is a definite scarcity of water and one must plan a trek around this need. There are lakes inside Rano Raraku and Rano Kau craters, and a small pond on Rano Aroi, but this water must be treated before using. There is drinking water only at Ana Kena and Rano Raraku, where the only authorized campsites exist, and there's livestock watering troughs at the estancia (ranch) headquarters of Vai Tea. There is water at no other place on the island—except at Hanga Roa. Scattered about the island are a number of eucalyptus groves which make for fine campsites, but one will need a large water bottle to camp in these places. The author was there one week and managed to walk around the entire island.

**Map:**  Tourist maps from souvenir shops or office of Parque Nacional Rapa Nui, Hanga Roa.

These are carved statues at the quarry on Rano Raraku.

Map 367-1, Rano Aroi, Rapa Nui (Easter Isl.), Chile

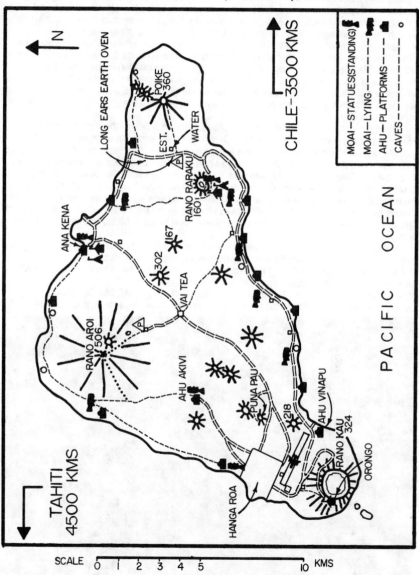

N

CHILE-3500 KMS

POIKE 360

LONG EARS EARTH OVEN

EST.

WATER

RANO RARAKU 160'

ANA KENA

167

302

VAI TEA

RANO AROI 506

PACIFIC OCEAN

AHU AKIVI

PUNA PAU

218

AHU VINAPU

RANO KAU 324

ORONGO

HANGA ROA

TAHITI 4500 KMS

MOAI – STATUES (STANDING)
MOAI – LYING
AHU – PLATFORMS
CAVES

SCALE   0  1  2  3  4  5        10   KMS

# Volcan Maipo, Andes Mts., Chile-Argentina

The region covered by this map is that directly south and southeast of Chile's capital, Santiago. The map's northern boundary is near Volcan San Jose, while the southern part is due east of the city of Curico.

The highest mountain on the map is Castillo, with its western peak having an altitude of 5485 meters, and its eastern summit at 5375 meters. The next highest peak and surely the most famous in this part of the Andes, is Volcan Maipo, with 5290 meters elevation. As with most of the mountains along the Chile-Argentina frontier, the ones in this section are volcanic in origin. Most have lost all signs of volcanism, but Maipo still retains a conal shape.

The most southerly 5000 meter peak in South America is also in this group, that's Sosneado, at 5189 meters. This area is in that part of Chile which has a changing weather system. It's still within the Mediterranean Climate, but receives heavy precipitation in the 6 months or so of winter. As a result, ice fields, even though small, are appearing on mountains with less elevation than others to the north. Note that all the glaciers and perpetual snow is on the western or Chilean side of the frontier. Moisture comes from the Pacific and west, leaving Argentina much dryer.

Approaching the area is best from the Chilean side, but few of the high peaks along the border are easily accessible. Fortunately, Castillo and the border area shown on the northern part of the map is easier to reach. There are many buses leaving Santiago going to as far as Volcan. From there it's about a 2 day walk to a base camp on Castillo, and perhaps 3 or 4 days to the base of Maipo. (See Tupungato map for more information on San Jose, 5821 meters.)

Maipo could also be reached from Rancagua and Sewell or Coya, but this is a real expedition. It could also be reached via the Argentina side and from an area south of San Carlos, but this too is a very long walk—unless there's been new roads built into that area in the last few years—and that seems unlikely. Probably best to reach Maipo from the electric plant west of Volcan.

For the ice fields around Arrieros, walk from Coya in the north, or from the end of the road running southeast from San Fernando, which is the southerly approach.

There's no big town shown on this map, so have all supplies before leaving Santiago. Carry snow and ice climbing equipment to all the higher peaks.

**Map:** Santiago and Volcan Tupungato, 1 : 500,000, from the IGM, 384 O'Higgins, Santiago. Or the Provincial map of Mendoza, from the Automovil Club Argentino, Buenas Aires.

Volcan Maipo, one of hundreds of volcanos dotting the Chilean landscape.

# Map 368-1, Maipo, Andes Mts., Chile-Argentina

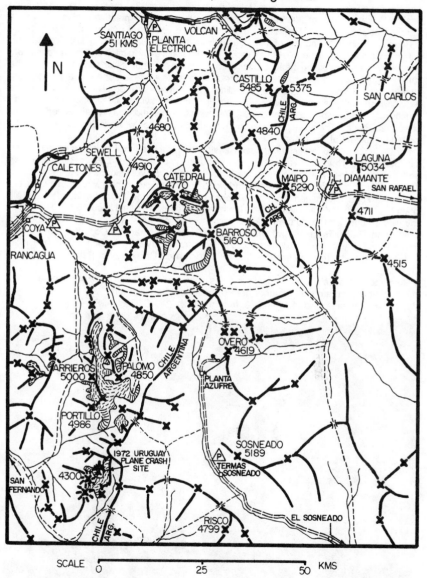

N

SANTIAGO
51 KMS

PLANTA
ELECTRICA

VOLCAN

P

CASTILLO
5485

5375

SAN CARLOS

4680

4840

CHILE ARG.

SEWELL

4910

CALETONES

CATEDRAL
4770

LAGUNA
5034

MAIPO
5290

L. DIAMANTE

SAN RAFAEL

COYA

P

P

CH. ARG.

4711

RANCAGUA

BARROSO
5160

4515

OVERO
4619

ARRIEROS
5000

PALOMO
4850

CHILE ARGENTINA

PLANTA
AZUFRE

PORTILLO
4986

SOSNEADO
5189

SAN
FERNANDO

4300

1972 URUGUAY
PLANE CRASH
SITE

P

TERMAS
SOSNEADO

EL SOSNEADO

CHILE ARG.

RISCO
4799

SCALE   0          25          50   KMS

# Antuco, Andes Mountains, Chile

In that part of Chile which forms the climatic boundry between the Mediterrean Climate to the north and the Marine West Coast Climate to the south, stands 3 more of the volcanos so prominent in the Chilean landscape. Shown on this map are three volcanos and another major summit, plus the Rio Bio Bio. It's this river that separates the dry from the wet climates in Chile. The highest summit here is the Sierra Velluda with one peak at 3385 meters. The most famous peak is Volcan Antuco at 2985 meters. Further to the south is an active volcano known as Callaqui, at 3164 meters. The last peak is another old volcano, Copahue at 2969 meters.

Reach Antuco by taking one of many buses from the rural bus terminal in Los Angeles and get off at Chacay. From there to the ski resort is 14 kms. It's easy to hitch on this part due to the several hydroelectric power stations in the area. From the ski resort it's an easy day climb to the summit. There is no snow on the normal route. From the ski resort one can also reach the eastern face of Velluda, by far the best climb on the mapped area. This peak will require experienced climbers with proper equipment, including snow and ice climbing gear. But it's mostly rock climbing on old volcanic rock. The north face can most easily be reached from the road near Chacay. There are places to buy food at Antuco, Chacay, Abanico and Rayenco, but no hotels, except at the resort in winter.

For Callaqui, take one of several buses leaving the rural bus terminal in Los Angeles each day, destined for Ralco. On various days some buses go on to Queuco. From Ralco one must walk the rest of the way to the hacienda house on the northwest slopes of the mountain, a distance of about 15 kms. Some cattle and wood hauling trucks go part way up this road, but they are few and far between. The house is one km past the bridge. From the house take an old logging road to the burned over area on the western slopes. The final ascent should be up the southwest ridge, as the northern slopes are sheer faces. This is about a 3 day climb for most—from Ralco. There are two small stores in Ralco and a bar. For Copahue, the simplest way is from the Argentine side where some traffic goes all the way to the Baños Copahue. It can also be reached by the trail from La Cueva—a long hike. Or by way of Ralco, Queuco and Trapatrapa.

Remember, this area is much drier than areas to the south, with less snow on the peaks. One can count on good summer weather here (December through April).

**Map:** Laguna de la Laja, 1 : 500,000, from the IGM, 240 O'Higgins, Santiago.

The old and eroded volcano, Velluda; as seen from the summit of Antuco.

# Map 369-1, Antuco, Andes Mountains, Chile

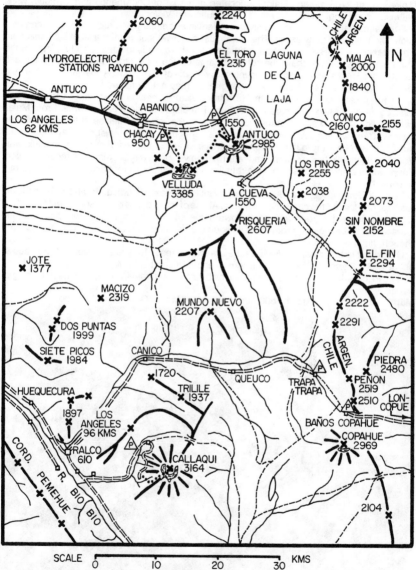

## Llaima, Andes Mountains, Chile

Shown on this map are three of the many volcanic cones which dot the landscape of southern Chile. The highest and most famous is Volcan Llaima, at about 3180 meters. The author was greeted to loud explosions at the summit of this peak in 1982. It's been active for many years. The second peak is Volcan Lonquimay at 2890 meters, and the third is Tolhuaca (Tolguaca) at 2708 meters. Llaima is located due east of Cherquenco and Temuco, while Tolhuaca and Lonquimay are east of Curacautin and Victoria.

For Llaima, take one of many daily buses leaving Temuco for Cherquenco. One can also hitch hike this route fairly easily. Then one must either walk or wait for a lift. It's 21 kms from Cherquenco to the Refugio Llaima, where an old ski resort is located; also buildings of the Parque Nacional. From there the ruta normal is up the west face—after crossing the ash covered glacier. It's very steep as volcanos go, with lots of falling rock. A one day climb from the refugio. Take ice ax and crampons—though they may not be needed.

For the other two peaks, take the tren from Victoria, getting off at either Curacautin or Malalcahuello. Or take a bus from Victoria or Temuco to either of these towns. From Malalcahuello, one must walk the remaining 13 kms to the Refugio Puelche at the base of Longuimay. Carry water from the refugio to the eastern ridge, then to the summit. An easy climb, but if you're there early in the season take an ice ax and crampons. A strong hiker could walk from Malalcahuello to the summit and return in one very long day but that's not recommended. For most it's a one day affair from the refugio. This is a small ski resort in winter and part of a national park.

To climb Tolhuaca, stop at Buena Vista, about 6 kms east of Curacautin, and walk up the old logging road toward the base of the volcano. At one of many points on the southwest face of the mountain, leave the road and climb toward the southwest ridge. One will pass Laguna Caracole at 1427 meters. From there walk up the ridge. Take an ice ax and crampons even though they may not be needed.

Of interest to botony specialists are the araucania trees. They are all over this area above about 1400 meters. Climbing season is from about December to March or April. Lots of black berries in the valleys in March and April. Hitch hiking is best from Christmas to the beginning of March.

**Map:**   Laguna de la Laja, 1 : 500,000, from the IGM 240 O'Higgins, Santiago.

The south side of Lonquemay, with the rare Arucana trees nearby.

# Map 370-1, Llaima, Andes Mountains, Chile

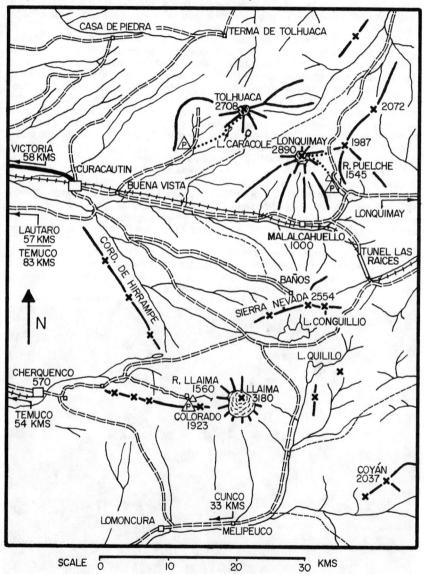

CASA DE PIEDRA  TERMA DE TOLHUACA

TOLHUACA
2708

2072

VICTORIA
58 KMS

L. CARACOLE  LONQUIMAY
2890  1987

R. PUELCHE
1545

CURACAUTIN

BUENA VISTA

LONQUIMAY

LAUTARO
57 KMS

TEMUCO
83 KMS

CORD. DE HIRRAMPE

MALALCAHUELLO
1000

TUNEL LAS
RAICES

BAÑOS

N

SIERRA NEVADA 2554

L. CONGUILLIO

L. QUILILO

CHERQUENCO
570

R. LLAIMA
1560

LLAIMA
3180

TEMUCO
54 KMS

COLORADO
1923

COYÁN
2037

CUNCO
33 KMS

LOMONCURA

MELIPEUCO

SCALE  0      10      20      30  KMS

# Lanin, Andes Mountains, Chile-Argentina

There are two major peaks on this map. First, the highest at 3845 meters is Volcan Lanin. This peak sits on the Chile-Argentine frontier about 55 kms from the resort town of Junin de Los Andes. The other major summit is Volcan Villarrica, located 12 kms from the Chilean summer resort of Pucon. Both of these peaks are volcanos with Lanin being semi-active and Villarrica active. The author was treated to thundering explosions of hot gases at the top of Villarrica in 1982. An eruption several years prior to '82 destroyed the ski resort on the north slopes of the peak.

To climb Lanin, one can take the three-times-weekly bus running from Junin to Temuco (returning on alternate days), and get off at the Argentine border station of Tromen. This is where the ruta normal begnis. Fewer buses and less traffic exist in winter on this route. In summer one can combine walking and hitching from Junin and with luck get there just as fast. From Tromen there's a trail to a new refugio on the northeast ridge at about 2525 meters. Because of various political problems between Chile and Argentina, one was required to have permission to climb this route and use the hut in 1982. Permission is granted at the army (ejercito) in Junin. The author didn't have it, so had to climb the east ridge route as shown. One need not have permission on southerly routes. The refugio and ruta normal are both on the border. Good glacier routes exist on the south face, but the normal route is a walk up. Take ice ax and crampons for this two day hike (3 or 4 days from Junin).

Take one of many daily buses or hitch hike from Temuco to Villarrica and Pucon. Just before reaching Pucon, turn right and walk or hitch hike up the gravel road to the refugio. On week-ends in summer there is lots of traffic on this road. Even some on weekdays. There's water at the refugio, and food and lodging in summer—December through March. There's also several picnic campgrounds just below the refugio. There's a trail running below the old ski lift up to near the glacier, then one must have ice ax and crampons to finish the climb, which has no crevasses on the north face.

Don't leave Junin without food—it's the last place to buy food if heading for Lanin. Buy food in Temuco, Villarrica of Pucon for climbing Villarrica. Lots of free black berries around Pucon in March and April. Both Junin and Temuco have fine tourist information offices for additional information. Araucania trees are found here especially around Lanin.

**Map:**  Volcan Villarrica, 1 : 500,000, from the IGM, 240 O'Higgins, Santiago.

Lanin from the east. Normal route and refugio are on the right-hand skyline.

# Map 371-1, Lanin, Andes Mountains, Chile-Argen.

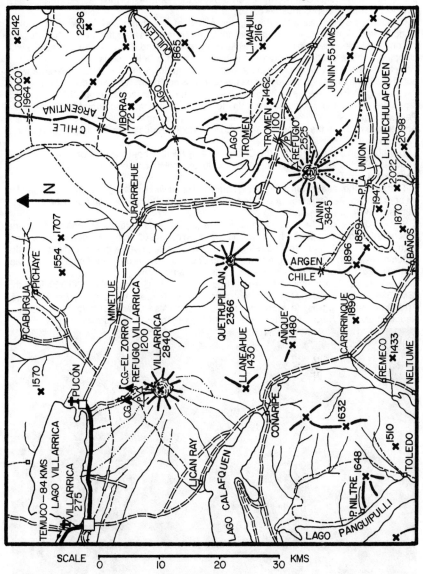

SCALE 0 10 20 30 KMS

# Tronador, Andes Mts., Chile-Argentina

On this map are two mountains of primary concern. The highest is Tronador, at 3554 meters, and Volcan Osorno at a height of 2661 meters. These are both of volcanic origin, Osorno being the younger and more conal shaped; Tronador is much higher and heavily glaciated.

The area covered by this map is on the boundary of Chile and Argentina with both summits very near 41 degree south latitude. On the Chilean side are the important cities of Puerto Montt, just to the southwest of Osorno, and Osorno City to the northwest of the mapped area. Largest city on the map is San Carlos de Bariloche.

Bariloche, on Lake Nahuel Huapi, is the center of a summer and winter resort region. Undoubtedly, it's the best known and best equipped ski resort in the southern hemisphere, with the only possible exception being some places in New Zealand. Summers are just as buy with camping, fishing, boating, hiking and climbing the most popular sports.

By far the easiest way of getting to the slopes of Tronador, is to drive or hitch hike southwest out of Bariloche to a place called Pampa Linda. This is not the end of the road, but this is where the trail begins, which ends at a refugio on the mountain's south face, at about 2270 meters. It's a one day hike to the refugio, another day for the summit climb, and a third for the return to Pampa Linda. Also from Pampa Linda is another trail heading in the direction of Laguna Frias. After three kms, take the left hand trail, which leads to the Refugio Otto Meiling. This is now the ruta normal.

Tronador can be climbed from the Chilean side by taking a boat from Petrohua across Lago Todos los Santos, then walking east from Peulla, to a point northwest of the peak, and up the northwest face.

There are other peaks with good hiking south and southwest of Bariloche. There are refugios on both Blanco, 2225 meters, and Catedral, 2388 meters. Buy supplies in Bariloche for these climbs as well as for Tronador.

Volcan Osorno can be reached best from a point 2 kms north of Ensenada. Take the secondary road at that point which leads to two refugios, at 900 and 1200 meters. It's 12 kms from the main road to the second refugio, which is a ski area. It's a one day climb from the Refugio Teski with ice ax and crampons. Get to Ensenada by the daily bus from Puerto Varas, or hitch hike. Buy all supplies in Puerto Varas or Puerto Montt.

**Map:** Valdivia, Puerto Montt, Volcan Villarrica, Lago Vidal Gomaz, all 1 : 500,000, from the IGM, 384 O'Higgins, Santiago. But best maps are in Toncek Arko's book, **Excursiones, Andinismo y Refugios de Montana en Bariloche.** Also Provincial map of La Pampa, Neuquen and Rio Negro, from the Automovil Club Argentino, Buenas Aires.

Located on the eastern side of Tronador is the Refugio Otto Meiling.

# Map 372-1, Tronador, Andes Mts., Chile-Argentina

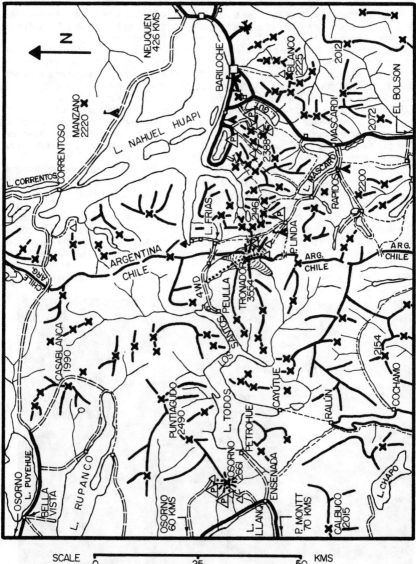

# Fitzroy, Campo de Hielo, Chile-Argentina

The location of this mapped area is in the south of Argentina in a region known as Patagonia and in the state or province of Santa Cruz. Many of the high peaks here are on the Chile-Argentina frontier, but all access is from the Argentina side.

The Chilean side shown on this map is a massive ice cap, known as the Campo de Hielo Sur. The ice and snow accumulate in Chile, part of which overflows east into Argentina, and into two lakes—Viedma and Argentino. One must visit the Glacier Moreno on Lago Argentino.

By far the most famous peak in this area is Fitzroy, with an altitude of 3441 meters. Next famous is the highest peak in another nearby group, Cerro Torre at 3122 meters. Each of these two groups have several peaks which cannot be shown in detail here.

The entire eastern half of the map, at least up to the Chilean border, shows part of the Parque Nacional Los Glacieres. The region is far from any large city so is rather remote. There's improved gravel roads into the area, but little traffic. There are many ranches or estancias with sheep and cattle grazing freely, and that's about all. However, in recent years, due to the national park status and an upsurge in tourism, the area now has some facilities.

The main road of access runs from Santa Cruz to Lago Viedma, then south to the only real town in the area, Calafate. From Calafate, the main road runs southeast to the small city of Rio Gallegos. A weekly bus runs from Rio Gallegos to Calafate. Hitch hiking (Dado) is a little slow. One can also take flights from either Rio Gallegos or Comodoro Rivadavia to Calafate. Once within the area, one must use a thumb or join a tour bus.

In summer there's lite traffic going in the direction of Fitzroy and the campground and park guardhouse as shown on the map. If you're going to the traditional base camp of Fitzroy, the Fitzroy River will have to be forded. Fitzroy is most often climbed from its east face. At Fitzroy is a hotel with a minimum of food.

For Torre and that group, walk west to Lago Torre, where base camps are normally set up. The normal route up Torre is on the northeast face. Some glacier travel is required for both of these peaks, before the peaks are actually reached. Buy all food before reaching this area, or pay high prices at Calafate, which is about the only place to buy food and supplies within the area. Go prepared for very bad weather.

**Map:**   Cerro Fitzroy, 1 : 500,000, from the IGM, 384 O'Higgins, Santiago, or the Provincia of Santa Cruz map by the Automovil Club Argentino, Buenas Aires.

Fitzroy, as seen from the Estancia Fitzroy, where is located a small hotel.

# Map 373-1, Fitzroy, Campo de Hielo, Chile-Argen.

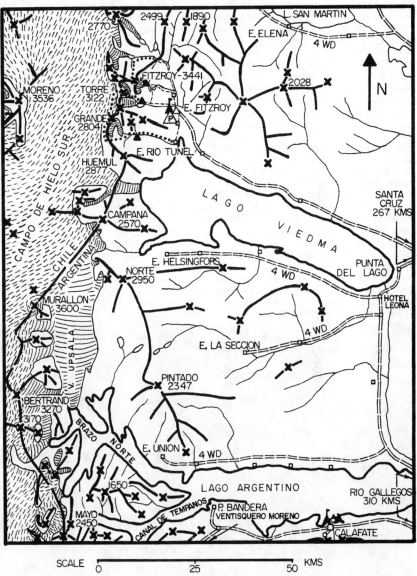

L. SAN MARTIN

E. ELENA
4 WD

2499

1890

2770

2028

FITZROY-3441

MORENO
3536

TORRE
3122

E. FITZROY

GRANDE
2804

P

HUEMUL
2877

E. RIO TUNEL

CAMPO DE HIELO SUR

LAGO VIEDMA

SANTA
CRUZ
267 KMS

CHILE

ARGENTINA

CAMPANA
2570

E. HELSINGFORS
4 WD

PUNTA
DEL LAGO

NORTE
2950

HOTEL
LEONA

MURALLON
3600

V. UPSALA

4 WD

E. LA SECCION

BERTRAND
3270

PINTADO
2347

3170

BRAZO NORTE

E. UNION
4 WD

1650

LAGO ARGENTINO

RIO GALLEGOS
310 KMS

MAYO
2450

CANAL DE TEMPANOS

P. BANDERA
VENTISQUERO MORENO

CALAFATE

N

SCALE  0        25        50   KMS

## Paine, Cordillera de Paine, Chile

Near the southern tip of South America in the region known as Patagonia, is a small compact massif or cordillera climbers call the Torres del Paine or Towers of Paine. These peaks present some of the best challenges for rock climbers in the world. These peaks are now part of a national park.

The highest peak is Paine Grande, at 3050 meters, largely covered with snow and ice. Several peaks which rise from the Lago Nordenskjold and in full view from Lago Sarmiento, are known as the Cuernos del Paine—the highest of which is about 2100 meters. Behind, or to the north of these, are the actual Torres del Paine, with Paine Sur, 2500, Central, 2460, and Torres Norte, 2250 meters. These last three are the most spectacular.

There are two problems with climbing or hiking in this region. First is getting there. The starting point for most people is Puerto Natalas, 254 kms north of Punta Arenas and 140 kms south of Paine by gravel road. This is the only city in the region and for the most part, the only place in which to buy food and supplies. The area between P. Natales and Paine is wind-swept and occupied only by a few scattered ranches or estancias with cattle and sheep. In other words it is isolated.

Transport is erratic. There's an occasional truck heading that way from P. Natales, and in summer buses make runs, but one may have to wait several days for either of these. It's best to first inquire at the tourist office in P. Natales, and if that doesn't help, stick out a thumb. Groups can hire vehicles. Before leaving P. Natales, have all food and supplies in your possession, as there's little if anything to buy in the park. Things should improve as time goes on as more people visit the area and create the demand for better services. If entering Chile from Argentina, there are daily buses from Rio Turbio to P. Natales.

The second problem is the weather. It's seemingly always bad, at least for those attempting the peaks. Storms come in one after another, and the wind is always present. Rain gear is the most important item of equipment.

Climbing for the most part is done on rock, but some snow is usually encountered. The map shows some of the access routes to the peaks. For those who are out for a good hike and perhaps fotography, there's a reasonably easy hike around the entire cordillera, which can be done in about one week to 10 days from any one of several starting points. The best time for visiting this region is from Christmas through about March.

**Map:** Cerro Fitzroy and Puerto Natales, 1 : 500,000, from the IGM, 384 O'Higgins, Santiago, or the Province map of Santa Cruz, from the Automovil Club Argentino, Buenas Aires.

Torres del Paine from the east. South (left), Central and North Towers.

# Map 374-3, Paine, Cordillera Paine, Chile

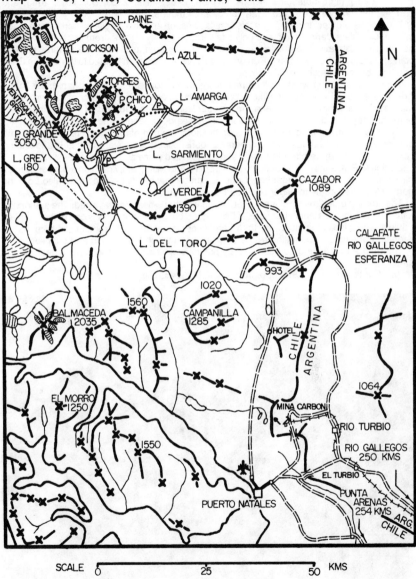

L. PAINE

L. DICKSON

L. AZUL

ARGENTINA
CHILE

N

TORRES

P. CHICO
P.

L. AMARGA

P. NORD

P. GRANDE
3050

VENTISQUERO GREY

L. GREY
180

L. SARMIENTO

CAZADOR
1089

CALAFATE
RIO GALLEGOS
ESPERANZA

L. VERDE

1390

L. DEL TORO

993

1020

1560

BALMACEDA
2035

CAMPANILLA
1285

HOTEL

CHILE
ARGENTINA

1064

EL MORRO
1250

MINA CARBON

RIO TURBIO

1550

RIO GALLEGOS
250 KMS

EL TURBIO

PUNTA
ARENAS
254 KMS ARG.
CHILE

PUERTO NATALES

SCALE  0                    25                    50   KMS

## Darwin, Cordillera Darwin, Chile

This map covers the most southern land masses in South America and Tierra del Fuego. Included here is the Cordillera Darwin, a heavily glaciated region (which almost resembles an ice cap) and the most southerly city in the world, Ushuaia. Most of the area shown is Chilean territory, but the eastern part is Argentina. The highest peak in the range is Darwin, at 2488 meters. Other high mountains include Shipton, 2469; Italia, 2350; Buckland, 2043; and perhaps the most climbed peak, Sarmiento, 2234 meters.

The biggest problem to climbing in this area is transport and accessibility. There are no roads into the Cordillera Darwin itself, and only a few trails—mostly in the extreme eastern sections, not far from Ushuaia. The only means of access is by boat, and from one of three starting points; Ushuaia in Argentina, and Porvenir and Punta Arenas, both located to the north in Chile and both on the Straights of Magallanes.

If you or your group want to climb mountains in the northern sections, then either Punta Arenas or Porvenir would be the likely starting point. P. Arenas is the larger of the two, which makes it the best choice. In P. Arenas, make your first inquiries at the tourist office in the center of town. They can direct climbers to tour companies or to people who have boats for hire.

Likewise, if you're interested in peaks on the southern part of the cordillera, go to Ushuaia and make inquires. Ushuaia is a very popular tourist spot these days, with hotels and touring companies that can be hired to take groups to isolated places.

Getting to P. Arenas can be done by boat from Puerto Montt; or by road on a bus, or by hitch hiking from the north and Argentina. Ushuaia can be reached via a good road also from the north. Climbers can fly to either of these places as well.

The next big problem with climbing here is the weather—nearly always bad. The author had a full week of fine weather in Ushuaia, in December, but that is rare. This is one of the foggiest, rainiest, and windiest spots on earth. It hardly seems necessary to remind climbers that P. Arenas, Porvenir and Ushuaia are the only places in which to buy food and supplies.

The map shows several routes taken by previous climbing parties to various peaks in the area.

**Map:** Punta Arenas, 1 : 500,000, from the IGM, 384 O'Higgins, Santiago.

From Ushuaia, Olivia on the left, then Cinco Hermanos in the center.

# Map 375-1, Darwin, Cordillera Darwin, Chile

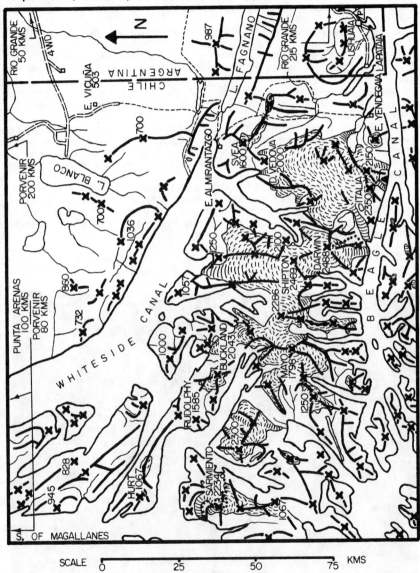

SCALE 0    25    50    75    KMS

# Mt. Usborne, Falkland Islands

The Falkland Islands are located in the South Atlantic, about 600 kms east of Tierra del Fuego, and about 1600 kms almost due south of Buenas Aires. There seems to be some dispute over the ownership of the islands; Argentina lays claim to them, called Islas Malvinas on Argentine maps. However, they are also claimed by the people in the Falklands as being part of the British Commonwealth. Great Britain officially claims them as part of the British Antarctic Territories, along with South Georgia, South Sandwich, South Shetlands, and the South Orkneys.

The people in the Falkland Islands are of British descent and speak English. About half of the total land area is owned by the Falkland Islands Company. Their only product is sheep, with sheep stations dotting the landscape. The only exports from the islands are wool and some hides—nothing more. All supplies and most food are imported. The company headquarters is in London.

Getting around the islands is not easy. Float planes have now replaced boats for taking most passengers and mail to the outlying areas. Boats are still used to transport wool and sheep, but nothing is scheduled.

Stanley is the only real town in the islands, and about half of the islands 2000 residents live there. The rest of the people live in the "camps" or sheep stations. Darwin is second to Stanley on an all-weather road. Stanley has but two hotels, several bars, and a couple of stores. There's now a few tourists visiting the islands, with one tour agency taking groups out in boats to view the wildlife.

The highest peak in this land of "peat bogs," is Mt. Usborne, 705 meters. Inquire around Stanley as to people heading in the direction of Darwin, as there are no buses in the islands. Before Darwin, head north to Darwin Hut, then the peak. It's a windy, wet place, these Falkland Islands—so go prepared with a good sturdy waterproof tent and rain clothing. (Some or many changes must be expected since the Falklands War in 1982. Now flights come in from London via Asension Island. Check civilian airlines for possible flights).

**Map:**  East and West Falklands (2 maps), 1 : 250,000, plus larger scale maps too, from the British Directorate of Overseas Surveys, Secretariat, Stanley.

This the Darwin Hut located at the bottom of Mt. Osborne.

# Map 376-1, Usborne, Falkland Islands

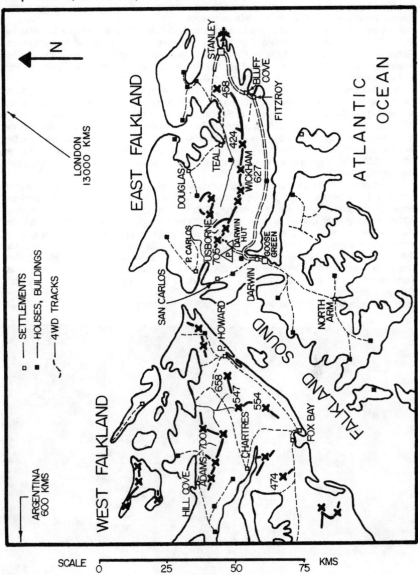

## Vinson Massif, Sentinal Range, Antarctica

If you've been dreaming about climbing the highest mountains on the snow continent of Antarctica, just keep on dreaming. The chances of getting the opportunity of climbing there are very slim. One would have to belong to a scientific expedition doing some kind of study in the mountains, or be filthy rich and hire someone to fly you and equipment there as a privately sponsored group. But since the mountains on this map are so high and present such challenges, they have been included in this book anyway.

The entire mountain range is called the Ellsworth Mountains. The one small part of that range on this map is called the Sentinel Range. Approximately the southern half of the Sentinel Range is included here. And the highest peak in the range, and the highest peak in all of Antarctica, is the Vinson Massif, reaching to 5140 meters. Next in height is Tyree, at 4965 meters; third is Shinn, at 4801; and fourth is Gardner, at 4688 meters.

The information about these mountains comes from National Geographic Magazine, June, 1967, and the American Alpine Club Journal, 1967. It was a 10 member American group sponsored by the National Geographic Society, the National Science Foundation, and the American Alpine Club, with the help of the US Navy, which went to this remote corner of the world and made 6 climbs in about one month back in 1966-67. If the author is not mistaken, this was the second and last expedition to visit the Sentinel Range. (In 1957 an American survey team established elevations of the important peaks, but make no ascents). This range was only discovered in 1957.

The American Exped, climbed the 4 highest peaks previously mentioned, then later climbed Ostenso, 4170 meters, and Long Gables, 4151 meters (just off the map). Their routes are shown on the map with the exception of Long Gables. The group was flown in to a point about 30 kms from the point where the mountains emerge from the ice. They used snowmobiles and Nansen sleds to haul supplies to the base of each peak. They then set up camps, three intermediate camps on Vinson, and reached the summits rather easily. Only Tyree was difficult, and only two climbers reached its summit. Long Gables was next most difficult. They had good weather for the most part, but howling blizzards pinned them down on occasions. Temperatures averages around -30 C. The obvious time to visit Antarctica is December through February.

**Map:**   Vinson Massif, 1 : 250,000, from the USGS, Washington D.C.

South face of Mt. Gardner, with Tyree on the far right.

# Map 377-3, Vinson M., Sentinal Ra., Antarctica

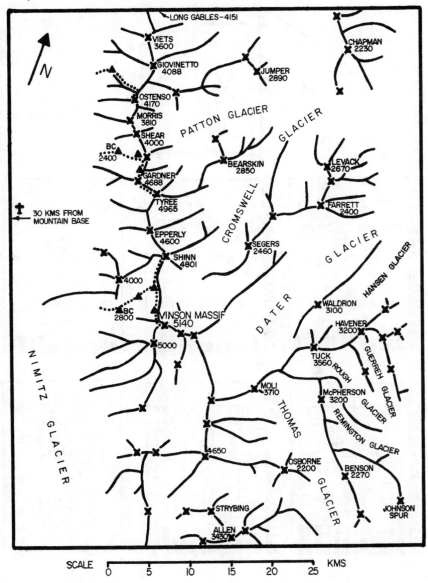

LONG GABLES – 4151

N

VIETS
3600

GIOVINETTO
4088

CHAPMAN
2230

JUMPER
2890

OSTENSO
4170

MORRIS
3810

PATTON GLACIER

SHEAR
4000

BC
2400

BEARSKIN
2850

GLACIER

LEVACK
2670

GARDNER
4688

TYREE
4965

CROMSWELL

FARRETT
2400

30 KMS FROM
MOUNTAIN BASE

EPPERLY
4600

SHINN
4801

SEGERS
2460

GLACIER

4000

HANSEN GLACIER

BC
2800

VINSON MASSIF
5140

DATER

WALDRON
3100

HAVENER
3200

5000

GUERREH GLACIER

TUCK
3560

ROUGH

N I M I T Z

MOLI
3710

McPHERSON
3200

REMINGTON GLACIER

G L A C I E R

4650

THOMAS

OSBORNE
2200

BENSON
2270

JOHNSON
SPUR

GLACIER

STRYBING

ALLEN
3430

SCALE          KMS

0     5     10     15     20     25

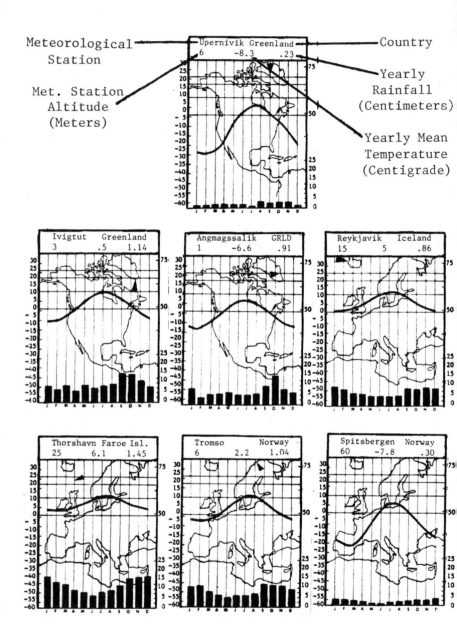

Meteorological Station

Met. Station Altitude (Meters)

Country

Yearly Rainfall (Centimeters)

Yearly Mean Temperature (Centigrade)

Upernivik    Greenland
6        -8.3        .23

Ivigtut    Greenland
3          .5        1.14

Angmagssalik    GRLD
1        -6.6        .91

Reykjavik    Iceland
15          5        .86

Thorshavn  Faroe Isl.
25        6.1        1.45

Tromso      Norway
6        2.2        1.04

Spitsbergen   Norway
60      -7.8        .30

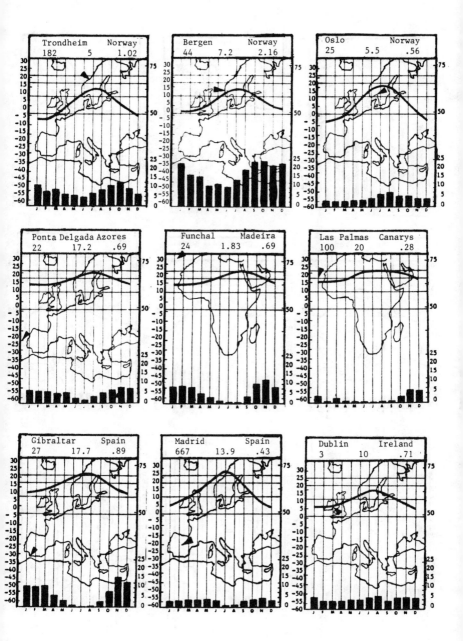

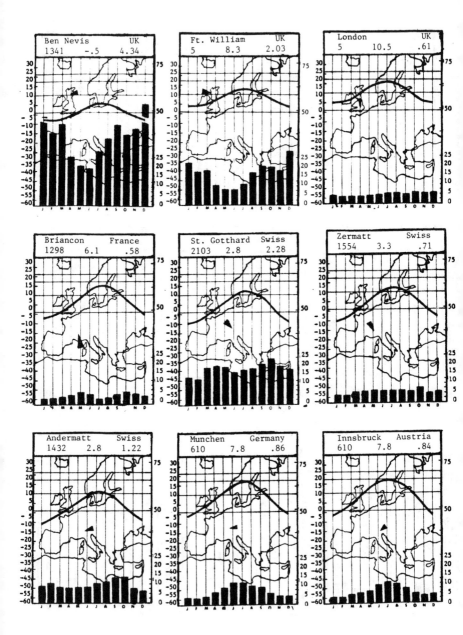

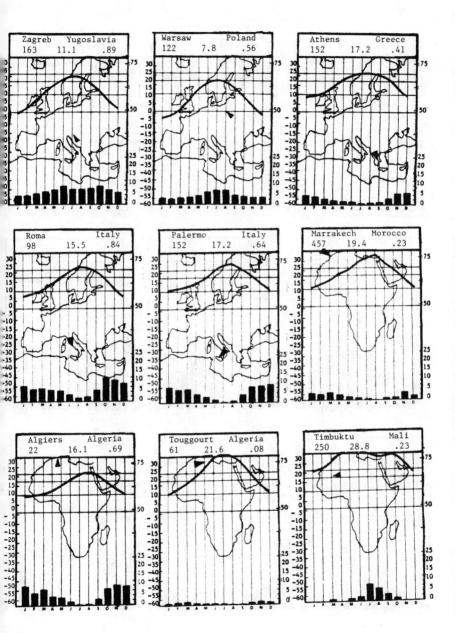

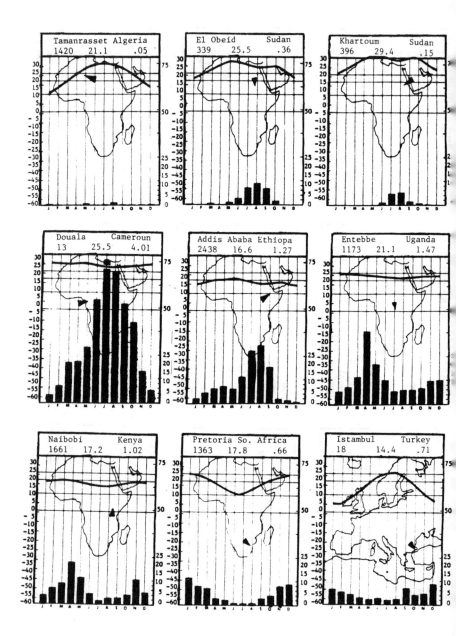

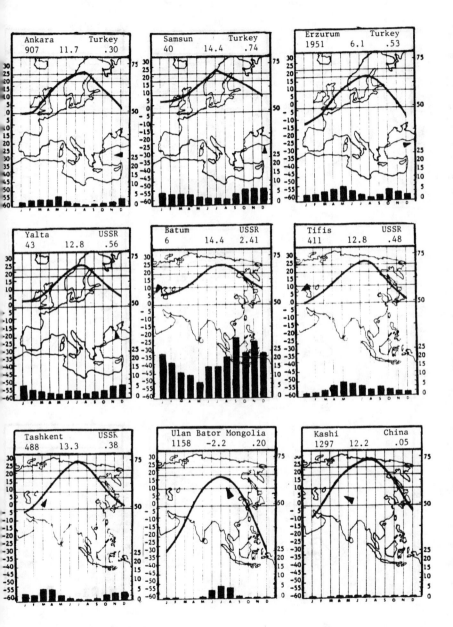

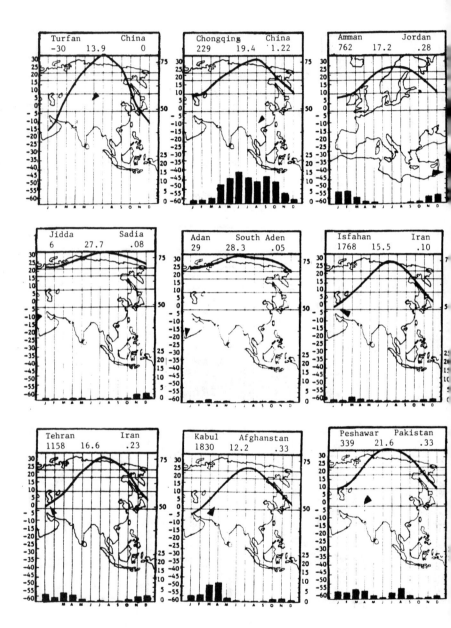

| Turfan | China |
| -30 | 13.9 | 0 |

| Chongqing | China |
| 229 | 19.4 | 1.22 |

| Amman | Jordan |
| 762 | 17.2 | .28 |

| Jidda | Sadia |
| 6 | 27.7 | .08 |

| Adan | South Aden |
| 29 | 28.3 | .05 |

| Isfahan | Iran |
| 1768 | 15.5 | .10 |

| Tehran | Iran |
| 1158 | 16.6 | .23 |

| Kabul | Afghanstan |
| 1830 | 12.2 | .33 |

| Peshawar | Pakistan |
| 339 | 21.6 | .33 |

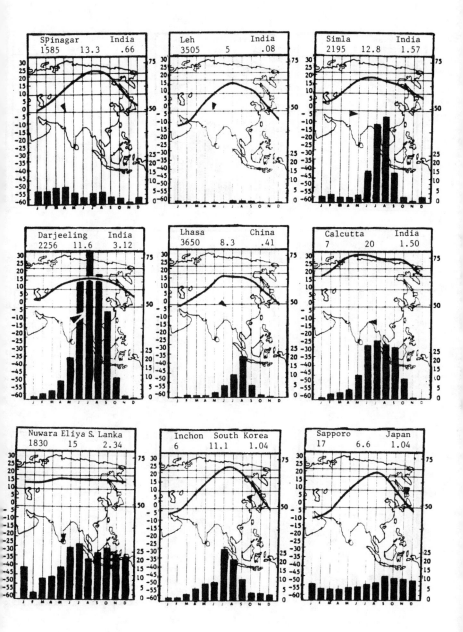

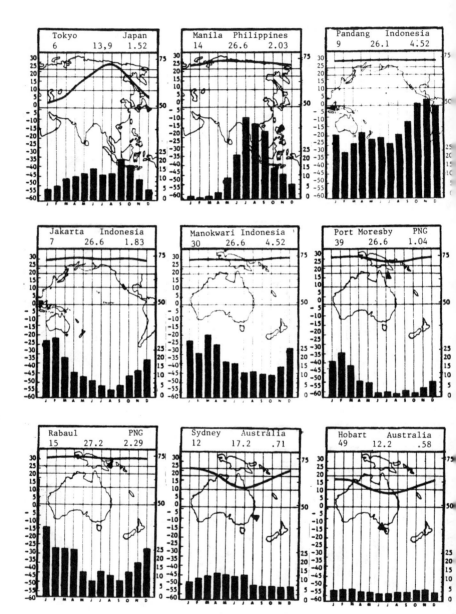

Tokyo        Japan
6      13,9    1.52

Manila   Philippines
14     26.6    2.03

Pandang   Indonesia
9      26.1    4.52

Jakarta   Indonesia
7      26.6    1.83

Manokwari  Indonesia
30     26.6    4.52

Port Moresby    PNG
39     26.6    1.04

Rabaul          PNG
15     27.2    2.29

Sydney     Australia
12     17.2    .71

Hobart     Australia
49     12.2    .58

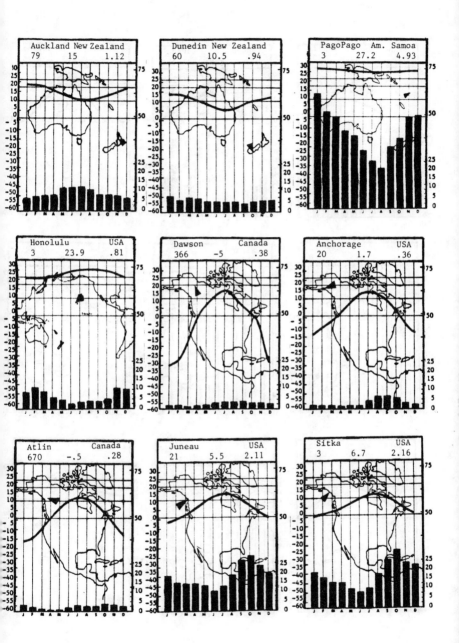

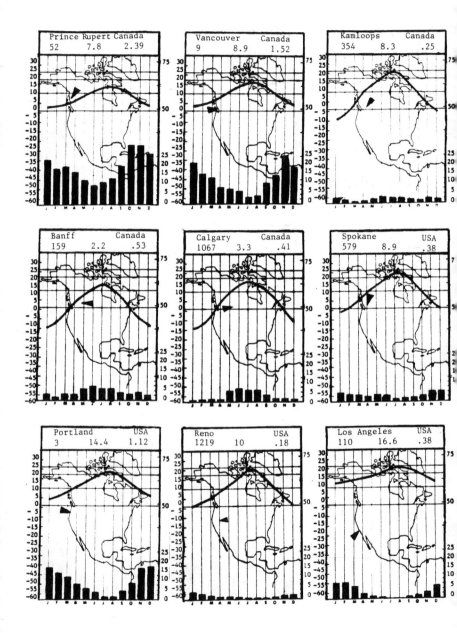

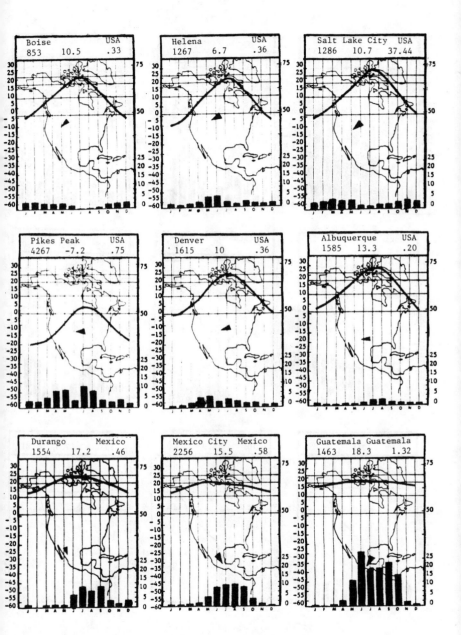

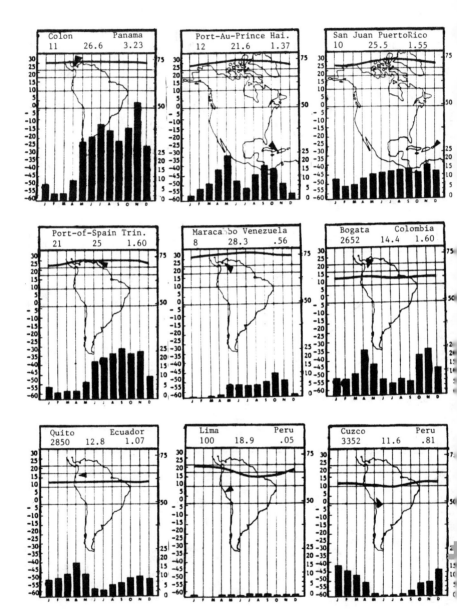

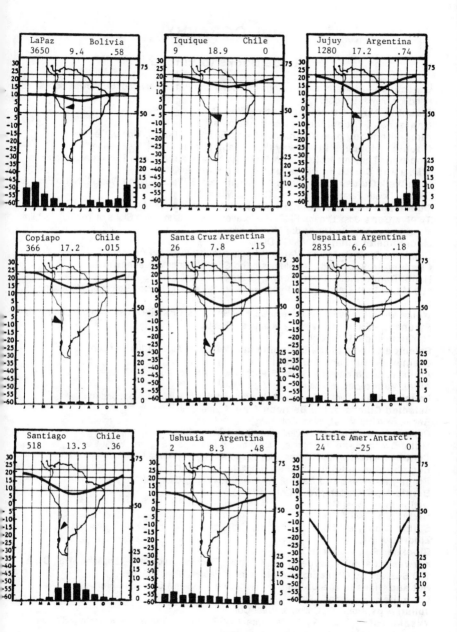

# BIBLIOGRAPHY

## Guide Books to Europe

**Landscapes of Madeira** (hiking guide), John and Pat Underwood, Sunflower Books, 12 Kendrick Mews, London.
**Stauning Alps—Greenland**,Gastons/West Col
**Montagne di Groenlandia** (Italian), Mario Fantin
**Atlas—Handbog over Gronland**, Arnold Busch Publishers, Viborg, Denmark
**Mountain Holidays in Norway** (Per Praag), Norway Travel Association, Oslo
**Mountain Touring Holidays in Norway**, Norwegian Mountain Touring Association
**Walks and Climbs in Romsdal**, Cicerone Press (UK)
**Irish Walk Guides**, (Six volumes—1. South West, 2. West, 3. North West, 4. North East, 5. East, 6. South East), Joss Lynam, Gill and Macmillan
**Dublin and Wicklow Mountains**, Irish Ramblers Club, Dublin
**Twelve Bens**, Joss Lynam, FMCI (Federation of Mountaineering Clubs of Ireland), Dublin
**Mountaineering in Ireland**, FMCI, Dublin
**Mountains of Killarney**, FMCI, Dublin
**Climbers Club Guide of Wales** (11 volumes), Cordee, Leicester
**Climbing in Scotland** (14 volumes), The Scottish Mountaineering Trust
**Haute Randonnee—Pyreneenne**, G. Veron, Club Alpin Grancais
**100 Hikes in the Alps (and Pyrenees)**, Ira Spring and Harvey Edwards, Mountaineers, Seattle,
**Walks and Climbs in the Pyrenees**, Kev Reynolds, Cicerone Press, Cumbria, England,
**Pyrenees—East and West** (2 volumes), West Col
**Maritime Alps**, West Col
**Selected Climbs in the Dauphine and Vercors**, Alpine Club, London
**Grainans—West and East** (2 volumes), West Col
**Alpes Valaisannes** (4 volumes-French) Swiss Alpine Club
**Alpes Vaudoises** (French) Swiss Alpine Club
**Pennine Alps** (3 volumes—East, Central and West), Alpine Club, London
**Selected Climbs in the Bernese Alps**, Alpine Club, London
**Bernese Alps West**, West Col
**Berner Alpen**(5 volumes—German), Swiss Alpine Club
**Mittel Switzerland** (Lepontine, Ticino and Adula Alps—English), West Col
**Central Switzerland** (Dammastock Region—English), West Col
**Engelhorner and Salbritschen** (English), West Col
**Bregaglia—West and East** (2 volumes—English), West Col
**Bernia Alps** (English), West Col
**Ortler Alps**, West Col
**Otztal Alps**, West Col
**Stubai Alps**, West Col
**Zillertal Alps**, West Col
**Glockner Region**, West Col
**Karwendel and Kaisergebirge** (Kalkalpen Region—2 volumes—English), West Col
**100 Scalate su Ghiaccio e Misto**, Walter Pause, Gorlich Editore,
**Hut and Hikes in the Dolomites**, Ruth Dudner, Sierra Club, Sân Francisco
**Dolomites** (2 volumes), Alpine Club, London
**Julian Alps**, Robin G. Collomb, West Col
**Vysoki Tatry,** Turisticky Sprievodca CSSR, Julius Andrasi a Kolektiv, Slovenske Telovychovne Vydavatelstvo, Bratislava, Czech.
**Backpackers Greece**, Marc S. Dubin, Bradt Enterprises, 95 Harvey Street, Cambridge, Mass., USA, and 41 Nortoft Rd., Chalfont St. Peter, Bucks England.

# Guide Books to Africa

**Guide Book to Mt. Kenya and Kilimanjaro**, Mountain Club of Kenya, Nairobi
**Guide to the Ruwenzori**, Osmaston and Pasteur, Mountain Club of Uganda and West Col
**Guide to Rock Climbs in Uganda**, Pasteur and Osmaston, Mountain Club of Uganda
**Backpackers Africa**, Hilary and George Bradt, Bradt Enterprizes, Boston (Overmead, Bucks England)
**Table Mountain Guide**, Mountain Club of South Africa
**Climbs on Table Mountain**, Mountain Club of South Africa
**The Drakensberg of Natal**, Liebenberg, Mountain Club of South Africa

# Guide Books to Asia

**Sivalaya—Explorations of the 8000 Metre Peaks of the Himalaya**, Baume, Mountaineers, Seattle
**Himalayan Trekking** (Japanese), Tokyo (Good maps only—little or no English)
**A Guide to Trekking in Nepal**, Stephen Bezruchka, Mountaineers, Seattle
**Japan Handbook,** J.D. Bisignani, Moon Publications, P.O. Box 1696, Chico California, USA.

**China on Your Own,** Russell and Penny Jennings, Open Road Publishers, 3415 West Broadway, Vancouver, B.C., Canada.

# Guide Books to the Pacific

**The Mount Aspiring Region**, Granam Bishop, New Zealand Alpine Club
**Mount Cook Alpine Regions**, Hewitt and Davidson, New Zealand Alpine Club
**Hiking Maui—The Valley Isle**, Robert Smith, Wilderness Press, Berkley
**Indonesian Handbook**, Bill Dalton, Moon Publications, South Yarra, Australia
**South Pacific Handbook**, Bill Dalton-David Stanley, Moon Publications, P.O. Box 1696, Chico California, USA.

# Guide Books to North America

**Climbing in North America**, Chris Jones, American Alpine Club, University of California Press
**Alaska Mountain Guide**, J. Vin Hoeman
**A Tourist's Guide to Mount McKinley**, Bradford Washburn, Alaska Northwest Publishing, Anchorage
**55 Ways to the Wilderness in Southcentral Alaska**, Simmerman and Nienheuser, Mountaineers, Seattle
**Exploring Manning Park**, Mountaineers, Seattle.
**Exploring the Purcell Wilderness**, Edwards, Morrow and Twomey, Mountaineers, Seattle
**103 Hikes in Southwestern British Columbia**, Macarees, Mountaineers, Seattle
**109 Walks in B.C.'s Lower Mainland**, Macarees, Mountaineers, Seattle
**50 Hikes in Mt. Rainier National Park**, Springs and Manning, Mountaineers, Seattle
**101 Hikes in the North Cascades**, Springs and Manning, Mountaineers, Seattle
**102 Hikes in the Alpine Lakes, South Cascades and Olympics**, Springs and Manning, Mountaineers, Seattle
**Climbers Guide to the Interior Ranges of British Columbia—North and South** (2 volumes), Putnam and others, American Alpine Club and Alpine Club of Canada
**Rocky Mountains of Canada—North and South** (2 volumes), Putnam and others, American Alpine Club and Alpine Club of Canada
**The Canadian Rookies Trail Guide,** Patton and Robinson, Devil's Head Press Ltd., P.O. Box 125, Canmore, Alberta, Canada.

**Climbers Guide to the Olympics**, Olympic M. R. C.
**Roads and Trails of Olympic National Park**, Frederick Leissler, University of Washington Press, Seattle
**Climbing History and Routes of Mount Rainier**, Dee Molenar
**North Cascades**, Miller, Mountaineers, Seattle
**Cascade Alpine Guide** (2 volumes), Fred Becky, Mountaineers, Seattle
**A Climbers Guide of Oregon**, N. A. Dodge
**South Cascades**, Sterling and Springs, Mountaineers, Seattle
**Climbers Guide to the High Sierra**, Steve Roper, Sierra Club, San Francisco
**Climbers Guide to Yosemite Valley**, Steve Roper, Sierra Club, San Francisco
**John Muir Trail Country**, Lew and Ginny Clark, Western Trails Publications
**Trail of the Sawtooth and Whitecloud Mountains,** Margaret Fuller, Signpost Books, 8912 192nd SW, Edmonds, Wash., USA.
**A Climbers Guide to Glacier National Park**, Edwards, Sierra Club, San Francisco
**A Climbers Guide to the Teton Range**, Ortenburger, Sierra Club, San Francisco
**Wind River Trails**, Finis Mitchell, Wasatch Publishers, Salt Lake City, Utah
**Guide to Wyoming Mountains and Wilderness Areas**, O. H. Bonney, Swallow Press
**Wasatch Trails**, Betty Bottcher, Wasatch Mountain Club
**Utah Valley Trails**, Paxmans and Taylors, Wasatch Publishers, Salt Lake City, Utah
**Utah Mountaineering Guide and the Best Canyon Hikes**, Michael R. Kelsey, Kelsey Publishing, Springville Utah.
**Hiker's Guide to Utah**, Dave Hall, Falcon Press Publishing Co., Billings and Helena, Montana.
**A Climbing Guide to Colorado's Fourteeners**, Borneman and Lampert, Pruett Publishing, Boulder, Colorado
**Guide to the Colorado Mountains**, Robert Ormes (Colorado Mountain Club), Swallow Press

## Guide Books to Mexico, Central America, Caribbean, and South America

**Backpacking in Mexico and Central America**, (second edition), H. Bradt and R. Rachowiechi, Bradt Enterprises, 95 Harvey St., Cambridge, Mass., USA, and 41 Nortoft Rd, Chalfont St. Peter, Bucks SL90LA, England.
**Mexico's Volcanoes; A Climber's Guide**, R. J. Secor, Mountaineers, Seattle
**Le Ande**, Mario Fantin, Club Alpino Italiano
**Backpacking in Venezuela, Colombia and Ecuador**, Hilary and George Bradt, Bradt Enterprises, Boston, Mass., and Bucks England
**The Fools Guide to Ecuador and Peru**, Michael Koerner, Birmingham, Michigan, USA
**El Volcanismo En El Ecuador**, Minard L. Hall, I.P.G.H. Seccion Nacional del Ecuador, Quito,
**Galapagos Guide**, White, Epler nad Gilbert, Charles Darwin Foundation for the Galapagos Islands, Ecuador
**Climbing and Hiking in Ecuador,** Rob Rachowiecki, Bradt Enterprises, 95 Harvey Street, Cambridge, Mass., USA, and 41 Nortuft Road, Chalfont St. Peter, Buck England, UK.
**Yuraq Janka—Guide to the Cordilleras Blanca and Rosko**, John Ricker, American and Canadian Alpine Clubs
**Trails of the Cordilleras Blanca, and Huayhuash of Peru**, Jim Bartle, Editorial Grafica Pacific Press, Lima, Peru
**Cordillera Blanca**, Kinzl and Schneider
**Backpacking and Trekking in Peru and Bolivia**, Hilary and George Bradt, Bradt Enterprises, Boston, Mass., and Bucks England
**The South Cordillera Real**, Pecher and Schmiemann, Plata Publishing, Chur Switzerland
**Backpacking in Chile and Argentina, Plus the Falkland Islands**, Hilary Bradt and John Pilkington, **Bradt Enterprises,** Boston Mass., and Bucks England
**Mi Amiga La Montana**, Jose Fadel, Fundacion Michel Torino, Salta, Argentina

A Patagonia Handbook, Ben Campbell-Kelly, Manchester, UK.
Excursiones, Andinismo y Refugios de Montaña, Toncek Arko, Guias Regionales Argentinas, Vidal 2321, Buenas Aires, and Neumeyer 60, Bariloche, Argentina.

Guia de Excursionismo Para La Cordillera de Santiago. Gaston San Roman Herbage, Editorial Universitaria, San Francisco 454, Casilla 10220, Santiago, Chile.

## World Guide Books

Mountains of the World, William M. Bueler, Mountaineers, Seattle
Encyclopedia of Mountaineering, Walt Unsworth, Penguin Books, Harmondsworth, England
The World Guide to Mountains and Mountaineering, John Cleare, Webb and Bower Books, Exeter, England
Standard Encyclopedia of the Worlds Mountains, Anthony Huxley, G. P. Putnam's Sons, New York
Atlante di Alpinismo Italiano Nel Mondo, Mario Fantin, Club Alpino Italiano.

The author and his father hiking in the Uinta Mountains of Utah (Map 256).

# FOTOGRAPHIC CREDITS

All fotos by the author except for (fotographer and page number):

W. Heiss 76
R. Bucher 92
F. Thorbecke 104, 118, 128
W. Pause 126, 130, 134, 136, 142, 148, 150
National Geographic 50, 186, 220, 604
Hunt and Brasher 200, 202
J. Tasker 246
B. Washburn 364, 374, 376
A. Post 368, 378
J. Cleare 204, 208, 382, 446, 774
B. Hagen 384
B. Spring 418
E. Bordogni 692
S. Calegari 738

S. Silverstein 780
B. Kimball 424
C. Fava 776
Chinese Mountaineering Association 206, 210, 212, 214, 256, 258, 260, 262
T. Kazami 250, 254
S. Hamza 166
Andalsnes Photo 34
C. Chisholm 260
Tasmanian National Parks 340
Tahiti Tourist Board 354
J. Underwood 52
Klondike Gold Rush National Park 380

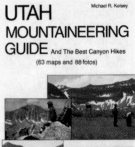